SHAPING ENTREPRENEURSHIP RESEARCH

Shaping Entrepreneurship Research: Made, as Well as Found is a collection of readings designed to support entrepreneurship research. Focused on a worldview in which the future is open-ended and shapeable through human action – i.e. "made", this collection reframes entrepreneurship as a science of the artificial rather than as a natural or social science. It posits an open-ended universe for the making of human artifacts even if large swathes of nature and society are not within the control of the people making them.

The book explores the notion of "made" through 25 foundational readings – classics from the history of ideas. Organized into five sections, each classic is individually introduced by the editors in one of five chapters written to explain its relevance and significance for a "made" view of entrepreneurship. Readers will benefit from exposure to these classic ideas and ongoing research in a variety of areas that fall somewhat outside the line-of-sight of traditional entrepreneurship research. Both individually and collectively, the readings suggest opportunities to ask new questions and develop new ways of framing entrepreneurship research that carry the discussion beyond worlds found to worlds made as well as found.

The book is crafted to be valuable to three groups of scholars: young scholars with limited or no access to research infrastructure but with a desire to participate in deep conversations; young scholars with access to research infrastructure who also desire to listen-in on a different kind of conversation; and established entrepreneurship scholars who are contemplating an alternative set of foundational ideas to support their conversations in the discipline.

Saras D. Sarasvathy is Professor of Business Administration at the Darden Graduate School of Business Administration, University of Virginia, USA and Jamuna Raghavan Chair Professor in Entrepreneurship, Indian Institute of Management, Bangalore.

Nicholas Dew is Associate Professor of Business and Public Policy at the Naval Postgraduate School, USA.

Sankaran Venkataraman is the MasterCard Professor of Business Administration and Senior Associate Dean at the Darden Graduate School of Business Administration, University of Virginia, USA.

SHAPING ENTREPRENEURSHIP RESEARCH

Made, as Well as Found

Edited by *Saras D. Sarasvathy, Nicholas Dew and Sankaran Venkataraman*

LONDON AND NEW YORK

First published 2020
by Routledge
2 Park Square, Milton Park, Abingdon, Oxon OX14 4RN

and by Routledge
52 Vanderbilt Avenue, New York, NY 10017

Routledge is an imprint of the Taylor & Francis Group, an informa business

© 2020 Saras D. Sarasvathy, Nicholas Dew and Sankaran Venkataraman;
individual chapters, the contributors

The right of Saras D. Sarasvathy, Nicholas Dew and Sankaran Venkataraman
to be identified as the authors of the editorial material, and of the authors
for their individual chapters, has been asserted in accordance with sections
77 and 78 of the Copyright, Designs and Patents Act 1988.

All rights reserved. No part of this book may be reprinted or reproduced or
utilized in any form or by any electronic, mechanical, or other means, now
known or hereafter invented, including photocopying and recording, or in
any information storage or retrieval system, without permission in writing
from the publishers.

Trademark notice: Product or corporate names may be trademarks or
registered trademarks, and are used only for identification and explanation
without intent to infringe.

British Library Cataloguing-in-Publication Data
A catalogue record for this book is available from the British Library

Library of Congress Cataloging-in-Publication Data
A catalog record has been requested for this book

ISBN: 978-1-138-06198-9 (hbk)
ISBN: 978-1-138-06199-6 (pbk)
ISBN: 978-1-315-16192-1 (ebk)

Typeset in Bembo
by Wearset Ltd, Boldon, Tyne and Wear

CONTENTS

Preface	*viii*
A short primer on engaging with this book	*xii*

PART I
Motivation: a pluralistic approach to entrepreneurship
research   **1**

1   Understanding the natural and the artificial worlds   17
    H. A. Simon

2   Three varieties of knowledge   35
    D. Davidson

3   The market as a creative process   47
    J. M. Buchanan and V. J. Vanberg

PART II
Maker: entrepreneurial agency   **65**

4   The embodied mind   80
    G. Lakoff and M. Johnson

5   The construction of preference   104
    P. Slovic

vi Contents

6 The technology of foolishness 120
J. March

7 Great men, great thoughts, and the environment 131
W. James

PART III
Making: entrepreneurial process **151**

8 Words, works, worlds 172
N. Goodman

9 Competition as a discovery procedure 185
F. A. Hayek

10 The transactional self 194
J. Bruner

11 The spandrels of San Marco and the Panglossian paradigm:
a critique of the adaptationist programme 204
S. J. Gould and R. C. Lewontin

12 The Coasian and Knightian theories of the firm 222
D. J. Boudreaux and R. G. Holcombe

PART IV
Made: entrepreneurial outcomes **237**

13 The state of humanity: introduction 254
J. L. Simon

14 From the past to the future 280
J. L. Simon

15 The possibility of social choice 298
A. Sen

16 The mystery of capital: by way of conclusion 340
H. De Soto

Contents **vii**

17 Beyond markets and states: polycentric governance of complex
economic systems 353
E. Ostrom

18 Social attitudes, entrepreneurship, and economic development 393
A. Gerschenkron

PART V
**Method: studying entrepreneurship as a three-legged
artifact** **409**

19 Economics as a historical science 429
H. A. Simon

20 The art and science of cause and effect 446
J. Pearl

21 Conceptual metaphor in everyday language 475
G. Lakoff and M. Johnson

22 Contingency, irony, and solidarity 505
R. Rorty

23 What pragmatism means 521
W. James

24 Conclusion: the creative powers of a free civilization 534
F. A. Hayek

Bibliography *550*
Index *552*

PREFACE

This book started as a conversation among the authors. That conversation eventually turned into a reading seminar, of sorts. Each of us had been working on the themes in this book for over a decade at least. In grappling with those themes, each of us had come to the readings in this book sometimes on our own and sometimes in conversation with each other and at other times through conversations with others. Those conversations gelled into the idea of developing a book composed of a set of readings that would support a PhD seminar. If we could design and teach a doctoral seminar focused on a worldview in which the future is open-ended and somewhat shapeable through human action – i.e. "made" – then how would we, as scholars, approach the study of such a world?

That task focused us on selecting a particular set of readings that we then began to think and talk together about in some depth. We also began to realize that most doctoral seminars are taught by individual faculty, and the temptation of all of us is to focus on what we already know and are expert in. By contrast we were reading and talking and thinking – sometimes individually and alone and sometimes in conversation with each other or others – about what we did not know but needed to grasp intellectually. As we began writing together about our thoughts and conversations, we realized that some young entrepreneurship scholars might be interested in the same thing we were interested in. This led to the notion that we could try to design and teach an "open-ended" doctoral seminar to explore the notion of the "made" through a selection of foundational readings that were the most useful in our own struggles.

One of us then began to take the readings "out on the road" to short intense one-week research seminars taught in several different countries. What you see in this book incorporates insights from teaching those seminars and the conversations that ensued in and out of those classrooms. One of the most important insights had to do with students' repeatedly asking a rather simple yet surprising question: *How* do you read such dense material? Unsaid behind that was the question, *Why* do we need to read such dense materials? We will tackle the first question in the primer section after this preface. Here let us examine the latter question from two different perspectives.

From the perspective of a young scholar with limited or no access to research infrastructure

Access to education is growing very fast and becoming a pressing problem in the world. On the one hand, literacy rates are increasing in most parts of the world, as are school enrolment rates and mean years of schooling. Yet, on the other hand, access to education is becoming a more pressing problem partly because of increasing income inequality and partly because of the dramatic increase in the number of school-age children − a result of declining child mortality rates. In other words, good news on the health front and good news in education data combine to increase the need and desire for more and better quality education. New technology has also contributed to this issue. The widespread use of mobile phones has brought an increased awareness of what's possible through education as well as the desire to learn and know more.

Everywhere in the world, educators are even more keenly aware of the need for and possibilities of research. The desire to participate in deeper conversations such as those available in doctoral seminars in the U.S. and Europe is palpable. This desire is visible in the popularity of TED talks, online courses, conferences and workshops in even the remotest parts of the globe. Concurrent with these desires to engage with more sophisticated tools and products of research is an insatiable demand to educate growing populations on the basics of every discipline and topic imaginable. We therefore concluded that a book such as the one we have written might be welcome and (hopefully) useful and hence appreciated. Our own engagement with educators and scholars in several different countries around the world provided some direct evidence of this as well.

From the perspective of a young scholar *with* access to research infrastructure

Social science research programs are more-or-less designed to train young scholars in empirical research skills that will contribute to their career prospects. These programs may spend less time helping young scholars think through the history of ideas with a view to connecting their own work to that history. As a result, opportunities to grapple with material of the sort contained in the readings here may not be as plentiful as classes on the latest statistical techniques. At Darden, where two of us have worked for a long time and the third is an alumnus of, we strive to provide opportunities for students to engage in complex texts from the history of ideas. For us, this is a matter of intellectual rigor as well as a matter of taste.

If you are a young scholar with less access to the kind of reading seminar materials that we present in this book, this book could be a way for you to listen in on a

x Preface

different kind of conversation and "taste" a different menu of ideas to see if you enjoy it. And hopefully to participate in this conversation through aspects of your own writing and teaching in the future.

For scholars of entrepreneurship

If you are already a scholar of entrepreneurship this book offers an alternative set of foundational readings for doing research in new and rising streams within the entrepreneurship discipline that views the world as being in-the-making and therefore makeable through human action (Alvarez & Barney, 2007; McMullen & Shepherd, 2006; Venkataraman et al., 2012). As Townsend et al. (2018) show in a recent *Annals* article, these streams of research embrace uncertainty (multiple multi-dimensional uncertainties to be more precise) as being at the core of entrepreneurial phenomena. In this book we also embrace entrepreneurship as a method of acting in the face of such uncertainties. And we seek to contribute to these streams some scaffolding of thinking from the history of ideas.

By "history of ideas" we mean the unbroken courses of large ideas that have not only explained but also shaped human experience since the beginning of recorded history. Ideas such as gravity and God, genetics and choice, evolution and free will, market and government. Even the idea of entrepreneurship itself, whether we trace that back to the coining of the term by Richard Cantillon or to the ancient Chinese concept of Dao that points to the possibility of transformation in everything in life.

The readings we have selected may come across as "dense" but only because the authors of each have spent decades, if not their entire lives, working on particular phenomena or viewpoints. Therefore, they present their ideas with clarity and eloquence yet without oversimplifications that would take away from the nuances of their topic. The joy of reading and building on these pieces is akin to the joy of listening to complex but clear melodies from classical music such as Pachelbel's canon or Niyamat Khan's Dhrupad gharana. Both branches of classical music require effortful cultivation and practice in listening, yet that investment leads to a deeper enjoyment of all kinds of music, including more popular varieties – even advertising jingles that inescapably – if unintentionally – build on classics. These kinds of developed tastes are not matters of elitism. Instead we think they foster humility without which it would be easy to jump too fast to unwarranted conclusions and reinvent wheels, as opposed to painstakingly building on prior works. The humility to grapple with the depths of foundational work allows us, in turn, to develop contributions that push forward productive possibilities for enhancing human experience and well-being. Many of us working in academia are ultimately funded through taxpayer money on the premise that we will contribute to this larger, cumulative intellectual enterprise that also has practical benefits to society. This book is an attempt to lay down some sod for such contributions in the field of entrepreneurship.

We have already mentioned that recent work in entrepreneurship has begun taking uncertainty more seriously. This dalliance with complex, multiple, multi-faceted uncertainties facing entrepreneurs and their stakeholders has led to some interesting debates in the literature about the nature of entrepreneurial phenomena such as opportunities. In this book we do not weigh in on whether opportunities are "out there" to be discovered or whether they are "created" through subjective perceptions, imagination and ideas. We chose the notions of made and found instead of discovery and creation because in this book we wish to consciously sidestep issues of ontology and epistemology. Discovery conjures up systematic processes of hypotheses testing that may lead to an (over)emphasis on the objective. Creation privileges subjectivism and social construction in ways that may serve to obscure, rather than clarify, the worldview we wish to expose through the readings in this book. However, we look forward to future conversations about overlaps or conflicts between the ideas exposed here and the ones that we have temporarily sidestepped.

All in all, we have enjoyed working on this book but we have enjoyed our conversations even more. If the book reads like there could be more, that the conversation is not quite finished and a closing chapter is yet to be written, we would simply agree. For we would argue that this is appropriate, that for this book it should be so. Future chapters are for *you* to write. It is up to you to continue the conversation as you "make" your own intellectual future. And ours.

Welcome!

References

Alvarez, S. A., & Barney, J. B. (2007). Discovery and creation: Alternative theories of entrepreneurial action. *Strategic Entrepreneurship Journal*, *1*(1–2), 11–26.

McMullen, J. S., & Shepherd, D. A. (2006). Entrepreneurial action and the role of uncertainty in the theory of the entrepreneur. *Academy of Management Review*, *31*(1), 132–152.

Townsend, D. M., Hunt, R. A., McMullen, J. S., & Sarasvathy, S. D. (2018). Uncertainty, knowledge problems, and entrepreneurial action. *Academy of Management Annals*, *12*(2), 659–687.

Venkataraman, S., Sarasvathy, S. D., Dew, N., & Forster, W. R. (2012). Reflections on the 2010 AMR decade award: Whither the promise? Moving forward with entrepreneurship as a science of the artificial. *Academy of Management Review*, *37*(1), 21–33.

A SHORT PRIMER ON ENGAGING WITH THIS BOOK

For those of you who are coming to this book as seasoned scholars, you have already developed a successful approach to reading, writing and engaging in a disciplined research conversation in the field of entrepreneurship. For those of you who are coming to this book as young scholars, we thought it might be helpful to briefly share some thoughts about how to engage with the material in this book so that you might get the best possible outcomes from your investment in it.

How to read this book

The readings in this book are classics that are often dense and can be difficult to comprehend. Therefore, it behooves the reader to develop reading strategies that get the best out of challenging material. Sometimes a scholar might commit to dwelling in particular materials and therefore simply read them from beginning to end. This may be the right approach when it is important to understand the whole idea. But scholars do not necessarily read from word one to the last word. An alternative strategy is to examine a chapter "inside out" rather than beginning to end. You might want to quickly scan a reading in two or three different ways in order to establish a mental map of the reading. You might read the opening and closing paragraphs or abstract and conclusions, and browse the flow of the material indicated by headings and subheadings. You might select particular sections of the material to examine in depth: the first section or sometimes even a particular section in the middle of a reading or portions of text around an important figure or table, and so on. Sometimes it may be helpful to replicate the argument of a chapter for yourself by constructing your own arguments and figuring through the logical flow of the material. If you have the time, you might then choose to read more sections more carefully or to invest in reading a piece from beginning to end.

A short primer on engaging with this book **xiii**

Whatever your reading strategy is for the material, every classic merits being read with at least three different purposes in mind:

- First, read from the point of view of the author(s) with the purpose of simply trying to understand what they are saying, on their own terms. Give them every opportunity to convince you – perhaps even seduce you – into accepting their argument.
- Second, read critically. The purpose of this way of reading is to break down the arguments made in a piece and think about how you would argue against them. It may be useful to test an argument with compelling examples, to closely examine its weakest assumptions, or to build persuasive, carefully thought-through counter-arguments.
- Third, read with constructive appreciation. Develop your own version of the piece by keeping what's useful upon which you can build a better set of arguments that push beyond the original text.

The structure of readings seminars

The entire philosophy behind this book is that scholarly research is a disciplined conversation between peers. Sometimes the conversation takes the written form of journal articles and books, sometimes it consists of conference presentations and classroom lectures or case studies and policy discussions, but all of these are conversations. Some of these conversations have been going on for many years – indeed, the readings in this book sometimes initiated them or were major contributions to them. New recruits to a particular conversation have to walk in the door, join in, engage and eventually shape and move these conversations in interesting new directions. However, since the conversation is between seasoned scholars who have typically devoted many years of their lives to developing the main threads of a conversation, new recruits need to learn how to engage in the conversation in bold yet acutely disciplined ways.

Reading seminars are a classic, structured method for introducing young scholars into particular research conversations. Seminars are built around three types of engagement: concurrent reading, writing and discussions. Therefore, to get the best experience out of seminars, young scholars need a writing strategy as well as a reading strategy for the materials. Regardless of the specific material, the three ways of reading described above may be reflected in three ways of writing, as follows:

1 The first reading approach translates into writing a faithful summary;
2 The second results in writing a respectful yet ruthless critique;
3 The third builds on the author's work and attempts to move the conversation beyond it. This approach may offer an alternative argument, i.e. be fundamentally critical; or it might offer ways to test the author's arguments, or apply it to new settings/phenomena, or otherwise add to it in an organic way.

xiv A short primer on engaging with this book

Note that while #1 above may be a necessary part of comprehending challenging material, what is even more beneficial is critical reflection or building efforts or a combination of them. Whichever writing strategy you take, it is important to bear in mind that reading, writing and discussing occur concurrently and often are not neatly organized. Furthermore, for many of us, writing is experimental and takes a lot of effort and practice to do well enough to be part of a disciplined conversation.

This brings us to a final point regarding how to engage in a disciplined conversation in a readings seminar. To engage in a discussion with others about the materials in this book, it may be helpful to prepare several questions or points you wish to debate with others. Generally speaking, these fall into a few natural categories: (a) clarification questions, namely things you did not understand or were struggling with in a reading; (b) things you understood exceptionally well given your particular background and competences; (c) things you think would really contribute to a discussion in a substantial way; and (d) anything and everything else that comes to mind. Preparing for how you want to engage in a discussion about the readings typically occurs concurrently with the process of reading and writing.

The consequences of making

A final word about engaging with the classics from the history of ideas that we chose to be part of this book. The immediate objective of this book – to support a readings seminar about the "made" worldview – is ultimately in support of the larger goal of encouraging new contributions to rising research streams that are already propelling the field of entrepreneurship forward, and even to help underpin the development of new research streams in the field. Yet despite this grander purpose, there is also an utterly selfish reason for engaging with these materials that we experience every time we go back and revisit them: they also remake you. To engage with them is to engage in a personal odyssey of making and remaking how you experience being in the world. And therefore, even if every other reason for engaging with these readings turns out to be downright worthless, every reader should feel very confident about the personal value of spending time with these classics.

PART I

Motivation

A pluralistic approach to entrepreneurship research

> *Is the game Siva plays one of skill or of chance? There are excellent reasons to renounce this formulation. Where Wittgenstein has argued that any true question must be capable of being answered, we would be tempted to invert the order: Most answers preexist in, or are predetermined by, the question's frame.*
>
> Don Handelman and David Shulman in God Inside Out:
> Siva's Game of Dice (1997: 198)

We are inspired to put together this book of readings by the desire to formulate new questions in entrepreneurship research and to frame the conversation differently. In particular, we hope to carry the discussion beyond worlds found to worlds *made* as well as found.

Like any area of scholarship driven by variance studies seeking to come to grips with a monistic reality, dichotomous formulations of questions abound in our field:

- Do opportunities exist "out there" in the world, or only in the perceptions of entrepreneurs?
- Is the entrepreneur Schumpeterian (one who creates disequilibrium) or is she Kirznerian (spots disequilibria and brings the economy back to equilibrium)?
- Are entrepreneurs risk-loving or risk-averse?
- Is the entrepreneur high in self-efficacy or merely overconfident?
- Are entrepreneurs born or made through their circumstances?
- Is entrepreneurship an independent force for change in the world or is it largely a product of institutional constraints and incentives?
- Is the entrepreneurial process goal-driven or means-driven?
- Is entrepreneurship a game of skill or of chance?

It is easy to insist entrepreneurship is all of the above. Or to rest in the evasive "it all depends". We strive in a more optimistic spirit of pluralism that does not sidestep

2 Motivation

the necessity to discriminate between better and worse formulations. And we seek to embrace contingency in ways that harden, not soften the precision and hence usefulness of our frames. We seek to embrace theoretical pluralism while eschewing naïve relativism. And we wish to investigate contingent phenomena without compromising useful generalizations.

Fortunately for our purpose, we find ample help in the history of ideas and in ongoing work in a variety of areas currently somewhat outside the line of sight of most entrepreneurship research. In particular, we use three seminal pieces that offer us the materials from which to make the worldview we wish to explore in this book. Each of these in itself advocates against three different classical dichotomies that underlie current theorizing. Buchanan and Vanberg (1991) show us how to move beyond the dichotomous role of the market either as an allocative process or as a discovery process and illuminates the value of formulating it as a creative process. Simon (1988) opens up the sciences of the artificial so we can escape the futile debate that pits the natural against the social sciences. And Davidson (2001) takes on the mother of all dichotomies – the subjective as opposed to the objective nature of knowledge – and exposes the inescapable tripod of subjective-intersubjective-objective that constitutes all of epistemology.

Of worlds found and made

While working as a management consultant in Washington, D.C., Jennifer Lovitt Riggs was sent to the Pentagon to brief a top-ranking defense official. As she walked across the parking lot in her beautiful high-heeled shoes, she developed a blister …

A short time later, Riggs started Nota Bene Shoes:

> Nota Bene is the only line of women's dress shoes that from the very first sketch combines smart design, high style, quality construction, and superior materials, to create a distinctive shoe – one that is not only beautiful, but also feels good enough to walk in all day. In short, *Nota Bene is beauty designed for motion.*
>
> *(Sarasvathy et al., 2007)*

Riggs claims she never wanted to be an entrepreneur. She just wanted beautiful shoes that were really comfortable. She could not find them on the market. So she decided to make them. In making the shoes of her dreams, she also remade herself into an entrepreneur.

This simple story contains several puzzles of particular interest to the entrepreneurship researcher. These puzzles can be examined using the two lenses of worlds found and made. If we assume opportunities, products and markets exist *in potentio* in a universe of all possible ventures, we would be led to organize the puzzles in a different way than if we approached new ventures as made *de novo* through the actions of entrepreneurs and their stakeholders. A large portion of current research assumes the former. The overall approach based on this assumption is embodied in themes such as the following:

- Riggs "recognized" the opportunity – that is, the potential market for beautiful, comfortable shoes. *Research question: How do entrepreneurs recognize opportunities?*
- Related puzzle: Why did the thousands of other suffering women before and after Riggs not recognize this opportunity? New theme: There was something in Riggs that made her one of the very few people capable of recognizing the opportunity. *New research question: What traits and abilities distinguish the successful entrepreneur and/or effective opportunity recognition?*
- Related puzzle: If there was something special about Riggs's abilities in terms of opportunity recognition, why was Nota Bene her first venture – why had she not discovered other opportunities and acted on them? New theme: A peculiar combination of circumstances along with Riggs' natural and idiosyncratic proclivities led to the discovery of the opportunity. *New research question: What necessary conditions lead to the discovery and successful exploitation of valuable opportunities?*

There is another way to approach the phenomenon. And that is to assume that Riggs' actions *created* the opportunity. Or more precisely, Riggs' actions included interactions with others who helped *co-create* the opportunity. This approach brings to light some new themes:

- Riggs acted to change her situation. *New research question: What experiences, actions, interactions and reactions lead to the development of new opportunities, ventures and markets?*
- Related puzzle: Not all actions lead to the development of new ventures. Possible responses to Riggs' situation include (a) passive adaptation (continue to suffer, or change jobs, or wear sensible shoes); (b) individual creativity (make new shoes for herself alone); (c) social movement (organize women to get new dress codes adopted in the workplace), and so on. New theme: Riggs acted *entrepreneurially* – that is, she fabricated a business model to produce and sell the shoes she designed. *New research questions: How does one act entrepreneurially? What are the antecedents and consequences of acting entrepreneurially?*
- Related puzzle: It is not enough for Riggs to make the shoes; other people have to buy them; other people have to help make them as well. New theme: Riggs not only made shoes, but also made a market for her shoes. *New research question: How does entrepreneurial action create new markets?*

Seeing the world of entrepreneurship as "made" not only allows us to ask new questions and bring additional perspectives to bear on the "found" universe, it also prompts us toward new ways of *doing* research. Rather than seeking necessary (but often insufficient) explanations as in the "found" world view, the task of research is expanded to include cases where only sufficient (even if unnecessary) explanations

4 Motivation

can be found. That Riggs actually made the shoes with the help of an adequate number of people who were willing to pay a sufficient price and invest enough with her in kind or in cash to enable her to continue making them is sufficient to explain Nota Bene Shoes. It could be argued that there is nothing "inevitable" or "necessary" about the creation of either the venture or even the market niche.

It is customary to argue that entrepreneurship is valuable because it creates jobs in the economy, positive returns for investors and increases GDP over time. Entrepreneurship research therefore is justified as an endeavor that seeks to identify the necessary conditions, such as technology and infrastructure development, for the sustenance and growth of productive entrepreneurship. Individual entrepreneurs can then be taught what they should and should not do to discover and exploit opportunities available to them and policy makers can enact the necessary conditions for the genesis of those opportunities. In terms of policy, the "made" world view instead allows us to rest on the minimal sufficient conditions for the creation of valuable opportunities, such as the freedoms and capabilities that enable human action in general and the removal of obstacles to entrepreneurial action in particular (Kukathas, 2003; Sen, 1999). Technologies, infrastructure and even institutions then become endogenous to the entrepreneurial process – that is, they are *made* by people acting entrepreneurially. Entrepreneurship research, in this view, is not only about discovering opportunities created by exogenous macrolevel factors. It also seeks to find good design principles and criteria for the fabrication of valuable opportunities at all levels – micro, meso and macro, including opportunities in public, social and every other imaginable sector in the economy – assuming nothing as given except basic freedoms and capabilities.

The collection of readings in this book have been chosen to help shape entrepreneurship research as an endeavor to study the making, as well as the finding of, valuable new opportunities, ventures and markets. In other words, they are meant to help us reframe entrepreneurship as a science of the artificial (Simon, 1988) rather than as a natural or social science. A science of the artificial is a science of design and fabrication. It takes natural laws (and perhaps certain structures of the social environment) as constraints but rejects the notion that that these determine our designs. It posits an open-ended universe for the making of human artifacts even if large swathes of Nature and society are not within the control of the humans making them.

To study entrepreneurship as a science of the artificial, we not only need to re-think our questions and methods, but also the philosophical foundations on which these rest. If natural laws and social conditions do not entirely determine the design of entrepreneurial opportunities and ventures, what would form the epistemological basis for entrepreneurial action? Davidson's *Three Varieties of Knowledge* provides the beginning of a powerful new synthesis that ties together the philosophy of American Pragmatism with what we have learned so far about the mind from biology, neuro- and cognitive sciences. Whereas the natural sciences have traditionally taken the "objective" nature of the universe as unquestionable fact, the social sciences seriously question this premise. Postmodern social constructionism continues to gain ground in all the social sciences (Pinch & Bijker, 1984; Goldman, 1999; Zajac & Westphal, 2004; Moore, 2006) and actively seeks to permanently retire the dream of an objective social science to the annals of history and even mythology. Davidson takes on the "myth of the subjective" instead and makes a compelling argument for embracing the inextricable tripod of the subjective, inter-subjective and objective nature of all human knowledge. This is relevant and useful for our purposes – for, as we will see through some of the foundational readings in this book, the maker of human artifacts *makes* his wares by acting upon the world and interacting with other makers, remaking himself in the process.

One of the economic consequences of such three-way making and remaking is a radical rearrangement of the role of the market in human affairs – both in practice and in theory. By recasting the market as a creative (rather than an allocative or discovery) process, Buchanan and Vanberg (1991) opens up new pathways to integrate an artifactual science of entrepreneurship with the macroeconomics of freedom, creativity and social choice.

Before we examine each of these three readings in greater detail, it may be useful to reiterate the reflexive relationship between made and found worlds. The materials for the new making are found in the actual world as it exists at the moment each making begins. And what is made today provides the materials found for tomorrow's making. Yet what we deem makeable and worth making and what we take as found and not makeable or transformable makes a real difference both in the world we live in and the questions we ask as scholars of entrepreneurship. In this regard, a brief examination of what we mean by "entrepreneurship" might be worthwhile.

On not defining entrepreneurship

"What is entrepreneurship, really?" is not a meaningful question for the pluralist. Nor do we believe it is necessary for everyone interested in entrepreneurship to agree upon a single definition. All that is necessary is for each scholar in each individual study to precisely explain what exactly he or she is aiming to understand and then operationalize key issues in measures that matter for the purpose of the particular study and with an eye to relate and cumulate results into a coherent body of ongoing research.

For example, entrepreneurship scholars have long argued for a view of entrepreneurship as a driver of innovation. Inspired by Schumpeter's conceptualization of "creative destruction" entrepreneurs are seen as disruptors. This also led to the distinction between opportunity entrepreneurship versus necessity entrepreneurship. More recently, a few scholars began contemplating the notion of the "ordinary" entrepreneur. One could argue then that the definition of entrepreneurship is murky and that the field is fragmented. Yet, when we examine the coherent streams of research emerging from each of these definitions, we can see how each adds texture and nuance to our understanding of entrepreneurship as a whole.

6 Motivation

We believe that scholars can gather around different fires in different rooms even as they seek to build a common roof on shared real estate. In other words, some scholars will gather around the notion of small business; others might be interested in firm formation; yet others in founding processes or founder characteristics; some will converge upon regional economic development and others will seek social and public enterprises or private opportunities and corporate spinoffs. So long as there exist communities of scholars who seek conversation and companionship on shared journeys and are willing to actively build upon each others' work, their provisional agreement on certain measures and ways of characterizing the phenomena they are interested in is sufficient to make real intellectual progress feasible.

For those who argue that we need to agree upon a single definition for all times and places, we merely point out the fact that biologists do not seek to agree upon a single definition of life before they study it in a variety of extraordinarily productive communities such as those of zoologists, paleontologists, molecular biologists, neuroscientists and evolutionists. Physicists, similarly, cannot all agree upon a definition for mass, nor do economists have a single definition of the market. Yet each of these variously-defined concepts – life, mass, market – is central to centuries of scientific coherence into useful fields of study that are intellectually exciting and socially valuable. Entrepreneurship, too, is a central concept that inspires, provokes and sustains a widening group of scholars wanting to tackle important issues impacting the world we live and work in (Shepherd, 2015).

We are of the view that entrepreneurship is a large beast – a phenomenon of considerable depth and possibility that merits the attention of a diverse set of scholars trained in a variety of disciplines. As Swedberg (2000) showed, virtually every social science has something valuable to bring to entrepreneurship. We would only add to that that entrepreneurship can offer valuable insights and new challenges to the various sciences that seek to understand it. Currently entrepreneurship scholars turn to psychology, sociology or economics for tools to tackles its problems. More recently, historians, anthropologists, philosophers and ethicists have also begun paying attention. With such a plethora of spotlights shining on the subject, it might be time for us to think through ways to highlight overlaps and distinctions and begin building integrated perspectives that make sense of our various understandings.

The three readings that motivate this book each provide ways of putting the pieces together into meaningful wholes. We will discuss each in turn next.

Simon: the sciences of the artificial

In the very first chapter of the book, Simon begins with characteristically simple statements that help define his subject.

> A natural science is a body of knowledge about some class of things – objects or phenomena – in the world: about the characteristics and properties that they have; about how they behave and interact with each other.
>
> *(1988: 3)*[1]

Motivation **7**

A science of the artificial studies

> … objects and phenomena in which human purpose as well as natural law are embodied.
>
> *(1988: 6)*

Therefore, an airplane would be a legitimate object of interest to a science of the artificial while a bird may not, unless the bird served specific human purposes such as pigeons bred for carrying messages. Note here that the interest is in *human* artifacts. It is for this reason that a field such as myrmecology (the study of ants) is not an artifactual science, even though ants build artifacts, namely, ant heaps. Moreover, the relationship between purpose and artifact goes both ways:

> As man's aims change, so too do his artifacts – and vice versa.
>
> *(1988: 6)*

In terms of entrepreneurship, the founder's motivations influence the kind of firm she builds, but the very process of building the firm often changes her motivations and goals. This reflexive relationship is carried forward to the environment in which the artifact operates – in building a firm, the entrepreneur may also transform markets and fabricate parts of the macroenvironment in which the new venture seeks to survive and grow. More generally, human beings not only construct artifacts that are well adapted to the environment within which they seek to fulfill their purposes, but their environment may be reconstituted and constructed through their artifice:

> The world we live in today is much more a man-made, or artificial, world than it is a natural world.
>
> *(1988: 4–5)*

Simon's artifact, then, lies on the interface between inner and outer environments:

> We can view the matter quite symmetrically. An artifact can be thought of as a meeting point – an "interface" in today's terms – between the "inner" environment, the substance and organization of the artifact itself, and an "outer" environment, the surroundings in which it operates.
>
> *(1988: 9)*

In the first extract we have selected for this book, Simon elaborates upon several advantages of factoring the artifact into its inner and outer environments, not the least of which has to do with the relationship between artifacts and natural laws. Throughout *The Sciences of the Artificial*, Simon repeatedly emphasized that *natural laws constrain, but do not dictate*, the fabrication of artifacts. That is, it is possible to *design* artifacts.

This seemingly innocuous statement is in fact utterly audacious. It suggests that a phenomenon like new venture creation can be studied on its own – beyond the

8 Motivation

sciences that govern the inner and outer environments that it forms the interface of. In other words, if we factor the founding of a firm into the motivations and psychological characteristics of its founders on the one hand, and the institutional and cultural characteristics of the society they live in on the other, we need not be limited to psychology and sociology or economics to study it. We can study new venture creation as a process of design that matches up psychology with sociology or economics, and even transforms relevant elements in each of these sciences. Let us briefly consider a few examples that clarify this claim.

A psychological approach to studying entrepreneurship may consist in identifying certain key characteristics of the successful entrepreneur, such as high need for autonomy or high self-efficacy. An artifactual science of entrepreneurship would ask instead: What kinds of firms could, should and would entrepreneurs with specific levels of need for autonomy or self-efficacy start? And how would these new ventures affect/change the economic and social climate of such an entrepreneurial community? Instead of asking whether optimism or pessimism leads to the better invention, an artifactual science points to the relevance and consequence of the fact that the optimist builds the airplane and the pessimist fabricates the parachute. And examines under what conditions the very act of invention reshapes the inventors' risk propensities as well as the dominant ethos of the culture they live in. Similarly, if social network theory suggests that entrepreneurs with larger structural holes (or more number of holes) in their networks are more likely to build enduring ventures, an artifactual science of entrepreneurship might then seek to develop principles and tactics for the entrepreneur to transform his or her given network into those that contain structural holes (Burt, 2009).

It would even posit that structural holes can be made, not only found. In sciences of the artificial, there are continual endeavors to transform natural phenomena and even social phenomena into grist for the artifactual mill. In one sense it could be argued that the history of humanity has been the history of bringing more and more phenomena within human control so much so that the human itself is beginning to be amenable to artifactual design through genetics, epigenetics, neuroscience and yes, artificial intelligence. A major and central task of a science of the artificial is to make highlight this trend and make it conscious that we can no longer leave things to chance or evolution. A startling example of this is the state and future of the planet we inhibit.

One way to operationalize this idea is to posit that a science of the artificial seeks to transform state descriptions culled from conceptions and findings in other sciences and through empirical investigations of the phenomenon at hand into process descriptions that can feed back to other disciplines. These process descriptions usually combine the descriptive and the normative, fact and value. To put it another way, sciences of the artificial provide design principles for *building* artifacts using the knowledge gleaned in the natural and social sciences.

In his book, Simon laid out several initial steps toward understanding what it would take to build a science of design including a list of topics that would form its core that he laid out in Chapters 5 and 6. Chapter 6[2] is particularly interesting to those of us studying entrepreneurship because it tackles what Simon calls "the evolving artifact." In this chapter Simon paints on a rather large canvas with broad brushstrokes that outline in vivid color the possibilities offered by sciences of the artificial – that is, studies of the process of design in a human societal setting. The opening lines lay out the ambitious scope of the chapter:

> In Chapter 5 I surveyed some of the modern tools of design that are used by planners and artificers. Even before most of those tools were available to them, ambitious planners often took whole societies and their environments as systems to be refashioned …
>
> As we look back on such design efforts and their implementation, and as we contemplate the tasks of design that are posed in the world today, our feelings are very mixed. We are energized by the great power our technological knowledge bestows on us. We are intimidated by the magnitude of the problems it creates or alerts us to. We are sobered by the very limited success – and sometimes disastrous failure – of past efforts to design on the scale of whole societies. We ask, "If we can go to the Moon, why can't we …?" not expecting an answer, for we know that going to the Moon was a simple task indeed, compared with some others we have set for ourselves, such as creating a humane society or a peaceful world.
>
> *(1988: 160)*

It is possible, particularly in business schools, to construe entrepreneurship very narrowly. Studying it as a science of the artificial allows us and even compels us to broaden the scope of our questions, without avoiding their depth and complexity. Simon emphasizes the feasibility and value of "designing artifacts on a societal scale" (1988: 163) and then rolls up his sleeves to tackle the complexities of such designing:

> Our first topic will be problem representation; our second, ways of accommodating to the inadequacies that can be expected in data; our third, how the nature of the client affects planning; our fourth, limits on the planner's time and attention; and our fifth, the ambiguity and conflict of goals in societal planning. These topics, which can be viewed as a budget of obstacles or alternatively as a budget of planning requirements, will suggest to us some additions to the curriculum in design outlined in the last chapter.
>
> *(1988: 164)*

After discussing these thorny issues in some depth, Simon ends the chapter on a note of optimism about the task ahead of us:

> Our age is one in which people are not reluctant to express their pessimism and anxieties. It is true that humanity is faced with many problems. It always has been but perhaps not always with such keen awareness of them as we

10 Motivation

have today. We might be more optimistic if we recognized that we do not have to solve all of these problems. Our essential task — a big enough one to be sure — is simply to keep open the options for the future or perhaps even to broaden them a bit by creating new variety and new niches. Our grandchildren cannot ask more of us than that we offer to them the same chance for adventures, for the pursuit of new and interesting designs, that we have had.

(1988: 190–191)

Ultimately, a science of the artificial assumes and entails an open-ended universe. The broad themes of an open-ended universe and the ability of human beings to build such a universe and deal with its attendant problems are echoed in all three selected readings that motivate this book. Each of the readings carefully outlines both the reasons for adopting such a world view as well as precise beginnings for our theorizing about how to build such a world and survive and thrive in it.

Davidson: subjective, intersubjective, objective (three varieties of knowledge)

Davidson, like other good philosophers of mind, and unlike Simon, is not easy to read. That is because the topic he takes up is not easy. But his treatment of it is careful, and his writing painstakingly crafted to embody that carefulness. Yet, like Simon, Davidson imbues his subject and its possibilities with a cheerful optimism that bodes well for us. Take the opening paragraph of his essay on the *Three Varieties of Knowledge:*

I know, for the most part, what I think, want, and intend, and what my sensations are. In addition, I know a great deal about the world around me, the locations and sizes and causal properties of the objects in it. I also sometimes know what goes on in other people's minds.

(2001: 205)

He then builds, brick by brick, a compelling edifice of arguments for why these three varieties of knowledge cannot all be unreliable:

It should now be clear what ensures that our view of the world is, in its plainest features, largely correct. The reason is that the stimuli that cause our most basic verbal responses also determine what those verbal responses mean, and the content of the beliefs that accompany them. The nature of interpretation guarantees both that a large number of our simplest perceptual beliefs are true, and that the nature of these beliefs is known to others. Of course many beliefs are given content by their relations to further beliefs, or are caused by misleading sensations; any particular belief or set of beliefs about the world around us may be false. What cannot be the case is that our general picture of the world and our place in it is mistaken, for it is this picture which informs the rest of our beliefs and makes them intelligible, whether they be true or false.

(2001: 213)

The concept of "opportunity" in entrepreneurship research provides fertile ground for the application of Davidson's thesis about the inextricable triple – subjective, intersubjective, objective – that constitutes all of epistemology (Venkataraman et al., 2012).

Venkataraman (1997) and Shane and Venkataraman (2000) made "opportunity" a central concept for entrepreneurship researchers. Their work led entrepreneurship scholars to develop more refined understandings about the nature of opportunities – what they are, how to define them theoretically, how to operationalize and measure them empirically – and so on. In particular, a sophisticated debate has developed in the literature around the ontology of opportunity, one drawing more on North American research traditions that have esteemed a positivist/realist position on opportunities, while the other has drawn more on European research traditions that have favored social constructionist positions (Gartner et al., 2003). The former position has chosen to view opportunities as existing independent of the entrepreneur, while the latter have preferred to scrutinize opportunities as being enacted based on the understandings of the entrepreneur and their stakeholders. Naturally this has also led to controversies about whether opportunities can be created *de novo* or can only be discovered or selected from the universe of opportunities available now.

An opportunity is an epistemological construct – a kind of knowledge about the world. Its ontological status is irrelevant. For, taking Davidson seriously requires taking the existence of the world as given. The social sciences have recently been obsessed by the slippery nature of "reality". Davidson puts that ontological angst to rest with one powerful statement:

Of course all three varieties of knowledge are concerned with aspects of the same reality; where they differ is in the mode of access to reality.

(2001: 205)

The question of opportunity then becomes merely whether a particular type of knowledge about the world, namely an opportunity, can exist and if so, what is it and how does one access it? At the minimum, for an opportunity to exist, it must be experienced by the entrepreneur as an opportunity, verified by others as so, and finally, it has to exist or be brought into actual existence in the world. There is nothing in Davidson that precludes the making as well as finding of knowledge in the world. The only caveat is that the three varieties of knowledge, namely – subjective, intersubjective, objective – cannot exist in isolation from one another.

The story of entrepreneurship, therefore, may begin with any one or more of the three legs of the tripod. The entrepreneur may "find" an opportunity in the world, or may even imagine one entirely subjectively – but in order for it to become an epistemological construct, i.e. a piece of knowledge about the actual

12 Motivation

world – he would have to embody it in such a way that other people also have access to it and experience it as an opportunity. Thus "making" an opportunity is implicit even in "finding" it.

Let's start with the easiest case, and the clearest one in terms of a "found" opportunity – say, finding a hundred dollar bill on the sidewalk. What makes this an opportunity consists in at least three things:

- First, someone has to find it
- Second, that someone has to know it is a hundred dollar bill
- Third, other people have to acknowledge its value as a true (not counterfeit) bill.

If any one of those three conditions does not hold, the opportunity would not in fact be an opportunity. In order for the third condition to hold, the person who found the bill has to pick it up and use the bill in some way – and that involves action and interaction that constitute the atomic units of "making" in the sense in which we have been using the word thus far.

Most entrepreneurial opportunities are, of course, not so simple. They are subject to uncertainties along all three legs of the Davidsonian tripod. Under conditions of uncertainty, the actions and interactions that the entrepreneur has to undertake, including the decision to take action at all, increase in complexity and ambiguity. In other words, most entrepreneurial opportunities in the world have to be *made* through the actions and interactions of stakeholders in the enterprise, using materials and concepts *found* in the world. Opportunities are, in fact, artifacts.

Some of these opportunities may lead to market transactions, profitable ventures and even new markets.[3] Others may lead to failed or aborted ventures. But almost always, entrepreneurial actions and interactions lead to the fabrication of other opportunities. Knowledge of any kind increases the perimeter of the circle of ignorance, bringing to light new questions to be answered and new problems to be solved. Knowledge, in other words, creates opportunities for new knowledge. And entrepreneurial fabrication of opportunities, even when it results in aborted ventures, provides fodder for the fabrication of other opportunities. In *The Sciences of the Artificial,* Simon explains this tendency of an artifactual universe toward open-endedness as follows:

> If there is a trend toward variety, then evolution is not to be understood as a series of tournaments for the occupation of a fixed set of environmental niches, each tournament won by the organism that is fittest for that niche. Instead evolution brings about a proliferation of niches. The environments to which most biological organisms adapt are formed mainly of other organisms, and the environments to which human beings adapt, mainly other human beings. Each new bird or mammal provides a niche for one or more new kind of flea.

(1988: 189)

This fact is even more salient in the realm of entrepreneurial action, especially effectual actions and interactions seeking to design and more consciously cocreate the environment (Sarasvathy, 2001, 2008). Viewed through the lens of artificiality, the subjective-intersubjective-objective tripod of epistemology necessarily drives the ontology of the artifacts we end up making. Furthermore, such artifacts necessarily add up to an open-ended universe or a universe always in-the-making, a universe partly found and mostly made. A market is such a universe. When we view "the" market as a pre-existing natural phenomenon, acting, for example, as a selection mechanism on our puny individual actions that offer mere random churn in a social evolutionary process, we miss noticing the creativity inherent in all market processes. But when we consider the artificiality of markets and the Davidsonian tripod enabling their making, markets become plural and open-ended. Markets are always in-the-making and hence amenable to sciences of the artificial. A strong case for such open-ended creativity of markets is made by Buchanan and Vanberg (1991). As we will see next, they locate this open-endedness directly in entrepreneurial action.

Buchanan and Vanberg: the market as a creative process

The Buchanan and Vanberg (henceforth B&V) article is particularly relevant for developing a "made" view of entrepreneurship because it not only explicates a creative view of the market, but offers an important critique of the "discovery" view of Israel Kirzner that informs much theorizing in entrepreneurship research.

Much of our recent conversation about entrepreneurial opportunities is based on Kirzner's work. Both Shane and Venkataraman's (2000) thesis about entrepreneurs bringing forth new products and services in the absence of current markets for them and Shane's (2003) definition of entrepreneurial opportunities as situations for the creation of new means-end frameworks can be traced to Kirzner's writings (1979, 1997). B&V's criticism of Kirzner is anchored in the inherent unknowability of the future that in turn is rooted in a *nonteleological* perspective on understanding the world. Their arguments build upon Lachmann's (1977: 85) thesis that "*Time and knowledge* belong together", and that "time cannot pass without modifying knowledge" (ibid.: 93):

> Whatever may be said about the knowability of divergences in the cross-sectional interpretation, it should be obvious that the notion of *intertemporal* divergences between markets at different points in time is inherently problematic. If, as we must assume, divergences between today's and tomorrow's markets are typically associated with differences between today's and tomorrow's *knowledge,* what does it mean to say that entrepreneurial alertness corrects the "failure to realize" divergences between *present* and *future* markets? What sense does it make to describe today's failure to possess tomorrow's knowledge as *error*?
>
> *(Buchanan & Vanberg, 1991: 176)*

14 Motivation

When we juxtapose B&V's thesis with Davidson's *Three Varieties of Knowledge* as applied to entrepreneurial opportunities, we see that between today and tomorrow new opportunities get made, new knowledge gets created and even new goals may be forged. In other words, entrepreneurs' artifactual intervention in the world makes foreknowledge of the future particularly futile. Further support for the non-teleological perspective is lent by Simon in the section titled "Designing without final goals":

> The idea of final goals is inconsistent with our limited ability to foretell or determine the future. The real result of our actions is to establish initial conditions for the next succeeding stage of action. What we call "final" goals are in fact criteria for choosing the initial conditions that we will leave to our successors.
>
> *(1988: 187)*

B&V emphasize the non-teleological nature of intertemporal choice and ground in it an unequivocal rejection of a "discovery" view of both entrepreneurship and the market process:

> Entrepreneurial activity, in particular, is not to be modeled as discovery of that which is "out there". Such activity, by contrast, *creates* a reality that will be different subsequent on differing choices. Hence, the reality of the future must be shaped by choices yet to be made, and this reality has no existence independent of these choices.
>
> *(1991: 178)*

They assert on page 180:

> There is, in our view, no systematically sustainable middle ground between a teleological and a nonteleological perspective.
>
> *(1991: 180)*

They then go on to illustrate the nonteleological perspective through the conceptualization of a market as a "game without goods". In contrast to conventional conceptualizations of markets as exchanges facilitating existent goods through the Walrasian auctioneer, a game without goods starts with the assumption

> … that no goods exist and that persons are described by certain talents, capacities, and skills that enable them to produce consumable goods from nature.
>
> *(1991: 181)*

Entrepreneurship may be modeled as such a game in which opportunities are novel epistemological constructs that help transform natural resources and human abilities into consumable goods. In sketching this illustration, B&V further assume that the

Motivation **15**

… rules of the game allow certain enforceable rights to the shares in natural endowments and to their own capacities and skills.

(1991: 181)

Based on some of the readings gleaned in this book, we can furthermore argue that entrepreneurship not only helps fabricate consumable goods from natural resources, but it also helps transform the rules of the game themselves to facilitate such fabrication. In other words, entrepreneurial action need not be limited to economics (Lounsbury et al., 2018). It impinges on and transforms society and history and turns those too into artifacts constituting an open-ended universe.

The found view – i.e. a teleological conception of market economics – suggests that opportunities are markets *in potentio* and the job of entrepreneurs is to find them. Entrepreneurship in this view is akin to an Easter egg hunt. The made view argues instead that what entrepreneurs *do* with what is found in the world, how they combine those raw materials with their own abilities, aspirations and experiences creates opportunities, that when attested to, bought into and co-shaped by others, can, under certain conditions of sufficiency, converge and coalesce into markets. Entrepreneurship, in this view, is akin to making a communal sculpture or co-painting a mural by sufficiently large groups of stakeholders.

How this making can, does and should happen, who makes it happen and the consequences of such making ought to form, in our opinion, the content of entrepreneurship research. The readings in this book have been selected so as to inform our research into the substantive and procedural aspects of this particular science of the artificial.

Notes

1 The page numbering used throughout refers to where the text was in the original version of the referenced publication.
2 Although we are not terribly enamored of the title of the chapter, "Social Planning," we believe much of the discussion is pertinent to developing the sort of entrepreneurship research that could provide the micro-foundations for a variety of macroeconomic and policy concerns that tie together business with social transformation.
3 As Olson (1984) argues, the most profitable opportunities require collective action on rather large scales. They are, in other words, social artifacts.

References

Buchanan, J. M. & Vanberg, V. J. (1991). The market as a creative process. *Economics and Philosophy* **7**: 167–186.

Burt, R. S. (2009). *Structural holes: The social structure of competition*. Cambridge, MA: Harvard University Press.

Davidson, D. (2001). *Subjective, intersubjective, objective*. New York, Oxford University Press Incorporated.

Gartner, W., Carter, N., Hills, G., Steyaert, C. & Hjorth, D. (2003). The language of opportunity. In C. Steyaert & D. Hjorth (Eds.), *New movements in entrepreneurship* (pp. 103–125). Cheltenham, UK: Edward Elgar.

16 Motivation

Goldman, A. I. (1999). *Knowledge in a social world*. Oxford University Press.

Handelman, D. & Shulman, D. D. (1997). *God inside out: *Siva's Game of Dice*. New York, Oxford University Press.

Kirzner, I. (1979). *Perception, opportunity, and profit: Studies in the theory of entrepreneurship*. University of Chicago Press.

Kirzner, I. (1997). Entrepreneurial discovery and the competitive market process: An Austrian approach. *Journal of Economic Literature* **35**: 60–85.

Kukathas, C. (2003). The liberal archipelago: A theory of diversity and freedom. Oxford University Press.

Lachmann, L. M. (1977). *Capital, expectations, and the market process*. Kansas City, Sheed Andrews and McMeel.

Lounsbury, M., Gehman, J., & Glynn, M. A. (2018). Beyond *Homo Entrepreneurus*: Judgment and the theory of cultural entrepreneurship. *Journal of Management Studies* **56**(6): 1214–1236.

Moore, K. (2006). Biology as technology: A social constructionist framework for an evolutionary psychology. *Review of general psychology* **10**(4): 285–301.

Olson, M. (1984). *The rise and decline of nations: Economic growth, stagflation, and social rigidities*. New Haven, CT: Yale University Press.

Pinch, T. J. & Bijker, W. E. (1984). The social construction of facts and artefacts: Or how the sociology of science and the sociology of technology might benefit each other. *Social Studies of Science* **14**(3): 399.

Sarasvathy, S. D. (2001). Causation and effectuation: Toward a theoretical shift from economic inevitability to entrepreneurial contingency. *Academy of Management Review*, **26**(2), 243–263.

Sarasvathy, S. D. (2008). *Effectuation: Elements of entrepreneurial expertise*. Edward Elgar Publishing.

Sarasvathy, S. D., Dew, N., Read, S. & Wiltbank, R. (2007). Empirical investigations of effectual logic: Implications for strategic entrepreneurship. Max Planck Ringberg Conference on Entrepreneurship. Ringberg Castle, Germany, www.effectuation.org.

Sen, A. (1999). The possibility of social choice. American Economic Review, **89**(3): 349–378.

Shane, S. (2003). *A general theory of entrepreneurship: The individual-opportunity nexus*. Northampton, MA: Edward Elgar Publishing Incorporated.

Shane, S. & Venkataraman, S. (2000). The promise of entrepreneurship as a field of research. *Academy of Management Review* **25**(1): 217–227.

Shepherd, D. A. (2015). Party On! A call for entrepreneurship research that is more interactive, activity based, cognitively hot, compassionate, and prosocial. Journal of Business Venturing, **30**(4): 489–507.

Simon, H. A. (1988). *The sciences of the artificial*. Cambridge, MA and London, MIT Press.

Swedberg, R. (Ed.). (2000). *Entrepreneurship: The social science view* (Vol. 1). Oxford University Press.

Venkataraman, S. (1997). The distinctive domain of entrepreneurship research. *Advances in Entrepreneurship, Firm Emergence and Growth* **3**(1): 119–138.

Venkataraman, S., Sarasvathy, S. D., Dew, N., & Forster, W. R. (2012). Reflections on the 2010 AMR decade award: Whither the promise? Moving forward with entrepreneurship as a science of the artificial. Academy of Management Review, **37**(1): 21–33.

Zajac, E. J. & Westphal, J. D. (2004). The social construction of market value: Institutionalization and learning perspectives on stock market reactions. *American Sociological Review* **69**(3): 433–457.

1

UNDERSTANDING THE NATURAL AND THE ARTIFICIAL WORLDS

H. A. Simon

About three centuries after Newton we are thoroughly familiar with the concept of natural science—most unequivocally with physical and biological science. A natural science is a body of knowledge about some class of things—objects or phenomena—in the world: about the characteristics and properties that they have; about how they behave and interact with each other.

The central task of a natural science is to make the wonderful commonplace: to show that complexity, correctly viewed, is only a mask for simplicity; to find pattern hidden in apparent chaos. The early Dutch physicist Simon Stevin, showed by an elegant drawing (Figure 1.1) that the law of the inclined plane follows in

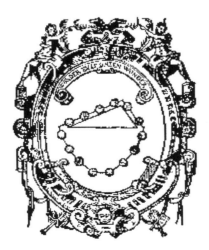

FIGURE 1.1 The vignette devised by Simon Stevin to illustrate his derivation of the law of the inclined plane

18   H. A. Simon

"self-evident fashion" from the impossibility of perpetual motion, for experience and reason tell us that the chain of balls in the figure would rotate neither to right nor to left but would remain at rest. (Since rotation changes nothing in the figure, if the chain moved at all, it would move perpetually.) Since the pendant part of the chain hangs symmetrically, we can snip it off without disturbing the equilibrium. But now the balls on the long side of the plane balance those on the shorter, steeper side, and their relative numbers are in inverse ratio to the sines of the angles at which the planes are inclined.

Stevin was so pleased with his construction that he incorporated it into a vignette, inscribing above it

> *Wonder, en is gheen wonder*
> that is to say: "Wonderful, but not incomprehensible."

This is the task of natural science: to show that the wonderful is not incomprehensible, to show how it can be comprehended—but not to destroy wonder. For when we have explained the wonderful, unmasked the hidden pattern, a new wonder arises at how complexity was woven out of simplicity. The aesthetics of natural science and mathematics is at one with the aesthetics of music and painting —both inhere in the discovery of a partially concealed pattern.

The world we live in today is much more a man-made,[1] or artificial, world than it is a natural world. Almost every element in our environment shows evidence of human artifice. The temperature in which we spend most of our hours is kept artificially at 20 degrees Celsius; the humidity is added to or taken from the air we breathe; and the impurities we inhale are largely produced (and filtered) by man.

Moreover for most of us—the white-collared ones—the significant part of the environment consists mostly of strings of artifacts called "symbols" that we receive through eyes and ears in the form of written and spoken language and that we pour out into the environment—as I am now doing—by mouth or hand. The laws that govern these strings of symbols, the laws that govern the occasions on which we emit and receive them, the determinants of their content are all consequences of our collective artifice.

One may object that I exaggerate the artificiality of our world. Man must obey the law of gravity as surely as does a stone, and as a living organism man must depend for food, and in many other ways, on the world of biological phenomena. I shall plead guilty to overstatement, while protesting that the exaggeration is slight. To say that an astronaut, or even an airplane pilot, is obeying the law of gravity, hence is a perfectly natural phenomenon, is true, but its truth calls for some sophistication in what we mean by "obeying" a natural law. Aristotle did not think it natural for heavy things to rise or light ones to fall (*Physics*, Book IV); but presumably we have a deeper understanding of "natural" than he did.

So too we must be careful about equating "biological" with "natural." A forest may be a phenomenon of nature; a farm certainly is not. The very species upon which we depend for our food—our corn and our cattle—are artifacts of our

The natural and the artificial worlds **19**

ingenuity. A plowed field is no more part of nature than an asphalted street—and no less.

These examples set the terms of our problem, for those things we call artifacts are not apart from nature. They have no dispensation to ignore or violate natural law. At the same time they are adapted to human goals and purposes. They are what they are in order to satisfy our desire to fly or to eat well. As our aims change, so too do our artifacts—and vice versa.

If science is to encompass these objects and phenomena in which human purpose as well as natural law are embodied, it must have means for relating these two disparate components. The character of these means and their implications for certain areas of knowledge—economics, psychology, and design in particular—are the central concern of this book.

The artificial

Natural science is knowledge about natural objects and phenomena. We ask whether there cannot also be "artificial" science—knowledge about artificial objects and phenomena. Unfortunately the term "artificial" has a pejorative air about it that we must dispel before we can proceed.

My dictionary defines "artificial" as, "Produced by art rather than by nature; not genuine or natural; affected; not pertaining to the essence of the matter." It proposes, as synonyms: affected, factitious, manufactured, pretended, sham, simulated, spurious, trumped up, unnatural. As antonyms, it lists: actual, genuine, honest, natural, real, truthful, unaffected. Our language seems to reflect man's deep distrust of his own products. I shall not try to assess the validity of that evaluation or explore its possible psychological roots. But you will have to understand me as using "artificial" in as neutral a sense as possible, as meaning man-made as opposed to natural.[2]

In some contexts we make a distinction between "artificial" and "synthetic." For example, a gem made of glass colored to resemble sapphire would be called artificial, while a man-made gem chemically indistinguishable from sapphire would be called synthetic. A similar distinction is often made between "artificial" and "synthetic" rubber. Thus some artificial things are imitations of things in nature, and the imitation may use either the same basic materials as those in the natural object or quite different materials.

As soon as we introduce "synthesis" as well as "artifice," we enter the realm of engineering. For "synthetic" is often used in the broader sense of "designed" or "composed." We speak of engineering as concerned with "synthesis," while science is concerned with "analysis." Synthetic or artificial objects—and more specifically prospective artificial objects having desired properties—are the central objective of engineering activity and skill. The engineer, and more generally the designer, is concerned with how things *ought* to be—how they ought to be in order to *attain goals*, and to *function*. Hence a science of the artificial will be closely akin to a science of engineering—but very different, as we shall see in my fifth chapter, from what goes currently by the name of "engineering science."

20 H. A. Simon

With goals and "oughts" we also introduce into the picture the dichotomy between normative and descriptive. Natural science has found a way to exclude the normative and to concern itself solely with how things are. Can or should we maintain this exclusion when we move from natural to artificial phenomena, from analysis to synthesis?[3]

We have now identified four indicia that distinguish the artificial from the natural; hence we can set the boundaries for sciences of the artificial:

1 Artificial things are synthesized (though not always or usually with full forethought) by human beings.
2 Artificial things may imitate appearances in natural things while lacking, in one or many respects, the reality of the latter.
3 Artificial things can be characterized in terms of functions, goals, adaptation.
4 Artificial things are often discussed, particularly when they are being designed, in terms of imperatives as well as descriptives.

The environment as mold

Let us look a little more closely at the functional or purposeful aspect of artificial things. Fulfillment of purpose or adaptation to a goal involves a relation among three terms: the purpose or goal, the character of the artifact, and the environment in which the artifact performs. When we think of a clock, for example, in terms of purpose we may use the child's definition: "a clock is to tell time." When we focus our attention on the clock itself, we may describe it in terms of arrangements of gears and the application of the forces of springs or gravity operating on a weight or pendulum.

But we may also consider clocks in relation to the environment in which they are to be used. Sundials perform as clocks *in sunny climates*—they are more useful in Phoenix than in Boston and of no use at all during the Arctic winter. Devising a clock that would tell time on a rolling and pitching ship, with sufficient accuracy to determine longitude, was one of the great adventures of eighteenth-century science and technology. To perform in this difficult environment, the clock had to be endowed with many delicate properties, some of them largely or totally irrelevant to the performance of a landlubber's clock.

Natural science impinges on an artifact through two of the three terms of the relation that characterizes it: the structure of the artifact itself and the environment in which it performs. Whether a clock will in fact tell time depends on its internal construction and where it is placed. Whether a knife will cut depends on the material of its blade and the hardness of the substance to which it is applied.

The artifact as "interface"

We can view the matter quite symmetrically. An artifact can be thought of as a meeting point—an "interface" in today's terms—between an "inner" environment,

The natural and the artificial worlds **21**

the substance and organization of the artifact itself, and an "outer" environment, the surroundings in which it operates. If the inner environment is appropriate to the outer environment, or vice versa, the artifact will serve its intended purpose. Thus, if the clock is immune to buffeting, it will serve as a ship's chronometer. (And conversely, if it isn't, we may salvage it by mounting it on the mantel at home.)

Notice that this way of viewing artifacts applies equally well to many things that are not man-made—to all things in fact that can be regarded as adapted to some situation; and in particular it applies to the living systems that have evolved through the forces of organic evolution. A theory of the airplane draws on natural science for an explanation of its inner environment (the power plant, for example), its outer environment (the character of the atmosphere at different altitudes), and the relation between its inner and outer environments (the movement of an airfoil through a gas). But a theory of the bird can be divided up in exactly the same way.[4]

Given an airplane, or *given* a bird, we can analyze them by the methods of natural science without any particular attention to purpose or adaptation, without reference to the interface between what I have called the inner and outer environments. After all, their behavior is governed by natural law just as fully as the behavior of anything else (or at least we all believe this about the airplane, and most of us believe it about the bird).

Functional explanation

On the other hand, if the division between inner and outer environment is not necessary to the analysis of an airplane or a bird, it turns out at least to be highly convenient. There are several reasons for this, which will become evident from examples.

Many animals in the Arctic have white fur. We usually explain this by saying that white is the best color for the Arctic environment, for white creatures escape detection more easily than do others. This is not of course a natural science explanation; it is an explanation by reference to purpose or function. It simply says that these are the kinds of creatures that will "work," that is, survive, in this kind of environment. To turn the statement into an explanation, we must add to it a notion of natural selection, or some equivalent mechanism.

An important fact about this kind of explanation is that it demands an understanding mainly of the outer environment. Looking at our snowy surroundings, we can predict the predominant color of the creatures we are likely to encounter; we need know little about the biology of the creatures themselves, beyond the facts that they are often mutually hostile, use visual clues to guide their behavior, and are adaptive (through selection or some other mechanism).

Analogous to the role played by natural selection in evolutionary biology is the role played by rationality in the sciences of human behavior. If we know of a business organization only that it is a profit-maximizing system, we can often predict how its behavior will change if we change its environment—how it will alter its prices if a sales tax is levied on its products. We can sometimes make this prediction —and economists do make it repeatedly—without detailed assumptions about the adaptive mechanism, the decision-making apparatus that constitutes the inner environment of the business firm.

Thus the first advantage of dividing outer from inner environment in studying an adaptive or artificial system is that we can often predict behavior from knowledge of the system's goals and its outer environment, with only minimal assumptions about the inner environment. An instant corollary is that we often find quite different inner environments accomplishing identical or similar goals in identical or similar outer environments—airplanes and birds, dolphins and tunafish, weight-driven clocks and battery-driven clocks, electrical relays and transistors.

There is often a corresponding advantage in the division from the standpoint of the inner environment. In very many cases whether a particular system will achieve a particular goal or adaptation depends on only a few characteristics of the outer environment and not at all on the detail of that environment. Biologists are familiar with this property of adaptive systems under the label of homeostasis. It is an important property of most good designs, whether biological or artifactual. In one way or another the designer insulates the inner system from the environment, so that an invariant relation is maintained between inner system and goal, independent of variations over a wide range in most parameters that characterize the outer environment. The ship's chronometer reacts to the pitching of the ship only in the negative sense of maintaining an invariant relation of the hands on its dial to the real time, independently of the ship's motions.

Quasi independence from the outer environment may be maintained by various forms of passive insulation, by reactive negative feedback (the most frequently discussed form of insulation), by predictive adaptation, or by various combinations of these.

Functional description and synthesis

In the best of all possible worlds—at least for a designer—we might even hope to combine the two sets of advantages we have described that derive from factoring an adaptive system into goals, outer environment, and inner environment. We might hope to be able to characterize the main properties of the system and its behavior without elaborating the detail of *either* the outer or inner environments. We might look toward a science of the artificial that would depend on the relative simplicity of the interface as its primary source of abstraction and generality.

Consider the design of a physical device to serve as a counter. If we want the device to be able to count up to one thousand, say, it must be capable of assuming any one of at least a thousand states, of maintaining itself in any given state, and of shifting from any state to the "next" state. There are dozens of different inner environments that might be used (and have been used) for such a device. A wheel notched at each twenty minutes of arc, and with a ratchet device to turn and hold it, would do the trick. So would a string of ten electrical switches properly connected to represent binary numbers. Today instead of switches we are likely to use transistors or other solid-state devices.[5]

The natural and the artificial worlds **23**

Our counter would be activated by some kind of pulse, mechanical or electrical, as appropriate, from the outer environment. But by building an appropriate transducer between the two environments, the physical character of the interior pulse could again be made independent of the physical character of the exterior pulse—the counter could be made to count anything.

Description of an artifice in terms of its organization and functioning—its interface between inner and outer environments—is a major objective of invention and design activity. Engineers will find familiar the language of the following claim quoted from a 1919 patent on an improved motor controller:

> What I claim as new and desire to secure by Letters Patent is:
> 1 In a motor controller, in combination, reversing means, normally effective field-weakening means and means associated with said reversing means for rendering said field-weakening means ineffective during motor starting and thereafter effective to different degrees determinable by the setting of said reversing means ...[6]

Apart from the fact that we know the invention relates to control of an electric motor, there is almost no reference here to specific, concrete objects or phenomena. There is reference rather to "reversing means" and "field-weakening means," whose further purpose is made clear in a paragraph preceding the patent claims:

> The advantages of the special type of motor illustrated and the control thereof will be readily understood by those skilled in the art. Among such advantages may be mentioned the provision of a high starting torque and the provision for quick reversals of the motor.[7]

Now let us suppose that the motor in question is incorporated in a planing machine (see Figure 1.2). The inventor describes its behavior thus:

> Referring now to [Figure 1.2], the controller is illustrated in outline connection with a planer (100) operated by a motor M, the controller being adapted to govern the motor M and to be automatically operated by the reciprocating bed of the planer. The master shaft of the controller is provided with a lever (102) connected by a link (103) to a lever (104) mounted upon the planer frame and projecting into the path of lugs and (106) on the planer bed. As will be understood, the arrangement is such that reverse movements of the planer bed will, through the connections described, throw the master shaft of the controller back and forth between its extreme positions and in consequence effect selective operation of the reversing switches (1) and (2) and automatic operation of the other switches in the manner above set forth.[8]

In this manner the properties with which the inner environment has been endowed are placed at the service of the goals in the context of the outer

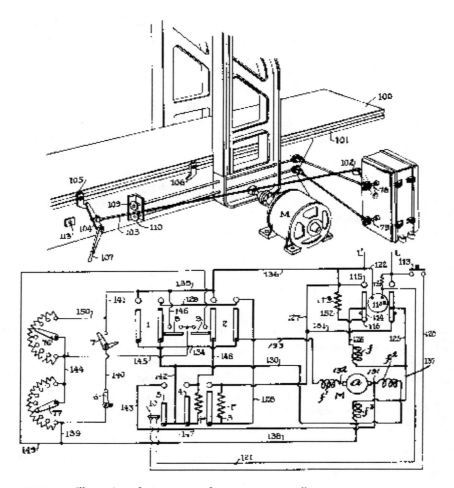

FIGURE 1.2 Illustrations from a patent for a motor controller

environment. The motor will reverse periodically under the control of the position of the planer bed. The "shape" of its behavior—the time path, say, of a variable associated with the motor—will be a function of the "shape" of the external environment—the distance, in this case, between the lugs on the planer bed.

The device we have just described illustrates in microcosm the nature of artifacts. Central to their description are the goals that link the inner to the outer system. The inner system is an organization of natural phenomena capable of attaining the goals in some range of environments, but ordinarily there will be many functionally equivalent natural systems capable of doing this.

The outer environment determines the conditions for goal attainment. If the inner system is properly designed, it will be adapted to the outer environment, so that its behavior will be determined in large part by the behavior of the latter, exactly as in the case of "economic man." To predict how it will behave, we need

The natural and the artificial worlds **25**

only ask, "How would a rationally designed system behave under these circumstances?" The behavior takes on the shape of the task environment.[9]

Limits of adaptation

But matters must be just a little more complicated than this account suggests. "If wishes were horses, all beggars would ride." And if we could always specify a protean inner system that would take on exactly the shape of the task environment, designing would be synonymous with wishing. "Means for scratching diamonds" defines a design objective, an objective that *might* be attained with the use of many different substances. But the design has not been achieved until we have discovered at least one realizable inner system obeying the ordinary natural laws—one material, in this case, hard enough to scratch diamonds.

Often we shall have to be satisfied with meeting the design objectives only approximately. Then the properties of the inner system will "show through." That is, the behavior of the system will only partly respond to the task environment; partly, it will respond to the limiting properties of the inner system.

Thus the motor controls described earlier are aimed at providing for "quick" reversal of the motor. But the motor must obey electromagnetic and mechanical laws, and we could easily confront the system with a task where the environment called for quicker reversal than the motor was capable of. In a benign environment we would learn from the motor only what it had been called upon to do; in a taxing environment we would learn something about its internal structure—specifically about those aspects of the internal structure that were chiefly instrumental in limiting performance.[10]

A bridge, under its usual conditions of service, behaves simply as a relatively smooth level surface on which vehicles can move. Only when it has been overloaded do we learn the physical properties of the materials from which it is built.

Understanding by simulating

Artificiality connotes perceptual similarity but essential difference, resemblance from without rather than within. In the terms of the previous section we may say that the artificial object imitates the real by turning the same face to the outer system, by adapting, relative to the same goals, to comparable ranges of external tasks. Imitation is possible because distinct physical systems can be organized to exhibit nearly identical behavior. The damped spring and the damped circuit obey the same second-order linear differential equation; hence we may use either one to imitate the other.

Techniques of simulation

Because of its abstract character and its symbol manipulating generality, the digital computer has greatly extended the range of systems whose behavior can be imitated.

26 H. A. Simon

Generally we now call the imitation "simulation," and we try to understand the imitated system by testing the simulation in a variety of simulated, or imitated, environments.

Simulation, as a technique for achieving understanding and predicting the behavior of systems, predates of course the digital computer. The model basin and the wind tunnel are valued means for studying the behavior of large systems by modeling them in the small, and it is quite certain that Ohm's law was suggested to its discoverer by its analogy with simple hydraulic phenomena.

Simulation may even take the form of a thought experiment, never actually implemented dynamically. One of my vivid memories of the Great Depression is of a large multicolored chart in my father's study that represented a hydraulic model of an economic system (with different fluids for money and goods). The chart was devised by a technocratically inclined engineer named Dahlberg. The model never got beyond the pen-and-paint stage at that time, but it could be used to trace through the imputed consequences of particular economic measures or events— provided the theory was right![11]

As my formal education in economics progressed, I acquired a disdain for that naive simulation, only to discover after World War II that a distinguished economist, Professor A. W. Phillips had actually built the Moniac, a hydraulic model that simulated a Keynesian economy.[12] Of course Professor Phillips's simulation incorporated a more nearly correct theory than the earlier one and was actually constructed and operated—two points in its favor. However, the Moniac, while useful as a teaching tool, told us nothing that could not be extracted readily from simple mathematical versions of Keynesian theory and was soon priced out of the market by the growing number of computer simulations of the economy.

Simulation as a source of new knowledge

This brings me to the crucial question about simulation: *How can a simulation ever tell us anything that we do not already know?* The usual implication of the question is that it can't. As a matter of fact, there is an interesting parallelism, which I shall exploit presently, between two assertions about computers and simulation that one hears frequently:

1 A simulation is no better than the assumptions built into it.
2 A computer can do only what it is programmed to do.

I shall not deny either assertion, for both seem to me to be true. But despite both assertions simulation can tell us things we do not already know.

There are two related ways in which simulation can provide new knowledge— one of them obvious, the other perhaps a bit subtle. The obvious point is that, even when we have correct premises, it may be very difficult to discover what they imply. All correct reasoning is a grand system of tautologies, but only God can

The natural and the artificial worlds **27**

make direct use of that fact. The rest of us must painstakingly and fallibly tease out the consequences of our assumptions.

Thus we might expect simulation to be a powerful technique for deriving, from our knowledge of the mechanisms governing the behavior of gases, a theory of the weather and a means of weather prediction. Indeed, as many people are aware, attempts have been under way for some years to apply this technique. Greatly over-simplified, the idea is that we already know the correct basic assumptions, the local atmospheric equations, but we need the computer to work out the implications of the interactions of vast numbers of variables starting from complicated initial conditions. This is simply an extrapolation to the scale of modern computers of the idea we use when we solve two simultaneous equations by algebra.

This approach to simulation has numerous applications to engineering design. For it is typical of many kinds of design problems that the inner system consists of components whose fundamental laws of behavior—mechanical, electrical, or chemical—are well known. The difficulty of the design problem often resides in predicting how an assemblage of such components will behave.

Simulation of poorly understood systems

The more interesting and subtle question is whether simulation can be of any help to us when we do not know very much initially about the natural laws that govern the behavior of the inner system. Let me show why this question must also be answered in the affirmative.

First, I shall make a preliminary comment that simplifies matters: we are seldom interested in explaining or predicting phenomena in all their particularity; we are usually interested only in a few properties abstracted from the complex reality. Thus, a NASA-launched satellite is surely an artificial object, but we usually do not think of it as "simulating" the moon or a planet. It simply obeys the same laws of physics, which relate only to its inertial and gravitational mass, abstracted from most of its other properties. It *is* a moon. Similarly electric energy that entered my house from the early atomic generating station at Shippingport did not "simulate" energy generated by means of a coal plant or a windmill. Maxwell's equations hold for both.

The more we are willing to abstract from the detail of a set of phenomena, the easier it becomes to simulate the phenomena. Moreover we do not have to know, or guess at, all the internal structure of the system but only that part of it that is crucial to the abstraction.

It is fortunate that this is so, for if it were not, the topdown strategy that built the natural sciences over the past three centuries would have been infeasible. We knew a great deal about the gross physical and chemical behavior of matter before we had a knowledge of molecules, a great deal about molecular chemistry before we had an atomic theory, and a great deal about atoms before we had any theory of elementary particles—if indeed we have such a theory today.

This skyhook-skyscraper construction of science from the roof down to the yet unconstructed foundations was possible because the behavior of the system at each

28 H. A. Simon

level depended on only a very approximate, simplified, abstracted characterization of the system at the level next beneath.[13] This is lucky, else the safety of bridges and airplanes might depend on the correctness of the "Eightfold Way" of looking at elementary particles.

Artificial systems and adaptive systems have properties that make them particularly susceptible to simulation via simplified models. The characterization of such systems in the previous section of this chapter explains why. Resemblance in behavior of systems without identity of the inner systems is particularly feasible if the aspects in which we are interested arise out of the *organization* of the parts, independently of all but a few properties of the individual components. Thus for many purposes we may be interested in only such characteristics of a material as its tensile and compressive strength. We may be profoundly unconcerned about its chemical properties, or even whether it is wood or iron.

The motor control patent cited earlier illustrates this abstraction to organizational properties. The invention consisted of a "combination" of "reversing means," of "field weakening means," that is to say, of components specified in terms of their functioning in the organized whole. How many ways are there of reversing a motor, or of weakening its field strength? We can simulate the system described in the patent claims in many ways without reproducing even approximately the actual physical device that is depicted. With a small additional step of abstraction, the patent claims could be restated to encompass mechanical as well as electrical devices. I suppose that any undergraduate engineer at Berkeley, Carnegie Mellon University, or MIT could design a mechanical system embodying reversibility and variable starting torque so as to simulate the system of the patent.

The computer as artifact

No artifact devised by man is so convenient for this kind of functional description as a digital computer. It is truly protean, for almost the only ones of its properties that are detectable in its behavior (when it is operating properly!) are the organizational properties. The speed with which it performs it basic operations may allow us to infer a little about its physical components and their natural laws; speed data, for example, would allow us to rule out certain kinds of "slow" components. For the rest, almost no interesting statement that one can make about an operating computer bears any particular relation to the specific nature of the hardware. A computer is an organization of elementary functional components in which, to a high approximation, only the function performed by those components is relevant to the behavior of the whole system.[14]

Computers as abstract objects

This highly abstractive quality of computers makes it easy to introduce mathematics into the study of their theory—and has led some to the erroneous conclusion that, as a computer science emerges, it will necessarily be a mathematical rather than an

The natural and the artificial worlds **29**

empirical science. Let me take up these two points in turn: the relevance of mathematics to computers and the possibility of studying computers empirically.

Some important theorizing, initiated by John von Neumann, has been done on the topic of computer reliability. The question is how to build a reliable system from unreliable parts. Notice that this is not posed as a question of physics or physical engineering. The components engineer is assumed to have done his best, but the parts are still unreliable! We can cope with the unreliability only by our manner of organizing them.

To turn this into a meaningful problem, we have to say a little more about the nature of the unreliable parts. Here we are aided by the knowledge that *any* computer can be assembled out of a small array of simple, basic elements. For instance, we may take as our primitives the so-called Pitts-McCulloch neurons. As their name implies, these components were devised in analogy to the supposed anatomical and functional characteristics of neurons in the brain, but they are highly abstracted. They are formally isomorphic with the simplest kinds of switching circuits—"and," "or," and "not" circuits. We postulate, now, that we are to build a system from such elements and that each elementary part has a specified probability of functioning correctly. The problem is to arrange the elements and their interconnections in such a way that the complete system will perform reliably.

The important point for our present discussion is that the parts could as well be neurons as relays, as well relays as transistors. The natural laws governing relays are very well known, while the natural laws governing neurons are known most imperfectly. But that does not matter, for all that is relevant for the theory is that the components have the specified level of unreliability and be interconnected in the specified way.

This example shows that the possibility of building a mathematical theory of a system or of simulating that system does not depend on having an adequate microtheory of the natural laws that govern the system components. Such a microtheory might indeed be simply irrelevant.

Computers as empirical objects

We turn next to the feasibility of an *empirical* science of computers—as distinct from the solid-state physics or physiology of their componentry.[15] As a matter of empirical fact almost all of the computers that have been designed have certain common organizational features. They almost all can be decomposed into an active processor (Babbage's "Mill") and a memory (Babbage's "Store") in combination with input and output devices. (Some of the larger systems, somewhat in the manner of colonial algae, are assemblages of smaller systems having some or all of these components. But perhaps I may oversimplify for the moment.) They are all capable of storing symbols (program) that can be interpreted by a program–control component and executed. Almost all have exceedingly limited capacity for simultaneous, parallel activity—they are basically one-thing-at-a-time systems. Symbols generally have to be moved from the larger memory components into the central processor

30 H. A. Simon

before they can be acted upon. The systems are capable of only simple basic actions: recoding symbols, storing symbols, copying symbols, moving symbols, erasing symbols, and comparing symbols.

Since there are now many such devices in the world, and since the properties that describe them also appear to be shared by the human central nervous system, nothing prevents us from developing a natural history of them. We can study them as we would rabbits or chipmunks and discover how they behave under different patterns of environmental stimulation. Insofar as their behavior reflects largely the broad functional characteristics we have described, and is independent of details of their hardware, we can build a general—but empirical—theory of them.

The research that was done to design computer time-sharing systems is a good example of the study of computer behavior as an empirical phenomenon. Only fragments of theory were available to guide the design of a time-sharing system or to predict how a system of a specified design would actually behave in an environment of users who placed their several demands upon it. Most actual designs turned out initially to exhibit serious deficiencies, and most predictions of performance were startlingly inaccurate.

Under these circumstances the main route open to the development and improvement of time-sharing systems was to build them and see how they behaved. And this is what was done. They were built, modified, and improved in successive stages. Perhaps theory could have anticipated these experiments and made them unnecessary. In fact it didn't, and I don't know anyone intimately acquainted with these exceedingly complex systems who has very specific ideas as to how it might have done so. To understand them, the systems had to be constructed, and their behavior observed.[16]

In a similar vein computer programs designed to play games or to discover proofs for mathematical theorems spend their lives in exceedingly large and complex task environments. Even when the programs themselves are only moderately large and intricate (compared, say, with the monitor and operating systems of large computers), too little is known about their task environments to permit accurate prediction of how well they will perform, how selectively they will be able to search for problem solutions.

Here again theoretical analysis must be accompanied by large amounts of experimental work. A growing literature reporting these experiments is beginning to give us precise knowledge about the degree of heuristic power of particular heuristic devices in reducing the size of the problem spaces that must be searched. In theorem proving, for example, there has been a whole series of advances in heuristic power based on and guided by empirical exploration: the use of the Herbrand theorem, the resolution principle, the set-of-support principle, and so on.[17]

Computers and thought

As we succeed in broadening and deepening our knowledge—theoretical and empirical—about computers, we discover that in large part their behavior is

The natural and the artificial worlds **31**

governed by simple general laws, that what appeared as complexity in the computer program was to a considerable extent complexity of the environment to which the program was seeking to adapt its behavior.

This relation of program to environment opened up an exceedingly important role for computer simulation as a tool for achieving a deeper understanding of human behavior. For if it is the organization of components, and not their physical properties, that largely determines behavior, and if computers are organized somewhat in the image of man, then the computer becomes an obvious device for exploring the consequences of alternative organizational assumptions for human behavior. Psychology could move forward without awaiting the solutions by neurology of the problems of component design—however interesting and significant these components turn out to be.

Symbol systems: rational artifacts

The computer is a member of an important family of artifacts called symbol systems, or more explicitly, physical symbol systems.[18] Another important member of the family (some of us think, anthropomorphically, it is the *most* important) is the human mind and brain. It is with this family of artifacts, and particularly the human version of it, that we will be primarily concerned in this book. Symbol systems are almost the quintessential artifacts, for adaptivity to an environment is their whole *raison d'être*. They are goal-seeking, information-processing systems, usually enlisted in the service of the larger systems in which they are incorporated.

Basic capabilities of symbol systems

A physical symbol system holds a set of entities, called symbols. These are physical patterns (e.g., chalk marks on a blackboard) that can occur as components of symbol structures (sometimes called "expressions"). As I have already pointed out in the case of computers, a symbol system also possesses a number of simple processes that operate upon symbol structures—processes that create, modify, copy, and destroy symbols. A physical symbol system is a machine that, as it moves through time, produces an evolving collection of symbol structures.[19] Symbol structures can, and commonly do, serve as internal representations (e.g., "mental images") of the environments to which the symbol system is seeking to adapt. They allow it to model that environment with greater or less veridicality and in greater or less detail, and consequently to reason about it. Of course, for this capability to be of any use to the symbol system, it must have windows on the world and hands, too. It must have means for acquiring information from the external environment that can be encoded into internal symbols, as well as means for producing symbols that initiate action upon the environment. Thus it must use symbols to *designate* objects and relations and actions in the world external to the system.

Symbols may also designate processes that the symbol system can interpret and execute. Hence the programs that govern the behavior of a symbol system can be

32 H. A. Simon

stored, along with other symbol structures, in the system's own memory, and executed when activated.

Symbol systems are called "physical" to remind the reader that they exist as real-world devices, fabricated of glass and metal (computers) or flesh and blood (brains). In the past we have been more accustomed to thinking of the symbol systems of mathematics and logic as abstract and disembodied, leaving out of account the paper and pencil and human minds that were required actually to bring them to life. Computers have transported symbol systems from the platonic heaven of ideas to the empirical world of actual processes carried out by machines or brains, or by the two of them working together.

Intelligence as computation

The three chapters that follow rest squarely on the hypothesis that intelligence is the work of symbol systems. Stated a little more formally, the hypothesis is that a physical symbol system of the sort I have just described has the necessary and sufficient means for general intelligent action.

The hypothesis is clearly an empirical one, to be judged true or false on the basis of evidence. One task of chapters 3 and 4 will be to review some of the evidence, which is of two basic kinds. On the one hand, by constructing computer programs that are demonstrably capable of intelligent action, we provide evidence on the sufficiency side of the hypothesis. On the other hand, by collecting experimental data on human thinking that tend to show that the human brain operates as a symbol system, we add plausibility to the claims for necessity, for such data imply that all known intelligent systems (brains and computers) are symbol systems.

Economics: abstract rationality

As prelude to our consideration of human intelligence as the work of a physical symbol system, chapter 2 introduces a heroic abstraction and idealization—the idealization of human rationality which is enshrined in modern economic theories, particularly those called neoclassical. These theories are an idealization because they direct their attention primarily to the external environment of human thought, to decisions that are optimal for realizing the adaptive system's goals (maximization of utility or profit). They seek to define the decisions that would be substantively rational in the circumstances defined by the outer environment.

Economic theory's treatment of the limits of rationality imposed by the inner environment—by the characteristics of the physical symbol system—tends to be pragmatic, and sometimes even opportunistic. In the more formal treatments of general equilibrium and in the so-called "rational expectations" approach to adaptation, the possibilities that an information-processing system may have a very limited capability for adaptation are almost ignored. On the other hand, in discussions of the rationale for market mechanisms and in many theories of decision making under uncertainty, the procedural aspects of rationality receive more serious treatment.

The natural and the artificial worlds **33**

In chapter 2 we will see examples both of neglect for and concern with the limits of rationality. From the idealizations of economics (and some criticisms of these idealizations) we will move, in chapters 3 and 4, to a more systematic study of the inner environment of thought—of thought processes as they actually occur within the constraints imposed by the parameters of a physical symbol system like the brain.

Notes

1 I will occasionally use "man" as an androgynous noun, encompassing both sexes, and "he," "his," and "him" as androgynous pronouns including women and men equally in their scope.

2 I shall disclaim responsibility for this particular choice of terms. The phrase "artificial intelligence," which led me to it, was coined, I think, right on the Charles River, at MIT. Our own research group at Rand and Carnegie Mellon University have preferred phrases like "complex information processing" and "simulation of cognitive processes." But then we run into new terminological difficulties, for the dictionary also says that "to simulate" means "to assume or have the mere appearance or form of, without the reality; imitate; counterfeit; pretend." At any rate, "artificial intelligence" seems to be here to stay, and it may prove easier to cleanse the phrase than to dispense with it. In time it will become sufficiently idiomatic that it will no longer be the target of cheap rhetoric.

3 This issue will also be discussed at length in my fifth chapter. In order not to keep readers in suspense, I may say that I hold to the pristine empiricist's position of the irreducibility of "ought" to "is," as in chapter 3 of my *Administrative Behavior* (New York: Macmillan, 1976). This position is entirely consistent with treating natural or artificial goal-seeking systems as phenomena, without commitment to their goals. *Ibid.*, appendix. See also the well-known paper by A. Rosenbluth, N. Wiener, and J. Bigelow, "Behavior, Purpose, and Teleology," *Philosophy of Science, 10* (1943):18–24.

4 A generalization of the argument made here for the separability of "outer" from "inner" environment shows that we should expect to find this separability, to a greater or lesser degree, in *all* large and complex systems, whether they are artificial or natural. In its generalized form it is an argument that all nature will be organized in "levels." My essay "The Architecture of Complexity," included in this volume as chapter 8, develops the more general argument in some detail.

5 The theory of functional equivalence of computing machines has had considerable development in recent years. See Marvin L. Minsky, *Computation: Finite and Infinite Machines* (Englewood Cliffs, N.J.: Prentice-Hall, 1967), chapters 1–4.

6 U.S. Patent 1,307,836, granted to Arthur Simon, June 24, 1919.

7 Ibid.

8 Ibid.

9 On the crucial role of adaptation or rationality—and their limits—for economics and organization theory, see the introduction to part IV, "Rationality and Administrative Decision Making," of my *Models of Man* (New York: Wiley, 1957); pp. 38–41, 80–81, and 240–244 of *Administrative Behavior*; and chapter 2 of this book.

10 Compare the corresponding proposition on the design of administrative organizations: "Rationality, then, does not determine behavior. Within the area of rationality behavior is perfectly flexible and adaptable to abilities, goals, and knowledge. Instead, behavior is determined by the irrational and nonrational elements that bound the area of rationality … administrative theory must be concerned with the limits of rationality, and the manner in which organization affects these limits for the person making a decision." *Administrative Behavior*, p. 241. For a discussion of the same issue as it arises in psychology, see my "Cognitive Architectures and Rational Analysis: Comment," in Kurt VanLehn (ed.), *Architectures for Intelligence* (Hillsdale, NJ: Erlbaum, 1991).

34 H. A. Simon

11 For some published versions of this model, see A. O. Dahlberg, *National Income Visualized* (N.Y.: Columbia University Press, 1956).

12 A. W. Phillips, "Mechanical Models in Economic Dynamics," *Economica*, New Series, *17* (1950):283–305.

13 This point is developed more fully in "The Architecture of Complexity," chapter 8 in this volume. More than fifty years ago, Bertrand Russell made the same point about the architecture of mathematics. See the "Preface" to *Principia Mathematica:* "... the chief reason in favour of any theory on the principles of mathematics must always be inductive, i.e., it must lie in the fact that the theory in question enables us to deduce ordinary mathematics. In mathematics, the greatest degree of self-evidence is usually not to be found quite at the beginning, but at some later point; hence the early deductions, until they reach this point, give reasons rather for believing the premises because true consequences follow from them, than for believing the consequences because they follow from the premises." Contemporary preferences for deductive formalisms frequently blind us to this important fact, which is no less true today than it was in 1910.

14 On the subject of this and the following paragraphs, see M. L. Minsky, *op. cit.*; then John von Neumann, "Probabilistic Logics and the Synthesis of Reliable Organisms from Unreliable Components," in C. E. Shannon and J. McCarthy (eds.), *Automata Studies* (Princeton: Princeton University Press, 1956).

15 A. Newell and H. A. Simon, "Computer Science as Empirical Inquiry," *Communications of the ACM, 19*(March 1976):113–126. See also H. A. Simon, "Artificial Intelligence: An Empirical Science," *Artificial Intelligence*, 77(1995):95–127.

16 The empirical, exploratory flavor of computer research is nicely captured by the account of Maurice V. Wilkes in his 1967 Turing Lecture, "Computers Then and Now," *Journal of the Association for Computing Machinery, 15*(January 1968):1–7.

17 Note, for example, the empirical data in Lawrence Wos, George A. Robinson, Daniel F. Carson, and Leon Shalla, "The Concept of Demodulation in Theorem Proving," *Journal of the Association for Computing Machinery, 14*(October 1967):698–709, and in several of the earlier papers referenced there. See also the collection of programs in Edward Feigenbaum and Julian Feldman (eds.), *Computers and Thought* (New York: McGraw-Hill, 1963). It is common practice in the field to title papers about heuristic programs, "Experiments with an *XYZ* Program."

18 In the literature the phrase *information-processing system* is used more frequently than symbol system. I will use the two terms as synonyms.

19 Newell and Simon, "Computer Science as Empirical Inquiry," p. 116.

2

THREE VARIETIES OF KNOWLEDGE

D. Davidson

I know, for the most part, what I think, want, and intend, and what my sensations are. In addition, I know a great deal about the world around me, the locations and sizes and causal properties of the objects in it. I also sometimes know what goes on in other people's minds. Each of these three kinds of empirical knowledge has its distinctive characteristics. What I know about the contents of my own mind I generally know without appeal to evidence or investigation. There are exceptions, but the primacy of unmediated self-knowledge is attested by the fact that we distrust the exceptions until they can be reconciled with the unmediated. My knowledge of the world outside of myself, on the other hand, depends on the functioning of my sense organs, and this causal dependence on the senses makes my beliefs about the world of nature open to a sort of uncertainty that arises only rarely in the case of beliefs about our own states of mind. Many of my simple perceptions of what is going on in the world are not based on further evidence; my perceptual beliefs are simply caused directly by the events and objects around me. But my knowledge of the propositional contents of other minds is never immediate in this sense; I would have no access to what others think and value if I could not note their behavior.

Of course all three varieties of knowledge are concerned with aspects of the same reality; where they differ is in the mode of access to reality.

The relations among the three sorts of empirical knowledge, particularly questions of conceptual priority, have long headed the list of philosopher's epistemological concerns, and they are my subject here. Many familiar approaches to the question how the three sorts of knowledge are related take self-knowledge as primary. perhaps because of its directness and relative certainty, and then attempt to derive knowledge of the external world from it; as a final step, they try to base knowledge of other minds on observations of behavior. This is not, needless to say, the only direction the derivation can take: one may instead accept knowledge of

36 D. Davidson

the external world, at least in some of its manifestations, as basic, and try to relate or reduce the other forms of knowledge to it. The elaboration of such reductive proposals, and the demonstration of their failure, constitutes much of the history of philosophy from Descartes to the present. If many philosophers have turned away from these problems in recent years, it is not because the problems are thought to have been solved, but because the problems seem intractable. There is also, of course, the wistful hope that the problems themselves are illusory.

This cannot be the case. There are compelling reasons for accepting the view that none of the three forms of knowledge is reducible to one or both of the others. Here I give my own reasons for believing this; but I take the hopelessness of finding effective modes of reduction to be apparent from the almost universal rejection of standard reductionist programs. Skepticism in various of its familiar guises is our grudging tribute to the apparent impossibility of unifying the three varieties of knowledge: one form of skepticism springs from the difficulty of accounting for our knowledge of the external world on the basis of our knowledge of our own minds; another recognizes that our knowledge of other minds cannot consist only in what we can observe from the outside. The intractability of the mind-body problem is another such tribute.

It is striking the extent to which philosophers, even those who have been skeptics about the possibility of justifying beliefs about the external world, have put aside these doubts when they have come to consider the problem of other minds; striking, since the latter problem can arise only if knowledge of behavior, and hence of the external world, is possible. Holding the problems apart has the unfortunate effect of obscuring the fact that the two problems rest on a common assumption. The assumption is that the truth concerning what a person believes about the world is logically independent of the truth of those beliefs. This certainly seems to be the case, for surely the totality of a person's beliefs and subjective experiences is logically consistent with the falsity of any of those beliefs. So no amount of knowledge of the contents of one's own mind insures the truth of a belief about the external world. The logical independence of the mental works equally in the other direction: no amount of knowledge of the external world entails the truth about the workings of a mind. If there is a logical or epistemic barrier between the mind and nature, it not only prevents us from seeing out; it also blocks a view from outside in.

It is sometimes thought that if we separate the problem of knowing what is in a mind from the problem of knowing about anything whatever outside of ourselves, then the problem of knowledge of other minds is solved when we recognize that it is part of the concept of a mental state or event that certain forms of behavior, or other outward signs, count as evidence for the existence of that mental state or event. No doubt it is true that it is part of the concept of a mental state or event that behavior is evidence for it. What is unclear is how this answers the sceptic. For the fact that behavior is evidence for what is in a mind offers no explanation of the asymmetry between the indirect knowledge we have of other minds and the direct knowledge we have of our own mind. The proffered solution insists that behavioral

Three varieties of knowledge **37**

evidence can suffice for the justified attribution of mental states to others, while it recognizes that such evidence is generally irrelevant to self-ascriptions of the same states. But if we are given no explanation of this striking asymmetry, we ought to conclude that there are really two kinds of concepts: mental concepts that apply to others, and mental concepts that apply to ourselves. If the mental states of others are known only through their behavioral and other outward manifestations, while this is not true of our own mental states, why should we think our own mental states are anything like those of others? We might also wonder why, if this answer to the problem of knowledge of other minds is satisfactory, we should not accept an analogous solution to the problem of our knowledge of the external world. Yet it is widely recognized that this answer to general skepticism is unacceptable. Do we distinguish between the problems because we suppose that while we have no access to the outside world except through experience, we nevertheless can intelligibly extrapolate to the experiences of others, since we have access to experience in our own case? But this supposition begs the question, since it assumes without argument that what we call the mental states of others are similar to what we identify as mental states in ourselves.

I have been rehearsing these problems and perplexities because I want, first of all, to stress the apparent oddity of the fact that we have three irreducibly different varieties of empirical knowledge. We need an overall picture which not only accommodates all three modes of knowing, but makes sense of their relations to one another. Without such a general picture we should be deeply puzzled that the same world is known to us in three such different ways. And, second, it is essential to appreciate the extent to which problems that have usually been taken one at a time are interrelated. There are three basic problems: how a mind can know the world of nature, how it is possible for one mind to know another, and how it is possible to know the contents of our own minds without resort to observation or evidence. It is a mistake, I shall urge, to suppose that these questions can be collapsed into two, or taken in isolation.

In trying to form a picture of the relations among the three kinds of knowledge we must do much more than show *that* they are mutually irreducible; we must see *why* they are irreducible. This in turn will involve bringing out the respective conceptual roles played by each of the forms of knowledge, and why each of these three sorts of knowledge is indispensable—why we could not get along without all of them. Of course, if I am right that each of the three varieties of knowledge is indispensable, scepticism of the senses and scepticism about other minds must be dismissed. For the Cartesian or Humean skeptic about the external world holds that it is all too obvious that we can get along without knowledge of the world of nature —what we know of our own mind is self-sufficient, and may be all the knowledge we have. The skeptic about other minds is equally convinced that we can get along without knowledge of other minds—this must be possible if we are forever uncertain whether we have it.

It may seem at first that we could rather easily get along without a form of words to express our beliefs about the mental states of others or of ourselves. I think this

38 D. Davidson

is imaginable; but the issue with which I am concerned is primarily epistemic, not linguistic. The epistemic question is whether we could get along without knowledge of minds, both our own and those of others. I shall argue that we could not. What we could not do is get along without a way of expressing, and thus communicating, our thoughts about the natural world. But if we can do this, the transition to also being able verbally to attribute thoughts is relatively simple, and it would be astonishing if this step were not taken. With respect to our own thoughts, it is no more than the difference between saying assertively 'Snow is white' and saying assertively 'I believe that snow is white'. The truth conditions of these assertions are not the same, but anyone who understands the first assertion knows the truth conditions of the second, even if he does not command a sentence with those truth conditions. This is because anyone who understands speech can recognize assertions, and knows that someone who makes an assertion represents himself as believing what he says. Similarly, someone who says to Jones that snow is white knows the truth conditions of 'Jones believes that snow is white' (even if he does not know English nor has a way of expressing belief).

Belief is a condition of knowledge. But to have a belief it is not enough to discriminate among aspects of the world, to behave in different ways in different circumstances; a snail or a periwinkle does this. Having a belief demands in addition appreciating the contrast between true belief and false, between appearance and reality, mere seeming and being. We can, of course, say that a sunflower has made a mistake if it turns towards an artificial light as if it were the sun, but we do not suppose the sunflower can think it has made a mistake, and so we do not attribute a belief to the sunflower. Someone who has a belief about the world—or anything else—must grasp the concept of objective truth, of what is the case independent of what he or she thinks. We must ask, therefore, after the source of the concept of truth.

Wittgenstein put us on the track of the only possible answer to this question, whether or not his problem was as broad as ours, and whether or not he believed in answers to philosophical problems. The source of the concept of objective truth is interpersonal communication. Thought depends on communication. This follows at once if we suppose that language is essential to thought and we agree with Wittgenstein that there cannot be a private language.[1] The central argument against private languages is that, unless a language is shared, there is no way to distinguish between using the language correctly and using it incorrectly; only communication with another can supply an objective check. If only communication can provide a check on the correct use of words, only communication can supply a standard of objectivity in other domains, or so I shall argue. We have no grounds for crediting a creature with the distinction between what is thought to be the case and what is the case unless the creature has the standard provided by a shared language; and without this distinction there is nothing that can clearly be called thought.

In communication, what a speaker and the speaker's interpreter must share is an understanding of what the speaker means by what he says. How is this possible? It might help if we knew how language came into existence in the first place, or at least could give an account of how an individual learns his first language, given that others in his environment are already linguistically accomplished. Failing such knowledge or account, what we can do instead is ask how a competent interpreter (one with adequate conceptual resources and a language of his own) might come to understand the speaker of an alien tongue. An answer to this question should reveal some important features of communication, and throw indirect light on what makes possible a first entry into language.

The intrepid interpreter, working without a bilingual trot, seeks to assign a propositional content to the utterances of a speaker. In effect he assigns a sentence of his own to each of the sentences of the speaker. To the extent that he gets things right, the interpreter's sentences provide the truth conditions of the speaker's sentences, and hence supply the basis for the interpretation of the speaker's utterances. The result can be thought of as a recursive characterization of truth, by the interpreter, of the sentences, and hence actual and potential utterances, of the speaker.

An interpreter cannot directly observe another person's propositional attitudes; beliefs, desires, and intentions, including the intentions which partly determine the meanings of utterances, are invisible to the naked eye. The interpreter can, however, attend to the outward manifestations of these attitudes, including utterances. Since we are all able to discover from such manifestations what an agent thinks and means, there must be an intelligible relation between evidence and attitude. How do we bridge this gap? I know of only one way: an interpreter can perceive, often enough, that an agent has a certain sort of attitude towards an object or event the interpreter perceives. If the interpreter could in this way directly *individuate* the attitudes of someone else, the problem would be solved, but only by assuming the interpreter is a mind reader. It would not beg the question, however, to assume the interpreter can detect one or more nonindividuating attitude. Examples of the kind of special attitude I have in mind are: holding a sentence true at a time, wanting a sentence to be true, or preferring that one sentence rather than another be true. The assumption that we can detect such an attitude does not beg the question of how we endow the attitudes with content, since a relation such as holding true between a speaker and an utterance is an extensional relation which can be known to hold without knowing what the sentence means. These attitudes are nonindividuative, for though they are psychological in nature, they do not distinguish the different propositional contents different utterances express.

In *Word and Object* Quine appealed to the nonindividuative attitude of prompted assent. Since someone assents to an utterance, or holds a sentence true, in part because of what he believes and in part because of what the utterance or sentence means in his language, Quine's problem was to separate out these two elements on the basis of evidence that combined their influence. If the separation succeeds, the result is a theory of both belief and meaning for the speaker, for it must yield an interpretation of the speaker's utterances, and if one knows both that the speaker assents to the utterance, and what it means in his mouth, one also knows what he believes.

The process of separating meaning and opinion invokes two key principles which must be applicable if a speaker is interpretable: the Principle of Coherence and the Principle of Correspondence. The Principle of Coherence prompts the

40 D. Davidson

interpreter to discover a degree of logical consistency in the thought of the speaker; the Principle of Correspondence prompts the interpreter to take the speaker to be responding to the same features of the world that he (the interpreter) would be responding to under similar circumstances. Both principles can be (and have been) called principles of charity: one principle endows the speaker with a modicum of logic, the other endows him with a degree of what the interpreter takes to be true belief about the world. Successful interpretation necessarily invests the person interpreted with basic rationality. It follows from the nature of correct interpretation that an interpersonal standard of consistency and correspondence to the facts applies to both the speaker and the speaker's interpreter, to their utterances and to their beliefs.

Two questions now obtrude. The first is: why should an interpersonal standard be an objective standard, that is, why should what people agree on be true? The second is: even if it is the case that communication assumes an objective standard of truth, why should this be the only way such a standard can be established?

Here is a way of answering these questions. All creatures classify objects and aspects of the world in the sense that they treat some stimuli as more alike than others. The criterion of such classifying activity is similarity of response. Evolution and subsequent learning no doubt explain these patterns of behavior. But from what point of view can these be called patterns? The criterion on the basis of which a creature can be said to be treating stimuli as similar, as belonging to a class, is the similarity of the creatures's responses to those stimuli; but what is the criterion of similarity of responses? *This* criterion cannot be derived from the creature's responses; it can only come from the responses of an observer to the responses of the creature. And it is only when an observer consciously correlates the responses of another creature with objects and events of the observer's world that there is any basis for saying the creature is responding to those objects or events rather than any other objects or events. As would-be interpreters of the verbal behavior of the speaker of an alien language, we group distinct verbal acts of the speaker together: 'Mother', 'Snow', 'Table', when repeated as one-word sentences, sound similar if we are appropriately attuned. When we discover kinds of objects or events in the world that we can correlate with the utterances of a speaker, we are on the way to interpreting the simplest linguistic behavior.

If we are teaching someone a language, the situation becomes more complex, but more clearly interpersonal. What seems basic is this: an observer (or teacher) finds (or instills) a regularity in the verbal behavior of the informant (or learner) which he can correlate with events and objects in the environment. This much can take place without developed thought on the part of the observed, of course, but it is the necessary basis for attributing thoughts and meanings to the person observed. For until the triangle is completed connecting two creatures, and each creature with common features of the world, there can be no answer to the question whether a creature, in discriminating between stimuli, is discriminating between stimuli at the sensory surfaces or somewhere further out, or further in. Without this sharing of reactions to common stimuli, thought and speech would have no particular content—that is, no content at all. It takes two points of view to give a location to the cause of a thought, and thus to define its content. We may think of it as a form of triangulation: each of two people is reacting differentially to sensory stimuli streaming in from a certain direction. Projecting the incoming lines outward, the common cause is at their intersection. If the two people now note each other's reactions (in the case of language, verbal reactions), each can correlate these observed reactions with his or her stimuli from the world. A common cause has been determined. The triangle which gives content to thought and speech is complete. But it takes two to triangulate.

Until a base line has been established by communication with someone else, there is no point in saying one's own thoughts or words have a propositional content. If this is so, then it is clear that knowledge of another mind is essential to all thought and all knowledge. Knowledge of another mind is possible, however, only if one has knowledge of the world, for the triangulation which is essential to thought requires that those in communication recognize that they occupy positions in a shared world. So knowledge of other minds and knowledge of the world are mutually dependent; neither is possible without the other. Ayer was surely right when he said, 'it is only with the use of language that truth and error, certainty and uncertainty, come fully upon the scene'.[2]

Knowledge of the propositional contents of our own minds is not possible without the other forms of knowledge since there is no propositional thought without communication. It is also the case that we are not in a position to attribute thoughts to others unless we know what we think since attributing thoughts to others is a matter of matching the verbal and other behavior of others to our own propositions or meaningful sentences. Knowledge of our own minds and knowledge of the minds of others are thus mutually dependent.

It should now be clear what insures that our view of the world is, in its plainest features, largely correct. The reason is that the stimuli that cause our most basic verbal responses also determine what those verbal responses mean, and the content of the beliefs that accompany them. The nature of interpretation guarantees both that a large number of our simplest perceptual beliefs are true, and that the nature of these beliefs is known to others. Of course many beliefs are given content by their relations to further beliefs, or are caused by misleading sensations; any particular belief or set of beliefs about the world around us may be false. What cannot be the case is that our general picture of the world and our place in it is mistaken, for it is this picture which informs the rest of our beliefs and makes them intelligible, whether they be true or false.

The assumption that the truth of what we believe is logically independent of what we believe is revealed as ambiguous. Any particular belief may indeed be false; but enough in the framework and fabric of our beliefs must be true to give content to the rest. The conceptual connections between our knowledge of our own minds and our knowledge of the world of nature are not definitional but holistic. The same is true of the conceptual connections between our knowledge of behavior and our knowledge of other minds.

42 D. Davidson

There are, then, no 'barriers', logical or epistemic, between the three varieties of knowledge. On the other hand, the very way in which each depends on the others shows why none can be eliminated, or reduced to the others.

As noted above, we may think of an interpreter who aims to understand a speaker as matching up sentences of his own with the utterances and states of mind of the speaker. The totality of evidence available to the interpreter determines no unique theory of truth for a given speaker, not just because actually available evidence is finite while the theory has an infinity of testable consequences, but because all possible evidence cannot limit acceptable theories to one. Given the richness of the structure represented by the set of one's own sentences, and the nature of the connections between the members of this set and the world, we should not be surprised if there are many ways of assigning our own sentences to the sentences and thoughts of someone else that capture everything of significance.

The situation is analogous to the measurement of weight or temperature by assigning numbers to objects. Even supposing there are no errors of measurement, and that all possible observations have been made, an assignment of numbers to objects that correctly registers their weights is not unique: given one such assignment, another can be produced by multiplying all the numbers by any positive constant. In the case of ordinary temperature (not absolute temperature), any correct assignment of numbers can be converted to another by a linear transformation. Because there are many different but equally acceptable ways of interpreting an agent we may say, if we please, that interpretation or translation is indeterminate, or that there is no fact of the matter as to what someone means by his or her words. In the same vein, we could speak of the indeterminacy of weight or temperature. But we normally accentuate the positive by being clear about what is invariant from one assignment of numbers to another, for it is what is invariant that is empirically significant. The invariant *is* the fact of the matter. We can afford to look at translation and the content of mental states in the same light.[3]

I once thought that the indeterminacy of translation supplied a reason for supposing there are no strict laws connecting mental and physical concepts, and so supported the claim that mental concepts are not even nomologically reducible to physical concepts. I was wrong: indeterminacy turns up in both domains. But one source of indeterminacy in the case of the mental is that the line between empirical truth and truth due to meaning cannot in general be clearly defined on behavioral grounds; and behavioral grounds are all we have for determining what speakers mean. It is here that the irreducible difference between mental concepts and physical concepts begins to emerge: the former, at least insofar as they are intentional in nature, require the interpreter to consider how best to render the creature being interpreted intelligible, that is, as a creature endowed with reason. As a consequence, an interpreter must separate meaning from opinion partly on normative grounds by deciding what, from his point of view, maximizes intelligibility. In this endeavor the interpreter has, of course, no other standards of rationality to fall back on than his own. When we try to understand the world as physicists, we necessarily employ our own norms, but we do not aim to discover rationality in the phenomena.

Three varieties of knowledge **43**

How does the normative element in mental concepts prevent their reduction to physical concepts? Perhaps it is obvious that definitional reduction is out of the question; but why can't there be laws—strict laws—that connect each mental event or state with events or states described in the vocabulary of an advanced physics? When writing about this twenty years ago I said, in effect, that one can hope for strict connecting laws only when the concepts connected by the laws are based on criteria of the same sort, and so a strict law could not combine normative with non-normative concepts.[4] This answer still seems to me right as far as it goes, but it has understandably been found inconclusive by critics. I now want to add some further considerations.

One further consideration is this: strict laws do not employ causal concepts, while most, if not all, mental concepts are irreducibly causal. An action, for example, must be intentional under some description, but an action is intentional only if it is caused by mental factors such as beliefs and desires. Beliefs and desires are identified in part by the sorts of action they are prone to cause, given the right conditions. Many of the concepts that feature in commonsense explanations are causal in this way. An accident was caused by the fact that the road was slippery; something is slippery if it causes appropriate objects to slip under appropriate circumstances. We explain why the wing of an airplane does not break when it bends by noting that it is made of elastic materials; a material is elastic if there is something about it that causes it, under appropriate conditions, to return to its original shape after deformation. Such explanations do not lend themselves to precision for two reasons: we cannot spell out in detail when the circumstances are appropriate, and the appeal to causality finesses part of what a full-scale explanation would make manifest. Descriptions of objects, states, and events that are needed to instantiate strict, exceptionless laws do not contain causal concepts (which is not to say that laws which contain only noncausal concepts are not causal laws).

In the case of causal properties like elasticity, slipperiness, malleability, or solubility, we tend to think, rightly or wrongly, that what they leave unexplained can be (or already has been) explained by the advance of science. We would not be changing the subject if we were to drop the concept of elasticity in favor of a specification of the microstructure of the materials in the airplane wing that cause it to return to its original shape when exposed to certain forces. Mental concepts and explanations are not like this. They appeal to causality because they are designed, like the concept of causality itself, to single out from the totality of circumstances which conspire to cause a given event just those factors that satisfy some particular explanatory interest. When we want to explain an action, for example, we want to know the agent's reasons, so we can see for ourselves what it was about the action that appealed to the agent. But it would be foolish to suppose that there are strict laws that stipulate that whenever an agent has certain reasons he will perform a given action.

The normative and the causal properties of mental concepts are related. If we were to drop the normative aspect from psychological explanations, they would no longer serve the purposes they do. We have such a keen interest in the subject's reasons for acting and for his or her changes of belief that we are willing to settle for explanations that cannot be made to fit perfectly with the laws of physics. Physics, on the other hand, has as an aim laws that are as complete and precise as we can make them; a different aim. The causal element in mental concepts helps make up for the precision they lack; it is part of the concept of an intentional action that it is caused and explained by beliefs and desires; it is part of the concept of a belief or a desire that it tends to cause, and so explain, actions of certain sorts.

Much of what I have said about what distinguishes mental concepts from the concepts of a developed physics could also be said to distinguish the concepts of many of the special sciences such as biology, geology, and meteorology. So even if I am right that the normative and causal character of mental concepts divides them definitionally and nomologically from the concepts of a developed physics, it may seem that there must be something more basic or foundational that accounts for this division. I think there is.

Knowledge of the contents of our own minds must, in most cases, be trivial. The reason is that, apart from special cases, the problem of interpretation cannot arise. When I am asked about the propositional contents of my mind, I must use my own sentences. The answer is usually absurdly obvious: my sentence 'Snow is white', like my thought that snow is white, is true if and only if snow is white. My knowledge of the contents of another mind is possible, I have argued, only in the context of a generally correct, and shared, view of the world. But such knowledge differs from the knowledge I have of my own mind since it is necessarily indirect in that it depends, among other things, on observed correlations between the speech and other behavior of the person, and of events in our communal environment.

The fundamental difference between my knowledge of another mind and of the shared physical world has a different source. Communication, and the knowledge of other minds that it presupposes, is the basis of our concept of objectivity, our recognition of a distinction between false and true belief. There is no going outside this standard to check whether we have things right, any more than we can check whether the platinum–iridium standard kept at the International Bureau of Weights and Standards in Sèvres, France, weighs a kilogram. (This comparison was valid when the standard in Sèvres defined the kilogram.) We can, of course, turn to a third party and a fourth to broaden and secure the interpersonal standard of the real, but this leads not to something intrinsically different, just to more of the same.

I spoke before of an analogy between how we assign numbers to keep track of the relations among objects with respect to temperature or weight and how we use our own sentences to identify the contents of the thoughts and utterances of others. But the analogy is imperfect: the nature of the scaling device differs in the two cases. We depend on our linguistic interactions with others to yield agreement on the properties of numbers and the sort of structures in nature that allow us to represent those structures in the numbers. We cannot in the same way agree on the structure of the sentences or thoughts we use to chart the thoughts and meanings of others, for the attempt to reach such an agreement simply sends us back to the very process of interpretation on which all agreement depends.

It is here, I suggest, that we come to the ultimate springs of the difference between understanding minds and understanding the world as physical. A community of minds is the basis of knowledge; it provides the measure of all things. It makes no sense to question the adequacy of this measure, or to seek a more ultimate standard.

We have dwelt at length on the inescapability of the objective aspect of all thought. What remains of the subjective aspect? Clearly we have not obliterated the difference between self-knowledge and knowledge of other minds: the first remains direct and the second indirect. Objectivity itself we have traced to the intersections of points of view—for each person, the relation between his own reactions to the world and the reactions of others. These differences are real. Our thoughts are 'inner' and 'subjective' in that we know what they are in a way no one else can. But though possession of a thought is necessarily individual, its content is not. The thoughts we form and entertain are located conceptually in the world we inhabit, and know we inhabit, with others. Even our thoughts about our own mental states occupy the same conceptual space and are located on the same public map.

The philosophical conception of subjectivity is burdened with a history and a set of assumptions about the nature of mind and meaning that sever the meaning of an utterance or the content of a thought from questions about external reality, 'my' world from the world as it appears to others. This popular conception holds that the subjective is prior to the objective, that there is a subjective world prior to knowledge of external reality. It is evident that the picture of thought and meaning I have sketched here leaves no room for such priority since it predicates self-knowledge on knowledge of other minds and of the world. The objective and the intersubjective are thus essential to anything we can call subjectivity, and constitute the context in which it takes form. Collingwood put it succinctly:

> The child's discovery of itself as a person is also its discovery of itself as a member of a world of persons ... The discovery of myself as a person is the discovery that I can speak, and am thus a *persona* or speaker; in speaking I am both speaker and hearer; and since the discovery of myself as a person is also the discovery of other persons around me, it is the discovery of speakers and hearers other than myself.[5]

It may seem that if sharing a general view of the world is a condition of thought, the differences in intellectual and imaginative character among minds and cultures will be lost to sight. If I have given this impression, it is because I have wanted to concentrate on what seems to me primary, and so apt to go unnoticed: the necessary degree of communality essential to understanding another individual, and the extent to which such understanding provides the foundation of the concept of truth and reality upon which all thought depends. But I do not want to suggest that we cannot understand those with whom we differ on vast tracts of physical and moral opinion. It is also the case that understanding is a matter of degree: others may

46 D. Davidson

know things we do not, or even perhaps cannot. What is certain is that the clarity and effectiveness of our concepts grows with the growth of our understanding of others. There are no definite limits to how far dialogue can or will take us.

Some philosophers worry that if all our knowledge, at least our propositional knowledge, is objective, we will lose touch with an essential aspect of reality: our personal, private outlook. I think this worry is groundless. If I am right, our propositional knowledge has its basis not in the impersonal but in the interpersonal. Thus, when we look at the natural world we share with others, we do not lose contact with ourselves, but rather acknowledge membership in a society of minds. If I did not know what others think, I would have no thoughts of my own and so would not know what I think. If I did not know what I think, I would lack the ability to gauge the thoughts of others. Gauging the thoughts of others requires that I live in the same world with them, sharing many reactions to its major features, including its values. So there is no danger that in viewing the world objectively we will lose touch with ourselves. The three sorts of knowledge form a tripod: if any leg were lost, no part would stand.

Notes

1 Of course there can be a private code based on a publicly acquired language. I have no idea how broadly Wittgenstein intended his thesis about private languages to be interpreted; perhaps he intended his argument to apply only to those concepts which are necessarily private. But I, like Saul Kripke in *Wittgenstein on Rules and Private Language*, think the argument applies to language quite generally, and so (I would say) to propositional thought. But while I accept the idea that communication is the source of objectivity, I do not think communication depends on speakers using the same words to express the same thoughts.
2 A. J. Ayer, *The Problem of Knowledge*, 54.
3 Here I accept Quine's thesis of the indeterminacy of translation, and extend it to the interpretation of thought generally. The analogy with measurement is my own.
4 In 'Mental Events', essay 11 in *Essays on Actions and Events*.
5 R. G. Collingwood, *The Principles of Art*, 248.

3

THE MARKET AS A CREATIVE PROCESS

J. M. Buchanan and V. J. Vanberg

GEORGE MASON UNIVERSITY

> Had Pyrrhus not fallen by a beldam's hand in Argos or Julius Caesar not been
> knifed to death? They are not to be thought away. Time has branded them
> and fettered they are lodged in the room of the infinite possibilities they have
> ousted. But can those have been possible, seeing that they never were? Or,
> was that only possible which came to pass?
>
> *James Joyce*[1]

Introduction

Contributions in modern theoretical physics and chemistry on the behavior of non-linear systems, exemplified by Ilya Prigogine's work on the thermodynamics of open systems (Prigogine and Stengers, 1984), attract growing attention in economics (Anderson, Arrow, and Pines, 1988; Arthur, 1990; Baumol and Benhabib, 1989; Mirowski, 1990; Radzicki, 1990). Our purpose here is to relate the new orientation in the natural sciences to a particular nonorthodox strand of thought within economics. All that is needed for this purpose is some appreciation of the general thrust of the enterprise, which involves a shift of perspective from the determinism of conventional physics (which presumably inspired the neoclassical research program in economics) to the nonteleological open-endedness, creative, and nondetermined nature of evolutionary processes.

Prigogine and Stengers (1984, p. 177) refer to this shift in perspective as "a reconceptualization of the physical sciences," as a move "from deterministic, reversible processes to stochastic and irreversible ones." The emphasis is shifted from equilibrium to nonequilibrium as a "source of spontaneous self-organization" (Prigogine, 1985, p. 108), to self-organizing processes in open systems far from thermodynamic equilibrium (Prigogine, 1985, p. 108). A characteristic feature of such systems is the presence of nonlinearities that can amplify "small causes" into "large effects." At critical points (referred to as "bifurcations"), very small events can have

48 J. M. Buchanan and V. J. Vanberg

significant macroeffects, in the sense that they "decide" which particular path — among a number of equally possible paths — the system will take, a fact that introduces a stochastic element and renders self-organizing processes in far-from-equilibrium conditions inherently un-determined.[2] Such processes exhibit a mixture of necessity and chance that, as Prigogine and Stengers note (1984, pp. 169ff.), produces a unique and irreversible " 'history' path along which the system evolves."

What is suggested here is a generalized perspective that brings into focus creativity and open-endedness in the evolution of nonequilibrium systems, a perspective that has as its *leitmotiv* "that the future is not given" (Prigogine, 1986, p. 493), but is created in an unfolding evolutionary process.[3] Authors like P. M. Allen (1988, p. 99) and J. S. Wicken (1987, p. 3) speak of a *new evolutionary synthesis*, a "unified view of the world which bridges the gap between the physical and the human sciences" (Allen, 1988, p. 118). In his discussion on the relevance of the "new evolutionary synthesis" for economic theory, Allen stresses the concern with *microscopic diversity* as the critical feature. The "cloudy, confused complexity of the real world" (1988, p. 99) is the essential subject of an evolutionary approach — in contrast to a perspective that looks for types and classes, and that views microscopic diversity and variation as negligible aberrations, to be averaged out through classification and aggregation.[4] Variability and individual diversity at the microscopic level drive evolutionary processes; they are the crucial ingredient to the "creativity" of these processes, of their potential to generate novelty. As Allen (1988, p. 108) puts it: "The fluctuations, mutations and apparently random movements which are naturally present in real complex systems constitute a sort of 'imaginative' and creative force which will explore around whatever exists at present." Allen sees here the critical difference between an evolutionary perspective and one that centers around the notion of predetermined equilibrium states, the difference between the new self-organization paradigm and a "Newtonian paradigm" in which any "representation of 'creative processes' was entirely absent" (*Ibid.*, p. 97).[5]

As noted, our purpose is, first, to identify a body of criticism of orthodox equilibrium theory in economics that seems to correspond closely with the developments noted in the natural sciences, and, second, to elaborate on the implications of this (the *radical subjectivist*) criticism in some detail and, particularly, in its relation to its near neighbor, the entrepreneurial conceptualization of Israel Kirzner.

Subjectivism, the growth of knowledge, and indeterminedness

P. M. Allen's article is but one example of the growing number of comments on the apparent relevance of the *new evolutionary synthesis* for a reorientation of economic theory. The reasons that limit the applicability of equilibrium models, even in the traditional realm of physics and chemistry, apply *a fortiori* to the domain of economics. The equilibrium concept is associated with a world view that treats the future as implied in the present. In principle, future states could be predicted based on sufficient knowledge of the present; that is, if it were not for *de facto* limits on

The market as a creative process **49**

our knowledge of an immensely complex reality. By contrast, a core insight of the new paradigm is that nature is creative, that novelty and genuinely unpredictable outcomes are generated as the evolutionary process unfolds over time. The creativity argument has all the more force where concern is with social processes that are driven by human choice and inventiveness.[6]

One criticism of economic orthodoxy that has been advanced from a strict *subjectivist* position (a criticism that has, to our knowledge, been developed independently of the literature discussed above) has, in some respects, a strikingly similar thrust.[7] It should be said at the outset that there is no clearly delineated body of thought that would fall under the rubric of *subjectivism*. The term has been adopted by, and used as a label for, a number of perspectives in economics that agree in their broad criticism of the neoclassical general equilibrium framework, but that are by no means theoretically homogeneous. With this proviso stated, we want to concentrate the discussion here on what is often referred to as "radical subjectivism," a position associated primarily with the name of G. L. S. Shackle (1979) as well as with the work of such other authors as L. M. Lachmann, J. Wiseman, and S. C. Littlechild. In section 3, we shall take a closer look at the modern Austrian version of subjectivism, represented by I. Kirzner's work on entrepreneurship, and we shall discuss the differences that Kirzner sees between his own position and "radical subjectivism."[8]

At the core of Shackle's attack on the "neoclassical citadel" (Lachmann, 1976, p. 54), and central to the radical subjectivist view in general, is the issue of what we can claim to know about the future in our efforts to understand the world of human affairs. The basic objection to neo-classical general equilibrium theory is that it embodies assumptions about the knowability of the future that are entirely unfounded, not only in their most extreme variant, the assumption of perfect knowledge, but also in their softer varieties, such as assumptions about rational expectations or Bayesian adaptive rationality. For radical subjectivism there is simply no way around the fundamental fact that whatever happens in the social realm is dependent on human choices, choices that – if they are *choices* – could be different, and could, if they were different, have different effects.[9] There can, therefore, be no "given" future, independent of the choices that will be made. Instead, there are innumerable potential futures of which only one will emerge as the choice-process unfolds. As Shackle puts it, "the content of time-to-come is not merely unknown but nonexistent, and the notion of foreknowledge of human affairs is vacuous" (1983, p. 33). Or in J. Wiseman's terms: "The essence of the radical subjectivist position is that the future is not simply 'unknown,' but is 'nonexistent' or 'indeterminate' at the point of decision" (1989, p. 230).[10]

The recognition that in human social affairs the future is undetermined but "created" in the process of choice, does not imply that the future is "beyond *conjecture*" (Wiseman, 1990, p. 104), nor does it ignore that individuals have *expectations* about the future on which they base their action. The subjectivist's understanding of the nature and role of such expectations is, however, critically different from their interpretation in a neoclassical framework. To the subjectivist, expectations

50 J. M. Buchanan and V. J. Vanberg

may be more or less reasonable (in the sense of being more or less defendable in the light of past experience), but they can, ultimately, not be more than conjectures about an undetermined and, therefore, unknowable future. To the neoclassical economist, by contrast, expectations are about a future that is, in principle, *knowable*, even if its knowability may be limited by imperfections of the "expecters." Ignorance of the future is essentially seen as a source of inefficiency, as a problem that can, in principle, be remedied by learning.[11] By contrast, from a subjectivist position, such ignorance is simply "an inescapable characteristic of the human condition" (Wiseman, 1989, p. 225). And "the possibility of learning does not imply that through learning the future will become knowable, but only that experience will change behavior" (*Ibid.*, p. 143).[12]

Arguing on the same theme, Shackle suggests that every person choosing among different courses of action can be seen "to be making history, on however small a scale, in some sense other than mere passive obedience to the play of all-pervasive causes" (1983, p. 28). Every choice can be seen as the beginning of a sequel that "will be partly the work of many people's choices-to-come whose character ... the chooser of present action cannot know" (*Ibid.*, pp. 28ff.).[13] Our "unknowledge" of the future is, from this perspective, not "a deficiency, a falling-short, a failure of search and study" (*Ibid.*, p. 33). Rather, it reflects a fundamental fact of human existence, "the imaginative and originative source and nature of the choosables, and the endless proliferant creation of hypothetical sequels of choosable action" (*Ibid.*, p. 36). It reflects, in other words, "*the plurality of rival possibles*" (*Ibid.*, p. 37).[14]

The emphasis on choice as an *originating* force, the notion of the *creativeness* of the human mind, and the outlook on history as an *open-ended*, evolving process, are intimately interconnected aspects of the same general theme that marks the critical difference between the subjectivist perspective and its neoclassical counterpart. It marks the difference between the *nonteleological* outlook on the human social realm that informs the subjectivist notion of an open-ended, creative-choice process, and the *teleological* thrust that underlies, if only implicitly, the neoclassical notion of an equilibrium solution that is "preordained by patterns of mineral resources, geography, population, consumer tastes and technological possibilities" (Arthur, 1990, p. 99).[15] To Shackle and other radical subjectivists, the whole general equilibrium concept is questionable when applied to a constantly changing social world that has no predeterminable telos, whether in the pompous sense of a Marxian philosophy of history or in the more pedestrian sense of a conceptually definable equilibrium toward which the process of socioeconomic change could be predicted to gravitate. In a world in which creative human choice is a constant source of an "unknowable future," the notion of a "social equilibrium" is, in J. Wiseman's words, a "pseudo-concept" (1989, p. 214), one that can "have only the most tenuous general meaning" (*Ibid.*, p. 265).[16]

Another way of stating the subjectivist objection against the neoclassical equilibrium concept is by saying that the latter does not provide for an adequate account of "real," historical time. It does not take seriously the fact that, as L. M. Lachmann puts it, "*Time* and *Knowledge* belong together" (1977, p. 85), that "time cannot pass

The market as a creative process **51**

without modifying knowledge" (*Ibid.*, p. 93)[17] The common argument that "simplifying assumptions" allow general equilibrium models to ignore the complexities of the "time and knowledge" problem is rejected by Wiseman as unconvincing. The simplifying assumptions about human knowledge are, he argues, "not legitimate simplifications but a gross perversion of the nature of the decision-problem faced by people living in the real world" (1989, p. 140), a defect that cannot be remedied by sophisticated refinements of the models that are based on such assumptions.[18]

The contrast is between two critically different perspectives by which efforts to understand the world can be guided: (1) a *teleological* perspective, and (2) a *nonteleological* perspective. We argue that it is its uncompromising nonteleological character that marks the critical difference between the understanding of the market process suggested by the subjectivist perspective and various standard conceptions of the market that, if only in a very subliminal fashion, have a teleological undertone. And, as an aside, we want to submit that this "residual teleology" constitutes somewhat of a hidden common link between standard economic teaching on the self-organizing nature of markets and the blatant teleology of the socialist planning mentality.

Kirzner's theory of entrepreneurship

Israel Kirzner's work, with its explicit emphasis on the entrepreneurial role in economic interaction, is of particular interest in the present context because of Kirzner's (1985, pp. 7ff.) claim that his own "alertness" theory of entrepreneurship keeps a balanced middle ground between "two extreme views," the neoclassical equilibrium view on the one side and Shackle's subjectivism on the other, or, in our terms, between a teleological and a nonteleological concept of the market process.[19] As we shall argue, however, in spite of his emphasis on innovative entrepreneurial dynamics and in spite of his verbal recognition of the *creative* and *open-ended* nature of the market process, Kirzner's approach fails to escape the subliminal teleology of the equilibrium framework.[20]

There is, as Littlechild (1979) has pointed out in some detail, a disharmonious mixture in Kirzner's work, between a basic affinity to, and remaining disagreements with, the radical subjectivist position. Kirzner explicitly recognizes the creative dynamics of the market process, and indeed, makes this the central theme of his work. He criticizes the neo-classical position for assigning "*no* role ... to the creative entrepreneur" (1985, p. 13); he talks of the role of entrepreneurship "in an open-ended, uncertain world (*Ibid.*, p. 52), a world in which we "find scope for the unpredictable, the creative, the imaginative expression of the human mind" (*Ibid.*, p. 58); and he talks of new products, new qualities of products, new methods of production, and new forms of organization that are endlessly generated in the course of the entrepreneurial process.[21] Yet, such emphasis on creativity, imagination, and novelty is combined with a theoretical perspective that located the essence of entrepreneurship in "the discovery of error" (Kirzner, 1985, p. 50), and the

52 J. M. Buchanan and V. J. Vanberg

scope for entrepreneurship "in the possibility of discovering error" (*Ibid.*, p. 51), a combination that can hardly be called harmonious.

Discovery of error means, in the context of Kirzner's theory, such things as the discovery of "erroneously low valuation" (*Ibid.*, p. 50) of resources, the "alertness to hitherto unperceived opportunities" (*Ibid.*, p. 52), or the noticing of "situations overlooked until now because of error" (*Ibid.*), phrases that all invite the same questions: If the essence of entrepreneurial discovery is to "provide protection" or "rescue" from "earlier" or "past error" (*Ibid.*, p. 53), what is then the benchmark or *reference-base* against which the failure to do something can be judged to be an "error"? And how does the notion of *creativity* square with such definition of entrepreneurial activity? Are creativity and imagination the same as discovery of errors?

There is, in our view, a fundamental inconsistency in Kirzner's attempt to integrate the innovativeness of entrepreneurial activity into an equilibrium framework – by modeling it as *discovery* of "erroneously overlooked opportunities."[22] The critical step in Kirzner's argument, the step that is intended to establish a "middle ground" between a teleological and a nonteleological understanding of the market process, is his extension of the notion of a divergence between "different parts of the market" (1985, p. 62) from a *cross-sectional* to an *intertemporal* interpretation.[23] According to the cross-sectional interpretation, the entrepreneur acts essentially as *arbitrageur:* By taking advantage of hitherto unnoticed divergences between different parts in a present market, he helps to bring about greater consistency (Kirzner, 1985, pp. 61ff.). According to the intertemporal interpretation, the entrepreneur takes advantage of yet unnoticed divergences between *today's* market and *tomorrow's* market, thus helping "to coordinate markets also across time" (*Ibid.*, p. 62).[24]

Whatever may be said about the knowability of divergencies in the cross-sectional interpretation, it should be obvious that the notion of *intertemporal* divergences between markets at different points in time is inherently problematic. If, as we must assume, divergences between today's and tomorrow's markets are typically associated with differences between today's and tomorrow's *knowledge*, what does it mean to say that entrepreneurial alertness corrects the "failure to realize" divergences between *present* and *future* markets? What sense does it make to describe today's failure to possess tomorrow's knowledge as *error*?[25] If, to use Lachmann's phrase, "*Time* and *Knowledge* belong together," a comparison between present and future markets cannot possibly be made in a sense that would make such terminology meaningful. The kind of comparison that can be made, at least conceptually, across contemporaneous markets cannot be made along the "intertemporal dimension" (Kirzner, 1985, p. 62). Time is not simply another "dimension," comparable to the spatial. Different parts of a present market exist, they are *present*, and differences in their characteristics can be discovered. Future parts of a market simply do not exist; they are, by definition, not present. There are, at any point in time, many *potential* futures imaginable, based on more or less informed reflections. Yet, which future will come into existence will depend on choices that are yet to be made. Of course, human beings aim to be "prepared for the future," and they act on their

The market as a creative process   **53**

expectations of what lies ahead. The subjectivist argument on the unknowability of the future is certainly not meant as a recommendation to merchants not to anticipate the coming of winter in their storekeeping. Yet, if, and to the extent that, human choices and their complex interactions shape the emerging future, the latter can be a matter of speculation, but not of foreknowledge.

The supposition that the future is foreknowable clearly seems implied when, in talking about the problem of intertemporal entrepreneurial alertness, Kirzner speaks of pictures of the future that may or may not "correspond to the truth as it will be realized" (1985, p. 55), of man's efforts to overcome uncertainty "by more accurate prescience" (*Ibid.*, p. 58), of "past failure to pierce correctly the fog of uncertainty" (*Ibid.*, p. 53), and so forth. It is far from obvious how such insinuation of a preknowable future can be consistent with a genuine appreciation of the creativity of the human mind. Indeed, when arriving at this issue, Kirzner simply retreats to the *ex cathedra* claim that his approach does encompass the two notions, without actually showing *how* this can be done. He emphasizes that intertemporal entrepreneurial alertness "does not consist merely in 'seeing' the unfolding of the tapestry of the future in the sense of seeing a preordained flow of events" (1985, p. 56). Indeed, he insists that such alertness must "embrace the awareness of the ways in which the human agent can ... in fact *create* the future" (*Ibid.*). Yet, as if the compatibility of the two arguments were obvious, he also insists that the function of market entrepreneurship in the multiperiod context is nonetheless still that of "discovery of errors" in the sense explained above (*Ibid.*).[26] And he leaves undiscussed the issue of what one entrepreneur's creativity means for the truthfulness of another entrepreneur's picture of the future.[27]

If, as Kirzner's construction seems to suggest, today's failure to possess tomorrow's knowledge qualifies as *error* from which entrepreneurial alertness is to provide rescue, one could conclude that the ultimate benchmark or reference base for such judgment is an imagined world in which everything that humans may ever imagine, think, or know will be revealed.[28] Judged against such a benchmark, every act, however imaginative and creative, can be seen as a discovery of something that was already waiting to be found. And failure to discover may be discussed in terms of error and overlooked opportunities. It seems questionable, however, whether the mental construct of such an imagined world is a helpful analytical guide when applied to the study of socioeconomic change.

What might be misleadingly suggestive here is the analogy to the scientific discovery process. To the extent that science is concerned with an objective reality "out there," our conjectural knowledge of this reality can be expected to grow over time, through a process of discovery. Although we cannot know at present what we will know in the future, any future increase in knowledge can, in some sense, be viewed as a finding of something that could, in principle, be currently discovered. There is something knowable out there, to be discovered sooner or later. Any such account of the discovery process in science is itself seriously challenged by the new conceptions advanced by Prigogine and others, because of its neglect of real time. But, even if, for the purpose of our discussion here, we should leave this issue aside, the analogous challenge advanced by the radical subjectivists to neoclassical equilibrium economics applies with full force to the concept of the market as a discovery process. Entrepreneurial activity, in particular, is not to be modelled as discovery of that which is "out there." Such activity, by contrast, *creates* a reality that will be different subsequent on differing choices. Hence, the reality of the future must be shaped by choices yet to be made, and this reality has no existence independent of these choices. With regard to a "yet to be created" reality, it is surely confusing to consider its emergence in terms of the discovery of "overlooked opportunities."[29]

Conceptions and misconceptions of the market

The essential characteristic of the radical subjectivist position that marks its critical departure from a neoclassical framework is, at the same time, the feature that it shares with the new evolutionary synthesis discussed at the beginning of this article: Its conception of "a world in which time plays a vital role" (Littlechild, 1979, p. 38), of history as an open-ended evolving process, and of a future that is not predetermined, merely waiting to be revealed, but that is "continuously *originated* by the pattern and sequence of human choice" (*Ibid.*). Such a conception has clear implications for the theory of the market that set it apart from various theoretical constructs that have been used to explain or to illustrate the adaptive nature of the market process. If the emphasis on the creativity of human choice is taken seriously, it is not only the standard neoclassical equilibrium notion that seems questionable, but also less orthodox conceptions of the market process, including Kirzner's more subliminally teleological perspective on markets and entrepreneurship. By stating this we certainly do not want to suggest that "radical subjectivism" exists as a well-specified theoretical paradigm ready for adoption – it clearly is not. What we want to suggest, however, is that the creativity of human choice poses a problem that any effective socioeconomic theory cannot evade.

The critical shift in perspective may be further illustrated by reference to three separate understandings of the spontaneous order of the market that have been advanced by scholars who have been generally supportive of market organization of the economy, no one of whom would ever have referred to the market as an "analogue computer" for the "computation of equilibrium prices."

(1) One of us (Buchanan) learned basic price theory at the University of Chicago in the 1940s, when all students, undergraduate and graduate, were required to master the Syllabus written by Henry Simons.[30] This Syllabus contained three well-known rent problems that were designed to provide an understanding of how a competitive economy allocates scarce resources among uses. And, as a test of the efficacy of competitive adjustment, one task given to the students was that of comparing the total product of the economy in competitive equilibrium with that which might be achieved under allocation by a benevolent and omniscient planner.

(2) In a deservedly famous article, "The Logic of Liberty," Michael Polanyi introduced the metaphor of a sack of potatoes that need only to be shaken to insure minimization of volume to demonstrate how localized, decentralized adjustment, akin to that which is characteristic of market organization, works better than centralized adjustment.[31]

(3) In a monograph-length essay devoted to an explication of the spontaneous order of the market, Norman Barry (1982) stated that the results of a market "appear to be a product of some omniscient, designing mind."[32]

In each of these illustrative examples, there is revealed, at least by inference, an understanding of the spontaneous ordering properties of a market process that is sharply different from the understanding held by the radical subjectivists. In each example, the efficacy of market adjustment is measured *teleologically* in terms of the relative achievement of some predefined goal or objective. In Simons' problems, the objective is, simply, economic product, which is wheat in his one-good economy. In Polanyi's case, the objective is explicitly stated to be minimization of volume. In Barry's essay, the argument is more sophisticated, but any conceptualization of an omniscient, designing mind must imply some well-defined objective that exists independently from the separate participants' own *creative* choices.

If the efficacy of market organization is, as insinuated in the above examples, evaluated teleologically, in terms of its capacity to approach an independently (that is, independent of the choice process itself) determinable state, then there remains only an ambiguous discourse over comparative performance as between such an organization and centralized economic planning. Even if Simons, Polanyi, and Barry, along with others, may have succeeded in demonstrating that decentralized arrangements are superior in achieving some objectively identifiable goal, their conceptualization of the market process forces them into a line of comparative defense that a radical subjectivist understanding of the market would have rendered unnecessary from the outset. If the market is genuinely perceived as an open-ended, nondetermined evolutionary process in which the essential driving force is human choice, any insinuation, however subtle, of a "telos" toward which the process can be predicted to move must be inherently misleading. There is, in our view, no systematically sustainable middle ground between a teleological and a nonteleological perspective. And all conceptualizations of the market process that suppose, whether explicitly or implicitly, a "something" toward which the process is moving are, by this very fact, *teleological*, whether the "something" is specified as an equilibrium or otherwise. This applies to the notion of a mechanical equilibrium as implied in the standard textbook models of intersecting demand and supply curves, as well as to the thermodynamic equilibrium concept that is implied where the market process is interpreted in terms of exhaustion of potential gains from trade. And it also applies to images of the market that are intended to capture the constant change in the equilibrium-telos, such as K. Boulding's image of the "dog chasing a cat" (Littlechild, 1986, p. 32).

It should be noted that to question the appropriateness of teleological conceptions of the market is not the same as denying the apparent fact that the human participants in the "catallaxy," the game of the market, reasonably *adapt* to the circumstances that they confront and to changes that they expect to occur. The predictive potential of microeconomic theory lies in the uniformity of such adaptive response among persons. But such adaptive behavior does not imply that the overall process is moving toward some determined goal, whether conceived as a predetermined equilibrium or as a "moving cat." The game described by the market may be misunderstood if interpreted in a teleological mind-set. The market economy, *as an aggregation*, neither maximizes nor minimizes anything. It simply allows participants to pursue that which they value, subject to the preferences and endowments of others, and within the constraints of general "rules of the game" that allow, and provide incentives for, individuals to try out new ways of doing things. There simply is no "external," independently defined objective against which the results of market processes can be evaluated.

We may illustrate the nonteleological perspective on market interaction by dropping the familiar presupposition that potential traders initially possess quantities of well-defined marketable goods. Assume that no goods exist, and that persons are described by certain talents, capacities, and skills that enable them to produce consumable goods from nature. Assume that the rules of the game allow persons to claim enforceable rights to the shares in natural endowments and to their own capacities and skills. In this model, trade will take place when persons recognize that their well-being can be enhanced by producing *and* exchanging rather than producing for their own consumption only. But the chain of choices is extended, and, also, there is an added requirement that any participant exercise *imagination* in choosing to specialize in production with the ultimate purpose of achieving an increase in well-being through exchange.

Think of the choice calculus of a person in this setting. What can I produce that will prove of exchange value to others? Response to this question allows the participant not only to select among a preexisting, set of goods, but, also and importantly, to *create* new goods that are expected to be of potential exchangeable value. Once the creative-inventive-imaginative element in choice is introduced into the game here, then any idealized omniscience on the part of a planner who might attempt to duplicate the market result would become patently absurd. Individuals would use their own imagination, their own assessment of the potential evaluations of others, in producing goods wholly divorced from their own consumption, goods that are anticipated to yield values when put on the market, values that, as income to the producers, can be used to purchase goods from others in the nexus. This seeking to satisfy others through producing marketable value as an indirect means of producing value for themselves – this characteristic behavioral element in a market order was central to Adam Smith's insight. And it is this feature that allows us to compare the performance of market organization with alternative social arrangements, even in the absence of an independently existing scalar. Markets tend to satisfy the preferences of persons, regardless of what their preferences might be,

The market conceived as a "game without goods" also suggests the tenuousness of the whole notion of equilibrium, defined as the exhaustion of gains from trade, which looms so important in the alternative teleological perspective. In the production and exchange of preexisting and well-defined goods, it is relatively easy to think of the game as having a definitive and final outcome once the goods have been so allocated that no participant seeks out further trades. Goods are, by definition, then allocated to their highest valued uses. But the usefulness of this equilibrium notion becomes less clear when we assume that there is no definite set of goods to be allocated. Conceptually, it remains possible to "freeze" the imaginative elements in individual choice at some point and allow the production-exchange process to work itself out to an equilibrium, where no further gains from trade, *and from imagination of new trading prospects*, are possible. The artificiality of such an equilibrium construction is apparent, however, since there seems nothing in the mind that is even remotely analogous to the cessation of exchange. There is no determinate limit to the potential of market value to be created as the process of human interaction proceeds.

What has made, and continues to make, the equilibrium concept attractive even to economists who, like Kirzner, are explicitly critical of the neoclassical orthodoxy is, it seems, its perceived capacity to readily capture the coordinative properties of markets, and the suspicion that the radical subjectivist critique may leave one incapable of systematically accounting for the orderliness of markets. Even if such suspicion may have been invited by some of the radical subjectivists, the emerging *new evolutionary synthesis* suggests a theoretical perspective that allows the subjectivist emphasis on the creativity of human choice, with all its implications, to be taken seriously, while, at the same time, it offers nonteleological explanations for the adaptiveness and coordinative properties that markets exhibit.

Conclusion

We have suggested that a perceptual vision of the market as a *creative process* offers more insight and understanding than the alternative visions that elicit interpretations of the market as a *discovery process*,[33] or, more familiarly, as an *allocative process*. In either of the latter alternatives, there is a telos imposed by the scientist's own perception, a telos that is nonexistent in the first stance. And removal of the teleological inference from the way of looking at economic interaction carries with it significant implications for any diagnosis of failure or success, diagnosis that is necessarily preliminary to any normative usage of scientific analysis.

We may illustrate the differing implications in application to the observed failure of the centrally planned economies of Eastern Europe and elsewhere. The neoclassical economist, trapped in the allocationist perception, tends to locate the source of failure in the distorted incentive structure that causes persons to be confronted with choice alternatives that do not reflect authentically derived evaluations.

58 J. M. Buchanan and V. J. Vanberg

Resources do not flow to their most highly valued uses because persons who make decisions about resource use do not find it privately in their own interest to shift allocation in such fashion as to accomplish this conceptually definable, and desirable, result.

Some of the modern Austrian economists, and notably Kirzner, add an important element to the neoclassical critique. They suggest that, even if the incentive problems could, somehow, be ignored or assumed corrected, there would still remain the epistemological or knowledge problem. Only a decentralized market structure of economic interaction can exploit fully the knowledge of localized circumstances required to allow a definition of the ultimate valuation that is placed on resource use. Only the market can allow persons the effective liberty to discover the particular localized eccentricities that give form to value. This extension of the neoclassical emphasis on incentive structures is important and relevant to any overall assessment of the central planning model for an economy.

We suggest, however, that the critique, even as extended, falls short of capturing an essential element in any comparative assessment of the market and the planning alternatives. The teleological feature remains to be exorcised. In the neoclassical setting, even as extended by Kirzner, an *omniscient* and *benevolent* monolithic planner could secure the ideally defined result. Omniscience would, of course, insure access to any and all knowledge; benevolence could be such as to match the objective function precisely with whatever it is that individuals desire. But even the planner so idealized cannot create that which is not there and will not be there save through the exercise of the creative choices of individuals, who themselves have no idea in advance concerning the ideas that their own imaginations will yield.

The fundamental misunderstandings of the theory of the market economy that provided the analytical-intellectual foundations for socialism as a principle for socioeconomic organization are exposed by any one of the three interpretations contrasted here. The market as an allocative process, responding to the structure of incentives that confront choice-makers; the market as a discovery process, utilizing localized information; or the market as a creative process that exploits man's imaginative potential – socialism cannot, organizationally, be made equivalent to any one of these idealized perceptions. But, the "fatal conceit" that was socialism, to use Hayek's descriptive term here, would have surely faced more difficulty in achieving dominance as an idea if the creative spontaneity of the market process had been more fully appreciated.

Acknowledgments

An earlier version of this paper was presented at a Liberty Fund Conference on "An Inquiry into Liberty and Self-Organizing Systems," April 26–29, 1990, Rio Rico, Arizona. We received helpful comments on previous drafts from Hartmut Kliemt, Karen Vaughn, Jack Wiseman, and an anonymous referee.

Notes

1 Joyce, 1960, p. 30.
2 Prigogine and Stengers: "Whenever we reach a bifurcation point, deterministic description breaks down. The type of fluctuation present in the system will lead to the choice of the branch it will follow. Crossing a bifurcation point is a stochastic process, such as the tossing of a coin" (1984, p. 177).
3 Prigogine: "[W]e come to a world which is open, in which the past is present and cumulative, in which the present is there but the future is not. ... The future does not exist yet, the future is in construction, a construction which is going on in all existing activities" (1985, p.117).
4 The critical importance of individual diversity and variation from an evolutionary perspective is similarly stressed by biologist E. Mayr, who uses in this context the term "population thinking": "Population thinkers stress the uniqueness of everything in the organic world. What is important for them is the individual, not the type. ... There is no 'typical' individual, and mean values are abstractions. ... The differences between biological individuals are real, while the mean values which we may calculate in the comparison of groups of individuals (species, for example) are man-made inferences" (Mayr, 1982, pp. 46ff.). Mayr contrasts "population thinking" with "essentialist thinking": "Adoption of population thinking is intimately tied up with a rejection of essentialist thinking. Variation is irrelevant and therefore uninteresting to the essentialist. Varying characters are 'mere accidents,' in the language of essentialism" (*Ibid.*, p. 487).
5 As P. Allen points out, one has to realize "that there is a critical difference between asking whether a system *obeys* the laws of physics, ... or whether its behavior can be predicted from a knowledge of those laws" (1985, pp. 268ff.). For nonlinear systems, Allen argues, the first can be the case without the second being possible, due to the mixture of deterministic and stochastic aspects of nonlinear systems (*Ibid.*, p. 270). Allen's argument parallels K. R. Popper's remark in *The Open Universe:* "[C]ausality has to be distinguished from determinism, and our world of uniqueness is – unlike Kant's noumenal world – in space and, even more important, in time; for I find it crucially important to distinguish between the determined *past* and the open *future*" (1982, p. 48). In reference to Prigogine's work, Popper argues in the same treatise: "We must not ... blind us to the fact that the universe that harbours life is creative in the best sense: creative in the sense in which the great poets, the great artists, the great musicians have been creative, as well as the great mathematicians, the great scientists, and the great inventors" (*Ibid.*, p. 174).
6 Prigogine: "Clearly, a social system is by definition a nonlinear one, as interactions between the members of the society may have a catalystic effect. At each moment fluctuations are generated, which may be damped or amplified by society. An excellent example of a huge amplification ... is the acquisition of knowledge. ... Instead of seeing human systems in terms of 'equilibrium' or as a 'mechanism,' we see a creative world of imperfect information and shifting values, in which different futures can be envisaged" (1986, p. 503).
7 This similarity has been explicitly noted by Fehl (1986); see also Witt (1985).
8 There are other versions of "economic subjectivism" that can be distinguished from both its "radical" and Austrian variety, in particular, the "opportunity costs approach" that has been systematically stated by one of the present authors (Buchanan, 1969, 1987). This version, as well as others that could be identified, will, however, not be discussed as such in the present article.
9 Allen: "The response to this question of 'choice,' which makes modelling and predicting difficult, can be of two kinds. Either we can suppose that choice is an illusion and that the mechanical analogy is in fact legitimate, or we must find some new scientific paradigm in which 'choice' really exists" (1985, p. 269).
10 Littlechild stresses that same point when he summarizes the "radical subjectivist" view as implying that the "as-yet-undetermined actions of other agents" make for "the essential

60 J. M. Buchanan and V. J. Vanberg

open-endedness of creativity" (1986, p. 31) in human affairs, that "the future is not so much unknown as it is nonexistent or indetermined at the time of decision" (*Ibid.*, p. 29).

11 Wiseman: "Mainstream economics deals with unknowability by assuming it away. In the simple model, this is done by assuming perfect knowledge of the future. ... The more sophisticated models assume knowledge of the possible number of future states of the world. ... They assume that *someone* has a knowledge of the future that no one can possibly have" (1990, p. 103). See also Wiseman (1989, p. 159).

12 Wiseman: "*The future* has not yet happened. About it, men can have only *opinions*, related to past experience (learning). Since men can (must) choose how to act, their chosen acts, together with the evolution of the physical world, are continuously creating the emerging future. If this is so (as it must be), then the future cannot be known 'now' (that is, in the continuous present)" (1989, p. 268).

13 As a summary of Shackle's position, Littlechild states, "Choice ... represents an origin, a beginning. ... [I]t does have a sequel. It makes a difference to what comes after. This sequel cannot be foreknown, because subsequent events will depend partly upon other such choices yet to be made" (1979, p. 33).

14 Shackle: "[I]f we had *all the data there are or could be* about the *present*, we might still not be able to infer what the sequel of any action now chosen would be. ... If history, past and to come, is all one book already written at the beginning of time, what is choice? ... But if choice is fertile, effective, truly *inceptive*, then there can be no foreknowledge. History-to-come, in that case, is not only unknown but *not yet existent*" (1981, p. 60).

15 We use the term "teleological" here in a more general sense than that of an explanation in terms of intended ends or purposeful design. We classify as "teleological" all theoretical perspectives that explain processes in terms of some predeterminable end point toward which they are supposed to move, rather than in terms of explicitly specified forces and principles that actually "drive" them. It is in this sense that we classify as "teleological" an equilibrium theory that describes economic processes in terms of "where they are going," namely, their end-point equilibria, but does not provide an explicit explanatory account of the dynamics of these processes themselves.

16 Littlechild: "[F]or G. L. S. Shackle, the relevance of the whole concept (of general equilibrium) is in question. Every act of choice embodies the chooser's creative imagination of the future. The market therefore follows a 'kaleidic' process, with moments of order interspersed with disintegration into a new pattern. The economy is changing and developing, but in no sense does it have a single goal" (1983, pp. 48ff.).

17 Lachmann: "The impossibility of prediction in economics follows from the fact that economic change is linked to change in knowledge, and future knowledge cannot be gained before its time. Knowledge is generated by spontaneous acts of the mind" (1977, p. 90).

18 Wiseman: "But if what is assumed away is the essence of the problem, then greater complexity will generate not greater insights but more sophisticated confusion" (1989, p. 227).

19 Kirzner: "I claim, indeed, that the 'alertness' view of entrepreneurship enables us to have the best of both worlds: we *can* incorporate entrepreneurship into the analysis without surrendering the heart of microeconomic theory" (1985, p. 11). Stated differently, Kirzner claims to avoid the neoclassical orthodoxy's failure to account for "the creative entrepreneur" (*Ibid.*, p. 13), without falling "into the seductive trap offered by the opposite extreme" (*Ibid.*), that is, by the radical subjectivist position.

20 G. P. O'Driscoll's and M. J. Rizzo's exposition of a modern Austrian-subjectivist economics is, in a similar way, characterized by a tension between the acceptance of basic tenets of radical subjectivism and the attempt to maintain "an appropriately revised idea of equilibrium" (1985, p. 79).

21 Kirzner: "In the course of this entrepreneurial process, new products may be introduced, new qualities of existing products may be developed, new methods of production may be ventured, new forms of industrial organization, financing, marketing, or tackling risk may be developed. All the ceaseless churning and agitation of the market is to be understood as the consequence of the never-ending discovery process of which the market consists" (1985, pp. 30ff.).

The market as a creative process **61**

22 Kirzner: "I postulate a continuous discovery process – an entrepreneurial discovery process – that in the absence of external changes in underlying conditions, fuels a tendency toward equilibrium" (1985, p. 12).

23 Kirzner: "What market entrepreneurship accomplishes is a tendency for transactions in different parts of the market (including the market at different dates) to become coordinated" (1985, p. 64).

24 Kirzner's crucial argument, in this context, is worth quoting at some length: "When we introduce the passage of time, the dimensions along which mutual ignorance may develop are multiplied. Market participants in one part of today's market may not only be imperfectly aware of the transactions available in another part of the market; they also may be imperfectly aware of the transactions that will be available in next year's market. Absence of consistency between different parts of today's market is seen as a special case of a more general notion of inconsistency that includes also inconsistency between today's transactions and those to be transacted next year. … It is still the case, as noted, that the entrepreneurial function is that of bringing about a tendency for transactions in different parts of the market (conceived broadly now as including transactions entered into at different times) to be made in greater mutual consistency. But whereas in the case of entrepreneurship in the single-period market (that is, the case of the entrepreneur as arbitrageur) entrepreneurial alertness meant alertness to present facts, in the case of multiperiod entrepreneurship alertness must mean alertness to the future" (1985, pp. 62ff.).

25 A well-known classical statement of the argument that we simply cannot anticipate future knowledge and, therefore, cannot predict future human choices that will be affected by such future knowledge, can be found in K. R. Popper's Preface to his *The Poverty of Historicism* (1957).

26 The same kind of tension between Kirzner's chosen theoretical framework and his attempt to incorporate the notion of entrepreneurial inventiveness in the creation of new products and new ways of doing things is also visible in his more recent discussion on the subject (Kirzner, 1989, pp. 84ff.). In her review of this book, K. Vaughn comments on Kirzner's attempts to account for the creative aspects of entrepreneurship while retaining his earlier language: "It has become obvious to this reviewer that the old language no longer fits his new theoretical insights" (1990, p. 185).

27 Kirzner indirectly refers to this issue without, however, discussing it: "In particular the futurity that entrepreneurship must confront introduces the possibility that the entrepreneur may, by his own creative actions, in fact *construct* the future as *he* wishes it to be. In the single-period case alertness can at best discover hitherto overlooked current facts. In the multiperiod case entrepreneurial alertness must include the entrepreneur's perception of the way in which creative and imaginative action may vitally shape the kind of transactions that will be entered into in future market periods" (1985, pp. 63ff.).

28 And, by implication, one could argue that the "equilibrium" toward which intertemporal coordination – as it is promoted by entrepreneurial discovery of error – tends to gravitate can only be some final state of universal enlightenment, at the end of all times. Support for such, admittedly exaggerated, interpretation may be seen in statements such as this: "My view, therefore, sees initial market ignorance indeed as an inescapable feature of the human condition in a world of change, but also as subject to continual erosion. … (Entrepreneurs) discover where existing decisions were in fact mistaken. Here lies the source for any equilibrating tendencies that markets display" (Kirzner, 1985, p. 13).

29 The discussion here, and elsewhere in this article, is related, at least indirectly, to a criticism of Michael Polanyi advanced by one of us in two related articles (Buchanan, 1977, 1985). Polanyi conceptualized the scientific process as exploration or discovery, and he argued persuasively that decentralized organization of the scientific enterprise would insure more rapid advance in "solving" the "jigsaw puzzle." From this conceptualization of the scientific process, Polanyi supported, by analogy, the spontaneous ordering properties of decentralized market processes.

Buchanan's criticism suggested that, even if the discovery-exploration metaphor remains applicable to the enterprise of the physical sciences, such a metaphor is misleading

62 J. M. Buchanan and V. J. Vanberg

when applied and extended to economic or political interaction among freely choosing individuals.

30 The Simons' Syllabus was circulated only in mimeographed form. Gordon Tullock, himself a student of Simons in the 1940s, edited and published a somewhat incomplete version in 1983 (Tullock, 1983).

31 This article was the title essay in the volume *The Logic of Liberty* (Polanyi, 1951).

32 For a commentary on Barry's essay, see Buchanan (1982).

33 Although the thrust of his work clearly supports the vision of the market as a creative process, Hayek's (1978) illuminating discussion on "Competition as a Discovery Procedure" is not entirely free of the ambiguities that the concept of *discovery* tends to invoke when applied to the market process. Potentially misleading are, in this regard, his comparison between the discovery processes in science and in the market (*Ibid.*, p. 181) and some of his comments on the problem of measuring market performance (*Ibid.*, pp. 185ff.).

References

Allen, Peter M. 1985. "Towards a New Science of Complex Systems." In *The Science and Praxis of Complexity*, by S. Aida et al., pp. 268–97. Tokyo: The United Nations University.

Allen, Peter M. 1988. "Evolution, Innovation and Economics." In *Technical Change and Economic Theory*, edited by G. Dosi, C. Freeman, R. Nelson, G. Silverberg, and L. Soete, pp. 95–119. London: Pinter Publishers Ltd.

Anderson, Philip W., Kenneth J. Arrow, and David Pines (editors). 1988. *The Economy as an Evolving Complex System*. New York: Addison-Wesley.

Arthur, W. Brian. 1990. "Positive Feedbacks in the Economy." *Scientific American* 262:92–99.

Barry, Norman. 1982. "The Tradition of Spontaneous Order." *The Literature of Liberty* 5:7–58.

Baumol, William, and Stephen Benhabib. 1989. "Chaos: Significance, Mechanism, and Economic Applications." *Journal of Economic Issues* 3:77–106.

Buchanan, James M. 1969. *Cost and Choice – An Inquiry in Economic Theory*. Chicago: Markham Publishing Company.

Buchanan, James M. 1977. "Politics and Science." In *Freedom in Constitutional Contract*, by J. M. Buchanan, pp. 64–77. College Station: Texas A&M University Press.

Buchanan, James M. 1982. "Order Defined in the Process of Its Emergence." *The Literature of Liberty* 5:5.

Buchanan, James M. 1985. "The Potential for Tyranny in Politics as Science." In *Liberty, Market and State*, by J. M. Buchanan, pp. 40–54. New York: New York University Press.

Buchanan, James M. 1987. "L. S. E. Cost Theory in Retrospect." In *Economics – Between Predictive Science and Moral Philosophy*, by J. M. Buchanan, pp. 141–51. College Station: Texas A&M University Press.

Fehl, Ulrich. 1986. "Spontaneous Order and the Subjectivity of Expectations: A Contribution to the Lachmann-O'Driscoll Problem." In *Subjectivism, Intelligibility, and Economic Understanding*, edited by I. M. Kirzner, pp. 72–86. New York: New York University Press.

Hayek, Friedrich A. 1978. "Competition as a Discovery Procedure." In *New Studies in Philosophy, Politics, Economics, and the History of Ideas*, by F. A. Hayek, pp. 179–90. Chicago: The University of Chicago Press.

Joyce, James. 1960. *Ulysses*. London: Bodley Head.

Kirzner, Israel M. 1985. *Discovery and the Capitalist Process*. Chicago: The University of Chicago Press.

The market as a creative process **63**

Kirzner, Israel M. 1989. *Discovery, Capitalism, Distributive Justice*. New York: Basil Blackwell.

Lachmann, Ludwig M. 1976. "From Mises to Shackle: An Essay on Austrian Economics and the Kaleidic Society." *Journal of Economic Literature* 14:54–62.

Lachmann, Ludwig M. 1977. "Professor Shackle on the Economic Significance of Time." In *Capital, Expectations, and the Market Process*, by L. M. Lachmann, pp. 81–93. Kansas City, MO: Sheed Andrews and McMeel.

Littlechild, Stephen C. 1979. "Comment: Radical Subjectivism or Radical Subversion." In *Time, Uncertainty and Disequilibrium: Exploration of Austrian Themes*, edited by M. Rizzo, pp. 32–49. Lexington, MA: Lexington Books.

Littlechild, Stephen C. 1983. "Subjectivism and Method in Economics." In *Beyond Positive Economics*, edited by J. Wiseman, pp. 38–49. London: Macmillan.

Littlechild, Stephen C. 1986. "Three Types of Market Process." In *Economics as a Process – Essays in the New Institutional Economics*, edited by Richard N. Langlois, pp. 27–39. Cambridge: Cambridge University Press.

Mayr, Ernst. 1982. *The Growth of Biological Thought – Diversity, Evolution, and Inheritance*. Cambridge, MA: Harvard University Press.

Mirowski, Philip. 1990. "From Mandelbrot to Chaos in Economic Theory." *Southern Economic Journal* 57:289–307.

O'Driscoll, Gerald P., and Mario J. Rizzo. 1985. *The Economics of Time and Ignorance*. New York: Basil Blackwell.

Polanyi, Michael. 1951. *The Logic of Liberty*. Chicago: The University of Chicago Press.

Popper, Karl R. 1957. *The Poverty of Historicism*. Boston: The Beacon Press.

Popper, Karl R. 1982. *The Open Universe – An Argument for Indeterminism*. Totowa, NJ: Rowan and Littlefield.

Prigogine, Ilya. 1985. "New Perspectives on Complexity." In *The Science and Praxis of Complexity*, by S. Aida et al., pp. 107–18. Tokyo: The United Nations University.

Prigogine, Ilya. 1986. "Science, Civilization and Democracy." *Futures* 18:493–507.

Prigogine, Ilya, and Isabelle Stengers. 1984. *Order out of Chaos – Man's New Dialogue with Nature*. Toronto: Bantam Books.

Radzicki, Michael J. 1990. "Institutional Dynamics, Deterministic Chaos, and Self-Organizing Systems." *Journal of Economic Issues* 24:57–102.

Shackle, G. L. S. 1979. *Imagination and the Nature of Choice*. Edinburgh: Edinburgh University Press.

Shackle, G. L. S. 1981. "Comments." In *Subjectivist Economics – The New Austrian School*, by A. H. Shand, pp. 59–67. Oxford: The Pica Press.

Shackle, G. L. S. 1983. "The Bounds of Unknowledge." In *Beyond Positive Economics*, edited by J. Wiseman, pp. 28–37. London: Macmillan.

Tullock, Gordon (editor). 1983. *The Simons' Syllabus*, by Henry Calvert Simons. Blacksburg, Virginia Polytechnic Institute and State University.

Vaughn, Karen I. 1990. "Profits, Alertness and Imagination" (review of I. M. Kirzner's *Discovery, Capitalism, and Distributive Justice*). *Journal des Economistes et des Etudes Humaines* 1:183–88.

Wicken, Jeffrey S. 1987. *Evolution, Thermodynamics, and Information – Extending the Darwinian Paradigm*. Oxford: Oxford University Press.

Wiseman, Jack. 1989. *Cost, Choice, and Political Economy*. Aldershot: Edward Elgar.

Wiseman, Jack. 1990. "Principles of Political Economy – An Outline Proposal, Illustrated by Application to Fiscal Feralism." *Constitutional Political Economy* 1:101–27.

Witt, Ulrich. 1985. "Coordination of Individual Economic Activities as an Evolving Process of Self-Organization." *Economie Appliquée* 37:569–95.

PART II

Maker

Entrepreneurial agency

> If we want to discover what man amounts to, we can only find it in what men are, and what men are, above all other things, is various. It is in understanding that variousness – its range, its nature, its basis, and its implications – that we shall come to construct a concept of human nature that is more than a statistical shadow and less than a primitive dream, has both substance and truth.
>
> *(Geertz, 1973: 52)*

"The entrepreneur" has been a key focus of entrepreneurship research almost from the day scholars decided to take up the task. The earliest description is attributed to Richard Cantillon who viewed the entrepreneur as a risk-bearer whose income consisted not in rent, wages or interest, but in profit. Hundreds of studies have since sought to isolate the psychological characteristics of the species "entrepreneur" with particular emphasis on his or her risk propensity (Stewart & Roth, 2001; Miner & Raju, 2004). More recently, attention has turned to the role of the entrepreneur as finder of opportunities (Kirzner, 1979; Shane, 2000; Baron & Ensley, 2006). To that we would like to add the notion of entrepreneur as "maker" of new opportunities. Not necessarily the lone entrepreneur who enacts a vision or creates opportunities from scratch, but entrepreneurs and their stakeholders as cocreators who view the future as worlds in-the-making.

What difference does it make whether we study entrepreneurs as finders of opportunities in extant worlds or makers of new worlds? (Goodman, 1978) One of the major differences can be traced back to the separation of the subjective from the objective, a separation that the found world view rather easily espouses and the made world view strives against. Makers seek to reshape themselves and the world around them. They are both agents and products of change. Making picks out those regularities in the environment that lend themselves to reshaping at the hands of the makers and their stakeholders. Finding, in contrast, seeks regularities that are

66 Maker

not easily subject to change. Whereas finders, like surfers, look for large waves they can get ahead of and ride to victory, makers seek to transform waves into electricity to solve energy problems for residents along the shoreline. Both finding and making may result in valuable contributions to human welfare. Moreover, the labors of one feed into and pave the way for value creation in the other. Yet whereas entrepreneurship research into finding has readily available to it both philosophical scaffolding and disciplinary blueprints, research into making is still in its fledgling state. In our efforts to enable building these, we begin by noticing that making puts interaction at the heart of the phenomenon – interaction with the world and interactions with others (Venkataraman et al., 2012). Instead of pitting organism against environment and individual against social, the readings we have selected for this part of the book develop a variety of interactional views of agency that help flesh out Davidson's epistemological tripod of subjective, intersubjective and objective:

- Todd and Gigerenzer (2003) develop an ecological view of human rationality that is interactionally constructed in an evolutionary sense.
- Lakoff and Johnson (1999) develop an embodied view of the mind, with all its perceptions and conceptions interactionally constructed through movements in physical and social space.
- Slovic (1995) shows how our preferences are not given and stable, but interactionally constructed in the very process of discovering them.
- March (1982) urges us to study the development of human goals in interaction with ethics, aesthetics and literary criticism.
- And James (1880) makes a compelling and eloquent argument for the interaction and intervention of human agency in social evolution itself.

It is customary to read chronologically. But we have arranged the readings in reverse order so that we can trace the making of mind, meaning, preferences and goals as products of interaction with physical and social space and then examine, through James's seminal essay, how we can create ample theoretical room for human designs within and in spite of seemingly overwhelming environmental and evolutionary constraints.

Todd and Gigerenzer: Bounding rationality to the world[1]

Todd and Gigerenzer (T&G) present a novel application of an idea that is already familiar to entrepreneurship scholars with a strategic management bent. That idea is strategic complementarities (sometimes referred to as synergy or mutualism). T&G argue that the mind and the environment should be seen as complementary, and that "fast and frugal heuristics" interact synergistically with "naturally" structured environments.

The study of ecological rationality thus involves analyzing the structure of environments, the structure of heuristics, and the match between them. The goal of the study of ecological rationality is an understanding of the particular decision mechanisms people and other animals use to make good decisions given particular structures of information in the environment. By letting the world do some of the work—by relying on and leveraging the presence of particular useful information patterns in the environment—human decision mechanisms themselves can be simpler (Clark, 2008).

For the entrepreneur this suggests a movement away from domain-independent success factors such as better market analyses and more involved financial calculations to a renewed focus on fast and frugal heuristics that leverage local and contingent factors that lead to novelty and iterative value creation. Of course, this is not to say that fast and frugal heuristics are all that it takes to explain cognitive performance, but clearly, we would expect to see that such simple heuristics often provide sufficient conditions for adequate levels of performance.

The T&G thesis about ecological rationality provides a rather broad and fundamental challenge to the external validity of results from psychology. Recent psychological research such as the work of Kahneman, Slovic, and Tversky (1982) and their collaborators has profoundly altered our view of rationality. However, T&G draw our attention to the fact that many of the lab experiments used in this line of research explicitly remove the synergy between the mind's heuristic tools and naturally occurring patterns in the environment. In particular, these studies systematically use inappropriate data representations and unnatural task environments that human cognition is not well adapted to. The result, not surprisingly, is that people can often be made to look "irrational" in these experiments. However, when problems are framed appropriately, the synergy between the mind's heuristic reasoning and the environment reappears, irrationality disappears, and people appear as pretty adept reasoners. As T&G put it (2003: 146-147):

> Bounded rationality is like a pair of scissors, with the mind as one blade, and the structure of the environment as the other. To understand behavior, one has to look at both and how they fit together. In other words, to evaluate cognitive strategies as rational or irrational, one needs also to analyze the environment, because a strategy is rational or irrational only with respect to a particular (physical and social) environment. The study of cognitive illusions and errors, however, focuses on the first blade, and compares it (the workings of the mind) with the laws of probability and logic rather than with the structure of the environment. One blade alone does not work as well as two; by introducing a properly fit second blade (crucial aspects of environmental structure), apparently stable cognitive illusions can be made to disappear.

As an example of such scissors-repair, Gigerenzer, Hoffrage, and Kleinbölting (1991) theoretically derived and experimentally demonstrated that two well-studied cognitive illusions, the overconfidence bias and the hard–easy effect, disappear when the underlying questions are randomly sampled from an environment rather than systematically selected—that is, when people face an appropriate environmental structure. (Juslin, Winman, and Olsson, (2000), confirmed this initial

68 Maker

demonstration in a quantitative review of over one hundred extant studies.) Note that this is different from the "de-biasing" approach often taken by those with the "error-prone" perspective of bounded rationality. Generally in de-biasing studies, rather than changing the information structure of the environment as above, broader methods such as providing greater incentives and greater learning opportunities are used in an attempt to help people overcome their reasoning biases. These efforts have typically met with limited success, leaving the negative impression that "biases are not fragile effects which easily disappear, but rather substantial and important behavioral regularities" (Conlisk, (1996: 671). Taking both blades of Simon's scissors into account mitigates the necessity to overcome so-called biases and shows instead how heuristics can leverage these to generate successful strategies in appropriate environments.

It might be particularly interesting to consider and test implications from ecological rationality to entrepreneurship research (Zhang and Cueto, 2017). Recent work in entrepreneurial cognition is largely skewed toward showing how "biased" entrepreneurs are—take, for example, work concerning overconfidence (Camerer and Lovallo 1999; Klayman, Soll et al. 1999; Forbes 2005; Bhandari and Deaves 2006) and hubris (Hayward, Shepherd et al. 2006).

> Other than the notable exception of Bryant (2007) that takes a positive stance toward bias using the ecological approaches to decision making, the majority of entrepreneurial bias studies explicitly or implicitly adopt the classical view of bias by Tversky and Kahneman (1973).
>
> *(Zhang and Cueto 2017: 439)*

What kinds of ecologically appropriate research designs might counter the results from these studies? T&G's arguments on the benefits of bounded rationality, although controversial, might be worth highlighting in this regard (2003: 160-1). The main thrust of their arguments is that whereas reasoning from small samples of data is traditionally thought to be bad, small samples actually increase the chances of detecting correlations (Kareev 2000). There is some evidence that expert entrepreneurs refuse to do market research or reject market research data, preferring instead to operate in environments characterized by Knightian uncertainty (Sarasvathy, Simon et al. 1998). Perhaps replicating such environments in the lab might make overconfidence effects disappear.

Of course, simple heuristics do not work well merely by using little information —they must use appropriate (little) information. This immediately raises the question of how we know which cues are the most informative ones to use in the first place. For some decisions, evolution has equipped us with knowledge of the most important cues to pay attention to (e.g., a food's taste or a parent's face). In other settings, we have mechanisms for learning useful cues, individually, in interaction with the environment or with other people and from our culture. Much research remains to be done to uncover these mechanisms, especially in the case of entrepreneurs. Moreover, we also design and construct our own environments, explicitly or implicitly, to include salient useful cues that reduce our need to search for information or to predict future behavior; for instance, as T&G point out, a wedding ring is a good cue of a married state, and a turn signal is a good cue of a driver's upcoming behavior (2003: 153). The cues that entrepreneurs and their stakeholders construct to structure their environments to yield favorable outcomes could form a productive line of future research in entrepreneurship.

Lakoff and Johnson: the embodied mind

Lakoff & Johnson (1980) sowed the seeds of a research endeavor that came to fruition with the publication of Lakoff & Johnson (1999). Here we see the full thesis: that the mind is embodied, not in the trivial sense that mind is a function of the brain, but in the sense that our reasoning capacity – the very thing that makes us human – in a nontrivial sense piggybacks or is an outgrowth of the brain's role in our physical functioning in the world. As a result:

> There is no ... autonomous faculty of reason separate from and independent of bodily capacities such as perception and movement.... What is important is not just that we have bodies and that thought is somehow embodied. What is important is that the peculiar nature of our bodies shapes our very possibilities for conceptualization and categorization.
>
> *(1999: 17, 19)*

Lakoff & Johnson's logic for this strong claim is that there is emerging empirical evidence in cognitive science of commonalities between the neural structures involved, for instance, in physical motor controls and in linguistic conceptual structures. On page 41 they outline Narayanan's model of motor schemas and linguistic aspect, which share the same basic structure. Since these very different functionings have common structures, they then suggest it is at least plausible to think that Mother Nature, a master opportunist (Dennett, 1995), built newer parts of the brain out of these older more primitive brain structures; that is, that at the neural level certain structures are built on a common pattern.

> From a biological perspective, it is eminently plausible that reason has grown out of the sensory and motor systems and that it still uses those systems or structures developed from them. This explains why we have the kind of concepts we have ...
>
> *(1999: 43)*

Both evolutionary biologists (Gould & Howard, 1991) and other philosophers (Skoyles, 1999) corroborate this by showing that the human brain grew in size extremely quickly in a rapid intergenerational burst covering maybe only 10,000 years, bootstrapping and exapting its way to more sophisticated functions. The logic is that the brain grew so fast by opportunistically coopting previously evolved

70 Maker

functions to do new things. So, whereas the notion of the embodied mind is a radical claim from the perspective of the traditional philosophical theories of the mind that inform contemporary scholarship in economics, sociology and management, it is not at all radical from a biological perspective: indeed, it is quite plausible and even highly likely.

Lakoff & Johnson's arguments, derived from empirical evidence in cognitive science, show how the emerging sciences of the mind turn upside down certain philosophical understandings that permeate all kinds of scholarship, including entrepreneurship. By establishing a common platform for intersubjective knowledge – namely, that people have similar bodies – these findings also connect strongly to Davidson's (2001) thesis that knowledge is a subjective–intersubjective–objective tripod. Like Davidson and T&G, Lakoff & Johnson mount a powerful attack on the idea that reality can be divided up into objective/subjective categories that are independent of the properties of the human body and brain, and that these concepts can be acquired by disembodied reason. They use the example of color to show that the claims of disembodied reason are wrong. Objectivism cannot explain color because color does not exist in objects, independent of bodies and brains. Social constructionism cannot explain color because color is created jointly by the world and human bodies and brains, not by culture. Instead, color is a function of human beings physically interacting with the world over a long period of biological history. As Lakoff & Johnson put it:

> Philosophically, color and color concepts make sense only in something like an embodied realism, a form of interactionism that is neither purely objective nor purely subjective.
>
> *(1999: 25)*

What emerges from this perspective is the idea that people are naturally in touch with the world because their basic conceptual structures and the bodily functioning match up. They are also naturally in touch with each other, because at the basic level people experience the same objective reality because they share the same bodily structure and structure of concepts (i.e. we all see trees – p. 18). They relate intersubjectively because they can reasonably know basic aspects of the minds of each other. This embodied realism therefore supports Davidson's collusion of objective, subjective and intersubjective. Yet at the same time it allows room for the idea that as concepts become more abstract, there is less congruence, and more room for conflicting concepts. People can, and do, talk across each other, at conceptual odds with one another in highly abstract situations (Kuhn, 1962). The idea of the embodied mind helps us understand at once why such misunderstandings do not occur at more basic levels, and how they might possibly be resolved, namely, through pluralistic approaches.

The embodied mind provides one sound philosophical plank on which to build a "made" view of entrepreneurship. In the process of *making* new opportunities – i.e. *fabricating* new value propositions – entrepreneurs and their stakeholders end up creating new conceptual categories and new ways of living in the world and interacting with it and with each other. These get embodied in the artifacts that entrepreneurs and their stakeholders design. Thus, Starbucks is not just about brewing a better cup of coffee, it embodies different habits of consumption and new modes of physical and social interaction. Instagram is not just about sharing photographs. It has become a way of building brands such as MVMT and new ventures such as HelloFresh. Bollywood stars influence the fate of blockbuster films through it and even FEMA uses it for disaster management. And brown has come to signify service ("What can brown do for you?") while environmental entrepreneurs are called "green" precisely because metaphors mean what they say when they get embodied in daily speech and use (Davidson, 1978).

Slovic: the construction of preferences

One of the major conceptual categories that get constructed through human interactions with the world and with other human beings is preferences. Traditional models of rationality, even those based on bounded rationality, often take preferences as given and well ordered. These assumptions have repeatedly been shattered empirically – both the article by Slovic and the one by March point out several instances of such empirical counter-evidence. But the interesting feature of Slovic's summary of these is the demonstration of "deep interplay between descriptive phenomena and normative principles". (1995: 370).

The construction of preferences is especially important to entrepreneurship research that looks into stakeholder interactions in new ventures as well as to the nexus between economic value creation and the personal values of those involved in building new ventures. Both notions of disembodied and acontextual individual preferences on the one hand, and structural determinism (whether through incentives or institutional pressures) on the other, break down in the face of the evidence being amassed in psychological studies of preferences. As Slovic puts it:

> [For] judgments and choices among options that are important, complex and perhaps unfamiliar … preferences are not simply read off some master list, but are constructed on the spot by an adaptive decision maker. Construction strategies include anchoring and adjustment, relying on the prominent dimension, eliminating common elements, discarding nonessential differences, adding new attributes into the problem frame in order to bolster one alternative, or otherwise restructuring the decision problem to create dominance and thus reduce conflict and indecision. As a result of these mental gymnastics, decision making is a highly contingent form of information processing … (emphasis added).

> (1995: 369)

Slovic highlights that psychologists have done "hundreds of studies" to try to understand preferences. This empirical evidence, painstakingly gathered and steadily

72 Maker

accumulated by the field, has led to at least one conclusion of particular importance for scholars of entrepreneurship namely, that for big decisions – such as the decision to become an entrepreneur – we should expect preference construction to be the norm. Instead of positing that entrepreneurs become entrepreneurs because of something inherent or already extant within them or due to external incentives and pressures, we need to explain the "making" of entrepreneurs as well as what they make and how (Harmeling, 2006). Even when they have clear preferences to become an entrepreneur, they may not be clear on their preferences for which particular venture to start.

This means that we may need to recast some of our hypotheses in favor of ambiguity and inchoate preferences. Researchers that base their studies on stable, given preferences – whether for financial profitability or other forms of psychic income – would have to justify why that assumption is relevant to the design of their study and/or to implications based on its findings. Learning to do research in the face of constructed preferences is only now beginning to be tackled by scholars. For entrepreneurship researchers, who have the perfect setting for designing studies based on constructed preferences, this could be a substantial boon, an important opportunity to push our contributions beyond our discipline into the broader history of ideas.

March: the technology of foolishness

March (1978) pointed out that rational choice involves two guesses, a guess about uncertain future consequences and a guess about uncertain future preferences. He called for the development of a technology of foolishness to complement the technologies of intelligence that have been developed to improve the first guess. In concluding that article he expressed the hope that efforts to develop a technology of foolishness would:

> … lead theories of choice to a slightly clearer understanding of the complexities of preference processing and to some modest links with the technologies of ethics, criticism, and aesthetics.
>
> *(1978: 605)*

March and his collaborators have since then taken several steps in this endeavor, yet researchers routinely ignore the issue of preference uncertainty. The reason why is explained by the fact that most scholars implicitly or explicitly take goals as given in their models. This assumption often takes the form of a *metagoal* assumption: economic theories, for example, assume that more wealth is better, because it is exchangeable for something else later; and sociological theories assume more power is better, because it can always be translated into other things later. "More" therefore constitutes a good meta-goal, because more of anything can always be traded in for what you really want, later. March's essay seeks to focus our attention on the precarious nature of such assumptions and urges us to reassess our ideas about preferences in a more realistic and valuable way. Moral philosophy has always taken the question of the goodness and rightness of goals as a central topic of debate; and psychologists – as the article by Slovic shows – have seriously taken up the question of preferences in the years since March originally wrote. Yet in the intervening period, rational choice has become even more entrenched as the "gold standard" for decision-making. Within entrepreneurship research it informs work on opportunity recognition, resource mobilization, institutional entrepreneurship, etc.

How do we begin constructing a technology of foolishness in entrepreneurship research? A technology of foolishness, as we noted above, is a way to grapple with the second guess of rational choice, i.e. the guess about uncertain preferences. A technology of foolishness therefore has to consist of strategies to make decisions in the presence of goal ambiguity. March's seemingly innocuous yet profoundly radical statements on page 75 are worth our attention in this regard:

> Perhaps we should explore a somewhat different approach to the normative question of how we ought to behave when our value premises are not yet (and never will be) fully determined. Suppose we treat action as a way of creating interesting goals at the same time as we treat goals as a way of justifying action. It is an intuitively plausible and simple idea, but one that is not immediately within the domain of standard normative theories of intelligent choice.
>
> Interesting people and interesting organizations construct complicated theories of themselves. In order to do this, they need to supplement the technology of reason with a technology of foolishness. Individuals and organizations need ways of doing things for which they have no good reason. Not always. Not usually. But sometimes. They need to act before they think.

In beginning to specify key elements of a technology that lets us act before we think, however, March argues *against* setting up a notion of "supergoals" in terms of which alternative goals are evaluated. Instead he takes up the more challenging, if almost nonsensical, idea of making decisions now in terms of goals that will only be knowable later – an idea evocative of the old Aristotelian problem of teleology. March seems to acknowledge the immensity of the challenge that he is suggesting we should undertake and says, "I do not know in detail what is required, but I think it will be substantial. As we challenge the dogma of pre-existent goals, we will be forced to reexamine some of our most precious prejudices" (1982: 75).

One of the major ways he suggests to begin this reexamination involves introducing some playfulness into reasoning processes, both in theory and practice (March, 1982: 76–81). In particular, he outlines five possible elements as a beginning in this direction:

1   We can treat goals as hypotheses.
2   We can treat intuition as real.
3   We can treat hypocrisy as a transition.
4   We can treat memory as an enemy.
5   We can treat experience as a theory.

74 Maker

As Sarasvathy and Dew (2005) point out, entrepreneurs do use these elements in their decision-making:

> They are only very loosely tethered to goals and do make frequent references to relying on their "gut feeling." Particularly in dealing with failures, they treat their own and their key peoples' mistakes as transitions. In fact, the experts even view them as important inputs into success. Furthermore, they have no problem re-interpreting their own histories in light of experience, or tackling new projects with renewed naivete, so that they may open themselves to productive failures and valuable surprises.
>
> *(2005: 392)*

Many of these ideas are still awaiting development. Thus, the technology of foolishness is both a thought piece in itself, as well as a continuing source of inspiration for scholars interested in understanding how entrepreneurs find, develop and construct their goals – a cornerstone in any entrepreneurship research that seeks to build on a "made" world view. Armed with insights from the readings above, we can now turn to a pivotal work on the role of the makers in a view of worlds in-the-making.

James: great men and evolution

Every once in a while, we come upon a piece of writing that is so evocative, so incisive and so beautifully argued that rereading it every few years is a treat one begins to earnestly look forward to. William James's article on the role of human agency within an evolutionary world view is such a piece. James, of course, was not talking about entrepreneurship, per se, in this article. But he just as well might be – we only need to replace Grant and Bismarck with Mohammed Yunus and Bill Gates in the following:

> Our problem is, What are the causes that make communities change …? I shall reply …, The difference is due to the accumulated influences of individuals, of the examples, their initiatives, and their decisions. The Spencerian school replies, The changes are irrespective of persons, and independent of individual control. They are due to the environment, to the circumstances, the physical geography, the ancestral conditions …; to everything, in fact, except the Grants and the Bismarcks, the Joneses and the Smiths.

We know from the above statement what James is taking aim at. Now let us see how he argues his case. James's argument is very simple:

> The human mind is essentially partial. It can be efficient at all only by picking out what to attend to and ignoring everything else – by narrowing its point of view.
>
> *(1880: 2)*

This comment is, of course, a precursor to Simon's (1957) articulation of bounded rationality, which was taken up and features prominently in the work of psychologists such as Kahneman, Gigerenzer and Slovic, who we have already been examining in some detail. The point here is that James's logic is based on the uncontestable notion of bounded rationality; he is one of the psychologists who planted this little acorn that grew into a great big tree. The implication of this bounded cognition is, for James, not that our judgment is somehow impaired by it. Instead it offers both the necessity and opportunity for us to choose, shape and construct our own boundaries by deciding what our purposes are. We can choose which cues to pay attention to and which causal factors to build our actions upon by working with one another to construct useful purposes. One of his examples is a man slipping on an icy step and dying of a cracked skull. If we want to save the next person from the same fate, it will do no good to take all possible explanations into account. Instead, we must focus on the proximate cause and remove the ice. More broadly, in the case of individual action, we cannot avoid a focus on the agents themselves, a point James captures eloquently – if somewhat tongue-in-cheek – in the opening paragraph of the essay (1880: 1):

> Not a sparrow falls to the ground but some of the remote conditions of his fall are to be found in the milky way … That is to say, alter the milky way … and the universe would so far be a different universe from what it is now. One fact involved in the difference might be that the particular little street boy who threw the stone which brought down the sparrow might not find himself opposite the sparrow at that particular moment … But true as all this is, it would be very foolish for any one who was inquiring the cause of the sparrow's fall to overlook the boy as too personal, proximate, and so to speak anthropomorphic an agent, and to say that the true cause is … the structure of the milky way.

The paragraph speaks for itself. Proximate causes matter. It is easy to find the cause of anything in something less immediate, but to do so is at the least unpragmatic, and more often than not, it is also unscientific.

> To believe that the cause of everything is to be found in its antecedents is the starting point, the initial postulate, not the goal and consummation, of science. If she is simply to lead us out of the labyrinth by the same hole we went in by three or four thousand years ago, it seems hardly worthwhile to have followed her through the darkness at all. If anything is humanly certain it is that the great man's society, properly so called, does not make him before he can remake it.

So how does James reconcile his insistence on the importance of individuals with an evolutionary world view that he fully accepts as well? He first separates out physiological evolution from social evolution:

76 Maker

> Physiological forces, with which the social, political, geographical, and to a great extent anthropological conditions have just as much and just as little do as conditions of the crater of Vesuvius has to do with the flickering of this gas by which I write, are what make him.

And then argues against a naïve transfer of Darwinian ideas to social evolution:

> The causes of production of great men lie in a sphere wholly inaccessible to the social philosopher. He must simply accept geniuses as data, just as Darwin accepts his spontaneous variations. For him, as for Darwin, the only problem is, these data being given, how does the environment affect them, and how do they affect the environment? Now, I affirm that the relation of the visible environment to the great man is in the main exactly what it is to the "variation" in the Darwinian philosophy. It chiefly adopts or rejects, preserves or destroys, in short selects him. And whenever it adopts and preserves the great man, it becomes modified by his influence in an entirely original and peculiar way. He acts as a ferment, and changes its constitution, just as the advent of a new zoölogical species changes the faunal and floral equilibrium of the region in which it appears. We all recollect Mr. Darwin's famous statement of the influence of cats on the growth of clover in their neighborhood. We all have read of the effects of the European rabbit in New Zealand, and we have many of us taken part in the controversy about the English sparrow here, whether he kills more canker worms, or drives away most native birds. Just so the great man, whether he be an important from without like Clive in India or Agassiz here, or whether he spring from the soil like Mahomet or Franklin, brings about a rearrangement, on a large or a small scale, of the pre-existing social relations.

In other words, Darwinian evolution is silent on where the particular variations or mutations come from on which selection does its magic. This is even more true in evolutionary perspectives in the social sciences. As Witt (2005) points out:

> Even though the very process of creating novelty is central to the understanding of evolution in general and economic change/increasing economic variety in particular, it is still an underinvestigated issue ... novelty and its emergence are neglected topics.
>
> *(1)*

We have unfortunately segmented the study of evolutionary processes in the social sciences into groups of scholars who study how variance is produced (innovation theorists) and other groups that study how it is selected (ecologists). James's point is not only that both need equal attention, but also that it makes a difference whether we see novelty as the result of randomness or of conscious purposeful behavior. After all, this was the man who resolved for himself the "free will" question and worked his way out of clinical depression by an act of true pragmatism: "My first act of free will is to believe in free will" (Dennett, 2004).

Just as the person who believes in free will may make different choices than the person who does not, the entrepreneur who accepts as fact the claim that individuals can only achieve random variation will make very different choices than entrepreneurs who believe they are actually making a difference in the world, in their own lives and in the lives of their stakeholders. In fact, it is rather difficult to see how the former could take any action at all, especially in an unpredictable situation with ambiguous preferences. It may be only by believing in the efficacy of action that entrepreneurs can act at all; and only by coming to grips with the simultaneous tripod of the subjective-intersubjective-objective that they can build new ventures and innovative artifacts that embody new conceptual categories and valuable new opportunities.

The picture of the maker that emerges from these readings is not a reflexive one, where organism acts on environment and then environment acts on individual, where separation between the two is preserved even as each changes the other. It is, instead, an interactive and transformative image in which the individual realizes and learns how she is shaped by forces outside her control, yet also refuses to give up faith in the efficacy of her own efforts to shape her future and to reshape her environment. In this new picture we see the outlook of entrepreneurs such as Alice Coles, who led the transformation of her utterly poverty-stricken community in Bayview, Virginia. When asked whether one person could change the world, she answered that one person could not make all the difference, but one person could surely be the hinge on which the door to new worlds may be opened (Coles, 2004).

Note

1 Todd and Gigerenzer (2003) is the only reading not included in this book due to exorbitant pricing for copyright permission. For a book length treatment of this idea, please see Todd, P. M., & Gigerenzer, G. E. (2012). Ecological rationality: Intelligence in the world. Oxford University Press.

References

Baron, R. A. & Ensley, M. D. (2006). Opportunity recognition as the detection of meaningful patterns: Evidence from comparisons of novice and experienced entrepreneurs. *Management Science* **52**(9): 1331–1344.

Bhandari, G. & Deaves, R. (2006). The demographics of overconfidence. *Journal of Behavioral Finance* **7**(1): 5–11.

Camerer, C. & Lovallo, D. (1999). Overconfidence and excess entry: An experimental approach. *American Economic Review* **89**(1): 306–318.

Clark, A. (2008). *Supersizing the mind: Embodiment, action, and cognitive extension.* Oxford University Press.

Coles, A. (2004). Alice Coles interview with Bill Bradley. CBS 60 Minutes, July 18.

Conlisk, J. (1996). Why Bounded Rationality? *Journal of Economic Literature* **34**(2): 669–700.

Davidson, D. (1978). What metaphors mean. *Critical Inquiry*, *5*(1), 31–47.

Davidson, D. (2001). *Subjective, intersubjective, objective*. New York, Oxford University Press Incorporated.

Dennett, D. (1995). *Darwin's dangerous idea*. New York, Simon and Schuster.

Dennett, D. C. (2004). *Freedom evolves*. London, Penguin.

Forbes, D. P. (2005). Are some entrepreneurs more overconfident than others? *Journal of Business Venturing* *20*(5): 623–640.

Geertz, C. (1973). *The interpretation of cultures: Selected essays*. New York, Basic Books.

Gigerenzer, G., Hoffrage, U. & Kleinbölting, H. (1991). Probabilistic mental models: A Brunswikian theory of confidence. *Psychological Review* *98*(4): 506–528.

Goodman, N. (1978). *Ways of worldmaking*. Indianapolis, IN: Hackett Publishing.

Gould, S. J. & Howard, S. (1991). An immunohistological study of macrophages in the human fetal brain. *Neuropathol Appl Neurobiol* *17*(5): 383–390.

Harmeling, S. (2006). Making entrepreneurs and worlds that entrepreneurs make: The entrepreneurial self as narrative process. Darden Graduate School of Business Administration. Charlottesville, VA, University of Virginia. Doctor of Philosophy in Business Administration.

Hayward, M. L. A., Shepherd, D. A. & Griffin, D. (2006). A hubris theory of entrepreneurship. *Management Science* *52*(2): 160–172.

James, W. (1880). Great men, great thoughts, and the environment. *Atlantic Monthly* *46*(276): 441–459.

Juslin, P., Winman, A. & Olsson, H. (2000). Naive empiricism and dogmatism in confidence research: a critical examination of the hard-easy effect. *Psychol Rev* *107*(2): 384–396.

Kahneman, D., Slovic, P. & Tversky, A. (1982). *Judgment under uncertainty: Heuristics and biases*. New York, Cambridge University Press.

Kareev, Y. (2000). Seven (indeed, plus or minus two) and the detection of correlations. *Psychological Review* *107*(2): 397–402.

Kirzner, I. (1979). *Perception, opportunity, and profit: Studies in the theory of entrepreneurship*. University of Chicago Press.

Klayman, J., Soll, J. B., Gonzalez-Vallejo, C. & Barlas, S. (1999). Overconfidence: It Depends on how, what, and whom you ask. *Organizational Behavior and Human Decision Processes* *79*(3): 216–247.

Kuhn, T. (1962). *The structure of scientific revolutions*. University of Chicago Press.

Lakoff, G. & Johnson, M. (1980). Conceptual metaphor in everyday language. *The Journal of Philosophy* *77*(8): 452–486.

Lakoff, G. & Johnson, M. (1999). *Philosophy in the flesh: The embodied mind and its challenge to western thought*. New York, Basic Books.

March, J. G. (1978). Bounded rationality, ambiguity, and the engineering of choice. *Bell Journal of Economics* *9*(2): 587.

March, J. G. (1982). The technology of foolishness. In March, J. G. & Olsen J. P. (Eds). *Ambiguity and choice in organizations*. (pp. 69–81) Bergen, Norway; Universitetsforlaget.

Miner, J. B. & Raju, N. S. (2004). When science divests itself of its conservative stance: The case of risk propensity differences between entrepreneurs and managers. *Journal of Applied Psychology* *89*(1): 14–21.

North, D. (2004). *Local knowledge and institutional reform*. Washington DC, Center for International Private Enterprise.

Sarasvathy, D. K., Simon, H. A. & Lave, L. (1998). Perceiving and managing business risks: Differences between entrepreneurs and bankers. *Journal of Economic Behavior and Organization* *33*(2): 207–225.

Sarasvathy, S. & Dew, N. (2005). Entrepreneurial logics for a technology of foolishness. *Scandinavian Journal of Management* **21**: 385–406.

Shane, S. (2000). Prior knowledge and the discovery of entrepreneurial opportunities. *Organization Science* **11**(4): 448–469.

Simon, H. (1957). Rational choice and the structure of the environment. Reprinted in Simon H. A. (1982). *Models of Bounded Rationality*. Cambridge, MA: MIT Press.

Skoyles, J. R. (1999). Neural plasticity and exaptation. *American Psychologist* **54**(6): 438–439.

Slovic, P. (1995). The construction of preference. *American Psychologist* **50**(5): 364–371.

Stewart, W. H. & Roth, P. L. (2001). Risk propensity differences between entrepreneurs and managers: A meta-analysis review. *Journal of Applied Psychology* **86**(1): 145–153.

Todd, P. M. & Gigerenzer, G. (2003). Bounding rationality to the world. *Journal of Economic Psychology* **24**(2): 143–165.

Venkataraman, S., Sarasvathy, S. D., Dew, N., & Forster, W. R. (2012). Reflections on the 2010 AMR decade award: Whither the promise? Moving forward with entrepreneurship as a science of the artificial. *Academy of Management Review*, **37**(1), 21–33.

Witt, U. (2005). On novelty and heterogeneity. In Witt, U. *Nonlinear Dynamics and Heterogeneous Interacting Agents*, (pp. 123–138). Cambridge University Press.

Zhang, S. X, & Cueto, J. (2017). The study of bias in entrepreneurship. *Entrepreneurship Theory and Practice* **41**(3): 419–454.

4

THE EMBODIED MIND

G. Lakoff and M. Johnson

What does it mean to say that concepts and reason are embodied? This chapter takes a first step toward answering that question. It takes up the role that the perceptual and motor systems play in shaping particular kinds of concepts: color concepts, basic-level concepts, spatial-relations concepts, and aspectual (event-structuring) concepts.

Any reasoning you do using a concept requires that the neural structures of the brain carry out that reasoning. Accordingly, the architecture of your brain's neural networks determines what concepts you have and hence the kind of reasoning you can do. Neural modeling is the field that studies which configurations of neurons carry out the neural computations that we experience as particular forms of rational thought. It also studies how such neural configurations are learned.

Neural modeling can show in detail one aspect of what it means for the mind to be embodied: how particular configurations of neurons, operating according to principles of neural computation, compute what we experience as rational inferences. At this point the vague question "Can reason make use of the sensorimotor system?" becomes the technically answerable question "Can rational inferences be computed by the same neural architecture used in perception or bodily movement?" We now know that, in some cases, the answer to this question is yes. Those cases will be discussed in this chapter.

How the body and brain shape reason

We have inherited from the Western philosophical tradition a theory of faculty psychology, in which we have a "faculty" of reason that is separate from and independent of what we do with our bodies. In particular, reason is seen as independent of perception and bodily movement. In the Western tradition, this autonomous capacity of reason is regarded as what makes us essentially human, distinguishing us

The embodied mind **81**

from all other animals. If reason were not autonomous, that is, not independent of perception, motion, emotion, and other bodily capacities, then the philosophical demarcation between us and all other animals would be less clearly drawn. This view was formulated prior to the emergence of evolutionary theory, which shows that human capacities grow out of animal capacities.

The evidence from cognitive science shows that classical faculty psychology is wrong. There is no such fully autonomous faculty of reason separate from and independent of bodily capacities such as perception and movement. The evidence supports, instead, an evolutionary view, in which reason uses and grows out of such bodily capacities. The result is a radically different view of what reason is and therefore of what a human being is. This chapter surveys some of the evidence for the view that reason is fundamentally embodied.

These findings of cognitive science are profoundly disquieting in two respects. First, they tell us that human reason is a form of animal reason, a reason inextricably tied to our bodies and the peculiarities of our brains. Second, these results tell us that our bodies, brains, and interactions with our environment provide the mostly unconscious basis for our everyday metaphysics, that is, our sense of what is real.

Cognitive science provides a new and important take on an age-old philosophical problem, the problem of what is real and how we can know it, if we can know it. Our sense of what is real begins with and depends crucially upon our bodies, especially our sensorimotor apparatus, which enables us to perceive, move, and manipulate, and the detailed structures of our brains, which have been shaped by both evolution and experience.

Neural beings must categorize

Every living being categorizes. Even the amoeba categorizes the things it encounters into food or nonfood, what it moves toward or moves away from. The amoeba cannot choose whether to categorize; it just does. The same is true at every level of the animal world. Animals categorize food, predators, possible mates, members of their own species, and so on. How animals categorize depends upon their sensing apparatus and their ability to move themselves and to manipulate objects.

Categorization is therefore a consequence of how we are embodied. We have evolved to categorize; if we hadn't, we would not have survived. Categorization is, for the most part, not a product of conscious reasoning. We categorize as we do because we have the brains and bodies we have and because we interact in the world the way we do.

The first and most important thing to realize about categorization is that it is an inescapable consequence of our biological makeup. We are neural beings. Our brains each have 100 billion neurons and 100 trillion synaptic connections. It is common in the brain for information to be passed from one dense ensemble of neurons to another via a relatively sparse set of connections. Whenever this happens, the pattern of activation distributed over the first set of neurons is too great to be represented in a one-to-one manner in the sparse set of connections. Therefore, the sparse set of connections necessarily groups together certain input patterns in mapping them across to the output ensemble. Whenever a neural ensemble provides the same output with different inputs, there is neural categorization.

To take a concrete example, each human eye has 100 million light-sensing cells, but only about 1 million fibers leading to the brain. Each incoming image must therefore be reduced in complexity by a factor of 100. That is, information in each fiber constitutes a "categorization" of the information from about 100 cells. Neural categorization of this sort exists throughout the brain, up through the highest levels of categories that we can be aware of. When we see trees, we see them as trees, not just as individual objects distinct from one another. The same with rocks, houses, windows, doors, and so on.

A small percentage of our categories have been formed by conscious acts of categorization, but most are formed automatically and unconsciously as a result of functioning in the world. Though we learn new categories regularly, we cannot make massive changes in our category systems through conscious acts of recategorization (though, through experience in the world, our categories are subject to unconscious reshaping and partial change). We do not, and cannot, have full conscious control over how we categorize. Even when we think we are deliberately forming new categories, our unconscious categories enter into our choice of possible conscious categories.

Most important, it is not just that our bodies and brains determine *that* we will categorize; they also determine what kinds of categories we will have and what their structure will be. Think of the properties of the human body that contribute to the peculiarities of our conceptual system. We have eyes and ears, arms and legs that work in certain very definite ways and not in others. We have a visual system, with topographic maps and orientation-sensitive cells, that provides structure for our ability to conceptualize spatial relations. Our abilities to move in the ways we do and to track the motion of other things give motion a major role in our conceptual system. The fact that we have muscles and use them to apply force in certain ways leads to the structure of our system of causal concepts. What is important is not just that we have bodies and that thought is somehow embodied. What is important is that the peculiar nature of our bodies shapes our very possibilities for conceptualization and categorization.

The inseparability of categories, concepts, and experience

Living systems must categorize. Since we are neural beings, our categories are formed through our embodiment. What that means is that the categories we form are *part of our experience!* They are the structures that differentiate aspects of our experience into discernible kinds. Categorization is thus not a purely intellectual matter, occurring after the fact of experience. Rather, the formation and use of categories is the stuff of experience. It is part of what our bodies and brains are constantly engaged in. We cannot, as some meditative traditions suggest, "get

The embodied mind **83**

beyond" our categories and have a purely uncategorized and unconceptualized experience. Neural beings cannot do that.

What we call *concepts* are neural structures that allow us to mentally characterize our categories and reason about them. Human categories are typically conceptualized in more than one way, in terms of what are called *prototypes*. Each prototype is a neural structure that permits us to do some sort of inferential or imaginative task relative to a category. Typical-case prototypes are used in drawing inferences about category members in the absence of any special contextual information. Ideal-case prototypes allow us to evaluate category members relative to some conceptual standard. (To see the difference, compare the prototypes for the ideal husband and the typical husband.) Social stereotypes are used to make snap judgments, usually about people. Salient exemplars (well-known examples) are used for making probability judgments. (For a survey of kinds of conceptual prototypes, see A4, Lakoff 1987.) In short, prototype-based reasoning constitutes a large proportion of the actual reasoning that we do. Reasoning with prototypes is, indeed, so common that it is inconceivable that we could function for long without it.

Since most categories are matters of degree (e.g., tall people), we also have graded concepts characterizing degrees along some scale with norms of various kinds for extreme cases, normal cases, not quite normal cases, and so on. Such graded norms are described by what are called *linguistic hedges* (A4, Lakoff 1972), for example, *very, pretty, kind of, barely*, and so on. For the sake of imposing sharp distinctions, we develop what might be called *essence prototypes*, which conceptualize categories as if they were sharply defined and minimally distinguished from one another.

When we conceptualize categories in this way, we often envision them using a spatial metaphor, as if they were containers, with an interior, an exterior, and a boundary. When we conceptualize categories as containers, we also impose complex hierarchical systems on them, with some category-containers inside other category-containers. Conceptualizing categories as containers hides a great deal of category structure. It hides conceptual prototypes, the graded structures of categories, and the fuzziness of category boundaries.

In short, we form extraordinarily rich conceptual structures for our categories and reason about them in many ways that are crucial for our everyday functioning. All of these conceptual structures are, of course, neural structures in our brains. This makes them embodied in the trivial sense that any mental construct is realized neurally. But there is a deeper and more important sense in which our concepts are embodied. What makes concepts concepts is their inferential capacity, their ability to be bound together in ways that yield inferences. *An embodied concept is a neural structure that is actually part of, or makes use of, the sensorimotor system of our brains. Much of conceptual inference is, therefore, sensorimotor inference.*

If concepts are, as we believe, embodied in this strong sense, the philosophical consequences are enormous. The locus of reason (conceptual inference) would be the same as the locus of perception and motor control, which are bodily functions. If this seems like a radical claim, it is radical only from the perspective of faculty psychology, a philosophy that posits a radical separation between rational abilities

84 G. Lakoff and M. Johnson

and the sensorimotor system. It is not at all radical from the point of view of the brain, which is the joint locus of reason, perception, and movement. The question from the viewpoint of the brain is whether conceptual inference makes use of the same brain structures as perceptual motor inference. In other words, does reason piggyback on perception and motor control? From the perspective of the brain, the locus of all three functions, it would be quite natural if it did.

Realism, inference, and embodiment

The question of what we take to be real and the question of how we reason are inextricably linked. Our categories of things in the world determine what we take to be real: trees, rocks, animals, people, buildings, and so on. Our concepts determine how we reason about those categories. In order to function *realistically* in the world, our categories and our forms of reason must "work" very well together; our concepts must characterize the structure of our categories sufficiently well enough for us to function.

Mainstream Western philosophy adds to this picture certain claims that we will argue are false. Not trivially false, but so false as to drastically distort our understanding of what human beings are, what the mind and reason are, what causation and morality are, and what our place is in the universe. Here are those claims:

1   Reality comes divided up into categories that exist independent of the specific properties of human minds, brains, or bodies.
2   The world has a rational structure: The relationships among categories in the world are characterized by a *transcendent* or *universal* reason, which is independent of any peculiarities of human minds, brains, and bodies.
3   The concepts used by mind-, brain-, and body-free reason correctly characterize the mind-, brain-, and body-free categories of reality.
4   Human reason is the capacity of the human mind to use transcendent reason, or at least a portion of it. Human reason may be performed by the human brain, but the structure of human reason is defined by transcendent reason, independent of human bodies or brains. Thus, the structure of human reason is disembodied.
5   Human concepts are the concepts of transcendent reason. They are therefore defined independent of human brains or bodies, and so they too are disembodied.
6   Human concepts therefore characterize the objective categories of mind-, brain, and body-free reality. That is, the world has a unique, fixed category structure, and we all know it and use it when we are reasoning correctly.
7   What makes us essentially human is our capacity for disembodied reason.
8   Since transcendent reason is culture-free, what makes us essentially human is not our capacity for culture or for interpersonal relations.
9   Since reason is disembodied, what makes us essentially human is not our relation to the material world. Our essential humanness has nothing to do with our connection to nature or to art or to music or to anything of the senses.

The embodied mind   **85**

Much of the history of mainstream Western philosophy consists of exploring variations on these themes and drawing out the consequences of these claims. A given philosopher may not hold all of these tenets in the strong form that we have stated them; however, together these claims form a picture of concepts, reason, and the world that any student of philosophy will be familiar with. If they are false, then large parts of the Western philosophical tradition and many of our most common beliefs have to be rethought.

These tenets were not adopted on the basis of empirical evidence. They arose instead out of a priori philosophy. Contemporary cognitive science calls this entire philosophical worldview into serious question on empirical grounds. Here is the reason why cognitive science has a crucial bearing on these issues.

At the heart of this worldview are tenets 4, 5, and 6—that human reason and human concepts are mind-, brain-, and body-free and characterize objective, external reality. If these tenets are false, the whole worldview collapses. Suppose human concepts and human reason are body- and brain-dependent. Suppose they are shaped as much by the body and brain as by reality. Then the body and brain are essential to our humanity. Moreover, our notion of what reality is changes. There is no reason whatever to believe that there is a disembodied reason or that the world comes neatly carved up into categories or that the categories of our mind are the categories of the world. If tenets 4, 5, and 6 are empirically incorrect, then we have a lot of rethinking to do about who we are and what our place is in the universe.

Embodied concepts

In this chapter and the next, we will review some of the results of cognitive science research that bear on these issues. We will suggest, first, that human concepts are not just reflections of an external reality, but that they are crucially shaped by our bodies and brains, especially by our sensorimotor system. We will do so by looking at three kinds of concepts: color concepts, basic-level concepts, and spatial-relations concepts. After that, we will use studies of neural modeling to argue that certain human concepts and forms of conceptual reasoning make use of the sensorimotor system.

The philosophical stakes here are high. As we shall see in later chapters, these arguments have far-reaching implications for who we are and what our role in the world is.

Color concepts

What could be simpler or more obvious than colors? The sky is blue. Fresh grass is green. Blood is red. The sun and moon are yellow. We see colors as inhering in things. Blue is in the sky, green in the grass, red in the blood, yellow in the sun. We see color, and yet it is false, as false as another thing we see, the moving sun rising past the edge of the stationary earth. Just as astronomy tells us that the earth moves around the sun, not the sun around a stationary earth, so cognitive science tells us that colors do not exist in the external world. Given the world, our bodies and brains have evolved to create color.

Our experience of color is created by a combination of four factors: wavelengths of reflected light, lighting conditions, and two aspects of our bodies: (1) the three kinds of color cones in our retinas, which absorb light of long, medium, and short wavelengths, and (2) the complex neural circuitry connected to those cones.

Here are some crucial things to bear in mind. One physical property of the surface of an object matters for color: its reflectance, that is, the relative percentages of high-, medium-, and low-frequency light that it reflects. That is a constant. But the actual wavelengths of light reflected by an object are not a constant. Take a banana. The wavelengths of light coming from the banana depend on the nature of the light illuminating it: tungsten or fluorescent, daylight on a sunny or a cloudy day, the light of dawn or dusk. Under different conditions the wavelengths of light coming from the banana will differ considerably, yet the color of the banana will be relatively constant; it will look pretty much the same. Color, then, is not just the perception of wavelength; color constancy depends on the brain's ability to compensate for variations in the light source. Moreover, there is not a one-to-one correspondence between reflectance and color; two different reflectances can both be perceived as the same red.

Another crucial thing to bear in mind is that light is not colored. Visible light is electromagnetic radiation, like radio waves, vibrating within a certain frequency range. It is not the kind of thing that could be colored. Only when this electromagnetic radiation impinges on our retinas are we able to see. We see a particular color when the surrounding lighting conditions are right, when radiation in a certain range impinges on our retina, and when our color cones absorb the radiation, producing an electrical signal that is appropriately processed by the neural circuitry of our brains. The qualitative experience that this produces in us is what we call "color."

One might suppose that color is an internal representation of the external reality of the reflectance properties of the surface of an object. If this were true, then the properties of colors and color categories would be representations of reflectances and categories of reflectances. But it is not true. Color concepts have internal structure, with certain colors being "focal." The category *red*, for instance, contains central red as well as noncentral, peripheral hues such as purplish red, pinkish red, and orangish red. The center-periphery structure of categories is a result of the neural response curves for color in our brains. Focal hues correspond to frequencies of maximal neural response. The internal structure of color categories is not out there in the surface reflectances. The same is true of the relationships among colors. The opposition between red and green or blue and yellow is a fact about our neural circuitry, not about the reflectance properties of surfaces. Color is not just the internal representation of external reflectance. And it is not a thing or a substance out there in the world.

To summarize, our color concepts, their internal structures, and the relationships between them are inextricably tied to our embodiment. They are a consequence

The embodied mind **87**

of four interacting factors: lighting conditions, wavelengths of electromagnetic radiation, color cones, and neural processing. Colors as we see them, say, the red of blood or the blue of the sky, are not out there in the blood or the sky. Indeed, the sky is not even an object. It has no surface for the color to be in. And without a physical surface, the sky does not even have a surface reflectance to be detected as color. The sky is blue because the atmosphere transmits only a certain range of wavelengths of incoming light from the sun, and of the wavelengths it does transmit, it scatters some more than others. The effect is like a colored lightbulb that only lets certain wavelengths of light through the glass. Thus, the sky is blue for a very different reason than a painting of the sky is blue. What we perceive as blue does not characterize a single "thing" in the world, neither "blueness" nor wavelength reflectance.

Color concepts are "interactional"; they arise from the interactions of our bodies, our brains, the reflective properties of objects, and electromagnetic radiation. Colors are not objective; there is in the grass or the sky no greenness or blueness independent of retinas, color cones, neural circuitry, and brains. Nor are colors purely subjective; they are neither a figment of our imaginations nor spontaneous creations of our brains.

The philosophical consequences are immediate. Since colors are not things or substances in the world, metaphysical realism fails. The meaning of the word *red* cannot be just the relation between the word and something in the world (say, a collection of wavelengths of light or a surface reflectance). An adequate theory of the conceptual structure of *red*, including an account of why it has the structure it has (with focal red, purplish red, orangish red, and so on) cannot be constructed solely from the spectral properties of surfaces. It must make reference to color cones and neural circuitry. Since the cones and neural circuitry are embodied, the internal conceptual properties of *red* are correspondingly embodied.

Subjectivism in its various forms—radical relativism and social constructionism —also fails to explain color, since color is created jointly by our biology and the world, not by our culture. This is not to say that color does not differ in its significance from culture to culture. It clearly does. Rather, color is a function of the world and our biology interacting.

Philosophically, color and color concepts make sense only in something like an embodied realism, a form of interactionism that is neither purely objective nor purely subjective. Color is also important for the "realism" of embodied realism. Evolution has worked with physical limitations: only certain wavelengths of light get through the atmosphere, only certain chemicals react to short, medium, and long wavelengths, and so on. We have evolved within these limitations to have the color systems we have, and they allow us to function well in the world. Plant life has been important to our evolution, and so the ability to place in one category the things that are green has apparent value for survival and flourishing. The same goes for blood and the color red, water and the sky and the color blue, and the sun and the moon and the color yellow. We have the color concepts we do because the physical limitations constraining evolution gave evolutionary advantages to beings with a color system that enabled them to function well in crucial respects.

Color, of course, does more than just help us recognize things in the world. It is an evolved aspect of the brain that plays many roles in our lives, cultural, aesthetic, and emotional. Thinking of color as merely the internal representation of the external reality of surface reflectance is not merely inaccurate; it misses most of the function of color in our lives.

At least since John Locke, philosophers have known that color is an interactional property of objects, what Locke called a "secondary quality" that does not exist in the object itself. Locke contrasted secondary qualities with "primary qualities," which were assumed to exist objectively in things independent of any perceiver. Primary qualities were seen as having metaphysical import, as determining what is real, while secondary qualities were seen as perceiver-dependent and therefore not constitutive of objective reality.

But giving up on color as a metaphysically real "primary quality" has profound philosophical consequences. It means abandoning the correspondence theory of truth, the idea that truth lies in the relationship between words and the metaphysically and objectively real world external to any perceiver. Since there is no color in the world in itself, a sentence like "Blood is red," which we all take to be true, would not be true according to the correspondence theory.

Since the correspondence theory of truth is the one thing many philosophers are not willing to give up, they go to extraordinary lengths to salvage it. Some attempt to see color as the internal representation of external reflectance of surfaces, and to say that "Blood is red" is true if and only if blood has such and such a surface reflectance. As we have seen, the same reasoning cannot work for "The sky is blue," since the sky cannot have a surface reflectance. Some philosophers have even been willing on these grounds to say that "The sky is blue" is false, granting that the sky has no surface reflectance but trying to keep the correspondence theory nonetheless. They claim that those of us who think that it is true that the sky is blue are simply being fooled by an optical illusion! Getting philosophers to give up on the correspondence theory of truth will not be easy. (For a thorough discussion of the details of the color debate in philosophy, see Thompson [A5, 1995]. For an account of the general philosophical implications of color research, see Varela, Thompson, and Rosch [C2, 1991], who argue, as we do, that color is interactional in nature and hence neither objective nor subjective. Defenses of objectivism and subjectivism can be found in Hilbert [A5, 1987, 1992] and Hardin [A5, 1988].)

As we are about to see, color is the tip of the iceberg. What Locke recognized as perceiver-dependence is a fully general phenomenon. Cognitive science and neuroscience suggest that the world as we *know* it contains *no* primary qualities in Locke's sense, because the qualities of things as we can experience and comprehend them depend crucially on our neural makeup, our bodily interactions with them, and our purposes and interests. For real human beings, the only realism is an embodied realism.

Basic-level categories

Why has metaphysical realism been so popular over the centuries? Why is it so common to feel that our concepts reflect the world as it is—that our categories of mind fit the categories of the world? One reason is that we have evolved to form at least one important class of categories that optimally fit our bodily experiences of entities and certain extremely important differences in the natural environment— what are called *basic-level categories*.

Our perceptual systems have no problem distinguishing cows from horses, goats from cats, or elephants from giraffes. In the natural world, the categories we distinguish among most readily are the folk versions of biological genera, namely, those that have evolved significantly distinct shapes so as to take advantage of different features of their environments. Go one level down in the biological hierarchy and it is a lot harder to distinguish one species of elephant from another (A4, Berlin et al. 1974). It's the same for physical objects. It's easy to tell cars from boats or trains, but a lot less easy to tell one kind of car from another.

Consider the categories *chair* and *car*, which are "in the middle" of the category hierarchies *furniture-chair-rocking chair* and *vehicle-car-sports car*. In the mid-1970s, Brent Berlin, Eleanor Rosch, Carolyn Mervis, and their coworkers discovered that such mid-level categories are cognitively "basic"—that is, they have a kind of cognitive priority, as contrasted with "superordinate" categories like *furniture* and *vehicle* and with "subordinate" categories like *rocking chair* and *sports car* (A4, Berlin et al. 1974; Mervis and Rosch 1981).

The body-based properties of basic-level categories

Basic-level categories are distinguished from superordinate categories by aspects of our bodies, brains, and minds: mental images, gestalt perception, motor programs, and knowledge structure. The basic level, as Berlin and Rosch found, is characterized by at least four conditions.

Condition 1: It is the highest level at which a single mental image can represent the entire category. For example, you can get a mental image of a chair. You can get mental images of other categories at the basic level such as tables and beds. But you cannot get a mental image of a general piece of furniture—a thing that is not a chair, table, or bed, but something more general. Similarly, you can get a mental image of a car. You can also get mental images of opposing categories at this level such as trains, boats, and planes. But you cannot get a mental image of a generalized vehicle—a thing that is not a car, train, boat, or plane, bur a vehicle in general. The basic level is the highest level at which we have mental images that stand for the entire category.

Condition 2: It is the highest level at which category members have similarly perceived overall shapes. You can recognize a chair or a car by its overall shape. There is no overall shape that you can assign to a generalized piece of furniture or a vehicle so that you could recognize the category from that shape. The basic level is the highest level at which category members are recognized by gestalt perception (perception of overall shape).

Condition 3: It is the highest level at which a person uses similar motor actions for interacting with category members. You have motor programs for interacting with objects at the basic level—for interacting with chairs, tables, and beds. But you have no motor programs for interacting with generalized pieces of furniture.

Condition 4: It is the level at which most of our knowledge is organized. You have a lot of knowledge at the basic level. Think for a moment of all that you know about cars versus what you know about vehicles. You know a handful of things about vehicles in general, but a great many things about cars. You know much less about lower-level categories, unless you are an expert.

As a result of these characteristics, the basic level has other priorities over the superordinate and subordinate levels: It is named and understood earlier by children, enters a language earlier in its history, has the shortest primary lexemes, and is identified faster by subjects. The basic level also tends to be used in neutral contexts, that is, contexts in which there is no explicit indication of which level is most appropriate. From the perspective of an overall theory of the human mind, these are important properties of concepts and cannot be ignored.

The philosophical significance of the basic level

The philosophical significance of these results follows directly. First, the division between basic-level and nonbasic-level categories is body-based, that is, based on gestalt perception, motor programs, and mental images. Because of this, classical metaphysical realism cannot be right, since the properties of categories are mediated by the body rather than determined directly by a mind-independent reality.

Second, the basic level is that level at which people interact optimally with their environments, given the kinds of bodies and brains they have and the kinds of environments they inhabit. How is this possible? The best answer we know, suggested by Tversky and Hemenway (A4, 1984), is that the properties that make for basic-level categories are responses to the part-whole structure of physical beings and objects. Gestalt perception is about overall part-whole structure, as is mental imagery. The use of motor schemas to interact with objects depends significantly on their overall part-whole structure. Moreover, the functions something can perform, and hence what we know about it, likewise depend to a significant degree on part-whole structure. That is why there is a basic-level category structure with respect to which we can function optimally.

Third, basic-level categorization tells us why metaphysical realism makes sense for so many people, where it seems to work, and where it goes wrong. Metaphysical realism seems to work primarily at the basic level. If you look only at examples of basic-level categories, at the level of category where we interact optimally with the world, then it appears as if our conceptual categories fit the categories of the world. If you look at categories at other levels, it does not (A4, Berlin et al. 1974). It is not surprising, therefore, that philosophical discussions about the

The embodied mind **91**

relationship between our categories and things in the world tend to use basic-level examples. Philosophical examples like "The cat is on the mat" or "The boy hit the ball" typically use basic-level categories like *cat, mat, boy,* and *ball* or basic-level substances like *water* and *gold*. It is no accident that philosophers do not try to make their argument with things farther down on the biological taxonomy: brown-capped chickadees, brown-headed nuthatches, Bewick's wrens, bushtits, and so on.

The basic level, of course, is not just about objects. There are basic-level actions, actions for which we have conventional mental images and motor programs, like swimming, walking, and grasping. We also have basic-level social concepts, like families, clubs, and baseball teams, as well as basic-level social actions, like arguing. And there are basic emotions, like happiness, anger, and sadness.

Fourth, the properties of the basic level explain an important aspect of the stability of scientific knowledge. For basic-level physical objects and basic-level actions or relations, the link between human categories and divisions of things in the world is quite accurate. We can think of scientific instruments as extending these basic-level abilities to perceive, image, and intervene. Telescopes, microscopes, cameras, and delicate probing instruments of all sorts extend our capacity for basic-level perception, imaging, and intervention. Such instruments allow us to greatly extend the range of our categories of mind to fit important distinctions in the world.

For basic-level categories, the idea that our categories of mind fit the categories of the world is not that far off. When our basic-level capacities are extended by scientific instrumentation, our ability to select useful real-world divisions is improved. Basic-level categories are the source of our most stable knowledge, and the technological capacity to extend them allows us to extend our stable knowledge.

In summary, our categories arise from the fact that we are neural beings, from the nature of our bodily capacities, from our experience interacting in the world, and from our evolved capacity for basic-level categorization—a level at which we optimally interact with the world. Evolution has not required us to be as accurate above and below the basic level as at the basic level, and so we are not.

There is a reason why our basic-level categorization and evolution march up. In the natural world, basic-level categories of organisms are genera. That means that they are for the most part determined by their overall part-whole structure. The part-whole structure of a class of organisms is, significantly, what determines whether it will survive and function well in a given environment. Thus, part-whole structure determines the natural categories of existing genera. And it is what our perceptual and motor systems have evolved to recognize at the basic level. That is why we have tended over our evolutionary history to function optimally in our basic-level interactions.

Though the facts of basic-level categorization do not fit metaphysical realism, they do provide us with the basis for embodied realism, which is an improvement over metaphysical realism in that it provides a link between our ideas and the world, at least

92 G. Lakoff and M. Johnson

at the level that matters most for our survival. The facts of basic-level categorization also remind us that our bodies contribute to our sense of what is real.

We turn next to spatial-relations concepts. These too are embodied. They have to be, because they allow us to negotiate space, to function in it as well as to conceptualize it and talk about it.

Spatial-relations concepts

Spatial-relations concepts are at the heart of our conceptual system. They are what make sense of space for us. They characterize what spatial form is and define spatial inference. But they do not exist as entities in the external world. We do not see spatial relations the way we see physical objects.

We do not see nearness and farness. We see objects where they are and we attribute to them nearness and farness from some landmark. The relations *in front of* and *in back of* are imposed by us on space in a complex way. When you go *in the front* of a church, you find yourself *in the back* of it. Or take the concept *across*. Suppose you are to row across a round pond. If you row "straight across" it (at a 90-degree angle from the shore), you have certainly rowed across it. If you row at a 45-degree angle, it is not as clear. If you row at a 15-degree angle, certainly not. Here, what counts as *across* varies with the shape of the area crossed and the angle of crossing and is also a matter of degree. Spatial-relations concepts are not simple or straightforward, and they vary considerably from language to language.

We use spatial-relations concepts unconsciously, and we impose them via our perceptual and conceptual systems. We just automatically and unconsciously "perceive" one entity as *in*, *on*, or *across from* another entity. However, such perception depends on an enormous amount of automatic unconscious mental activity on our part. For example, to see a butterfly as *in* the garden, we have to project a nontrivial amount of imagistic structure onto a scene. We have to conceptualize the boundaries of the garden as a three-dimensional container with an interior that extends into the air. We also have to locate the butterfly as a figure (or *trajector*) relative to that conceptual container, which serves as a ground (or *landmark*). We perform such complex, though mundane, acts of imaginative perception during every moment of our waking lives.

Most spatial relations are complexes made up of elementary spatial relations. English *into* is a composite of the English elementary spatial relations *in* and *to*. English *on* in its central sense is a composite of *above, in contact with*, and *supported by*. Each of these is an elementary spatial relation. Elementary spatial relations have a further internal structure consisting of an *image schema, a profile*, and a *trajector-landmark structure*.

To see what these terms mean, let us take a simple example.

The container schema

English *in* is made up of a container schema (a bounded region in space), a profile that highlights the interior of the schema, and a structure that identifies the boundary of the interior as the landmark (LM) and the object overlapping with the interior as a trajector (TR). In "Sam is in the house," the house is the landmark (LM) relative to which Sam, the trajector (TR), is located.

Spatial relations also have built-in spatial "logics" by virtue of their image-schematic structures. Figure 4.1 illustrates the spatial logic built into the container schema:

- Given two containers, *A* and *B*, and an object, *X*, if *A* is *in B* and *X* is *in A*, then *X* is *in B*.

We don't have to perform a deductive operation to compute this. It is self-evident simply from the image in Figure 4.1.

A container schema has the following structure: an inside, a boundary, and an outside. This is a gestalt structure, in the sense that the parts make no sense without the whole. There is no inside without a boundary and an outside, no outside without a boundary and an inside, and no boundary without sides. The structure is topological in the sense that the boundary can be made larger, smaller, or distorted and still remain the boundary of a container schema.

A container schema, like any other image schema, is conceptual. Such a container schema can, however, be physically instantiated, either as a concrete object, like a room or a cup, or as bounded region in space, like a basketball court or a football field.

Suppose the boundary of a container schema is physically instantiated in a concrete object, say, a box. A physical boundary can impose forceful and visual constraints: It can protect the container's contents, restrict their motion, and render them inaccessible to vision. It is important to distinguish a purely conceptual schema from a physically instantiated one; they have different properties.

Container schemas, like other image schemas, are cross-modal. We can impose a conceptual container schema on a visual scene. We can impose a container schema on something we hear, as when we conceptually separate out one part of a piece of music from another. We can also impose container schemas on our motor movements, as when a baseball coach breaks down a batter's swing into component parts and discusses what goes on "inside" each part.

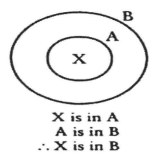

FIGURE 4.1 (Container Schema Logic)

The source-path-goal schema

As with a container schema, there is a spatial logic built into the source-path-goal schema (Figure 4.2). The source-path-goal schema has the following elements (or "roles"):

> A trajector that moves
> A source location (the starting point)
> A goal, that is, an intended destination of the trajector
> A route from the source to the goal
> The actual trajectory of motion
> The position of the trajector at a given time
> The direction of the trajector at that time
> The actual final location of the trajector, which may or may not be the intended destination

Extensions of this schema are possible: a vehicle, the speed of motion, obstacles to motion, forces that move one along a trajectory, additional trajectors, and so on.

This schema is topological in the sense that a path can be expanded, shrunk, or deformed and still remain a path. Trajectories are imaginative insofar as they are not entities in the world; they are conceptualized as a linelike "trail" left by an object as it moves and projected forward in the direction of motion.

As with the container schema, we can form spatial relations from this schema by the addition of profiling (also called *highlighting*) and a trajector-landmark relation. The concept expressed by *to* profiles the goal and identifies it as the landmark relative to which the motion takes place. The concept expressed by *from* profiles the source, taking the source as the landmark relative to which the motion takes place.

The source-path-goal schema also has an internal spatial "logic" and built-in inferences:

- If you have traversed a route to a current location, you have been at all previous locations on that route.
- If you travel from A to B and from B to C, then you have traveled from A to C.
- If there is a direct route from A to B and you are moving along that route toward B, then you will keep getting closer to B.
- If X and Y are traveling along a direct route from A to B and X passes Y, then X is further from A and closer to B than Y is.
- If X and Y start from A at the same time moving along the same route toward B and if X moves faster than Y, then X will arrive at B before Y.

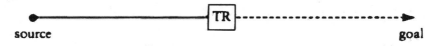

FIGURE 4.2 (Source-Path-Goal Schema)

The embodied mind **95**

Our most fundamental knowledge of motion is characterized by the source–path–goal schema, and this logic is implicit in its structure. Many spatial-relations concepts are defined using this schema and depend for their meaning on its inherent spatial logic, for example, *toward, away, through,* and *along*.

Bodily projections

Bodily projections are especially clear instances of the way our bodies shape conceptual structure. Consider examples such as *in front of* and *in back of*. The most central senses of these terms have to do with the body. We have inherent fronts and backs. We see from the front, normally move in the direction the front faces, and interact with objects and other people at our fronts. Our backs are opposite our fronts; we don't directly perceive our own backs, we normally don't move backwards, and we don't typically interact with objects and people at our backs.

We project fronts and backs onto objects. What we understand as the front of a stationary artifact, like a TV or a computer or a stove, is the side we normally interact with using our fronts. What we take to be the front of a moving object like a car is that part of the object that "faces" the direction in which it normally moves. We project fronts onto stationary objects without inherent fronts such as trees or rocks. English speakers project fronts onto such objects so the front faces the speaker. In other languages (e.g., Hausa), speakers project fronts onto such objects in the opposite direction, facing away from the speaker.

The concepts *front* and *back* are body-based. They make sense only for beings with fronts and backs. If all beings on this planet were uniform stationary spheres floating in some medium and perceiving equally in all directions, they would have no concepts of *front* or *back*. But we are not like this at all. Our bodies are symmetric in some ways and not in others. We have faces and move in the direction in which we see. Our bodies define a set of fundamental spatial orientations that we use not only in orienting ourselves, but in perceiving the relationship of one object to another.

When we perceive a cat as being in front of a car or behind a tree, the spatial relationships *in front of* and *behind*, between cat and car or between cat and tree, are not objectively there in the world. The spatial relation is not an entity in our visual field. The cat is behind the tree or in front of the car only relative to our capacity to project fronts and backs onto cars and trees and to impose relations onto visual scenes relative to such projections. In this way, perceiving the cat as being behind the tree requires an imaginative projection based on our embodied nature.

Compared to certain other languages, English is relatively impoverished in its use of bodily projections to conceptualize spatial relations. By contrast, languages of the Otomonguean family, such as Mixtec, use bodily projections as their primary means of characterizing spatial relations (A1, Brugman 1985).

For example, in Mixtec, there is no unitary concept or word corresponding to English *on*. The range of cases covered by English *on* is instead described by using body-part projections. Suppose you want to say "He is on top of the hill." You say the equivalent of "He is located head hill." If you want to say "I was on the roof of the house," you say the Mixtec equivalent of "I was located animal-back house," in which an animal back, being canonically oriented horizontally, is projected onto the house. If you want to say "I am sitting on the branch of the tree," you say the equivalent of "I am sitting arm tree."

One way in which languages differ is that, while some have mainly body-centered relations like *in front of*, others have mainly externally based relations, like *to the north of*, and still others have mixed systems (A8, Levinson 1992–present).

Other image schemas and elements of spatial relations

The study of spatial-relations concepts within cognitive linguistics has revealed that there is a relatively small collection of primitive image schemas that structure systems of spatial relations in the world's languages. Here are some examples, without the full detail given above: part-whole, center-periphery, link, cycle, iteration, contact, adjacency, forced motion (e.g., pushing, pulling, propelling), support, balance, straight-curved, and near-far. Orientations also used in the spatial-relations systems of the world's languages include vertical orientation, horizontal orientation, and front-back orientation. (For a fuller discussion see A4, Lakoff 1987, case study 2; A1, Johnson 1987; A8, Talmy 1983; and B2, Regier 1996.)

One of the important discoveries of cognitive science is that the conceptual systems used in the world's languages make use of a relatively small number of basic image schemas, though the range of complex spatial relations that can be built out of these schemas is very large. As we shall see when we get to the discussion of conceptual metaphor, the spatial logics of these body-based image schemas are among the sources of the forms of logic used in abstract reason.

The embodied nature of spatial-relations concepts

Spatial-relations concepts are embodied in various ways. Bodily projections are obviously based on the human body. Concepts like *front* and *back* and those in Mixtec arise from the body, depend on the body, and would not exist if we did not have the kinds of bodies we have. The same is true of fundamental force-dynamic schemas: pushing, pulling, propelling, supporting, and balance. We comprehend these through the use of our body parts and our ability to move them, especially our arms, hands, and legs.

Other image schemas are also comprehended through the body. Our bodies are containers that take in air and nutrients and emit wastes. We constantly orient our bodies with respect to containers—rooms, beds, buildings. We spend an inordinate amount of time putting things in and taking things out of containers. We also project abstract containers onto areas in space, as when we understand a swarm of bees as being *in* the garden. Similarly, every time we see something move, or move ourselves, we comprehend that movement in terms of a source-path-goal schema and reason accordingly.

The embodied mind **97**

These forms of embodiment arise from the way we schematize our own bodies and things we interact with daily (C2, Gallagher 1995). We will refer to this as *phenomenological embodiment*. But there is also *neural embodiment*, as we saw in the case of color. Neural embodiment characterizes the neural mechanisms that give rise to concepts—for example, the neural circuitry connected to the color cones that brings color into existence and characterizes the structure of color categories. These neural mechanisms explain why color categories have many of the phenomenological properties they have.

We do not yet know the exact neural mechanisms that give rise to spatial-relations concepts, but a beginning has been made. A computational neural model has been constructed that characterizes certain image schemas neurally, explains why they should exist, and accounts for their topological and orientational properties. Let us now turn to this research.

The neural modeling of spatial and motor concepts

As we mentioned above, much of the Western philosophical tradition assumes a form or faculty psychology, according to which we have a faculty of reason separate from our faculties of perception and bodily movement. Concepts and the forms of reason based on them are assumed to be purely part of the faculty of reason. Perception may inform reason, and movement may be a consequence of reason, but in the tradition no aspect of perception or movement is *part* of reason.

Consequently, there is assumed to be an absolute dichotomy between *perception* and *conception*. While *perception* has always been accepted as bodily in nature, just as movement is, *conception*—the formation and use of concepts—has traditionally been seen as purely mental and wholly separate from and independent of our abilities to perceive and move.

We have already begun to get intimations that this picture is false. We have seen that basic-level concepts depend on motor movement, gestalt perception, and mental imagery, which is carried out in the visual system of the brain. We have seen that color is anything but purely mental, that our color concepts are intimately shaped not merely by perception as a faculty of mind but by such physical parts of our bodies as color cones and neural circuitry. And we have seen that spatial-relations concepts like *front* and *back* are not characterized by some abstract, disembodied mental capacity but rather in terms of bodily orientation. In these cases, the body is not merely somehow involved in conceptualization but is shaping its very nature.

Embodiment not as realization but as shaping

What is the view that the mind is disembodied? It is the view that the contents of mind, the actual concepts, are not crucially shaped or given any significant inferential content by the body. It is the view that concepts are formal in nature and arise from the mind's capacity to generate formal structure in such a way as to derive further, inferred, formal structures. Advocates of the disembodied mind will, of course, say that conceptual structure must have a neural *realization* in the brain, which just *happens* to reside in a body. But they deny that anything about the body is essential for characterizing what concepts are.

The claim that the mind is embodied is, therefore, far more than the simple-minded claim that the body is needed if we are to think. Advocates of the disembodied-mind position agree with *that*. Our claim is, rather, that the very properties of concepts are created as a result of the way the brain and body are structured and the way they function in interpersonal relations and in the physical world.

The embodied-mind hypothesis therefore radically undercuts the *perception/conception* distinction. In an embodied mind, it is conceivable that the same neural system engaged in *perception* (or in bodily movement) plays a central role in *conception*. That is, the very mechanisms responsible for perception, movements, and object manipulation could be responsible for conceptualization and reasoning. Indeed, in recent neural modeling research, models of perceptual mechanisms and motor schemas can actually do *conceptual* work in language learning and in reasoning. This is a startling result. It flies in the face of time-honored philosophical theories of faculty psychology and their recent reincarnation in strong modularity theories of mind and language, each of which insists on a separation of the mechanisms for perception and conception.

Neural modeling as an existence proof for the embodiment of mind

As yet, we do not have any strong neurophysiological evidence, say from PET scan or functional MRI results, that the same neural mechanisms used in perception and movement are also used in abstract reasoning. What we do have is an existence proof that this is possible and good reasons to believe that it is plausible. The existence proof comes from the field of neural modeling, and it comes in the following form. A neural model of a perceptual or motor mechanism is constructed, and that very same mechanism is used for conceptual tasks as well. The conceptual tasks are of two sorts: (1) learning the structure of a semantic field of lexical items so as to get the relationships among the lexical items correct and (2) performing abstract inferences.

These models are existence proofs in the sense that they show that neural structures that can carry out sensorimotor functions in the brain can in principle do both jobs at once—the job of perception or motor control, on the one hand, and the job of conceptualizing, categorizing, and reasoning, on the other.

What is particularly impressive about these models is that they are computational. The field of computational neuroscience is concerned not merely with *where* the neural computations are done but with *how*, that is, with precise neural computational mechanisms that perform sensorimotor operations and that carry out conceptualizing, categorizing, reasoning, and language learning. Each of the models we will discuss does such jobs in detail.

The embodied mind **99**

Models have been constructed for three kinds of concepts:

1   Spatial-relations concepts, for example, those named by English words like *in, on, over, through,* and *under.*
2   Concepts of bodily movement, represented by verbs like *grasp, pull, lift, tap,* and *punch.*
3   Concepts indicating the structure of actions or events (what linguists call *aspectual concepts*) like *starting, stopping, resuming, continuing, finishing,* including those indicated grammatically as in process (in English *is/are* plus the verb stem plus *-ing: is running*) or completed (*has/have* plus the verb stem plus *-ed: has lifted*).

Since these concepts are about what the body does, namely, perceive and move, one would expect that what the body actually does should shape these concepts. In particular:

•   Since spatial-relations concepts are about space, it should not be surprising if our capacities for vision and negotiating space are used in constituting spatial-relations concepts and their logics.
•   Since concepts of bodily movement are about motor actions, it should not be surprising if our motor schemas and parameters of bodily movement structure those concepts and their logics.
•   Since moving the body is our most common form of action, it should not be surprising if the general structure of control schemas for bodily movements should be used to characterize aspectual structure, the structure we find in actions and events in general.

These models suggest some things that make eminently good sense: The visual systems of our brains are used in characterizing spatial-relations concepts. Our actual motor schemas and motor synergies are involved in what verbs of motor movement mean. And the general form of motor control gives general form to all our actions and the events we perceive. The point is this: In such models, there is no absolute perceptual/conceptual distinction, that is, the conceptual system makes use of important parts of sensorimotor system that impose crucial conceptual structure.

The three models

The three models we are about to discuss are highly complex, and we can give only a very brief overview of them here. A more detailed discussion is found in the Appendix. (For full discussions of all the technical details, see B2, Regier 1996; Bailey 1997; and Narayanan 1997a, b.)

Regier's model for learning spatial-relations terms

Terry Regier (B2, 1996) constructed a neural model for learning spatial-relations terms in the world's languages. Given a model of retinal input with geometric figures in various spatial configurations together with a linguistic description correctly describing the configuration in a given language, the neural model was to learn the system of spatial-relations concepts and terms so that it could correctly categorize and label novel configurations. It was to do this both in cases of static spatial configurations (e.g., *on*) and in cases involving motion (e.g., *onto*). The model learned using no negative evidence, that is, no incorrectly labeled cases, only correctly labeled ones.

Here is the idea behind the model: Though spatial-relations terms differ wildly across the world's languages, they have to categorize using structures found in the visual system of the brain. Spatial-relations concepts should therefore depend on neural structures found in the brain's visual system. Consequently, Regier's model is designed to make maximal use of the types of structures known to exist in the human visual system. Regier's major insights were, first, that topographic maps of the visual field should be instrumental in the computation of image schemas that have topological properties (e.g., the container schema); second, that orientation-sensitive cell assemblies should be able compute the orientational aspects of spatial concepts that rely on bodily orientation (e.g., *above*); third, that center-surround receptive fields should be crucial to characterizing concepts like *contact*; and finally that the "filling-in" architecture discovered by Ramachandran and Gregory (B1, 1991) should play a central role in characterizing the notion of *containment*.

The Regier model is simultaneously both perceptual and conceptual. By virtue of the way the perceptual mechanisms work, it accomplishes the conceptual task of categorizing spatial configurations adequately to fit the conceptual distinctions and contrasts among spatial-relations terms in natural languages. It thereby gives us some insight into how the neural structures in the brain that do perceptual work might be recruited to do conceptual work as well.

Bailey's model for learning verbs of hand motion

David Bailey's model (B2, 1997) learns not only how to categorize and name hand motions in the world's languages but also how to use those verbs correctly to give orders to produce the corresponding hand motion in a computer model of the body. At the heart of Bailey's model are models of high-level motor-control schemas that operate dynamically in time to control motor synergies—subcortical neural circuits that act automatically to produce small, low-level movements. These synergies provide the parameters used by the motor-control schemas, called *X-schemas* (for *executing schemas*).

The idea behind the model is this: Verbs of hand action differ considerably around the world, categorizing actual hand actions in markedly different ways from language to language. Yet the categorization should depend on the actual motor

The embodied mind **101**

schemas used in moving things with the hand and on parameters given by actual motor synergies. Thus, the actual motor mechanisms should also be doing the conceptual work of categorizing actions for the purpose of naming them. The success of the Bailey model suggests how neural circuitry used for motor control can be recruited for conceptual purposes.

Narayanan's model of motor schemas, linguistic aspect, and metaphor

Srini Narayanan (B2, 1997a, b), working with Bailey on modeling motor schemas, discovered that all motor schemas have the same high-level control structure:

> Getting into a state of readiness
> The initial state
> The starting process
> The main process (either instantaneous or prolonged)
> An option to stop
> An option to resume
> An option to iterate or continue the main process
> A check to see if a goal has been met
> The finishing process
> The final state

This should come as no surprise. Any high-level motor activity you undertake, from scratching your head to turning on a light switch to sipping a cup of tea, will have this structure. (It is actually more complex; for the sake of a brief presentation, we have simplified it a bit.) Narayanan then constructed a model of this control structure so that it could be structured separately from the individual special cases (e.g., lifting a cup). That permitted a great simplification in characterizing neural control structures.

Linguists should recognize this model immediately. It characterizes the semantic structure of events in general, what linguists call *aspect*. Any action one undertakes, whether a bodily movement or a more abstract undertaking like planning what to have for dinner, has such a structure. And each language has a linguistic means of highlighting aspects of such a structure. In English, for example, the present imperfect form of the verb (*is/are* plus the present stem of the verb plus *-ing*, as in *is walking*) focuses on the main process as it is happening.

Aspect—the general structure of events—has a conceptual structure and a logic. What Narayanan discovered was that exactly the same neural structure that can perform motor control also characterizes the conceptual structure of linguistic aspect, and the same neural mechanism that can control bodily movements can perform logical inferences about the structure of actions in general.

Narayanan devised an ingenious way to test whether his model of general high-level motor control could handle purely abstract inferences, inferences having nothing to do with bodily movement. He constructed a neural model of conceptual metaphor and then found cases in which body-based metaphors were used in an abstract domain, in this case, international economics. Prominent newspapers and journals use such metaphors every day in economic news reports; for example, "India loosened its stranglehold on business," "France fell into a recession and Germany pulled it out." Narayanan then showed that models of the motor schemas for physical actions can—under metaphoric projection—perform the appropriate abstract inferences about international economics.

The body in the mind

Each of these neural modeling studies constitutes an existence proof. Spatial-relations concepts *can* be represented and spatial-relations terms learned on the basis of neural perceptual apparatus in the brain's visual system (topographic maps of the visual field, orientation-sensitive cells, and so on). Concepts for hand motions *can* be represented and hand-motion terms learned on the basis of detailed models of high-level motor control and motor synergies. Aspectual concepts that characterize the structure of events *can* be adequately represented in terms of general motor-control schemas, and abstract reasoning using those schemas can be carried out using neural motor-control simulations. None of this proves that people actually use those parts of the brain involved in perception and motor control to do such reasoning, but it is in principle possible. At present, these systems that use neural models of motor-control schemas are the only ones capable of carrying out the given tasks.

Now that we know that there can be such a direct embodiment of reason, the question becomes an empirical one, to be settled in experimental neuroscience, not in the arena of philosophical argumentation. The evidence so far favors embodied cognition, and there are general reasons for believing that something like the embodied cognition theory will turn out to be true.

Brains tend to optimize on the basis of what they already have, to add only what is necessary. Over the course of evolution, newer parts of the brain have built on, taken input from, and used older parts of the brain. Is it really plausible that, if the sensorimotor system can be put to work in the service of reason, the brain would build a whole new system to duplicate what it could do already?

Regier has shown that the topological properties of spatial relations can be explained on the basis of the topological properties arising from applying center-surround receptive fields and Ramachandran's filling-in process to topographic maps of the visual field. Is it really plausible that the brain would develop another, nonvisual system with the same topological properties to reason about space, when we obviously already use vision to get around in space?

Narayanan has shown that the neural structure of motor control must already have all the capacities necessary to characterize aspect (the structure of events) and its logic. If the brain can reason about actions using the structure already present to perform actions, is it plausible that the brain would build another system to do the same thing? And if it did, is it plausible that it would take a significantly different neural form?

The embodied mind **103**

From a biological perspective, it is eminently plausible that reason has grown out of the sensory and motor systems and that it still uses those systems or structures developed from them. This explains why we have the kinds of concepts we have and why our concepts have the properties they have. It explains why our spatial-relations concepts should be topological and orientational. And it explains why our system for structuring and reasoning about events of all kinds should have the structure of a motor-control system.

It is only from a conservative philosophical position that one would want to believe in the old faculty psychology—in the idea that the human mind has nothing about it that animals share, that reason has nothing about it that smells of the body.

Philosophically, the embodiment of reason via the sensorimotor system is of great importance. It is a crucial part of the explanation of why it is possible for our concepts to fit so well with the way we function in the world. They fit so well because they have evolved from our sensorimotor systems, which have in turn evolved to allow us to function well in our physical environment. The embodiment of mind thus leads us to a philosophy of embodied realism. Our concepts cannot be a direct reflection of external, objective, mind–free reality because our sensorimotor system plays a crucial role in shaping them. On the other hand, it is the involvement of the sensorimotor system in the conceptual system that keeps the conceptual system very much in touch with the world.

5

THE CONSTRUCTION OF PREFERENCE

P. Slovic

DECISION RESEARCH AND UNIVERSITY OF OREGON

One of the main themes that has emerged from behavioral decision research during the past 2 decades is the view that people's preferences are often constructed in the process of elicitation. This concept is derived in part from studies demonstrating that normatively equivalent methods of elicitation often give rise to systematically different responses. These "preference reversals" violate the principle of procedure invariance that is fundamental to theories of rational choice and raise difficult questions about the nature of human values. If different elicitation procedures produce different orderings of options, how can preferences be defined and in what sense do they exist? Describing and explaining such failures of invariance will require choice models of far greater complexity than the traditional models.

The meaning of preference and the status of value may be illuminated by this well-known exchange among three baseball umpires. "I call them as I see them," said the first. "I call them as they are," claimed the second. The third disagreed, "They ain't nothing till I call them." Analogously, we can describe three different views regarding the nature of values. First, values exist—like body temperature—and people perceive and report them as best they can, possibly with bias ("I call them as I see them"). Second, people know their values and preferences directly—as they know the multiplication table ("I call them as they are"). Third, values or preferences are commonly constructed in the process of elicitation ("They ain't nothing till I call them"). The research reviewed in this article is most compatible with the third view of preference as a constructive, context-dependent process. (Tversky & Thaler, 1990, p. 210)

The expression of preference by means of choice and decision making is the essence of intelligent, purposeful behavior. Although decision making has been studied for centuries by philosophers, mathematicians, economists, and statisticians, it has a relatively short history within psychology. The first extensive review of the theory of decision making was published in the *Psychological Bulletin* by Edwards

The construction of preference **105**

(1954), whose article introduced psychologists to the "exceedingly elaborate, mathematical and voluminous" (p. 380) economic literature on choice and reviewed the handful of relevant experimental studies then in existence.

Edwards's (1954) review was followed by a rapid proliferation of theories of choice and decision making, along with carefully controlled experiments designed to test those theories. This work followed two parallel streams. One, the *theory of riskless choice*, had its origins in the notions of utility maximization put forth by Jeremy Bentham and James Mill. The first formal economic theories based on these notions assumed that decision makers are (a) completely informed about the possible courses of action and their consequences, (b) infinitely sensitive to differences among alternatives, and (c) rational in the sense that they can rank order the possible choices and make decisions that maximize some subjective measure of value or welfare—usually designated by the term *utility*.

The second stream, the *theory of risky choice*, deals with decisions made in the face of uncertainty about the events that determine the outcomes of one's actions. Maximization also plays a key role in these theories, but the quantity to be maximized becomes, because of the uncertainty involved, *expected utility*. Tests of the theory that individuals behave so as to maximize expected utility have been the topic of hundreds of experiments, many of which studied reactions to well-defined manipulations of simple gambles as their basic research paradigm.

A basic assumption of rational theories of choice is the principle of *invariance* (Tversky & Kahneman, 1986; Tversky, Sattath, & Slovic, 1988), which states that the relation of preference should not depend on the description of the options (description invariance) or on the method of elicitation (procedure invariance). Without stability across equivalent descriptions and equivalent elicitation procedures, one's preferences cannot be represented as maximization of utility.

Between 1950 and 1960 another development was taking place that was to have a profound influence on the study of decision making. This was the work of Simon (1956), who sharply criticized the assumption of maximization in utility theory. Simon argued that actual decision-making behavior is better described in terms of *bounded* rationality. A boundedly rational decision maker attempts to attain some satisfactory, although not necessarily maximal, level of achievement. Simon's conceptualization highlighted the role of perception, cognition, and learning in decision making and directed researchers to examine the psychological processes by which decision problems are represented and information is processed.

In recent years the information-processing view has dominated the empirical study of decision making. Both streams of research, on risky and on riskless choice, have been merged in a torrent of studies aimed at describing and understanding the mental operations associated with judgment and decision making. The result has been a far more complicated portrayal of decision making than that provided by utility maximization theory. It is now generally recognized among psychologists that utility maximization provides only limited insight into the processes by which decisions are made.

106 P. Slovic

In particular, a sizable body of research shows that description invariance and procedure invariance do not hold. Preferences appear to be remarkably labile, sensitive to the way a choice problem is described or "framed" and to the mode of response used to express the preference (Fischhoff, Slovic, & Lichtenstein, 1980; Kahneman & Tversky, 1979; Tversky & Kahneman, 1981). These failures of invariance have contributed to a new conception of judgment and choice in which beliefs and preferences are often constructed—not merely revealed—in the elicitation process.

Psychologists' claims that people do not behave according to the dictates of utility theory are particularly troubling to economists, whose theories assume that people are rational in the sense of having preferences that are complete and transitive[1] and in the sense that they choose what they most prefer.

This article reviews the history of research on preference reversals, a line of information-processing theories and experiments that has demonstrated the failure of procedure invariance and has contributed to a view of preference starkly different from the view embodied in economic theories of choice.

Preference reversals among gambles: early studies

The principle of procedure invariance is violated by preference reversals that are induced by changing from one mode of eliciting a preference to another, formally equivalent, mode of response.

An early demonstration of response-mode effects by Slovic and Lichtenstein (1968) used simple gambles as stimuli (e.g., .3 chance to win $16 and .7 chance to lose $4). Slovic and Lichtenstein observed that ratings of a gamble's attractiveness and choices between pairs of gambles were influenced primarily by the probabilities of winning and losing, whereas buying and selling prices (e.g., "What's the most you would pay for a chance to play this gamble?" or "What's the least amount for which you would sell a ticket to play it?") were primarily determined by the dollar amounts that could be won or lost. When participants found a bet attractive, their prices correlated predominantly with the amount that could be won; when they disliked a bet, their prices correlated primarily with the amount that could be lost. This pattern of correlations was explained as the result of a starting point (anchoring) and an adjustment procedure used when setting prices. Respondents setting a price on an attractive gamble appeared to start with the amount they could win and adjust it downward to account for the probabilities of winning and losing as well as for the amount that could be lost. The adjustment process was relatively imprecise, with the price response greatly influenced by the starting point payoff. Ratings and choices, on the other hand, appeared to be governed by different rules, leading to greater emphasis on probabilities.

Lichtenstein and Slovic (1971) hypothesized that if people process information differently when making choices and setting prices, it should be possible to construct pairs of gambles so that a person would choose one member of the pair but would set a higher price on the other. They demonstrated this predicted effect in

The construction of preference **107**

several studies, including one conducted on the floor of the Four Queens Casino in Las Vegas (Lichtenstein & Slovic, 1973). A typical pair of gambles in that study (shown below) consisted of one bet with a high probability to win a modest amount (called the P bet) and one bet with a lower probability of winning a larger payoff (called the $ bet):

> P bet: 11/12 chance to win 12 chips;
> 1/12 chance to lose 24 chips;
> $ bet: 2/12 chance to win 79 chips;
> 10/12 chance to lose 5 chips,

where each chip was worth 25 cents. Each participant first made a choice and later indicated a minimum selling price for each bet. For this pair of gambles, the two bets were chosen about equally often across respondents. However, the $ bet received a higher selling price about 88% of the time. Of the participants who chose the P bet, 87% gave a higher selling price to the $ bet. This is no minor inconsistency. Lichtenstein and Slovic (1971) showed that persons who persisted in this pattern of preferences (and some did) could be turned into "money pumps," continuously giving money to the experimenters without ever playing the gambles.

These early studies captured the attention of a few psychologists and other decision researchers who replicated and extended the findings. Economists were introduced to the preference reversal phenomenon by Grether and Plott (1979), who clearly recognized the threat this phenomenon posed to economic theories of choice: "The inconsistency is deeper than the mere lack of transitivity. ... It suggests that no optimization principles of any sort lie behind even the simplest of human choices" (p. 623). Accordingly, they carried out a series of experiments "designed to discredit the psychologists' works as applied to economics" (p. 623). Their design was based on 13 criticisms and potential artifacts that would render preference reversals irrelevant to economic theory, including the fact that the experimenters were psychologists, which might have led the participants to behave peculiarly. Their manipulations included using special incentives to heighten motivation, controlling for income and order effects, allowing indifference in the choice responses, testing the influence of strategic or bargaining biases, and having economists conduct the study. To their surprise, preference reversals remained much in evidence despite their determined effort to eradicate them.

Grether and Plott's (1979) careful experiment served only to motivate more extreme attempts by economists to make preference reversals disappear. Pommerehne, Schneider, and Zweifel (1982) attempted to increase motivation by raising the face value of the payoffs and creating differences in expected value between the P and $ bets in a pair. They too found a substantial proportion of reversals, leading them to conclude, "Even when the subjects are exposed to strong incentives for making motivated, rational decisions, the phenomenon of preference reversal does not vanish" (p. 573).

108 P. Slovic

Reilly (1982) was also skeptical of the adequacy of Grether and Plott's (1979) controls. To maximize respondents' understanding of the task, he conducted a study in which the money at risk was placed on a desk in front of the respondent and the size of potential losses in the gambles was increased to enhance motivation. Although the rate of preference reversals was somewhat lower than that observed by Grether and Plott, the phenomenon persisted to a substantial extent. Reilly conceded that these results provided "further confirmation of preference reversal as a persistent behavioral phenomenon in situations where economic theory is generally applied" (p. 582). Nevertheless, he maintained the hope that further strengthening of monetary incentives and the provision of additional information to the participants would make this troublesome phenomenon disappear, thus salvaging preference theory.

Preference reversals were also observed by Knez and Smith (1987), who allowed their participants to trade bets in an experimental market, and by Berg, Dickhaut, and O'Brien (1985), who used an arbitrage procedure that turned participants whose prices and preferences were inconsistent into money pumps. Chu and Chu (1990) and Cox and Grether (1994) were finally able to eradicate preference reversals in market settings characterized by repetition, feedback, and harsh penalties for being inconsistent.

Some economists have attempted to save utility theory by arguing that preference reversals can be accommodated by eliminating less central axioms rather than by abandoning transitivity (see, e.g., Holt, 1986; Karni & Safra, 1987). Other theorists, however, proposed more radical departures from utility theory. Both Loomes and Sugden (1983) and Fishburn (1985) designed theories that abandoned the requirement of transitivity.

Slovic and Lichtenstein (1983) responded to economists' repeated attacks and defensive posture by attempting to show how preference reversals fit into a larger picture of framing and information-processing effects that, as a whole, pose a collective challenge to preference theories far exceeding the challenge from reversals alone. They urged economists not to resist these developments but, instead, to examine them for insights into how people make decisions and the ways that the practice of decision making can be improved.

Hausman (1991) was also critical of economists' refusal to take preference reversals seriously. Writing "On Dogmatism in Economics: The Case of Preference Reversals," he traced economists' reactions to their reluctance to abandon a single systematic and parsimonious theory of choice that is also a theory of rational choice, in favor of psychologists' narrower and more complex theories. Nevertheless, he concluded, economists' reactions were hard to defend, creating "unreasonable barriers to theoretical and empirical progress" (p. 223).

Causes of preference reversals

Although the early studies established the robustness of the preference reversal phenomenon, its interpretation and explanation remained unclear, leading to a second wave of studies starting in the mid-1980s.

The construction of preference **109**

Tversky, Slovic, and Kahneman (1990) formulated the explanatory problem as follows. First, they defined a preference reversal as the following combination of responses:

$$H > L \text{ and } C_L > C_H,$$

where H refers to the high-probability gamble (earlier called the P bet), L refers to the low-probability gamble (the $ bet); C_H and C_L denote, respectively, the cash equivalent (or minimum selling price) of H and L; and $>$ and $\approx$ denote strict preference and indifference, respectively. Note that $>$ refers to the ordering of cash amounts and $X > Y$ implies $X > Y$; in other words, more money is preferred to less.

A preference reversal can be shown to imply either the intransitivity of the preference relation $>$, the failure of procedure invariance, or both.

If procedure invariance holds, an individual will be indifferent between his or her stated price (cash equivalent) X and the bet B; that is,

$$B > X \text{ iff } C_B > X \text{ and } C_B = X \text{ iff } B \approx X.$$

Therefore, if invariance holds, preference reversal implies the following intransitive cycle:

$$C_H \approx H > L \approx C_L > C_H,$$

where the two inequalities follow from the preference reversal, and the two equivalences follow from procedure invariance.

But two types of discrepancies between choice and pricing (i.e., failures of invariance) could also produce preference reversals: overpricing of L and underpricing of H. Overpricing of L is said to occur if the decision maker prefers the price over the bet when offered a choice between them (i.e., $C_L > L$). Underpricing of H occurs when $H > C_H$. Overpricing and underpricing merely identify the sign of the discrepancy between pricing and choice; the labels do not imply that choice represents one's true preference and that the bias resides only in pricing.

Tversky et al. (1990) developed a procedure for diagnosing whether any observed preference reversal was due to intransitivity, overpricing of L, underpricing of H, or both overpricing of L and underpricing of H, and they used this procedure in a new study.[2] The results were clear. The experiment yielded the usual rate of preference reversal (between 40% and 50%), but only 10% of preference reversal patterns were intransitive, and the remaining 90% violated procedure invariance. By far the major source of preference reversal was the overpricing of the L bet, which accounted for nearly two thirds of the observed patterns. These conclusions were further supported in a study by Bostic, Herrnstein, and Luce (1990), who used a somewhat different methodology.

110 P. Slovic

The compatibility hypothesis

In the earliest studies on preference reversals, two information-processing concepts were proposed to account for the dependence on payoff cues in pricing gambles. These were starting point and adjustment strategies (e.g., starting with the amount to win and adjusting it downward) and the concept of compatibility. Lichtenstein and Slovic (1973) proposed a "general hypothesis that the compatibility or commensurability between a cue dimension and the required response will affect the importance of the cue in determining the response" (p. 20).

The finding by Tversky et al. (1990) that preference reversals were due primarily to overpricing the high payoff bets led to a reexamination and more precise formulation of the compatibility hypothesis by them and by Slovic, Griffin, and Tversky (1990). Slovic et al. proposed that the weight of a stimulus attribute in judgment or in choice is enhanced by its compatibility with the response mode.[3] The rationale for this *scale compatibility hypothesis* is twofold. First, if the stimulus scale and the response scale do not match, additional mental operations are needed to map the former onto the latter. This increases effort and error and may reduce the impact of the stimulus scale. Second, a response mode tends to focus attention on the compatible features of the stimulus.

The hypothesized link between compatibility and preference reversals was supported in a number of new studies reported by Slovic et al. (1990). In one of these studies, participants were presented with six pairs of H and L bets. Three pairs involved monetary payoffs, and three pairs involved nonmonetary outcomes, such as a one-week pass for all movie theaters in town, or a dinner for two at a good restaurant. If preference reversals are due primarily to the compatibility of prices and payoffs, which are both expressed in dollars, their incidence should be substantially reduced by the use of nonmonetary outcomes. This prediction was confirmed; the overall incidence of reversals decreased from 41% (monetary bets) to 24% (nonmonetary bets).

Although the compatibility hypothesis can explain preference reversals between pairs of bets, the explanation does not depend on the presence of risk. Indeed, this hypothesis implies a similar discrepancy between choice and pricing for riskless options with a monetary component, such as delayed payments. Let (X, T) be a prospect that offers a payment of $\$X$, T years from now. Consider a long-term prospect L ($2,500, 5 years from now) and a short-term prospect $>$ ($1,600, 1.5 years from now). Suppose that respondents (a) choose between L and S and (b) price both prospects by stating the smallest immediate cash payment for which they would be willing to exchange the delayed payment. According to the compatibility hypothesis, the monetary component X would weigh more heavily in pricing than in choice. As a consequence, respondents should produce preference reversals in which the short-term option is preferred over the long-term option in a direct choice, but the latter is priced higher than the former (i.e., $S > L$ and $C_L > C_S$). This was precisely the pattern observed by Tversky et al. (1990). Their participants chose the short-term option 74% of the time but priced the long-term option above the short-term option 75% of the time; the rate of reversals exceeded 50%. Further analysis revealed that—as in the risky case—the major source of preference reversal was the overpricing of the long-term option, as entailed by compatibility.

Additional support for the role of compatibility in preference reversals came from a study by Schkade and Johnson (1989). This study used "mouselab," a computer-based method for monitoring the time spent by each participant looking at probabilities and at payoffs as they priced bets, rated their attractiveness, or made choices. They found that the percentage of time spent on payoffs was significantly greater in pricing than in choice when respondents produced preference reversals, but there was little difference when respondents did not exhibit reversals. A second experiment produced a high percentage of reversals between pricing responses and attractiveness ratings, along with strong evidence demonstrating the use of anchoring and adjustment strategies. The selection of anchors (e.g., payoffs for pricing and probabilities for rating) appeared to be guided by compatibility.

Goldstein and Einhorn (1987) also found reversals between pricing and attractiveness ratings and attributed them to the way in which the subjective value of a gamble was mapped onto the response scale. Although their model can accommodate reversals of preference, it does not predict the variety of compatibility effects that other studies have observed.

Choice, matching, and the prominence effect

Parallel to the early work on preference reversals, what appeared at the time to be a separate line of research was investigating of the difference between choice and matching responses through the use of a diverse array of two-dimensional stimuli, such as baseball players described in terms of their batting averages and number of home runs, typists described by their speed and accuracy, and so forth. The results, reported in Slovic (1975), were framed in terms of the ancient philosophical puzzle of how to choose between equally attractive alternatives. In these studies, participants first matched different pairs of options (making them equal in value), and, in a later session, chose between the matched options. Slovic found that participants did not choose randomly but rather tended to select the option that was superior on the more important dimension (e.g., batting average and typing accuracy). About a decade later, Tversky saw in this finding the seeds of a general theory of response-mode effects that had the potential to explain a wide variety of empirical findings, including preference reversals. This theory was explicated and tested by Tversky et al. (1988).

Tversky et al. (1988) noted that choice and matching operations were fundamental to measurement in both the physical and the social sciences. To determine the heavier of two objects, for example, one can place them on two sides of a pan balance and observe which side goes down. Alternatively, one can place each object separately on a sliding scale and observe the position at which the sliding scale is balanced. Similarly, to determine the preference order between options, one can use either choice or matching (where matching includes rating scales, cash

112 P. Slovic

equivalents, etc.). Note that the pan balance is analogous to binary choice, whereas the sliding scale resembles matching. In proper physical measurement, procedure invariance holds: The ordering of two objects with regard to weight is identical with either the pan balance or the sliding scale. However, as previously seen, choice and matching often disagree when used to measure preferences.

Generalizing from the results of Slovic (1975), Tversky et al. (1988) formulated the *prominence hypothesis:* The more prominent (important) attribute will weigh more heavily in choice than in matching. This hypothesis was tested and supported through a series of problems, including the highway safety problem shown in Table 5.1. Number of casualties was presumed to be the prominent dimension in this problem. When asked to choose between the two safety programs, 67% of the respondents chose X, the program that saved more lives at a higher cost per life saved. Other groups of respondents received the same problem except that one of the four values was missing. They were asked to fill in the missing value to make the two programs equally attractive. It is possible to infer a person's response to the choice task from their response to the matching task. For example, if the cost for Program X was missing and the respondent filled in a value less than $55 million to make the two programs equally attractive, one would infer that this person would choose Y over X when the cost for X was $55 million. In fact, the overwhelming number of matches favored the more economical Program Y that saves fewer lives. Only 4% of the inferred choices favored Program X. Similar responses were observed across a variety of other problems. In every case, the primary dimension was given more weight in choice than in matching. This effect gives rise to a marked discrepancy between the preferences derived from choice and from matching, thus violating procedure invariance. Because pricing a gamble or judging its cash equivalent is a matching response, one can view preference reversals among bets as a special case of the choice-matching discrepancy, in which probability of winning is the prominent dimension that receives greater weight in choice.[4]

Table 5.1 Highway Safety Problem Used to Assess the Prominence Effect

Problem: About 600 people are killed each year in Israel in traffic accidents. The ministry of transportation investigates various programs to reduce the number of casualties. Consider the following two programs, described in terms of yearly costs in millions of dollars [M]) and the number of casualties per year that is expected following the implementation of each program. Which program do you favor?

Program	Expected number of casualties	Cost	Percentage of respondents choosing
X	500	$55M	67
Y	570	$12M	33

Note

From "Contingent Weighting in Judgment and Choice" by A. Tversky, S. Sattath, and P. Slovic, 1988, Psychological Review, 95, p. 373. Copyright 1988 by the American Psychological Association.

The construction of preference **113**

Tversky et al. (1988) suggested that different heuristics or computational schemes appear to be used in the two kinds of tasks. Choice invokes more qualitative reasoning, such as the use of a lexicographic strategy (i.e., selecting the alternative that is ordinally superior on the most important attribute). Lexicographic reasoning is cognitively easier than making explicit tradeoffs and is also easier to justify to oneself and to others. Matching, on the other hand, requires a more quantitative assessment. Tversky et al. proposed that ordinal considerations loom larger in the ordinal procedure of choice than in the cardinal procedure of matching. The prominence effect may thus be seen as an example of a general principle that Fischer and Hawkins (1993) later labeled *strategy compatibility*.

Tversky et al. (1988) also developed a hierarchy of contingent trade-off models to accommodate the various compatibility effects observed in studies of judgment and preference. In these models, the trade-offs between attributes depend on the nature of the response.

Reliance on the prominent dimension makes a good reason for choice. Demonstration of the prominence effect thus focused attention on the importance of reasons, arguments, and justifications in choice. In earlier work, the search for good reasons to eliminate options from consideration had been shown to guide the choice strategies observed and modeled by Tversky (1969). Slovic (1975) also invoked justifiability to explain people's preferences for the option that was superior on the prominent dimension when faced with a choice among equally valued alternatives. Montgomery (1983) argued that people search for and construct dominance structures[5] in decision problems because they provide a compelling reason for choice. The axioms of utility theory may act as compelling arguments or reasons for making a particular decision when their applicability is detected or pointed out (Tversky & Kahneman, 1986).

Additional evidence for a reason-based conception of choice is provided by Tversky and Simonson (1993) and Shafir, Simonson, and Tversky (1993). Shafir et al. argued that a reason-based conception fits well with a constructive interpretation of choice. Different frames, contexts, and elicitation procedures highlight different aspects of the options and bring forth different reasons and considerations that influence the decision.

Construction of preference

The study of preference reversals has been one of several lines of research leading to a conception of choice quite different from the classical assumption that the decision maker has a complete preference order for all options and selects the option highest in that order. This new conception applies to judgments and choices among options that are important, complex, and perhaps unfamiliar, such as gambles, jobs, careers, homes, automobiles, surgical treatments, and environments. In these decisions, preferences are not simply read off some master list but are constructed on the spot by an adaptive decision maker (Payne, Bettman, & Johnson, 1992, 1993). Construction strategies include anchoring and adjustment, relying on the

114 P. Slovic

prominent dimension, eliminating common elements, discarding nonessential differences, adding new attributes into the problem frame in order to bolster one alternative, or otherwise restructuring the decision problem to create dominance and thus reduce conflict and indecision. As a result of these mental gymnastics, decision making is a highly contingent form of information processing, sensitive to task complexity, time pressure, response mode, framing, reference points, and numerous other contextual factors.

Krantz (1991) portrayed this new conception of decision making as attempting to solve several distinct problems in the absence of firm trade-offs or values. He challenged the normative status of utility theory as well as its descriptive status:

> The normative assumption that individuals *should* maximize *some* quantity may be wrong. Perhaps ... there exists nothing to be maximized. Ordering may be partial ... because the calculations are impossible in principle: People do and should act as *problem solvers, not maximizers*, because they have many different and incommensurable ... goals to achieve. (p. 34)

Practical implications of preference construction

The study of preference aims not only to understand decision making but to improve it. The constructive view has much to offer in this regard. For as Delquié (1993) has observed, prescriptive decision analysis basically concerns constructing preferences in situations in which the right choice is not readily apparent. The analysis requires a process that is transparent, logical, and free of arbitrariness. Truth ultimately resides in the process, rather than in the outcome.

Valuing the environment

One practical application of preference construction addresses the method of contingent valuation (CV), which has been used by economists for more than 25 years to value environmental actions such as wetlands protection, water and air quality improvements, and wildlife resources. The CV method posits a hypothetical market and asks people to imagine what they would pay in this market for a proposed change in the environmental state of interest. However, valuing environmental changes is exactly the kind of complex, unfamiliar task in which one would not expect to find stable, well-articulated preferences, making it a likely candidate for constructive processes. Irwin, Slovic, Lichtenstein, and McClelland (1993) used knowledge of constructive preferences to examine and critique the CV approach. They developed a preference reversal experiment in which they asked participants to choose between improved air quality and an upgraded computer and to indicate their cash equivalents for each improvement. Irwin et al. found, as predicted by the prominence hypothesis, that participants chose improved air quality as more valuable, presumably because choice invokes reasons, and there are stronger, more noble reasons for preferring air quality over a computer upgrade. They also predicted, and found, that people placed a higher monetary value on the computer upgrade, presumably because of the strong implicit price cues associated with a better computer. Preference reversals (preference for improved air quality in choice and the computer upgrade in pricing) were observed in 41% of the respondents.

Kahneman and Ritov (1994) also hypothesized and found prominence effects leading to reversals between choices and monetary values for environmental interventions, although the specific nature of these effects was somewhat different from that observed by Irwin et al. (1993).

With the findings of Irwin et al. (1993) in mind, Gregory, Lichtenstein, and Slovic (1993) launched a critique of the CV paradigm. They argued that if monetary values are constructed during the elicitation process in a way that is strongly influenced by context, one should take a deliberate approach to value construction, in a manner designed to rationalize the process. They recommended the use of multiattribute utility theory (von Winterfeldt & Edwards, 1986), which provides a systematic framework for eliciting and integrating the multiple dimensions of complex values. In this way, a CV survey would serve as an active process of value construction, rather than a neutral process of value discovery, and the designers of a CV study would function "not as archaeologists, carefully uncovering what is there, but as architects, working to build a defensible expression of value" (Gregory et al., 1993, p. 179).

Informed consent

The role of preference construction as an active process was perceived in a very different way by MacLean (1991), a philosopher interested in the role of informed consent in clinical medicine. MacLean described the move away from the traditional model whereby authority is delegated by the patient to the physician toward a new model of shared decision making, in which enlightened physicians give primary responsibility to the patient. The physician thus acts as an expert advisor, providing information and counseling. The shared decision-making model thus respects the patient's autonomy in the face of decisions that are difficult and momentous. It also protects the physician against the charge of imposing an unwanted treatment on the patient.

MacLean (1991) argued that if preferences are constructed in the process of informing, framing the options, and eliciting the response, the rationale behind the shared model of consent cannot be defended. Rather, this model makes the physician's role more difficult and risky. The physician is helping to construct preferences, which he or she should do consciously yet in a way that avoids domination. MacLean offered no simple guidelines for the physician but argued that the process must be more involved and interactive than the normal approach, if the value of informed consent is to be realized.

Preference management

The fact that preferences are highly labile, which psychologists have worked so hard to demonstrate, has been known to practical philosophers for ages. If preferences are so readily manipulable, why not manage them for one's own benefit? For example, people can choose their goals and aspiration levels. Thus, the Talmud asks, "Who is it that is rich?" and answers, "One who is content with his portion."[6] People are advised by those wiser than themselves to "put things in perspective," by comparing their misfortunes with far worse troubles or by considering how unimportant some present problem will seem 10 years from now.

The constructive theory may help people do a better job of managing their preferences. Thus MacLean's patients and physicians might be advised to sift and weigh alternative reasons or justifications, to work toward developing a rationale for action. A strong rationale might buffer the patient from regret and make it easier for him or her to accept the consequences of the decision. If the patient is an intuitive decision theorist, this process could invoke utility functions and maximization rules. However, quite different justifications could be equally legitimate if they have been thoughtfully derived.

An appreciation of framing effects could also help people manage their preferences more effectively (Thaler, 1985). Suppose, for example, that a person with $5,600 in a bank account misplaces a $100 bill. Rather than isolating and dwelling on this painful loss, assimilating it into one's total account may ease the sting by exploiting the perception that $5,500 is not that different from $5,600.

The concepts of preference construction and preference management reflect the deep interplay between descriptive phenomena and normative principles. The experimental study of decision processes appears to be forging a new conception of preference, one that may require serious restructuring of normative theories and approaches toward improving decision making.

Notes

Editor's note. Articles based on APA award addresses that appear in the *American Psychologist* are scholarly articles by distinguished contributors to the field. As such, they are given special consideration in the *American Psychologist's* editorial process.

This article was originally presented as part of a Distinguished Scientific Contributions award address at the 102nd Annual Convention of the American Psychological Association in Los Angeles, California, in August 1994.

Daniel Kahneman served as action editor for this article.

Author's note. I am indebted to Sarah Lichtenstein, Baruch Fischhoff, Amos Tversky, and Danny Kahneman, who made immense contributions to the research described in this article and who made the conduct of my own research in this area a truly pleasurable and exciting venture.

Correspondence concerning this article should be addressed to Paul Slovic, Decision Research, 1201 Oak Street, Eugene, OR 97401.

1 Persons' preferences are complete if, for all options x and y, they prefer x to y or y to x or are indifferent between them. Their preferences are transitive if, for all options x, y, and z, if they prefer x to y and y to z, then they prefer x to z. Completeness and transitivity are fundamental to utility theories.

2 In this diagnostic procedure, the original preference reversal design was extended to include, in addition to the standard H and L bets, a cash amount X that was compared with both of them. That is, participants indicated their preferences between each of the pairs in the triple {H, L, X}. Participants also produced cash equivalents, C_L and C_H for both of the bets. By focusing on standard preference reversal patterns in which the prespecified cash amount X has been set to lie between the values of C_L and C_H generated by the respondent (i.e., $H > L$ and $C_L > X > C_H$), it is possible to diagnose each preference reversal pattern according to whether it was produced by an intransitivity, by an overpricing of L, by an underpricing of H, or by both. For example, if respondents indicated that $L > X$ and that $X > H$, then their preferences are intransitive because the method analyzes only those cases in which $H > L$. Alternatively, if respondents overprice the L bet, then their pattern of responses will be $X > L$ and $X > H$. (The respondents produce a price for L that is greater than X, but when offered a choice between X and L, they choose X.) This pattern is transitive, although it is a preference reversal.

3 The significance of the compatibility between input and output has long been recognized by students of human performance. Engineering psychologists have discovered that responses to visual displays of information, such as an instrument panel, will be faster and more accurate if the response structure is compatible with the arrangement of the stimuli (Fitts & Seeger, 1953). For example, the response to a pair of lights will be faster and more accurate if the left light is assigned to the left key and the right light to the right key. Similarly, a square array of four burners on a stove is easier to control with a matching square array of knobs than with a linear array.

4 A nice example of prominence is the finding that personal safety looms larger in choices between options that vary in both safety and cost than in the pricing of such options (Magat, Viscusi, & Huber, 1988). Safety is more prominent than money and, thus, is given greater weight in choice than in pricing.

5 A dominance structure is a choice situation in which one option is as good or better than another on all relevant aspects.

6 Not being a Talmudic scholar, I am indebted to David Krantz (1991) for this example.

References

Berg, J., Dickhaut, J., & O'Brien, J. (1985). Preference reversal and arbitrage. In V. Smith (Ed.), *Research in experimental economics* (pp. 31–72). Greenwich, CT: JAI Press.

Bostic, R., Herrnstein, R., & Luce, R. (1990). The effect on the preference–reversal phenomenon of using choice indifferences. *Journal of Economic Behavior and Organization, 13*, 193–212.

Chu, Y., & Chu, R. (1990). The subsidence of preference reversals in simplified and market-like experimental settings: A note. *American Economic Review, 80*, 902–911.

Cox, J., & Grether, D. M. (1994). *The preference reversal phenomenon: Response mode, markets, and incentives.* Unpublished manuscript, California Institute of Technology, Department of Economics.

Delquié, P. (1993, August). *Eliciting preferences free of compatibility and prominence biases.* Unpublished manuscript, University of Texas at Austin.

Edwards, W. (1954). The theory of decision making. *Psychological Bulletin, 51*, 380–417.

Fischer, G., & Hawkins, S. (1993). Strategy compatibility, scale compatibility, and the prominence effect. *Journal of Experimental Psychology: Human Perception and Performance, 19*, 580–597.

Fischhoff, B., Slovic, P., & Lichtenstein, S. (1980). Knowing what you want: Measuring labile values. In T. S. Wallsten (Ed.), *Cognitive processes in choice and decision behavior.* Hillsdale, NJ: Erlbaum.

118 P. Slovic

Fishburn, P. (1985). Nontransitive preference theory and the preference reversal phenomenon. *Rivista Internazionale di Scienze Economiche e Commerciali, 32*, 39–50.

Fitts, P., & Seeger, C. (1953). S-R compatibility: Spatial characteristics of stimulus and response codes. *Journal of Experimental Psychology, 46*, 199–210.

Goldstein, W., & Einhorn, H. (1987). Expression theory and the preference reversal phenomena. *Psychological Review, 94*, 236–254.

Gregory, R., Lichtenstein, S., & Slovic, P. (1993). Valuing environmental resources: A constructive approach. *Journal of Risk and Uncertainty, 7*, 177–197.

Grether, D. M., & Plott, C. (1979). Economic theory of choice and the preference reversal phenomena. *American Economic Review, 69*, 623–638.

Hausman, D. (1991). On dogmatism in economics: The case of preference reversals. *Journal of Socio-Economics, 20*, 205–225.

Holt, C. (1986). Preference reversals and the independence axiom. *American Economic Review. 76*, 508–515.

Irwin, J., Slovic, P., Lichtenstein, S., & McClelland, G. (1993). Preference reversals and the measurement of environmental values. *Journal of Risk and Uncertainty, 6*, 5–18.

Kahneman, D., & Ritov, I. (1994). Determinants of stated willingness to pay for public goods. A study in the headline method. *Journal of Risk and Uncertainty, 9*, 5–38.

Kahneman, D., & Tversky, A. (1979). Prospect theory: An analysis of decision under risk. *Econometrica, 47*, 263–291.

Karni, E., & Safra, Z. (1987). "Preference reversal" and the observability of preferences by experimental methods. *Econometrica, 55*, 675–685.

Knez, M., & Smith, V. L. (1987). Hypothetical valuations and preference reversals in the context of asset trading. In A. Roth (Ed.), *Laboratory experiments in economics.* Cambridge, England: Cambridge University Press.

Krantz, D. H. (1991). From indices to mappings: The representational approach to measurement. In D. Brown & J. Smith (Eds.), *Frontiers of mathematical psychology* (pp. 1–52). New York: Springer-Verlag.

Lichtenstein, S., & Slovic, P. (1971). Reversals of preference between bids and choices in gambling decisions. *Journal of Experimental Psychology, 89*, 46–55.

Lichtenstein, S., & Slovic, P. (1973). Response-induced reversals of preference in gambling: An extended replication in Las Vegas. *Journal of Experimental Psychology, 101*, 16–20.

Loomes, C., & Sugden, R. (1983). A rationale for preference reversal. *American Economic Review, 73*, 428–432.

MacLean, D. (1991). *A critical look at informed consent.* Unpublished manuscript, University of Maryland at Baltimore County, Catonsville, MD.

Magat, W. A., Viscusi, W. K., & Huber, J. (1988). Paired comparison and contingent valuation approaches to morbidity risk evaluation. *Journal of Experimental Economics and Management, 15*, 395–411.

Montgomery, H. (1983). Decision rules and the search for a dominance structure: Towards a process model of decision making. In P. Humphreys, O. Svenson, & A. Vari (Eds.), *Analyzing and aiding decision processes* (pp. 343–369). Amsterdam: North-Holland.

Payne, J., Bettman, J., & Johnson, E. (1992). Behavioral decision research: A constructive processing perspective. *Annual Review of Psychology, 43*, 87–131.

Payne, J., Bettman, J., & Johnson, E. (1993). *The adaptive decision maker.* New York: Cambridge.

Pommerehne, W., Schneider, F., & Zweifel, P. (1982). Economic theory of choice and the preference reversal phenomenon: A reexamination. *American Economic Review, 72*, 569–574.

Reilly, R. (1982). Preference reversal: Further evidence and some suggested modifications in experimental design. *American Economic Review, 72*, 576–584.

Schkade, D., & Johnson, E. (1989). Cognitive processes in preference reversals. *Organizational Behavior and Human Performance, 44*, 203–231.

Shafir, E., Simonson, I., & Tversky, A. (1993). Reason-based choice. *Cognition, 49*, 11–36.

Simon, H. (1956). Rational choice and the structure of the environment. *Psychological Review, 63*, 129–138.

Slovic, P. (1975). Choice between equally valued alternatives. *Journal of Experimental Psychology: Human Perception and Performance, 1*, 280–287.

Slovic, P., Griffin, D., & Tversky, A. (1990). Compatibility effects in judgment and choice. In R. Hogarth (Ed.), *Insights in decision making: A tribute to Hillel J. Einhorn* (pp. 5–27). Chicago: University of Chicago Press.

Slovic, P., & Lichtenstein, S. (1968). Relative importance of probabilities and payoffs in risk-taking. *Journal of Experimental Psychology Monographs, 78*, 1–18.

Slovic, P., & Lichtenstein, S. (1983). Preference reversals: A broader perspective. *American Economic Review, 73*, 596–605.

Thaler, R. (1985). Mental accounting and consumer choice. *Marketing Science, 4*, 199–214.

Tversky, A. (1969). Intransitivity of preferences. *Psychological Review, 76*, 31–48.

Tversky, A., & Kahneman, D. (1981). The framing of decisions and the psychology of choice. *Science, 211*, 453–458.

Tversky, A., & Kahneman, D. (1986). Rational choice and the framing of decisions. *Journal of Business, 59*, 251–278.

Tversky, A., Sattath, S., & Slovic, P. (1988). Contingent weighting in judgment and choice. *Psychological Review, 95*, 371–384.

Tversky, A., & Simonson, I. (1993). Context-dependent preferences. *Management Science, 39*, 1179–1189.

Tversky, A., Slovic, P., & Kahneman, D. (1990). The causes of preference reversal. *American Economic Review, 80*, 204–217.

Tversky, A., & Thaler, R. H. (1990). Anomalies: Preference reversals. *Journal of Economic Perspectives, 4*, 201–211.

von Winterfeldt, D., & Edwards, W. (1986). *Decision analysis and behavioral research*. New York: Cambridge.

6

THE TECHNOLOGY OF FOOLISHNESS

J. March

STANFORD UNIVERSITY

Choice and rationality[1]

The concept of choice as a focus for interpreting and guiding human behavior has rarely had an easy time in the realm of ideas. It is beset by theological disputations over free will, by the dilemmas of absurdism, by the doubts of psychological behaviorism, by the claims of historical, economic, social, and demographic determinism. Nevertheless, the idea that humans make choices has proven robust enough to become a major matter of faith in important segments of contemporary western civilization. It is a faith that is professed by virtually all theories of social policy making.

The major tenets of this faith run something like this:

> Human beings make choices. If done properly, choices are made by evaluating alternatives in terms of goals on the basis of information currently available. The alternative that is most attractive in terms of the goals is chosen. The process of making choices can be improved by using the technology of choice. Through the paraphernalia of modern techniques, we can improve the quality of the search for alternatives, the quality of information, and the quality of the analysis used to evaluate alternatives. Although actual choice may fall short of this ideal in various ways, it is an attractive model of how choices should be made by individuals, organizations, and social systems.

These articles of faith have been built upon, and have stimulated, some scripture. It is the scripture of theories of decision making. The scripture is partly a codification of received doctrine and partly a source for that doctrine. As a result, our cultural ideas of intelligence and our theories of choice bear some substantial resemblance. In particular, they share three conspicuous interrelated ideas:

The first idea is the *pre-existence of purpose*. We find it natural to base an interpretation of human choice behavior on a presumption of human purpose. We have, in fact, invented one of the most, elaborate terminologies in the professional literature: "values", "needs", "wants", "goods", "tastes", "preferences", "utility", "objectives", "goals", "aspirations", "drives". All of these reflect a strong tendency to believe that a useful interpretation of human behavior involves defining a set of objectives that (a) are prior attributes of the system, and (b) make the observed behavior in some sense intelligent *vis-à-vis* those objectives.

Whether we are talking about individuals or about organizations, purpose is an obvious presumtion of the discussion. An organization is often defined in terms of its purpose. It is seen by some as the largest collectivity directed by a purpose. Action within an organization is justified (or criticized) in terms of the purpose. Individuals explain their own behavior, as well as the behavior of others, in terms of a set of value premises that are presumed to be antecedent to the behavior. Normative theories of choice begin with an assumption of a pre-existent preference ordering defined over the possible outcomes of a choice.

The second idea is the *necessity of consistency*. We have come to recognize consistency both as an important property of human behavior and as a prerequisite for normative models of choice. Dissonance theory, balance theory, theories of congruency in attitudes, statuses, and performances have all served to remind us of the possibilities for interpreting human behavior in terms of the consistency requirements of a limited capacity information-processing system.

At the same time, consistency is a cultural and theoretical virtue. Action should be made consistent with belief. Actions taken by different parts of an organization should be consistent with each other. Individual and organizational activities are seen as connected with each other in terms of their consequences for some consistent set of purposes. In an organization, the structural manifestation of the dictum of consistency is the hierarchy with its obligations of coordination and control. In the individual, the structural manifestation is a set of values that generates a consistent preference ordering.

The third idea is the (*primacy of rationality*). By rationality I mean a procedure for deciding what is correct behavior by relating consequences systematically to objectives. By placing primary emphasis on rational techniques, we implicitly have rejected – or seriously impaired – two other procedures for choice: (a) The processes of intuition, by means of which people may do things without fully understanding why. (b) The processes of tradition and faith, through which people do things because that is the way they are done.

Both within the theory and within the culture we insist on the ethic of rationality. We justify individual and organizational action in terms of an analysis of means and ends. Impulse, intuition, faith, and tradition are outside that system and viewed as antithetical to it. Faith may be seen as a possible source of values. Intuition may be seen as a possible source of ideas about alternatives. But the analysis and justification of action lie within the context of reason.

122 J. March

These ideas are obviously deeply imbedded in the culture. Their roots extend into ideas that have conditioned much of modern western history and interpretations of that history. Their general acceptance is probably highly correlated with the permeation of rationalism and individualism into the style of thinking within the culture. The ideas are even more obviously imbedded in modern theories of choice. It is fundamental to those theories that thinking should precede action; that action should serve a purpose; that purpose should be defined in terms of a consistent set of pre-existent goals; and that choice should be based on a consistent theory of the relation between action and its consequences.

Every tool of management decision that is currently a part of management science, operations research, or decision theory assumes the prior existence of a set of consistent goals. Almost the entire structure of micro-economic theory builds on the assumption that there exists a well-defined, stable, and consistent preference ordering. Most theories of individual or organizational choice behavior accept the idea that goals exist and that (in some sense) an individual or organization acts on those goals, choosing from among some alternatives on the basis of available information. Discussions of educational policy, for example, with the emphasis on goal setting, evaluation, and accountability, are directly in this tradition.

From the perspective of all of man's history, the ideas of purpose, consistency, and rationality are relatively new. Much of the technology currently available to implement them is extremely new. Over the past few centuries, and conspicuously over the past few decades, we have substantially improved man's capability for acting purposively, consistently, and rationally. We have substantially increased his propensity to think of himself as doing so. It is an impressive victory, won – where it has been won – by a happy combination of timing, performance, ideology, and persistence. It is a battle yet to be concluded, or even engaged, in many cultures of the world; but within most of the western world, individuals and organizations see themselves as making choices.

The problem of goals

The tools of intelligence as they are fashioned in modern theories of choice are necessary to any reasonable behavior in contemporary society. It is difficult to see how we could, and inconceivable that we would, fail to continue their development, refinement, and extension. As might be expected, however, a theory and ideology of choice built on the ideas outlined above is deficient in some obvious, elementary ways, most conspicuously in the treatment of human goals.

Goals are thrust upon the intelligent man. We ask that he act in the name of goals. We ask that he keep his goals consistent. We ask that his actions be oriented to his goals. We ask that a social system amalgamate individual goals into a collective goal. But we do not concern ourselves with the origin of goals. Theories of individual organizational and social choice assume actors with pre-existent values.

Since it is obvious that goals change over time and that the character of those changes affects both the richness of personal and social development and the

The technology of foolishness   123

outcome of choice behavior, a theory of choice must somehow justify ignoring the phenomena. Although it is unreasonable to ask a theory of choice to solve all of the problems of man and his development, it is reasonable to ask how something as conspicuous as the fluidity and ambiguity of objectives can plausibly be ignored in a theory that is offered as a guide to human choice behavior.

There are three classic justifications. The first is that goal development and choice are independent processes, conceptually and behaviorally. The second is that the model of choice is never satisfied in fact and that deviations from the model accommodate the problems of introducing change. The third is that the idea of changing goals is so intractable in a normative theory of choice that nothing can be said about it. Since I am unpersuaded of the first and second justifications, my optimism with respect to the third is somewhat greater than most of my fellows.

The argument that goal development and choice are independent behaviorally seems clearly false. It seems to me perfectly obvious that a description that assumes goals come first and action comes later is frequently radically wrong. Human choice behavior is at least as much a process for discovering goals as for acting on them. Although it is true enough that goals and decisions are "conceptually" distinct, that is simply a statement of the theory. It is not defense of it. They are conceptually distinct if we choose to make them so.

The argument that the model is incomplete is more persuasive. There do appear to be some critical "holes" in the system of intelligence as described by standard theories of choice. There is incomplete information, incomplete goal consistency, and a variety of external processes impinging on goal development – including intuition and tradition. What is somewhat disconcerting about the argument, however, is that it makes the efficacy of the concepts of intelligent choice dependent on their inadequacy. As we become more competent in the techniques of the model, and more committed to it, the "holes" become smaller. As the model becomes more accepted, our obligation to modify it increases.

The final argument seems to me sensible as a general principle, but misleading here. Why are we more reluctant to ask how human beings might find "good" goals than we are to ask how they might make "good" decisions? The second question appears to be a relatively technical problem. The first seems more pretentious. It claims to say something about alternative virtues. The appearance of pretense, however, stems directly from the theory and the ideology associated with it.

In fact, the conscious introduction of goal discovery as a consideration in theories of human choice is not unknown to modem man. For example, we have two kinds of theories of choice behavior in human beings. One is a theory of children. The other is a theory of adults. In the theory of childhood, we emphasize choices as leading to experiences that develop the child's scope, his complexity, his awareness of the world. As parents, or psychologists, we try to lead the child to do things that are inconsistent with his present goals because we know (or believe) that he can only develop into an interesting person by coming to appreciate aspects of experience that he initially rejects.

124 J. March

In the theory of adulthood, we emphasize choices as a consequence of our intentions. As adults, or economists, we try to take actions that (within the limits of scarce resources) come as close as possible to achieving our goals. We try to find improved ways of making decisions consistent with our perceptions of what is valuable in the world.

The asymmetry in these models is conspicuous. Adults have constructed a model world in which adults know what is good for themselves, but children do not. It is hard to react positively to the conceit. The asymmetry has, in fact, stimulated a rather large number of ideologies and reforms designed to allow children the same moral prerogative granted to adults – the right to imagine that they know what they want. The efforts have cut deeply into traditional child-rearing, traditional educational policies, traditional politics, and traditional consumer economics.

In my judgment, the asymmetry between models of choice for adults and models of choice for children is awkward; but the solution we have adopted is precisely wrong-headed. Instead of trying to adapt the model of adults to children, we might better adapt the model of children to adults. For many purposes, our model of children is better. Of course, children know what they want. Everyone does. The critical question is whether they are encouraged to develop more interesting "wants". Values change. People become more interesting as those values and the interconnections made among them change.

One of the most obvious things in the world turns out to be hard for us to accommodate in our theory of choice: A child of two will almost always have a less interesting set of values (yes, indeed, a *worse* set of values) than a child of 12. The same is true of adults. Values develop through experience. Although one of the main natural arenas for the modification of human values is the area of choice, our theories of adult and organizational decision making ignore the phenomenon entirely.

Introducing ambiguity and fluidity to the interpretation of individual, organizational, and societal goals, obviously has implications for behavioral theories of decision making. The main point here, however, is not to consider how we might describe the behavior of systems that are discovering goals as they act. Rather it is to examine how we might improve the quality of that behavior, how we might aid the development of interesting goals.

We know how to advise a society, an organization, or an individual if we are first given a consistent set of preferences. Under some conditions, we can suggest how to make decisions if the preferences are only consistent up to the point of specifying a series of independent constraints on the choice. But what about a normative theory of goal-finding behavior? What do we say when our client tells us that he is not sure his present set of values is the set of values in terms of which he wants to act?

It is a question familiar to many aspects of ordinary life. It is a question that friends, associates, students, college presidents, business managers, voters, and children ask at least as frequently as they ask how they should act within a set consistent and stable values.

Within the context of the normative theory of choice as it exists, the answer we give is: First determine the values, then act. The advice is frequently useful.

The technology of foolishness 125

Moreover, we have developed ways in which we can use conventional techniques for decision analysis to help discover value premises and to expose value inconsistencies. These techniques involve testing the decision implications of some successive approximations to a set of preferences. The object is to find a consistent set of preferences with implications that are acceptable to the person or organization making the decisions. Variations on such techniques are used routinely in operations research, as well as in personal counseling and analysis.

The utility of such techniques, however, apparently depends on the assumption that a primary problem is the amalgamation or excavation of preexistent values. The metaphors – "finding oneself", "goal clarification", "self-discovery", "social welfare function", "revealed preference" – are metaphors of search. If our value premises are to be "constructed" rather than "discovered", our standard procedures may be useful; but we have no *a priori* reason for assuming they will.

Perhaps we should explore a somewhat different approach to the normative question of how we ought to behave when our value premises are not yet (and never will be) fully determined. Suppose we treat action as a way of creating interesting goals at the same time as we treat goals as a way of justifying action. It is an intuitively plausible and simple idea, but one that is not immediately within the domain of standard normative theories of intelligent choice.

Interesting people and interesting organizations construct complicated theories of themselves. In order to do this, they need to supplement the technology of reason with a technology of foolishness. Individuals and organizations need ways of doing things for which they have no good reason. Not always. Not usually. But sometimes. They need to act before they think.

Sensible foolishness

In order to use the act of intelligent choice as a planned occasion for discovering new goals, we apparently require some idea of sensible foolishness. Which of the many foolish things that we might do now will lead to attractive value consequences? The question is almost inconceivable. Not only docs it ask us to predict the value consequences of action, it asks us to evaluate them. In what terms can we talk about "good" changes in goals?

In effect, we are asked either to specify a set of super-goals in terms of which alternative goals are evaluated, or to choose among alternatives *now* in terms of the unknown set of values we will have at some future time (or the distribution over time of that unknown set of future values). The former alternative moves us back to the original situation of a fixed set of values – now called "super-goals" – and hardly seems an important step in the direction of inventing procedures for discovering new goals. The latter alternative seems fundamental enough, but it violates severely our sense of temporal order. To say that we make decisions now in terms of goals that will only be knowable later is non sensical – as long as we accept the basic framework of the theory of choice and its presumptions of pre-existent goals.

126 J. March

I do not know in detail what is required, but I think it will be substantial. As we challenge the dogma of pre-existent goals, we will be forced to reexamine some of our most precious prejudices: the strictures against imitation, coercion, and rationalization. Each of those honorable prohibitions depends on the view of man and human choice imposed on us by conventional theories of choice.

Imitation is not necessarily a sign of moral weakness. It is a prediction. It is a prediction that if we duplicate the behavior or attitudes of someone else, the chances of our discovering attractive new goals for ourselves are relatively high. In order for imitation to be normatively attractive we need a better theory of who should be imitated. Such a theory seems to be eminently feasible. For example, what are the conditions for effectiveness of a rule that you should imitate another person whose values are in a close neighborhood of yours? How do the chances of discovering interesting goals through imitation change as the number of other people exhibiting the behavior to be imitated increases?

Coercion is not necessarily an assault on individual autonomy. It can be a device for stimulating individuality. We recognize this when we talk about parents and children (at least sometimes). What has always been difficult with coercion is the possibility for perversion that it involves, not its obvious capability for stimulating change. What we require is a theory of the circumstances under which entry into a coercive system produces behavior that leads to the discovery of interesting goals. We are all familiar with the tactic. We use it in imposing deadlines, entering contracts, making commitments. What are the conditions for its effective use? In particular, what are the conditions for coercion in social systems?

Rationalization is not necessarily a way of evading morality. It can be a test for the feasibility of a goal change. When deciding among alternative actions for which we have no good reason, it may be sensible to develop some definition of how "near" to intelligence alternative "unintelligent" actions lie. Effective rationalization permits this kind of incremental approach to changes in values. To use it effectively, however, we require a better idea of the kinds of metrics that might be possible in measuring value distances. At the same time, rationalization is the major procedure for integrating newly discovered goals into an existing structure of values. It provides the organization of complexity without which complexity itself becomes indistinguishable from randomness.

There are dangers in imitation, coercion, and rationalization. The risks are too familiar to elaborate. We should, indeed, be able to develop better techniques. Whatever those techniques may be, however, they will almost certainly undermine the superstructure of biases erected on purpose, consistency, and rationality. They will involve some way of thinking about action now as occurring in terms of a set of unknown future values.

Play and reason

A second requirement for a technology of foolishness is some strategy for suspending rational imperatives toward consistency. Even if we know which of several

The technology of foolishness **127**

foolish things we want to do, we still need a mechanism for allowing us to do it. How do we escape the logic of our reason?

Here, I think, we are closer to understanding what we need. It is playfulness. Playfulness is the deliberate, temporary relaxation of rules in order to explore the possibilities of alternative rules. When we are playful, we challenge the necessity of consistency. In effect, we announce – in advance – our rejection of the usual objections to behavior that does not fit the standard model of intelligence.

Playfulness allows experimentation. At the same time, it acknowledges reason. It accepts an obligation that at some point either the playful behavior will be stopped or it will be integrated into the structure of intelligence in some way that makes sense. The suspension of the rules is temporary.

The idea of play may suggest three things that are, in my mind, quite erroneous in the present context. First, play may be seen as a kind of Mardi Gras for reason, a release of emotional tensions of virtue. Although it is possible that play performs some such function, that is not the function with which I am concerned. Second, play may be seen as part af some mystical balance of spiritual principles: Fire and water, hot and cold, weak and strong. The intention here is much narrower than a general mystique of balance. Third, play may be seen as an antithesis of intelligence, so that the emphasis on the importance of play becomes a support for simple self-indulgence. My present intent is to propose play as an instrument of intelligence, not a substitute.

Playfulness is a natural outgrowth of our standard view of reason. A strict insistence on purpose, consistency, and rationality limits our ability to find new purposes. Play relaxes that insistence to allow us to act "unintelligently" or "irrationally", or "foolishly" to explore alternative ideas of possible purposes and alternative concepts of behavioral consistency. And it does this while maintaining our basic commitment to the necessity of intelligence.

Although play and reason are in this way functional complements, they are often behavioral competitors. They are alternative styles and alternative orientations to the same situation. There is no guarantee that the styles will be equally well-developed. There is no guarantee that all individuals, all organizations, or all societies will be equally adept in both styles. There is no guarantee that all cultures will be equally encouraging to both.

Our design problem is either to specify the best mix of styles or, failing that, to assure that most people and most organizations most of the time use an alternation of strategies rather than perseverate in either one. It is a difficult problem. The optimization problem looks extremely difficult on the face of it, and the learning situations that will produce alternation in behavior appear to be somewhat less common than those that produce perseveration.

Consider, for example, the difficulty of sustaining playfulness as a style within contemporary American society. Individuals who are good at consistent rationality are rewarded early and heavily. We define it as intelligence, and the educational rewards of society are associated strongly with it. Social norms press in the same direction, particularly for men. Many of the demands of modern organizational life reinforce the same abilities and style preferences.

128 J. March

The result is that many of the most influential, best educated, and best placed citizens have experienced a powerful overlearning with respect to rationality. They are exceptionally good at maintaining consistent pictures of themselves, of relating action to purposes. They are exceptionally poor at a playful attitude toward their own beliefs, toward the logic of consistency, or toward the way they see things as being connected in the world. The dictates of manliness, forcefulness, independence, and intelligence are intolerant of playful urges if they arise. The playful urges that arise are weak ones.

The picture is probably overdrawn, but not, I believe, the implications. For societies, for organizations, and for individuals reason and intelligence have had the unnecessary consequence of inhibiting the development of purpose into more complicated forms of consistency. In order to move away from that position, we need to find some ways of helping individuals and organizations to experiment with doing things for which they have no good reason, to be playful with their conception of themselves. It is a facility that requires more careful attention than I can give it, but I would suggest five things as a small beginning:

First, we can treat *goals as hypotheses*. Conventional decision theory allows us to entertain doubts about almost everything except the thing about which we frequently have the greatest doubt – our objectives. Suppose we define the decision process as a time for the sequential testing of hypotheses about goals. If we can experiment with alternative goals, we stand some chance of discovering complicated and interesting combinations of good values that none of us previously imagined.

Second, we can treat *intuition as real*. I do not know what intuition is, or even if it is any one thing. Perhaps it is simply an excuse for doing something we cannot justify in terms of present values or for refusing to follow the logic of our own beliefs. Perhaps it is an inexplicable way of consulting that part of our intelligence that is not organized in a way anticipated by standard theories of choice. In either case, intuition permits us to see some possible actions that are outside our present scheme for justifying behavior.

Third, we can treat *hypocrisy as a transition*. Hypocrisy is an inconsistency between expressed values and behavior. Negative attitudes about hypocrisy stem from two major things. The first is a general onus against inconsistency. The second is a sentiment against combining the pleasures of vice with the appearance of virtue. Apparently, that is an unfair way of allowing evil to escape temporal punishment. Whatever the merits of such a position as ethics, it seems to me distinctly inhibiting toward change. A bad man with good intentions may be a man experimenting with the possibility of becoming good. Somehow it seems to me more sensible to encourage the experimentation than to insult it.

Fourth, we can treat *memory as an enemy*. The rules of consistency and rationality require a technology of memory. For most purposes, good memories make good choices. But the ability to forget, or overlook, is also useful. If I do not know what I did yesterday or what other people in the organization are doing today, I can act within the system of reason and still do things that are foolish.

Fifth, we can treat *experience as a theory*. Learning can be viewed as a series of conclusions based on concepts of action and consequences that we have invented.

The technology of foolishness **129**

Experience can be changed retrospectively. By changing our interpretive concepts now, we modify what we learned earlier. Thus, we expose the possibility of experimenting with alternative histories. The usual strictures against "self-deception" in experience need occasionally to be tempered with an awareness of the extent to which all experience is an interpretation subject to conscious revision. Personal histories, and national histories, need to be rewritten rather continuously as a base for the retrospective learning of new self-conceptions.

Each of these procedures represents a way in which we temporarily suspend the operation of the system of reasoned intelligence. They are playful. They make greatest sense in situations in which there has been an overlearning of virtues of conventional rationality. They are possibly dangerous applications of powerful devices more familiar to the study of behavioral pathology than to the investigation of human development. But they offer a few techniques for introducing change within current concepts of choice.

The argument extends easily to the problems of social organization. If we knew more about the normative theory of acting before you think, we could say more intelligent things about the functions of management and leadership when organizations or societies do not know what they are doing. Consider, for example, the following general implications.

First, we need to reexamine the functions of management decision. One of the primary ways in which the goals of an organization are developed is by interpreting the decisions it makes, and one feature of good managerial decisions is that they lead to the development of more interesting value premises for the organization. As a result, decisions should not be seen as flowing directly or strictly from a pre-existent set of objectives. Managers who make decisions might well view that function somewhat less as a process of deduction or a process of political negotiation, and somewhat more as a process of gently upsetting preconceptions of what the organization is doing.

Second, we need a modified view of planning. Planning in organizations has many virtues, but a plan can often be more effective as an interpretation of past decisions than as a program for future ones. It can be used as a part of the efforts of the organization to develop a new consistent theory of itself that incorporates the mix of recent actions into a moderately comprehensive structure of goals. Procedures for interpreting the meaning of most past events are familiar to the memoirs of retired generals, prime ministers, business leaders, and movie stars. They suffer from the company they keep. In an organization that wants to continue to develop new objectives, a manager needs to be relatively tolerant of the idea that he will discover the meaning of yesterday's action in the experiences and interpretations of today.

Third, we need to reconsider evaluation. As nearly as I can determine, there is nothing in a formal theory of evaluation that requires that the criterion function for evaluation be specified in advance. In particular, the evaluation of social experiments need not be in terms of the degree to which they have fulfilled our *a priori* expectations. Rather we can examine what they did in terms of what we now

130 J. March

believe to be important. The prior specification of criteria and the prior specification of evaluational procedures that depend on such criteria are common presumptions in contemporary social policy making. They are presumptions that inhibit the serendipitous discovery of new criteria. Experience should be used explicitly as an occasion for evaluating our values as well as our actions.

Fourth, we need a reconsideration of social accountability. Individual preferences and social action need to be consistent in some way. But the process of pursuing consistency is one in which both the preferences and the actions change over time. Imagination in social policy formation involves systematically adapting to and influencing preferences. It would be unfortunate if our theories of social action encouraged leaders to ignore their responsibilities for anticipating public preferences through action and for providing social experiences that modify individual expectations.

Fifth, we need to accept playfulness in social organizations. The design of organizations should attend to the problems of maintaining both playfulness and reason as aspects of intelligent choice. Since much of the literature on social design is concerned with strengthening the rationality of decision, managers are likely to overlook the importance of play. This is partly a matter of making the individuals within an organization more playful by encouraging the attitudes and skills of inconsistency. It is also a matter of making organizational structure and organizational procedure more playful. Organizations can be playful even when the participants in them are not. The managerial devices for maintaining consistency can be varied. We encourage organizational play be permitting (and insisting on) some temporary relief from control, coordination, and communication.

Intelligence and foolishness

Contemporary theories of decision making and the technology of reason have considerably strengthened our capabilities for effective social action. The conversion of the simple ideas of choice into an extensive technology is a major achievement. It is, however, an achievement that has reinforced some biases in the underlying models of choice in individuals and groups. In particular, it has reinforced the uncritical acceptance of a static interpretation of human goals.

There is little magic in the world, and foolishness in people and organizations is one of the many things that fail to produce miracles. Under certain conditions, it is one of several ways in which some of the problems of our current theories of intelligence can be overcome. It may be a good way. It preserves the virtues of consistency while stimulating change. If we had a good technology of foolishness, it might (in combination with the technology of reason) help in a small way to develop the unusual combinations of attitudes and behaviors that describe the interesting people, interesting organizations, and interesting societies of the world.

Note

1 This chapter is based on March (1972).

7

GREAT MEN, GREAT THOUGHTS, AND THE ENVIRONMENT

W. James

LECTURE DELIVERED BEFORE THE HARVARD NATURAL HISTORY SOCIETY.
PUBLISHED IN THE *ATLANTIC MONTHLY*, OCTOBER, 1880

A remarkable parallel, which I think has never been noticed, obtains between the facts of social evolution on the one hand, and of zoölogical evolution as expounded by Mr. Darwin on the other.

It will be best to prepare the ground for my thesis by a few very general remarks on the method of getting at scientific truth. It is a common platitude that a complete acquaintance with any one thing, however small, would require a knowledge of the entire universe. Not a sparrow falls to the ground but some of the remote conditions of his fall are to be found in the milky way, in our federal constitution, or in the early history of Europe. That is to say, alter the milky way, alter our federal constitution, alter the facts of our barbarian ancestry, and the universe would so far be a different universe from what it now is. One fact involved in the difference might be that the particular little street-boy who threw the stone which brought down the sparrow might not find himself opposite the sparrow at that particular moment; or, finding himself there, he might not be in that particular serene and disengaged mood of mind which expressed itself in throwing the stone. But, true as all this is, it would be very foolish for any one who was inquiring the cause of the sparrow's fall to overlook the boy as too personal, proximate, and so to speak anthropomorphic an agent, and to say that the true cause is the federal constitution, the westward migration of the Celtic race, or the structure of the milky way. If we proceeded on that method, we might say with perfect legitimacy that a friend of ours, who had slipped on the ice upon his door-step and cracked his skull, some months after dining with thirteen at the table, died because of that ominous feast. I know, in fact, one such instance; and I might, if I chose, contend with perfect logical propriety that the slip on the ice was no real accident. "There are no accidents," I might say, "for science. The whole history of the world converged to produce that slip. If anything had been left out, the slip would not have occurred just there and then. To say it would is to deny the relations of cause and effect

132 W. James

throughout the universe. The real cause of the death was not the slip, *but the conditions which engendered the slip,* — and among them his having sat at a table, six months previous, one among thirteen. *That* is truly the reason why he died within the year."

It will soon be seen whose arguments I am, in form, reproducing here. I would fain lay down the truth without polemics or recrimination. But unfortunately we never fully grasp the import of any true statement until we have a clear notion of what the opposite untrue statement would be. The error is needed to set off the truth, much as a dark background is required for exhibiting the brightness of a picture. And the error which I am going to use as a foil to set off what seems to me the truth of my own statements is contained in the philosophy of Mr. Herbert Spencer and his disciples. Our problem is, What are the causes that make communities change from generation to generation, — that make the England of Queen Anne so different from the England of Elizabeth, the Harvard College of to-day so different from that of thirty years ago?

I shall reply to this problem, The difference is due to the accumulated influences of individuals, of their examples, their initiatives, and their decisions. The Spencerian school replies, The changes are irrespective of persons, and independent of individual control. They are due to the environment, to the circumstances, the physical geography, the ancestral conditions, the increasing experience of out relations; to everything, in fact, except the Grants and the Bismarcks, the Joneses and the Smiths.

Now, I say that these theorizers are guilty of precisely the same fallacy as he who should ascribe the death of his friend to the dinner with thirteen, or the fall of the sparrow to the milky way. Like the dog in the fable, who drops his real bone to snatch at its image, they drop the real causes to snatch at others, which from no possible human point of view are available or attainable. Their fallacy is a practical one. Let us see where it lies. Although I believe in free-will myself, I will waive that belief in this discussion, and assume with the Spencerians the predestination of all human actions. On that assumption I gladly allow that were the intelligence investigating the man's or the sparrow's death omniscient and omnipresent, able to take in the whole of time and space at a single glance, there would not be the slightest objection to the milky way or the fatal feast being invoked among the sought-for causes. Such a divine intelligence would see instantaneously all the infinite lines of convergence towards a given result, and it would, moreover, see impartially: it would see the fatal feast to be as much a condition of the sparrow's death as of the man's; it would see the boy with the stone to be as much a condition of the man's fall as of the sparrow's.

The human mind, however, is constituted on an entirely different plan. It has no such power of universal intuition. Its finiteness obliges it to see but two or three things at a time. If it wishes to take wider sweeps it has to use 'general ideas,' as they are called, and in so doing to drop all concrete truths. Thus, in the present case, if we as men wish to feel the connection between the milky way and the boy and the dinner and the sparrow and the man's death, we can do so only by falling back on

Great men, great thoughts, and the environment **133**

the enormous emptiness of what is called an abstract proposition. We must say, All things in the world are fatally predetermined, and hang together in the adamantine fixity of a system of natural law. But in the vagueness of this vast proposition we have lost all the concrete facts and links; and in all practical matters the concrete links are the only things of importance. The human mind is essentially partial. It can be efficient at all only by *picking out* what to attend to, and ignoring everything else, – by narrowing its point of view. Otherwise, what little strength it has is dispersed, and it loses its way altogether. Man always wants his curiosity gratified for a particular purpose. If, in the case of the sparrow, the purpose is punishment, it would be idiotic to wander off from the cats, boys, and other possible agencies close by in the street, to survey the early Celts and the milky way: the boy would meanwhile escape. And if, in the case of the unfortunate man, we lose ourselves in contemplation of the thirteen-at-table mystery, and fail to notice the ice on the step and cover it with ashes, some other poor fellow, who never dined out in his life, many slip on it in coming to the door, and fall and break his head too.

It is, then, a necessity laid upon us as human beings to limit our view. In mathematics we know how this method of ignoring and neglecting quantities lying outside a certain range has been adopted in the differential calculus. The calculator throws out all the "infinitesimals of the quantities he is considering. He treats them (under certain rules) as if they did not exist. In themselves they exist perfectly all the while; but they are as if they did not exist for the purposes of his calculation. Just so an astronomer, dealing with the tidal movements of the ocean, takes no account of the waves made by the wind, or by the pressure of all the steamers which day upon night are moving their thousands of tons upon its surface. Just so the marksman, in sighting his rifle, allows for the motion of the wind, but not for the equally real motion of the earth and solar system. Just so a business man's punctuality may overlook an error of five minutes, while a physicist, measuring the velocity of light, must count each thousandth of a second.

There are, in short, *different cycles of operation* in nature; different departments, so to speak, relatively independent of one another, so that what goes on at any moment in one may be compatible with almost any condition of things at the same moment in the next. The mould on the biscuit in the store-room of a man-of-war vegetates in absolute indifference to the nationality of the flag, the direction of the voyage, the weather, and the human dramas that may go on on board; and a mycologist may study it in complete abstraction from all these larger details. Only by so studying it, in fact, is there any chance of the mental concentration by which alone he may hope to learn something of its nature. On the other hand, the captain who in maneuvering the vessel through a naval fight should think it necessary to bring the mouldy biscuit into his calculations would very likely lose the battle by reason of the excessive "thoroughness" of his mind.

The causes which operate in these incommensurable cycles are connected with one another only *if we take the whole universe into account.* For all lesser points of view it is lawful – nay, more, it is for human wisdom necessary – to regard them as disconnected and irrelevant to one another.

134 W. James

And this brings us nearer to our special topic. If we look at an animal or a human being, distinguished from the rest of his kind by the possession of some extra-ordinary peculiarity, good or bad, we shall be able to discriminate between the causes which originally *produced* the peculiarity in him and the causes that *maintained* it after it is produced; and we shall see, if the peculiarity be one that he was born with, that these two sets of causes belong to two such irrelevant cycles. It was the triumphant originality of Darwin to see this, and to act accordingly. Separating the causes of production under the title of 'tendencies to spontaneous variation,' and relegating them to a physiological cycles which he forthwith agreed to ignore alto-gether, he confined his attention to the causes of preservation, and under the names of natural selection and sexual selection studied them exclusively as functions of the cycle of the environment.

Pre-Darwinian philosophers had also tried to establish the doctrine of descent with modification; but they all committed the blunder of clumping the two cycles of causation into one. What preserves an animal with his peculiarity, if it be a useful one, they saw to be the nature of the environment to which the peculiarity was adjusted. The giraffe with his peculiar neck is preserved by the fact that there are in his environment tall trees whose leaves he can digest. But these philosophers went further, and said that the presence of the trees not only maintained an animal with a long neck to browse upon their branches, but also produced him. They *made* his neck long by the constant striving they aroused in him to reach up to them. The environment, in short, was supposed by these writers to mould the animal by a kind of direct pressure, very much as a seal presses the wax into harmony with itself. Numerous instances were given of the way in which this goes on under our eyes. The exercise of the forge makes the right arm strong, the palm grows callous to the oar, the mountain air distends the chest, the chased fox grows cunning and the chased bird shy, the arctic cold stimulates the animal combustion, and so forth. Now these changes, of which many more examples might be adduced, are at present distinguished by the special name of *adaptive* changes. Their peculiarity is that that very feature in the environment to which the animal's nature grows adjusted, itself produces the adjustment. The 'inner relation,' to use Mr. Spencer's phrase, 'corresponds' with its own efficient cause.

Darwin's first achievement was to show the utter insignificance in amount of these changes produced by direct adaptation, the immensely greater mass of changes being produced by internal molecular accidents, of which we know nothing. His next achievement was to define the true problem with which we have to deal when we study the effects of the visible environment on the animal. That problem is simply this: Is the environment more likely to *preserve or to destroy him,* on account of this or that peculiarity with which he may be born? In giving the name of "acci-dental variations" to those peculiarities with which an animal is born, Darwin does not for a moment mean to suggest that they are not the fixed outcome of natural law. If the total system of the universe be taken into account, the causes of these variations and the visible environment which preserves or destroys them, undoubt-edly do, in some remote and round-about way, hang together. What Darwin means is, that, since the environment is a perfectly known thing, and its relations to the organism in the way of destruction or preservation are tangible and distinct, it would utterly confuse our finite understandings and frustrate our hopes of science to mix in with it facts from such a disparate and incommensurable cycle as that in which the variations are produced. This last cycle is that of occurrences before the animal is born. It is the cycle of influences upon ova and embryos; in which lie the causes that tip them and tilt them towards masculinity or femininity, towards strength or weakness, towards health or disease, and towards divergence from the parent type. What are the causes there?

In the first place, they are molecular and invisible, – inaccessible, therefore, to direct observation of any kind. Secondly, their operations are compatible with any social, political and physical conditions of the environment. The same parents, living in the same environing conditions, may at one birth produce a genius, at the next an idiot or a monster. The visible external conditions are therefore not direct determinants of this cycle; and the more we consider the matter, the more we are forced to believe that two children of the same parents ar made to differ from each other by causes as disproportionate to their ultimate effects as is that famous pebble on the Rocky Mountain crest, which separates two rain-drops, to the Gulf of St. Lawrence and the Pacific Ocean towards which it makes them severally flow.

The great mechanical distinction between transitive forces and discharging forces is nowhere illustrated on such a scale as in physiology. Almost all causes there are forces of *detent,* which operate by simply unlocking energy already stored up. They are upsetters of unstable equilibria, and the resultant effect depends infinitely more on the nature of the materials upset than on that of the particular stimulus which joggles them down. Galvanic work, equal to unity, done on a frog's nerve will discharge from the muscle to which the nerve belongs mechanical work equal to seventy thousand; and exactly the same muscular effect will emerge if other irritants than galvanism are employed. The irritant has merely started or provoked something which then went on of itself, – as a match may start a fire which consumes a whole town. And qualitatively as well as quantitatively the effect may be absolutely incommensurable with the cause. We find this condition of things in all organic matter. Chemists are distracted by the difficulties which the instability of albuminoid compounds opposes to their study. Two specimens, treated in what outwardly seem scrupulously identical conditions, behave in quite different ways. You know about the invisible factors of fermentation, and how the fate of a jar of milk – whether it turn into a sour clot or a mass of koumiss – depends on whether the lactic acid ferment or the alcoholic is introduced first, and gets ahead of the other in starting the process. Now, when the result is the tendency of an ovum, itself invisible to the naked eye, to tip towards this direction or that in its further evolution, – to bring forth a genius or a dunce, even as the rain-drop passes east or west of the pebble, – is it not obvious that the deflecting cause must lie in a region so recondite and minute, must be such a ferment of a ferment, an infinitesimal of so high an order, that surmise itself may never succeed even in attempting to frame an image of it?

136 W. James

Such being the case, was not Darwin right to turn his back upon that region altogether, and to keep his own problem carefully free from all entanglement with matters such as these? The success of his work is a sufficient affirmative reply.

And this brings us at last to the heart of our subject. The causes of production of great men lie in a sphere wholly inaccessible to the social philosopher. He must simply accept geniuses as data, just as Darwin accepts his spontaneous variations. For him, as for Darwin, the only problem is, these date being given, How does the environment affect them, and how do they affect the environment? Now, I affirm that the relation of the visible environment to the great man is in the main exactly what it is to the "variation" in the Darwinian philosophy. It chiefly adopts or rejects, preserves or destroys, in short *selects* him. And whenever it adopts and preserves the great man, it becomes modified by his influence in an entirely original and peculiar way. He acts as a ferment, and changes its constitution, just as the advent of a new zoölogical species changes the faunal and floral equilibrium of the region in which it appears. We all recollect Mr. Darwin's famous statement of the influence of cats on the growth of clover in their neighborhood. We all have read of the effects of the European rabbit in New Zealand, and we have many of us taken part in the controversy about the English sparrow here, – whether he kills more canker worms, or drives away most native birds. Just so the great man, whether he be an important from without like Clive in India or Agassiz here, or whether he spring from the soil like Mahomet or Franklin, brings about a rearrangement, on a large or a small scale, of the pre-existing social relations.

The mutations of societies, then, from generation to generation, are in the main due directly or indirectly to the acts or the examples of individuals whose genius was so adapted to the receptivities of the moment, or whose accidental position of authority was so critical that they became ferments, initiators of movements, setters of precedent or fashion, centers of corruption, or destroyers of other persons, whose gifts, had they had free play, would have led society in another direction.

We see this power of individual initiative exemplified on a small scale all about us, and on a large scale in the case of the leaders of history. It is only following the common-sense method of a Lyell, a Darwin and a Whitney to interpret the unknown by the known, and reckon up cumulatively the only causes of social change we can directly observe. Societies of men are just like individuals, in that both at any given moment offer ambiguous potentialities of development. Whether a young man enters business or the ministry may depend on a decision which has to be made before a certain day. He takes the place offered in the counting-house, and is *committed*. Little by little, the habits, the knowledges, of the other career, which once lay so near, cease to be reckoned even among his possibilities. At first, he may sometimes doubt whether the self he murdered in that decisive hour might not have been the better of the two; but with the years such questions themselves expire, and the old alternative *ego,* once so vivid, fades into something less substantial than a dream. It is no otherwise with nations. They may be committed by kings and ministers to peace or war, by generals to victory or defeat, by prophets to this religion or that, by various geniuses to fame in art, science or industry. A war is a true point of bifurcation of future possibilities. Whether it fail or succeed, its declaration must be the starting-point of new policies. Just so does a revolution, or any great civic precedent, become a deflecting influence, whose operations widen with the course of time. Communities obey their ideals; and an accidental success fixes an ideal, as an accidental failure blights it.

Would England have to-day the "imperial" ideal which she now has, if a certain boy named Bob Clive had shot himself, as he tried to do, at Madras? Would she be the drifting raft she is now in European affairs if a Frederic the Great had inherited her throne instead of a Victoria, and if Messrs. Bentham, Mill, Cobden, and Bright had all been born in Prussia? England has, no doubt, to-day precisely the same intrinsic value relatively to the other nations that she ever had. There is no such fine accumulation of human material upon the globe. But in England the material has lost effective form, while in Germany it has found it. Leaders give the form. Would England be crying forward and backward at once, as she does now, "letting I will not wait upon I would," wishing to conquer but not to fight, if her ideal had in all these years been fixed by a succession of statesmen of supremely commanding personality, working in one direction? Certainly not. She would have espoused, for better or worse, either one course or another. Had Bismarck died in his cradle, the Germans would still be satisfied with appearing to themselves as a race of spectacled *Gelehrten* and political herbivora, and to the French as *ces bons,* or *ces naïfs, Allemands.* Bismarck's will showed them, to their own great astonishment, that they could play a far livelier game. The lesson will not be forgotten. Germany may have many vicissitudes, but they –

> *"will never do away, I ween*
> *The marks of that which once hath been"* –

of Bismarck's initiative, namely, from 1860 to 1873.

The fermentative influence of geniuses must be admitted as, at any rate, one factor in the changes that constitute social evolution. The community *may* evolve in many ways. The accidental presence of this or that ferment decides in which way it *shall* evolve. Why, the very birds of the forest, the parrot, the mino, have the power of human speech, but never develop it of themselves; some one must be there to teach them. So with us individuals. Rembrandt must teach us to enjoy the struggle of light with darkness, Wagner to enjoy peculiar musical effects; Dickens gives a twist to our sentimentality, Artemus Ward to our humor; Emerson kindles a new moral light within us. But it is like Columbus's egg. "All can raise the flowers now, for all have got the seed." But if this be true of individuals in the community, how can it be false of the community as a whole? If shown a certain way, a community may take it; if not, it will never find it. And the ways are to a large extent indeterminate in advance. A nation may obey either of many alternative impulses given by different men of genius, and still live and be prosperous, just as a man may enter either of many businesses. Only, the prosperities may differ in their type.

138 W. James

But the indeterminism is not absolute. Not every "man" fits every "hour." Some incompatabilites there are. A given genius may come either too early or too late. Peter the Hermit would now be sent to an insane asylum. John Mill in the tenth century would have lived and died unknown. Cromwell and Napoleon need their revolutions, Grant his civil war. An Ajax gets no fame in the day of telescopic-sighted rifles; and, to express differently an instance which Spencer uses, what could a Watt have effected in a tribe which no precursive genius had taught to smelt iron or to turn a lathe?

Now, the important thing to notice is that what makes a certain genius now incompatible with his surroundings is usually the fact that some previous genius of a different strain has warped the community away from the sphere of his possible effectiveness. After Voltaire, now Peter the hermit; after Charles IX and Louis XIV, no general protestantization of France; after a Manchester school, a Beacons-field's success is transient; after a Philip II, a Castelar makes little headway; and so on. Each bifurcation cuts off certain sides of the field altogether, and limits the future possible angles of deflection. A community is a living thing, and in words which I can do no better than quote from Professor Clifford, "it is the peculiarity of living things not merely that they change under the influence of surrounding circumstances, but that any change which takes place in them is not lost but retained, and as it were built into the organism to serve as the foundation for future actions. If you cause any distortion in the growth of a tree and make it crooked, whatever you may do afterwards to make the tree straight the mark of your distortion is there; it is absolutely indelible; it has become part of the tree's nature. ... Suppose, however, that you take a lump of gold, melt it, and let it cool. ... No one can tell by examining a piece of gold how often it has melted and cooled in geologic ages, or even in the last year by the hand of man. Any one who cuts down an oak can tell by the rings of its trunk how many times winter has frozen it into widowhood, and how many times summer has warmed it into life. A living being must always contain within itself the history, not merely of its own existence, but of all its ancestors."

Every painter can tell us how each added line deflects his picture in a certain sense. Whatever lines follow must be built on those first laid down. Every author who starts to rewrite a piece of work knows how impossible it becomes to use any of the first-written pages again. The new beginning has already excluded the possib-ility of those earlier phrases and transitions, while it has at the same time created the possibility of an indefinite set of new ones, no one of which, however, is com-pletely determined in advance. Just so the social surroundings of the past and present hour exclude the possibility of accepting certain contributions from individuals; but they do not positively define what contributions shall be accepted, for in them-selves they are powerless to fix what the nature of the individual offerings shall be.

Thus social evolution is a resultant of the interaction of two wholly distinct factors, – the individual, deriving his peculiar gifts from the play of physiological and infra-social forces, but bearing all the power of initiative and origination in his hands; and, second, the social environment, with its power of adopting or rejecting

Great men, great thoughts, and the environment   **139**

both him and his gifts. Both factors are essential to change. The community stagnates without the impulse of the individual. The impulse dies away without the sympathy of the community.

All this seems nothing more than common-sense. All who wish to see it developed by a man of genius should read that golden little work, Bagehot's *Physics and Politics,* in which (it seems to me) the complete sense of the way in which concrete things grow and change is as livingly present as the straining after a pseudo-philosophy of evolution is livingly absent. But there are never wanting minds to whom such views seem personal and contracted, and allied to an anthropomorphism long exploded in other fields of knowledge. "The individual withers, and the world is more and more," to these writers; and in a Buckle, a Draper, and a Taine we all know how much the "world" has come to be almost synonymous with the *climate.* We all know, too, how the controversy has been kept up between the partisans of a "science of history" and those who deny the existence of anything like necessary "laws" where human societies are concerned. Mr. Spencer, at the opening of his *Study of Sociology,* makes an onslaught on the "great-man theory" of history, from which a few passages may be quoted:

> "The genesis of societies by the action of great man may be comfortably believed so long as, resting in general notions, you do not ask for particulars. But now, if, dissatisfied with vagueness, we demand that our ideas shall be brought into focus and exactly defined, we discover the hypothesis to be utterly incoherent. If, not stopping at the explanation of social progress as due to the great man, we go back a step and ask, Whence comes the great man? we find that the theory breaks down completely. The question has two conceivable answers: his origin is supernatural, or it is natural. Is his origin supernatural? Then he is a deputy god, and we have theocracy once removed, – or, rather, not removed at all. ... Is this an unacceptable solution? Then the origin of the great man is natural; and immediately this is recognized, he must be classed with all other phenomena in the society that gave him birth as a product of hits antecedents. Along with the whole generation of which he forms a minute part, along with its institutions, language, knowledge, manners, and its multitudinous arts and appliances, he is a *resultant.* ... You must admit that the genesis of the great man depends on the long series of complex influences which has produced the race in which he appears, and the social state into which that race has slowly grown. ... Before he can remake his society, his society must remake him. all those changes of which he is the proximate initiator have their chief causes in the generations he descended from. If there is to be anything like a real explanation of those changes, it must be sought in that aggregate of conditions out of which both he and they have arisen."

Now, it seems to me that there is something which one might almost call impudent in the attempt which Mr. Spencer makes, in the fist sentence of this extract, to pin

140 W. James

the reproach of vagueness upon those who believe in the power of initiative of the great man.

Suppose I say that the singular moderation which now distinguishes social, political and religious discussion in England, and contrasts so strongly with the bigotry and dogmatism of sixty years ago, is largely due to J. S. Mill's example. I may possibly be wrong about the facts; but I am, at any rate, "asking for particulars," and not "resting in general notions." And if Mr. Spencer should tell me it started from no personal influence whatever, but from the "aggregate of conditions," the "generations," Mill and all his contemporaries "descended from," the whole past order of nature in short, surely he, not I, would be the person "satisfied with vagueness."

The fact is that Mr. Spencer's sociological method is identical with that of one who would invoke the zodiac to account for the fall of the sparrow, and the thirteen at table to explain the gentleman's death. It is of little more scientific value than the Oriental method of replying to whatever question arises by the unimpeachable truism, "God is great." *Not* to fall back on the gods, where a proximate principle may be found, has with us Westerners long since become the sign of an efficient as distinguished from an inefficient intellect.

To believe that the cause of everything is to be found in its antecedents is the starting-point, the initial postulate, not the goal and consummation, of science. If she is simply to lead us out of the labyrinth by the same whole we went in by three or four thousand years ago, it seems hardly worth while to have followed her through the darkness at all. If anything is humanly certain it is that the great man's society, properly so called, does *not* make him before he can remake it. Physiological forces, with which the social, political, geographical, and to a great extent anthropological conditions have just as much and just as little do as conditions of the crater of Vesuvius has to do with the flickering of this gas by which I write, are what make him. Can it be that Mr. Spencer holds the convergence of sociological pressures to have so impinged on Stratford-upon-Avon about the 26th of April, 1564, that a W. Shakespeare, with all his mental peculiarities, had to be born there, – as the pressure of water outside a certain boat will cause a stream of a certain form to ooze into a particular leak? And does he mean to say that if the aforesaid W. Shakespeare had died of cholera infantum, another mother at Stratford-upon-Avon would needs have engendered a duplicate copy of him, to restore the sociologic equilibrium? Or might the substitute arise at "Stratford-atte-Bowe"? Here, as elsewhere, it is very hard, in the midst of Mr. Spencer's vagueness, to tell what he does mean at all.

We have, however, in his disciple, Mr. Grant Allen, one who leaves us in no doubt whatever of his precise meaning. This widely informed, suggestive, and brilliant writer published last year a couple of articles in the *Gentleman's Magazine,* in which he maintained that individuals have no initiative in determining social change.

> "The differences between one nation and another, whether in intellect, commerce, art, morals, or general temperament, ultimately depend, not upon any

mysterious properties of race, nationality, or any other unknown and unintelligible abstractions, but simply and solely upon the physical circumstances to which they are exposed. If it be a fact, as we know it to be, that the French nation differs recognizably from the Chinese, and the people of Hamburg differ recognizably from the people of Timbuctoo, then the notorious and conspicuous differences between them are wholly due to the geographical position of the various races. If the people who went to Hamburg had gone to Timbuctoo, they would now be indistinguishable from the semi-barbarian negroes who inhabit that central African metropolis; and if the people who went to Timbuctoo had gone to Hamburg, they would now have been white-skinned merchants driving a roaring trade in imitation sherry and indigestible port. … The differentiating agency must be sought in the great permanent geographical features of land and sea; … these have necessarily and inevitably moulded the characters and histories of every nation upon the earth. … We cannot regard any nation as an active agent in differentiating itself. Only the surrounding circumstances can have any effect in such a direction. [These two sentences dogmatically deny the existence of the relatively independent physiological cycle of causation. WJ] To suppose otherwise is to suppose that the mind of man is exempt from the universal law of causation. There is no caprice, no spontaneous impulse, in human endeavors. Even tastes and inclinations *must* themselves be the result of surrounding causes."

Elsewhere Mr. Allen, writing of the Greek culture, says:

"It was absolutely and unreservedly the product of the geographical Hellas, acting upon the given factor of the undifferentiated Aryan brain. … To me it seems a self-evident proposition that nothing whatsoever can differentiate one body of men from another, except the physical conditions in which they are set, – including, of course, under the term *physical conditions* the relations of place and time in which they stand with regard to other bodies of men. To suppose otherwise is to deny the primordial law of causation. To imagine that the mind can differentiate itself is to imagine that it can be differentiated without a cause."

This outcry about the law of universal causation being undone, the moment we refuse to invest in the kind of causation which is peddled round by a particular school, makes one impatient. These writers have no imagination of alternatives. With them there is no *tertium quid* between outward environment and miracle. *Aut Cæsar, aut nullus! Aut* Spencerism, *aut* catechism!

If by "physical conditions" Mr. Allen means what he does mean, the outward cycle of visible nature and man, his assertion is simply physiologically false. For a national m,ind differentiates "itself" whenever a genius is born in its midst by causes acting in the invisible and molecular cycle. But if Mr. Allen means by "physical

142 W. James

conditions" the whole of nature, his assertion, though true, forms but the vague Asiatic profession of belief in an all-enveloping fate, which certainly need not plume itself on any specially advanced or scientific character.

★ ★ ★

And how can a thinker so clever as Mr. Allen fail to have distinguished in these matters between *necessary* conditions and *sufficient* conditions of a given result? The French say that to have an omelet we must break our eggs; that is, the breaking of eggs is a necessary condition of the omelet. But is it a sufficient condition? Does an omelet appear whenever three eggs are broken? So of the Greek mind. To get such versatile intelligence it may be that such commercial dealings with the world as the geographical Hellas afforded are a necessary condition. But if they are a sufficient condition, why did not the Phoenicians outstrip the Greeks in intelligence? No geographical environment can produce a given type of mind. It can only foster and further certain types fortuitously produced, and thwart and frustrate others. Once again, its function is simply selective, and determines what shall actually be only by destroying what is positively incompatible. An Arctic environment is incompatible with improvident habits in its denizens; but whether the inhabitants of such a region shall unite with their thrift the peacefulness of the Eskimo or the pugnacity of the Norseman is, so far as the climate is concerned, an accident. Evolutionists should not forget that we all have five fingers not because four or six would not do just as well, but merely because the first vertebrate above the fishes *happened* to have that number. He owed his prodigious success in founding a line of descent to some entirely other quality, – we know not which, – but the inessential five fingers were taken in tow and preserved to the present day. So of most social peculiarities. Which of them shall be taken in tow by the few qualities which the environment necessarily exacts is a matter of what physiological accidents shall happen among individuals. Mr. Allen promises to prove his thesis in detail by the examples of China, India, England, Rome, etc. I have not the smallest hesitation in predicting that he will do no more with these examples than he has done with Hellas. He will appear upon the scene after the fact, and show that the quality developed by each race was, naturally enough, not incompatible with its habitat. But he will utterly fail to show that the particular form of compatibility fallen into in each case was the one necessary and only possible form.

Naturalists know well enough how indeterminate the harmonies between a fauna and its environment are. An animal may better his chances of existence in either of many ways, – growing aquatic, arboreal, or subterranean; small and swift, or massive and bulky; spiny, horny, slimy, or venomous; more timid or more pugnacious; more cunning or more fertile of offspring; more gregarious or more solitary; or in other ways besides, – and any one of these ways may suit him to many widely different environments.

Readers of Mr. A. R. Wallace will well remember the striking illustration of this in his *Malay Archipelago*:

Great men, great thoughts, and the environment **143**

"Borneo closely resembles New Guinea not only in its vast size and its freedom from volcanoes, but in its variety of geological structure, its uniformity of climate, and the general aspect of the forest vegetation that clothes its surface; the Moluccas are the counterpart of the Philippines in their volcanic structure, their extreme fertility, their luxuriant forests, and their frequent earthquakes; and Bali, with the east end of Java, has a climate almost as dry and a soil almost as arid as that of Timor. Yet between these corresponding groups of islands, constructed, as it were, after the same pattern, subjected to the same climate, and bathed by the same oceans, there exists the greatest possible contrast when we compare their animal productions. Nowhere does the ancient doctrine that differences or similarities in the various forms of life that inhabit different countries are due to corresponding physical differences or similarities in the countries themselves, meet with so direct and palpable a contradiction. Borneo and New Guinea, as alike physically as two distinct countries can be, are zoölogically wide as the poles asunder; while Australia, with its dry winds, its open plains, its stony deserts, and its temperate climate, yet produces birds and quadrupeds which are closely related to those inhabiting the hot, damp, luxuriant forests which everywhere clothe the plains and mountains of New Guinea."

Here we have similar physical-geographical environments harmonizing with widely differing animal lives, and similar animal lives harmonizing with widely differing geographical environments. A singularly accomplished writer, E. Gryzanowski, in the *North America Review,* uses the instance of Sardinia and Corsica in support of this thesis with great effect. He says:

"These sister islands, lying in the very center of the Mediterranean, at almost equal distances from the centers of Latin and Neo-Latin civilization, within easy reach of the Phoenician, the Greek, and the Saracen, with a coast-line of more than a thousand miles, endowed with obvious and tempting advantages, and hiding untold sources of agricultural and mineral wealth, have nevertheless remained unknown, unheeded, and certainly uncared for during the thirty centuries of European history. ... These islands have dialects, but no language; records of battles, but no history. They have customs, but no laws; the *vendetta,* but no justice. They have wants and wealth, but no commerce; timber and ports, but no shipping. They have legends, but no poetry; beauty, but no art; and twenty years ago it could still be said that they had universities, but no students. ... That Sardinia, with all her emotional and picturesque barbarism, has never produced a single artists is almost as strange as her barbarism itself. ... Near the focus of European civilization, in the very spot which an *à priori* geographer would point out as the most favorable place for material and intellectual, commercial and political development, these strange sister islands have slept their secular sleep, like *nodes* on the sounding-board of history."

144 W. James

This writer then goes on to compare Sardinia and Sicily with some detail. All the material advantages are in favor of Sardinia, "and the Sardinian population, being of an ancestry more mixed than [even] that of the English race, would justify far higher expectations than that of Sicily." Yet Sicily's past history has been brilliant in the extreme, and her commerce to-day is great. Dr. Gryzanowiski [sic] has his own theory of the historic torpor of these favored isles. He thinks they stagnated because they never gained political autonomy, being always owned by some Continental power. I will not dispute the theory; but I will ask, Why did they not gain it? and answer immediately: Simply because no individuals were born there with patriotism and ability enough to inflame their countrymen with national pride, ambition, and thirst for independent life. Corsicans and Sardinians are probably as good stuff as any of their neighbors. But the best wood-pile will not blaze till a torch is applied, and appropriate torches seem to have been wanting.

Sporadic great men come everywhere. But for a community to get vibrating through and through with intensely active life, many geniuses coming together and in rapid succession are required. This is why great epochs are so rare, — why the sudden bloom of a Greece, an early Rome, a Renaissance, is such a mystery. Blow must follow blow so fast that no cooling can occur in the intervals. Then the mass of the nation glows incandescent, and may continue to glow by pure inertia long after the originators of its internal movement have passed away. We often hear surprise expressed that in these high tides of human affairs not only the people should be filled with stronger life, but that individual geniuses should seem so exceptionally abundant. This mystery is just about as deep as the time-honored conundrum as to why great rivers flow by great towns. It is true that great public fermentations awaken and adopt many geniuses, who in more torpid times would have had no chance to work. But over and above this there must be an exceptional concourse of genius about a time, to make the fermentation begin at all. The unlikeliness of the concourse is far greater than the unlikeliness of any particular genius; hence the rarity of these periods and the exceptional aspect which they always wear.

It is folly, then, to speak of the "laws of history" as of something inevitable, which science has only to discover, and whose consequences any one can then foretell but do nothing to alter or avert. Why, the very laws of physics are conditional, and deal with *ifs*. The physicist does not say, "The water will boil anyhow"; he only says it will boil if a fire is kindled beneath it. And so the utmost the student of sociology can ever predict is that *if* a genius of a certain sort show the way, society will be sure to follow. It might long ago have been predicted with great confidence that both Italy and Germany would reach a stable unity if some one could but succeed in starting the process. It could not have been predicted, however, that the *modus operandi* in each case would be subordination to a paramount state rather than federation, because no historian could have calculated the freaks of birth and fortune which gave at the same moment such positions of authority to three such peculiar individuals as Napoleon III, Bismarck, and Cavour. So of our own politics. It is certain now that the movement of the independents, reformers, or whatever one pleases to call them, will triumph. But whether ti do so by converting

Great men, great thoughts, and the environment   **145**

the Republican party to its ends, or by rearing a new party on the ruins of both our present factions, the historian cannot say. There can be no doubt that the reform movement would make more progress in one year with an adequate personal leader than as now in ten without one. Were there a great citizen, splendid with every civic gift, to be its candidate, who can doubt that he would lead us to victory? But, at present, we, his environment, who sigh for him and would so gladly preserve and adopt him if he came, can neither move without him, nor yet do anything to bring him forth.

To conclude: The evolutionary view of history, when it denies the vital importance of individual initiative, is, then, an utterly vague and unscientific conception, a lapse from modern scientific determinism into the most ancient oriental fatalism. The lesson of the analysis that we have made (even on the completely deterministic hypothesis with which we started) forms an appeal of the most stimulating sort to the energy of the individual. Even the dogged resistance of the reactionary conservative to changes which he cannot hope entirely to defeat is justified and shown to be effective. He retards the movement; deflects it a little by the concessions he extracts; gives it a resultant momentum, compounded of his inertia and his adversaries' speed; and keeps up, in short, a constant lateral pressure, which, to be sure, never heads it round about, but brings it up at last at a goal far to the right or left of that to which it would have drifted had he allowed it to drift alone.

$\star \star \star$

I now pass to the last division of my subject, the function of the environment in *mental* evolution. After what I have already said, I may be quite concise. Here, if anywhere, it would seem at first sight as if that school must be right which makes the mind passively plastic, and the environment actively productive of the form and order of its conceptions; which, in a word, thinks that all mental progress must result from a series of adaptive changes, in the sense already defined of that word. We know what a vast part of our mental furniture consists of purely remembered, not reasoned, experience. The entire field of our habits and associations by contiguity belongs here. The entire field of those abstract conceptions which were taught us with the language into which we were born belongs here also. And, more than this, there is reason to think that the order of "outer relations" experienced by the individual may itself determine the order in which the general characters imbedded therein shall be noticed and extracted by his mind. The pleasures and benefits, moreover, which certain parts of the environment yield, and the pains and hurts which other parts inflict, determine the direction of our interest and our attention, and so decide at which points the accumulation of mental experiences shall begin. It might, accordingly, seem as if there were no room for any agency other than this; as if the distinction we have found so useful between "spontaneous variation," as the producer of changed forms, and the environment, as their preserver and destroyer, did not hold in the case of mental progress; as if, in a word, the parallel with Darwinism might no longer obtain, and Spencer might be quite right with his fundamental law of intelligence, which says, "The cohesion between psychical

146 W. James

states is proportionate to the frequency with which the relation between the answering external phenomena has been repeated in experience."

But, in spite of all these facts, I have no hesitation whatever in holding firm to the Darwinian distinction even here. I maintain that the facts in question are all drawn from the lower strata of the mind, so to speak, – from the sphere of its least evolved functions, from the region of intelligence which man possesses in common with the brutes. And I can easily show that throughout the whole extent of those mental departments which are highest, which are most characteristically human, Spencer's law is violated at every step; and that as a matter of fact the new conceptions, emotions, and active tendencies which evolve are originally produced in the shape of random images, fancies, accidental out-births of spontaneous variation in the functional activity of the excessively instable human brain, which the outer environment simply confirms or refutes, adopts or rejects, preserves or destroys, – selects, in short, just as it selects morphological and social variations dues to molecular accidents of an analogous sort.

It is one of the tritest truisms that human intelligences of a simple order are very literal. They are slaves of habit, doing what they have been taught without variation; dry, prosaic, and matter-of-fact in their remarks; devoid of humor, except of the coarse physical kind which rejoices in a practical joke; taking the world for granted; and possessing in their faithfulness and honesty the single gift by which they are sometimes able to warm us into admiration. But even this faithfulness seems to have a sort of inorganic ring, and to remind us more of the immutable properties of a piece of inanimate matter than of the steadfastness of a human will capable of alternative choice. When we descend to the brutes, all these peculiarities are intensified. No reader of Schopenhauer can forget his frequent allusions to the *trockener ernst* of dogs and horses, nor to their *ehrlichkeit*. And every noticer of their ways must receive a deep impression of the fatally literal character of the few, simple, and treadmill-like operations of their minds.

But turn to the highest order of minds, and what a change! Instead of thoughts of concrete things patiently following one another in a beaten track of habitual suggestion, we have the most abrupt cross-cuts and transitions from one idea to another, the most rarefied abstractions and discriminations, the most unheard-of combinations of elements, the subtlest associations of analogy; in a word, we seem suddenly introduced into a seething caldron of ideas, where everything is fizzling and bobbing about in a state of bewildering activity, where partnerships can be joined or loosened in an instant, treadmill routine is unknown, and the unexpected seems the only law. According to the idiosyncrasy of the individual, the scintillations will have one character or another. They will be sallies of wit and humor; they will be flashes of poetry and eloquence; they will be constructions of dramatic fiction or of mechanical devices, logical or philosophic abstractions, business projects, or scientific hypotheses, with trains of experimental consequences based thereon; they will be musical sounds, or images of plastic beauty or picturesqueness, or visions of moral harmony. But, whatever their differences may be, they will all agree in this, – that their genesis is sudden and, as it were, spontaneous. That is to

Great men, great thoughts, and the environment **147**

say, the same premises would not, in the mind of another individual, have engendered just that conclusion; although, when the conclusion is offered to the other individual, he may thoroughly accept and enjoy it, and envy the brilliancy of him to whom it first occurred.

To Professor Jevons is due the great credit of having emphatically pointed out how the genius of discovery depends altogether on the number of these random notions and guesses which visit the investigator's mind. To be fertile in hypotheses is the first requisite, and to be willing to throw them away the moment experience contradicts them is the next. The Baconian method of collating tables of instance may be a useful aid at certain times. But one might as well expect a chemist's notebook to write down the name of the body analyzed, or a weather table to sum itself up into a prediction of probabilities of its own accord, as to hope that the mere fact of mental confrontation with a certain series of facts will be sufficient to make *any* brain conceive their law. The conceiving of the law is a spontaneous variation in the strictest sense of the term. It flashes out of one brain, and no other, because the instability of that brain is such as to tip and upset itself in just that particular direction. But the important thing to notice is that the good flashes and the bad flashes, the triumphant hypotheses and the absurd conceits, are on an exact equality in respect of their origin. Aristotle's absurd Physics and his immortal Logic flow from one source: the forces that produce the one produce the other.

When walking along the street, thinking of the blue sky or the fine spring weather, I may either smile at some grotesque whim which occurs to me, or I may suddenly catch an intuition of the solution of a long-unsolved problem, which at that moment was far from my thoughts. Both notions are shaken out of the same reservoir, – the reservoir of a brain in which the reproduction of images in the relations of their outward persistence or frequency has long ceased to be the dominant law. But to the thought, when it is once engendered, the consecration of agreement with outward relations may come. The conceit perishes in a moment, and is forgotten. The scientific hypothesis arouses in me a fever of desire for verification. I read, write, experiment, consult experts. Everything corroborates my notion, which being then published in a book spreads from review to review and from mouth to mouth, till at last there is no doubt I am enshrined in the Pantheon of the great diviners of nature's ways. The environment *preserves* the conception which it was unable to *produce* in any brain less idiosyncratic than my own.

Now, the spontaneous upsettings of brains this way and that at particular moments into particular ideas and combinations are matched by their equally spontaneous permanent tiltings or saggings towards determinate directions. The humorous bent is quite characteristic; the sentimental one equally so. And the personal tone of each mind, which makes it more alive to certain impressions, more open to certain reasons, is equally the result of that invisible and imaginable play of the forces of growth within the nervous system which, irresponsibly [sic; "irresponsive"?] to the environment, makes the brain peculiarly apt to function in a certain way. Here again the selection goes on. The products of the mind with the determined æsthetic bent please or displease the community. We adopt Wordsworth,

148 W. James

and grow unsentimental and serene. We are fascinated by Schopenhauer, and learn from him the true luxury of woe. The adopted bent becomes a ferment in the community, and alters its tone. The alteration may be a benefit or a misfortune, for it is (*pace* Mr. Allen) a differentiation from within, which has to run the gauntlet of the larger environment's selective power. Civilized Langeudoc, taking the tone of its scholars, poets, princes, and theologians, fell a prey to its rude Catholic environment in the Albigensian crusade. France in 1792, taking the tone of its St. Justs and Marats, plunged into its long career of unstable outward relations. Prussia in 1806, taking the tone of its Humboldts and its Steins, proved itself in the most signal way "adjusted" to its environment in 1872.

Mr. Spencer, in one of the strangest chapters of his *Psychology,* tries to show the necessary order in which the development of conceptions in the human race occurs. No abstract conception can be developed, according to him, until the outward experiences have reached a certain degree of heterogeneity, definiteness, coherence, and so forth.

> "Thus the belief in an unchanging order, the belief in *law,* is a belief of which the primitive man is absolutely incapable. ... Experiences such as he receives furnish but few data for the conception of uniformity, whether as displayed in things or in relations. ... The daily impressions which the savage gets yield the notion very imperfectly, and in but few cases. Of all the objects around – trees, stones, hills, pieces of water, clouds and so forth, – most differ widely, ... and few approach complete likeness so nearly as to make discrimination difficult. Even between animals of the same species it rarely happens that, whether alive or dead, they are presented in just the same attitudes. ... It is only along with a gradual development of the arts ... that there come frequent experiences of perfectly straight lines admitting of complete apposition, bringing the perceptions of equality and inequality. Still more devoid is savage life of the experiences which generate the conception of the uniformity of succession. The sequences observed from hour to hour and day to day seems anything but uniform; difference is a far more conspicuous trait among them. ... So that if we contemplate primitive human life as a whole, we see that multiformity of sequence, rather than uniformity, is the notion which it tends to generate. ... Only as fast as the practice of the arts develops the idea of measure can the consciousness of uniformity simultaneously make possible the notion of *exactness.* ... Hence the primitive man has little experience which cultivates the consciousness of what we call *truth.* How closely allied this it to the consciousness which the practice of the arts cultivates is implied even in language. We speak of a true surface as well as a true statement. Exactness describes perfection in a mechanical fit, as well as perfect agreement between the results of calculations."

The whole burden of Mr. Spencer's book is to show the fatal way in which the mind, supposed passive, is moulded by its experiences of "outer relations." In this

Great men, great thoughts, and the environment **149**

chapter the yard-stick, the balance, the chronometer, and other machines and instruments come to figure among the "relations" external to the mind. Surely they are so, after they have been manufactured; but only because of the preservative power of the social environment. Originally all these things and all other institutions were flashes of genius in an individual head, of which the outer environment showed no sign. Adopted by the race and become its heritage, they then supply instigations to new geniuses whom they environ to make new inventions and discoveries; and so the ball of progress rolls. But take out the geniuses, or alter their idiosyncrasies, and what increasing uniformities will the environment show? We defy Mr. Spencer or any one else to reply.

The plain truth is that the "philosophy" of evolution (as distinguished from our special information about particular cases of change) is a metaphysical creed, and nothing else. It is a mood of contemplation, an emotional attitude, rather than a system of thought, – a mood which is as old as the world, and which no refutation of any one incarnation of it (such as the Spencerian philosophy) will dispel; the mood of fatalistic pantheism, with its intuition of the One and All, which was, and is, and ever shall be, and from whose womb each single thing proceeds. Far be it from us to speak slightingly here of so hoary and mighty a style of looking on the world as this. What we at present call scientific discoveries had nothing to do with bringing it to birth, nor can one easily conceive that they should eve give it its *quietus,* no matter how logically incompatible with its spirit the ultimate phenomenal distinctions which science accumulates should turn out to be. It can laugh at the phenomenal distinctions on which science is based, for it draws its vital breath from a region which – whether above or below – is at least altogether different from that in which science dwells. A critic, however, who cannot disprove the truth of the metaphysic creed, can at least raise his voice in protest against its disguising itself in "scientific" plumes. I think that all who have had the patience to follow me thus far will agree that the Spencerian "philosophy" of social and intellectual progress is an obsolete anachronism, reverting to a pre-Darwinian type of thought, just as the Spencerian philosophy of "Force," effacing all the previous distinctions between actual and potential energy, momentum, work, force, mass, etc., which physicists have with so much agony achieved, carries us back to a pre-Galilean age.

PART III

Making

Entrepreneurial process

> The School of Higher Neantical Nillity is in fact wholly unconcerned with what does exist. Indeed, the banality of existence has been so amply demonstrated, there is no need for us to discuss it any further here. The brilliant Cerebron, attacking the problem analytically, discovered three distinct kinds of dragon: the mythical, the chimerical, and the purely hypothetical. They were all, one might say, nonexistent, but each nonexisted in an entirely different way ...
>
> [Trurl and Klaupaucius, the great constructors,] were the first to apply probability theory to this area ... They found that for the spontaneous manifestation of an average dragon, one would have to wait a good sixteen quintoquadrillion heptillion years. In other words, the whole problem would have remained a mathematical curiosity had it not been for that famous tinkering passion of Trurl, who decided to examine the nonphenomenon empirically. First, as he was dealing with the highly improbable, he invented a probability amplifier and ran tests in his basement ... To this day those who (sadly enough) have no knowledge of the General Theory of Improbability ask why Trurl probabilized a dragon and not an elf or goblin. The answer is simply that dragons are more probable than elves or goblins to begin with.
>
> *(Lem, 1974: 85)*

Trurl, the Constructor, knows a thing or two about the entrepreneurial process that begins with the possible and ends up making the improbable. In this part of the book we begin to think through how such a process might work and what it might take to understand it.

Our selections here begin with the grand quest outlined by Nelson Goodman (1978) in *Ways of Worldmaking,* in which he strives[1] to get his arms around the notion of a pluralistic universe:

> In just what sense are there many worlds? What distinguishes genuine from spurious worlds? What are worlds made of? How are they made? What role

152 Making

do symbols play in the making? And how is worldmaking related to knowing? These questions must be faced even if full and final answers are far off.

(Goodman, 1978: 1)

If we are to take up Goodman's quest and pursue it through the fertile field of entrepreneurship, we need to intrepidly push the boundaries on a variety of related fields including:

- Beyond new combinations in entrepreneurship theories
- Beyond current exogenous markets in economic theories
- Beyond egocentric or structural views of social psychology
- Beyond adaptation in evolutionary theories, and
- Beyond Coasian and Knightian bases for theories of the firm.

To come to grips with these topics, we have selected individual readings, each of which (irrespective of when it was written) has only recently begun gaining ground against mainstream ideologies. Yet our aim in exploring these is not merely to embrace them, but to climb upon them to reach farther, to *use* them to set an even more audacious agenda for entrepreneurship research.

Goodman: ways of worldmaking

The selection we have included offers the merest tantalizing glimpse of what we, as theorists, might be able to construct, should we choose to pick up the ideas and arguments Goodman has strewn about with casual yet profound generosity. The most important of these, of course, is the very notion of worldmaking. In particular:

We are not speaking in terms of multiple possible alternatives to a single actual world but of multiple actual worlds.

(978: 2)

At first encounter, this seems like utter nonsense, sheer philosophical snake oil. But a variety of careful thinkers have been working at these ideas long enough for it to be dispensed by prescription. Take for instance, Hilary Putnam's (1979) clarification that to posit the making of multiple worlds is not to posit that all worlds are equally possible. Instead the argument comes from the other direction:

If I am right, then this is another illustration of a theme to which Goodman constantly returns: that even where reduction [to one world] is possible it is typically non-unique.

(609)

Putnam goes on to show that whether the monism is that of the physicalist, namely, that ultimately Reality (with a capital R) is made up of particles, or whether it is the monism of the phenomenalist, namely, that the only Reality (again with a capital R) is the one made up of sense-data or perceptions, both will still be left with non-unique realities after removing all spurious or inferior conceptions using whatever set of criteria the two may come up with. In other words, physicalism and phenomenalism are themselves analogues! For those more interested in grappling with this difficult idea in more detail, please see bibliography at the end of this chapter. For now, we can turn to those sections of *Ways of Worldmaking* that are more immediately applicable to entrepreneurship research. And these have to do with *processes* for making new worlds. Here Goodman's main argument is very simple:

> The many stuffs … that worlds are made of are made along with the worlds. But made of what? Not from nothing, after all, but *from other worlds*. Worldmaking as we know it always starts from worlds already on hand; the making is a remaking.
>
> *(1978: 6)*

As intellectual descendants of Schumpeter, for entrepreneurship researchers this immediately conjures up the notion of "new combinations". Schumpeter's conception of new combinations derives from mathematics and evolutionary biology. However, there are strong reasons for thinking that human design processes are *not* the same as biological ones and the making of entrepreneurial ventures is not in any way an abstract process. More importantly, as Goodman points out, the products of human design – that is, artifacts – are not easily combined as we might imagine combining genes in biology or words in languages:

> The difference between juxtaposing and conjoining two statements has no evident analogue for two pictures or for a picture and a statement.

What we need are processes that transform existing worlds into new ones, processes that go beyond the notion of combinations. In mathematics, a combination is defined as follows: Given S, the set of all possible unique elements, a combination is a subset of the elements of S. This definition implies a search and selection process that picks out relevant elements and combines them into new sets. But the new set is always a subset of the larger set S that we began with. A transformation, in contrast, is any of a variety of different operations from geometry. Transformations can increase the dimensionality of the original space. See Figure III.1.

Interaction in space is an essential element of transformations. That is why the notion of transformative processes may better capture applications of Goodman's ideas to entrepreneurship than Schumpeterian combinations. Moreover, once we move from abstract mathematics into the realm of physical space and time, not to mention social space and history, it is easy to see that there are more processes in heaven and earth, Horatio, than are dreamt of by combinatorics.[2]

Goodman outlines five candidates for worldmaking processes. This list is not meant to be exhaustive or mutually exclusive; it is just meant to illustrate the many

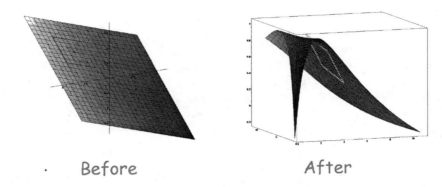

Before   After

FIGURE III.1

different kinds of transformational operations that can help make worlds. In the following discussion, we briefly articulate each transformation type, using an anecdotal example to illustrate the relevance of each for entrepreneurship:

1. Composition and decomposition
   In *The Sciences of the Artificial,* Simon (1988) went to some length to show that near-decomposability is essential to designing complex systems that endure over time. Most lasting designs whether in nature or in the realm of human artifacts, have this structural feature. The central idea in this type of transformation involves disassembly, reorganization and re-composition, yet it is not merely a matter of recombination, for the whole created out of this process is more than the sum of its parts. It is in this sense that Starbucks is not simply a collection of coffee shops. *Composing* the venture Starbucks consisted in a variety of transformative operations on people's tastes and habits, on sourcing coffee beans, on creating a unique identity and so on. This included *decomposing* the Italian ambience into its constitutive parts, *distorting* habits of beverage consumption into a social aesthetic that could then be *woven* into the urban landscape in ways that have *recomposed* entire neighborhoods. Worldmaking spotlights the richness and complexity of transformative, as contrasted with the cleaner and simpler lines of combinatorial, processes.

2. Weighting
   Weighting can be conceptualized as transforming a product or market by decreasing and increasing the relative emphasis of features or attributes. Weightings can be dichotomous or on scales or along specific dimensions. The Atkins diet for example, transformed the diet market and even markets for regular food products by overweighting proteins against carbohydrates.

3. Ordering
   Ordering involves deciding what is prior versus what's latter, what's in front versus what's behind, what's proximate versus what's far away, how things are sequenced, and so on. We have already seen the importance of ordering in the very construction of our conceptual categories (Lakoff & Johnson, 1999).

Ordering also depends critically on how measurement is done, and what criteria are used in determining value and price. An anecdotal example of the use of ordering as a transformative process in generating new markets is the Body Shop, which reordered the attributes of personal beauty products by putting "no animal testing" at the top of the list.

4   Deletion and supplementation

A focus on new combinations often obscures the effects on things *not* combined. Sometimes worlds get transformed simply by deleting things in them. The excision of old material, i.e. weeding out, is not much studied in our literature as compared to combinatorial processes (Goldenberg et al., 2001). For example, entrepreneur Henry Ford (reminiscent of Giacometti's paintings cited by Goodman) weeded out everything that was not essential in order to come up with a cheap design of automobiles – the Model T. The literature on the subject, however, almost always emphasizes his creative recombination of technologies to create the production line.

5   Deformation

Goodman (1978) describes deformation as akin to smoothing out a rough curve or caricaturing artifacts or people. Improvised jazz is an example: artists "deform" the melody in various ways with different notes, rhythm and tempo. Entrepreneurs engage in deformation, both metaphorically and literally in products and services. One could easily argue that The Hummer is a deformed tank or a jeep gone wild.[3]

An important assumption underlying these (and other yet-to-be-discovered) processes of worldmaking is that of the freedom to choose one's ends as well as one's courses of action. This freedom, however, is not arbitrary or unconstrained. There are self-imposed constraints as well as those imposed by physical laws and the aspirations and endowments of other actors. Yet these constraints themselves are not deterministic. At any given point in time, they provide stable boundaries within which human designs work to make new worlds. As Goodman cautions:

> Moreover, while readiness to recognize alternative worlds may be liberating, and suggestive of new avenues of exploration, a willingness to welcome all worlds builds none. Mere acknowledgement of the many available frames of reference provides us with no map of the motions of heavenly bodies; acceptance of the eligibility of alternative bases produces no scientific theory or philosophical system; awareness of varied ways of seeing paints no pictures. A broad mind is no substitute for hard work.
>
> *(1978: 21)*

In other words, Goodman is arguing that relativism (or unbridled pluralism) is not a sufficient condition for worldmaking; yet monism (whether physicalist or phenomenalist) is not a necessary condition. Harking back to Buchanan and Vanberg and leaping forward to Hayek and Bruner, this argument really boils

156 Making

down to two claims: (a) the freedom to choose one's ends provides the necessary condition for making new worlds; and (b) commitment to specific courses of action within particular frames of reference provides the sufficient condition. Together choice and commitment provide the motor power for all worldmaking enterprises. The next two readings elaborate upon these claims.

Hayek: (beyond) competition as a discovery procedure

The free market system has arguably become the only game in town in the twenty-first-century political economy. In entrepreneurship research, Kirzner's views advocating the efficacy of the free market process and the role in it of the entrepreneur as "discoverer" of new opportunities have become entrenched. Yet, it is the very taken-for-grantedness of these ideas that makes it important to revisit and reformulate them in light of a "made" view of entrepreneurship. Our selection from Hayek is seminal in this regard. Notice that this article was originally written in 1968, delivered as a lecture, and later that same year published in German, and then in Hayek's collected essays – again in German – in 1969. In this article, we can see the original seeds of the idea of discovery, sown by Hayek, which were then developed in Kirzner's work in 1973, 1979, 1985 and 1997.[4]

This piece also provides the antecedents for a major theme we examined in the Buchanan and Vanberg article in Part I, a theme that forms a core element of the made view we are trying to construct, namely the notion of the market as a game without goods:

> [E]conomic market theory often prevents access to a true understanding of competition by proceeding from the assumption of a "given" quantity of scarce goods. Which goods are scarce, however, or which things are goods, or how scarce or valuable they are, is precisely one of the conditions that competition should discover: in each case it is the preliminary outcomes of the market process that inform individuals where it is worthwhile to search.
>
> *(Hayek, 2002: 13)*

In other words, the "discovery procedure" that Hayek is talking about is not a simple search and selection process given a space of goods, but it is the procedure by which we arrive at the spaces within which to search. If goods are not taken as already existing, and we do not know before the market process begins producing outcomes where to search, what kind of "discovery" process is this? Hayek does not clarify. Instead he relegates the job to future scholarship:

> This suggestion must suffice here to clarify the kind of knowledge I am speaking of when I call competition a discovery procedure. Much more would have to be added if I wanted to formulate this outline so concretely that the meaning of this process emerged clearly.
>
> *(13)*

We have seen at least one attempt at clarification of this process in Buchanan and Vanberg that has to do with modeling the market as a *creative* rather than as a discovery process in the Kirznerian sense. However, what Hayek *is* very much concerned with in this article, much more than spelling out the internal details of the process, is its external validation – that is, how *well* it works compared with other processes of economic organization in society. In this connection, his definition of "catallaxy" and its contrast with "economy" is worth clarifying:

> An economy in the strong sense of the word is an organization or an arrangement in which someone consciously uses means in the service of a uniform hierarchy of ends…. Contrast this with the two advantages of a spontaneous market order or catallaxy; it can use the knowledge of all participants, and the objectives it serves are the particular objectives of all its participants in all their diversity and polarity.
>
> *(14)*

> The fact that catallaxy serves no uniform system of objectives gives rise to all the familiar difficulties that disturb not only socialists, but all economists endeavoring to evaluate the performance of the market order.
>
> *(14)*

Exactly how Hayek came across the term and adapted it for himself is (to the best of our knowledge) unknown, but the term derives from the Greek word katal-latein, which means "barter" as well as "to join a community", both of which, as we have argued in terms of Davidson's epistemological tripod earlier and as we will see in the next reading by Bruner, are essential aspects of intersubjective worldmaking. In particular, the negotiations involved at the intersubjective level in a catallaxy may have as much to do with the reformulation of individual aims as well as choice of and commitment to particular communities as it has to do with the achievement of well-articulated individual ends. It is here that Hayek cracks open the door to a truly "made" world view when he says:

> It is an outcome of the market mechanism that someone is induced to fill the gap that arises when someone else does not fulfill the expectations on the basis of which a third party has made plans. In this sense all the collective supply and demand curves that we use so happily are not really data, but rather *outcomes* of the constantly ongoing process of competition [emphasis added].
>
> *(2002: 18)*

Yet Hayek's conceptualization of the market process is not a Utopian one – nor is it simply a matter of "leaving it" to free markets. It takes work and sometimes a toll in human suffering to *make* markets work. Hayek demonstrates he is aware of the work when he urges us to confront the role of failure in the process. Entrepreneurship research, perhaps understandably, has largely been obsessed with success. However,

158 Making

there is also some interest in studying failure (McGrath, 1999; Shepherd, 2004; Shepherd, 2009). But even these studies are focused on the *causes* of failure so failure can be avoided rather than in understanding failure as an essential ingredient of success, both for the entrepreneur's career over several firms and also for the economy's growth and prosperity over robust innovations in technologies and institutions, many of which will consist in failed experiments – or as Hayek points out in the quote from Hardin about Adam Smith's insight in this regard – negative feedback:

> The invisible hand that regulates prices appears to express this idea. Smith says in essence that in a free market, prices are determined by negative feedback.
>
> *(2002: 15)*

At several places in the article Hayek returns to the importance of failure as an essential input into the market process and connects it to Adam Smith's ideas about the relative roles of skill and chance in the game of catallaxy.[5] But at the heart of his treatment of failure is the recurring emphasis on the non-zero-sum nature of the game. Hayek's discussion of negative feedback, therefore, is essentially optimistic and anticipates research on integrative negotiation, where the focus of negotiation is not on dividing the pie, but on increasing its size (Walton & McKersie, 1965; Pruitt & Lewis, 1975; Bazerman, Curhan et al., 2000):

> In modern terminology we can say that we are playing a non-zero-sum game whose rules have the objective of increasing the payoff but leave the share of the individuals partly to chance.
>
> *(Hayek, 2002: 16)*

Failure is particularly pertinent to entrepreneurship research. Yet the literature stream on this topic mostly focuses either on "fear of failure" where success and failure are assumed to constitute a 0–1 variable (Morgan & Sisak, 2016; Cacciotti et al., 2016) or cognition and emotions related to dealing with it and hopefully learning from it (Cope, 2011; Ucbasaran et al., 2013; Byrne & Shepherd, 2015; Shepherd, 2009). In contrast, Hayek's conceptualization of failure with a special emphasis on its role in making markets non-zero-sum games opens new doors for research into entrepreneurship failure at a whole new level of analysis.

We turn next to yet another level focusing on the negotiated nature of worldmaking.

Bruner: (beyond) egocentric and structural views of social psychology

Whereas psychology in general concerns itself with mental processes internal to individual agents, social psychology studies the individual as largely determined by his or her position in social space. With decades of experimental work under his belt, social psychologist Jerome Bruner began grappling with Nelson Goodman's ideas about worldmaking in his book *Actual Minds, Possible Worlds*. As he explicitly states in a review of Goodman's ideas in Chapter 7 of the book:

> So whatever the limitations of Goodman's proposals, he has made clearer a concept of mind to be specified not in terms of properties but rather as an instrument for producing worlds. His point of view has obviously had a strong influence in the preceding chapters of this book and will in later ones.
>
> *(Bruner, 1986: 104)*

Our selection from the same book titled *The Transactional Self* sheds light on a path toward building an intersubjective social psychology. The core concept at the heart of such a discipline would be the transactional self:

> If you engage for long in the study of how human beings relate to one another, especially through the use of language, you are bound to be struck by the importance of "transactions." This is not an easy word to define. I want to signify those dealings which are premised on a mutual sharing of assumptions and beliefs about how the world is, how mind works, what we are up to, and how communications should proceed.
>
> *(Bruner, 1986: 57)*

Bruner begins by refuting the solely egocentric view of interaction, including experimental results that show that children (and adults too) are locked in their own individual perspectives and unable to take the perspective of other participants in an interaction:

> To show that a child (or an adult) cannot, for example, figure out what three mountains he sees before him might look like to somebody viewing them from their "back" sides (to take as our whipping boy one of the classic experiments demonstrating egocentrism), does not mean he cannot take another's perspective into account *in general*.
>
> *(Bruner, 1986: 60) [Emphasis original]*

He then goes on to argue against a strict culture-centered view also:

> It would not be an exaggeration to say that in the last decade there has been a revolution in the definition of human culture. It takes the form of a move away from the strict structuralism that held that culture was a set of interconnected rules from which people derive particular behaviors to fit particular situations, to the idea of culture as implicit and only semiconnected knowledge of the world from which, through negotiation, people arrive at satisfactory ways of acting in given contexts.
>
> *(Bruner, 1986: 65)*

160 Making

In this regard, Bruner's reference to the anthropologist Clifford Geertz's analogy of likening acting in a culture to interpreting an ambiguous text is particularly telling.[6] Geertz's point is that culture is not like a steel cage within which we act, nor is it like the rules of grammar that determine whether a sentence is good or bad or valid or invalid. Instead, culture is like ambiguous text. It provides ample room for interpretation and re-interpretation through individual acts and interpersonal interactions. Geertz's and Bruner's arguments about culture are evocative of Herbert Simon's argument for the relationship between human design and physical law, namely that the latter constrains but does not determine our designs. The *ambiguity* in the text that is cultural context pushes the door open and provides adequate room for Goodman's worldmaking.

We could make a similar "design hypothesis" for the entrepreneur's vision or "story" of the new venture, namely, that enduring entrepreneurial stories will provide room for the stakeholder acquisition process to negotiate new possibilities. These new possibilities will usually be embodied in specific transformations of the venture's business model. These changes would therefore be empirically observable and verifiable. In other words, entrepreneurial worldmaking could be a viable line of future research. What Goodman and Bruner claim for the artist, the child and the transactional self in general may be instanced very clearly in the entrepreneurial construction of new ventures and new markets. For example, the "story of the money" that venture capitalists seek or the promising "vision" that key employees and others look for may be modeled as negotiated realities observable in changes over time in the entrepreneur's narratives and in the venture's business models.

To summarize the vision of worldmaking so far: If worldmaking is essentially a negotiated process through which the self is transacted for, culture is reinterpreted, product markets are designed and existing worlds are transformed into actual new ones, it seems obvious that we should be paying closer attention to stakeholder negotiations in the entrepreneurial setting. Yet most of our work continues to focus on "pitches" from entrepreneurs and investment "decisions" from venture capitalists. When we do look deeper into the storytelling aspects, we begin to observe the paradox of formulating unambiguous projections in the pitches that become the source of future disappointments (Garud et al., 2014) Even the literature on negotiations in social psychology has mostly neglected new venture creation processes. Consider for example, that Bazerman et al.'s (2000) classic and comprehensive review of the growing literature on negotiations does not include the words "venture" or "entrepreneur" at all. Also, the very idea of "transformation" as opposed to "bargaining" is new to the literature on negotiations. Note for example, Linda Putnam's (2004) exhortation to negotiation scholars to incorporate transformative notions from the literature on international conflicts:

> In traditional bargaining, the goal of the process is to get a settlement or to resolve the conflict. Viewing negotiation from the lens of transformations shifts this focus to changing the definition of a conflict, altering the level of abstraction in which a dispute is managed, and/or recasting how parties view their

relationship.... Contrasting the two processes, one sees that integrative and distributive bargaining involve making a choice and legitimating this choice among preset options while transformation leads to generating and enlarging options by presenting the conflict in an entirely new way (Pearce and Littlejohn 1997). Even though integrative bargaining and the search for mutual gains has always entailed the creation of choices, traditional approaches to negotiation operate with assumptions that may not facilitate transformations.

(Putnam, 2004: 292)

On the one hand, negotiation research has shown that people often fail to reach mutually beneficial agreements even when they may be readily available (e.g. (Bazerman & Neale, 1992; Thompson, Gentner et al., 2000)). On the other hand, research has also begun to show that such agreements are reached and even new and unanticipated ones forged through repeated exchanges between the same negotiators (Pruitt & Rubin, 1986; Thompson, Gentner et al., 2000). Indeed, Lawler and his collaborators have shown that commitment leading to stable group formation occurs through a process of repeated negotiated exchanges:

The development of relational cohesion and commitment is an endogenous process that emerges from the interaction between actors.

(Lawler & Yoon, 1996: 90)

In the abstract to the paper, Lawler and Yoon (1996) summarize the results of their laboratory experiments as follows:

The behavioral consequences are a tendency for actors to (1) stay in the exchange relation despite attractive alternatives, (2) provide each other token gifts, and (3) contribute to a new joint venture.

(89)

All these examples from sociological and psychological literatures on relational exchanges and interpersonal negotiations point to fertile untapped resources for future entrepreneurship research. Furthermore, fully embracing the proposition that "Most of our approaches to the world are mediated through negotiation with others," (Bruner, 1986: 68) has important implications not only for new research, but also for reexamining and challenging existing dogma in our field. The following selection challenges one such particularly pervasive dogma, namely, the role of *adaptation* in an evolutionary view of competitive market processes.

Gould and Lewontin: (beyond) adaptation in evolutionary theories

Conventional views of evolutionary adaptation tend to keep selection processes completely separate from the processes that create variation. Selection is deemed to

162 Making

act *upon* variations that are presumed to be randomly generated. In such a view of evolutionary adaptation, everything that exists (i.e. has survived) can be explained as a product of environmental selection. As Gould and Lewontin (1979) point out in their argument against such a monolithic view:

> This [strict adaptationist] programme regards natural selection as so powerful and the constraints upon it so few that direct production of adaptation through its operation becomes the primary cause of nearly all organic form, function, and behavior.
>
> *(Gould & Lewontin, 1979: 150–151)*

In arguing for a more pluralistic view of evolutionary processes, Gould and Lewontin hark back to Darwin's own battle against the monolith:

> Although Darwin regarded selection as the most important of evolutionary mechanisms (as do we), no argument from opponents angered him more than the common attempt to caricature and trivialize his theory by stating that it relied exclusively upon natural selection. In the last edition of the Origin, he wrote (1872: 395):
> As my conclusions have lately been much misrepresented, and it has been stated that I attribute the modification of species exclusively to natural selection, I may be permitted to remark that in the first edition of this work, and subsequently, I placed in a most conspicuous position-namely at the close of the introduction-the following words: "I am convinced that natural selection has been the main, but not the exclusive means of modification." This has been of no avail. Great is the power of steady misinterpretation.
> We do not now regard all of Darwin's subsidiary mechanisms as significant or even valid, though many, including direct modification and correlation of growth, are very important. But we should cherish his consistent attitude of pluralism in attempting to explain Nature's complexity.
>
> *(Gould & Lewontin, 1979: 590)*

Gould and Lewontin have encountered considerable criticism for their staunch embrace of a more pluralistic view. But Gould's (2002) opus on multilevel selection and other alternatives to the monolithic view provides ample answers to the critics. Even the tiny selection we have included here has become a classic in the literature precisely because of the careful way Gould and Lewontin go about making their point.

The pluralistic nature of evolution – the idea that there are many processes through which evolution occurs – ought to be an important theme for entrepreneurship researchers who wish to build on the notion of entrepreneurship as worldmaking. Because a "made" view of entrepreneurship is as much concerned with changing the economic and social environment as finding and exploiting opportunities within it, we find a natural comradeship with Gould and Lewontin's

Making **163**

pluralistic approach to evolutionary processes. Entrepreneurship is a promising locus for the investigation of non-adaptationist processes, particularly since economic evolution involves novelty produced through human intent as well as random variations.

There is an important consequence to the widespread and rather unquestioning adoption of the conventional view of evolutionary processes. On the one hand, the adaptationist view provides good explanations for the survival and success of entrepreneurial firms (almost too good when we take into account the panglossian nature of such explanations – as in the example of Barash's work that Gould and Lewontin examine). On the other hand, it provides very little useful guidance for individual entrepreneurs starting new ventures, since the conventional view assumes random variation at the micro-level. What really matters in the adaptationist view then is exogenous environmental selection, over which individual entrepreneurs usually have very little control, unless they happen to occupy certain central positions in social networks that enable easier access to resources or to legitimizing institutions. Ironically, just as in the case of the psychological traits literature, the entrepreneurial game then becomes one of "either you have it, or you don't" – and the focus of both research and pedagogy is to sort potential entrepreneurs into predetermined probabilistic bins rather than to build theories about *doing* entrepreneurship better.

This concern is also echoed by sociologists such as Lawler and Emirbayer who argue that structural views, be they of social networks or legitimizing institutions, are stuck in static dichotomies and the only way out is through a focus on a "transactional" (Lawler, 2002) or "relational" (Emirbayer, 1997; Emirbayer & Mische, 1998) view of intersubjective interactions:

> The key question confronting sociologists in the present day is not "material versus ideal," "structure versus agency," "individual versus society," or any of the other dualisms so often noted; rather, it is the choice between substantialism and relationalism.
>
> *(Emirbayer, 1997: 282)*

Gould and Lewontin point to five nonexhaustive alternatives to the adaptationist program. We examine each and provide examples from the history of technological entrepreneurship:

1 No adaptation and no selection at all

   Of the five alternate mechanisms listed by Gould and Lewontin, the first one will be perhaps the most familiar to entrepreneurship researchers – that is, no adaptation or selection at all. Scholars have frequently argued that "random walks" might better explain entrepreneurial performance than any hypothesis under consideration (Arrow in Sarasvathy, 2000; Denrell, 2004). Anecdotally, one could argue that products such as Beanie Babies succeed simply because they do and not due to any systematic causal chains that entail their success.

164 Making

2   No adaptation and no selection on the part at issue; form of the part is a correlated consequence of selection directed elsewhere.

"Bundling" as a strategy often results in this type of survival. Most of us use Powerpoint® for our presentations, not because CorelDraw® is an inferior product, but because Powerpoint® comes bundled with other Microsoft® products. And we use those, of course, mostly due to externalities – that is, because all our colleagues are using them.

3   The decoupling of selection and adaptation.

   i   Selection without adaptation. Any monopolistic firm can exercise market power (even if only for limited periods of time) to get their products and services "selected" by the market, irrespective of whether they are "adaptive" along relevant criteria or not.

   ii   Adaptation without selection. Similarly, there exist well-adapted products from the point of view of customer ease-of-use and economic efficiencies, such as the Dvorak keyboard, that do not get selected-out owing to path dependencies or other reasons.

4   Adaptation and selection but no selective basis for differences among adaptations.

Note for example the Ice Hotel in Sweden and the one in Canada. The founder of the Ice Hotel in Sweden (the first one to be built) chose not to franchise his idea. As a result we have two ice hotels, each well adapted for its environment, and successful in terms of market selection. Yet there were not particular features on the basis of which they competed or were selected for.

5   Adaptation and selection, but the adaptation is a secondary utilization of parts present for reasons of architecture, development or history.

This is one of the most interesting, useful and widely evidenced alternative to adaptation in technological entrepreneurship. In fact, this idea was so interesting and valid to biological evolution that it was given a name of its own, "exaptation" and developed in much greater detail by Gould and Vrba (1982). Exaptive processes are especially pertinent for entrepreneurship researchers, because exaptation is one way to make links between the evolutionary processes and ideas about true uncertainty that feature so prominently in the work of Knight (1921). Mokyr defined exaptation as follows:

> The basic idea is that a technique that was originally selected for one trait owes its later success and survival to another trait which it happens to possess.
>
> *(2000: 57)*

Exaptation transforms resources by converting them from established uses (things they were designed for) to new uses (things they weren't designed for). Aspirin and Viagra are well-known examples of exaptation (Andriani, Ali, & Mastrogiorgio, 2017). Another example is Riverdale Mills Aquamesh lobster traps, made from plastic-dipped galvanized wire mesh. Aquamesh has such tiny openings that it is virtually impossible to scale or cut through, which made it perfect for security fencing after the September 11 terrorist attacks in New York. So Riverdale started selling Wirewall (Crowley, 2002).

In sum, when we push our theorizing beyond adaptive evolution, we come upon a variety of other evolutionary mechanisms, many of which do not involve a central role for selection at all (Odling-Smee et al., 2003). This coheres well with the themes we have repeatedly emphasized in this book, namely, that (a) we need not posit markets as the primary driver of selection at the macro-level and (b) we cannot "leave it" to markets to do the job at the micro-level. This means we have to develop theories and heuristics of entre-preneurial decision making that do not begin and end with the parameters of exogenous demand functions. We turn to that problem next.

Boudreaux and Holcomb (B&H): (beyond) the Coasian and Knightian firm

Before we introduce and critically examine B&H (Boudreaux & Holcombe, 1989), it is important to point out the usefulness of reading the classics in the original. Knight (1921) is particularly relevant as an exemplar of a seminal idea several decades before its time. Note the clarity and compelling feel of the following passage from the original:

> Universal foreknowledge would leave no place for an "entrepreneur" … The word "uncertainty" seemed best for distinguishing the defects of mana-gerial knowledge from the ordinary "risks" of business activity, which can feasibly be reduced if not eliminated by applying the insurance principle through some organization or grouping of cases. Thus uncertainty explains profit and loss; but profit, when it occurs, is not properly a "reward for risk-taking", though the expectation of gain is the incentive for assuming the entrepreneurial role. Nor is entrepreneurship to be treated as a "factor of production" on par with others, since it is not at all in the same sense measur-able or subject to varying proportions and marginal imputation. Profit (when positive) is not the price of the service of its recipient, but a "residual", the one true residual in distribution.
>
> *(Knight, 2002: lix)*

The reason we have included B&H instead of Knight in the original is so we can leverage the large body of research based on Coase's seminal work that already informs entrepreneurship and strategic management research to get a better handle on Knight's ideas. It is easy to forget that Knight *preceded* Coase. And in B&H's review of the literature we can clearly grasp why contemporary economics still has no real role for the entrepreneur and why strategic management research are as yet unable to explain the genesis of new markets. B&H provide a very accessible

166 Making

account of what is important about Knight's thesis in terms of the entrepreneurial process of making. They answer the obvious question: *Making what?* Their answer (as ours) is: *Making markets*. B&H present a complete yet concise review of the literature of Coasian theories to demonstrate that Knight is important for those of us who are interested in how markets are made. Note, for example, the following quotations:

- [T]he primary function of the Knightian firm is entrepreneurial; it is a necessary component of the creation of markets (Boudreaux & Holcombe, 1989: 147)
- [F]or Knight, the firm is not superimposed upon an already-existing technical production structure; instead, firms are integral to the formation of this structure (1989: 152)

Note how these insights link to our earlier arguments about choice and commitment and the constraints that such choice and commitment impose on selection mechanisms.

- The kinds of goods and services that will be available in the future are the results of decisions made by entrepreneurs ... The Knightian firm is directed by entrepreneurs whose individual decisions help determine the future course of the economy (1989: 152).
- In Knight's model, entrepreneurs decide what to do rather than have the market dictate the activities of the firm.... The fact remains that firms act as if they can choose their outputs (1989: 153).

This point about the nonexistence of markets until someone commits to producing particular goods is expressly linked with the arguments of James and Gould and Lewontin about the less than omnipotent power of selection mechanisms. Knight's insight about the decision-making role of the entrepreneur highlights the fact that selection mechanisms can only work on alternatives that are already available: *they determine what survives, not which alternatives are offered*. The general thrust of recent economic literature on innovation has also demonstrated that new goods are pushed up from the supply side, rather than being pulled through by demand (Dosi, 1982; Geroski, 2003). In fact, good historical accounts of innovation (e.g. Mowery & Rosenberg, 1979) have amassed evidence against demand-pull theories of the genesis of new product markets. It is in light of these recent arguments for modeling the market process as a game without goods (a la Buchanan and Vanberg and Hayek earlier) that Knight's thesis about the centrality of the entrepreneur as constructor of new markets becomes inescapable.

The argument against demand-pull is simply that "market demand" is not a precise or pre-existent target that entrepreneurs shoot at. Demand might sometimes need to be invented (Schumpeter, 1934: 65), or it might change so rapidly as to be meaningless as a "target" (Christensen, Raynor et al., 2001), or it might be inchoate (Geroski, 2003); or just so dispersed (Hayek, 1991) that there is no clear "signal" about it in existing marketplaces. As Hayek (Hayek, 1978a) and B&V (1991) point out, the market process at the macro-level is perhaps better thought of as enabling the discovery and creation of new demand as well as ways to fulfill that demand. In other words, the macro-market provides the necessary freedoms for entrepreneurial choice. What the entrepreneur commits to construct at the micro-level determines what becomes available for selection at the macro-level. The *market,* therefore, does not determine the micro-level choices of the entrepreneur with regard to particular product markets. Instead, a well-functioning market process at the macro-level ensures ample room for the entrepreneur to design new product markets at the micro-level that are ex-ante unknowable, or subject to Knightian uncertainty to such an extent that it is meaningless to discuss the "foresight" of the Knightian entrepreneur.

We have noted earlier the importance of *Knightian uncertainty*, as opposed to *calculable risk*, to entrepreneurial decisions and actions. But it might be worth re-iteration in the context of B&H's arguments about the entrepreneurial firm as driver of the market process at the micro-level. In the following quote, note the use of the word "unknowable" – the value of the final output is not merely unknown, it is *unknowable*:

> An alternative, which corresponds to Knight's concept of the firm, is to model the entrepreneur as choosing to bring new goods and services to market or to use new production processes where the outcome is uncertain. The Knightian entrepreneur is subject to uncertainty in selecting ways to allocate resources because the value of the final output is unknowable at the time the resources are committed to particular production processes.
>
> *(1989: 148)*

Earlier, we mentioned one reason why this value is unknowable, namely, that demand signals are either too weak, changing too fast or non-existent. A second reason stems from the temporal dimension of the problem. All production processes take time, particularly those based on innovations, technological or otherwise. So uncertainty enters the picture in yet another way because resource values can change unpredictably during the time lags in the production and commercialization processes (B&H, 1989: 151). Third, the process of production itself often gets constructed through the entrepreneurial process. Novel production methods will involve real uncertainty as to the final value of the output. Consider Gordon Moore's invention of the planar process of semiconductor fabrication. Intel's founding team did not know what they were going to get in terms of outputs, or what it would take to make the manufacturing process work. For all these reasons, offering new goods in the market entails the assumption of Knightian uncertainty by the entrepreneur. In B&H's words:

> The essential point is that all time-consuming production processes are inescapably bound up with Knightian uncertainty.
>
> *(1989: 151)*

168 Making

And so:

> [T]he problem of decision making under uncertainty … formed the crux of
> the matter in Knight's view.
>
> *(1989: 152)*

Under Knightian uncertainty, the entrepreneur cannot, by definition, use "fore-sight" to make better decisions. The literature on this subject, therefore, tends to substitute the notion of "judgment" instead. Following Knight himself, this line of research posits entrepreneurs as specialists in certain types of "judgment", which allows them to position themselves in situations that are likely to lead to value creation through the exercise of such specialized judgment (Casson, 2003; Langlois, 2003; Langlois, 2005; Foss & Klein, 2012). Of course, this can be deliberate or assumed, i.e. entrepreneurs can create a firm in order to make certain "bets" that leverage their specialized judgment, or they can create a firm and de facto assume certain "bets" as a result of that.

The bottom line of this line of research so far, however, is to follow Knight in black boxing the concept of "judgment". Langlois (2005: 15), for example defined judgment as follows:

> Judgment is the (largely tacit) ability to make, under conditions of structural uncertainty, decisions that turn out to be reasonable or successful ex post.

And again:

> [Entrepreneurship] depends on intuition, the capacity of seeing things in a way which afterwards process to be true …

Like Trurl, the intrepid constructor who let out the dragons of improbability to roam free, we find opening the black box of Knightian "judgment" an irresistible agenda for future research in entrepreneurship (Sarasvathy & Dew, 2013). We believe that Goodman's philosophy, Hayek's economics, Bruner's social psychology and Gould and Lewontin's pluralistic quarrels with dominant evolutionary theories will all come in handy in prising open that rusty old artifact and move us toward a deeper investigation of *making* through entrepreneurship.

Notes

1 We use the word "strives" because (as he himself would be the first to acknowledge), we do not believe he achieved his objectives. But Goodman is a careful philosopher – a subtle and bold thinker whose attempt, even when sketchy and unfinished, heralds a whole new world of intellectual promise of particular import to entrepreneurship research.

2 Given the topic, we hope Shakespeare will allow us this distortion of his sentence.

3 Actual quotation from a friend and wonderful Mexican cook.

4 This short article is also of a piece with the "Creative Powers" article in Part IV of this book. The two pieces together make a precis of Hayek's *The Constitution of Liberty*. It is a curious fact that the article itself is not much cited, considering Hayek's fame and how long it has been around. Yet it appears to be on the comeback trail in some circles – note, for example, a new translation of it by Snow.
5 Very reminiscent of the quote we began this book with.
6 Recall our quotation from Geertz at the beginning of Part II of the book.

References

Andriani, P., Ali, A., & Mastrogiorgio, M. (2017). Measuring exaptation and its impact on innovation, search, and problem solving. *Organization Science*, *28*(2), 320–338.

Bazerman, M. H., Curhan, J. R., Moore, D. A. & Valley, K. L. (2000). Negotiation. *Annual Review of Psychology* *51*(1): 279–314.

Bazerman, M. H. & Neale, M. A. (1992). *Negotiating rationally*, New York, Free Press.

Boudreaux, D. J. & Holcombe, R. G. (1989). The Coasian and Knightian theories of the firm. *Managerial and Decision Economics* *10*: 147–154.

Bruner, J. (1986). *Actual minds, possible worlds*. Cambridge, MA: Harvard University Press.

Buchanan, J. M. & Vanberg, V. J. (1991). The market as a creative process. *Economics and Philosophy* 7: 167–186.

Byrne, O. & Shepherd, D. A. (2015). Different strokes for different folks: Entrepreneurial narratives of emotion, cognition, and making sense of business failure. *Entrepreneurship Theory and Practice* *39*(2): 375–405.

Cacciotti, G., Hayton, J. C., Mitchell, J. R. & Giazitzoglu A. (2016). A reconceptualization of fear of failure in entrepreneurship. *Journal of Business Venturing* *31*(3): 302–325.

Casson, M. (2003). *The entrepreneur: An economic theory*. Northampton, MA: Edward Elgar Publishing Incorporated.

Christensen, C. M., Raynor, M. E. & Verlinden, M. C. (2001). Skate to where the money will be. *Harvard Business Review* *79*(10): 72.

Cope, J. (2011). Entrepreneurial learning from failure: An interpretative phenomenological analysis. *Journal of Business Venturing* *26*(6): 604–623.

Crowley, P. (2002). Good lobster traps make good fences. *Newsweek*, April 29.

Darwin, C. (1872). *The origin of species*. 6th London ed. Chicago: Thomas and Thomas.

Denrell, J. (2004). Random walks and sustained competitive advantage. *Management Science* *50*(7): 922–934.

Dew, N. (2004). *The birth of the new rfid industry: Microfoundations for sociological and economic views of new market creation*. Working Paper.

Dosi, G. (1982). Technological paradigms and technological trajectories: A suggested interpretation of the determinants and directions of technical change. *Research Policy* *11*(3): 147.

Emirbayer, M. (1997). Manifesto for a relational sociology. *American Journal of Sociology* *103*(2): 281–317.

Emirbayer, M. & Mische, A. (1998). What is agency? *American Journal of Sociology* *103*(4): 962–1023.

Foss, N. J. & Klein P. G. (2012). *Organizing entrepreneurial judgment: A new approach to the firm*: Cambridge University Press.

Garud, R., Schildt, H. A. & Lant, T. K. (2014). Entrepreneurial storytelling, future expectations, and the paradox of legitimacy. *Organization Science* *25*(5): 1479–1492.

Geroski, P. (2003). *The evolution of new markets*. New York, Oxford University Press.

170 Making

Goldenberg, J., Lehmann, D. R., & Mazursky, D. (2001). The idea itself and the circumstances of its emergence as predictors of new product success. *Management Science*, *47*(1), 69–84.

Goodman, N. (1978). *Ways of worldmaking*. Indianapolis,, Hackett Pub. Co.

Gould, S. J. (2002). *The structure of evolutionary theory*. Cambridge, MA: Belknap Press.

Gould, S. J. & Lewontin, R. C. (1979). The spandrels of San Marco and the Panglossian paradigm: A critique of the adaptationist programme. *Proceedings of the Royal Society of London. Series B, Biological Sciences 205*(1161): 581–598.

Gould, S. J. & Vrba, E. S. (1982). Exaptation – a missing term in the science of form. *Paleobiology 8*(1): 4–15.

Hayek, F. A. (1978a). *The constitution of liberty*. University of Chicago Press.

Hayek, F. A. (1978b). *New studies in philosophy, politics, economics, and the history of ideas*. London, Routledge and K. Paul.

Hayek, F. A. (1984). Competition as a discovery procedure. In Nishiyama, C. & Leube, K. R. *The essence of Hayek*. Stanford, CA: Stanford University Press: 257.

Hayek, F. A. (1991). The use of knowledge in society. In *Individualism and economic order*, Chicago University Press: 77.

Hayek, F. A. (2002). Competition as a discovery procedure. *Quarterly Journal of Austrian Economics 5*(3): 9–23.

Knight, F. H. (1921/2002). *Risk, uncertainty and profit*. New York, Houghton Mifflin.

Lakoff, G. & Johnson, M. (1999). *Philosophy in the flesh: The embodied mind and its challenge to western thought*. New York, Basic Books.

Langlois, R. N. (2003). Cognitive comparative advantage and the organization of work: Lessons from Herbert Simon's vision of the future. *Journal of Economic Psychology 24*(2): 167.

Langlois, R. N. (2005). The entrepreneurial theory of the firm and the theory of the entrepreneurial firm. *University of Connecticut, Department of Economics Working Paper Series*: 1–37.

Lawler, E. J. (2002). Micro social orders. *Social Psychology Quarterly 65*(1): 4–17.

Lawler, E. J. & Yoon, J. (1996). Commitment in exchange relations: Test of a theory of relational cohesion. *American Sociological Review 61*(1): 89–108.

Lem, S. (1974). *The seventh sally. The Cyberiad: Fables for the cybernetic age*. San Diego, CA: Harcourt Brace Jovanovich.

McGrath, R. G. (1999). Falling forward: Real options reasoning and entrepreneurial failure. *The Academy of Management Review 24*(1): 13–30.

Mokyr, J. (2000). Evolutionary phenomena in technological change. In Ziman, J. *Technological innovation as an evolutionary process*. Cambridge University Press: 52–65.

Morgan, J. & Sisak, D. (2016). Aspiring to succeed: A model of entrepreneurship and fear of failure. *Journal of Business Venturing 31*(1): 1–21.

Mowery, D. & Rosenberg, N. (1979). The influence of market demand upon innovation: A critical review of some recent empirical studies. *Research Policy 8*: 102–153.

Odling-Smee, F. J., Laland, K. N., & Feldman, M. W. (2003). *Niche construction: the neglected process in evolution* (No. 37). Princeton, NJ: Princeton University Press.

Pruitt, D. G. & Lewis, S. A. (1975). Development of integrative solutions in bilateral negotiation. *Journal of Personality and Social Psychology 31*(4): 621–633.

Pruitt, D. G. & Rubin, J. Z. (1986). *Social conflict*. Boston. McGraw-Hill.

Putnam, H. (1979). Reflections on Goodman's ways of worldmaking. *The Journal of Philosophy 76*(11): 603–618.

Putnam, L. L. (2004). Transformations and critical moments in negotiations. *Negotiation Journal 20*(2): 275–295.

Sarasvathy, S. (2000). Report on the seminar on research perspectives in entrepreneurship. *Journal of Business Venturing* **15**: 1–57.

Sarasvathy, S. D. & Dew N. (2013). Without judgment: An empirically-based entrepreneurial theory of the firm. *Review of Austrian Economics* **26**(3): 277–296.

Schumpeter, J. (1934). *The theory of economic development.* Oxford University Press.

Shepherd, D. A. (2004). Educating entrepreneurship students about emotion and learning from failure. *Academy of Management Learning and Education* **3**(3): 274–287.

Shepherd, D. A. (2009). *From lemons to lemonade: Squeeze every last drop of success out of your mistakes.* Upper Saddle River, NJ: Pearson Prentice Hall.

Simon, H. A. (1988). *The sciences of the artificial.* Cambridge, MA and London, MIT Press.

Snow, M. (2002). Notes on the translation of F.A. Hayek's 'Competition as a discovery procedure'. *Quarterly Journal of Austrian Economics* **5**(3): 7–8.

Thompson, L., Gentner, D. & Loewenstein, J. (2000). Avoiding missed opportunities in managerial life: Analogical training more powerful than individual case training. *Organizational Behavior and Human Decision Processes* **82**(1): 60–75.

Ucbasaran, D., Shepherd, D. A., Lockett, A. & Lyon, S. J. (2013). Life after business failure: The process and consequences of business failure for entrepreneurs. *Journal of Management* **39**(1): 163–202.

Walton, R. E. & McKersie, R. B. (1965). *A behavioral theory of labor negotiations.* New York, McGraw-Hill.

8

WORDS, WORKS, WORLDS

N. Goodman

Questions

Countless worlds made from nothing by use of symbols—so might a satirist summarize some major themes in the work of Ernst Cassirer. These themes—the multiplicity of worlds, the speciousness of 'the given', the creative power of the understanding, the variety and formative function of symbols—are also integral to my own thinking. Sometimes, though, I forget how eloquently they have been set forth by Cassirer,[1] partly perhaps because his emphasis on myth, his concern with the comparative study of cultures, and his talk of the human spirit have been mistakenly associated with current trends toward mystical obscurantism, anti-intellectual intuitionism, or anti-scientific humanism. Actually these attitudes are as alien to Cassirer as to my own skeptical, analytic, constructionalist orientation.

My aim in what follows is less to defend certain theses that Cassirer and I share than to take a hard look at some crucial questions they raise. In just what sense are there many worlds? What distinguishes genuine from spurious worlds? What are worlds made of? How are they made? What role do symbols play in the making? And how is worldmaking related to knowing? These questions must be faced even if full and final answers are far off.

Versions and visions

As intimated by William James's equivocal title *A Pluralistic Universe*, the issue between monism and pluralism tends to evaporate under analysis. If there is but one world, it embraces a multiplicity of contrasting aspects; if there are many worlds, the collection of them all is one. The one world may be taken as many, or the many worlds taken as one; whether one or many depends on the way of taking.[2]

Words, works, worlds **173**

Why, then, does Cassirer stress the multiplicity of worlds? In what important and often neglected sense are there many worlds? Let it be clear that the question here is not of the possible worlds that many of my contemporaries, especially those near Disneyland, are busy making and manipulating. We are not speaking in terms of multiple possible alternatives to a single actual world but of multiple actual worlds. How to interpret such terms as "real", "unreal", "fictive", and "possible" is a subsequent question.

Consider, to begin with, the statements "The sun always moves" and "The sun never moves" which, though equally true, are at odds with each other. Shall we say, then, that they describe different worlds, and indeed that there are as many different worlds as there are such mutually exclusive truths? Rather, we are inclined to regard the two strings of words not as complete statements with truth-values of their own but as elliptical for some such statements as "Under frame of reference A, the sun always moves" and "Under frame of reference B, the sun never moves"— statements that may both be true of the same world.

Frames of reference, though, seem to belong less to what is described than to systems of description: and each of the two statements relates what is described to such a system. If I ask about the world, you can offer to tell me how it is under one or more frames of reference; but if I insist that you tell me how it is apart from all frames, what can you say? We are confined to ways of describing whatever is described. Our universe, so to speak, consists of these ways rather than of a world or of worlds.

The alternative descriptions of motion, all of them in much the same terms and routinely transformable into one another, provide only a minor and rather pallid example of diversity in accounts of the world. Much more striking is the vast variety of versions and visions in the several sciences, in the works of different painters and writers, and in our perceptions as informed by these, by circumstances, and by our own insights, interests, and past experiences. Even with all illusory or wrong or dubious versions dropped, the rest exhibit new dimensions of disparity. Here we have no neat set of frames of reference, no ready rules for transforming physics, biology, and psychology into one another, and no way at all of transforming any of these into Van Gogh's vision, or Van Gogh's into Canaletto's. Such of these versions as are depictions rather than descriptions have no truth-value in the literal sense, and cannot be combined by conjunction. The difference between juxtaposing and conjoining two statements has no evident analogue for two pictures or for a picture and a statement. The dramatically contrasting versions of the world can of course be relativized: each is right under a given system—for a given science, a given artist, or a given perceiver and situation. Here again we turn from describing or depicting 'the world' to talking of descriptions and depictions, but now without even the consolation of intertranslatability among or any evident organization of the several systems in question.

Yet doesn't a right version differ from a wrong one just in applying to the world, so that rightness itself depends upon and implies a world? We might better say that 'the world' depends upon rightness. We cannot test a version by comparing it with a world undescribed, undepicted, unperceived, but only by other means that I shall

174 N. Goodman

discuss later. While we may speak of determining what versions are right as 'learning about the world', 'the world' supposedly being that which all right versions describe, all we learn about the world is contained in right versions of it; and while the underlying world, bereft of these, need not be denied to those who love it, it is perhaps on the whole a world well lost. For some purposes, we may want to define a relation that will so sort versions into clusters that each cluster constitutes a world, and the members of the cluster are versions of that world; but for many purposes, right world-descriptions and world-depictions and world-perceptions, the ways-the-world-is, or just versions, can be treated as our worlds.[3]

Since the fact that there are many different world-versions is hardly debatable, and the question how many if any worlds-in-themselves there are is virtually empty, in what non-trivial sense are there, as Cassirer and like-minded pluralists insist, many worlds? Just this, I think: that many different world-versions are of independent interest and importance, without any requirement or presumption of reducibility to a single base. The pluralist, far from being anti-scientific, accepts the sciences at full value. His typical adversary is the monopolistic materialist or physicalist who maintains that one system, physics, is preeminent and all-inclusive, such that every other version must eventually be reduced to it or rejected as false or meaningless. If all right versions could somehow be reduced to one and only one, that one might with some semblance of plausibility[4] be regarded as the only truth about the only world. But the evidence for such reducibility is negligible, and even the claim is nebulous since physics itself is fragmentary and unstable and the kind and consequences of reduction envisaged are vague. (How do you go about reducing Constable's or James Joyce's world-view to physics?) I am the last person likely to underrate construction and reduction.[5] A reduction from one system to another can make a genuine contribution to understanding the interrelationships among world-versions; but reduction in any reasonably strict sense is rare, almost always partial, and seldom if ever unique. To demand full and sole reducibility to physics or any other one version is to forego nearly all other versions. The pluralists' acceptance of versions other than physics implies no relaxation of rigor but a recognition that standards different from yet no less exacting than those applied in science are appropriate for appraising what is conveyed in perceptual or pictorial or literary versions.

So long as contrasting right versions not all reducible to one are countenanced, unity is to be sought not in an ambivalent or neutral *something* beneath these versions but in an overall organization embracing them. Cassirer undertakes the search through a cross-cultural study of the development of myth, religion, language, art, and science. My approach is rather through an analytic study of types and functions of symbols and symbol systems. In neither case should a unique result be anticipated; universes of worlds as well as worlds themselves may be built in many ways.

How firm a foundation?

The non-Kantian theme of multiplicity of worlds is closely akin to the Kantian theme of the vacuity of the notion of pure content. The one denies us a unique world, the other the common stuff of which worlds are made. Together these theses defy our intuitive demand for something stolid underneath, and threaten to leave us uncontrolled, spinning out our own inconsequent fantasies.

The overwhelming case against perception without conception, the pure given, absolute immediacy, the innocent eye, substance as substratum, has been so fully and frequently set forth—by Berkeley, Kant, Cassirer, Gombrich,[6] Bruner,[7] and many others—as to need no restatement here. Talk of unstructured content or an unconceptualized given or a substratum without properties is self-defeating; for the talk imposes structure, conceptualizes, ascribes properties. Although conception without perception is merely *empty*, perception without conception is *blind* (totally inoperative). Predicates, pictures, other labels, schemata, survive want of application, but content vanishes without form. We can have words without a world but no world without words or other symbols.

The many stuffs—matter, energy, waves, phenomena—that worlds are made of are made along with the worlds. But made from what? Not from nothing, after all, but *from other worlds*. Worldmaking as we know it always starts from worlds already on hand; the making is a remaking. Anthropology and developmental psychology may study social and individual histories of such world-building, but the search for a universal or necessary beginning is best left to theology.[8] My interest here is rather with the processes involved in building a world out of others.

With false hope of a firm foundation gone, with the world displaced by worlds that are but versions, with substance dissolved into function, and with the given acknowledged as taken, we face the questions how worlds are made, tested, and known.

Ways of worldmaking

Without presuming to instruct the gods or other worldmakers, or attempting any comprehensive or systematic survey, I want to illustrate and comment on some of the processes that go into worldmaking. Actually, I am concerned more with certain relationships among worlds than with how or whether particular worlds are made from others.

Composition and decomposition

Much but by no means all worldmaking consists of taking apart and putting together, often conjointly: on the one hand, of dividing wholes into parts and partitioning kinds into subspecies, analyzing complexes into component features, drawing distinctions; on the other hand, of composing wholes and kinds out of parts and members and subclasses, combining features into complexes, and making connections. Such composition or decomposition is normally effected or assisted or consolidated by the application of labels: names, predicates, gestures, pictures, etc. Thus, for example, temporally diverse events are brought together under a proper name or identified as making up 'an object' or 'a person'; or snow is sundered into

176 N. Goodman

several materials under terms of the Eskimo vocabulary. Metaphorical transfer—for example, where taste predicates are applied to sounds—may effect a double reorganization, both re-sorting the new realm of application and relating it to the old one (*LA*: II).

Identification rests upon organization into entities and kinds. The response to the question "Same or not the same?" must always be "Same what?"[9] Different soandsos may be the same such-and-such: what we point to or indicate, verbally or otherwise, may be different events but the same object, different towns but the same state, different members but the same club or different clubs but the same members, different innings but the same ball game. 'The ball-in-play' of a single game may be comprised of temporal segments of a dozen or more baseballs. The psychologist asking the child to judge constancy when one vessel is emptied into another must be careful to consider *what* constancy is in question—constancy of volume or depth or shape or kind of material, etc.[10] Identity or constancy in a world is identity with respect to what is within that world as organized.

Motley entities cutting across each other in complicated patterns may belong to the same world. We do not make a new world every time we take things apart or put them together in another way; but worlds may *differ* in that not everything belonging to one belongs to the other. The world of the Eskimo who has not grasped the comprehensive concept of snow differs not only from the world of the Samoan but also from the world of the New Englander who has not grasped the Eskimo's distinctions. In other cases, worlds differ in response to theoretical rather than practical needs. A world with points as elements cannot be the Whiteheadian world having points as certain classes of nesting volumes or having points as certain pairs of intersecting lines or as certain triples of intersecting planes. That the points of our everyday world can be equally well defined in any of these ways does not mean that a point can be identified in any one world with a nest of volumes and a pair of lines and a triple of planes; for all these are different from each other. Again the world of a system taking minimal concrete phenomena as atomic cannot admit qualities as atomic parts of these concreta.[11]

Repetition as well as identification is relative to organization. A world may be unmanageably heterogeneous or unbearably monotonous according to how events are sorted into kinds. Whether or not today's experiment repeats yesterday's, however much the two events may differ, depends upon whether they test a common hypothesis; as Sir George Thomson puts it:

> There will always be something different. ... What it comes to when you say you repeat an experiment is that you repeat all the features of an experiment which a theory determines are relevant. In other words you repeat the experiment as an example of the theory.[12]

Likewise, two musical performances that differ drastically are nevertheless performances of the same work if they conform to the same score. The notational system distinguishes constitutive from contingent features, thus picking out the performance-kinds that count as works (*LA*, pp. 115–130). And things 'go on in the same way' or not according to what is regarded as the same way; 'now I can go on',[13] in Wittgenstein's sense, when I have found a familiar pattern, or a tolerable variation of one, that fits and goes beyond the cases given. Induction requires taking some classes to the exclusion of others as relevant kinds. Only so, for example, do our observations of emeralds exhibit any regularity and confirm that all emeralds are green rather than that all are grue (i.e. examined before a given date and green, or not so examined and blue—*FFF*, pp. 72–80). The uniformity of nature we marvel at or the unreliability we protest belongs to a world of our own making.

In these latter cases, worlds differ in the relevant kinds they comprise. I say "relevant" rather than "natural" for two reasons: first, "natural" is an inapt term to cover not only biological species but such artificial kinds as musical works, psychological experiments, and types of machinery; and second, "natural" suggests some absolute categorical or psychological priority, while the kinds in question are rather habitual or traditional or devised for a new purpose.

Weighting

While we may say that in the cases discussed some relevant kinds[14] of one world are missing from another, we might perhaps better say that the two worlds contain just the same classes sorted differently into relevant and irrelevant kinds. Some relevant kinds of the one world, rather than being absent from the other, are present as irrelevant kinds; some differences among worlds are not so much in entities comprised as in emphasis or accent, and these differences are no less consequential. Just as to stress all syllables is to stress none, so to take all classes as relevant kinds is to take none as such. In one world there may be many kinds serving different purposes; but conflicting purposes may make for irreconcilable accents and contrasting worlds, as may conflicting conceptions of what kinds serve a given purpose. Grue cannot be a relevant kind for induction in the same world as green, for that would preclude some of the decisions, right or wrong, that constitute inductive inference.

Some of the most striking contrasts of emphasis appear in the arts. Many of the differences among portrayals by Daumier, Ingres, Michelangelo, and Rouault are differences in aspects accentuated. What counts as emphasis, of course, is departure from the relative prominence accorded the several features in the current world of our everyday seeing. With changing interests and new insights, the visual weighting of features of bulk or line or stance or light alters, and yesterday's level world seems strangely perverted—yesterday's realistic calendar landscape becomes a repulsive caricature.

These differences in emphasis, too, amount to a difference in relevant kinds recognized. Several portrayals of the same subject may thus place it according to different categorial schemata. Like a green emerald and a grue one, even if the same emerald, a Piero della Francesca *Christ* and a Rembrandt one belong to worlds organized into different kinds.

178 N. Goodman

Works of art, though, characteristically illustrate rather than name or describe relevant kinds. Even where the ranges of application—the things described or depicted—coincide, the features or kinds exemplified or expressed may be very different. A line drawing of softly draped cloth may exemplify rhythmic linear patterns; and a poem with no words for sadness and no mention of a sad person may in the quality of its language be sad and poignantly express sadness. The distinction between saying or representing on the one hand and showing or exemplifying on the other becomes even more evident in the case of abstract painting and music and dance that have no subject-matter but nevertheless manifest—exemplify or express —forms and feelings. Exemplification and expression, though running in the opposite direction from denotation—that is, from the symbol to a literal or metaphorical feature of it instead of to something the symbol applies to—are no less symbolic referential functions and instruments of worldmaking.[15]

Emphasis or weighting is not always binary as is a sorting into relevant and irrelevant kinds or into important and unimportant features. Ratings of relevance, importance, utility, value often yield hierarchies rather than dichotomies. Such weightings are also instances of a particular type of ordering.

Ordering

Worlds not differing in entities or emphasis may differ in ordering; for example, the worlds of different constructional systems differ in order of derivation. As nothing is at rest or is in motion apart from a frame of reference, so nothing is primitive or is derivationally prior to anything apart from a constructional system. However, derivation unlike motion is of little immediate practical interest; and thus in our everyday world, although we almost always adopt a frame of reference at least temporarily, we seldom adopt a derivational basis. Earlier I said that the difference between a world having points as pairs of lines and a world having lines as composed of points is that the latter but not the former admits as entities nonlinear elements comprised within lines. But alternatively we may say that these worlds differ in their derivational ordering of lines and points of the not-derivationally-ordered world of daily discourse.

Orderings of a different sort pervade perception and practical cognition. The standard ordering of brightness in color follows the linear increase in physical intensity of light, but the standard ordering of hues curls the straight line of increasing wavelength into a circle. Order includes periodicity as well as proximity; and the standard ordering of tones is by pitch and octave. Orderings alter with circumstances and objectives. Much as the nature of shapes changes under different geometries, so do perceived patterns change under different orderings; the patterns perceived under a twelve-tone scale are quite different from those perceived under the traditional eight-tone scale, and rhythms depend upon the marking off into measures.

Radical reordering of another sort occurs in constructing a static image from the input on scanning a picture, or in building a unified and comprehensive image of an object or a city from temporally and spatially and qualitatively heterogeneous observations and other items of information.[16] Some very fast readers recreate normal word-ordering from a series of fixations that proceed down the left-hand page and then up the right-hand page of a book.[17] And spatial order in a map or a score is translated into the temporal sequence of a trip or a performance.

All measurement, furthermore, is based upon order. Indeed, only through suitable arrangements and groupings can we handle vast quantities of material perceptually or cognitively. Gombrich discusses the decimal periodization of historical time into decades, centuries, and millennia.[18] Daily time is marked off into twenty-four hours, and each of these into sixty minutes of sixty seconds each. Whatever else may be said of these modes of organization, they are not 'found in the world' but *built into a world*. Ordering, as well as composition and decomposition and weighting of wholes and kinds, participates in worldmaking.

Deletion and supplementation

Also, the making of one world out of another usually involves some extensive weeding out and filling—actual excision of some old and supply of some new material. Our capacity for overlooking is virtually unlimited, and what we do take in usually consists of significant fragments and clues that need massive supplementation. Artists often make skillful use of this: a lithograph by Giacometti fully presents a walking man by sketches of nothing but the head, hands, and feet in just the right postures and positions against an expanse of blank paper; and a drawing by Katharine Sturgis conveys a hockey player in action by a single charged line.

That we find what we are prepared to find (what we look for or what forcefully affronts our expectations), and that we are likely to be blind to what neither helps nor hinders our pursuits, are commonplaces of everyday life and amply attested in the psychological laboratory.[19] In the painful experience of proof-reading and the more pleasurable one of watching a skilled magician, we incurably miss something that is there and see something that is not there. Memory edits more ruthlessly; a person with equal command of two languages may remember a learned list of items while forgetting in which language they were listed.[20] And even within what we do perceive and remember, we dismiss as illusory or negligible what cannot be fitted into the architecture of the world we are building.

The scientist is no less drastic, rejecting or purifying most of the entities and events of the world of ordinary things while generating quantities of filling for curves suggested by sparse data, and erecting elaborate structures on the basis of meagre observations. Thus does he strive to build a world conforming to his chosen concepts and obeying his universal laws.

Replacement of a so-called analog by a so-called digital system through the articulation of separate steps involves deletion; for example, to use a digital thermometer with readings in tenths of a degree is to recognize no temperature as lying between 90 and 90.1 degrees. Similar deletion occurs under standard musical notation, which recognizes no pitch between c and $c\#$ and no duration between a

180 N. Goodman

sixty-fourth and a one hundred-and-twenty-eighth note. On the other hand, supplementation occurs when, say, an analog replaces a digital instrument for registering attendance, or reporting money raised, or when a violinist performs from a score.

Perhaps the most spectacular cases of supplementation, though, are found in the perception of motion. Sometimes motion in the perceptual world results from intricate and abundant fleshing out of the physical stimuli. Psychologists have long known of what is called the 'phi phemomenon': under carefully controlled conditions, if two spots of light are flashed a short distance apart and in quick succession, the viewer normally sees a spot of light moving continuously along a path from the first position to the second. That is remarkable enough in itself since of course the direction of motion cannot have been determined prior to the second flash; but perception has even greater creative power. Paul Kolers has recently shown[21] that if the first stimulus spot is circular and the second square, the seen moving spot transforms smoothly from circle to square; and transformations between two-dimensional and three-dimensional shapes are often effected without trouble. Moreover, if a barrier of light is interposed between the two stimulus spots, the moving spot detours around the barrier. Just why these supplementations occur as they do is a fascinating subject for speculation (see further V below).

Deformation

Finally, some changes are reshapings or deformations that may according to point of view be considered either corrections or distortions. The physicist smooths out the simplest rough curve that fits all his data. Vision stretches a line ending with arrowheads pointing *in* while shrinking a physically equal line ending with arrowheads pointing *out*, and tends to expand the size of a smaller more valuable coin in relation to that of a larger less valuable one.[22] Caricaturists often go beyond overemphasis to actual distortion. Picasso starting from Velasquez's *Las Meninas*, and Brahms starting from a theme of Haydn's, work magical variations that amount to revelations.

These then are ways that worlds are made. I do not say *the* ways. My classification is not offered as comprehensive or clearcut or mandatory. Not only do the processes illustrated often occur in combination but the examples chosen sometimes fit equally well under more than one heading; for example, some changes may be considered alternatively as reweightings or reorderings or reshapings or as all of these, and some deletions are also matters of differences in composition. All I have tried to do is to suggest something of the variety of processes in constant use. While a tighter systematization could surely be developed, none can be ultimate; for as remarked earlier, there is no more a unique world of worlds than there is a unique world.

Trouble with truth

With all this freedom to divide and combine, emphasize, order, delete, fill in and fill out, and even distort, what are the objectives and the constraints? What are the criteria for success in making a world?

Insofar as a version is verbal and consists of statements, truth may be relevant. But truth cannot be defined or tested by agreement with 'the world'; for not only do truths differ for different worlds but the nature of agreement between a version and a world apart from it is notoriously nebulous. Rather—speaking loosely and without trying to answer either Pilate's question or Tarski's—a version is taken to be true when it offends no unyielding beliefs and none of its own precepts. Among beliefs unyielding at a given time may be long-lived reflections of laws of logic, short-lived reflections of recent observations, and other convictions and prejudices ingrained with varying degrees of firmness. Among precepts, for example, may be choices among alternative frames of reference, weighlings, and derivational bases. But the line between beliefs and precepts is neither sharp nor stable. Beliefs are framed in concepts informed by precepts; and if a Boyle ditches his data for a smooth curve just missing them all, we may say either that observational volume and pressure are different properties from theoretical volume and pressure or that the truths about volume and pressure differ in the two worlds of observation and theory. Even the staunchest belief may in time admit alternatives; "The earth is at rest" passed from dogma to dependence upon precept.

Truth, far from being a solemn and severe master, is a docile and obedient servant. The scientist who supposes that he is single-mindedly dedicated to the search for truth deceives himself. He is unconcerned with the trivial truths he could grind out endlessly; and he looks to the multifaceted and irregular results of observations for little more than suggestions of overall structures and significant generalizations. He seeks system, simplicity, scope; and when satisfied on these scores he tailors truth to fit (*PP*:VII, 6–8). He as much decrees as discovers the laws he sets forth, as much designs as discerns the patterns he delineates.

Truth, moreover, pertains solely to what is said, and literal truth solely to what is said literally. We have seen, though, that worlds are made not only by what is said literally but also by what is said metaphorically, and not only by what is said either literally or metaphorically but also by what is exemplified and expressed—by what is shown as well as by what is said. In a scientific treatise, literal truth counts most; but in a poem or novel, metaphorical or allegorical truth may matter more, for even a literally false statement may be metaphorically true (*LA*, pp. 51, 68–70) and may mark or make new associations and discriminations, change emphases, effect exclusions and additions. And statements whether literally or metaphorically true or false may show what they do not say, may work as trenchant literal or metaphorical examples of unmentioned features and feelings. In Vachel Lindsay's *The Congo*, for example, the pulsating pattern of drumbeats is insistently exhibited rather than described.

Finally, for nonverbal versions and even for verbal versions without statements, truth is irrelevant. We risk confusion when we speak of pictures or predicates as

182 N. Goodman

"true of" what they depict or apply to; they have no truth-value and may represent or denote some things and not others, while a statement does have truth-value and is true of everything if of anything.[23] A nonrepresentational picture such as a Mondrian says nothing, denotes nothing, pictures nothing, and is neither true nor false, but shows much. Nevertheless, showing or exemplifying, like denoting, is a referential function; and much the same considerations count for pictures as for the concepts or predicates of a theory: their relevance and their revelations, their force and their fit—in sum their *rightness*. Rather than speak of pictures as true or false we might better speak of theories as right or wrong; for the truth of the laws of a theory is but one special feature and is often, as we have seen, overridden in importance by the cogency and compactness and comprehensiveness, the informativeness and organizing power of the whole system.

"The truth, the whole truth, and nothing but the truth" would thus be a perverse and paralyzing policy for any worldmaker. The whole truth would be too much; it is too vast, variable, and clogged with trivia. The truth alone would be too little, for some right versions are not true—being either false or neither true nor false—and even for true versions rightness may matter more.

Relative reality

Shouldn't we now return to sanity from all this mad proliferation of worlds? Shouldn't we stop speaking of right versions as if each were, or had, its own world, and recognize all as versions of one and the same neutral and underlying world? The world thus regained, as remarked earlier, is a world without kinds or order or motion or rest or pattern—a world not worth fighting for or against.

We might, though, take the real world to be that of some one of the alternative right versions (or groups of them bound together by some principle of reducibility or translatability) and regard all others as versions of that same world differing from the standard version in accountable ways. The physicist takes his world as the real one, attributing the deletions, additions, irregularities, emphases of other versions to the imperfections of perception, to the urgencies of practice, or to poetic license. The phenomenalist regards the perceptual world as fundamental, and the excisions, abstractions, simplifications, and distortions of other versions as resulting from scientific or practical or artistic concerns. For the man-in-the-street, most versions from science, art, and perception depart in some ways from the familiar serviceable world he has jerry-built from fragments of scientific and artistic tradition and from his own struggle for survival. This world, indeed, is the one most often taken as real; for reality in a world, like realism in a picture, is largely a matter of habit.

Ironically, then, our passion for *one* world is satisfied, at different times and for different purposes, in *many* different ways. Not only motion, derivation, weighting, order, but even reality is relative. That right versions and actual worlds are many does not obliterate the distinction between right and wrong versions, does not recognize merely possible worlds answering to wrong versions, and does not imply that all right alternatives are equally good for every or indeed for any purpose.

Not even a fly is likely to take one of its wing-tips as a fixed point; we do not welcome molecules or concreta as elements of our everyday world, or combine tomatoes and triangles and typewriters and tyrants and tornadoes into a single kind; the physicist will count none of these among his fundamental particles; the painter who sees the way the man-in-the-street does will have more popular than artistic success. And the same philosopher who here metaphilosophically contemplates a vast variety of worlds finds that only versions meeting the demands of a dogged and deflationary nominalism suit his purposes in constructing philosophical systems.

Moreover, while readiness to recognize alternative worlds may be liberating, and suggestive of new avenues of exploration, a willingness to welcome all worlds builds none. Mere acknowledgement of the many available frames of reference provides us with no map of the motions of heavenly bodies; acceptance of the eligibility of alternative bases produces no scientific theory or philosophical system; awareness of varied ways of seeing paints no pictures. A broad mind is no substitute for hard work.

Notes on knowing

What I have been saying bears on the nature of knowledge. On these terms, knowing cannot be exclusively or even primarily a matter of determining what is true. Discovery often amounts, as when I place a piece in a jigsaw puzzle, not to arrival at a proposition for declaration or defense, but to finding a fit. Much of knowing aims at something other than true, or any, belief. An increase in acuity of insight or in range of comprehension, rather than a change in belief, occurs when we find in a pictured forest a face we already knew was there, or learn to distinguish stylistic differences among works already classified by artist or composer or writer, or study a picture or a concerto or a treatise until we see or hear or grasp features and structures we could not discern before. Such growth in knowledge is not by formation or fixation or belief[24] but by the advancement of understanding.[25]

Furthermore, if worlds are as much made as found, so also knowing is as much remaking as reporting. All the processes of worldmaking I have discussed enter into knowing. Perceiving motion, we have seen, often consists in producing it. Discovering laws involves drafting them. Recognizing patterns is very much a matter of inventing and imposing them. Comprehension and creation go on together.

I shall return in Chapters VI and VII to many of the questions surveyed here. Now I want to consider two much more specific topics: in Chapter II, a subtle categorization peculiarly significant for the arts; and in Chapter III, a sample tracing of a notion across versions in various systems and media.

Notes

1 E.g. in *Language and Myth*, translated by Susanne Langer (Harper, 1946).
2 But see further VII: 1 below.
3 Cf. "The Way the World Is" (1960), *PP*, pp. 24–32, and Richard Rorty, "The World Well Lost", *Journal of Philosophy*, Vol. 69 (1972), pp. 649–665.

184 N. Goodman

4 But not much, for no one type of reducibility serves all purposes.

5 Cf. "The Revision of Philosophy" (1956), *PP*, pp. 5–23; and also *SA*.

6 In *Art and Illusion* (Pantheon Books, 1960), E. H. Gombrich argues in many passages against the notion of 'the innocent eye'.

7 See the essays in Jerome S. Bruner's *Beyond the Information Given* [hereinafter *BI*], Jeremy M. Anglin, ed. (W. W. Norton, 1973). Chap. I.

8 Cf. *SA*, pp. 127–145; and "Sense and Certainty" (1952) and "The Epistemological Argument" (1967), *PP*, pp. 60–75. We might take construction of a history of successive development of worlds to involve application of something like a Kantian regulative principle, and the search for a first world thus to be as misguided as the search for a first moment of time.

9 This does not, as sometimes is supposed, require any modification of the Leibniz formula for identity, but merely reminds us that the answer to a question "Is this the same as that?" may depend upon whether the "this" and the "that" in the question refer to thing or event or color or species, etc.

10 See *BI*, pp. 331–340.

11 See further *SA*, pp. 3–22, 132–135, 142–145.

12 In "Some Thoughts on Scientific Method" (1963), in *Boston Studies in the Philosophy of Science*, Vol. 2 (Humanities Press, 1965), p. 85.

13 Discussion of what this means occupies many sections, from about Sec. 142 on, of Ludwig Wittgenstein's *Philosophical Investigations*, translated by C. E. M. Anscombe, (Blackwell, 1953). I am not suggesting that the answer I give here is Wittgenstein's.

14 I speak freely of kinds here. Concerning ways of nominalizing such talk, see *SA*: II and *PP*:IV.

15 On exemplification and expression as referential relations see *LA*, pp. 50–57, 87–95.

16 See *The Image of the City* by Kevin Lynch (Cambridge, Technology Press, 1960).

17 See E. Llewellyn Thomas, "Eye Movements in Speed Reading", in *Speed Reading: Practices and Procedures* (University of Delaware Press, 1962), pp. 104–114.

18 In "Zeit, Zahl, und Zeichen", delivered at the Cassirer celebration in Hamburg, 1974.

19 See "On Perceptual Readiness" (1957) in *BI*, pp. 7–42.

20 See Paul Kolers, "Bilinguals and Information Processing", *Scientific American* 218 (1968), 78–86.

21 *Aspects of Motion Perception* (Pergamon Press, 1972), pp. 47ff.

22 See "Value and Need as Organizing Factors in Perception" (1947), in *BI*, pp. 43–56.

23 E.g., "2+2=4" is true of everything in that for every x, x is such that 2+2=4. A statement S will normally not be *true about* x unless S is about x in one of the senses of "about" defined in "About" (*PP*, pp. 246–272); but definition of "about" depends essentially on features of statements that have no reasonable analogues for pictures. See further: Joseph Ullian and Nelson Goodman, "Truth about Jones", *Journal of Philosophy*, Vol. 74 (1977), pp. 317–338; also VII:5 below.

24 I allude here to Charles S. Peirce's paper, "The Fixation of Belief" (1877), in *Collected Papers of Charles Sanders Peirce*, Vol. 5 (Harvard University Press, 1934), pp. 223–247.

25 On the nature and importance of understanding in the broader sense, see M. Polanyi, *Personal Knowledge* (University of Chicago Press, 1960).

9

COMPETITION AS A DISCOVERY PROCEDURE

F. A. Hayek

I

It is difficult to defend economists against the charge that for some 40 to 50 years they have been discussing competition on assumptions that, *if* they were true of the real world, would make it wholly uninteresting and useless. If anyone really knew all about what economic theory calls the *data*, competition would indeed be a very wasteful method of securing adjustment to these facts. It is thus not surprising that some people have been led to the conclusion that we can either wholly dispense with the market, or that its results should be used only as a first step towards securing an output of goods and services which we can then manipulate, correct, or redistribute in any manner we wish. Others, who seem to derive their conception of competition solely from modern textbooks, have not unnaturally concluded that competition does not exist.

Against this, it is salutary to remember that, *wherever* the use of competition can be rationally justified, it is on the ground that we do *not* know in advance the facts that determine the actions of competitors. In sports or in examinations, no less than in the award of government contracts or of prizes for poetry, it would clearly be pointless to arrange for competition, if we were certain beforehand who would do best. As indicated in the title of this lecture, I propose to consider competition as a procedure for the discovery of such facts as, without resort to it, would not be known to anyone, or at least would not be utilised.[1]

This may at first appear so obvious and incontestable as hardly to deserve attention. Yet, some interesting consequences that are not so obvious immediately follow from the explicit formulation of the above apparent truism. One is that competition is valuable *only* because, and so far as, its results are unpredictable and on the whole different from those which anyone has, or could have, deliberately aimed at. Further, that the generally beneficial effects of competition must include disappointing or defeating some particular expectations or intentions.

186 F. A. Hayek

Closely connected with this is an interesting methodological consequence. It goes far to account for the discredit into which the micro-economic approach to theory has fallen. Although this theory seems to me to be the only one capable of explaining the role of competition, it is no longer understood, even by some professed economists. It is therefore worthwhile to say at the outset a few words about the methodological peculiarity of any theory of competition, because it has made its conclusions suspect to many of those who habitually apply an over-simplified test to decide what they are willing to accept as scientific. The necessary consequence of the reason why we use competition is that, *in those cases in which it is interesting*, the validity of the theory can never be tested empirically. We can test it on conceptual models, and we might conceivably test it in artificially created real situations, where the facts which competition is intended to discover are already known to the observer. But in such cases it is of no practical value, so that to carry out the experiment would hardly be worth the expense. If we do not know the facts we hope to discover by means of competition, we can never ascertain how effective it has been in discovering those facts that might be discovered. All we can hope to find out is that, on the whole, societies which rely for this purpose on competition have achieved their aims more successfully than others. This is a conclusion which the history of civilisation seems eminently to have confirmed.

The peculiarity of competition — which it has in common with scientific method — is that its performance cannot be tested in particular instances where it is significant, but is shown only by the fact that the market will prevail in comparison with any alternative arrangements. The advantages of accepted scientific procedures can never be proved scientifically, but only demonstrated by the common experience that, on the whole, they are better adapted to delivering the goods than alternative approaches.[2]

The difference between economic competition and the successful procedures of science consists in the fact that the former is a method of discovering particular facts relevant to the achievement of specific, temporary purposes, while science aims at the discovery of what are sometimes called 'general facts', which are regularities of events. Science concerns itself with unique, particular facts only to the extent that they help to confirm or refute theories. Because these refer to general, permanent features of the world, the discoveries of science have ample time to prove their value. In contrast, the benefits of particular facts, whose usefulness competition in the market discovers, are in a great measure transitory. So far as the theory of scientific method is concerned, it would be as easy to discredit it on the ground that it does not lead to testable predictions about what science will discover, as it is to discredit the theory of the market on the ground that it fails to predict particular results the market will achieve. This, in the nature of the case, the theory of competition cannot do in any situation in which it is sensible to employ it. As we shall see, its capacity to predict is necessarily limited to predicting the kind of pattern, or the abstract character of the order that will form itself, but does not extend to the prediction of particular facts.[3]

II

Having relieved myself of this pet concern, I shall return to the central subject of this lecture, by pointing out that economic theory sometimes appears at the outset to bar its way to a true appreciation of the character of the process of competition, because it starts from the assumption of a 'given' supply of scarce goods. But which goods are scarce goods, or which things are goods, and how scarce or valuable they are — these are precisely the things which competition has to discover. Provisional results from the market process at each stage alone tell individuals what to look for. Utilisation of knowledge widely dispersed in a society with extensive division of labour cannot rest on individuals knowing all the particular uses to which well-known things in their individual environment might be put. Prices direct their attention to what is worth finding out about market offers for various things and services. This means that the, in some respects always unique, combinations of individual knowledge and skills, which the market enables them to use, will not merely, or even in the first instance, be such knowledge of facts as they could list and communicate if some authority asked them to do so. The knowledge of which I speak consists rather of a capacity to find out particular circumstances, which becomes effective only if possessors of this knowledge are informed by the market which kinds of things or services are wanted, and how urgently they are wanted.[4]

This must suffice to indicate what kind of knowledge I am referring to when I call competition a discovery procedure. Much would have to be added to clothe the bare bones of this abstract statement with concrete flesh, so as to show its full practical importance. But I must be content with thus briefly indicating the absurdity of the usual procedure of starting the analysis with a situation in which all the facts are supposed to be known. This is a *state* of affairs which economic theory curiously calls 'perfect competition'. It leaves no room whatever for the *activity* called competition, which is presumed to have already done its task. However, I must hurry on to examine a question, on which there exists even more confusion — namely, the meaning of the contention that the market adjusts activities spontaneously to the facts it discovers — or the question of the purpose for which it uses this information.

The prevailing confusion here is largely due to mistakenly treating the order which the market produces as an 'economy' in the strict sense of the word, and judging results of the market process by criteria which are appropriate only to such a single organised community serving a given hierarchy of ends. But such a hierarchy of ends is not relevant to the complex structure composed of countless individual economic arrangements. The latter, unfortunately, we also describe by the same word 'economy', although it is something fundamentally different, and must be judged by different standards. An economy, in the strict sense of the word, is an organisation or arrangement in which someone deliberately allocates resources to a unitary order of ends. Spontaneous order produced by the market is nothing of the kind; and in important respects it does not behave like an economy proper. In particular, such spontaneous order differs because it does *not* ensure that what general

188 F. A. Hayek

opinion regards as more important needs are always satisfied before the less important ones. This is the chief reason why people object to it. Indeed, the whole of socialism is nothing but a demand that the market order (or catallaxy, as I like to call it, to prevent confusion with an economy proper)[5] should be turned into an economy in the strict sense, in which a common scale of importance determines which of the various needs are to be satisfied, and which are not to be satisfied.

The trouble with this socialist aim is a double one. As is true of every deliberate organisation, only the knowledge of the organiser can enter into the design of the economy proper, and all the members of such an economy, conceived as a deliberate organisation, must be guided in their actions by the unitary hierarchy of ends which it serves. On the other hand, advantages of the spontaneous order of the market, or the catallaxy, are correspondingly two. Knowledge that is used in it is that of all its members. Ends that it serves are the separate ends of those individuals, in all their variety and contrariness.

Out of this fact arise certain intellectual difficulties which worry not only socialists, but all economists who want to assess the accomplishments of the market order; because, if the market order does not serve a definite order of ends, indeed if, like any spontaneously formed order, it cannot legitimately be said to *have* particular ends, it is also not possible to express the value of the results as a sum of its particular individual products. What, then, do we mean when we claim that the market order produces in some sense a maximum or optimum?

The fact is, that, though the existence of a spontaneous order not made for a particular purpose cannot be properly said to have a purpose, it may yet be highly conducive to the achievement of many different individual purposes not known as a whole to any single person, or relatively small group of persons. Indeed, rational action is possible only in a fairly orderly world. Therefore it clearly makes sense to try to produce conditions under which the chances for any individual taken at random to achieve his ends as effectively as possible will be very high — even if it cannot be predicted which particular aims will be favoured, and which not.

As we have seen, the results of a discovery procedure are in their nature unpredictable; and all we can expect from the adoption of an effective discovery procedure is to improve the chances for unknown people. The only common aim which we can pursue by the choice of this technique of ordering social affairs is the general kind of pattern, or the abstract character, of the order that will form itself.

III

Economists usually ascribe the order which competition produces as an equilibrium — a somewhat unfortunate term, because such an equilibrium presupposes that the facts have already all been discovered and competition therefore has ceased. The concept of an 'order' which, at least for the discussion of problems of economic policy, I prefer to that of equilibrium, has the advantage that we can meaningfully speak about an order being approached to various degrees, and that order can be preserved throughout a process of change. While an economic equilibrium never really exists, there is some justification for asserting that the kind of order of which our theory describes an ideal type, is approached in a high degree.

This order manifests itself in the first instance in the circumstance that the expectations of transactions to be effected with other members of society, on which the plans of all the several economic subjects are based, can be mostly realised. This mutual adjustment of individual plans is brought about by what, since the physical sciences have also begun to concern themselves with spontaneous orders, or 'self-organising systems', we have learnt to call 'negative feedback'. Indeed, as intelligent biologists acknowledge, 'long before Claude Bernard, Clerk Maxwell, Walter B. Cannon, or Norbert Wiener developed cybernetics, Adam Smith has just as clearly used the idea in *The Wealth of Nations*. The 'invisible hand' that regulated prices to a nicety is clearly this idea. In a free market, says Smith in effect, prices are regulated by negative feedback'.[6]

We shall see that the fact that a high degree of coincidence of expectations is brought about by the systematic disappointment of some kind of expectations is of crucial importance for an understanding of the functioning of the market order. But to bring about a mutual adjustment of individual plans is not all that the market achieves. It also secures that whatever is being produced will be produced by people who can do so more cheaply than (or at least as cheaply as) anybody who does not produce it (and cannot devote his energies to produce something else comparatively even more cheaply), and that each product is sold at a price lower than that at which anybody who in fact does not produce it could supply it. This, of course, does not exclude that some may make considerable profits over their costs if these costs are much lower than those of the next efficient potential producer. But it does mean that of the combination of commodities that is in fact produced, as much will be produced as we know to bring about by any known method. It will of course not be as much as we might produce if all the knowledge anybody possessed or can acquire were commanded by some one agency, and fed into a computer (the cost of finding out would, however, be considerable). Yet we do injustice to the achievement of the market if we judge it, as it were, from above, by comparing it with an ideal standard which we have no known way of achieving. If we judge it, as we ought to, from below, that is, if the comparison in this case is made against what we could achieve by any other method — especially against what would be produced if competition were prevented, so that only those to whom some authority had conferred the right to produce or sell particular things were allowed to do so. All we need to consider is how difficult it is in a competitive system to discover ways of supplying to consumers better or cheaper goods than they already get. Where such unused opportunities seem to exist we usually find that they remain undeveloped because their use is either prevented by the power of authority (including the enforcement of patent privileges), or by some private misuse of power which the law ought to prohibit.

It must not be forgotten that in this respect the market only brings about an approach towards some point on that n-dimensional surface, by which pure economic theory represents the horizon of all possibilities to which the production of any one proportional combination of commodities and services could conceivably be carried. The market leaves the particular combination of goods, and its distribution among individuals, largely to unforeseeable circumstances — and, in this sense, to accident. It is, as Adam Smith already understood,[7] as if we had agreed to play a game, partly of skill and partly of chance. This competitive game, at the price of leaving the share of each individual in some measure to accident, ensures that the real equivalent of whatever his share turns out to be, is as large as we know how to make it. The game is, to use up-to-date language, not a zero-sum game, but one through which, by playing it according to the rules, the pool to be shared is enlarged, leaving individual shares in the pool in a great measure to chance. A mind knowing all the facts could select any point he liked on the surface and distribute this product in the manner he thought right. But the only point on, or tolerably near, the horizon of possibilities which we know how to reach is the one at which we shall arrive if we leave its determination to the market. The so-called 'maximum' which we thus reach naturally cannot be defined as a sum of particular things, but only in terms of the chances it offers to unknown people to get as large a real equivalent as possible for their relative shares, which will be determined partly by accident. Simply because its results cannot be assessed in terms of a single scale of values, as is the case in an economy proper, it is very misleading to assess the results of a catallaxy as if it were an economy.

IV

Misinterpretation of the market order as an economy that can and ought to satisfy different needs in a certain order of priority, shows itself particularly in the efforts of policy to correct prices and incomes in the interest of what is called 'social justice'. Whatever meaning social philosophers have attached to this concept, in the practice of economic policy it has almost always meant one thing, and one thing only: the protection of certain groups against the necessity to descend from the absolute or relative material position which they have for some time enjoyed. Yet this is not a principle on which it is possible to act generally without destroying the foundations of the market order. Not only continuous increase, but in certain circumstances even mere maintenance of the existing level of incomes, depends on adaptation to unforeseen changes. This necessarily involves the relative, and perhaps even the absolute, share of some having to be reduced, although they are in no way responsible for the reduction.

The point to keep constantly in mind is that *all* economic adjustment is made necessary by unforeseen changes; and the whole reason for employing the price mechanism is to tell individuals that what they are doing, or can do, has for some reason for which they are not responsible become less or more demanded. Adaptation of the whole order of activities to changed circumstances rests on the remuneration derived from different activities being changed, without regard to the merits or faults of those affected.

The term 'incentives' is often used in this connection with somewhat misleading connotations, as if the main problem were to induce people to exert themselves

Competition as a discovery procedure **191**

sufficiently. However, the chief guidance which prices offer is not so much how to act, but *what to do*. In a continuously changing world even mere maintenance of a given level of wealth requires incessant changes in the direction of the efforts of some, which will be brought about only if the remuneration of some activities is increased and that of others decreased. With these adjustments, which under relatively stable conditions are needed merely to maintain the income stream, no 'surplus' is available which can be used to compensate those against whom prices turn. Only in a rapidly growing system can we hope to avoid absolute declines in the position of some groups.

Modern economists seem in this connection often to overlook that even the relative stability shown by many of those aggregates which macro-economics treats as data, is itself the result of a micro-economic process, of which changes in relative prices are an essential part. It is only thanks to the market mechanism that someone else is induced to step in and fill the gap caused by the failure of anyone to fulfil the expectations of his partners. Indeed, all those aggregate demand and supply curves with which we like to operate are not really objectively given facts, but results of the process of competition going on all the time. Nor can we hope to learn from statistical information what changes in prices or incomes are necessary in order to bring about adjustments to the inevitable changes.

The chief point, however, is that in a democratic society it would be wholly impossible by commands to bring about changes which are not felt to be just, and the necessity of which could never be clearly demonstrated. Deliberate regulation in such a political system must always aim at securing prices which appear to be just. This means in practice preservation of the traditional structure of incomes and prices. An economic system in which each gets what others think he deserves would necessarily be a highly inefficient system — quite apart from its being also an intolerably oppressive system. Every 'incomes policy' is therefore more likely to prevent than to facilitate those changes in the price and income structures that are required to adapt the system to new circumstances.

It is one of the paradoxes of the present world that the communist countries are probably freer from the incubus of 'social justice', and more willing to let those bear the burden against whom developments turn, than are the 'capitalist' countries. For some Western countries at least the position seems hopeless, precisely because the ideology dominating their politics makes changes impossible that are necessary for the position of the working class to rise sufficiently fast to lead to the disappearance of this ideology.

V

If even in highly developed economic systems competition is important as a process of exploration in which prospectors search for unused opportunities that, when discovered, can also be used by others, this is to an even greater extent true of underdeveloped societies. My first attention has been deliberately given to problems of preserving an efficient order for conditions in which most resources and

192 F. A. Hayek

techniques are generally known, and constant adaptations of activities are made necessary only by inevitably minor changes, in order to maintain a given level of incomes. I will not consider here the undoubted role competition plays in the advance of technological knowledge. But I do want to point out how much more important it must be in countries where the chief task is to discover yet unknown opportunities of a society in which in the past competition has not been active. It may not be altogether absurd, although largely erroneous, to believe that we can foresee and control the structure of society which further technological advance will produce in already highly developed countries. But it is simply fantastic to believe that we can determine in advance the social structure in a country where the chief problem still is to discover what material and human resources are available, or that for such a country we can predict the particular consequences of any measures we may take.

Apart from the fact that there is in such countries so much more to be discovered, there is still another reason why the greatest freedom of competition seems to be even more important there than in more advanced countries. This is that required changes in habits and customs will be brought about only if the few willing and able to experiment with new methods can make it necessary for the many to follow them, and at the same time to show them the way. The required discovery process will be impeded or prevented, if the many are able to keep the few to the traditional ways. Of course, it is one of the chief reasons for the dislike of competition that it not only shows how things can be done more effectively, but also confronts those who depend for their incomes on the market with the alternative of imitating the more successful or losing some or all of their income. Competition produces in this way a kind of impersonal compulsion which makes it necessary for numerous individuals to adjust their way of life in a manner that no deliberate instructions or commands could bring about. Central direction in the service of so-called 'social justice' may be a luxury rich nations can afford, perhaps for a long time, without too great an impairment of their incomes. But it is certainly not a method by which poor countries can accelerate their adaptation to rapidly changing circumstances, on which their growth depends.

Perhaps it deserves mention in this connection that possibilities of growth are likely to be greater the more extensive are a country's yet unused opportunities. Strange though this may seem at first sight, a high rate of growth is more often than not evidence that opportunities have been neglected in the past. Thus, a high rate of growth can sometimes testify to bad policies of the past rather than good policies of the present. Consequently it is unreasonable to expect in already highly developed countries as high a rate of growth as can for some time be achieved in countries where effective utilisation of resources was previously long prevented by legal and institutional obstacles.

From all I have seen of the world the proportion of private persons who are prepared to try new possibilities, if they appear to them to promise better conditions, and if they are not prevented by the pressure of their fellows, is much the same everywhere. The much lamented absence of a spirit of enterprise in many of the new countries is not an unalterable characteristic of the individual inhabitants, but the consequence of restraints which existing customs and institutions place upon them. This is why it would be fatal in such societies for the collective will to be allowed to direct the efforts of individuals, instead of governmental power being confined to protecting individuals against the pressures of society. Such protection for private initiatives and enterprise can only ever be achieved through the institution of private property and the whole aggregate of libertarian institutions of law.

Notes

The University of Chicago Press. © 1978 by F. A. Hayek.

This lecture was originally delivered, without the present section II, to a meeting of the Philadelphia Society at Chicago on 29 March 1968 and later, on 5 July 1968, in German, without the present final section, to the Institut für Weltwirtschaft of the University of Kiel. Only the German version has been published before, first in the series of 'Kieler Vorträge', N.S. 56, Kiel, 1968, and then reprinted in my collected essays entitled *Freiburger Studien*, Tübingen, 1969.

1 Since I wrote this my attention has been drawn to a paper by Leopold von Wiese on 'Die Konkurrenz, vorwiegend in soziologisch-systematischer Betrachtung', *Verhandlungen des 6. Deutschen Soziologentages*, 1929, where, on p. 27, he discusses the 'experimental' nature of competition.
2 Cf. the interesting studies of the late Michael Polanyi in *The Logic of Liberty*, London, 1951, which show how he has been led from the study of scientific method to the study of competition in economic affairs; and see also K. R. Popper, *The Logic of Scientific Discovery*, London, 1959.
3 On the nature of 'pattern prediction' see my essay on 'The theory of complex phenomena' in *Studies in Philosophy, Politics and Economics*, London and Chicago, 1967.
4 Cf. Samuel Johnson in J. Boswell, *Life of Samuel Johnson*, L. F. Powell's revision of G. B. Hill's edition, Oxford, 1934, vol. II, p. 365 (18 April 1775): 'Knowledge is of two kinds. We know a subject ourselves, or we know where we can find information about it'.
5 For a fuller discussion see now my *Law, Legislation and Liberty*, vol. II, *The Mirage of Social Justice*, London and Chicago, 1976, pp. 107–20.
6 G. Hardin, *Nature and Man's Fate* (1951), Mentor ed. 1961, p. 54.
7 Adam Smith, *The Theory of Moral Sentiments*, London, 1759, part VI, chapter 2, penultimate paragraph, and part VII, section II, chapter 1.

10

THE TRANSACTIONAL SELF

J. Bruner

If you engage for long in the study of how human beings relate to one another, especially through the use of language, you are bound to be struck by the importance of "transactions." This is not an easy word to define. I want to signify those dealings which are premised on a mutual sharing of assumptions and beliefs about how the world is, how mind works, what we are up to, and how communication should proceed. It is an idea captured to some extent by Paul Grice's maxims about how to proceed in conversation, by Deirdre Wilson and Dan Sperber's notion that we always assume that what others have said must make *some* sense, by Hilary Putnam's recognition that we usually assign the right level of ignorance or cleverness to our interlocutors. Beyond these specifics, there remains a shady but important area of sharing—Colwyn Trevarthen calls it "intersubjectivity"—that makes the philosopher's query about how we know Other Minds seem more practical than the philosopher ever intended it to be.

One knows intuitively as a psychologist (or simply as a human being) that the easy access we have into each other's minds, not so much in the particulars of what we are thinking but in general about what minds are like, cannot be explained away by invoking singular concepts like "empathy." Nor does it seem sufficient to perform a miracle of phenomenology, as did the German philosopher Max Scheler, and subdivide *Einfuhlung* into a half-dozen "feelable" classes. Or to take the route of nineteenth-century psychologists and elevate "sympathy" to the status of an instinct. More typically, the contemporary student of mind will try to unravel the mystery by exploring how we develop this sense of what other minds are about, or by examining its pathologies, as in autistic children and in young schizophrenics. Or he will try to unravel the details of interpersonal knowledge among adults by conducting experiments on facets of this knowledge, as have Fritz Heider and his students. Or, yet another alternative, he will dismiss the issue of intersubjective knowledge as "nothing but" projection, for whatever smug satisfaction that may give him.

The transactional self **195**

I first became caught up in this issue through work I did in collaboration with Renato Tagiuri, and we ended up writing a chapter on "person perception" in one of the standard Handbooks-treating it as a perceptual problem. Along the way to that chapter we did some of those little experiments which are the craft of psychology. We asked people who were parts of small groups or cliques and who knew each other well two very simple questions: who in the group would they (each individual) most like to spend more time with, and who in the group did they think would most like to spend more time with them. I should say at the outset that this is a procedure fraught with statistical problems, particularly if one wants to study the "accuracy" of interpersonal perceptions or to determine whether people's choices are "transparent" to others. But the statistical hurdles can be jumped by using what are called "Monte Carlo procedures," which consist of allocating each person's choices and guesses of others' choices with the aid of a roulette wheel. One can then compare the subjects' real performance with the wheel's allocation of choices and guesses by chance. Yes, on average people are more accurate and more transparent than would be expected by chance—a not very startling finding. They know better than chance who likes them, or to put it inversely, people's preferences are transparent.

But there is something very curious about how people operate in such situations that is not so obvious after all. For one thing, a person who chooses another will (in excess of chance) believe that the other person chooses him back. Or, since the direction of cause is never clear in human affairs, if we *feel* chosen by somebody, we will choose that person in return whether our feeling is correct or not. There is simply a human bias: feeling liked by somebody begets liking him back. To this add the fact that we know better than chance who likes us. Now, is this a matter of "accuracy" or of "vanity"? Are we "victims" of vanity or beneficiaries of our sensitivity? If we bias our Monte Carlo wheels with these same "human" tendencies, they will perform indistinguishably from humans. Does that mean that humans are simply biased robots? Is that a meaningful question, really? It smacks altogether too much of those early Cartesian questions about man as a machine with a human soul added to it, perhaps making its will known through the pineal gland just as we can make "humanness" available to the Monte Carlo robot by rigging the wheel.

The model we had been using seemed wrong—or at least it led us down dead ends where we did not want to travel. What it told us—and it was not trivial—was that shared sensitivities and biases can produce some strikingly social consequences. For one thing, they produce astonishing stability within groups. People act in accordance with their perceptions and their choices, and they reciprocate accordingly. We created a little discussion group of seven members, to discuss "psychology and life" (they were all undergraduates). And we administered our test four or five times over a term. Some interesting things happened to the dyads or pairs that composed that group. Certain patterns virtually disappeared over time or occurred eventually at levels *below* chance. Instances of pairs in which each chose the other with neither feeling chosen in return were gone by the end of the term. So too were cases where both felt chosen by the other but did not choose in return.

196 J. Bruner

The transactional process seemed to intensify over time. We left it at that and went off to pursue other matters.

But the problem was to return, and it did so, more than a decade later, when I began a series of studies on growth in human infancy and particularly on the development of human language and its precursors. My first brush with it was in studying the development of exchange games in infancy, when I was struck with how quickly and easily a child, once having mastered the manipulation of objects, could enter into "handing back and forth," handing objects around a circle, exchanging objects for each other. The competence seemed there, as if *ab ovum*; the performance was what needed some smoothing out. Very young children had something clearly in mind about what others had in mind, and organized their actions accordingly. I thought of it as the child achieving mastery of one of the precursors of language use: a sense of mutuality in action.

So too in a second study (which I shall tell about more fully later) in which we were interested in how the child came to manage his attention jointly with others —a prerequisite of linguistic reference. We found that by their first birthday children are already adept at following another's line of regard to search for an object that is engaging their partner's attention. That surely requires a sophisticated conception of a partner's mind.

Yet why should we have been surprised? The child has such conceptions "in mind" in approaching language. Children show virtually no difficulty in mastering pronouns and certain demonstratives, for example, even though these constitute that confusing class of referring expressions called deictic shifters. A deictic shifter is an expression whose meaning one can grasp only through appreciating the interpersonal context in which it is uttered and by whom it is uttered. That is to say, when I use the pronoun *I*, it means me; when my partner uses it, it refers to him. A spatial shifter pair like *here* and *there* poses the same problem: *here* used by me is close to me; *here* used by you is close to you. The shifter ought to be hard to solve for the child, and yet it isn't.

It *ought* to be, that is, if the child were as "self-centered" as he is initially made out to be by current theories of child development. For our current theories (with notable exceptions carried over from the past, like the views of George Herbert Mead) picture the child as starting his career in infancy and continuing it for some years after, locked in his own perspective, unable to take the perspective of another with whom he is in interaction. And, indeed, there are even experimental "demonstrations" to prove the point. But *what* point? Surely not that we can take any perspective of anybody in any plight at any time. We would not have been so slow in achieving the Copernican revolution if that were the case, or in understanding that to the Indians North America must have seemed like *their* homeland. To show that a child (or an adult) cannot, for example, figure out what three mountains he sees before him might look like to somebody viewing them from their "back" sides (to take as our whipping boy one of the classic experiments demonstrating egocentrism), does not mean he cannot take another's perspective into account *in general*.

The transactional self **197**

It is curious, in view of the kinds of considerations I have raised, that psychological theories of development have pictured the young child as so lacking in the skills of transaction. The prevailing view of initial (and slowly waning) egocentrism is, in certain respects, so grossly, almost incongruously wrong and yet so durable, that it deserves to be looked at with care. Then we can get back to the main issue—what it is that readies the child so early for transacting his life with others on the basis of some workable intuitions about Other Minds and, perhaps, about Human Situations as well. The standard view seems to have four principal tenets:

1 *Egocentric perspective.* That initially young children are incapable of taking the perspective of others, have no conception of Other Minds, and must be brought to sociality or allocentrism through development and learning. In its baldest form, this is the doctrine of initial primary process in terms of which even the first perceptions of the child are said to be little more than hallucinatory wish-fulfillments.
2 *Privacy.* That there is some inherently individualistic Self that develops, determined by the universal nature of man, and that it is beyond culture. In some deep sense, this Self is assumed to be ineffable, private. It is socialized, finally, by such processes as identification and internalization: the outer, public world becoming represented in the inner, private one.
3 *Unmediated conceptualism.* That the child's growing knowledge of the world is achieved principally by direct encounters with that world rather than mediated through vicarious encounters with it in interacting and negotiating with others. This is the doctrine of the child going it alone in mastering his knowledge of the world.
4 *Tripartism.* That cognition, affect, and action are represented by separate processes that, with time and socialization, come to interact with one another. Or the opposite view: that the three stem from a common process and that, with growth, they differentiate into autonomous systems. In either case, cognition is the late bloomer, the weak vessel, and is socially blind.

I do not want to argue that these four premises are "wrong," only that they are arbitrary, partial, and deeply rooted in the morality of our own culture. They are true under certain conditions, false under others, and their "universalization" reflects cultural bias. Their acceptance as universals, moreover, inhibits the development of a workable theory of the nature of social transaction and, indeed, even of the concept of Self. One could argue against the tenet of privacy, for example (inspired by anthropologists), that the distinction between "private self" and "public self" is a function of the culture's conventions about when one talks and negotiates the meanings of events and when one keeps silent, and of the ontological status given to that which is kept silent and that which is made public. Cultures and subcultures differ in this regard; so even do families.

198 J. Bruner

But let us return now to the main point: to the nature of transaction and the "executive processes" necessary to effect it, to those transactional selves hinted at in the title of this chapter. Consider in more detail now what the mastery of language entails with respect to these ideas.

Take *syntax* first. We need not pause long over it. The main point that needs making is that the possession of language gives us rules for generating well-formed utterances, whether they depend on the genome, upon experience, or upon some interaction of the two. Syntax provides a highly abstract system for accomplishing communicative functions that are crucial for regulating joint attention and joint action, for creating topics and commenting upon them in a fashion that segments "reality," for forefronting and imposing perspectives on events, for indicating our stance toward the world to which we refer and toward our interlocutors, for triggering presuppositions, and so on. We may not "know" all these things about our language in any explicit way (unless we happen to have that special form of consciousness which linguists develop), but what we do know from the earliest entry into language is that others can be counted upon to use the same rules of syntax for forming and for comprehending utterances as we use. It is so pervasive a system of calibration that we take it for granted. It entails not just the formulas of Grice, or of Sperber and Wilson, or of Putnam to which I referred, but the assurance that mind is being used by others as we use it. Syntax indeed entails a particular use of mind, and however much one may argue (as Joseph Greenberg in his way and Noam Chomsky in his have argued) that we cannot even conceive of alternative ways of using our minds, that language expresses our natural "organs of thought," it is still the case that the joint and mutual use of language gives us a huge step in the direction of understanding other minds. For it is not simply that we all *have* forms of mental organization that are akin, but that we *express* these forms constantly in our transactions with one another. We can count on constant transactional calibration in language, and we have ways of calling for repairs in one another's utterances to assure such calibration. And when we encounter those who do not share the means for this mutual calibration (as with foreigners), we regress, become suspicious, border on the paranoid, shout.

Language is also our principal means of *referring*. In doing so, it uses cues to the context in which utterances are being made and triggers presuppositions that situate the referent (matters discussed in Chapter 2). Indeed, reference plays upon the shared presuppositions and shared contexts of speakers. It is to the credit of Gareth Evans that he recognized the profound extent to which referring involves the mapping of speakers' subjective spheres on one another. He reminds us, for example, that even a failed effort to refer is not just a failure, but rather that it is an offer, an invitation to another to search possible contexts with us for a possible referent. In this sense, referring to something with the intent of directing another's attention to it requires even at its simplest some form of negotiation, some hermeneutic process. And it becomes the more so when the reference is not present or accessible to pointing or to some other ostensive maneuver. Achieving joint reference is achieving a kind of solidarity with somebody. The achievement by the child of such

The transactional self **199**

"intersubjective" reference comes so easily, so naturally, that it raises puzzling questions.

The evidence from early pointing (usually achieved before the first birthday) and from the infant's early following of another's line of regard suggests that there must be something preadapted and prelinguistic that aids us in achieving initial linguistic reference. I do not doubt the importance of such a biological assist. But this early assist is so paltry in comparison to the finished achievement of reference that it cannot be the whole of the story. The capacity of the average speaker to handle the subtleties of ellipsis, of anaphora—to know that, in the locution "Yesterday I saw *a* bird; *the* bird was singing," the shift from indefinite to definite article signals that the same bird is referred to in the second phrase as in the first—is too far removed from its prelinguistic beginnings to be accounted for by them. One has to conclude that the subtle and systematic basis upon which linguistic reference itself rests must reflect a natural organization of mind, one into which we *grow* through experience rather than one we achieve by learning.

If this is the case—and I find it difficult to resist—then human beings must come equipped with the means not only to calibrate the workings of their minds against one another, but to calibrate the worlds in which they live through the subtle means of reference. In effect, then, this is the means whereby we know Other Minds and their possible worlds.

The relation of words or expressions to other words or expressions constitutes, along with reference, the sphere of *meaning*. Because reference rarely achieves the abstract punctiliousness of a "singular, definite referring expression," is always subject to *polysemy*, and because there is no limit on the ways in which expressions can relate to one another, meaning is always underdetermined, ambiguous. To "make sense" in language, as David Olson argued persuasively some years ago, always requires an act of "disambiguation." Young children are not expert at such disambiguation, but procedures for effecting it are there from the earliest speech. They negotiate—even at two years of age—not only what is being referred to by an expression, but what other expressions the present one relates to. And children's early monologues, reported by Ruth Weir a generation ago and more recently by Katherine Nelson and her colleagues in the New York Language Acquisition Group, all point to a drive to explore and to overcome ambiguities in the meaning of utterances. The young child seems not only to negotiate sense in his exchanges with others but to carry the problems raised by such ambiguities back into the privacy of his own monologues. The realm of meaning, curiously, is not one in which we ever live with total comfort. Perhaps it is this discomfort that drives us finally to construct those larger-scale products of language—drama and science and the disciplines of understanding—where we can construct new forms in which to transact and negotiate this effort after meaning.

To create hypothetical entities and fictions, whether in science or in narrative, requires yet another power of language that, again, is early within reach of the language user. This is the capacity of language to create and stipulate realities of its own, its *constitutiveness*. We create realities by warning, by encouraging, by dubbing

200 J. Bruner

with titles, by naming, and by the manner in which words invite us to create "realities" in the world to correspond with them. Constitutiveness gives an externality and an apparent ontological status to the concepts words embody: for example, the law, gross national product, antimatter, the Renaissance. It is what makes us construct proscenia in our theater and still be tempted to stone the villain. At our most unguarded, we are all Naive Realists who believe not only that *we* know what is "out there," but also that it is out there for *others* as well. Carol Feldman calls it "ontic dumping," converting our mental processes into products and endowing them with a reality in some world. The private is rendered public. And thereby, once again, we locate ourselves in a world of shared reality. The constitutiveness of language, as more than one anthropologist has insisted, creates and transmits culture and locates our place in it—a matter to which I turn next.

Language, as we know, consists not only of a locution, of what is actually said, but of an illocutionary force—a conventional means of indicating what is intended by making that locution under those circumstances. These together constitute the speech acts of ordinary language, and they might be considered as much the business of the anthropologist as of the linguist. I will revisit the psychological implications of speech acts in a later chapter; here we need only take them for granted as a phenomenon. As a phenomenon, they imply that learning how to use language involves both learning the culture and learning how to express intentions in congruence with the culture. This brings us to the question of how we may conceive of "culture" and in what way it provides means not only for transacting with others but for conceiving of ourselves in such transactions.

It would not be an exaggeration to say that in the last decade there has been a revolution in the definition of human culture. It takes the form of a move away from the strict structuralism that held that culture was a set of interconnected rules from which people derive particular behaviors to fit particular situations, to the idea of culture as implicit and only semiconnected knowledge of the world from which, through negotiation, people arrive at satisfactory ways of acting in given contexts. The anthropologist Clifford Geertz likens the process of acting in a culture to that of interpreting an ambiguous text. Let me quote a paragraph written by one of his students, Michelle Rosaldo:

> In anthropology, I would suggest, the key development ... is a view of culture ... wherein meaning is proclaimed a public fact—or better yet, where culture and meaning are described as processes of interpretive apprehension by individuals of symbolic models. These models are both "of" the world in which we live and "for" the organization of activities, responses, perceptions and experiences by the conscious self. For present purposes, what is important here is first of all the claim that meaning is a fact of public life, and secondly, that cultural patterns—social facts—provide the template for all human action, growth and understanding. Culture so construed is, furthermore, a matter less of artifacts and propositions, rules, schematic programs, or beliefs,

than of associative chains and images that tell what can be reasonably linked up with what; we come to know it through collective stories that suggest the nature of coherence, probability and sense within the actor's world. Culture is, then, always richer than the traits recorded in the ethnographer's accounts because its truth resides not in explicit formulations of the rituals of daily life but in the daily practices of persons who in acting take for granted an account of who they are and how to understand their fellows' moves.

I have already discussed the linguistics, so to speak, by which this is accomplished. What of the "cultural" side of the picture? *How* we decide to enter into transaction with others linguistically and by what exchanges, how *much* we wish to do so (in contrast to remaining "detached" or "silent" or otherwise "private"), will shape our sense of what constitutes culturally acceptable transactions and our definition of our own scope and possibility in doing so—our "selfhood." As Rosaldo reminds us (using the Ilongot people as contrast) our Western concern with "individuals and with their inner hidden selves may well be features of *our* world of action and belief—itself to be explained and not assumed as the foundation of cross-cultural study." Indeed, the images and stories that we provide for guidance to speakers with respect to when they may speak and what they may say in what situations may indeed be a first constraint on the nature of selfhood. It may be one of the many reasons why anthropologists (in contrast to psychologists) have always been attentive not only to the content but to the form of the myths and stories they encounter among their "subjects."

For stories define the range of canonical characters, the settings in which they operate, the actions that are permissible and comprehensible. And thereby they provide, so to speak, a map of possible roles and of possible worlds in which action, thought, and self-definition are permissible (or desirable). As we enter more actively into the life of a culture around us, as Victor Turner remarks, we come increasingly to play parts defined by the "dramas" of that culture. Indeed, in time the young entrant into the culture comes to define his own intentions and even his own history in terms of the characteristic cultural dramas in which he plays a part —at first family dramas, but later the ones that shape the expanding circle of his activities outside the family.

It can never be the case that there is a "self" independent of one's cultural-historical existence. It is usually claimed, in classical philosophical texts at least, that Self rises out of our capacity to reflect upon our own acts, by the operation of "metacognition." But what is strikingly plain in the promising research on metacognition that has appeared in recent years—work by Ann Brown, by J. R. Hayes, by David Perkins, and others—is that metacognitive activity (self-monitoring and self-correction) is very unevenly distributed, varies according to cultural background, and, perhaps most important, can be taught successfully as a skill. Indeed, the available research on "linguistic repairs," self-corrections in utterances either to bring one's utterances into line with one's intent or to make them comprehensible to an interlocutor, suggests that an *Anlage* of metacognition is present as early as the eighteenth month of life. How much and in what form it develops will, it seems reasonable to suppose, depend upon the demands of the culture in which one lives —represented by particular others one encounters and by some notion of a "generalized other" that one forms (in the manner so brilliantly suggested by writers as various and as separated in time as St. Augustine in the *Confessions* and George Herbert Mead in *Mind, Self, and Society*).

It would seem a warranted conclusion, then, that our "smooth" and easy transactions and the regulatory self that executes them, starting as a biological readiness based on a primitive appreciation of other minds, is then reinforced and enriched by the calibrational powers that language bestows, is given a larger-scale map on which to operate by the culture in which transactions take place, and ends by being a reflection of the history of that culture as that history is contained in the culture's images, narratives, and tool kit.

In the light of the foregoing, we would do well to reexamine the tenets of the classical position on egocentrism with which we began:

Egocentric perspective. Michael Scaife and I discovered, as I mentioned in passing, that by the end of the first year of life, normal children habitually follow another's line of regard to see what the other is looking at, and when they can find no target out there, they turn back to the looker to check gaze direction again. At that age the children can perform none of the classic Piagetian tasks indicating that they have passed beyond egocentrism. This finding led me to take very seriously the proposals of both Katherine Nelson and Margaret Donaldson that when the child understands the event structure in which he is operating he is not that different from an adult. He simply does not have as grand a collection of scripts and scenarios and event schemas as adults do. The child's mastery of deictic shifters suggests, moreover, that egocentrism per se is not the problem. It is when the child fails to grasp the structure of events that he adopts an egocentric framework. The problem is not with competence but with performance. It is not that the child does not have the capacity to take another's perspective, but rather that he cannot do so without understanding the situation in which he is operating.

Privacy. The notion of the "private" Self free of cultural definition is part of the stance inherent in our Western conception of Self. The nature of the "untold" and the "untellable" and our attitudes toward them are deeply cultural in character. Private impulses are defined as such by the culture. Obviously, the divide between "private" and "public" meanings prescribed by a given culture makes a great difference in the way people in that culture view such meanings. In our culture, for example, a good deal of heavy emotional weather is made out of the distinction, and there is (at least among the educated) a push to get the private into the public domain —whether through confession or psychoanalysis. To revert to Rosaldo's Ilongot, the pressures are quite different for them, and so is the divide. How a culture defines privacy plays an enormous part in what people feel private *about* and when and how —as we have already seen in Amélie Rorty's account of personhood in Chapter 2.

Unmediated conceptualism. In the main, we do not construct a reality solely on the basis of private encounters with exemplars of natural states. Most of our approaches

The transactional self **203**

to the world are mediated through negotiation with others. It is this truth that gives such extraordinary force to Vygotsky's theory of the zone of proximal development, to which I shall turn in the next chapter. We know far too little about learning from vicarious experience, from interaction, from media, even from tutors.

Tripartism. I hope that all of the foregoing underlines the poverty that is bred by making too sharp a distinction between cognition, affect, and action, with cognition as the late-blooming stepsister. David Krech used to urge that people "perfink" —perceive, feel, and think at once. They also *act* within the constraints of what they "perfink." We *can* abstract each of these functions from the unified whole, but if we do so too rigidly we lose sight of the fact that it is one of the functions of a culture to keep them related and together in those images, stories, and the like by which our experience is given coherence and cultural relevance. The scripts and stories and "loose associative chains" that Rosaldo spoke of are templates for canonical ways of fusing the three into self-directing patterns—ways of being a Self in transaction. In Chapter 8, on the relation of thought and emotion, I shall take up this matter in more detail.

Finally, I want briefly to relate what I have said in this chapter to the discussions of narrative in the chapters of Part One. Insofar as we account for our own actions and for the human events that occur around us principally in terms of narrative, story, drama, it is conceivable that our sensitivity to narrative provides the major link between our own sense of self and our sense of others in the social world around us. The common coin may be provided by the forms of narrative that the culture offers us. Again, life could be said to imitate art.

11

THE SPANDRELS OF SAN MARCO AND THE PANGLOSSIAN PARADIGM

A critique of the adaptationist programme

S. J. Gould and R. C. Lewontin

MUSEUM OF COMPARATIVE ZOOLOGY, HARVARD UNIVERSITY, CAMBRIDGE, MASSACHUSETTS 02138, U.S.A.

An adaptationist programme has dominated evolutionary thought in England and the United States during the past 40 years. It is based on faith in the power of natural selection as an optimizing agent. It proceeds by breaking an organism into unitary 'traits' and proposing an adaptive story for each considered separately. Trade-offs among competing selective demands exert the only brake upon perfection; non-optimality is thereby rendered as a result of adaptation as well. We criticize this approach and attempt to reassert a competing notion (long popular in continental Europe) that organisms must be analysed as integrated wholes, with *Baupläne* so constrained by phyletic heritage, pathways of development and general architecture that the constraints themselves become more interesting and more important in delimiting pathways of change than the selective force that may mediate change when it occurs. We fault the adaptationist programme for its failure to distinguish current utility from reasons for origin (male tyrannosaurs may have used their diminutive front legs to titillate female partners, but this will not explain *why* they got so small); for its unwillingness to consider alternatives to adaptive stories; for its reliance upon plausibility alone as a criterion for accepting speculative tales; and for its failure to consider adequately such competing themes as random fixation of alleles, production of non-adaptive structures by developmental correlation with selected features (allometry, pleiotropy, material compensation, mechanically forced correlation), the separability of adaptation and selection, multiple adaptive peaks, and current utility as an epiphenomenon of non-adaptive structures. We support Darwin's own pluralistic approach to identifying the agents of evolutionary change.

Introduction

The great central dome of St Mark's Cathedral in Venice presents in its mosaic design a detailed iconography expressing the mainstays of Christian faith. Three circles of figures radiate out from a central image of Christ: angels, disciples, and virtues. Each circle is divided into quadrants, even though the dome itself is radially symmetrical in structure. Each quadrant meets one of the four spandrels in the arches below the dome. Spandrels – the tapering triangular spaces formed by the intersection of two rounded arches at right angles (Figure 11.1) – are necessary architectural by-products of mounting a dome on rounded arches. Each spandrel contains a design admirably fitted into its tapering space. An evangelist sits in the upper part flanked by the heavenly cities. Below, a man representing one of the four Biblical rivers (Tigris, Euphrates, Indus and Nile) pours water from a pitcher into the narrowing space below his feet.

The design is so elaborate, harmonious and purposeful that we are tempted to view it as the starting point of any analysis, as the cause in some sense of the surrounding architecture. But this would invert the proper path of analysis. The system begins with an architectural constraint: the necessary four spandrels and their tapering triangular form. They provide a space in which the mosaicists worked; they set the quadripartite symmetry of the dome above.

FIGURE 11.1 One of the four spandrels of St Mark's; seated evangelist above, personification of river below.

Such architectural constraints abound and we find them easy to understand because we do not impose our biological biases upon them. Every fan vaulted ceiling must have a series of open spaces along the mid-line of the vault, where the sides of the fans intersect between the pillars (Figure 11.2). Since the spaces must exist, they are often used for ingenious ornamental effect. In King's College Chapel in Cambridge, for example, the spaces contain bosses alternately embellished with the Tudor rose and portcullis. In a sense, this design represents an 'adaptation', but the architectural constraint is clearly primary. The spaces arise as a necessary by-product of fan vaulting; their appropriate use is a secondary effect. Anyone who tried to argue that the structure exists because the alternation of rose and portcullis makes so much sense in a Tudor chapel would be inviting the same ridicule that Voltaire heaped on Dr Pangloss: 'Things cannot be other than they are ... Everything is made for the best purpose. Our noses were made to carry spectacles, so we have spectacles. Legs were clearly intended for breeches, and we wear them.' Yet evolutionary biologists, in their tendency to focus exclusively on immediate adaptation to local conditions, do tend to ignore architectural constraints and perform just such an inversion of explanation.

FIGURE 11.2 The ceiling of King's College Chapel.

As a closer example, recently featured in some important biological literature on adaptation, anthropologist Michael Hamer has proposed (1977) that Aztec human sacrifice arose as a solution to chronic shortage of meat (limbs of victims were often consumed, but only by people of high status). E. O. Wilson (1978) has used this explanation as a primary illustration of an adaptive, genetic pre-disposition for carnivory in humans. Hamer and Wilson ask us to view an elaborate social system and a complex set of explicit justifications involving myth, symbol, and tradition as mere epiphenomena generated by the Aztecs as an unconscious rationalization masking the 'real' reason for it all: need for protein. But Sahlins (1978) has argued that human sacrifice represented just one part of an elaborate cultural fabric that, in its entirety, not only represented the material expression of Aztec cosmology, but also performed such utilitarian functions as the maintenance of social ranks and systems of tribute among cities.

We strongly suspect that Aztec cannibalism was an 'adaptation' much like evangelists and rivers in spandrels, or ornamented bosses in ceiling spaces: a secondary epiphenomenon representing a fruitful use of available parts, not a cause of the entire system. To put it crudely: a system developed for other reasons generated an increasing number of fresh bodies; use might as well be made of them. Why invert the whole system in such a curious fashion and view an entire culture as the epiphenomenon of an unusual way to beef up the meat supply. Spandrels do not exist to house the evangelists. (Moreover, as Sahlins argues, it is not even clear that human sacrifice was an adaptation at all. Human cultural practices can be orthogenetic and drive towards extinction in ways that Darwinian processes, based on genetic selection, cannot. Since each new monarch had to outdo his predecessor in even more elaborate and copious sacrifice, the practice was beginning to stretch resources to the breaking point. It would not have been the first time that a human culture did itself in. And, finally, many experts doubt Harner's premise in the first place (Ortiz de Montellano 1978). They argue that other sources of protein were not in short supply, and that a practice awarding meat only to privileged people who had enough anyway, and who used bodies so inefficiently (only the limbs were consumed, and partially at that) represents a mighty poor way to run a butchery.)

We deliberately chose non-biological examples in a sequence running from remote to more familiar: architecture to anthropology. We did this because the primacy of architectural constraint and the epiphenomenal nature of adaptation are not obscured by our biological prejudices in these examples. But we trust that the message for biologists will not go unheeded: if these had been biological systems, would we not, by force of habit, have regarded the epiphenomenal adaptation as primary and tried to build the whole structural system from it?

The adaptationist programme

We wish to question a deeply engrained habit of thinking among students of evolution. We call it the adaptationist programme, or the Panglossian paradigm. It is

208 S. J. Gould and R. C. Lewontin

rooted in a notion popularized by A. R. Wallace and A. Weismann (but not, as we shall see, by Darwin) towards the end of the nineteenth century: the near omnipotence of natural selection in forging organic design and fashioning the best among possible worlds. This programme regards natural selection as so powerful and the constraints upon it so few that direct production of adaptation through its operation becomes the primary cause of nearly all organic form, function, and behaviour. Constraints upon the pervasive power of natural selection are recognized of course (phyletic inertia primarily among them, although immediate architectural constraints, as discussed in the last section, are rarely acknowledged). But they are usually dimissed as unimportant or else, and more frustratingly, simply acknowledged and then not taken to heart and invoked.

Studies under the adaptationist programme generally proceed in two steps:

1   An organism is atomized into 'traits' and these traits are explained as structures optimally designed by natural selection for their functions. For lack of space, we must omit an extended discussion of the vital issue: 'what is a trait?' Some evolutionists may regard this as a trivial, or merely a semantic problem. It is not. Organisms are integrated entities, not collections of discrete objects. Evolutionists have often been led astray by inappropriate atomization, as D'Arcy Thompson (1942) loved to point out. Our favourite example involves the human chin (Gould 1977, pp. 381–382; Lewontin 1978). If we regard the chin as a 'thing', rather than as a product of interaction between two growth fields (alveolar and mandibular), then we are led to an interpretation of its origin (recapitulatory) exactly opposite to the one now generally favoured (neotenic).

2   After the failure of part-by-part optimization, interaction is acknowledged via the dictum that an organism cannot optimize each part without imposing expenses on others. The notion of 'trade-off' is introduced, and organisms are interpreted as best compromises among competing demands. Thus, interaction among parts is retained completely within the adaptationist programme. Any suboptimality of a part is explained as its contribution to the best possible design for the whole. The notion that suboptimality might represent anything other than the immediate work of natural selection is usually not entertained. As Dr Pangloss said in explaining to Candide why he suffered from venereal disease: 'It is indispensable in this best of worlds. For if Columbus, when visiting the West Indies, had not caught this disease, which poisons the source of generation, which frequently even hinders generation, and is clearly opposed to the great end of Nature, we should have neither chocolate nor cochineal.' The adaptationist programme is truly Panglossian. Our world may not be good in an abstract sense, but it is the very best we could have. Each trait plays its part and must be as it is.

At this point, some evolutionists will protest that we are caricaturing their view of adaptation. After all, do they not admit genetic drift, allometry, and a variety of

San Marco and the Panglossian paradigm **209**

reasons for non–adaptive evolution? They do, to be sure, but we make a different point. In natural history, all possible things happen sometimes; you generally do not support your favoured phenomenon by declaring rivals impossible in theory. Rather, you acknowledge the rival, but circumscribe its domain of action so narrowly that it cannot have any importance in the affairs of nature. Then, you often congratulate yourself for being such an undogmatic and ecumenical chap. We maintain that alternatives to selection for best overall design have generally been relegated to unimportance by this mode of argument. Have we not all heard the catechism about genetic drift: it can only be important in populations so small that they are likely to become extinct before playing any sustained evolutionary role (but see Lande 1976).

The admission of alternatives in principle does not imply their serious consideration in daily practice. We all say that not everything is adaptive; yet, faced with an organism, we tend to break it into parts and tell adaptive stories as if trade-offs among competing, well designed parts were the only constraint upon perfection for each trait. It is an old habit. As Romanes complained about A. R. Wallace in 1900: 'Mr. Wallace does not expressly maintain the abstract impossibility of laws and causes other than those of utility and natural selection … Nevertheless, as he nowhere recognizes any other law or cause …, he practically concludes that, on inductive or empirical grounds, there *is* no such other law or cause to be entertained.'

The adaptationist programme can be traced through common styles of argument. We illustrate just a few; we trust they will be recognized by all:

1   If one adaptive argument fails, try another. Zig-zag commissures of clams and brachiopods, once widely regarded as devices for strengthening the shell, become sieves for restricting particles above a given size (Rudwick 1964). A suite of external structures (horns, antlers, tusks) once viewed as weapons against predators, become symbols of intraspecific competition among males (Davitashvili 1961). The eskimo face, once depicted as 'cold engineered' (Coon *et al.* 1950), becomes an adaptation to generate and withstand large masticatory forces (Shea 1977). We do not attack these newer interpretations; they may all be right. We do wonder, though, whether the failure of one adaptive explanation should always simply inspire a search for another of the same general form, rather than a consideration of alternatives to the proposition that each part is 'for' some specific purpose.

2   If one adaptive argument fails, assume that another must exist; a weaker version of the first argument. Costa & Bisol (1978), for example, hoped to find a correlation between genetic polymorphism and stability of environment in the deep sea, but they failed. They conclude (1978, pp. 132, 133): 'The degree of genetic polymorphism found would seem to indicate absence of correlation with the particular environmental factors which characterize the sampled area. The results suggest that the adaptive strategies of organisms belonging to different phyla are different.'

210 S. J. Gould and R. C. Lewontin

3 In the absence of a good adaptive argument in the first place, attribute failure to imperfect understanding of where an organism lives and what it does. This is again an old argument. Consider Wallace on why all details of colour and form in land snails must be adaptive, even if different animals seem to inhabit the same environment (1899, p. 148): 'The exact proportions of the various species of plants, the numbers of each kind of insect or of bird, the peculiarities of more or less exposure to sunshine or to wind at certain critical epochs, and other slight differences which to us are absolutely immaterial and unrecognizable, may be of the highest significance to these humble creatures, and be quite sufficient to require some slight adjustments of size, form, or colour, which natural selection will bring about.'

4 Emphasize immediate utility and exclude other attributes of form. Fully half the explanatory information accompanying the full-scale Fibreglass *Tyrannosaurus* at Boston's Museum of Science reads: 'Front legs a puzzle: how *Tyrannosaurus* used its tiny front legs is a scientific puzzle; they were too short even to reach the mouth. They may have been used to help the animal rise from a lying position.' (We purposely choose an example based on public impact of science to show how widely habits of the adaptationist programme extend. We are not using glass beasts as straw men; similar arguments and relative emphases, framed in different words, appear regularly in the professional literature.) We don't doubt that *Tyrannosaurus* used its diminutive front legs for something. If they had arisen *de novo*, we would encourage the search for some immediate adaptive reason. But they are, after all, the reduced product of conventionally functional homologues in ancestors (longer limbs of allosaurs, for example). As such, we do not need an explicitly adaptive explanation for the reduction itself. It is likely to be a developmental correlate of allometric fields for relative increase in head and hindlimb size. This non-adaptive hypothesis can be tested by conventional allometric methods (Gould (1974) in general; Lande (1978) on limb reduction) and seems to us both more interesting and fruitful than untestable speculations based on secondary utility in the best of possible worlds. One must not confuse the fact that a structure is used in some way (consider again the spandrels, ceiling spaces and Aztec bodies) with the primary evolutionary reason for its existence and conformation.

Telling stories

> 'All this is a manifestation of the rightness of things, since if there is a volcano at Lisbon it could not be anywhere else. For it is impossible for things not to be where they are, because everything is for the best' (Dr Pangloss on the great Lisbon earthquake of 1755 in which up to 5/1 /200 people lost their lives).

We would not object so strenuously to the adaptationist programme if its invocation, in any particular case, could lead in principle to its rejection for want of evidence. We might still view it as restrictive and object to its status as an argument

San Marco and the Panglossian paradigm **211**

of first choice. But if it could be dismissed after failing some explicit test, then alternatives would get their chance. Unfortunately, a common procedure among evolutionists does not allow such definable rejection for two reasons. First, the rejection of one adaptive story usually leads to its replacement by another, rather than to a suspicion that a different kind of explanation might be required. Since the range of adaptive stories is as wide as our minds are fertile, new stories can always be postulated. And if a story is not immediately available, one can always plead temporary ignorance and trust that it will be forthcoming, as did Costa & Bisol (1978), cited above. Secondly, the criteria for acceptance of a story are so loose that many pass without proper confirmation. Often, evolutionists use *consistency* with natural selection as the sole criterion and consider their work done when they concoct a plausible story. But plausible stories can always be told. The key to historical research lies in devising criteria to identify proper explanations among the substantial set of plausible pathways to any modern result.

We have, for example (Gould 1978) criticized Barash's (1976) work on aggression in mountain bluebirds for this reason. Barash mounted a stuffed male near the nests of two pairs of bluebirds while the male was out foraging. He did this at the same nests on three occasions at 10 day intervals: the first before eggs were laid, the last two afterwards. He then counted aggressive approaches of the returning male towards both the model and the female. At time one, aggression was high towards the model and lower towards females but substantial in both nests. Aggression towards the model declined steadily for times two and three and plummeted to near zero towards females. Barash reasoned that this made evolutionary sense since males would be more sensitive to intruders before eggs were laid than afterwards (when they can have some confidence that their genes are inside). Having devised this plausible story, he considered his work as completed (1976, pp. 1099, 1100):

> 'The results are consistent with the expectations of evolutionary theory. Thus aggression toward an intruding male (the model) would clearly be especially advantageous early in the breeding season, when territories and nests are normally defended ... The initial aggressive response to the mated female is also adaptive in that, given a situation suggesting a high probability of adultery (i.e. the presence of the model near the female) and assuming that replacement females are available, obtaining a new mate would enhance the fitness of males ... The decline in male-female aggressiveness during incubation and fledgling stages could be attributed to the impossibility of being cuckolded after the eggs have been laid ... The results are consistent with an evolutionary interpretation.'

They are indeed consistent, but what about an obvious alternative, dismissed without test by Barash? Male returns at times two and three, approaches the model, tests it a bit, recognizes it as the same phoney he saw before, and doesn't bother his female. Why not at least perform the obvious test for this alternative to

212 S. J. Gould and R. C. Lewontin

a conventional adaptive story: expose a male to the model for the *first* time after the eggs are laid.

Since we criticized Barash's work, Morton *et al.* (1978) repeated it, with some variations (including the introduction of a female model), in the closely related eastern bluebird *Sialia sialis.* 'We hoped to confirm', they wrote, that Barash's conclusions represent 'a widespread evolutionary reality, at least within the genus *Sialia.* Unfortunately, we were unable to do so.' They found no 'anticuckoldry' behaviour at all: males never approached their females aggressively after testing the model at any nesting stage. Instead, females often approached the male model and, in any case, attacked female models more than males attacked male models. 'This violent response resulted in the near destruction of the female model after presentations and its complete demise on the third, as a female flew off with the model's head early in the experiment to lose it for us in the brush' (1978, p. 969). Yet, instead of calling Barash's selected story into question, they merely devise one of their own to render both results in the adaptationist mode. Perhaps, they conjecture, replacement females are scarce in their species and abundant in Barash's. Since Barash's males can replace a potentially 'unfaithful' female, they can afford to be choosy and possessive. Eastern bluebird males are stuck with uncommon mates and had best be respectful. They conclude: 'If we did not support Barash's suggestion that male bluebirds show anticuckoldry adaptations, we suggest that both studies still had "results that are consistent with the ex-pectations of evolutionary theory" (Barash 1976, p. 1099), as we presume any careful study would.' But what good is a theory that cannot fail in careful study (since by 'evolutionary theory', they clearly mean the action of natural selection applied to particular cases, rather than the fact of transmutation itself).

The master's voice re-examined

Since Darwin has attained sainthood (if not divinity) among evolutionary biologists, and since all sides invoke God's allegiance, Darwin has often been depicted as a radical selectionist at heart who invoked other mechanisms only in retreat, and only as a result of his age's own lamented ignorance about the mechanisms of heredity. This view is false. Although Darwin regarded selection as the most important of evolutionary mechanisms (as do we), no argument from opponents angered him more than the common attempt to caricature and trivialize his theory by stating that it relied exclusively upon natural selection. In the last edition of the *Origin*, he wrote (1872, p. 395):

> 'As my conclusions have lately been much misrepresented, and it has been stated that I attribute the modification of species exclusively to natural selection, I may be permitted to remark that in the first edition of this work, and subsequently, I placed in a most conspicuous position – namely at the close of the Introduction – the following words: "I am convinced that natural selection has been the main, but not the exclusive means of modification." This has been of no avail. Great is the power of steady misinterpretation.'

San Marco and the Panglossian paradigm **213**

Romanes, whose once famous essay (1900) on Darwin's pluralism versus the panselectionism of Wallace and Weismann deserves a resurrection, noted of this passage (1900, p. 5): 'In the whole range of Darwin's writings there cannot be found a passage so strongly worded as this: it presents the only note of bitterness in all the thousands of pages which he has published.' Apparently, Romanes did not know the letter Darwin wrote to *Nature* in 1880, in which he castigated Sir Wyville Thomson for caricaturing his theory as panselectionist (1880, p. 32):

> 'I am sorry to find that Sir Wyville Thomson does not understand the principle of natural selection … If he had done so, he could not have written the following sentence in the Introduction to the Voyage of the Challenger: "The character of the abyssal fauna refuses to give the least support to the theory which refers the evolution of species to extreme variation guided only by natural selection." This is a standard of criticism not uncommonly reached by theologians and metaphysicians when they write on scientific subjects, but is something new as coming from a naturalist … Can Sir Wyville Thomson name any one who has said that the evolution of species depends only on natural selection? As far as concerns myself, I believe that no one has brought forward so many observations on the effects of the use and disuse of parts, as I have done in my "Variation of Animals and Plants under Domestication"; and these observations were made for this special object. I have likewise there adduced a considerable body of facts, showing the direct action of external conditions on organisms.'

We do not now regard all of Darwin's subsidiary mechanisms as significant or even valid, though many, including direct modification and correlation of growth, are very important. But we should cherish his consistent attitude of pluralism in attempting to explain Nature's complexity.

A partial typology of alternatives to the adaptationist programme

In Darwin's pluralistic spirit, we present an incomplete hierarchy of alternatives to immediate adaptation for the explanation of form, function, and behaviour.

1   No adaptation and no selection at all. At present, population geneticists are sharply divided on the question of how much genetic polymorphism within populations and how much of the genetic differences between species is, in fact, the result of natural selection as opposed to purely random factors. Populations are finite in size and the isolated populations that form the first step in the speciation process are often founded by a very small number of individuals. As a result of this restriction in population size, frequencies of alleles change by *genetic drift*, a kind of random genetic sampling error. The stochastic process of change in gene frequency by random genetic drift, including the very strong sampling process that goes on when a new isolated population is formed from

214 S. J. Gould and R. C. Lewontin

a few immigrants, has several important consequences. First, populations and species will become genetically differentiated, and even fixed for different alleles at a locus in the complete absence of any selective force at all.

Secondly, alleles can become fixed in a population *in spite of natural selection.* Even if an allele is favoured by natural selection, some proportion of population, depending upon the product of population size N and selection intensity s, will become homozygous for the less fit allele because of genetic drift. If $N s$ is large this random fixation for unfavourable alleles is a rare phenomenon, but if selection coefficients are on the order of the reciprocal of population size ($Ns = 1$) or smaller, fixation for deleterious alleles is common. If many genes are involved in influencing a metric character like shape, metabolism or behaviour, then the intensity of selection on each locus will be small and $N s$ per locus may be small. As a result, many of the loci may be fixed for non–optimal alleles.

Thirdly, new mutations have a small chance of being incorporated into a population, even when selectively favoured. Genetic drift causes the immediate loss of most new mutations after their introduction. With a selection intensity s, a new favourable mutation has a probability of only $2s$ of ever being incorporated. Thus, one cannot claim that, eventually, a new mutation of just the right sort for some adaptive argument will occur and spread. 'Eventually' becomes a very long time if only one in 1000 or one in 1/1 /200 of the 'right' mutations that do occur ever get incorporated in a population.

2   No adaptation and no selection on the part at issue; form of the part is a correlated consequence of selection directed elsewhere. Under this important category, Darwin ranked his 'mysterious' laws of the 'correlation of growth'. Today, we speak of pleiotropy, allometry, 'material compensation' (Rensch 1959, pp. 179–187) and mechanically forced correlations in D'Arcy Thompson's sense (1942; Gould 1971). Here we come face to face with organisms as integrated wholes, fundamentally not decomposable into independent and separately optimized parts.

Although allometric patterns are as subject to selection as static morphology itself (Gould 1966), some regularities in relative growth are probably not under immediate adaptive control. For example, we do not doubt that the famous 0.66 interspecific allometry of brain size in all major vertebrate groups represents a selected 'design criterion,' though its significance remains elusive (Jerison 1973). It is too repeatable across too wide a taxonomic range to represent much else than a series of creatures similarly well designed for their different sizes. But another common allometry, the 0.2 to 0.4 intraspecific scaling among homeothermic adults differing in body size, or among races within a species, probably does not require a selectionist story though many, including one of us, have tried to provide one (Gould 1974). R. Lande (personal communication) has used the experiments of Falconer (1973) to show that selection upon *body size alone* yields a brain–body slope across generations of 0.35 in mice.

More compelling examples abound in the literature on selection for altering the timing of maturation (Gould 1977). At least three times in the evolution of arthropods (mites, flies and beetles), the same complex adaptation has evolved, apparently for rapid turnover of generations in strongly r-selected feeders on superabundant but ephemeral fungal resources: females reproduce as larvae and grow the next generation within their bodies. Offspring eat their mother from inside and emerge from her hollow shell, only to be devoured a few days later by their own progeny. It would be foolish to seek adaptive significance in paedomorphic morphology *per se*; it is primarily a by-product of selection for rapid cycling of generations. In more interesting cases, selection for small size (as in animals of the interstitial fauna) or rapid maturation (dwarf males of many crustaceans) has occurred by progenesis (Gould 1977, pp. 324–336), and descendant adults contain a mixture of ancestral juvenile and adult features. Many biologists have been tempted to find primary adaptive meaning for the mixture, but it probably arises as a by-product of truncated maturation, leaving some features 'behind' in the larval state, while allowing others, more strongly correlated with sexual maturation, to retain the adult configuration of ancestors.

3   The decoupling of selection and adaptation.

    i   Selection without adaptation. Lewontin (1979) has presented the following hypothetical example: 'A mutation which doubles the fecundity of individuals will sweep through a population rapidly. If there has been no change in efficiency of resource utilization, the individuals will leave no more offspring than before, but simply lay twice as many eggs, the excess dying because of resource limitation. In what sense are the individuals or the population as a whole better adapted than before? Indeed, if a predator on immature stages is led to switch to the species now that immatures are more plentiful, the population size may actually decrease as a consequence, yet natural selection at all times will favour individuals with higher fecundity.'

    ii   Adaptation without selection. Many sedentary marine organisms, sponges and corals in particular, are well adapted to the flow régimes in which they live. A wide spectrum of 'good design' may be purely phenotypic in origin, largely induced by the current itself. (We may be sure of this in numerous cases, when genetically identical individuals of a colony assume different shapes in different microhabitats.) Larger patterns of geographic variation are often adaptive and purely phenotypic as well. Sweeney & Vannote (1978), for example, showed that many hemimetabolous aquatic insects reach smaller adult size with reduced fecundity when they grow at temperatures above and below their optima. Coherent, climatically correlated patterns in geographic distribution for these insects – so often taken as *a priori* signs of genetic adaptation – may simply reflect this phenotypic plasticity.

'Adaptation' – the good fit of organisms to their environment – can occur at three hierarchical levels with different causes. It is unfortunate that our language

216 S. J. Gould and R. C. Lewontin

has focused on the common result and called all three phenomena 'adaptation': the differences in process have been obscured and evolutionists have often been misled to extend the Darwinian mode to the other two levels as well. First, we have what physiologists call 'adaptation': the phenotypic plasticity that permits organisms to mould their form to prevailing circumstances during ontogeny. Human 'adaptations' to high altitude fall into this category (while others, like resistance of sickling heterozygotes to malaria, are genetic and Darwinian). Physiological adaptations are not heritable, though the capacity to develop them presumably is. Secondly, we have a 'heritable' form of non-Darwinian adaptation in humans (and, in rudimentary ways, in a few other advanced social species): cultural adaptation (with heritability imposed by learning). Much confused thinking in human sociobiology arises from a failure to distinguish this mode from Darwinian adaptation based on genetic variation. Finally, we have adaptation arising from the conventional Darwinian mechanism of selection upon genetic variation. The mere existence of a good fit between organism and environment is insufficient evidence for inferring the action of natural selection.

4   Adaptation and selection but no selective basis for differences among adaptations. Species of related organisms, or subpopulations within a species, often develop different adaptations as solutions to the same problem. When 'multiple adaptive peaks' are occupied, we usually have no basis for asserting that one solution is better than another. The solution followed in any spot is a result of history; the first steps went in one direction, though others would have led to adequate prosperity as well. Every naturalist has his favourite illustration. In the West Indian land snail *Cerion*, for example, populations living on rocky and windy coasts almost always develop white, thick and relatively squat shells for conventional adaptive reasons. We can identify at least two different developmental pathways to whiteness from the mottling of early whorls in all *Cerion*, two paths to thickened shells and three styles of allometry leading to squat shells. All 12 combinations can be identified in Bahamian populations, but would it be fruitful to ask why – in the sense of optimal design rather than historical contingency – *Cerion* from eastern Long Island evolved one solution, and *Cerion* from Acklins Island another?

5   Adaptation and selection, but the adaptation is a secondary utilization of parts present for reasons of architecture, development or history. We have already discussed this neglected subject in the first section on spandrels, spaces and cannibalism. If blushing turns out to be an adaptation affected by sexual selection in humans, it will not help us to understand why blood is red. The immediate utility of an organic structure often says nothing at all about the reason for its being.

Another, and unfairly maligned, approach to evolution

In continental Europe, evolutionists have never been much attracted to the Anglo-American penchant for atomizing organisms into parts and trying to explain each as a direct adaptation. Their general alternative exists in both a strong and a weak form. In the strong form, as advocated by such major theorists as Schindewolf (1950), Remane (1971), and Grassé (1977), natural selection under the adaptationist programme can explain superficial modifications of the *Bauplan* that fit structure to environment: why moles are blind, giraffes have long necks, and ducks webbed feet, for example. But the important steps of evolution, the construction of the *Bauplan* itself and the transition between *Baupläne*, must involve some other unknown, and perhaps 'internal', mechanism. We believe that English biologists have been right in rejecting this strong form as close to an appeal to mysticism.

But the argument has a weaker – and paradoxically powerful – form that has not been appreciated, but deserves to be. It also acknowledges conventional selection for superficial modifications of the *Bauplan*. It also denies that the adaptationist programme (atomization plus optimizing selection on parts) can do much to explain *Baupläne* and the transitions between them. But it does not therefore resort to a fundamentally unknown process. It holds instead that the basic body plans of organisms are so integrated and so replete with constraints upon adaptation (categories 2 and 5 of our typology) that conventional styles of selective arguments can explain little of interest about them. It does not deny that change, when it occurs, may be mediated by natural selection, but it holds that constraints restrict possible paths and modes of change so strongly that the constraints themselves become much the most interesting aspect of evolution.

Rupert Riedl, the Austrian zoologist who has tried to develop this thesis for English audiences (1977 and 1975, now being translated into English by R. Jefferies), writes:

> 'The living world happens to be crowded by universal patterns of organization which, most obviously, find no direct explanation through environmental conditions or adaptive radiation, but exist primarily through universal requirements which can only be expected under the systems conditions of complex organization itself ... This is not self-evident, for the whole of the huge and profound thought collected in the field of morphology, from Goethe to Remane, has virtually been cut off from modern biology. It is not taught in most American universities. Even the teachers who could teach it have disappeared.'

Constraints upon evolutionary change may be ordered into at least two categories. All evolutionists are familiar with *phyletic* constraints, as embodied in Gregory's classic distinction (1936) between habitus and heritage. We acknowledge a kind of phyletic inertia in recognizing, for example, that humans are not optimally designed for upright posture because so much of our *Bauplan* evolved for quadrupedal life. We also invoke phyletic constraint in explaining why no molluscs fly in air and no insects are as large as elephants.

Developmental constraints, a subcategory of phyletic restrictions, may hold the most powerful rein of all over possible evolutionary pathways. In complex

218 S. J. Gould and R. C. Lewontin

organisms, early stages of ontogeny are remarkably refractory to evolutionary change, presumably because the differentiation of organ systems and their integration into a functioning body is such a delicate process, so easily derailed by early errors with accumulating effects. Von Baer's fundamental embryological laws (1828) represent little more than a recognition that early stages are both highly conservative and strongly restrictive of later development. Haeckel's biogenetic law, the primary subject of late nineteenth century evolutionary biology, rested upon a misreading of the same data (Gould 1977). If development occurs in integrated packages, and cannot be pulled apart piece by piece in evolution, then the adaptationist programme cannot explain the alteration of developmental programmes underlying nearly all changes of *Bauplan*.

The German palaeontologist A. Seilacher, whose work deserves far more attention than it has received, has emphasized what he calls '*bautechnischer*', or *architectural*, constraints (Seilacher 1970). These arise not from former adaptations retained in a new ecological setting (phyletic constraints as usually understood), but as architectural restrictions that never were adaptations, but rather the necessary consequences of materials and designs selected to build basic *Baupläne*. We devoted the first section of this paper to non-biological examples in this category. Spandrels must exist once a blueprint specifies that a dome shall rest on rounded arches. Architectural constraints can exert a far-ranging influence upon organisms as well. The subject is full of potential insight because it has rarely been acknowledged at all.

In a fascinating example, Seilacher (1972) has shown that the divaricate form of architecture (Figure 11.3) occurs again and again in all groups of molluscs, and in brachiopods as well. This basic form expresses itself in a wide variety of structures: raised ornamental lines (not growth lines because they do not conform to the mantle margin at any time), patterns of coloration, internal structures in the mineralization of calcite, and incised grooves. He does not know what generates this pattern and feels that traditional and nearly exclusive focus on the adaptive value of each manifestation has diverted attention from questions of its genesis in growth and also prevented its recognition as a general phenomenon. It must arise from some characteristic pattern of inhomogeneity in the growing mantle, probably from the generation of interference patterns around regularly spaced centres; simple computer simulations can generate the form in this manner (Waddington & Cowe 1969). The general pattern may not be a direct adaptation at all.

Seilacher then argues that most manifestations of the pattern are probably nonadaptive. His reasons vary, but seem generally sound to us. Some are based on field observations: colour patterns that remain invisible because clams possessing them either live buried in sediments or remain covered with a periostracum so thick that the colours cannot be seen. Others rely on more general principles: presence only in odd and pathological individuals, rarity as a developmental anomaly, excessive variability compared with much reduced variability when the same general structure assumes a form judged functional on engineering grounds.

In a distinct minority of cases, the divaricate pattern becomes functional in each of the four categories (Figure 11.3). Divaricate ribs may act as scoops and anchors

San Marco and the Panglossian paradigm 219

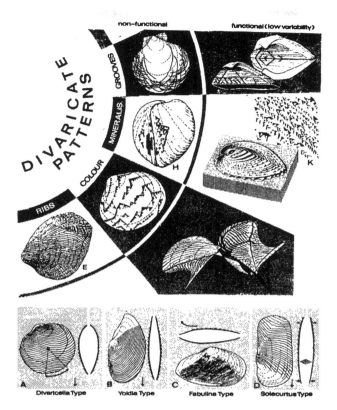

FIGURE 11.3 The range of divaricate patterns in molluscs. E, F, H, and L are non-functional in Seilacher's judgement. A-D are functional ribs (but these are far less common than non-functional ribs of the form E). G is the mimetic *Arca zebra*. K is Corculum. See text for details.

in burrowing (Stanley 1970), but they are not properly arranged for such function in most clams. The colour chevrons are mimetic in one species *(Pteria zebra)* that lives on hydrozoan branches; here the variability is strongly reduced. The mineralization chevrons are probably adaptive in only one remarkable creature, the peculiar bivalve *Corculum cardissa* (in other species, they either appear in odd specimens or only as post-mortem products of shell erosion). This clam is uniquely flattened in an anterio-posterior direction. It lies on the substrate, posterior up. Distributed over its rear end are divaricate triangles of mineralization. They are translucent, while the rest of the shell is opaque. Under these windows dwell endosymbiotic algae!

All previous literature on divaricate structure has focused on its adaptive significance (and failed to find any in most cases). But Seilacher is probably right in representing this case as the spandrels, ceiling holes and sacrificed bodies of our first section. The divaricate pattern is a fundamental architectural constraint. Occasionally, since it is there, it is used to beneficial effect. But we cannot understand the

220 S. J. Gould and R. C. Lewontin

pattern or its evolutionary meaning by viewing these infrequent and secondary adaptations as a reason for the pattern itself.

Galton (1909, p. 257) contrasted the adaptationist programme with a focus on constraints and modes of development by citing a telling anecdote about Herbert Spencer's fingerprints:

> 'Much has been written, but the last word has not been said, on the rationale of these curious papillary ridges; why in one man and in one finger they form whorls and in another loops. I may mention a characteristic anecdote of Herbert Spencer in connection with this. He asked me to show him my Laboratory and to take his prints, which I did. Then I spoke of the failure to discover the origin of these patterns, and how the fingers of unborn children had been dissected to ascertain their earliest stages, and so forth. Spencer remarked that this was beginning in the wrong way; that I ought to consider the purpose the ridges had to fulfil, and to work backwards. Here, he said, it was obvious that the delicate mouths of the sudorific glands required the protection given to them by the ridges on either side of them, and therefrom he elaborated a consistent and ingenious hypothesis at great length. I replied that his arguments were beautiful and deserved to be true, but it happened that the mouths of the ducts did not run in the valleys between the crests, but along the crests of the ridges themselves.'

We feel that the potential rewards of abandoning exclusive focus on the adaptationist programme are very great indeed. We do not offer a council of despair, as adaptationists have charged; for non-adaptive does not mean non-intelligible. We welcome the richness that a pluralistic approach, so akin to Darwin's spirit, can provide. Under the adaptationist programme, the great historic themes of developmental morphology and *Bauplan* were largely abandoned; for if selection can break any correlation and optimize parts separately, then an organism's integration counts for little. Too often, the adaptationist programme gave us an evolutionary biology of parts and genes, but not of organ-isms. It assumed that all transitions could occur step by step and underrated the importance of integrated developmental blocks and pervasive constraints of history and architecture. A pluralistic view could put organisms, with all their recalcitrant, yet intelligible, complexity, back into evolutionary theory.

References

Baer, K. E. von 1828 *Entwicklungsgeschichte der Tiere*. Königsberg: Bornträger.

Barash, D. P. 1976 Male response to apparent female adultery in the mountain bluebird: an evolutionary interpretation. *Am. Nat.* **110**, 1097–1101.

Coon, C. S., Garn, S. M. & Birdsell, J. B. 1950 *Races*. Springfield, Ohio: C. Thomas.

Costa, R. & Bisol, P. M. 1978 Genetic variability in deep-sea organisms. *Biol. Bull.* **155**, 125–133.

Darwin, C. 1872 *The origin of species*. London: John Murray.

Darwin, C. 1880 Sir Wyville Thomson and natural selection. *Nature, Lond.* **23**, 32.

San Marco and the Panglossian paradigm 221

Davitashvili, L. S. 1961 *Teoriya polovogo otbora* [Theory of sexual selection]. Moscow: Akademii Nauk.

Falconer, D. S. 1973 Replicated selection for body weight in mice. *Genet. Res.* **22**, 291–321.

Galton, F. 1909 *Memories of my life*. London: Methuen.

Gould, S. J. 1966 Allometry and size in ontogeny and phylogeny. *Biol. Rev.* **41**, 587–640.

Gould, S. J. 1971 D'Arcy Thompson and the science of form. *New Literary Hist.* **2**(2), 229–258.

Gould, S. J. 1974 Allometry in primates, with emphasis on scaling and the evolution of the brain. In *Approaches to primate paleobiology. Contrib. Primatol.* **5**, 244–292.

Gould, S. J. 1977 *Ontogeny and phylogeny*. Cambridge, Mass.: Belknap Press.

Gould, S. J. 1978 Sociobiology: the art of storytelling. *New Scient.* **80**, 530–533.

Grassé, P.-P. 1977 *Evolution of living organisms*. New York: Academic Press.

Gregory, W. K. 1936 Habitus factors in the skeleton of fossil and recent mammals. *Proc. Am. phil. Soc.* **76**, 429–444.

Harner, M. 1977 The ecological basis for Aztec sacrifice. *Am. Ethnologist* **4**, 117–135.

Jerison, H. J. 1973 *Evolution of the brain and intelligence*. New York: Academic Press.

Lande, R. 1976 Natural selection and random genetic drift in phenotypic evolution. *Evolution* **30**, 314–334.

Lande, R. 1978 Evolutionary mechanisms of limb loss in tetrapods. *Evolution* **32**, 73–92.

Lewontin, R. C. 1978 Adaptation. *Scient. Am.* **239** (3), 156–169.

Lewontin, R. C. 1979 Sociobiology as an adaptationist program. *Behav. Sci.* (In the press.)

Morton, E. S., Geitgey, M.S. & McGrath, S. 1978 On bluebird 'responses to apparent female adultery'. *Am. Nat.* **112**, 968–971.

Ortiz de Montellano, B. R. 1978 Aztec cannibalism: an ecological necessity? *Science N.Y.* **200**, 611–617.

Remane, A. 1971 *Die Grundlagen des natürlichen Systems der vergleichenden Anatomie und der Phylogenetik*. Königstein-Taunus: Koeltz.

Rensch, B. 1959 *Evolution above the species level*. New York: Columbia University Press.

Riedl, R. 1975 *Die Ordnung des Lebendigen*. Hamburg: Paul Parey.

Riedl, R. 1977 A systems-analytical approach to macro-evolutionary phenomena. *Q. Rev. Biol.* **52**, 351–370.

Romanes, G. J. 1900 The Darwinism of Darwin and of the post-Darwinian schools. In *Darwin, and after Darwin*, vol. 2, new edn. London: Longmans, Green & Co.

Rudwick, M. J. S. 1964 The function of zig-zag deflections in the commissures of fossil brachiopods. *Palaeontology* **7**, 135–171.

Sahlins, M. 1978 Culture as protein and profit. *New York review of books*, 23 Nov., pp. 45–53.

Schindewolf, O. H. 1950 *Grundfragen der Paläontologie*. Stuttgart: Schweizerbart.

Seilacher, A. 1970 Arbeitskonzept zur Konstruktionsmorphologie. *Lethaia* **3**, 393–396.

Seilacher, A. 1972 Divaricate patterns in pelecypod shells. *Lethaia* **5**, 325–343.

Shea, B. T. 1977 Eskimo craniofacial morphology, cold stress and the maxillary sinus. *Am. J. phys. Anthrop.* **47**, 289–300.

Stanley, S. M. 1970 Relation of shell form to life habits in the Bivalvia (Mollusca). *Mem. geol. Soc. Am.* no. 125, 296 pp.

Sweeney, B. W. & Vannote, R. L. 1978 Size variation and the distribution of hemimetabolous aquatic insects: two thermal equilibrium hypotheses. *Science, N.Y.* **200**, 444–446.

Thompson, D. W. 1942 *Growth and form*. New York: Macmillan.

Waddington, C. H. & Cowe, J. R. 1969 Computer simulation of a molluscan pigmentation pattern. *J. theor. Biol.* **25**, 219–225.

Wallace, A. R. 1899 *Darwinism*. London: Macmillan.

Wilson, E. O. 1978 *On human nature*. Cambridge, Mass.: Harvard University Press.

12

THE COASIAN AND KNIGHTIAN THEORIES OF THE FIRM

D. J. Boudreaux

DEPARTMENT OF ECONOMICS, GEORGE MASON UNIVERSITY, FAIRFAX, VA, USA

and

R. G. Holcombe

DEPARTMENT OF ECONOMICS, FLORIDA STATE UNIVERSITY, TALLAHASSEE, FL, USA

The theory of the firm is one of the fundamental building blocks of microeconomic theory, yet there is no single generally accepted theory of the firm that explains what firms do or even why they exist (Archibald, 1987). The lack of a well–defined economic theory of the firm stems from the static equilibrium models that form the foundation of economics. Economists are aware of the fact that the competitive model shows the results of competition but does not depict the competitive process itself. Resources are allocated efficiently in the competitive model because entrepreneurs, prompted by economic profits, have directed them to their highest-valued uses. However, the equilibrium shows the results of entrepreneurship without explaining what entrepreneurs do in the process of resource allocation. Moreover, no role remains for the entrepreneur once equilibrium is attained.

This fact has been recognized by economists for over half a century. Coase (1937) noted that a smoothly functioning price system leaves no room for firms, which in his definition organize resources by command. He argued that, in reality, there are costs to using the price system, and in balancing these costs and benefits it is often cheaper to organize production through administrative direction rather than through the price system. Although Coase sought to explain the nature of firms using Marshall's analytics (Coase, 1937, pp. 331–2), his theory is built solidly on the general-equilibrium framework within which economists conceptualize the competitive model. Recent contributions to the theory of the firm follow in this tradition.

In contrast, Knight's theory of the firm (1921) builds upon his conception of uncertainty and, hence, is not based on the assumptions of general-equilibrium theory. His entrepreneur is a decision maker who pursues profits by making decisions under uncertainty. Whereas the Coasian firm implies a general-equilibrium framework, Knight's firm exists to solve problems that arise only because the real world is never in general equilibrium. The extent of the distinction may not be

The Coasian and Knightian theories of the firm **223**

immediately apparent, because even when working with partial-equilibrium models economists tend to have a Walrasian view of the economy. However, as argued below, the primary function of the Knightian firm is entrepreneurial; it is a necessary component of the creation of markets. In contrast, the Coasian firm emerges only after markets exist; it engages in management rather than true entrepreneurship. Because of the equilibrium nature of neoclassical microeconomics, the contemporary theory of the firm has developed along Coasian rather than Knightian lines.

The paper is organized as follows. First, the general-equilibrium nature of Coase's firm is discussed. Then a brief review of the theory of the firm up to 1970 illustrates how the theory of the firm developed in the Coasian tradition. Next, some more recent contributions to the theory of the firm are analyzed to show that, despite their differences, these theories continue in the general-equilibrium tradition. At this point the Knightian theory of the firm is examined in order to contrast it with the contemporary Coasian theory. After reviewing Coase's criticisms of Knight's theory we contrast the Coasian and Knightian theories on the basis of the distinction between managerial functions and entrepreneurial functions. The conclusion is that by retaining its general-equilibrium foundations the contemporary theory of the firm has slighted the entrepreneurial role that is a fundamental reason for the existence of firms.

The Coasian theory of the firm

Neoclassical price theory models firms as production functions that transform inputs into outputs. Hirshleifer's (1988) statement is typical: 'Firms are the crucial *productive* agents of society, engaged in the conversion of resources into final goods' (p. 160; original emphasis). Machlup (1987, p. 9) endorsed this definition. In his critique of the 'anti-marginalisits' who call for more realism in the theory of the firm, he argued

> that there is widespread confusion regarding the purposes of the 'theory of the firm' as used in traditional price theory ... The model of the firm in that theory is not, as so many writers believe, designed to serve to explain and predict the behavior of real firms; instead, it is designed to explain and predict changes in observed prices (quoted, paid, received) as effects of particular changes in conditions (wage rates, interest rates, import duties, excise taxes, technology, etc.). In the causal connection the firm is only a theoretical link, a mental construct helping to explain how one gets from the cause to the effect.

Machlup noted that the neoclassical firm is a set of simplifying assumptions designed to illuminate the way that *markets* work rather than to understand the function of firms themselves. This is a valid methodological position for explaining as simply as possible the essential features of competitive price determination.[1] However, at the same time, this argument reveals why neoclassical price theory leaves no room for a theory of the firm because firms in this model are an assumption. This methodological position is not adequate for explaining the origin, nature and operation of real-world firms.

Real-world firms allocate the resources under their control by conscious administrative command. However, if the competitive price system is an efficient allocator of resources, why do firms exist? Coase employed the neoclassical framework to answer this question. The entrepreneur's profits are derived from the cost reductions he achieves by taking a transaction out of the market and putting it under his administrative direction. According to Coase, the entrepreneur's task is to notice where the costs of transferring resources from one stage to the next via the price system are high relative to the costs of achieving the same resource-allocation pattern via administrative direction. The entrepreneur internalizes excessive costs hindering the movement of resources from one stage of production to another by bringing them under one roof of common ownership. Coase's entrepreneur is a low-cost substitute for the price mechanism. According to Coase (1937, p. 333), the entrepreneur is 'the person or persons who, in a competitive system, take the place of the price mechanism in the direction of resources'.

Of course, there are costs involved not only with using the price system but also with reliance upon administrative direction. The entrepreneur in Coase's firm balances these costs to make the optimal use of administrative direction in the allocation of resources while leaving the remainder of resource-allocation decisions' to the market. For Coase, these two opposing costs are the relevant factors in the determination of the number of production stages under the control of a single firm. The greater the costs of exchanging resources across lines of ownership, the greater the number of production stages that will be under the control of one firm. Optimal firm size is achieved by equating at the margin the costs of administrative direction with those of using the price system.

Implicit in Coase's description of the firm is a general-equilibrium conception of the economy. Entrepreneurship in Coase's model is a factor of production whose function is to reduce the costs of combining other factors into some *given* final output. The return to entrepreneurship comes from these savings in cost. However, within Coase's framework the goods to be produced and the methods of production are given, and are not determined by the decisions of the entrepreneur.[2] It is the assumption of a given vector of inputs, outputs and prices in the economy that implies a general equilibrium in the Coasian theory of the firm, even though only a subset of the economy (a firm) is being examined. A theory that casts the role of the entrepreneur as minimizing the cost of producing a given output with given inputs can only make sense if it takes place within a general equilibrium, which provides the mechanism for operating the production processes that are assumed to be given and upon which Coase's entrepreneur acts to change, at the margin, the institutional method of allocating resources.

An alternative, which corresponds to Knight's concept of the firm, is to model the entrepreneur as choosing to bring new goods to market or to use new production processes where the outcome is uncertain. The Knightian entrepreneur is

Other contributions to the theory of the firm

It is commonly accepted that little work was done by economists on the theory of the firm between the appearance of Coase's article and the early 1970s. Wiggins (1984, p. 255) notes that 'After Coase's seminal analysis the field lay dormant until Williamson and Alchian and Demsetz renewed interest in the area'. However, even though economists did not have an ongoing research agenda on the economic nature of the firm during this 30-odd-year period, members of the Carnegie school of behavioral economics were, along with organization theorists, building models of firms and other types of organizational hierarchies (Cyert and March, 1959; Cohen and Cyert, 1965; Downs and Monson, 1965; Simon, 1976, 1952–3, 1962). This work skirted the edges of neoclassical economics, but in addition there were notable, if isolated, contributions by neoclassical economists during this period that deserve mention.

Plant (1974), one of Coase's professors at the London School, explored the forces working within business firms to encourage and discourage centralization of control over the production process. Plant's discussion provides more empirical content than Coase regarding the costs of using the price system and the results on firm size, but Plant's underlying theory is remarkably similar to Coase's. According to Plant (p. 186):

> centralization is the means by which the collaborating enterprises secure the advantage of specialized services or equipment which would not otherwise be available to them on such favorable terms, if at all. If the service or merchandise in question is freely bought and sold on any scale in a well-organized market, there will be no need for centralization of firms.

Plant, also like Coase, assumes that firms exist only to lower the cost of producing given outputs with given inputs.

Another notable contribution is Penrose's *The Theory of the Growth of the Firm* (1959) and Chandler's *Strategy and Structure* (1962). The main premise of this theory is that firms exist in a dynamic state of rivalrous competition.[3] Penrose and Chandler both recognized that at any point in time a firm is composed of a certain stock of capital, including human capital, and that its current investments are, in large part, determined by the particular attributes of the firm's existing stock of capital. Over time, the production process benefits from learning by doing, and production that requires deliberate rational mental processes when it is first undertaken eventually becomes routine. The firm then finds itself with an excess of entrepreneurial and managerial capacity, and naturally attempts to put this capacity to productive use by searching for new and different activities.

The Penrose-Chandler theory differs from Coase's at a fundamental level. According to the former, firms are not organizational forms serving only to minimize the costs of attaining 'the' optimal pattern of resource allocation that is selected by a process that is conceptually distinct from the process that determines the existence and size of firms. For Penrose and Chandler these two processes are inseparable. The entrepreneurial decisions that determine what to produce are intimately connected to decisions regarding the size and scope of firms. In contrast to Coase, but similar to Knight, Penrose and Chandler model the entrepreneur as an active participant in the competitive process that selects what products will be available for consumers to evaluate on the market.

Another contribution to the theory of the firm prior to the resurgence of interest in the early 1970s was made by Malmgren (1961). Following Coase in defining the firm as a substitute for the price system, Malmgren argued that the firm exists in order to reduce uncertainty about input prices and supply availability. Like Coase, he takes the final end of the production process as given and fixed, thereby removing from consideration any role the firm might play, apart from reducing the transaction costs of given production processes.

With few exceptions, theorists of the firm have followed Coase in accepting a general-equilibrium framework in which inputs, technical production processes, and outputs are data. In this framework the only role of the firm is to minimize the total costs—which include transaction costs—of producing given outputs.

The contemporary theory of the firm

The contemporary theory of the firm remains in the Coasian tradition because it assumes given technical production processes that use given inputs to produce a given set of outputs. In the influential article by Alchian and Demsetz (1972) the firm emerges because of the transaction costs attendant upon organizing team production processes. In team production processes 'The output is yielded by a team, by definition, and is not a *sum* of separable outputs of each of its members' (p. 779; original emphasis).

The problem with team production is that each member of the team has an incentive to shirk, resulting in inefficient production. If a method could be devised to monitor effectively and efficiently the behavior of each team member the problem would be solved, because the shirkers would then be required to bear the full cost of their shirking. In the Alchian and Demsetz model one team member has the job of monitoring the other members. To assure that the monitor himself does not shirk, he is given title to the residual earnings of the team as well as the right to adjust individually the remuneration of each of the team members. As residual claimant, the monitor is thereby forced by the competitive pressures of the market to ensure that the team output is at its profit-maximizing level.[4]

Alchian and Demsetz begin their article by distancing themselves from Coase's conception of the firm as a substitute for the market. They argue that it is 'delusion' to believe that firms

The Coasian and Knightian theories of the firm **227**

are characterized by the power to settle issues by fiat, by authority, or by disciplinary action superior to that available in the conventional market … The firm [has] no authority, no disciplinary action any different in the slightest degree from ordinary market contracting between two people (p. 777).

Despite this difference with Coase, Alchian and Demetz build their theory on the same implied framework of given inputs and given outputs. Indeed, Alchian and Demsetz are even more explicit than is Coase in modeling entrepreneurship as a factor of production that minimizes the cost of producing a given output. The entrepreneur is the monitor.

In the Alchian and Demsetz model the monitor is not a genuine decision maker but a type of laborer who has a comparative advantage in monitoring the individual contributions to team production processes and in determining the appropriate rewards and punishments. In light of this fact, the use by Alchian and Demsetz of the term 'residual claimant' differs from the typical way in which this term is used. The residual in the Alchian and Demsetz model has nothing to do with uncertainty or entrepreneurial decision making, but is rather a fully determinate return that exists in equilibrium and can be perfectly foreseen in an equilibrated world, just as the return to any other factor of production is implicit in the general-equilibrium framework.

Jensen and Meckling (1976) extended and generalized the Alchian and Demsetz concept of the firm. They realized that the crucial insight of Alchian and Demsetz is not limited to team production processes, but that the conception of the firm as a set of contracts among the owners of various cooperating factors of production is applicable to all firms in market economies. In this 'nexus of contracts' view, firms are considered to be nothing but special types of market arrangements:

> Viewing firms as the nexus of a set of contracting relationships among individuals also serves to make it clear that the personalization of the firm implied by asking questions such as 'what should be the objective function of the firm' or 'does the firm have a social responsibility' is seriously misleading. *The firm is not an individual* … We seldom fall into the trap of characterizing the wheat or stock market as an individual, but we often make this error by thinking about organizations as if they were persons with motivations and intentions (p. 311; original emphasis).

Coase was trying to explain why firms exist as 'islands of conscious power' in a decentralized market economy, but the Jensen and Meckling conception of the firm removes the conscious decision-making aspect from the firm and returns the theory of the firm—at least in this respect—to its pre-Coasian state. The inherent contradiction between characterizing firms as islands of conscious power while remaining in a general-equilibrium framework was recognized, if only implicitly, by Alchian and Demsetz and Jensen and Meckling. However, rather than abandon the general-equilibrium framework these theorists chose instead to abandon the

228 D. J. Boudreaux and R. G. Holcombe

notion of discretionary decision making by entrepreneurs. Thus, the idea of firms as 'islands of conscious power' was jettisoned. In these nexus–of–contracts models, as in Coase's model, the entrepreneur has his task assigned to him by the general-equilibrium system.[5]

Williamson's studies of the allocation of resources via alternative institutional and contractual arrangements have shed much light on the nature of firms and other organizations. Williamson (1975, p. 8) also builds on the foundation laid by Coase and models internal organizations as substitutes for markets: 'Markets and firms are alternative instruments for completing a related set of transactions'. He adds that 'a presumption of market failure is warranted where it is observed that transactions are shifted out of a market and into a firm ...' (1975, p. 20; see also 1985, p. 87).[6] The task at hand, then, is to identify the real–world forces that cause the costs of using the price system to be higher or lower than those of using hierarchical organizations. This task clearly is within the Coasian tradition.

The purpose of this section has been to illustrate that at least one crucial aspect of the contemporary theory of the firm is based squarely on the foundation laid by Coase. The theory of the firm presumes a general-equilibrium setting in which the optimal allocation of resources is implied as a solution to an equilibrium model. Regardless of the specific model of the firm, the entrepreneur takes as given the inputs to be used and the outputs to be produced. The entrepreneurial task is to combine these resources in a way that minimizes total costs of production, including transaction costs. In this general-equilibrium setting the entrepreneur is simply another factor of production that, in equilibrium, receives a market rate of return for his services. This Coasian theory of the firm contrasts with the Knightian theory, in which the entrepreneur makes decisions under uncertainty and in which the decisions of entrepreneurs are crucial in determining what particular goods and services will be available on the market.

The Knightian theory of the firm

Undoubtedly the best–known aspect of Knight's work is his distinction between risk and uncertainty. Each of these terms, when modified by Knight's name, has a precise meaning in today's literature. Knight (1921, p. 51) notes that a perfectly competitive market is characterized by the absence of uncertainty, but that if activities occur repeatedly, statistical calculation can transform the ignorance about particular outcomes into a measure of risk, resulting in a world characterized only by Knightian risk.

In his chapter on epistemology, Knight distinguishes between what he calls the ignorance theory of probability and the doctrine of real probability (pp. 219–20). The ignorance theory holds that the entire universe is completely determined and all future events could be predicted with apodictic certainty if man's knowledge were complete. The doctrine of real probability, on the contrary, holds that the universe is characterized in some measure by genuine indeterminacy. According to the doctrine of real probability there is not even the conceptual possibility of

The Coasian and Knightian theories of the firm   **229**

knowing the future in all of its details. Knight quite clearly accepted the doctrine of real probability (pp. 218–22). Thus, the source of Knightian uncertainty is not simply man's ignorance of the future. Rather, Knightian uncertainty arises mainly because the future is not bound or determined to emerge from the present in a stochastically predictable way. By assuming man to possess perfect knowledge is implicitly to make a further restrictive assumption about the nature of economic processes—i.e. that there is some optimal pattern of resource allocation that is independent of the actual choices made by people.

The distinction here is, on the one hand, outside the traditional bounds of economics,[7] but, on the other, it has implications for the way in which the firm is modeled. The general-equilibrium framework at the base of Coase's theory implicitly accepts the ignorance theory of probability because a general equilibrium today in an economy that produces capital goods must correctly forecast the demand for these goods. Such correct forecasts presume that next period's equilibrium is implied in the vector of equilibrium prices and outputs in the current period. Because the same argument applies for any number of periods into the future, a determinate general equilibrium today embodies within it the information sufficient to determine all future prices and outputs. Such information, in turn, requires a complete array of markets for all economically relevant present and future commodities.[8] If this were not the case there could not be a unique determinate equilibrium in the present, especially when we consider intertemporal transactions such as the production and purchase of capital goods.

It is in this general-equilibrium setting that the contemporary theory of the firm, following Coase, depicts the entrepreneur as an input that reduces the costs of production for the already-determined set of outputs. However, Knight's theory recognizes that human consciousness severs any rigid connection between the present and the future (p. 51). The uncertainty inherent in economic reality causes the future to diverge from the present in ways that cannot be completely anticipated, even actuarially, in the present.

Knight considered consciousness itself to be a product of man's inability to foresee perfectly the details of the future:

> The role of consciousness is to give the organism this 'knowledge' about the future. For all that we can see or for all that science can tell us, we might as well be unconscious automata, but we are not … We *perceive* the world before we react to it, and we react not to what we perceive, but always to what we *infer* … The universal form of conscious behavior is thus action designed to change a future situation inferred from a present one (pp. 201–2; original emphasis).

If man's actions are in the slightest way the product of his own conscious volition, rather than purely the result of the operation of physical or psychological laws, the future is not fully determined by the present. Individuals can and do make choices today that alter the course of future events in ways that are impossible to predict.[9]

For Knight, the goods to be produced are not taken as given. Rather, it is the role of the entrepreneur in Knight's theory to make these decisions regarding what to produce. Although, for simplicity, he assumed the entrepreneur to face no uncertainty as an input buyer, Knight argued that the essence of entrepreneurship stems from the fact that the prices of outputs are uncertain because of changing consumer tastes and because the activities of other suppliers are uncertain (pp. 257, 317–18). These uncertainties do not exist in general equilibrium and, hence, do not apply to firms in a world of general equilibrium.

In the second half of *Risk, Uncertainty, and Profit* Knight emphasizes that the entrepreneurial role mainly involves the exercise of judgment. All of the information-providing aids that an entrepreneur has access to only serve to increase 'the value of the intuitive "judgments" on the basis of which his decisions are finally made ...' (p. 261). Entrepreneurs are distinguished from non-entrepreneurs by the fact that the former have positioned themselves to receive the returns from the exercise of judgment, while the latter have sold to entrepreneurs the right to any changes in the value of their resource services that occur during the production process.

Entrepreneurial judgment is the real-world substitute for the hypothetical perfect foresight exercised by producers in static equilibrium models. If the vectors of future outputs and prices were known, production plans would be made on that basis. However, because of uncertainty, good judgment is the best tool available for forging profitable production plans. The initial act of entrepreneurship is imagining a specific good or service that consumers might be willing to spend a profitable enough portion of their incomes on in competition with what other entrepreneurs might make available and then in acting on this judgment.

In the real world of change there necessarily are unforeseen future consequences of actions taken in the current period. Moreover, these actions themselves are a source of the changes that render the future uncertain. Given the fact that uncertainty is a part of real-world economies, the role of the entrepreneur is to make decisions about resource allocation where there is not enough information, even in a probabilistic sense, to maximize profits in the way described by neoclassical price theory.

If the assumption of given outputs is dropped, new goods do not have markets with existing prices sufficient to provide the necessary information for efficient resource allocation. Market prices can provide information only if markets already exist, but the origination of each market currently in existence was the result of an earlier entrepreneurial decision to produce and market the good. New goods can only be produced on the basis of entrepreneurial judgment, without the guidance of market prices. Uncertainty implies that resource values will change in unpredictable ways as the process of production unwinds. It is therefore necessary for someone to take responsibility for the outcomes of production process. This responsible agent is the Knightian entrepreneur. The entrepreneur's return is the residual (positive or negative) left by the excess of sales revenue over (or under) the costs incurred by the entrepreneur at the time the production decision was made.

The distinguishing characteristic of the Knightian entrepreneur, then, is that he makes decisions under uncertainty about how resources will be allocated. This role

The Coasian and Knightian theories of the firm **231**

is not found in the contemporary theory of the firm[10] in which the general-equilibrium framework—because it takes outputs and demands as given—leaves no room for such decisions to be made.[11]

Coase's criticisms of Knight's theory

Coase (1937) criticized Knight's theory of the firm, concluding that 'nowhere does Professor Knight give a reason why the price mechanism should be superseded' (p. 347). His criticism arises because he examined the world through general-equilibrium lenses and failed to recognize the problem of decision making under uncertainty that formed the crux of the matter in Knight's view.

Coase's criticism of Knight stems from his assumption that 'We can imagine a system where all advice or knowledge was bought as required' (p. 346). An entrepreneur need not speculate, in Coase's view, because all knowledge is available for purchase. He then points out that:

> A large proportion of jobs are done to contract, that is, the contractor is guaranteed a certain sum providing he performs certain acts. But this does not involve any direction … The fact that Professor Knight mentions that 'the second party would not place himself under the direction of the first without such a guarantee' is irrelevant to the problem we are considering (p. 347).

Coase adds in a footnote (n. 12, p. 347) 'that it is possible to have a private enterprise system without the existence of firms'.

These criticisms are valid for a world in which the task of the economic system is given to it in the form of fixed (or at least actuarially predictable) technology, resource constraints, and consumer demands. Entrepreneurship then involves minimizing the cost of producing given outputs with a given production process. However, for Knight, the firm is not superimposed upon an already-existing technical production structure; instead, firms are integral to the formation of this structure. The essential point is that all time-consuming production processes are inescapably bound up with Knightian uncertainty. Coase's criticisms, however, are made from within a framework where Knightian uncertainty does not exist.

Management and entrepreneurship

Although there are fundamental differences between the Coasian and Knightian theories of the firm, the theories are not mutually inconsistent. Both are correct in the sense that they each describe some part of the process by which firms contribute to the pattern of resource allocation. The differences in the theories amount to what is normally thought of as those between management and entrepreneurship. The Coasian firm is run by managers while the Knightian firm is run by entrepreneurs.

While there are differences among the theories of the firm developed by Coase, Alchian and Demsetz, Jensen and Meckling, and Williamson, these theories all consider the role of the firm to be one of minimizing the costs of production by lowering transaction costs, agency costs, shirking, and so forth. This contemporary theory of the firm is about how, due to various imperfections in allocating resources, the firm (as an alternative contracting institution) can lower the cost of producing a given output using a given technique. The theory of the firm evolved in this way because the general-equilibrium framework provides the analytical backdrop for the theory, even though many of the specific models are couched in the language of partial-equilibrium analysis.

However, activities within the firm to hold costs down—such as deciding whether to produce in house or contract out—are those that typically are associated with management. The contemporary theory of the firm is thus an economic theory of the domain of *management*. The activities that Knight attributed to the firm are those of entrepreneurship, where the firm exists in order to facilitate decision making under uncertainty. In Knight's theory, the kinds of goods and services that will be available in the future are a result of the decisions made by entrepreneurs. In Coase's theory, however, the particular array of outputs are not the result of individual decisions at all but are instead taken as given. The Knightian firm is directed by entrepreneurs whose individual decisions help determine the future course of the economy. The Coasian firm is managed by persons who follow market signals that lead them toward a determinate outcome.

To summarize: the Knightian theory of the firm is directed by a theory of entrepreneurship, whereas the Coasian theory embodies a theory of management that contains no room for genuine entrepreneurship.

Conclusion

The static equilibrium models that form the foundation of neoclassical economics have little need for a well-developed theory of the firm. In neoclassical theory firms are production functions that transform inputs into outputs, and if competitive markets can allocate resources efficiently, there appears to be no reason why firms should exist at all. All resource allocation can take place through decentralized markets without the intervention of firms. The role of the theory of the firm is to explain why it is efficient for firms to exist in a market economy.

The Coasian and Knightian theories of the firm deal with the issue from two different vantage points. The Coasian theory takes the inputs and outputs in the firm's production process as given, and models the firm as an organization that acts to minimize the costs of transforming these inputs into outputs. While contemporary theorists have found a number of significant issues on which to differ with Coase, the theory of the firm as it stands today does share with Coase the general-equilibrium framework as a starting point for examining why firms exist. The contemporary theory of the firm rests on the Coasian foundation which models firms as institutions that reduce total production costs of given outputs by reducing transaction costs.

The Coasian and Knightian theories of the firm **233**

In the Knightian theory the outputs to be produced are a product of decision making within the firm. The entrepreneur in Knight's theory is the individual within the firm who makes those decisions. Thus, the decisions made by Knight's entrepreneur are those about variables that are taken as given in the Coasian framework. It is not surprising, then, that Coase, when analyzing Knight's theory, was unable to discover within Knight's work an explanation of why firms exist. Knight's reasons are assumed away in the Coasian framework.

In Coase's model, the role of the firm amounts to what would usually be considered management. The firm's managers act to minimize the costs of production. However, in Knight's model, entrepreneurship is the primary role of the firm, as Knight's entrepreneurs decide what the firm will do rather than have the market dictate the activities of the firm. One could digress into an epistemological discussion about whether entrepreneurs really are able to decide what their firms will do or whether they just have the illusion of discretion. However, such a discussion would serve no purpose, because top-level executives in firms (perhaps as agents for shareholders) *do* spend an extensive amount of time deciding what goods and services to produce.

Knight's neglected theory of the firm provides insight into important activities of firms, and if one is trying to understand the activities of firms it matters little whether the firms act in a discretionary way and, following Alchian's (1950) model of evolution, the inefficient are weeded out, or whether there really is no discretion because everything is determined as the result of some general-equilibrium arrangement of data. The fact remains that firms act as if they can choose their outputs, and a theory of the firm cannot be complete unless it incorporates these entrepreneurial decisions into the firm's activities.

One need not choose between the Knightian and Coasian frameworks for 'the' correct theory of the firm, as they are not mutually inconsistent. Indeed, firms undertake the Coasian managerial functions just as they are formed by the Knightian entrepreneurial ones. However, a fully adequate theory of the firm cannot be developed within a general-equilibrium setting because one of the key characteristics of a firm is decision making under uncertainty—i.e. where vectors of outputs and prices are not known by decision makers. By working implicitly within the framework of general equilibrium, contemporary theorists, following Coase, have assumed away some important aspects of the firm's environment. These aspects are the fundamental building blocks of Knight's theory of the firm, and their explicit recognition promises a richer and more complete theory of enterprise and of the firm.

Acknowledgements

We appreciate the helpful suggestions offered by Pete Boettke, James Buchanan, Roger Garrison, Jack High, David Kaserman, and William Shughart. The remaining errors are our responsibility.

Notes

1 Machlup's argument follows along the lines of Friedman's (1953) discussion of the role of assumptions in economic theory. See Musgrave (1981) for an insightful elaboration of the uses of assumptions in economics.

2 McNulty (1984) offers a similar criticism of the neoclassical theory of the firm.

3 This is the same rivalrous competition that is the driving force in Schumpeter's (1942) process of creative destruction.

4 See Barzel (1987) for a discussion of the characteristics of input owners who have a comparative advantage in being the monitor.

5 Fama (1980) takes tho nexus–of–contracts theory to its logical conclusion by calling for an end to use of the concepts 'ownership' and 'entrepreneurship' in the economic theory of the firm.

6 Arrow (1974, p. 33) shares Williamson's belief that firms arise only because markets fail. As Arrow says, 'organizations are a means of achieving the benefits of collective action in situations where the price system fails'.

7 Proponents of the ignorance theory must argue, for example, that there is no free will, but that all behavior is the result of past influences (genetic and environmental) on the individual. If the ignorance theory were valid, one would have no choice but to read this note because one's current actions are dictated *only* by past events. Likewise, no person's current actions can change the future state of the world. It seems that issues such as free-will versus predestination are outside the set of issues normally thought of as economic.

8 See Radner (1970) for a discussion of why general equilibrium requires a complete array of markets for all commodities. Radner notes that commodities are distinguished from each other not only by their physical, spatial, and temporal characteristics but also by the specific contingent circumstances under which commodities are produced and sold (for example, umbrellas on a rainy day are a different commodity than those on a dry one). Also, our interpretation of Knight squares with LeRoy and Singell's (1987, p. 405) recent conclusion that 'the central idea of Knight's *Risk, Uncertainty, and Profit* is the presence or absence of markets'.

9 The reader may recognize similarities between our 'Knightian' position and the position of Shackle (1972). We agree with Shackle that the future is not fully determined and that economic models built on the presumption of full determination are incomplete. However, we differ in at least three respects. First, we believe that equilibrium (i.e. deterministic) models are useful heuristic tools for illuminating important subject matter. Second, we believe that it is possible to incorporate Knightian uncertainty into economic models. Third, we are not nihilists; we do not believe that the absence of complete determination implies the existence of social chaos which is impossible for man to understand.

10 An exception to this is Kirzner's (1973) theory of the firm, in which entrepreneurs are people who happen upon opportunities for profitable activity and then act on those discoveries. However, Kirzner's entrepreneurial discoveries differ from Knight's purposeful decision making under uncertainty. Also, Buchanan (1980) recognizes uncertainty as inseparably associated with entrepreneurship.

11 One of the tenets of Friedman's (1953) methodological positivism is that the realism of assumptions is not a relevant criterion for judging a model. All theory involves abstraction from unimportant details, but a theory's assumptions define its starting point and circumscribe its tasks, and a theory can never explain more than its starting point allows. To this extent, a theory can bo judged by its assumptions. In the standard theory of the firm there are certain assumptions that cover up facts of reality that are important determinants of the role—and even of the existence—of firms. A general-equilibrium theory of the firm that begins by assuming a complete vector of goods and prices has no chance of detecting the effect of uncertainty on the organization of the production process.

References

A. A. Alchian (1950). Uncertainty, evolution, and economic theory. *Journal of Political Economy* **58**, June, 211–21.

A. A. Alchian and H. Demsetz (1972). Production, information costs, and economic organization. *American Economic Review* **62**, December, 777–95.

G. C. Archibald (1987). Theory of the firm. In *The New Palgrave: A Dictionary of Economics*, Vol. 2, edited by J. Eatwell, M. Milgate and P. Newman, London: Macmillan, pp. 357–63.

K. J. Arrow (1974). *The Limits of Organization*, New York: W. W. Norton.

Y. Barzel (1987). The entrepreneur's reward for self-policing. *Economic Inquiry* **25**, January, 103–16.

J. M. Buchanan (1980). Resource allocation and entrepreneurship. *The Swedish Journal of Political Science* **5**, 285–92.

A. D. Chandler (1962). *Strategy and Structure*, Cambridge, Mass.: MIT Press.

R. H. Coase (1937). The nature of the firm. Reprinted from *Economica*, in *A. E. A. Readings in Price Theory*, edited by G. J. Stigler and K. E. Boulding, Homewood, IL: Richard D. Irwin (1952).

K. J. Cohen and R. M. Cyert (1965). *The Theory of the Firm*, Englewood Cliffs, NJ: Prentice-Hall.

R. M. Cyert and J. G. March (1959). A behavioral theory of organizational objectives. In *Modern Organization Theory*. edited by M. Haire. New York: John Wiley.

E. F. Fama (1980). Agency problems and the theory of the firm. *Journal of Political Economy* **88**, April, 288–307.

M. Friedman (1953). The methodology of positive economics. In *Essays in Positive Economics*, Chicago: University of Chicago Press.

J. Hirshleifer (1988). *Price Theory and Applications*, 4th edn, Englewood Cliffs, NJ: Prentice-Hall.

M. Jensen and W. Meckling (1976). The theory of the firm: managerial behavior, agency costs and ownership structure. *Journal of Financial Economics* **3**, October, 305–60.

I. M. Kirzner (1973). *Competition and Entrepreneurship*, Chicago: University of Chicago Press.

F. H. Knight (1921). *Risk, Uncertainty, and Profit*, Boston: Houghton Mifflin.

S. F. LoRoy and L. D. Singell (1987). Knight on risk and uncertainty. *Journal of Political Economy* **95**, April, 394–406.

F. Machlup (1967). Theories of the firm: marginalist, bohavioral, managerial. *American Economic Review* **57**, March, 1–33.

H. B. Malmgren (1961). Information, expectations and the theory of the firm. *Quarterly Journal of Economics* **75**, Auguat, 399–421.

P. J. McNulty (1984). On the nature and theory of economic organization: the role of the firm reconsidered. *History of Political Economy* **16**, Summer, 233–53.

R.J. Monson and A. Downs (1965). A theory of large managerial firms. *Journal of Political Economy* **73**, June, 221–36.

A. Musgrave (1981). Unreal assumptions in economic theory: the F-twist revisited. *Kyklos* **34**, 377–87.

E. Penrose (1959). *The Theory of the Growth of the Firm*, New York: John Wiley.

A. Plant (1974). Centralise or decentralise. In A. Plant, *Selected Economic Essays and Addresses*, London: Routledge and Kegan Paul.

R. Radner (1970). Problems in the theory of markets under uncertainty. *American Economic Review* **60**, May, 454–60.

236 D. J. Boudreaux and R. G. Holcombe

J. A. Schumpeter (1942). *Capitalism, Socialism, and Democracy*, New York: Harper and Row.

G. L. S. Shackle (1972). *Epistemics and Economics*, Cambridge: Cambridge University Press.

H. A. Simon (1952–3). A comparison of organization theories. *Review of Economic Studies* **20**, 1–9.

H. A. Simon (1962). New developments in the theory of the firm. *American Economic Review* **52**, May, 1–15.

H. A. Simon (1976). *Administrative Behavior*, 3rd edn, New York: The Free Press.

S. N. Wiggins (1984). Organizational structures and economic efficiency: comment. *Journal of Institutional and Theoretical Economics* **140**, 224–6.

O. E. Williamson (1975). *Markets and Hierarchies*, New York: The Free Press.

O. E. Williamson (1985). *The Economic Institutions of Capitalism*, New York: The Free Press.

PART IV

Made

Entrepreneurial outcomes

> The conceptions by the light of which men will judge our own ideas in a thousand years – or perhaps even in 50 years – are beyond our guess. If a library of the year 3000 came into our hands today, we could not understand its contents. How should we consciously determine a future which is, by its very nature, beyond our comprehension? Such presumption reveals only the narrowness of an outlook uninformed by humility.
>
> *M. Polanyi (1951: 199)*

This part of the book is devoted to exploring key institutions that may enable worldmaking and sorting through macroissues related to a made view of entrepreneurial opportunities. Interestingly, the *outcomes* of worldmaking as we have described it through the readings in this book so far already imply intrinsic links between micro and macro issues. For example, a made world is neither *made*, nor *a* world. It is always pluralistic and always unfinished. Yet the micromaking of worlds today rests (arguably) on macropillars made yesterday. Moreover, the micromaking of worlds results in macropillars even when unintended. Through the readings in this part of the book, we examine possible candidates for pillar-hood and how the pillars themselves may be made.

Julian Simon (1995) is the quintessential optimist when it comes to human affairs. Our two selections from *The State of Humanity* bookend his detailed demonstration that people are the ultimate resource for building better worlds – the fount and basin of all value. Ergo, the fostering and enhancing of human freedoms have to be the primary task of any macro–pillar we might choose for the worldmaking enterprise. But which freedoms? And how do the macropillars themselves get made? The next two selections from Sen (1999) and de Soto (2000) address the former question; then Ostrom (2010) offers empirical evidence answering the latter. Gerschenkron (1962) reinforces her findings with evidence from history. And with

238 Made

Gerschenkron, Julian Simon's optimism comes full circle, for he shows how entrepreneurship can make opportunities *even in the absence of* macropillars and often has in history.

Simon: *The State of Humanity* – introduction chapter

At first glance, it is counterintuitive to think of increasing population as the key to building a better world. It appears even more bizarre to think of shortages as the key to prosperity. But that is exactly Simon's point:

> The key theoretical idea again: the growth of population and of income create actual and expected shortages, and hence lead to price run-ups. A price increase represents an opportunity that attracts profit-minded entrepreneurs to seek new ways to satisfy the shortages. Some fail, at a cost to themselves. A few succeed, and the final result is that we end up better off than if the original shortages had never arisen.
>
> *(1995: 27)*

As we pointed out through the readings in Part III, this is far from a complete picture either of innovation or of entrepreneurship. Innovations are driven as much by the supply-side push of scientific and technological progress as by demand-pull generated through shortages. Entrepreneurs too do not wait for shortages to appear before they act. Yet, the general thrust of Simon's analysis is still valid – namely, that the overall rate of increase in value creation from innovation and entrepreneurship has been enough to outstrip value lost due to the increase in population. This holds even in cases such as healthcare, where innovation and entrepreneurship have been directly or indirectly involved in the increase in population in the first place.

One of the most important ways value creation outruns value consumption is through the entrepreneurial transformation of problems into opportunities. However, this transformation, as Simon points out, is neither inevitable nor costless:

> ... a better future does not happen "automatically" and without effort. It will happen because women and men will struggle with problems with their muscles and minds, and will probably overcome most of them – as people always have eventually overcome economic problems in the past – if the social and economic system gives them the opportunity to do so.
>
> *(1995: 21)*

Whether we readily share Simon's irrepressible optimism about the likelihood (not inevitability) of human achievement driven by adversity or not, we can begin to appreciate his larger thesis about the role of entrepreneurship in seeking to create and participate in a virtuous circle of sorts. We can also begin to see a clearer picture of where entrepreneurship research fits in within this thesis. At least one important objective of entrepreneurship research is to clarify and specify how exactly problems may be transformed into opportunities in the plaiting together of this virtuous circle.

> ... Adding more people causes problems. But people are also the means to solve these problems ... The ultimate resource is people ... who will exert their wills and imaginations for their own benefit, and so inevitably they will benefit the rest of us as well.
>
> *(Simon, 1995: 27)*

In a world in which people are the ultimate resource, entrepreneurship is the currency that puts both sides of the coin (problem making and solution finding) to work in the realm of long run value creation. Furthermore, this value creation often happens *in spite of* narrow individual motivations and, as we will see in the following readings from de Soto and Gerschenkron, is perhaps only temporarily repressed even in the face of pervasive institutional hindrances. Simon, however, emphasizes the importance of three institutions conducive to the freedoms that unleash rather than restrain the ultimate resource, an argument also echoed by Ostrom's extensive empirical observations:

> The extent to which the political-social-economic system provides freedom from government coercion is a crucial element in the economics of resources and population. Skilled persons require an appropriate social and economic framework that provides incentives for working hard and taking risks, enabling their talents to flower and come to fruition. The key elements of such a framework are economic liberty, respect for property and fair and sensible rules of the market that are enforced equally for all.
>
> *(1995: 26)*

Simon also has some things to say about how such a freedom from government coercion might be achieved. For that we turn to our second selection, namely the last chapter of *The State of Humanity*.

Simon: *The State of Humanity* – final chapter: from the past to the future

> All of us like to think we are important – intellectuals certainly as much as anyone ... But in the longer run, the elemental forces of people's desires to carve out a good living for themselves and for their families, to have children and raise them happy and well-educated, to employ one's talents and energies and to enjoy their fruits – these forces will eventuate in government policies that allow people these fundamental freedoms.
>
> All that is required of philosophers and economists is that they manage to prise from rulers a small chink of living and operating room for individuals,

240 Made

> and some degree of rule of law. All the rest will be done by individuals themselves, without recourse to any grand ideas.
>
> *(1995: 658–659)*

Simon is making two important claims here. First, that when ordinary people are free to pursue their ordinary ambitions for living well, they will make macropillars that enable and enhance basic freedoms. This claim reoccurs and is reinforced by arguments from Sen, de Soto and Gerschenkron, and persuasive empirical evidence from Ostrom in the ensuing readings. And second, Simon is making a powerful restatement of the basic philosophy of Adam Smith and Friedrich Hayek: in economic matters, things work from the bottom up. Fundamental to these bottom–up processes is entrepreneurship. Both claims are encapsulated in the last sentence: *All the rest will be done by individuals themselves, without recourse to any grand ideas.*

In making irrepressibly confident and even outrageously optimistic forecasts for humankind's future, what is Simon relying on? A thorough perusal of his book suggests: large quantities of data over huge swathes of human history. But in the final section of the final chapter of his book, it becomes clear that the thin but unbreakable thread holding all the data together can be drawn out into one key observation: *it is just ordinary people going around doing ordinary things that collectively results in relentless progress.* And the ordinary people driving this process, of course, are entrepreneurs as well as their stakeholders; and the method they use "to carve out a good living for themselves and their families" is the process of trade, exchange and the carving together of new opportunities and new institutions.

In Simon's data, as in Adam Smith's observations of the pin factory and Hayek's lucid arguments, trade is almost an inescapable *algorithm*, very simple and basic, yet universal and eternal – a machine that just keeps grinding on relentlessly – in butcher and baker shops, in Wal-Mart and on eBay, even among prisoners and in concentration camps – there is always trade and organization and room for entrepreneurship.

A key insight that some of the readings in this book add to the mass of theorizing and observation over several centuries of the development of free market economics is that there are at least three layers to the inexorable process of trade:

- The outermost consists in the simplest form of exchange and trade. This is market-making in the ordinary sense of Braudel (1992) and others. It consists in arbitraging between given goods and services or bringing together given means and ends, either through long distance trade or overcoming a variety of barriers that keep markets from working – be those government suppression or transaction costs.
- The middle layer extends trade to innovation, particularly on the supply side. Exchange begets specialization, and this begets incentives to innovate in the form of improved production processes. This is what Adam Smith's pin factory did. And with the development and spread of the scientific method, it now encompasses a wide variety of markets based on technological innovations.

- We could go one layer deeper than this – and the readings in this book show how. Once supply-side innovation becomes part of the exchange equation, the role of demand-side innovation follows easily. In other words, the incentive to ask "what else can I offer to exchange with others" becomes irresistible. This, of course, leads to Buchanan and Vanberg's (1991) conceptualization of the market as a game without goods. Simon points this out when he quotes Frank Knight

> Frank Knight once wrote that what most people most seek is not to have their wants fulfilled, but bigger and better wants.
>
> *(1995: 656)*

And so we move from simple exchange to innovation to shifting outward the very frontiers of human aspirations out of which are fashioned new institutions, the macropillars scaffolding the making of new worlds. Economics, at this point, becomes more than the textbook definition of allocating scarce resources to meet unlimited (given) wants. It becomes about the genesis of these wants as well as the making of resources to fulfill them. And in this, it goes beyond resources, technologies and efficiency to become intertwined with ethics, esthetics and ecology as well. As such, this economics cannot run on auto-pilot. It cannot escape flesh and blood human beings whose values and tastes as well as the fulfillment of those values and tastes become dependent variable of interest. In a game without goods – i.e. an economics without pre-existent demand functions, volitional action and free agency become the very core of the engine of progress. And the central institution of economic development, as Sen argues next, has to constitute those freedoms that enable the generation as well as fulfillment of human ends.

Sen: the possibility of social choice

One of the most compelling ideas that burgeons out from reading Sen's Nobel lecture is that social choice ought to be an area of particular interest to entrepreneurship researchers; and social choice theorists ought to be taking more serious note of entrepreneurship as a mechanism of reconciling inconsistencies in social choice. Yet there is very little traffic between the two at this point in time.

The intellectual field of social choice has to do with the relationship between individual welfare and social judgments and the processes that lead to better judgment at the macro-level. As Sen points out:

> If there is a central question that can be seen as the motivating issue that inspires social choice theory, it is this: how can it be possible to arrive at cogent aggregative judgments about the society (for example, about "social welfare" or "the public interest" or "aggregate poverty"), given the diversity of preferences, concerns, and predicaments of the different individuals *within* the society? How can we find any rational basis for making such aggregative

242 Made

> judgments as "the society prefers this to that" or "the society should choose this over that" or "this is socially right"?
>
> *(1999: 349)*

Why should entrepreneurship researchers care about social choice? And why should social choice theorists care about entrepreneurship?

The answer to the first question, namely why entrepreneurship researchers should care about social choice theory, is easy: Because social choice offers us an interesting new set of dependent variables that help move our level of analysis beyond individuals and firms to society as a whole. The macro-agenda for entrepreneurship research is not confined to the role of entrepreneurship in achieving societal objectives (such as economic growth and employment given institutional constraints) but can now encompass the generation of those societal objectives. Entrepreneurial opportunities can therefore be expanded to include opportunities to experiment with and even engineer better social choices. And entrepreneurship researchers, like entrepreneurs themselves, have a choice: to see and analyze how profitability is linked to the good life – i.e. to overcome the separation thesis that Freeman (1984) identified, or to see the two as at loggerheads with each other, and therefore in incompatible realms of scholarship.

The answer to the second question, namely, why social choice theorists should care about entrepreneurship, is at once more complicated and more interesting. It is directly related to the main themes discussed in Sen's Nobel lecture as well as to the central issues we are grappling with in this book: intersubjectivity, pluralism and partially made worlds.

An important thing to notice in the selection is Sen's optimism with regard to broadening the informational basis for social choice and thereby rejuvenating a field populated by "obituary notices". The cause for the initial pessimism was rooted in ignoring the intersubjective. By adhering to the Utilitarian calculus of objectively aggregating purely subjective (given) individual preferences, good social choice becomes impossible. Therefore, the first step is to take intersubjectivity seriously. As Sen asserts:

> ... how much of a change in the possibility of social choice is brought about by systematic use of interpersonal comparisons? Does Arrow's impossibility, and related results, go away with the use of interpersonal comparisons in social welfare judgments? The answer briefly is, yes.
>
> *(1999: 357)*

In the ensuing discussion, Sen explicitly cites Davidson (on page 358) to argue for the feasibility of comparing mental states and then goes on to a more pluralistic basis for carrying out the comparisons – not merely in terms of happiness or utility or even income or wealth, but in terms of a diverse set of capabilities that allow one to live well according to one's own choice of ends and environments. The development of Sen's arguments leading up to the necessity for criteria based on freedoms rather than on outcomes per se is worth tracing in more detail from an entrepreneurial standpoint. Let us begin that trace with Sen's own words:

> Indeed, I have tried to argue in favor of judging individual advantage in respect of the respective capabilities, which the person has, to live the way he or she has reason to value. This approach focuses on the substantive freedoms that people have rather than only on the particular outcomes with which they end up. For responsible adults, the concentration on freedom rather than only achievement has some merit, and it can provide a general framework for analyzing individual advantage and deprivation in a contemporary society. The extent of interpersonal comparisons may only be partial – often based on the intersections of difference points of view. But the use of such partial comparability can make a major difference to the informational basis for reasoned social judgments.
>
> *(1999: 364)*

How can interpersonal comparisons be carried out? Utilitarianism's answer to this question has been through a formal aggregative calculus. Sen's answer has to do with the measurement of inequalities, be they inequalities in income (poverty), environmental conditions or social climate and so on (1999: 360). But entrepreneurship offers yet another basis – not only for carrying out such comparisons, but also for carrying out local *transformations* of both individual preferences and inequalities across individuals through a process of negotiations. Our arguments with regard to worldmaking in the previous section of this book are pertinent in this regard. In a world not yet fully made, consisting of selves (including preferences and capabilities) that are capable of being at least partially reconstructed, there is enough room for individuals to negotiate each others' preferences and improve each others' capabilities as well as to simply carry out profitable exchanges that mop up existing gains from trade. As we will see later in this chapter, Ostrom's observations about "cheap talk" are also relevant and useful here.

Preferences and capabilities as outcomes of negotiations is a tricky and important point worth belaboring. With entrepreneurship in the picture, economics becomes not only about trade and innovation, but also about the entrepreneurial construction of preferences and demand functions. And social choice becomes not only about policy solutions to measure and overcome inequalities but also about the entrepreneurial transformation of those inequalities into new opportunities and new markets. Entrepreneurship, in short, provides mechanisms not only for broadening the information base for social choice solutions but also provides guiding criteria for negotiated transformations *without* government intervention. Taking entrepreneurship seriously requires us to confront the question of when to use public policy to lead to better solutions and when and how to enable entrepreneurs to tackle issues of social choice – a topic currently non-existent in the social choice literature. This question is especially important with regard to the liberal paradox that Sen discusses toward the end of his speech.

244 Made

After a satisfying resolution to the problem of interpersonal comparisons that helps overcome impossibility results in social choice, Sen points out fertile areas for more work to be done. In particular, he outlines the liberal paradox that consists in the conflict between what he terms the "opportunity" and "process" aspects of liberty. Put another way, this refers to the fact that liberty involves both choices *within* particular domains and choices *between* those domains (1999: 364). A simplistic example may be that of an individual wanting to make more money, but also wanting to spend more time with the family. Liberty, therefore, involves not only the freedom to choose between jobs within one's occupation but also the freedom to choose between occupation and family. And the freedom to put these two together in unexpected ways, as female entrepreneurship around the globe illustrates (Eddleston & Powell, 2012). Obviously, there may be conflicts or trade-offs between these two choices, both at the level of the individual and that of the society. As Sen points out toward the end of his speech:

> This too calls for an informational enrichment (taking note of people's political values as well as individual desires), but this enrichment is of a rather different kind from that of using interpersonal comparisons of well-being and overall advantage.
>
> *(1999: 364)*

Entrepreneurship, more than most other fields, provides mechanisms for reconciling these types of conflicts. By *designing* (in the sense of *The Science of the Artificial*) rather than *selecting between* jobs, *fabricating* and not only *finding* business models and market opportunities, entrepreneurs can overcome the liberal paradox. As Venkataraman (2002) argued, entrepreneurship provides a viable exit option to the moral manager faced with unpalatable trade-offs. Similarly, entrepreneurship can also provide alternative design palettes for policy makers and communities faced with the liberal paradox. In other words, when it comes to changing institutions, political or policy measures are not the only game in town. Entrepreneurs can help transform as well as create institutions that foster and enhance those very capabilities and freedoms that form the informational basis for good social choice. Of course, at this point in time, this claim is only a hypothesis. But it opens the door to a set of solutions at the micro and meso levels that current social choice theorists focused on the macro or policy level are completely ignoring. The next three readings in this section begin to lay firmer foundation for the efficacy and importance of this hypothesis.

De Soto: the mystery of capital – by way of conclusion

Take for example, Hernando de Soto. He was an economist, businessman, consultant and policy advisor, who became an entrepreneur when he decided to open a garment workshop on the outskirts of Lima to empirically demonstrate the importance of an effective property rights system to the economic development of a poor country. In particular, he focused on the titling of untitled assets and the microdetails of what it took to transform physical resources into "capital" in a country without working legal institutions that create and enforce property rights. In doing so, he also illustrated the difference between entrepreneurship that takes institutions as given and works within the constraints of those institutions (i.e. creates the "extralegal" or shadow economies of countries like Peru) and entrepreneurship that seeks to make those institutions (i.e. de Soto's own brand of institutional entrepreneurship). In sum, de Soto embodies the contrasts between "found" and "made" views of institutions, even as he theorizes about the importance of property rights as an essential macro-pillar for entrepreneurship and economic development.

De Soto begins by making the same criticism of policymakers that we made earlier of social choice theorists – namely, that an exclusive focus on macro issues blinds one to the problems and opportunities at the micro level:

> Too many policymakers have taken an Olympian view of the globalizations process. Once they stabilized and adjusted at the macro level, allowing legal business and foreign investors to proper and orthodox economists to control the treasury, they felt they had fulfilled their duty. Because they concentrated only on policies dealing with the aggregates, they did not inquire whether people had the means to participate in an expanded market system.
>
> *(2000: 211)*

To the above two groups of economists who missed the entrepreneurial microfoundations of capitalism, de Soto adds a provocatively interesting name, the author of *Das Kapital* himself:

> Marx would probably be shocked to find how in developing countries much of the teeming mass does not consist of oppressed legal proletarians but of oppressed extralegal small entrepreneurs with a sizeable amount of assets.
>
> *(2000: 216)*

The root of this "oppression" is also the root of the "mystery" of capital. The mere existence of physical resources even when combined with free markets is not sufficient to produce the kind of economic development that has been achieved by Western capitalist societies. As Edith Penrose pointed out, what people *do* with those resources matters. And what they can do with them depends in turn on whether they are embedded in a "mind-friendly" property rights system:

> People have always produced surplus value: pyramids, cathedrals, expensive armies, to name a few examples. Clearly much of today's surplus value in the West has originated not in scandalously expropriated labor time but in the way that property has given minds the mechanisms with which to extract additional work from commodities.
>
> *(2000: 217)*

246 Made

De Soto argues that property rights are in essence a representational system – similar to Arabic numerals, musical notations and computer languages. As such a good property rights system embraces Davidson's epistemological tripod. It is subjective, intersubjective and objective all at once. It empowers our interactions with the world and with other people while working with and not against our innate cognitive abilities and limitations:

> What distinguishes a good legal property system is that it is "mind-friendly." It obtains and organizes knowledge about recorded assets in forms we can control.
>
> *(2000: 218)*

> A good property system is a medium that allows us to understand each other, make connections, and synthesize knowledge about our assets to enhance our productivity.
>
> *(2000: 219)*

Moreover, it takes into account the fact that the creativity at the heart of the market process is powered by human beings seeking to shape and control their local environments.

> The capacity of property to reveal the capital that is latent in the assets we accumulate is born out of the best intellectual tradition of controlling our environment in order to prosper.
>
> *(2000: 220)*

Buchanan and Vanberg's arguments about the creative nature of market process and Simon's notion of a science of the artificial are naturally combined with Davidson's tripod in de Soto's vision of a "mind-friendly" property rights system.

While arguing *for* a legal property rights system at the macro level that is in sync with a central role for entrepreneurship in micro theories of development, de Soto also argues *against* a pivotal role for culture per se. His argument is echoed and elaborated upon in both readings (Ostrom and Gerschenkron) that come next. Nonetheless, de Soto's argument is worth highlighting on its own merit. By espousing a nonadaptationist or exaptive view of the evolution of social artifacts, it evokes the Gould and Lewontin reading from Part III of this book:

> Throughout history people have confused the efficiency of the representational tools they have inherited to create surplus value with the inherent values of their culture. They forget that often what gives an edge to a particular group of people is the innovative use they make of a representational system developed by another culture.
>
> *(De Soto, 2000: 224)*

Culture, in this view, is not a cage. It is an input into value creation. And like any other input into fabrication processes, any given culture can be decomposed and recombined with elements from other cultures as well as with internally generated innovations to create new cultural elements. One culture can be adapted to another, absorbed into another – and bits and pieces of either may be spatially and temporally exapted to new uses. Culture, in short, is also *made*. It follows then that culture may be transformed and reshaped through intentional and serendipitous human actions, reactions and interactions.

Hence de Soto cautions us about assuming that entrepreneurship is a product of a certain culture. Instead, let us try to understand if institutions such as property rights are enough to explain the differences in entrepreneurship between societies. Certainly entrepreneurship occurs despite the absence of the basic institutions of capitalism, i.e. entrepreneurs will trade and build small businesses whether the institutional frameworks are available or not. Moreover, entrepreneurs will even strive to fabricate these institutions. But when key market-augmenting institutions (Olson, 1984) such as a mind-friendly property system is in place, entrepreneurship becomes more productive and creates the sort of virtuous circle of value creation that Julian Simon and others point to. Baumol's exposition of productive, unproductive and even destructive entrepreneurship (1990) is familiar to entrepreneurship researchers. De Soto shows one way to channel entrepreneurship into a productive circle. His thesis is consistent with theorizing by public choice economists such as Gordon Tullock and James Buchanan, as well as the ideas of institutionalists such as Douglas North and Mancur Olson. What makes it powerful is its rich embrace of the empirical reality of flesh and blood entrepreneurs from a variety of different cultures seeking to create value *despite* institutional constraints:

> I humbly suggest that before any Brahmin who lives in a bell jar tries to convince us that succeeding at capitalism requires certain cultural traits, we should first try to see what happens when developing and former communist countries establish property rights systems that can create capital for everyone … Much behavior that is today attributed to cultural heritage is not the inevitable result of people's ethnic or idiosyncratic traits but of their rational evaluation of the relative costs and benefits of entering the legal property system.
>
> *(De Soto, 2000: 224)*

For more on the relative unimportance of culture as a necessary macro-pillar for a made view of entrepreneurship, we will turn to Gerschenkron's detailed historical analysis that inveighs against culture-based explanations for economic development (or the lack thereof). But before we get to that, let us examine the overwhelming prolificity of empirical findings in the work of Elinor Ostrom that compel us to reconsider the endless of potential of what can indeed be *made* through entrepreneurial action.

248 Made

Ostrom: polycentric governance of common pool resources

The intellectual journey of the first female to win the Nobel prize in economics, is itself a journey of "making" in exactly the sense in which we have been using the term in this book. In the reading, Elinor Ostrom traces that journey that paints a surprising empirical tapestry of what can be made once we move away from the dichotomy of markets versus governments. At the time she began her journey, economic theorizing was caught in a dichotomy that persists to this day:

> In his classic definitional essay, Paul Samuelson (1954) divided goods into two types. Pure private goods are both excludable (individual A can be excluded from consuming private goods unless paid for) and rivalrous (whatever individual A consumes, no one else can con sume). Public goods are both nonexcludable (impossible to keep those who have not paid for a good from consuming it) and nonrivalrous (whatever individual A consumes does not limit the consumption by others). This basic division was consistent with the dichotomy of the institutional world into private property exchanges in a market setting and government-owned property organized by a public hierarchy. The people of the world were viewed primarily as consumers or voters.
>
> *(Ostrom, 2010: 643)*

Over decades of studying public goods ranging from the policing of metropolitan cities to the governance of common pool resources such as ground water and forests, Ostrom came to the realization that;

> The classic assumptions about rational individuals facing a dichotomy of organizational forms and of goods hide the potentially productive efforts of individuals and groups to organize and solve social dilemmas such as the overharvesting of common-pool resources and the underprovision of local public goods.
>
> *(Ostrom, 2010: 648)*

Ostrom also empirically discovered what Sen had argued as the primary instrument for overcoming the central dilemma in social choice, namely that socially valuable preferences can be constructed through intersubjective interactions. Ostrom's empirical observations led her to conclude that something as simple as "cheap talk" can lead to the making of polycentric institutions that go beyond the dichotomy of market and government to govern really complex common pool resources:

> Public investigators purposely keep prisoners separated so they cannot communicate. The users of a common-pool resource are not so limited.
>
> When analysts perceive the human beings they model as being trapped inside perverse situations, they then assume that other human beings external

to those involved – scholars and public officials – are able to analyze the situation, ascertain why counterproductive outcomes are reached, and posit what changes in the rules-in-use will enable participants to improve outcomes. Then, external officials are expected to impose an optimal set of rules on those individuals involved. It is assumed that the momentum for change must come from outside the situation rather than from the self-reflection and creativity of those within a situation to restructure their own patterns of interaction.

(Ostrom, 2010: 648)

Ostrom's own empirical work and studies by hundreds of scholars using dozens of methods ranging from lab and field experiments to longitudinal case studies piled up evidence against standard assumptions of noncooperative behavior. In doing so they also cumulated evidence for a more positive view of the human capacity to develop complex governance systems – including the generation of trust – where none should exist within the framework of conventional assumptions, leading Ostrom to conclude:

The surprising but repeated finding that users of resources that are in relatively good condition or even improving do invest in various ways of monitoring one another relates to the core problem of building trust. Unfortunately, policy analysts, public officials, and scholars who still apply simple mathematical models to the analysis of field settings have not yet absorbed the central lessons articulated here.

(Ostrom, 2010: 664)

The most important lesson for public policy analysis derived from the intellectual journey I have outlined here is that humans have a more complex motivational structure and more capability to solve social dilemmas than posited in earlier rational-choice theory. Designing institutions to force (or nudge) entirely self-interested individuals to achieve better outcomes has been the major goal posited by policy analysts for governments to accomplish for much of the past half century. Extensive empirical research leads me to argue that instead, a core goal of public policy should be to facilitate the development of institutions that bring out the best in humans.

(Ostrom, 2010: 664–665)

Ostrom's findings are of great importance to entrepreneurship researchers seeking to study social entrepreneurship and entrepreneurship dealing with sustainability issues. These phenomena are pushing against extant assumptions about what can be made through entrepreneurship, indicating a need for scholarship that reconsiders the theoretical assumptions we have borrowed from other disciplines to study these phenomena. An explicit argument about this last issue comes from Gerschenkron, whom we turn to next.

250 Made

Gerschenkron: social attitudes, entrepreneurship and economic development

Gerschenkron's essay is as relevant today as it was in the 1950s when it was first published. The essay targets a fundamental issue in sociological approaches to entrepreneurship: the influence of social attitudes, or the general climate of opinion, on entrepreneurial action. This issue is just as pertinent today as it was in the 1950s, since we are living through the new institutional movement in sociology and its spillovers into management and entrepreneurship, which focuses on the background institutions, or different kinds of embeddedness, of economic action (Powell & DiMaggio, 1991). The central thesis of these theories is that the cultural landscape shapes entrepreneurial action in fundamental ways. The thesis bears close resemblance to the Parsonian thesis that Gerschenkron takes up. Gerschenkron's critique of the Parsonian thesis therefore is very relevant to entrepreneurship research today on both conceptual and empirical grounds.

In terms of the conceptual critique, Gerschenkron finds a fundamental problem in the Parsonian idea of sociological "roles," i.e. the notion that entrepreneurs are fulfilling predefined roles in a social play, where social expectations – and the positive and negative sanctioning therein – defines what entrepreneurs do. He starts the critique with the static nature of roles:

> One cannot suppress some wonderment as to why these particular concepts should have proven attractive to those interested in explaining the process of economic *change*. It does seem that these concepts essentially pertain to a static system.
>
> *(1962: 54; emphasis original)*

How, in such a theoretical system, where individual action is always socially sanctioned or in today's terminology institutionally embedded, is change to take place? Is the very existence of deviant behavior (variations from the norm) enough to explain entrepreneurial behavior? Gerschenkron argues – not:

> For, though it may make sense in certain historical situations to take a dominant system of social values for granted, it is much less satisfactory to accept the deviant behavior as given. If we deal with an agricultural community based on century-long traditions, we may be willing to accept those traditions as given. But if suddenly deviant values make their entry upon the economic scene, the urge for further explanation is irresistible. We cannot help asking whence the change in value orientations: what caused their sudden outburst? There is nothing within the theoretical framework that provides the elements of such an explanation beyond, perhaps, some implicit and inchoate ideas about the tolerable degree of tension between deviant and generally accepted behavior.
>
> *(1962: 58)*

And so we are led back once more to James (1880) and to the other accounts in this volume of how differences and variation come to be in the economic system in the first place. To associate the entrepreneur with difference is one thing; to explain how these differences come about is another thing entirely. Gerschenkron's point was that Parsonianism wasn't up to the task: it is a form of selectionism, a process of ironing out wrinkles and removing novelty. It cannot explain novelty generation. It has very little to say about the *making* of new worlds.

Gerschenkron fortifies his conceptual thesis with empirical illustrations uncovered through historical analyses of entrepreneurship and industrialization in several European countries. After elaborating upon detailed examples from France, Russia and Germany, Gerschenkron brings us to inescapable conclusions about the inadequacy of explanations based on social attitudes:

> [S]erious doubts are permissible about whether the theory of roles in its present form and everything that it implies can be of much use for understanding processes in the economies within which a rapid change in *economic systems* is in the making.
>
> *(1962: 67–68)*

The historical reality Gerschenkron points to instead is one in which entrepreneurs do not appear as disciplined actors playing their pre-assigned social roles. Instead, there is wide variation in normative value systems, and variation also in the rates of change of these values. In market economies, this variation is further exacerbated by the very dominance of free market or capitalistic "values."

Take for example, Leonard Read's toy essay *I, Pencil* (1958). The miracle of the humble pencil, as Read pointed out, is that "not a single person on the face of this earth knows how to make me". Instead, the billions of pencils that are made every year depend on many individuals specializing and trading with each other. None of them have to approve of each other in order for this to happen. Of course, this is reminiscent of the point Adam Smith made about the butcher and the baker: no one in town needs to like them nor do they need to like the townspeople in order for everyone to benefit from trade with them. In fact, we customarily trade with people we don't like: it is one of the beauties of capitalism that one does not need to like someone in order to trade with them.

Gains from trade in general are so beneficial irrespective of and often because of variations in values as well as preferences and traits, that entrepreneurship occurs despite attempts to suppress it. This means social sanctions against entrepreneurship must be at least as varied as entrepreneurial activities, as well as severe enough to outweigh obvious gains from trade. This is hard to do: even Stalinist Russia could not suppress trade, whether in shadowy street corners or in the Gulag. Much trade is simple and self-enforcing, not relying on embeddedness, trust or relationships between buyer and seller. And in more complex cases, entrepreneurship makes new networks and institutions as well as leverages existing ones. Moreover, entrepreneurs throughout history have sought to make new social norms as

252 Made

well as new products and services; they have actively tried to shape and negotiate values as well as terms of trade (McCloskey, 2006). In fact, values and products do not exist in separate and mutually exclusive realms – they too interact and shape each other. In introducing new methods to sell cosmetics, Mary Kay made new kinds of women who learned to value financial independence as much as beautiful faces and clean homes. The eighteenth-century entrepreneur Wedgwood wrote to his partner Bentley that their task was to make artists of "mere men". Carnegie and Hershey not only made steel and chocolate, but also built towns, colleges and libraries.

As Gerschenkron is careful to point out, none of this means that the social environment does not materially impact entrepreneurship. As we saw with de Soto and Julian Simon, a few carefully engineered institutions such as a mind-friendly property rights system can make a big difference both in the quality and quantity of entrepreneurship. The question then becomes: what is the role of social attitudes and broad notions of institutional embeddedness? Gerschenkron proffers a strong conclusion:

> Perhaps the generalization may be ventured that adverse social attitudes toward entrepreneurs do not significantly affect the processes of industrialization unless they are allowed to become crystallized in governmental action.
>
> *(1962: 71)*

And that is precisely why it is important for scholars in general and entrepreneurship scholars in particular to help pick and choose exactly what kind of governmental interventions are enforced. Entrepreneurship research itself, therefore, has to become a science of the artificial in the fashioning of design criteria for the making of macropillars on which microaspects of entrepreneurial worldmaking can rest. In this regard, Gerschenkron's essay is worth studying for its *method* as well for its contents. It exhorts us to eschew monism and embrace pluralism (Rodrik, 2009); to de-emphasize rigid but empty generalizations in favor of rich precision in setting bounds and limits both in our questions and answers:

> A rigid conceptual framework is no doubt useful in formulating questions, but at all times it evokes the peril that those questions will be mistaken for answers. There is a deep-seated yearning in the social sciences for discovery of one general approach, one general law valid for all times and all climes. But these attitudes must be outgrown. They overestimate both the degree of simplicity of economic reality and the quality of scientific tools.
>
> *(1962: 67)*

> The question cannot be: are social values important or unimportant? It must read first of all: what is the degree of persistence in value systems, what is their propensity to change in response to what factors?
>
> *(1962: 68)*

The hard work that Gerschenkron urges of us scholars in formulating our questions takes seriously Michael Polanyi's warnings against "the narrowness of an outlook uninformed by humility" (quoted at the beginning of this chapter). The actual unfolding of history often humbles the most confident predictions of its best historians. In a world of entrepreneurial making and remaking, humility is an essential ingredient that no research method can do without. The final part of the book is devoted to exploring a few methods that take pluralism, contingency and humility seriously.

References

Baumol, W. J. (1990). Entrepreneurship: Productive, unproductive, and destructive. *Journal of Political Economy* **98**(5): 893–921.

Braudel, F. (1992). *Civilization and capitalism, 15th–18th century*. Berkeley, CA: University of California Press.

Buchanan, J. M. & Vanberg, V. J. (1991). The market as a creative process. *Economics and Philosophy* **7**: 167–186.

De Soto, H. (2000). *The mystery of capital: Why capitalism triumphs in the west and fails everywhere else*. New York, Basic Books.

Eddleston, K. A. & Powell, G. N. (2012). Nurturing entrepreneurs' work–family balance: A gendered perspective. *Entrepreneurship Theory and Practice* **36**(3): 513–541.

Freeman, R. E. (1984). *Strategic management: A stakeholder approach*. Boston, Pitman.

Gerschenkron, A. (1962). *Economic backwardness in historical perspective: A book of essays*. Cambridge, MA: Belknap Press.

James, W. (1880). Great men, great thoughts, and the environment. *Atlantic Monthly* **46**(276): 441–459.

McCloskey, D. N. (2006). *Bourgeois Virtues: Ethics for an age of commerce*. University of Chicago Press.

Olson, M. (1984). *The rise and decline of nations: Economic growth, stagflation, and social rigidities*. New Haven, CT: Yale University Press.

Ostrom, E. (2010). Beyond markets and states: polycentric governance of complex economic systems. American Economic Review, 100(3), 641-72.

Polanyi, M. (1951). *The logic of liberty*. London: Routledge.

Powell, W. W. & DiMaggio, P. J. (1991). *The new institutionalism in organizational analysis*. University of Chicago Press.

Read, L. E. (1958). I, pencil: My family tree as told to Leonard E. Read. *The Freeman* **8**(12): 32–37.

Rodrik, D. (2009). *One economics, many recipes: Globalization, institutions, and economic growth*. Princeton, NJ: Princeton University Press.

Sen, A. (1999). The possibility of social choice. *The American Economic Review* **89**(3): 349–378.

Simon, J. L. (1995). *The state of humanity*. Oxford. Blackwell in association with the Cato Institute.

Venkataraman, S. (2002). Stakeholder value equilibration and the entrepreneurial process. In Freeman, R. E. & Venkataraman, S. (Eds.) *Ethics and entrepreneurship: The Ruffin series*: (pp. 45–57). Charlottesville, VA: Philosophy Documentation Center.

13

THE STATE OF HUMANITY

Introduction

J. L. Simon

Executive summary

> If present trends continue, the world in 2000 will be more crowded, more polluted, less stable ecologically, and more vulnerable to disruption than the world we live in now. Serious stresses involving population, resources, and environment are clearly visible ahead. Despite greater material output, the world's people will be poorer in many ways than they are today.
>
> For hundreds of millions of the desperately poor, the outlook for food and other necessities of life will be no better. For many it will be worse. Barring revolutionary advances in technology, life for most people on earth will be more precarious in 2000 than it is now – unless the nations of the world act decisively to alter current trends.

The above quotation from page one of the 1980 *Global 2000 Report to the President* began the Introduction to this volume's predecessor, *The Resourceful Earth*, which I edited with the late Herman Kahn. Then, in order "to highlight our differences as much as possible," we restated that paragraph with our substitutions in italics, as follows:

> If present trends continue, the world in 2000 will be *less crowded* (though more populated), *less polluted, more stable ecologically, and less vulnerable to resource-supply disruption* than the world we live in now. Stresses involving population, resources, and environment *will be less in the future than now* ... The World's people will be richer in most ways than they are today ... The outlook for food and other necessities of life will be better ... life for most people on earth will be *less precarious* economically than it is now.

The years have been kind to our forecasts – or more importantly, the years have been good for humanity. The benign trends we then observed have continued until the time of writing this volume. Our species is better off in just about every measurable material way. And there is stronger reason than ever to believe that these progressive trends will continue past the year 2000, past the year 2100, and indefinitely.

The outlook portrayed in this volume is even more happy than before for two reasons: (1) conditions have improved in the phenomena we discussed a decade ago, and (2) we now document a much wider range of phenomena pertaining to human welfare than in the previous volume, and almost all of these additional trends also point in a positive direction.

More specifically, the trends toward greater cleanliness and less pollution of our air and water are even sharper than before, and cover a longer historical period and more countries (though the environmental disaster in Eastern Europe has only recently become public knowledge). The increase in availability and the decrease in scarcity of raw materials have continued unabated, and have even speeded up. None of the catastrophes in food supply and famine that were forecast by the doomsayers has occurred; rather, the world's people are eating better than ever.

When we widen our scope beyond such physical matters as natural resources and the environment – to mortality, the standard of living, slavery and freedom, housing, and the like – we find that these trends pertaining to economic welfare are heartening, also. Most important, fewer people are dying young. And life expectancy in the rich countries has increased most sharply in the older age cohorts, among which many thought that there was no improvement. Perhaps most exciting, the quantities of education that people obtain all over the world are sharply increasing, which means less tragic waste of human talent and ambition.

The extrapolation of these trends into the future is discussed in chapter 58. The long-run prospects are so favorable and so certain that I am prepared to bet on them; the terms of the wager I offer are below.

Please notice that this benign assessment does not imply that there will not be increases in *some* troubles – AIDS at present, for example, and other diseases in the future, as well as social and political upheavals. New problems always will arise. Indeed, the solution to any existing problem usually creates new – albeit usually lesser – problems. But the assessment refers to broad aggregate measures of *effects upon people* rather than the bad phenomena themselves – life expectancy rather than AIDS, skin cancers (or even better, lifetime healthy days) rather than a hole in the ozone layer (if that is indeed a problem), and agriculture rather than global warming.

The complete failure of the dire forecasts of the doomsayers, starting in the 1960s and continuing through the 1980 *Global 2000 Report* until now, should confer credibility on the assessment given here. Regrettably, however, the doomsayers' failure has not reduced the frequency of forecasts of doom, or sapped the reputations or influence of the forecasters. This disregard of contrary evidence is one more sign of the absence of true science – whose essence is the comparison of theories and forecasts against the data – in the conventional literature of impending doom.

256 J. L. Simon

Introduction to the introduction

> The humour of blaming the present, and admiring the past, is strongly rooted in human nature, and has an influence even on persons endued with the profoundest judgment and most extensive learning. (David Hume, 'Of the Populousness of Ancient Nations,' in 1777/1987, 464)

This introduction charts humanity's welfare in the past, and shows where we are now. The concluding chapter forecasts the future.

The following long quotation from William Petty tells in a seventeenth-century context the central message of this book:

> I have therefore thought fit to examin the following Perswasions, which I find too currant in the World, and too much to have affected the Minds of some, to the prejudice of all, viz.
>
> ... the whole Kingdom grows every day poorer and poorer; that formerly it abounded with Gold, but now there is a great scarcity both of Gold and Silver; that there is no Trade nor Employment for the People ... that Trade in general doth lamentably decay; that the Hollanders are at our heels, in the race of Naval Power; the French grow too fast upon both, and appear so rich and potent, that it is but their Clemency that they do not devour their Neighbors; and finally, that the Church and State of England, are in the same danger with the Trade of England; with many other dismal Suggestions, which I had rather stifle than repeat.
>
> ... But notwithstanding all this (the like whereof was always in all Places), the Buildings of London grow great and glorious; the American Plantations employ four Hundred Sail of Ships; Actions in the East-India Company are near double the principal Money; those who can give good Security, may have Money under the Statute-Interest; Materials for building (even Oaken-Timber) are little the dearer, some cheaper for the rebuilding of London; the Exchange seems as full of Merchants as formerly; no more Beggars in the Streets, nor executed for Thieves, than heretofore; the Number of Coaches, and Splendor of Equipage exceeding former Times; the publique Theatres very magnificent; the King has a greater Navy, and stronger Guards than before our Calamites; the Clergy rich, and the Cathedrals in repair; much Land has been improved, and the Price of Food so reasonable, as that Men refuse to have it cheaper by admitting of Irish Cattle; And in brief, no Man needs to want that will take moderate pains. That some are poorer than others, ever was and ever will be: And that many are naturally querulous and envious, is an Evil as old as the World.
>
> These general Observations, and that Men eat, and drink, and laugh as they use to do, have encouraged me to try if I could also comfort others, being satisfied my self, that the Interest and Affairs of England are in no deplorable Condition.

The state of humanity **257**

> The Method I take to do this, is not yet very usual; for instead of using only comparative and superlative Words and intellectual Arguments, I have taken the course (as a Specimen of the Political Arithmetick I have long aimed at) to express my self in Terms of Number, Weight, or Measure; ...
>
> ... I hope all ingenious and candid Persons will rectifie the Errors, Defects, and Imperfections, which probably may be found in any of the Positions, upon which these Ratiocinations were grounded. (Petty, Hull ed., 1986, pp. 241–5)

This volume portrays extraordinary progress for the human enterprise, especially in the past two centuries. Yet many people believe that conditions of life are generally worse than in the past, rather than better. We must therefore begin by discussing this perception, because it affects a reader's reaction to the factual material presented in this book.

Please ask yourself: Is a big wheat harvest a good thing? It would seem so; more wheat brought in implies more and cheaper food for consumers. Yet you'll often see such headlines as: "Good harvest, bad news."

Yes, a big harvest is unwelcome to farmers because they receive low prices; that is the "bad news." But is a small harvest better *on balance* than a big harvest? Not many people would say so. Still, *The Washington Post* headline just quoted is negative. And that "news" contributes to a widespread perception that the overall course of events is bad.

Certainly the public view (or at least the public view of the public view) is not wildly optimistic. At the time of writing, a major *Newsweek* story of November 4, 1991, is headlined "That Sinking Feeling," and goes on to say, "Americans feel gloomy, almost desperate, about the future of the economy" (pp. 18, 28). And the front-page headline of *The Washington Post* is "A Tide of Pessimism and Political Powerlessness Rises" (November 3, 1991); the story cites a poll saying that "seven in 10 Americans think the country is off track." Pessimism about the environment and resources is so universal that it needs no documentation.

The choice of comparison one makes always is crucial. A premise of this book is that it usually makes sense to compare our present state of affairs with *how it was before*. This is the comparison that is usually relevant for policy purposes because it measures our progress. But many private and public discussions instead compare a present state of *one group* to the present state of *other groups*, as a supposed measure of "equity," or as the basis for indignation and righteousness, or to support their political positions. Others compare the actual situation to the *best* possible, or to ideal purity, ostensibly to motivate improvement. A typical front-page story from *The Washington Post* (July 5, 1991) does both; it headlines a complaint of blacks that a nearby county "Isn't Drawing Upscale Stores," and the caption under a picture says "Prince George's resident Howard Stone is angered by the shortage of upscale retail stores in his community." (Yes, that was on the front page.) This issue is very different from the sorts of problems that most of humanity has faced throughout most of its history, the sorts of problems that are addressed in this book.

Many events that, on first reaction, people tend to consider bad have more good than bad about them. And if we act on that first negative reaction instead of a balanced assessment, we risk making unsound social decisions.

Consider this example: Is the trend of black infant mortality encouraging? I've asked this question of many audiences, both laypeople and professionals – even demographers. Almost everyone's reaction in the United States is that black infant mortality is a bad situation. But look at Figure 13.1, on infant mortality by race in the United States since 1915. White infant mortality in 1915 was almost 100 deaths per 1,000 births, and black infant mortality was fully 180 deaths per 1,000 births. Both rates are horrifying. And the rates were even worse in earlier years in some places – up to 300 or 400 deaths per thousand births. Nowadays, white infant mortality is about nine per thousand, and black infant mortality is about 18 per thousand. Of course it is bad that mortality is higher for blacks than for whites. But should we not be mainly impressed by the tremendous improvement for *both races* – rates falling to about ten percent of what they were – with the black rate coming ever closer to the white rate? Is not this extraordinary improvement for the entire population the most important story – and a most happy story? Yet the press gives us the impression that we should be mainly distressed about the state of black infant mortality.

Someone said to Voltaire, "Life is hard." Voltaire replied, "Compared to what?" Every evaluation requires that we make some comparison. The comparisons one

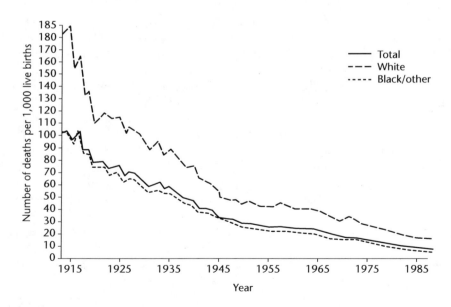

FIGURE 13.1 Infant mortality rate, total and by race, USA, 1915–1989

Sources: Historical Statistics of the US, Colonial Times to 1970, Series B 136–147; Statistical Abstract of the US, 1982–92 edn, Table 111; Statistical Abstract of the US, 1992 edn, Table 109.

chooses are decisive in the judgments one makes about whether things are getting better or worse. (Here we have the old joke. Woman 1: "How is your husband?" Woman 2: "Compared to what?" Or in another version, "Compared to whom?")

Proof of the distorting effect of the negative slant in the press is seen in polls where people are asked about their own situations and about the situations of the public at large. If the poll is representative and people's assessment of others is accurate, the averages for assessments of self and of others should be equal. But Figure 13.2 shows the typical result: that self-assessment is much more positive than assessment of others' situations; the gap between the two is a measure of the distortion. And the same result is found in poll after poll, of the state of the environment, economic welfare, crowdedness of neighborhood and nation, and so on; people have a more gloomy view of the situation at large than the objective facts warrant, by their own testimony.

The path of material human welfare

Let us distinguish three types of economic change: (a) Change that is *mainly absolute rather than relative*. An example is a health improvement that benefits everyone worldwide. (b) Change that is *mainly relative*, but where there is also an important overall effect. An example is a productivity improvement in one country due to people working smarter, which allows that country to greatly increase its exports to

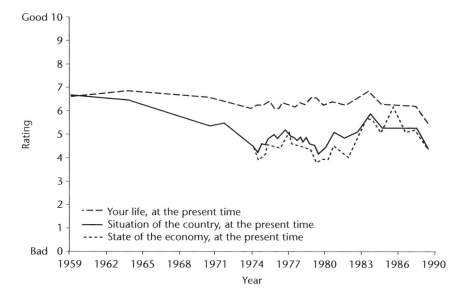

FIGURE 13.2 Ratings of own life, country, and economy, 1959–89

Source: Seymour and Schneider, 1983, pp. 142, 143; data for 1980s courtesy of Cambridge Reports International.

Note: No survey questions were asked after 1989.

260 J. L. Simon

the benefit of both exporters and importers, but causing problems for some other exporting countries. (c) Change that is *wholly relative*. An example is a change in the price charged by one trading partner to another, or the terms of trade between raw materials and consumer goods, or the dollar–yen exchange rate; in such zero–sum situations there is no on–balance change for bad or good. It is only the third category where one finds bad news, and indeed bad news is inevitable for one party or the other.

This is the central assertion of this book: Almost every absolute change, and the absolute component of almost every economic and social change or trend, points in a positive direction, as long as we view the matter over a reasonably long period of time. That is, all aspects of material human welfare are improving in the aggregate.

Most changes are like the infant mortality situation – some absolute or relative losers, but more mostly absolute gainers. However, many of the things that people worry about are purely relative, like the exchange rate of the dollar, or women's wages relative to men's. And this focus on the relative and the short run often misleads us into thinking that the overall course of things is bad, when in general just about every long–run trend in human welfare points in a positive direction.

For proper understanding of the important aspects of an economy we should look at the long–run movement. But the short–run comparisons – between the sexes, age groups, races, political groups, which are usually purely relative – make more news. And to repeat, just about every important long–run measure of human welfare shows improvement over the decades and centuries, in the United States as well as in the rest of the world. And there is no persuasive reason to believe that these trends will not continue indefinitely.

Would I bet on it? For sure. I'll bet a week's or month's pay (my winnings go to fund research) that just about any trend pertaining to human welfare will improve rather than get worse. First come, first served. But be warned that in economics, unlike the weather, it is easier to forecast the long run than the short run. (More about this in the epilogue, chapter 58.)

Amartya Sen has written that the standard of living is best measured, not by per capita income, but by a collection of measures of human welfare that he calls "functionings." This entire volume may be thought of as an operationalization of that notion. It contains essays on the long–run trends of all the important measures of human welfare for which there are sensible data and about which I could find a competent scholar to write. The volume contains essays on other relevant subjects as well, but long–run measures of human welfare comprise the core of the matter.

As soon as it is seen that the news is good even though the news stories are bad, the question arises: Why do we hear all these bad reports? Explaining why threats of doom are made, and why we choose to read and hear about them and then believe them, is a difficult subject about which there are many speculations but is beyond our scope here.

Some key material trends

Let's start with the longest and deepest trends. Surprising though they may be, please be aware that these trends – documented in the chapters of the volume – represent the uncontroversial settled findings of the economists and other experts who work in these fields (except for the case of population growth). What you will read below on that subject was an unusual viewpoint until sometime in the 1980s, at which time the mainstream scientific opinion shifted almost all the way to the position set forth here.

Length of life

Let's begin with the all-important issue, life itself. The most important and amazing demographic fact – the greatest human achievement in history, in my view – is the decrease in the world's death rate (chapters 2 and 3). The stylized graph in Figure 13.3a shows that it took thousands of years to increase life expectancy at birth from just over 20 years to the high 20s. Then in just the past two centuries, the length of life one could expect for a newborn in the advanced countries jumped from less than 30 years to perhaps 75 years (Figure 13.3b).

Starting well after World War II, length of life in the poor countries has leaped upward by perhaps 15 or even 20 years since the 1950s, caused by advances in agriculture, sanitation, and medicine. (China has excelled in this respect before developing her economy, which is exceptional.)

The extraordinary decline in child mortality shown in Figure 13.4 is an important element in increased life expectancy, for which every parent must give fervent

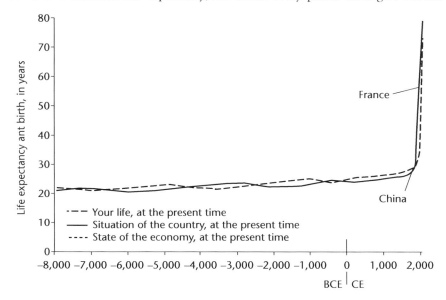

FIGURE 13.3a Trends in life expectancy over the millennia (stylized)

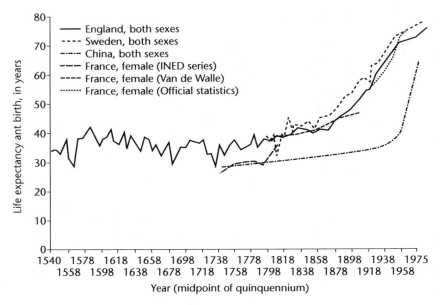

FIGURE 13.3b Life expectancy, England, Sweden, France, and China, 1541–1985

Sources: Preston in this volume for England and Sweden; Lee, 1979, p. 142 for France.

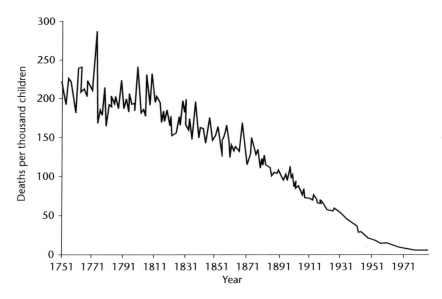

FIGURE 13.4 Child mortality, 1751 to present

Source: Hill in this volume.

The state of humanity **263**

thanks. But contrary to common belief, in the rich countries such as the United States the gains in life expectancy among the *oldest* cohorts have been particularly large in recent years. For example, among US males aged 65–74, mortality fell 26 percent from 1970 to 1988, and among females of that age, mortality fell 29 percent and 21 percent from 1960 and 1970 to 1988, respectively (*US Statistical Abstract*, 1990, p. 75).

The decrease in the death rate is the root cause of there being a much larger world population nowadays than in former times. In the nineteenth century the planet Earth could sustain only one billion people. Ten thousand years ago, only four million could keep themselves alive. Now, more than five billion people are living longer and more healthily than ever before, on average. This increase in the world's population represents humanity's victory against death.

The trends in health are more complex. The decline in mortality is the most important overall indicator of health, of course. And the increase in height in the Western countries in the past century is another strong index of health and nutrition (chapter 5). But whether the process of keeping more people alive into older age is accompanied by better or poorer health on average in those older years is in doubt (chapter 6).

Proportion of the labor force in agriculture

The best simple measure of a country's standard of living is the proportion of the labor force devoted to agriculture. When everyone must work at farming, as was the case only two centuries ago, there can be little production of non-agricultural goods. Figure 13.5 shows the astonishing decline over the centuries in the advanced countries in the proportion of the population working in agriculture, now only about one person in fifty. This shift has enabled consumption per person to multiply by a factor of twenty or forty.

Raw materials

People have since antiquity worried about running out of natural resources – flint, game animals, what-have-you. Yet, amazingly, all the historical evidence shows that raw materials – all of them – have become less scarce rather than more. Chapter 27 (Hausman) shows beyond any doubt that natural resource scarcity – as measured by the economically meaningful indicator of cost or price – has been decreasing rather than increasing in the long run for all raw materials, with only temporary and local exceptions. Copper gives typical evidence that the trend of falling prices has continued throughout all of history. In Babylonia under Hammurabi – almost 4,000 years ago – the price of copper was about a thousand times its price in the US now, relative to wages. At the time of the Roman Empire the price was a hundred times higher. And there is no reason why this trend should not continue forever.

The trend toward greater availability includes the most counter-intuitive case of all – oil. (See Adelman, chapter 28.) Concerning energy in general, there is no

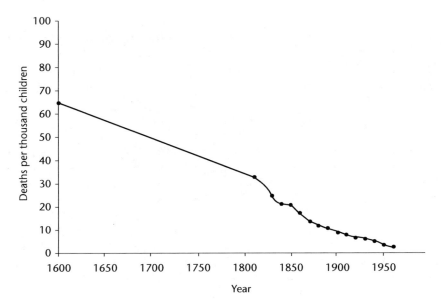

FIGURE 13.5 Percent of population employed in agriculture, Great Britain, 1600 to the present

Source: Mitchell and Deane.

reason to believe that the supply of energy is finite, or that the price of energy will not continue its long-run decrease forever.

Food is an especially important resource. The evidence is particularly strong that the trend in nutrition is benign despite rising population. The long-run price of food is down sharply, even relative to consumer products, due to increased productivity (Figures 13.6a–b). And per-person food consumption is up over the last 30 years. The increase of height in the West, documented in chapter 5 (Fogel), is another mark of improved nutrition.

(Africa's food production per person is down, but by the 1990s, few any longer claim that Africa's suffering has anything to do with a shortage of land or water or sun. Hunger in Africa clearly stems from civil wars and government interference with agriculture, which periodic droughts have made more murderous.)

Only one important resource has shown a trend of increasing scarcity rather than increasing abundance. It is the most important and valuable resource of all – human beings. Certainly there are more people on earth now than ever before. But if we measure the scarcity of people the same way that we measure the scarcity of other economic goods – by how much we must pay to obtain their services – we see that wages and salaries have been going up all over the world, in poor countries as well as in rich countries. The amount that one must pay to obtain the services of a barber or a professor has risen in India, just as the price of a barber or professor has risen in the United States over the decades. This increase in the price of people's services is a clear indication that people are becoming more scarce even though there are more of us.

The state of humanity 265

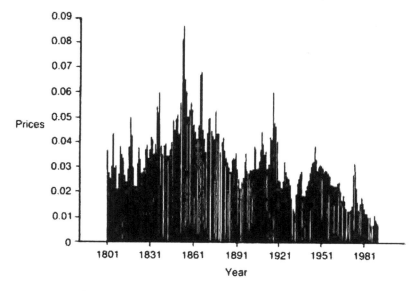

FIGURE 13.6a   Wheat prices indexed by consumer price index, USA, 1801–1990

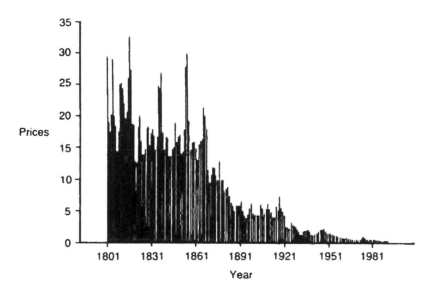

FIGURE 13.6b   Wheat prices indexed by wages, USA, 1801–1990

The standard of living

The pure purchasing-power aspect of the standard of living is difficult to measure. Consider, for example, that before the collapse of communism, the conventional-data estimate of per-capita income in East Germany was 79 percent of that in West Germany, and the "purchasing power parity" estimate was fully 90 percent. It is now clear to all that these computations were misleading. And the clearest evidence comes from data on individual elements of consumption and wealth.

Chapters 13, 14 and 24 (by Burnett and Mokyr; by Lebergott; and by Rector) show unmistakably how the standard of living has increased in the world and in the United States through the recent centuries and decades, right up through the 1980s.

Aggregate data always bring forth the question: But are not the gains mainly by the rich classes, and at the expense of the poor? Chapter 18 (by Lindert and Williamson) shows that for a portion of US history, income distribution did widen (though this is hardly proof that the rich were exploiting the poor). But there has been little or no such tendency during, say, the twentieth century. And a widening gap does not negate the fact of a rising absolute standard of living for the poor. Nor is there evidence in chapter 23 (by Blank) that an increasing proportion of the population lives below some fixed absolute poverty line. And chapter 24 (by Rector) shows extraordinary gains by the US poor in consumption during this century, as well as a high standard of living by any historical and cross-national standards.

A related question concerns possible exploitation by the rich countries that might cause misery for the poor countries. But the distribution of the most important element of "real wealth" – life expectancy – has narrowed between rich and poor countries (as well as between the rich and poor segments of populations within countries) over previous decades – to wit, the extraordinary reduction in the gap between the mortality of China and the rich countries since World War II. The reduction in the gap between literacy rates and other measures of amount of education in rich and poor countries corroborates this convergence. Figures in chapter 13 (by Mokyr), showing convergence in economic productivity in the rich countries along with general growth, dovetail with the other measures of income distribution. Data on the *absolute* gap between yearly incomes of the rich and poor countries are beside the point; widening is inevitable if all get rich at the same proportional rate, and the absolute gap can increase even if the poor improve their incomes at a faster proportional rate than the rich. Here one should notice that increased life expectancy among the poor relative to the rich reduces the gap in lifetime income, which is a more meaningful measure than yearly income.

It is important that the convergence among nations be properly interpreted as a spreading of a better standard of living to the entire world, rather than as a leveling down of the rich.

Cleanliness of the environment

Ask an average roomful of people if our environment is becoming dirtier or cleaner, and most will say "dirtier." Yet the air in the US and in other rich countries is irrefutably safer to breathe now than in decades past; the quantities of pollutants – especially particulates, which are the main threat to health – have been declining. And water quality has improved; the proportion of monitoring sites in the US with water of good drink-ability has increased since the data began in 1961. More generally, the environment is increasingly healthy, with every prospect that this trend will continue. (See Figures 13.7a–d)

When considering the state of the environment, we should think first of the terrible pollutions that were banished in the past century or so – the typhoid that polluted such rivers as the Hudson, smallpox that humanity has finally pursued to the ends of the earth and just about eradicated, the dysentery that distressed and killed people all over the world as it still does in India, the plagues and other epidemics that trouble us much less than in generations past, or not at all. Not only are we in the rich countries free of malaria (largely due to our intensive occupation of the land), but even the mosquitoes, that do no more than cause itches with their bites, are so absent from many urban areas that people no longer need screens for their homes and can have garden parties at dusk. It is a mark of our extraordinary success that these are no longer even thought of as pollutions.

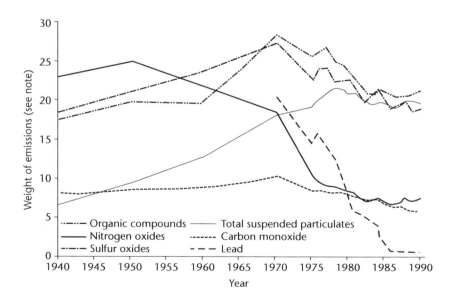

FIGURE 13.7a Emissions of major air pollutants in the USA, 1940–90

Source: Council on Environmental Quality, *Environmental Quality, 22nd Annual Report*, 1992, 273.

Note: In millions of metric tons per year, except lead in ten thousands of metric tons per year, and carbon monoxide in 10 million metric tons per year.

268 J. L. Simon

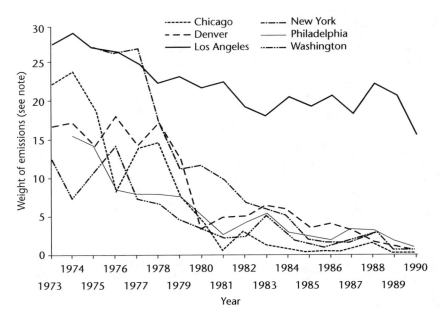

FIGURE 13.7b Air quality trends in major urban areas, USA (number of PSI days greater than 100)

Sources: Council on Environmental Quality, *Environmental Quality, 22nd Annual Report,* 1992, 277; id., *Environmental Quality, 12th Annual Report,* 1981, 244.

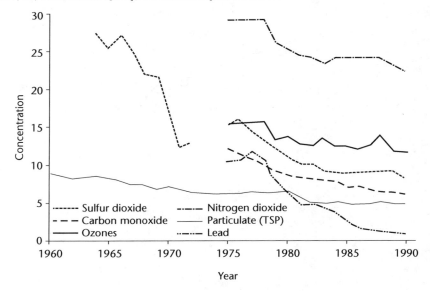

FIGURE 13.7c Pollutants in the air, USA, 1960–90

Sources: Council on Environmental Quality, *Environmental Quality, 12th Annual Report,* 1981, 243; Sulfur 1964 through 1972: EPA (1973): 32 stations.

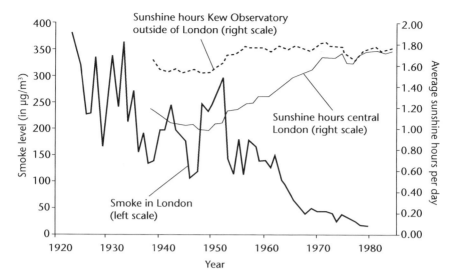

FIGURE 13.7d Smoke level and mean hours of winter sunshine in London, 1923–84

Sources: P. Brimblecombe and H. Rohde, "Air Pollution: Historical Trends," *Durability of Building Materials*, 5 (1988), 291–308; Derek Elsom, this volume.

The root cause of these victorious campaigns against the harshest pollutions was the nexus of increased technical capacity and increased affluence – wealth being the capacity to deal effectively with one's surroundings (see Wildavsky, 1988).

Species extinction

Fear is rampant about rapid rates of species extinction. The fear has little or no basis. The highest rate of observed extinctions is one species per year, in contrast to the 40,000 per year some ecologists have been forecasting for the year 2000. Species matter, and deserve thought. But the facts should matter, too, in deciding whether to spend tens of billions for research, "debt for nature" swaps, and other expensive programs. Furthermore, the new possibilities for genetic engineering, and for storage of seeds, reduce the dangers of extinctions that do occur. Chapter 34 (by Wildavsky and me) discusses how an issue of legitimate interest and concern has turned into an environmentalist scam.

Population growth

The predecessor volume did not discuss population growth because the topic was so controversial that we feared it would distract readers from the other topics. This volume follows the same policy, even though there have been major changes in the intellectual status of the topic. Only two comments will be made:

1 A score of competent statistical studies, starting in 1967 with an analysis by Nobel prizewinner Simon Kuznets, agree that there is no negative statistical relationship between economic growth and population growth for periods up to a century. And there is strong reason to believe that more people have a positive effect in the even longer run. That is, population growth does not lower the standard of living; it raises it in the long run.

2 There was a major turnaround in the 1980s in population economics. After decades of "Everyone knows ..." that population growth hampers economic development, there has been a revolution in scientific thought on the matter. The consensus now is close to the position in the paragraph above, though it runs against intuitive "common sense." This turnaround was made "official" in 1986 by a report of the National Academy of Sciences, but the public and the media have not yet gotten the word on this.

The greenhouse effect, the ozone layer, and acid rain

What about the greenhouse effect? The ozone layer? Acid rain? The one certainty is that on all of these issues there is major scientific controversy and lack of consensus about what has happened until now, why it happened, and what might happen in the future. All of these scares are recent, and there has not yet been time for proper research to be done and for the intellectual dust to settle. There may be hard problems here, or there may not, as chapters 47–50 (Kulp, Singer, Michaels and Lave) discuss.

An important aspect of these atmospheric issues is that no threatening trend in *human welfare* has been connected to changes in these phenomena. There has been no increase in skin cancers from ozone, no damage to agriculture from a greenhouse effect, and slight or no damage to lakes from acid rain. It may even be that a greenhouse effect would benefit us on balance by warming some areas we'd like warmer and by increasing the carbon dioxide stimulus to agriculture.

Perhaps the most important aspect of these as well as the yet-unknown atmospheric scares that will surely be brought before the public is that we now have ever-increasing capacities to reverse such trends if necessary. And we can do so at costs that are manageable rather than being an insuperable constraint upon growth or an ultimate limit upon the increase of productive output or of population. So we can look these issues squarely in the eye and move on.

In summary of this section, I'll dramatize these trends toward a better life – which can be seen in most of our own families if we look – with an anecdote. I have mild asthma. Sometime ago I slept in a home where there was a dog, and in the middle of the night I woke with a bad cough and shortness of breath. When I realized that dog dander was the cause, I found my 12 dollar pocket inhaler, good for 3,000 puffs, and took one puff. Within ten minutes my lungs were clear. A small miracle. Forty years ago I would have been sleepless and miserable all night, and I would have had to give up the squash–playing that I love so much, because exercise causes my worst asthma in the absence of an inhaler. Or consider diabetes. If your child had diabetes a hundred years ago, you had to watch helplessly as the child went blind and died early. Now injections, or even pills, can give the child as long and healthy a life as other children. Or glasses. Centuries ago you had to give up reading when your eyes dimmed as you got to be 40 or 50. Now you can buy magnifying eyeglasses at the drugstore for ten dollars. And you can even wear contact lenses for eye problems and keep your vanity intact. Is there not some condition in your family that in earlier times would have been a lingering misery or a tragedy, that nowadays our increasing knowledge has rendered easily bearable? Does it not bear out the abstract trends presented above?

Other aspects of human welfare

People alive now are living in the midst of what may be seen as the most extraordinary three or four centuries in human history – the period before us and probably the period after us as well. The Industrial Revolution and the gross material aspects of life are only a tiny part of the change.

Some advances need only to be mentioned to be assented to. Consider the amount of physically-caused pain that people suffered in their lives without any help from scientific medicine. Childbirth was a nightmare for every woman; now anesthetics allow a woman to choose a level of pain that is tolerable to her. People whose limbs were injured in peace or war often had to have them amputated, with only liquor as painkiller. Those who lived long enough to die of cancer had no way to dull their agony. Nowadays, it is miraculously different.

So far only material aspects of life have been mentioned. Now let us consider some of the important non-material trends.

Education and opportunity

Consider the astounding increase since World War II in the amount of education that the youth of the world are acquiring (chapter 21, by Boggs and me). This trend implies a vast increase in young people's opportunities to use their talents for their own and their families' benefits, and hence to the benefit of others in society as well. In my view, this trend is one of the most important, and one of the most happy, of all the trends experienced by the human enterprise. Already one can see results in the names on professors' doors in departments of computer science and chemistry, for example, in universities all over the United States, and in the Nobel Prize awards – Asian and African names that would not have been seen a decade or two ago. Less and less often will people of genius and strong character live out their lives in isolated villages unable to contribute to civilization at large.

The process of providing educational opportunity will not be complete for decades, at least. One can still see children sharing rickety desks and scarce books in a Colombian fishing village – just two miles from a busy modern international airport. But even this is vastly better than the way it was just a few years ago – no

272 J. L. Simon

school at all. And we can be confident that a century from now, scenes like that will be quite scarce.

The spread of reading material is manifest – all in the period of time since Gutenberg, so short relative to the history of humanity that it seems only an eyeblink. The recent spread may be measured by the increased amount of newsprint used in the world from decade to decade, and in the prices of advertising – data that this volume regrettably could not collect. And though access to libraries is not yet universal, with the aid of computers and electronic communications, that day is not far away. To dramatize this progress, reflect on the childhood only two centuries ago of Abraham Lincoln, who could not afford paper and pencil. Among a world's population five times as large as it was then, there are almost no children so stricken with educational poverty.

Work, leisure, and boredom

Leisure is surely greater now than since our days as hunters and gatherers when people worked perhaps 10 or 20 hours a week. The marked increase in leisure time in modern countries is documented in chapter 22 (Robinson); compare this to the 80-hour work weeks in industrial jobs a century or two ago, backbreaking labor in mines and factories from before dawn to after dusk.

There is some evidence that work time has increased for some groups in the past decade or two. But for many people, work is a good in itself in the sense that its goal is not the production of additional income, which confuses the issue quantitatively; the opportunity to do this additional rewarding work is a great good in itself, rather than a bad thing (as is the case of the work that goes into this volume, for me and surely for many of the other authors).

Indeed, one of the greatest boons to humanity in recent decades is the diminution in the boring factory tasks that robotized and dehumanized workers. No one who has not experienced eight-hour shifts of such mind–numbing jobs as lifting cases of beer onto or off a conveyor belt, or stacking double, triple, or quadruple sets of empty cans eleven-high in a truck that requires petty arithmetic so that the worker cannot even daydream, can understand how bad the mind–torture is. (Postal workers who sort mail and move bags of it are some of the last of these sufferers in a modern society. And of course workers in poor countries still suffer this because their muscle power is cheaper than machines.)

Though I have no data to document the observation, we apparently do not suffer another of the old painful ills – leisure boredom with nothing to do – that people experienced in earlier times. Indeed, even people who work less than 40 hours a week complain that they have too many things that they want to do.

Boredom also is dispelled by electronic entertainment. This is an extraordinary gift to the old and shut–in; anyone who has been in a hospital bed suffering too much pain even to be able to read a newspaper knows the value of taped music and books, and even junk television. (I'll forever be grateful for the surcease that the two National Football League playoff games brought to me on my first postoperative day.)

The state of humanity **273**

Mobility and travel

Mobility and travel speed constitute another aspect of life that shows extraordinary improvement (chapter 15, by Atack). Only two centuries ago, horse and sailing ship were the fastest modes of movement. Now there are bullet trains and super-sonic flight. The 1992 price of much faster space travel is $6 million per trip, but that price is sure to fall rapidly.

These changes, along with the breathtaking gains in communications speed, are society-altering aids to the spread of human opportunity and liberty all over the world. They also ease the curse most of humanity has suffered – the boredom in isolated villages. Music was a rare pleasure only a century ago. Now there are few people on earth too poor to purchase music around the clock on a transistor radio.

Qualifications to the argument

I am not saying that all is well everywhere, and I do not predict that all will be rosy in the future. Children are hungry and sick; people live out lives of physical or intellectual poverty, and lack of opportunity; irrational war (not even for economic gain) or some new pollution may finish us off. What this book does show is that for most relevant economic matters, the aggregate trends are improving rather than deteriorating.

Please note, too, that a better future does not happen "automatically" and without effort. It will happen because women and men will struggle with problems with their muscles and minds, and will probably overcome most of them – as people always have eventually overcome economic problems in the past – if the social and economic system gives them opportunity to do so.

This volume deals with material and economic welfare, but not with emotional or sexual or spiritual welfare. Whether people are happier than in earlier times as a result of material progress is outside our scope. (To the extent that we can measure happiness, it does increase with the standard of living; see Simon, 1974; Easterlin, 1974.) Many of those non-economic matters are, however, connected to economic welfare, as political freedom is inevitably intertwined with an advanced economy; still, they are not the subject here.

Some supposedly worsening non-economic trends are negative only by one interpretation. Two related examples are: (a) decline in the proportion of the elect-orate who vote, and (b) decline in newspaper readership. Not surprisingly, print journalists consider both of these trends to be baneful signs of community and indi-vidual degeneracy. The interpretation that I favor, however, is that these are signs of an absence of really bad news. When there is no war or natural disaster, there is lots of space for political news. And if the political issues have relatively small bearing upon our personal welfare, they lose our attention to other entertainment, and we devote to other purposes the time and energy required to vote. (It is the church or the academic department that is in crisis that attracts all its members to the monthly meeting.) That is, these signs that the journalists fuss about I take to be

274 J. L. Simon

the signs of a well-off and unthreatened public – to be greeted with smiles rather than with lament. But this is speculation beyond the scope of this volume.

And we now have a problem to which a solution is not visible: the lack of problems that will well challenge women and men. Anecdotal accounts suggest that in the 1950s, when it had the problem of rebuilding from the war and constructing a wholly modern society, Holland was a happier and more vibrant place to live in than now, when the problem people are most vocal about is the disposal of tens of millions of pig excrement each year.

The doomsayers' forecasts

Every forecast of the doomsayers has turned out to be wholly wrong. Metals, foods, and other natural resources have become more available rather than more scarce throughout the centuries. The famous *Famine 1975* forecast by the Paddock brothers – that we would see millions of famine deaths in the US on television – was followed instead by gluts in agricultural markets. Paul Ehrlich's primal scream about "What will we do when the [gasoline] pumps run dry?" was followed by gasoline cheaper than since the 1930s. The Great Lakes are not dead; instead they offer better sport fishing than ever. The main pollutants, especially the particulates that have killed people for years, have lessened in our cities.

The false forecasts have not been harmless, however. They have caused economic disasters for (just a few examples) mining companies and for the poor countries which depend upon natural resources, by misleading them with unsound expectations of increased prices for metals; wasted expenditures for aircraft manufacturers and airlines who planned on high prices for gasolines; and chaos in the auto market for auto makers and for consumers, as a result of laws about fuel economy premised upon a growing scarcity. But neither their personal embarrassment nor their public damage has reduced the doomsayers' credibility with the press, or their command over the funding resources of the federal government.

Not much more than one century ago – after more than 50 centuries of recorded history and hundreds of centuries of unrecorded history – for the first time people had something better than a firelight or oil lamp to break the darkness after dusk. And the absence of electricity continued almost into the second half of the twentieth century for substantial portions of the population of the richest country in the world. Now all of us Americans take Edison's gift for granted.

Less than two centuries ago there appeared the first land transportation that did not depend entirely on animal muscles. Now we complain about the ubiquity of cars. In the last two centuries the first anesthetics other than alcohol became available to provide surcease from the hellish pains of hospital and dental operations, and of diseases such as cancer, as well as to give those women in childbirth who want it another option besides deep breathing. How can one *not* recognize that this is truly a new age of the liberation of humanity from the bonds in which nature has kept us shackled throughout all of our history? And what liberation in the future could possibly match this one?

Can all this good news be true?

Some of the chapters reach documented conclusions that are unbelievable to most journalists and the public. For example, a Sunday *Washington Post* headline (November 10, 1991) reads "A House of Their Own is Out of Most Renters' Reach," and the article quotes young people saying that it is harder now to buy homes than it was for their parents. Richard Muth's chapter 20 shows that the contrary is true; the same quantity and quality house is much more easily affordable now for the representative young couple than it was for earlier generations. How many will believe that?

Hearers of the messages in this book often ask, "But what about the other side's data?" There are no other data. Test for yourself the assertion that the physical conditions of humanity have gotten better. Pick up the US Census Bureau's *Statistical Abstract of the United States* and *Historical Statistics of the United States* at the nearest library and consult the data on the measures of human welfare that depend upon physical resources, for the US or for the world as a whole. See the index for such topics as pollution, life expectancy, and the price indexes, plus the prices of the individual natural resources. While you're at it, check the amount of space per person in our homes, and the presence of such amenities as inside toilets and telephones. You will find "official" data showing that just about every single measure of the quality of life shows improvement rather than the deterioration that the doomsayers claim has occurred.

The long-run trends are mostly presented here in graphs rather than tables because graphs enable one to see trends especially well, and also because the volume reaches out beyond scholars in particular fields. But for scholars who wish to pursue these topics further, the underlying tables will (with luck) be published both in print and in computer files not long after this volume is out. And it is hoped that this collection of data will later be expanded to include material and subjects not included here, and that it will be updated regularly, to become an encyclopedia of how the human enterprise has fared throughout recent millennia. Inquiries from scholars who might participate in this project are warmly invited.

What is the mechanism that produces progress rather than increasing misery?

How can it be that economic welfare grows in time along with population, rather than humanity being reduced to misery and poverty as population grows and we use more and more resources? We need some theory to explain this controversion of common sense.

The Malthusian theory of increasing scarcity, based on supposedly fixed resources, which is the theory that the doomsayers rely upon, runs exactly contrary to the evidence from the long sweep of history. This is because Malthusianism and contemporary doomsters omit from their accounts the positive long-run effects of the problems induced by additional people and economic activity. Maybe neighborhood kids running over your lawn do not benefit you by causing improvements

276 J. L. Simon

in lawn care technology. But more people putting pollutants into the air eventually lead to agitation and the search for ways to prevent and clean up pollutions, a process that eventuates in our having a cleaner environment than before the pollution began to be bad. It is this crucial adjustment mechanism – the reason England's air and water are cleaner than they have been for centuries – that is too often left out of thinking on these matters.

More generally, the process operates as follows: More people and increased income cause problems in the short run – shortages and pollutions. Short-run scarcity raises prices and pollution causes outcries. These problems present opportunity and prompt the search for solutions. In a free society, solutions are eventually found, though many people seek and fail to find solutions at cost to themselves. In the long run the new developments leave us better off than if the problems had not arisen. This theory fits the facts of history.

Technology exists now to produce in virtually inexhaustible quantities just about all the products made by nature – foodstuffs, oil, even pearls and diamonds – and make them cheaper in most cases than the cost of gathering them in the wild natural state. And the standard of living of commoners is higher today than that of royalty only two centuries ago – especially their health and life expectancy, and their mobility to all parts of the world.

Consider this prototypical example of the process by which people wind up with increasing availability rather than decreasing availability of resources. England was full of alarm in the 1600s about an impending shortage of energy due to the deforestation of the country. People feared a scarcity of wood for both heating and the iron industry. This impending scarcity led to the development of coal.

Then in the mid-1800s the English came to worry about an impending coal crisis. The great English economist, Stanley Jevons, calculated that a shortage of coal would bring England's industry to a standstill by 1900; he carefully assessed that oil could never make a decisive difference. Triggered by the impending scarcity of coal (and of whale oil, whose story comes next), ingenious profit-minded people developed oil into a more desirable fuel than coal ever was. And in 1992 we find England exporting both coal and oil.

Another element in the story: Because of increased demand due to population growth and increased income, the price of whale oil for lamps jumped in the 1840s, and the US Civil War pushed it even higher, leading to a whale oil "crisis." This provided incentive for enterprising people to discover and produce substitutes. First came oil from rapeseed, olives and linseed, and camphene oil from pine trees. Then inventors learned how to get coal oil from coal. Other ingenious persons produced kerosene from the rock oil that seeped to the surface, a product so desirable that its price then rose from $0.75 a gallon to $2.00. This high price stimulated enterprisers to focus on the supply of oil, and finally Edwin L. Drake brought in his famous well in Titusville, Pennsylvania. Learning how to refine the oil took a while. But in a few years there were hundreds of small refiners in the US, and soon the bottom fell out of the whale oil market, the price falling from $2.50 or more at its peak around 1866 to well below a dollar.

The state of humanity   **277**

Here we should note that it was not the English or American government that developed coal or oil, because governments are not effective developers of new technology. Rather, it was individual entrepreneurs and inventors who sensed the need, saw opportunity, used all kinds of available information and ideas, made lots of false starts that were very costly to many of those individuals but not to others, and eventually arrived at coal and oil as viable fuels – because there were enough independent individuals investigating the matter for at least some of them to arrive at sound ideas and methods. This happened in the context of a competitive enterprise system that worked to produce what was needed by the public. And the entire process of impending shortage and new solution left us better off than if the shortage problem had never arisen.

The extent to which the political-social-economic system provides personal freedom from government coercion is a crucial element in the economics of resources and population. Skilled persons require an appropriate social and economic framework that provides incentives for working hard and taking risks, enabling their talents to flower and come to fruition. The key elements of such a framework are economic liberty, respect for property, and fair and sensible rules of the market that are enforced equally for all.

What happens if we should not continue to make new discoveries?

We have in our hands now – actually, in our libraries – the technology to feed, clothe, and supply energy to an ever-growing population for the next seven billion years. Most amazing is that most of this specific body of knowledge was developed within just the past two centuries or so, though it rests on basic knowledge that had accumulated for millennia, of course.

Indeed, the last necessary additions to this body of technology – nuclear fission and space travel – occurred decades ago. Even if no new knowledge were ever invented after those advances, we would be able to go on increasing our population forever, while improving our standard of living and our control over our environment. The discovery of genetic manipulation certainly enhances our powers greatly, but even without it we could have continued our progress forever.

Conclusion

The decrease in the death rate, and the attendant increase in life expectancy – more than doubling – during the last two centuries in the richer countries, and in the twentieth century in the poorer countries, is the most stupendous feat in human history. The decline in mortality is the cause of the rapid increases in human population during these periods. This triumph against death would seem the occasion for great rejoicing. Instead we find gloom. One reason for this peculiar outcome is focusing on short-run inter-group comparisons rather than on long-run changes for the human group as a whole.

278 J. L. Simon

In the short run, all resources are limited. An example of such a finite resource is the amount of time you will devote to reading this introduction. The longer run, however, is a different story. The standard of living has risen along with the size of the world's population since the beginning of recorded time. There is no convincing economic reason why these trends toward a better life should not continue indefinitely.

The key theoretical idea again: The growth of population and of income create actual and expected shortages, and hence lead to price run-ups. A price increase represents an opportunity that attracts profit-minded entrepreneurs to seek new ways to satisfy the shortages. Some fail, at cost to themselves. A few succeed, and the final result is that we end up better off than if the original shortages had never arisen. That is, we need our problems, though this does not imply that we should purposely create additional problems for ourselves.

Progress toward a more abundant material life does not come like manna from heaven, however. My message certainly is not one of complacency. In this I agree with the doomsayers: our world needs the best efforts of all humanity to improve our lot. I part company with the doomsters in that they expect us to come to a bad end despite the efforts we make, whereas I expect a continuation of humanity's history of successful efforts. And I believe that their message is self-fulfilling, because if you expect your efforts to fail because of inexorable natural limits, then you are likely to feel resigned, and therefore to literally resign. But if you recognize the possibility − in fact the probability − of success, you can tap large reservoirs of energy and enthusiasm.

Adding more people causes problems. But people are also the means to solve these problems. The main fuel to speed the world's progress is our stock of knowledge; the brakes are our lack of imagination and unsound social regulations of these activities. The ultimate resource is people − especially skilled, spirited, and hopeful young people endowed with liberty − who will exert their wills and imaginations for their own benefit, and so inevitably they will benefit the rest of us as well.

Recommended reading

Other very useful references for more material on the subject of this book include Lebergott (1984), from which several of the chapters in this volume draw, Clark (1957 and 1967), and Clark and Haswell (1967).

References

Clark, Colin (1957): *Conditions of economic progress*. 3d edn. New York: Macmillan.
—— (1967): *Population growth and land use*. New York: St Martin's.
—— and Margaret Haswell (1967): *The economics of subsistence agriculture*. New York: St Martin's.
Easterlin, Richard A. (1974): "Does Economic Growth Improve the Human Lot? Some Empirical Evidence," in P. A. David and W. R. Melvin (eds), *Nations and Households in Economic Growth*. Palo Alto: Stanford University Press.

Lebergott, Stanley (1984): *The Americans – An Economic Record*. New York: W. W. Norton & Company.

Simon, Julian L. (1974): "Interpersonal Comparisons Can Be Made – and Used for Redistribution Decisions," *Kyklos*, vol. XXVII, No. 1, pp. 63–98.

Wildavsky, Aaron (1988): *Searching for Safety*. New Brunswick: Transaction Press.

14

FROM THE PAST TO THE FUTURE

J. L. Simon

> No food, one problem. Much food, many problems.
>
> *(Anonymous)*

This is my long-run forecast in brief: The material conditions of life will continue to get better for most people, in most countries, most of the time, indefinitely. Within a century or two, all nations and most of humanity will be at or above today's Western living standards. The basis for this forecast is the set of trends contained in this volume, together with the simple economic theory stated in the Introduction.

I also speculate, however, that many people will continue to *think and say* that the material conditions of life are getting *worse*. This assessment will only become more cheerful when (or if) humanity invents or evolves or stumbles into an invigorating set of new challenges that will (a) capture peoples' imaginations and hearts and wills, and (b) replace the intergroup political struggles that now increasingly supplant the struggle against nature for a better material life.

This pessimistic outlook for our *world* does not mean, however, that people will be less "happy" about their own lives; about that I have no prediction. I do not predict how the changed material conditions will affect struggles between good and evil, or how increased affluence will change life in the future emotionally, sexually, socially, or spiritually.

Why should you believe this forecast rather than the forecasts made by the doomsayers? Three reasons:

1   My colleagues and I have been right across the board in the forecasts we have made in the past few decades, whereas the doomsayers have been wrong across the board.

2   Throughout the long sweep of history, forecasts of resource scarcity have always been heard, and – just as now – the doomsayers have always claimed that the past was no guide to the future because they stood at a turning point in history. But the turning-point forecasts have been wrong; there have been ups and downs, but no permanent reversals. In every period those who would have bet on improvement rather than deterioration in fundamental aspects of material life — such as the availability of natural resources – would usually have been right.

3   I'll bet my money and my reputation on these forecasts, whereas the doomsayers back off from putting their money where their mouths are; they refuse to put either their cash or their names on the line to back what they say. (Indeed, the credibility of the most famous of the doomsayers suffered greatly when in 1980 his group actually did wager on some of his forecasts, which turned out to be wrong at the expiration of the wager period in 1990.) Their unwillingness to wager should call into question whether (a) they really believe the dire forecasts they make, or (b) they just make statements they don't believe in order to scare the public and mobilize the government to do their will.

The purpose and the method of the forecasts

The recorded past of the human enterprise presented in this volume can help us forecast the future. And sound forecasts can help us evolve wise policies so that the future will be to our liking.

The rationale for statistical evidence far back into the past was given by (or attributed to) Winston Churchill: The further backward you look, the further forward you can see.

A crucial premise for using the past to forecast the future is the constancy of human nature. Along with David Hume and Adam Smith and their Scottish colleagues, and with William James and Friedrich Hayek, I assume that human propensities and appetites, as well as human relationships, will continue to be much the same as they have been; people will change their behavior when changes in conditions give them strong incentive to do so, but only then. This is a fundamental difference from many social commentators of the 1960s who forecast the disappearance of the nuclear family, the decline in the importance of physical beauty and other major changes in the relationship of the sexes, rejection of formal traditions such as the senior prom and evening dress, and the like. This is also unlike the assumption made by Karl Marx – an assumption which, as part of the general theory of communism, might rank as the worst intellectual blunder of all time – that human motivation can be altered so that collective incentives would substitute effectively for individual incentives and private property in inducing hard work and cooperation in impersonal relationships.

It is largely because of these differences in views of human nature that the forecasts to follow differ sharply from the forecasts of most of those who call themselves "futurists." The "futurists" base their predictions mainly on theories drawn from

282 J. L. Simon

physics, biology, and social science while paying little or no attention to the long time series of history.

It is commonly believed that human activities are less predictable than are phenomena in the physical and biological sciences – that is, that unlike natural-scientific events, human events cannot be forecast accurately. But this common observation is entirely unfounded – and indeed, it is baffling that this is said by anyone who has ever confidently expected a friend to show up for a scheduled date, or gone to a movie whose time and place were advertised in the newspaper. It is true that *some* human events cannot be predicted well – the winner of the next World Series, and tomorrow's interest rate. But some *physical* events cannot be predicted well, either – which side a well-flipped coin will fall on, or what the weather will be a year from today.

It also is commonly believed that long-run prediction is more difficult than short-run prediction. Martin Gardner, famous for his writings about mathematical puzzles and scientific fallacies, says that prediction "is like a chess game. You can predict a couple of moves ahead, but it's almost impossible to predict 30 moves ahead" "If it's so hard to be right about a decade, imagine the howlers in store a century hence," says the *Wall Street Journal*. The *Wall Street Journal*'s columnist Lindley H. Clark put the matter thusly: "Economists have a great deal of trouble predicting the future, and it's unlikely that this unhappy situation ever will change."

It is true that economists cannot predict *short-run trends* of interest rates, exchange rates, and security prices. The incapacity to forecast short-run economic events is well established scientifically, and there is sound reason *in principle* for the incapacity.

It is, however, possible to forecast *long-run trends* with great reliability. Indeed, the most important long-run economic predictions – those I make below – are almost a sure thing, subject only to the qualification that there be no global war or political upheaval.

The method which underlies most of my forecasts is as follows: (1) Array the longest available time series of the phenomenon, and decide whether there is a convincing reason not to consider those data to be a representative sample of the "universe" of experience from which the future experience also is likely to be derived. (2) If there is no compelling reason to reject this past experience as a basis for forecasting the future, consider whether there is a convincing theory to explain the trends it shows. (3) If the long-run data seem relevant, and there is a sound theory to explain them – or even if there is no theory but the data are very many and very consistent – extrapolate the long-run trend as the prediction.

Forecasts about human welfare

These are my most important long-run predictions, contingent on there being no global war or political upheaval: (1) People will live longer lives than now; fewer will die young. (2) Families all over the world will have higher incomes and better standards of living than now. (3) The costs of natural resources will be lower than at present. (4) Agricultural land will continue to become less and less important as an economic asset, relative to the total value of all other economic assets. These four predictions are quite certain because the very same predictions, made at all earlier times in history, would have turned out to be right. And sound theory explains these benign trends, as discussed in the Introduction to the book.

Almost as certain is that (5) the environment will be healthier than now – that is, the air and water people consume will be cleaner – because as nations continue to get richer, they will increasingly buy more cleanliness as one of the good things that wealth can purchase. People will probably continue to be worried about pollution nevertheless, both because new sorts of pollutions will occur as new kinds of economic activities develop, and because ability to detect pollutions increases. But the danger of the pollutions that catch our attention will diminish, because we address the worst pollutions first and leave the lesser ones for later, and because our capacity to foresee newly created pollutions in advance will increase. And (6) not only will accidents such as fires continue to diminish in number, but losses to natural disasters such as hurricanes and earthquakes will get smaller, as our buildings become stronger and our methods of mitigating disasters improve.

Perhaps the easiest and surest prediction is that (7) nuclear power from fission will account for a growing proportion of our electricity supply, and probably our total energy supply as well, until it is displaced by some other cheaper source of energy (perhaps fusion). (8) Nuclear power will never be displaced by solar energy using the kinds of technology that are currently available, or by any ordinary development of those kinds of technology.

Can one really make almost surefire long-run predictions? Check for yourself: Though the stock market gyrates from day to day and week to week, its course from decade to decade has almost always been upward. The story is the same in reverse with natural resource prices. Copper, iron, wheat, rice, sugar, and every other natural resource have fallen in price, and therefore risen in availability, throughout the two hundred years of US history, and over the thousands of years of human history wherever records exist. Indeed, the history of civilization is a history of increased knowledge to produce goods more efficiently and cheaply. This goes hand in hand with liberty becoming more widespread, and with increased mobility and communication. All this progress is reflected in the long-run trends of human welfare.

The reader may remark on the absence of forecasts about the ozone layer, the warmth of the surface of the earth, and related atmospheric issues, despite the high current interest in them. There are several reasons: (1) My interest is about human welfare and not about physical conditions – that is, skin cancers but not the ozone layer, agriculture but not the warmth of the earth. And I predict that each of the related human welfare measures will show improvement. If the ozone layer or the warmth of the earth truly does threaten aspects of human life, society will use its large modern capacities to alter those conditions, either in the atmosphere or by protecting individuals directly. (2) The record of the doomsayers in forecasting such matters is atrocious. Remember that only a decade or so before the global

284 J. L. Simon

warming scare got going – in the middle 1970s – the very persons and institutions that now scold us about taking action to reduce global warming were raising the alarm about global cooling. That is, it took only about a decade for the switch from one scenario of doom to the opposite. The worriers about cooling included *Science*, the most influential scientific journal in the world, quoting an official of the World Meteorological Organization; the National Academy of Sciences worrying about the onset of a 10,000 year ice age; *Newsweek*, warning that food production could be adversely affected within a decade; the *New York Times* quoting an official of the National Center for Atmospheric Research; and *Science Digest*, the science periodical with the largest circulation, writing that

> [T]he world's climatologists are agreed on only two things: That we do not have the comfortable distance of tens of thousands of years to prepare for the next ice age, and that how carefully we monitor our atmospheric pollution will have direct bearing on the arrival and nature of this weather crisis. The sooner man confronts these facts, these scientists say, the safer he'll be. Once the freeze starts, it will be too late. (Cited in Bray, 1991.)

Now ask yourself: How reliable could the evidence for the cooling alarm have been? And in connection with that answer, how reliable could be the evidence for the warming alarm of the 1990s, given that it is mostly composed of exactly the same records over many centuries that made up the evidence for the earlier cooling alarm? (Of course the doomsters err by ignoring most of this history and focusing only on the past few years or decades.) And most important, what would have been the results if we had acted on the recommendations made in connection with the cooling scare?

Will progress continue?

Some wonder: How can we be sure that scientific and technical progress will continue indefinitely? Related to this question is another: What will be the rate of economic growth in the future? Elsewhere (Simon, 1992, chapter 19) I conclude that no sensible answer about future rates of advance is possible in principle, in considerable part because of the inherent impossibility of comparative measurement of the value of progress in science from one period to the next.

But uncertainty about the rate of advance in technology does not imply uncertainty about the direction of the future of humankind. Our future material welfare is already assured by our knowledge of how to obtain energy from nuclear fission in unlimited quantities at constant or declining cost, even if no other source of energy is discovered until fissionable material runs out at some almost infinitely distant time. And energy is the only strong constraint on the supplies of all other raw materials.

Assurance about our raw-material future does not imply absence of need for more technology in the short run or the long run, however. There are, and always

From the past to the future **285**

will be, endless ways to improve human life, and plenty of pressing problems to challenge us. But we can confidently face the future without worrying about threats to the end of civilization from "over-consumption" and raw-materials shortages that technology is unable to deal with.

The rate of technical advance with respect to raw materials is not crucial for the long run, because the world's raw-material problems have been resolved for all time with technology already developed. (In brief, if energy is sufficiently cheap, all other raw materials can be obtained at low prices, because energy allows extra-ordinary transformations of many kinds (see Goeller and Weinberg, 1978). And nuclear fission with the breeder – and even more so, nuclear fusion if it becomes practical – provides an unlimited amount of energy at constant or declining cost forever (or at least for billions of years beyond the horizon of any conceivable con-temporary social decision).

Space for living and working is the only other resource requiring attention here. Construction technology now provides us space in huge quantity relative to the amount used until now, by building multistory buildings and by heating and cooling areas of the earth heretofore considered unusable for human habitation because of their extreme climates. If we wish to imagine a bit further, the sea and outer space can provide vast additional living space, and even now they are not impracticably costly. An evaluation of future technical advance might tell us how fast the costs of space and energy will fall, but those rates are not crucial to any decision about population growth. For more details, see Barnett and Morse (1963), or Simon (1981, and second edition forth-coming).

Of course it was not always so. In past eras, natural resources constrained human progress. In the present and immediate future, too, additional technology can improve the standard of living more rapidly than otherwise. Nothing said here implies that our future *economic* problems have been solved, or can be solved for all time. But the problems are less and less those of physical resources.

This leads us to ask what kinds of needs will make technical advance important in the very long run. Health and life come first to mind, of course. But if we accept the contention that our bodies inevitably wear out around age 90 no matter how effectively individual diseases are prevented or controlled, then we are already almost as far as we can go, without much possibility of further advance (see Fries and Crapo, 1981). Of course, biogenetics might engineer different bodies for us, making us a different sort of species. It is not obvious that we would consider this an advance, however, and it is too complex and controversial a matter to discuss here.

We certainly would value advances that would help us live our lives with more serenity, more excitement, and more enjoyment, in greater harmony with our fellows. We also would greatly value advances that would improve teaching and learning in such fashion that individuals could more fully take advantage of the talents with which they are born, in order to make a greater contribution to others and to live more satisfying lives than otherwise. Science may be able to help. But such knowledge is likely to come from fields other than physical science. Once we

286 J. L. Simon

enlarge the concept of technology to include social and psychological knowledge, we move to a different sphere of discourse – one in which, for example, the concept of "breakthrough" must have a very different meaning than it has in the physical sciences.

The argument, then, boils down to this: The crucial contributions to living that advances in productive technique might make in the long future differ fundamentally from those that it has made in the past and in the immediate future. We now possess knowledge about resource locations and materials processing that allows us to satisfy our physical needs and desires for food, drink, heat, light, clothing, longevity, transportation, and the recording and transmission of information and entertainment. We can perform these tasks sufficiently well that additional knowledge on these subjects will not revolutionize life on earth. It still remains to us to organize our institutions, economies, and societies in such fashion that the benefits of this knowledge are available to the vast majority rather than a minority of all people. And our desires for (among other things) leisure, wisdom, love, spirituality, sexuality, adventure, and personal beauty are quite unsatiated, and perhaps must always be so. But the sort of advances in productive knowledge that in the past brought us the possibility of satisfaction for our physical needs cannot sensibly be measured in a fashion comparable to future advances in beneficial knowledge, given our present skills in measurement. Therefore, we should not concern ourselves about the rate of future advances in physical knowledge compared with the rates in the past.

Though I predict that the future of physical discovery will not be like its past, I do not believe that we are at a turning point now. The shift I describe has been going on for at least a century and perhaps much longer, depending on how you view it, and should continue indefinitely. There is no discontinuity to be seen here.

This is not an argument for neglect of scientific and engineering research, of course. I hope that we vigorously continue to increase our technology, and thereby reduce the cost and increase the distribution of the means of satisfaction of our physical needs as, for example, in agricultural research. Furthermore, science is a great human adventure, worthwhile for the observers as well as the participants; space exploration may serve as an example. And even if we do not "need" the technical advances that may occur in the future, we may well find that they are worth far more to us than we would individually be willing to pay for their fruits, in which case there is justification for government support of such activities; space exploration, with the economic benefits it already has begun to provide, may again serve as an example.

One more qualification: Some writers such as Robert Higgs (1987) believe that governments will increase the sizes of their roles in modern economies and societies, which in turn will choke economic progress and even reverse it. In contrast, such writers as George Gilder (1984) and Richard McKenzie and Dwight Lee (1991), believe that technical progress and competition will force governments to play a smaller role. In choosing between these assessments about the future of

From the past to the future **287**

government there is little historical experience to rely upon. It seems to me relevant, as Stanley Engerman's essay in this volume documents, that slavery has diminished over the centuries. Less reliably, the evidence seems to point toward more freedom and democracy throughout the world since World War II, but the record is scrappy. Hence in this matter we are forced to rely heavily on analysis – that is, the combination of various theoretical arguments and selected supporting factual evidence. And in my judgment, the analysis of Gilder and McKenzie-Lee is more convincing, given the evidence since the mid-1980s.

The two main reasons that I think government will become less powerful are these: (1) The rapid movement across borders of capital and information facilitates sharp competition for resources among firms in different countries, which reduces the power of governments to tax captive businesses and individuals. (2) These new technologies of movement strengthen small enterprises relative to large enterprises, continuing the process that began when electricity became available as a substitute for steam or water power, and the truck became available as a substitute for the railroad. Smaller enterprises are harder for governments to control – both their locations and their activities.

Future fertility in modern countries is another important element about which we lack historical evidence. Will affluent couples continue to have children at a rate that will not increase the population? Or will procreation in rich countries increase sufficiently, while the proportion of the population in now poor countries falls, to continue the long-run expansion of population on Earth and perhaps elsewhere? More about this below.

Where are we in the long sweep of human existence?

People alive now are living in the midst of what may well be the most extraordinary three or four centuries in human history. The "industrial revolution" and its technical aftermath – even including the spectacular rise in living standards for most human beings from near subsistence to the level of today's modern nations – is only pan of the upheaval. The process has already been completed for perhaps a third of humanity, as described in various chapters in this book, and within a century or two (unless there is a holocaust) the rest of humanity is almost sure to attain the amenities of modern living standards; the worst holocaust imaginable could only delay the process by a century or so.

The most spectacular development, and by far the most meaningful in both human and economic terms, is the revolution in health that we are witnessing in the second part of the twentieth century. Barring catastrophic surprises in the first half of the twenty-first century, most of humanity will come to share the long healthy life that is now enjoyed by the middle-class contemporary residents of the advanced countries.

The technical developments of the past two centuries certainly depended on earlier discoveries. But the knowledge that emerged before the last two centuries was only infrastructure. Until the most recent generations, most people could not

288 J. L. Simon

observe the effects or gain the benefits of this progress in their own lives. Now we are reaping the full fruits of that earlier investment.

The spreading of a high level of living will be speeded by another phenomenon that can be predicted for sure: increased migration from poor to rich countries. The lure of a higher standard of living pushes migrants from their native countries and pulls them to richer places. And the felt need in the richer countries for youthful persons in the labor force to balance the ever greater concentrations in the older age cohorts fuels the deman for them. One can see the drama of this process in the youthful medical and custodial staffs in big-city hospitals who came from abroad to tend to the aged natives and the veterans of earlier migrations.

Might there not be even more and faster and more radical change in future? In human terms, I doubt it. Life expectancy and child mortality cannot fall much faster unless we change genetically. Concorde-like supersonic speed of travel demonstrably does not matter very much (and the trip to and from airport will take a long time to speed up). Communications cannot become much faster, many being at the speed of light now. The distances one can travel – to the planets and beyond – will eventually increase greatly, and this may alter life significantly, though I cannot imagine how.

The only impending shortage is a shortage of economic shortages. (For investors this implies that profitable investments lie in the economic sectors that profit from affluence. Stay away from commodities; their prices will fall, as they have been falling for hundreds and thousands of years. Sell marginal farm land; it will become less valuable as productivity per acre increases. Buy acreage that was wasteland in the past because it is mountainous or inaccessible; it will now become more profitable for those very characteristics, its recreational value.)

In *The Next Two Hundred Years*, Herman Kahn, my coauthor of the predecessor volume, decades ago foresaw this four-century emergence from isolated subsistence farming in which most of humanity has lived throughout history (Kahn, Brown, and Martel, 1976). Herman was frequently "accused" of being an optimist. He would reply, "I'm not an optimist, I'm a realist." Indeed, it is realistic to forecast improving long-run material trends for humanity, forever.

The future growth in education and opportunity

Chapter 21 shows the astounding increase in the amount of education that young people in the poorer countries of the world have been acquiring. This education implies an increase in opportunities to use their talents for their own and their families' benefits; the realization of these talents benefits others in society as well as those persons. This trend is to me one of the most important, and one of the most happy, of all trends in the human enterprise. One can see the results in the nameplates on professors' doors in departments of computer science and chemistry (for example) in universities all over the United States – Asian and African names that would not have been there a decade or two ago. Less and less often will people of genius and strong character live out their entire lives in isolated villages where they cannot contribute to civilization.

Quantitative evidence for the spread of education and of access to knowledge can be seen in the statistics of world education in chapter 21. But the most compelling evidence is found in the stories of individuals such as William Owens (see his astounding autobiography), who grew up just after the turn of the century in Pin Hook, Texas, so poor that he could not get more than a few months of schooling in each of the few years when he got any at all, and could obtain literally nothing to read–some old newspapers pasted onto the walls of a shack in which he lived, to keep out drafts, were the most he could find for a while. By the time Owens had miraculously become a professor of literature and folklore at Columbia University, access to reading material had become universal in the United States, and there were good schools and even wonderful junior colleges within the reach of just about every American.

Yes, Gutenberg's invention of printing was crucial. But it was the rise in economic productivity that has brought the benefits of that invention within reach of humanity at large. Aside from our victory against premature death in the past century, this spread of education and knowledge may be the most important alteration of all time in human welfare.

As with other aspects of the globalization of a modern standard of living, the process of providing enough education to liberate all young people and to empower them to exercise their talents to the fullest is far from complete. One can still see children sharing rickety desks and scarce books in a near-subsistence Colombian fishing village, just two miles from a busy international airport. Yet the situation there is better than it was just a few years ago when there was no school at all. We can be confident that a century from now scenes like that poor school will be few and far between. The children will have become too valuable to others to allow them to grow up that way.

Increased education does not imply that the public will be more enlightened on crucial issues than now. For example, I do not expect that most people and their political leaders will be much more in favor of truly free trade than now; the idea is simply too counter-intuitive for wide belief; for 200 years the public has shown that it does not rapidly learn this idea. I do expect that trade will become freer anyway, however, simply because of the pressure of international competition among countries. This is one of the many issues where we can expect that the inherent advantages of certain sorts of regimes – free trade, nuclear power, personal freedom – will gradually win against ideas and desires that run in the opposite direction. Ideas do have consequences, even if they are bad ideas, but the counterproductive consequences are limited and are eventually overcome by economic reality.

The likelihood of catastrophic disease

What about the possibility of a catastrophic disease that could devastate humanity? Many thoughtful people worry that increased human mobility might raise the chance of global disease transmission.

Before considering this possibility, we should note that even a disease of greater magnitude than has ever occurred would only reverse contemporary human progress for a relatively short time. The demographic and economic losses from the worst disaster in history – the Black Death, which killed perhaps a quarter of the population of major European countries – had been recovered after only a century or so; the population size and the standard of living soon were back almost to where they would have been otherwise.

Furthermore, even a disaster of unprecedented scale – say, a devastation of 90 percent or even 99 percent of humanity – would not have permanent effects. The only essential element for a modern economy and society is the knowledge that resides in libraries. With the books housed there, a small number of people could create what they would need in a matter of decades.

The necessary characteristics of a catastrophic disease

These are the characteristics that a disease would require to be catastrophic: (1) There must be a "vector" – a mechanism that spreads the disease – of great rapidity and efficiency. (2) The disease must kill or debilitate a large proportion of those who become infected. (3) Most important, the disease must show symptoms and be diagnosed only many years after people become infected.

The importance of a time lag between the infection and the appearance of symptoms is that humanity now has enormous capacity to protect itself against almost any conceivable vector once the disease is known and the vector is sought. The causes of new diseases of the sorts that have occurred in the past – bacterial, viral, environmental, even genetic – nowadays can be determined quickly; it would seem that most imaginable (and even unimaginable) diseases also would reveal their causes to scientists within a very few years. (The main mode of transmission of AIDS was discovered within weeks or months of the diagnosis of the first cases.) And once the vector has been identified – whether it be by air or water or insect bite or whatever – nowadays it is within our capabilities to block that transmission effectively. (Sexual transmission is the most difficult to prevent, but because a large proportion of the population is either monogamous or not sexually active, a sexually-transmitted disease could not kill a majority of the human population, let alone almost everyone.) Therefore, only if there is a long lag could a disease transmitted through the air or water manage to infect a large proportion of humanity. (If the elapsed time between being infected and showing symptoms were not so long in the case of AIDS, it would have done less harm.)

Our growing ability to deal with catastrophic disease

It is also relevant that our capacity to learn quickly and deal rapidly with new diseases has expanded enormously over the centuries and the last few decades. The first AIDS case was diagnosed only a decade before the time of writing this in 1992.

And we should note the beneficial spin-offs of new knowledge due to the onset of new diseases that will help check diseases in the future.

Absolute and relative progress

The predictions in this chapter are for the *absolute* progress of humanity as a whole, in keeping with the spirit and title of this volume. The public and the press are often – much too often, in my view – interested in the *relative* achievements of particular countries and groups, as discussed in the Introduction to the volume. The historical trends that are the foundations for the predictions in this chapter do not support solid predictions for particular countries and groups except in one respect: In light of data in the appendix to chapter 15, communities may be expected to converge in their standards of living in the long run.

Nevertheless, I hazard a few weak predictions about relative progress: With respect to Eastern Europe, the former Soviet Union has the benefit of a large educated class. But even so, it and the other Eastern European nations will need decades to create the legal and institutional infrastructure to support solid economic growth; this is the key element, in my view. Indeed, I expect the former Soviet Union republics to lag far behind several of the other Eastern European countries.

A hundred years from now China or India could be the leading nation in the world. If freedom wins out fairly soon in China, and if people in those two countries are reasonably wise about reconstructing their economic institutions to enable enterprise to flourish, a century could be more than enough time for them to nearly catch up economically with the leading countries in the world. After all, Hong Kong caught up more than halfway in less than half a century, and events are likely to move even faster in the future. If so, the sheer demographic weight of China and India is likely to dominate all other countries. They are then likely to exert leadership in various international forums.

Bets are off if India and China break up into smaller nations, of course. To my mind, there is little bad about such breakups, and it may benefit the individuals in the smaller units. But as Europe has shown, such splitting does not make for world dominance. Perhaps with enough splitting, no nation will be a super power. That might be the best world of all.

(Is international leadership a good thing? Maybe not. But if one does want the leadership role for the United States or another country, one should wish that its population increases rapidly rather than slowly, because that may be the only way to delay India's and China's surge to leadership.)

A shocking last prediction: The economic reasons for war diminish as land becomes less important relative to other assets and therefore less worth spending money and lives to annex. I predict that this trend will reduce the incidence of war in the long run, though I agree with writers who argue that the economic element is not the only crucial determinant of war.

292   J. L. Simon

Conditions getting better, perceptions getting worse

Even though the material conditions of life have been getting better, many people believe that conditions have been getting worse. The Introduction began by illustrating this process. The title of a news article conveys the flavor of the matter: "Down in the Dumps – The Glooming of America: If the numbers aren't so bad, why is the country feeling so lousy?" (*Newsweek*, January 13, 1992).

A curiosity: My mother's life spanned almost half of the past two-century revolutionary period. She was born in 1900 and saw her only child saved from death at age seven by the first new wonder drug. In her eighties she knew that her friends had mostly lived extraordinarily long lives. She recognized the convenience and comfort provided by such modern inventions as the telephone, air conditioning, and air-planes. And yet she disagreed when I said the conditions of life had markedly improved. When I asked Mother why she still thought things have gotten worse, she replied: "The headlines in the newspaper are all bad."

Journalism will get worse for at least a while into the future, as it covers a smaller proportion of its traditional stories – fires, politics, and local events – and covers more events for which its traditional techniques are not fitted – scientific developments, especially concerning the environment, social scientific trends, and other matters that require more than first-hand observation and individual interviews. Where this will end is not clear to me. Training of journalists in nontraditional techniques may be in the cards, but probably will never cure this problem because it is inherent in covering stories quickly as "news" without historical digging.

Scientific research will become more and more involved in advanced technique, which will mean that fewer exciting problems will be worked on, and science will become a less attractive field for creative persons.

We will always find grounds for worry. Apparently it is a built-in property of our mental systems that no matter how good things become, our aspiration levels ratchet up so that our anxiety levels decline hardly at all, and we focus on ever smaller actual dangers. Parents manage to worry about their kids' health and safety even though the mortality of children is spectacularly lower than in prior decades and centuries. And orthodox Jews and Muslims in the United States continue to worry about whether their food is ritually pure even though the protections against ritual contamination are remarkably better than in the past. (Once upon a time orthodox Jews said that "A Jew eats a small pig every year without knowing it." Nowadays, with plastic wrapping at the factory, and the microscopic examination techniques of modern science, the level of purity is much higher than in the past. But the level of concern does not abate.)

Remember please that there are fewer life-threatening disasters from decade by decade. Some evidence for this is found in statistics of accidents (see chapter 9). Other evidence may be seen in the headlines of newspapers, which less and less frequently concern earthquakes, fires, and floods, and more and more are about political and social issues. Surely this trend will continue for the foreseeable future. Fewer and fewer of our struggles will be against nature, and more and more will be

From the past to the future **293**

battles of one group versus another. This suggests that until we find new challenges
– such as terraforming other planets – we will be caught up in zero-sum issues that
are less likely to satisfy the spirit than are the battles against nature that society tends
to win.

The belief in progress

A hundred years ago belief in continued progress and a bright future was commonplace. Why not now?

One reason for the loss of belief in progress is the focus of the media on bad
things happening, a phenomenon discussed in the Introduction and the section
above. But another reason might well be the shattering blow to people's confidence that World War II inflicted. As the novelist Stefan Zweig wrote in his autobiography, *The World of Yesterday:*

> Against my will, I have witnessed the most terrible defeat of reason and the
> wildest triumph of brutality in the chronicle of the ages. Never – and I say
> this without pride, but rather with shame – has any generation experienced
> such a moral retrogression from such a spiritual height as our generation
> has. ...
>
> In the short interval between the time when my beard began to sprout and
> now, when it is beginning to turn gray, in this half-century more radical
> changes and transformations have taken place than in ten generations of
> mankind; and each of us feels it is almost too much. (p. xviii, University of
> Nebraska Press/Viking Press, 1943/1964)

Since Zweig wrote those lines during World War II, just about every change
important to humankind has been for the better-and the trends have been dramatic
in their extents. But this apparently has not been enough to convince people that
World War II was not an anomaly and is not likely to happen again in the foreseeable future.

But this may be wrong, too. A generally thoughtful columnist recently wrote:
"We have lost our conviction that things will always get better" (Richard Cohen,
"Progress Ain't What It Used to Be." *Washington Post Magazine*, October 13, 1991,
p. 7). Maybe people *never* had the conviction that things would always get better.

The crucial need for important challenges

Frank Knight once wrote that what people most seek is not to have their wants
fulfilled, but bigger and better wants. This may not be true of those who are cold
and hungry at the moment, or of adolescents driven wild by their hormones, or of
harried parents trying to be in three places at once. But it certainly is true of many
middle-class people who have acquired the physical appurtenances they consider
they need, and who have succeeded in their own eyes in their professions. And it

294 J. L. Simon

is true of many young people who do not see on their horizons exciting challenges to their talents and ambitions – no crusades or jihads to defeat an infidel, no new continents to discover, no frontier from which to hack out a homestead. As James Buchanan put it, "I do not envy the youngsters in modern suburbia, who lack a sense of scarcity along any [material] dimension" (1992, 23).

Anecdotal history shows the need for challenging problems. I heard Dutch people say about themselves in the 1990s that they are gloomy now but that in the 1950s, when Holland was still rebuilding after the war, the national mood was very much more cheery. Today every corner of the Netherlands seems already to have been improved and neatened. And there is discussion there of removing from agricultural use some of the fertile land that earlier was taken at such great effort from the sea, because the agricultural produce from that acreage is no longer needed. The Netherlands' worst problem, they say, is the disposal of millions of tons of pig excrement that they have not yet found uses for. This is not the sort of problem that fires the imaginations of the young.

More and more, as affluence spreads throughout humanity, our species' biggest problem will be a lack of satisfying challenges – opportunities to sacrifice, to make a large contribution to a larger cause, to be part of a team, to achieve nobility – truly William James's "moral equivalent of war." That's what the environmental activities now seem to offer. But they are flawed because they are mainly retentive, rather than creative (a subject I discuss in more detail in Simon, 1981; 1995).

A vast expansion of the human population could present such a challenge and might lead to buccaneering expeditions to conquer outer space. But the future course of fertility (upon which population growth will depend almost solely, because further mortality reduction will not be great) is not predictable as of now.

Only such new challenges, I believe, can prevent us from descending into C. S. Lewis's vision of the netherworld: "We must picture Hell as a state where everyone is perpetually concerned about his own dignity and advancement [and I would add, the dignity and advancement of the racial, religious, ethnic, national, and other groups one is a member of], where everyone has a grievance, and where everyone lives the deadly serious passion of envy, self-importance and resentment." (From *The Screwtape Letters*, quoted in *Washington Post*, January 17, 1993, C4.)

In the past, family resources constrained family size. But the evidence suggests that as average income continues to grow, it is likely – though by no means certain – that fertility and money income are becoming increasingly separated. That is, family size at incomes much higher than now in the USA might still be of the same order as in average American or European families today. Indeed, the family size of those on the highest income today is not particularly large. Families in the super-wealthy future may be bigger, or smaller, than now. Income is not likely to be a good predictor of what would happen if incomes climb to the point at which additional income does not matter. And if income and fertility do become increasingly separated, the biggest changes in fertility may then be associated with one or the other sort of fear: either the fear of depopulation, as in the 1930s, or the fear of overpopulation, as in the late 1960s and into the 1970s, in the United States and

China. The overall result may be a series of rises and falls in fertility, triggered by, and in turn triggering, these fears. This sequence might bear little or no relationship to basic economic conditions, just as in fact there was no basic economic difference in the two periods that would explain the depopulation and overpopulation fears in the 1930s and 1960s.

It may be that *relative* income is the key factor, as Richard Easterlin (1968) has argued. If so, fertility may continue to be affected by fluctuations over time and by the shape of income distribution. Only the far future will give the answers to these speculations, however.

What will determine the future?

> The history of mankind is the history of ideas. For it is ideas, theories, and doctrines that guide human action, determine the ultimate ends men aim at, and the choice of the means employed for the attainment of these ends.
>
> *(Ludwig von Mises, quoted in The Freeman, Feb 1993, p. 42)*

Though I greatly admire much of von Mises' economics, I consider the above remark as exemplifying the megalomania of the intellectual class. Curiously, von Mises agrees on this point with J. M. Keynes. And Hayek in 1944 said, "I agree with Lord Keynes that 'the ideas of economists and political philosophers, both when they are right and when they are wrong, are more powerful than is commonly understood. Indeed, the world is ruled by little else'" (Hayek, 1991, p. 36).

All of us like to think we are important — intellectuals certainly as much as anyone. And yes, ideas can be powerful in the intermediate run — witness the disaster caused by Marxist thinking for 70 years in Eastern Europe and China. But in the longer run, the elemental forces of peoples' desires to carve out a good living for themselves and for their families, to have children and raise them happy and well-educated, to employ one's talents and energies and to enjoy their fruits — these forces will eventuate in government policies that allow people these fundamental freedoms. There probably always will be temporary reversals and reversions to totalitarianism for a while. But we can hope that in an ever-ramified world where people can move ever more freely, these reversions will be of shorter duration and of lesser magnitude.

If ideas were all-important, the horde of more-or-less sensible economists descending (literally) on Eastern Europe should be able to put things straight in a hurry. But we will see that decades of evolutionary institutional rebuilding will be necessary; there is no single set of grand ideas that can replace that necessary work.

All that is required of philosophers and economists is that they manage to prise from rulers a small chink of living and operating room for individuals, and some degree of rule of law. All the rest will be done by individuals themselves, without recourse to any grand ideas. Indeed, this is the very doctrine of von Mises and Hayek — and Friedman, Smith, and Hume. In this rare respect, Hayek and von

296 J. L. Simon

Mises contradict themselves. They all know the power of black markets even in the teeth of the most fearsome sanctions. Such markets are not driven by grand ideas, but by human desires and economic incentives.

The more that humanity progresses, the less these ideas will matter, because the variety of régimes offered competitively by the various countries, and the easy mobility among them, will provide the necessary opportunities for entrepreneurs and other talented persons. The need grows less for philosophers of liberty to eke out a bit of freedom for society from the clutches of politicians intoxicated with the chance to put into operation their delusions of improvement by central control (theirs). People will achieve it anyway.

On the other hand, with greater progress comes greater freedom from pressing survival needs, which in turn enables people to indulge themselves in foolish, irrational, and counter-productive thinking, and can lead to mass movements that impede progress. (We might note that farmers and small retailers, who are of necessity in exceedingly close touch with economic reality, are – at least I so think – relatively free of foolish economic thinking, if only as the result of a Darwinian process.)

The brief forecast again

Whatever nature has produced that we make use of – food, oil, diamonds – humankind now can also produce, and faster than nature. An expectancy of health and a standard of living higher than that which any prince enjoyed 200 years ago is the birthright of every middle-class and working-class person in developed countries, and of most people in poverty as well. What is still to come is to bring these material gains to all groups of humanity. That may take half a century or a century. Yet that benign outcome may be predicted with a high degree of likelihood – a happy vision, indeed.

The future for the correct perception of these trends looks bleak, due to their portrayal in the press, however. The techniques that journalists use so well to cover fires and local politics do not work well for matters that go beyond first-hand observation. This includes scientific matters, as illustrated nowadays by environmental questions. And the bad-news bias in journalism transforms every story into a negative one, even if the underlying facts are positive. This in turn leads the public to think that conditions in general are getting worse. The press then reports this as pessimism. All this could have increasingly dire effects upon the public mood.

As to the non-material aspects of human existence – good luck to us.

References

Barnett, Harold J., and Chandler Morse (1963): *Scarcity and Growth: The Economics of Natural Resource Availability*. Baltimore: Johns Hopkins.

Bray, Anna J. (1991): "The Ice Age Cometh." *Policy Review*, Fall, 82–4.

Buchanan, James (1992): *Better Than Plowing, And Other Essays*. Chicago: University of Chicago Press.

From the past to the future **297**

Easterlin, Richard A. (1968): *Population, Labor Force, and Long Swings in Economic Growth*. New York: National Bureau of Economic Research.

Fries, James F., and Lawrence M. Crapo (1981): *Vitality and Aging*. San Francisco: W. H. Freeman and Company.

Gilder, George (1984): *The Spirit of Enterprise*. New York: Simon and Schuster.

Goeller, H. E., and A. M. Weinberg (1978): "The Age of Substitutability," *Science* 191, 683–9.

Hayek, Friedrich (1991): "On Becoming an Economist." In Hayek's *The Trend of Economic Thinking*. Chicago: University of Chicago Press.

Higgs, Robert (1987): *Crisis and Leviathan*. New York, Oxford: Oxford University Press.

Kahn, Herman, with William Brown and Leon Martel (1976): *The Next 200 Years*. New York: Morrow.

McKenzie, Richard B., and Dwight R. Lee (1991): *Quicksilver Capital*. New York: Free Press.

Owens, William (1986): *This Stubborn Soil*. New York: Vintage.

Simon, Julian L. (1981): *The Ultimate Resource*. Princeton: Princeton University Press. Second edn. forthcoming 1995.

———— (1992): *Population Growth and Economic Development in Poor Countries*. Princeton: Princeton University Press.

Weisbrod, Burton A. (1962): "An Expected-Income Measure of Economic Welfare." *The Journal of Political Economy*, August, 355–67.

15

THE POSSIBILITY OF SOCIAL CHOICE[†]

A. Sen[*]

"A camel," it has been said, "is a horse designed by a committee." This might sound like a telling example of the terrible deficiencies of committee decisions, but it is really much too mild an indictment. A camel may not have the speed of a horse, but it is a very useful and harmonious animal—well coordinated to travel long distances without food and water. A committee that tries to reflect the diverse wishes of its different members in designing a horse could very easily end up with something far less congruous: perhaps a centaur of Greek mythology, half a horse and half something else—a mercurial creation combining savagery with confusion.

The difficulty that a small committee experiences may be only greater when it comes to decisions of a sizable society, reflecting the choices "of the people, by the people, for the people." That, broadly speaking, is the subject of "social choice," and it includes within its capacious frame various problems with the common feature of relating social judgments and group decisions to the views and interests of the individuals who make up the society or the group. If there is a central question that can be seen as the motivating issue that inspires social choice theory, it is this: how can it be possible to arrive at cogent aggregative judgments about the society (for example, about "social welfare," or "the public interest," or "aggregate poverty"), given the diversity of preferences, concerns, and predicaments of the different individuals *within* the society? How can we find any rational basis for making such aggregative judgements as "the society prefers this to that," or "the society should choose this over that," or "this is socially right"? Is reasonable social choice at all possible, especially since, as Horace noted a long time ago, there may be "as many preferences as there are people"?

Social choice theory

In this lecture, I shall try to discuss some challenges and foundational problems faced by social choice theory as a discipline.[1] The immediate occasion for this lecture is, of course, an award, and I am aware that I am expected to discuss, in one form or another, my own work associated with this event (however immodest that attempt might otherwise have been). This I will try to do, but it is, I believe, also a plausible occasion to address some general questions about social choice as a discipline—its content, relevance, and reach—and I intend to seize this opportunity. The Royal Swedish Academy of Sciences referred to "welfare economics" as the general field of my work for which the award was given, and separated out three particular areas: social choice, distribution, and poverty. While I have indeed been occupied, in various ways, with these different subjects, it is social choice theory, pioneeringly formulated in its modem form by Arrow (1951),[2] that provides a general approach to the evaluation of, and choice over, alternative social possibilities (including inter alia the assessment of social welfare, inequality, and poverty). This I take to be reason enough for primarily concentrating on social choice theory in this Nobel lecture.

Social choice theory is a very broad discipline, covering a variety of distinct questions, and it may be useful to mention a few of the problems as illustrations of its subject matter (on many of which I have been privileged to work). When would *majority rule* yield unambiguous and consistent decisions? How can we judge how well a *society as a whole* is doing in the light of the disparate interests of its different members? How do we measure *aggregate poverty* in view of the varying predicaments and miseries of the diverse people that make up the society? How can we accommodate *rights and liberties* of persons while giving adequate recognition to their preferences? How do we appraise social valuations of public goods such as the *natural environment*, or *epidemiological security?* Also, some investigations, while not directly a part of social choice theory, have been helped by the understanding generated by the study of group decisions (such as the causation and prevention of *famines and hunger*, or the forms and consequences of *gender inequality*, or the demands of *individual freedom* seen as a "social commitment"). The reach and relevance of social choice theory can be very extensive indeed.

Origins of social choice theory and constructive pessimism

How did the subject of social choice theory originate? The challenges of social decisions involving divergent interests and concerns have been explored for a long time. For example, Aristotle in ancient Greece and Kautilya in ancient India, both of whom lived in the fourth century B.C., explored various constructive possibilities in social choice in their books respectively entitled *Politics* and *Economics*.[3]

However, social choice theory as a systematic discipline first came into its own around the time of the French Revolution. The subject was pioneered by French mathematicians in the late eighteenth century, such as J. C. Borda (1781) and

300 A. Sen

Marquis de Condorcet (1785), who addressed these problems in rather mathematical terms and who initiated the formal discipline of social choice in terms of voting and related procedures. The intellectual climate of the period was much influenced by European Enlightenment, with its interest in reasoned construction of social order. Indeed, some of the early social choice theorists, most notably Condorcet, were also among the intellectual leaders of the French Revolution.

The French Revolution, however, did not usher in a peaceful social order in France. Despite its momentous achievements in changing the political agenda across the whole world, in France itself it not only produced much strife and bloodshed, it also led to what is often called, not inaccurately, a "reign of terror." Indeed, many of the theorists of social coordination, who had contributed to the ideas behind the Revolution, perished in the flames of the discord that the Revolution itself unleashed (this included Condorcet who took his own life when it became quite likely that others would do it for him). Problems of social choice, which were being addressed at the level of theory and analysis, did not wait, in this case, for a peacefully intellectual resolution.

The motivation that moved the early social choice theorists included the avoidance of both instability and arbitrariness in arrangements for social choice. The ambitions of their work focused on the development of a framework for rational and democratic decisions for a group, paying adequate attention to the preferences and interests of all its members. However, even the theoretical investigations typically yielded rather pessimistic results. They noted, for example, that majority rule can be thoroughly inconsistent, with A defeating B by a majority, B defeating C also by a majority, and C in turn defeating A, by a majority as well.[4]

A good deal of exploratory work (often, again, with pessimistic results) continued in Europe through the nineteenth century. Indeed, some very creative people worked in this area and wrestled with the difficulties of social choice, including Lewis Carroll, the author of *Alice in Wonderland* (under his real name, C. L. Dodgson, 1874, 1884).

When the subject of social choice was revived in the twentieth century by Arrow (1951), he too was very concerned with the difficulties of group decisions and the inconsistencies to which they may lead. While Arrow put the discipline of social choice in a structured—and axiomatic—framework (thereby leading to the birth of social choice theory in its modern form), he deepened the pre-existing gloom by establishing an astonishing—and apparently pessimistic—result of ubiquitous reach.

Arrow's (1950, 1951, 1963) "impossibility theorem" (formally, the "General Possibility Theorem") is a result of breathtaking elegance and power, which showed that even some very mild conditions of reasonableness could not be simultaneously satisfied by any social choice procedure, within a very wide family. Only a dictatorship would avoid inconsistencies, but that of course would involve: (1) in politics, an extreme sacrifice of participatory decisions, and (2) in welfare economics, a gross inability to be sensitive to the heterogeneous interests of a diverse population. Two centuries after the flowering of the ambitions of social rationality, in Enlightenment thinking and in the writings of the theorists of the French Revolution, the subject

The possibility of social choice **301**

seemed to be inescapably doomed. Social appraisals, welfare economic calculations, and evaluative statistics would have to be, it seemed, inevitably arbitrary or unremediably despotic.

Arrow's "impossibility theorem" aroused immediate and intense interest (and generated a massive literature in response, including many other impossibility results).[5] It also led to the diagnosis of a deep vulnerability in the subject that overshadowed Arrow's immensely important *constructive* program of developing a systematic social choice theory that could actually work.

Welfare economics and obituary notices

Social choice difficulties apply to welfare economics with a vengeance. By the middle 1960's, William Baumol (1965) judiciously remarked that "statements about the significance of welfare economics" had started having "an ill-concealed resemblance to obituary notices" (p. 2). This was certainly the right reading of the prevailing views. But, as Baumol himself noted, we have to assess how sound these views were. We have, especially, to ask whether the pessimism associated with Arrovian structures in social choice theory must be seen to be devastating for welfare economics as a discipline.

As it happens, traditional welfare economics, which had been developed by utilitarian economists (such as Francis T. Edgeworth, 1881; Alfred Marshall, 1890; Arthur C. Pigou, 1920), had taken a very different track from the vote-oriented social choice theory. It took inspiration not from Borda (1781) or Condorcet (1785), but from their contemporary, Jeremy Bentham (1789). Bentham had pioneered the use of utilitarian calculus to obtain judgments about the social interest by aggregating the personal interests of the different individuals in the form of their respective utilities.

Bentham's concern—and that of utilitarianism in general—was with the *total utility* of a community. This was irrespective of the distribution of that total, and in this there is an informational limitation of considerable ethical and political importance. For example, a person who is unlucky enough to have a uniformly lower capability to generate enjoyment and utility out of income (say, because of a handicap) would also be given, in the utilitarian ideal world, a *lower* share of a given total. This is a consequence of the single-minded pursuit of maximizing the sum-total of utilities (on the peculiar consequences of this unifocal priority, see Sen, 1970a, 1973a; John Rawls, 1971; Claude d'Aspremont and Louis Gevers, 1977). However, the utilitarian interest in taking comparative note of the gains and losses of different people is not in itself a negligible concern. And this concern makes utilitarian welfare economics deeply interested in using a class of information—in the form of comparison of utility gains and losses of different persons—with which Condorcet and Borda had not been directly involved.

Utilitarianism has been very influential in shaping welfare economics, which was dominated for a long time by an almost unquestioning adherence to utilitarian calculus. But by the 1930's utilitarian welfare economics came under severe fire.

It would have been quite natural to question (as Rawls [1971] would masterfully do in formulating his theory of justice) the utilitarian neglect of distributional issues and its concentration only on utility sum-totals in a distribution-blind way. But that was not the direction in which the antiutilitarian critiques went in the 1930's and in the decades that followed. Rather, economists came to be persuaded by arguments presented by Lionel Robbins and others (deeply influenced by "logical positivist" philosophy) that interpersonal comparisons of utility had no scientific basis: "Every mind is inscrutable to every other mind and no common denominator of feelings is possible" (Robbins, 1938 p. 636). Thus, the epistemic foundations of utilitarian welfare economics were seen as incurably defective.

There followed attempts to do welfare economics on the basis of the different persons' respective orderings of social states, without any interpersonal comparisons of utility gains and losses (nor, of course, any comparison of the total utilities of different persons, which are neglected by utilitarians as well). While utilitarianism and utilitarian welfare economics are quite indifferent to the *distribution* of utilities between different persons (concentrating, as they do, only on the *sum-total* of utilities), the new regime without any interpersonal comparisons in any form, further reduced the informational base on which social choice could draw. The already-limited informational base of Benthamite calculus was made to shrink even further to that of Borda and Condorcet, since the use of different persons' utility rankings without any interpersonal comparison is analytically quite similar to the use of voting information in making social choice.

Faced with this informational restriction, utilitarian welfare economics gave way, from the 1940's onwards, to a so-called "new welfare economics," which used only one basic criterion of social improvement, viz, the "Pareto comparison." This criterion only asserts that an alternative situation would be definitely better if the change would increase the utility of everyone.[6] A good deal of subsequent welfare economics restricts attention to "Pareto efficiency" only (that is, only to making sure that no further Pareto improvements are possible). This criterion takes no interest whatever in *distributional* issues, which cannot be addressed without considering conflicts of interest and of preferences.

Some *further* criterion is clearly needed for making social welfare judgments with a greater reach, and this was insightfully explored by Abram Bergson (1938) and Paul A. Samuelson (1947). This demand led directly to Arrow's (1950, 1951) pioneering formulation of social choice theory, relating social preference (or decisions) to the set of individual preferences, and this relation is called a "social welfare function." Arrow (1951, 1963) went on to consider a set of very mild-looking conditions, including: (1) Pareto efficiency, (2) nondictatorship, (3) independence (demanding that social choice over any set of alternatives must depend on preferences *only* over those alternatives), and (4) unrestricted domain (requiring that social preference must be a complete ordering, with full transitivity, and that this must work for every conceivable set of individual preferences).

Arrow's impossibility theorem demonstrated that it is impossible to satisfy these conditions simultaneously.[7] In order to avoid this impossibility result, different ways

The possibility of social choice **303**

of modifying Arrow's requirements were tried out in the literature that followed, but other difficulties continued to emerge.[8] The force and widespread presence of impossibility results generated a consolidated sense of pessimism, and this became a dominant theme in welfare economics and social choice theory in general. Is this reading justified?

Complementarity of formal methods and informal reasoning

Before I proceed further on substantive matters, it may be useful to comment briefly on the nature of the reasoning used in answering this and related questions. Social choice theory is a subject in which formal and mathematical techniques have been very extensively used. Those who are suspicious of formal (and in particular, of mathematical) modes of reasoning are often skeptical of the usefulness of discussing real-world problems in this way. Their suspicion is understandable, but it is ultimately misplaced. The exercise of trying to get an integrated picture from diverse preferences or interests of different people does involve many complex problems in which one could be seriously misled in the absence of formal scrutiny. Indeed, Arrow's (1950, 1951, 1963) impossibility theorem—in many ways the "locus classicus" in this field—can hardly be anticipated on the basis of common sense or informal reasoning. This applies also to extensions of this result, for example to the demonstration that an exactly similar impossibility to Arrow's holds even without any imposed demand of internal consistency of social choice (see Sen, 1993a Theorem 3). In the process of discussing some substantive issues in social choice theory, I shall have the opportunity to consider various results which too are not easily anticipated without formal reasoning. Informal insights, important as they are, cannot replace the formal investigations that are needed to examine the congruity and cogency of combinations of values and of apparently plausible demands.

This is not to deny that the task of widespread public communication is crucial for the use of social choice theory. It is centrally important for social choice theory to relate formal analysis to informal and transparent examination. I have to confess that in my own case, this combination has, in fact, been something of an obsession, and some of the formal ideas I have been most concerned with (such as an adequate framework for informational broadening, the use of partial comparability and of partial orderings, and the weakening of consistency conditions demanded of binary relations and of choice functions) call simultaneously for formal investigation and for informal explication and accessible scrutiny.[9] Our deeply felt, real-world concerns have to be substantively integrated with the analytical use of formal and mathematical reasoning.

Proximity of possibility and impossibility

The general relationship between possibility and impossibility results also deserves some attention, in order to understand the nature and role of impossibility theorems.

304 A. Sen

When a set of axioms regarding social choice can all be simultaneously satisfied, there may be several possible procedures that work, among which we have to choose. In order to choose between the different possibilities through the use of discriminating axioms, we have to introduce *further* axioms, until only one possible procedure remains. This is something of an exercise in brinkmanship. We have to go on cutting down alternative possibilities, moving—implicitly—*towards* an impossibility, but then stop just before all possibilities are eliminated, to wit, when one and only one option remains.

Thus, it should be clear that a full axiomatic determination of a particular method of making social choice must inescapably lie next door to an impossibility—indeed just short of it. If it lies far from an impossibility (with various positive possibilities), then it cannot give us an axiomatic derivation of any specific method of social choice. It is, therefore, to be expected that constructive paths in social choice theory, derived from axiomatic reasoning, would tend to be paved on one side by impossibility results (opposite to the side of multiple possibilities). No conclusion about the fragility of social choice theory (or its subject matter) emerges from this proximity.

In fact, the literature that has followed Arrow's work has shown classes of impossibility theorems and of positive possibility results, all of which lie quite close to each other.[10] The real issue is not, therefore, the ubiquity of impossibility (it will always lie close to the axiomatic derivation of any specific social choice rule), but the reach and reasonableness of the axioms to be used. We have to get on with the basic task of obtaining workable rules that satisfy reasonable requirements.

Majority decisions and coherence

In the discussion so far, I have made no attempt to confine attention to particular configurations of individual preferences, ignoring others. Formally, this is required by Arrow's condition of "unrestricted domain," which insists that the social choice procedure must work for every conceivable cluster of individual preferences. It must, however, be obvious that, for any decision procedure, some preference profiles will yield inconsistencies and incoherence of social decisions while other profiles will not produce these results.

Arrow (1951) himself had initiated, along with Black (1948, 1958), the search for adequate restrictions that would guarantee consistent majority decisions. The necessary and sufficient conditions for consistent majority decisions can indeed be identified (see Sen and Pattanaik, 1969).[11] While much less restrictive than the earlier conditions that had been identified, they are still quite demanding; indeed it is shown that they would be easily violated in many actual situations.

The formal results on necessary or sufficiency conditions of majority decisions can only give as much hope—or generate as much disappointment—about voting-based social choice as the extent of social cohesion and confrontation (in the actual patterns of individual preferences) would allow. Choice problems for the society come in many shapes and sizes, and there may be less comfort in these results for some types

The possibility of social choice **305**

of social choice problems than for others. When distributional issues dominate and when people seek to maximize their own "shares" without concern for others (as, for example, in a "cake division" problem, with each preferring any division that increases her own share, no matter what happens to the others), then majority rule will tend to be thoroughly inconsistent. But when there is a matter of national outrage (for example, in response to the inability of a democratic government to prevent a famine), the electorate may be reasonably univocal and thoroughly consistent.[12] Also, when people cluster in parties, with complex agendas and dialogues, involving give and take as well as some general attitudes to values like equity or justice, the ubiquitous inconsistencies can yield ground to more congruous decisions.[13]

So far as welfare economics is concerned, majority rule and voting procedures are particularly prone to inconsistency, given the centrality of distributional issues in welfare-economic problems. However, one of the basic questions to ask is whether voting rules (to which social choice procedures are effectively restricted in the Arrovian framework) provide a reasonable approach to social choice in the field of welfare economics. Are we in the right territory in trying to make social welfare judgments through variants of voting systems?

Informational broadening and welfare economics

Voting-based procedures are entirely natural for some kinds of social choice problems, such as elections, referendums, or committee decisions.[14] They are, however, altogether unsuitable for many other problems of social choice.[15] When, for example, we want to get some kind of an aggregative index of social welfare, we cannot rely on such procedures for at least two distinct reasons.

First, voting requires active participation, and if someone decides not to exercise her voting right, her preference would find no direct representation in social decisions. (Indeed, because of lower participation, the interests of substantial groups —for example of African Americans in the United States—find inadequate representation in national politics.) In contrast, in making reasonable social welfare judgments, the interests of the less assertive cannot be simply ignored.

Second, even with the active involvement of every one in voting exercises, we cannot but be short of important information needed for welfare-economic evaluation (on this see Sen, 1970a, 1973a). Through voting, each person can rank different alternatives. But there is no direct way of getting interpersonal comparisons of different persons' well-being from voting data. We must go beyond the class of voting rules (explored by Borda and Condorcet as well as Arrow) to be able to address distributional issues.

Arrow had ruled out the use of interpersonal comparisons since he had followed the general consensus that had emerged in the 1940's that (as Arrow put it) "interpersonal comparison of utilities has no meaning" (Arrow, 1951 p. 9). The totality of the axiom combination used by Arrow had the effect of confining social choice procedures to rules that are, broadly speaking, of the voting type.[16] His impossibility result relates, therefore, to this class of rules.

306 A. Sen

To lay the foundations of a constructive social choice theory, if we want to reject the historical consensus against the use of interpersonal comparisons in social choice, we have to address two important—and difficult—questions. First, can we systematically incorporate and use something as complex as interpersonal comparisons involving many persons? Will this be a territory of disciplined analysis, rather than a riot of confusing (and possibly confused) ideas? Second, how can the analytical results be integrated with practical use? On what kind of information can we sensibly base interpersonal comparisons? Will the relevant information be actually available, to be used?

The first is primarily a question of analytical system building, and the second that of epistemology as well as practical reason. The latter issue requires a reexamination of the informational basis of interpersonal comparisons, and I would presently argue that it calls for an inescapably qualified response. But the first question can be addressed more definitively through constructive analysis. Without going into technicalities of the literature that has emerged, I would like to report that interpersonal comparisons of various types can be fully axiomatized and exactly incorporated in social choice procedures (through the use of "invariance conditions" in a generalized framework, formally constructed as "social welfare functionals," on which see Sen, 1970a, 1977c).[17] Indeed, interpersonal comparisons need not even be confined to "all-or-none" dichotomies. We may be able to make interpersonal comparisons to some extent, but not in every comparison, nor of every type, nor with tremendous exactness (see Sen, 1970a, c).

We may, for example, have no great difficulty in accepting that Emperor Nero's utility gain from the burning of Rome was smaller than the sum-total of the utility loss of all the other Romans who suffered from the fire. But this does not require us to feel confident that we can put everyone's utilities in an exact one-to-one correspondence with each other. There may, thus, be room for demanding "partial comparability"—denying both the extremes: full comparability and no comparability at all. The different extents of partial comparability can be given mathematically exact forms (precisely articulating the exact extent of inexactness).[18] It can also be shown that there may be no general need for terribly refined interpersonal comparisons for arriving at definite social decisions. Quite often, rather limited levels of partial comparability will be adequate for making social decisions.[19] Thus the empirical exercise need not be as ambitious as it is sometimes feared.

Before proceeding to the informational basis of interpersonal comparisons, let me ask a big analytical question: how much of a change in the possibility of social choice is brought about by systematic use of interpersonal comparisons? Does Arrow's impossibility, and related results, go away with the use of interpersonal comparisons in social welfare judgments? The answer briefly is, yes. The additional informational availability allows sufficient discrimination to escape impossibilities of this type.

There is an interesting contrast here. It can be shown that admitting cardinality of utilities *without* interpersonal comparisons does not change Arrow's impossibility theorem at all, which can be readily extended to cardinal measurability of utilities (see Theorem 8★2 in Sen, 1970a). In contrast even ordinal interpersonal comparisons is adequate to break the exact impossibility. We knew of course that with some types of interpersonal comparisons demanded in a full form (including cardinal interpersonal comparability), we can use the classical utilitarian approach.[20] But it turns out that even weaker forms of comparability would still permit making consistent social welfare judgments, satisfying all of Arrow's requirements, in addition to being sensitive to distributional concerns (even though the possible rules will be confined to a relatively small class).[21]

The distributional issue is, in fact, intimately connected with the need to go beyond voting rules as the basis of social welfare judgments. As was discussed earlier, utilitarianism too is in an important sense distribution indifferent: its program is to maximize the *sum-total* of utilities, no matter how unequally that total may be distributed (the extensive implications of this distributional indifference are discussed in Sen, 1973a). But the use of interpersonal comparisons can take other forms as well, allowing public decisions to be sensitive to *inequalities* in well-being and opportunities.

The broad approach of social welfare functionals opens up the possibility of using many different types of social welfare rules, which differ in the treatment of equity as well as efficiency, and also in their informational requirements.[22] Further, with the removal of the artificial barrier that had prohibited interpersonal comparisons, many other fields of normative measurement have also been investigated with the axiomatic approach of social welfare analysis. My own efforts in such fields as the evaluation and measurement of *inequality* (Sen, 1973a, 1992a, 1997b), *poverty* (Sen, 1976b, 1983b, 1985a, 1992a), *distribution-adjusted national income* (Sen, 1973b, 1976a, 1979a), and *environmental evaluation* (Sen, 1995a), have drawn solidly on the broadened informational framework of recent social choice theory.[23]

VIII Informational basis of interpersonal comparisons

While the analytical issues in incorporating interpersonal comparisons have been, on the whole, well sorted out, there still remains the important practical matter of finding an adequate approach to the empirical discipline of making interpersonal comparisons and then using them in practice. The foremost question to be addressed is this: interpersonal comparison of *what?*

The formal structures of social welfare functions are not, in any sense, specific to utility comparisons only, and they can incorporate other types of interpersonal comparisons as well. The principal issue is the choice of some accounting of individual advantage, which need not take the form of comparisons of mental states of happiness, and could instead focus on some other way of looking at individual well-being or freedom or substantive opportunities (seen in the perspective of a corresponding evaluative discipline).

The rejection of interpersonal comparisons of utilities in welfare economic and in social choice theory that followed positivist criticism (such as that of Robbins, 1938) was firmly based on interpreting them entirely as comparisons of mental

308 A. Sen

states. As it happens, even with such mental state comparisons, the case for unqualified rejection is hard to sustain.[24] Indeed, as has been forcefully argued by the philosopher Donald Davidson (1986), it is difficult to see how people can understand anything much about other people's minds and feelings, without making some comparisons with their own minds and feelings. Such comparisons may not be extremely precise, but then again, we know from analytical investigations that very precise interpersonal comparisons may not be needed to make systematic use of interpersonal comparisons in social choice (on this and related issues, see Sen, 1970a, c, 1997b; Blackorby, 1975).

So the picture is not so pessimistic even in the old home ground of mental state comparisons. But, more importantly, interpersonal comparisons of personal welfare, or of individual advantage, need not be based only on comparisons of mental states. In fact, there may be good ethical grounds for not concentrating too much on mental-state comparisons—whether of pleasures or of desires. Utilities may sometimes be very malleable in response to persistent deprivation. A hopeless destitute with much poverty, or a downtrodden laborer living under exploitative economic arrangements, or a subjugated housewife in a society with entrenched gender inequality, or a tyrannized citizen under brutal authoritarianism, may come to terms with her deprivation. She may take whatever pleasure she can from small achievements, and adjust her desires to take note of feasibility (thereby helping the fulfilment of her adjusted desires). But her success in such adjustment would not make her deprivation go away. The metric of pleasure or desire may sometimes be quite inadequate in reflecting the extent of a person's substantive deprivation.[25]

There may indeed be a case for taking incomes, or commodity bundles, or resources more generally, to be of direct interest in judging a person's advantage, and this may be so for various reasons—not merely for the mental states they may help to generate.[26] In fact, the Difference Principle in Rawls's (1971) theory of "justice as fairness" is based on judging individual advantage in terms of a person's command over what Rawls calls "primary goods," which are general-purpose resources that are useful for anyone to have no matter what her exact objectives are.

This procedure can be improved upon by taking note not only of the ownership of primary goods and resources, but also of interpersonal differences in converting them into the capability to live well. Indeed, I have tried to argue in favor of judging individual advantage in terms of the respective capabilities, which the person has, to live the way he or she has reason to value.[27] This approach focuses on the substantive freedoms that people have, rather than only on the particular outcomes with which they end up. For responsible adults, the concentration on freedom rather than only achievement has some merit, and it can provide a general framework for analyzing individual advantage and deprivation in a contemporary society. The extent of interpersonal comparisons may only be partial—often based on the intersection of different points of view.[28] But the use of such partial comparability can make a major difference to the informational basis of reasoned social judgments.

The possibility of social choice **309**

However, given the nature of the subject and the practical difficulties of informational availability and evaluation, it would be overambitious to be severely exclusive in sticking only to one informational approach, rejecting all others. In the recent literature in applied welfare economics, various ways of making sensible interpersonal comparisons of well-being have emerged. Some have been based on studying expenditure patterns, and using this to surmise about comparative well-being of different persons (see Pollak and Terence J. Wales, 1979; Dale W. Jorgenson et al., 1980; Jorgenson, 1990; Daniel T. Slesnick, 1998), while others have combined this with other informational inputs (see Angus S. Deaton and John Muellbauer, 1980; Atkinson and Francois Bourguignon, 1982, 1987; Fisher, 1987, 1990; Pollak, 1991; Deaton, 1995).[29] Others have tried to use questionnaires and have looked for regularities in people's answers to questions about relative well-being (see, for example, Arie Kapteyn and Bernard M. S. van Praag, 1976).

There have also been illuminating works in observing important features of living conditions and in drawing conclusions on quality of life and comparative living standards on that basis; indeed there is a well-established tradition of Scandinavian studies in this area (see, for example, Allardt et al. [1981] and Robert Erikson and Rune Aberg [1987]). The literature on "basic needs" and their fulfilment has also provided an empirical approach to understanding comparative deprivations.[30] Further, under the intellectual leadership of Mahbub ul Haq (1995), the United Nations Development Programme (UNDP) has made systematic use of a particular type of informational broadening to make comparisons based on observed features of living conditions (reported in UNDP, *Human Development Reports*).[31]

It is easy enough to pick holes in each of these methodologies and to criticize the related metrics of interpersonal comparisons. But there can be little doubt about the welfare-economic interest in the far-reaching uses of empirical information that have emerged from these works. They have substantially broadened our understanding of individual advantages and their empirical correlates. Each of these methodologies clearly has some limitations as well as virtues, and our evaluation of their relative merits may well diverge, depending on our respective priorities. I have had the occasion to argue elsewhere (and briefly also in this lecture, earlier on) in favor of partial comparabilities based on evaluation of capabilities,[32] but beyond that specific issue (on which others may well take a different view), I want to emphasize here the more general point that the possibilities of practical welfare economics and social choice have been immensely widened through these innovative, empirical works.

In fact, despite their differences, they fit in general into the overall pattern of informational widening to which recent analytical work in social choice theory has forcefully pointed. The analytical systems explored in the recent literature on welfare economics and social choice are broader than those in the Arrovian model (and correspondingly less uptight, and less "impossible," on which see Sen, 1970a, 1977c).[33] They are also analytically general enough to allow different empirical interpretations and to permit alternative informational bases for social choice. The diverse empirical methodologies, considered here, can all be seen in this broader

310 A. Sen

analytical perspective. The movements in "high theory" have been, in this sense, closely linked to the advances in "practical economics." It is the sustained exploration of constructive possibilities—at the analytical as well as practical levels—that has helped to dispel some of the gloom that was associated earlier with social choice and welfare economics.

Poverty and famine

The variety of information on which social welfare analysis can draw can be well illustrated by the study of poverty. Poverty is typically seen in terms of the lowness of incomes, and it has been traditionally measured simply by counting the number of people below the poverty-line income; this is sometimes called the head-count measure. A scrutiny of this approach yields two different types of questions. First, is poverty adequately seen as low income? Second, even if poverty is seen as low income, is the aggregate poverty of a society best characterized by the index of the head-count measure?

I take up these questions in turn. Do we get enough of a diagnosis of individual poverty by comparing the individual's income with a socially given poverty-line income? What about the person with an income well above the poverty line, who suffers from an expensive illness (requiring, say, kidney dialysis)? Is deprivation not ultimately a lack of opportunity to lead a minimally acceptable life, which can be influenced by a number of considerations, including of course personal income, but also physical and environmental characteristics, and other variables (such as the availability and costs of medical and other facilities)? The motivation behind such an exercise relates closely to seeing poverty as a serious deprivation of certain basic capabilities. This alternative approach leads to a rather different diagnosis of poverty from the ones that a purely income-based analysis can yield.[34]

This is not to deny that lowness of income can be very important in many contexts, since the opportunities a person enjoys in a market economy can be severely constrained by her level of real income. However, various contingencies can lead to variations in the "conversion" of income into the capability to live a minimally acceptable life, and if that is what we are concerned with, there may be good reason to look beyond income poverty. There are at least four different sources of variation: (1) personal heterogeneities (for example, proneness to illness), (2) environmental diversities (for example, living in a storm-prone or flood-prone area), (3) variations in social climate (for example, the prevalence of crime or epidemiological vectors), and (4) differences in relative deprivation connected with customary patterns of consumption in particular societies (for example, being relatively impoverished in a rich society, which can lead to deprivation of the absolute capability to take part in the life of the community).[35]

There is, thus, an important need to go beyond income information in poverty analysis, in particular to see poverty as capability deprivation. However (as was discussed earlier), the choice of the informational base for poverty analysis cannot really be dissociated from pragmatic considerations, particularly informational

The possibility of social choice **311**

availability. It is unlikely that the perspective of poverty as income deprivation can be dispensed with in the empirical literature on poverty, even when the limitations of that perspective are entirely clear. Indeed, in many contexts the rough-and-ready way of using income information may provide the most immediate approach to the study of severe deprivation.[36]

For example, the causation of famines is often best seen in terms of a radical decline in the real incomes of a section of the population, leading to starvation and death (on this see Sen, 1976d, 1981).[37] The dynamics of income earning and of purchasing power may indeed be the most important component of a famine investigation. This approach, in which the study of causal influences on the determination of the respective incomes of different groups plays a central part, contrasts with an exclusive focus on agricultural production and food supply, which is often found in the literature on this subject.

The shift in informational focus from food supply to entitlements (involving incomes as well as supply, and the resulting relative prices) can make a radical difference, since famines can occur even without any major decline—possibly without *any* decline at all—of food production or supply.[38] If, for example, the incomes of rural wage laborers, or of service providers, or of craftsmen collapse through unemployment, or through a fall of real wages, or through a decline in the demand for the relevant services or craft products, the affected groups may have to starve, even if the overall food supply in the economy is undiminished. Starvation occurs when some people cannot establish entitlement over an adequate amount of food, through purchase or through food production, and the overall supply of food is only one influence among many in the determination of the entitlements of the respective groups of people in the economy. Thus, an income-sensitive entitlement approach can provide a better explanation of famines than can be obtained through an exclusively production-oriented view. It can also yield a more effective approach to the remedying of starvation and hunger (on this see particularly Drèze and Sen, 1989).

The nature of the problem tends to identify the particular "space" on which the analysis has to concentrate. It remains true that in explaining the exact patterns of famine deaths and sufferings, we can get additional understanding by supplementing the income-based analysis with information on the conversion of incomes into nourishment, which will depend on various other influences such as metabolic rates, proneness to illness, body size, etc.[39] These issues are undoubtedly important for investigating the incidence of nutritional failures, morbidities, and mortalities. However, in a general analysis of the occurrence and causation of famines, affecting large groups, these additional matters may be of secondary importance. While I shall not enter further into the famine literature here, I would like to emphasize that the informational demands of famine analysis give an important place to income deprivation which have more immediacy and ready usability than the more subtle —and ultimately more informed—distinctions based on capability comparisons (on this see Sen [1981] and Drèze and Sen [1989]).

I turn now to the second question. The most common and most traditional measure of poverty had tended to concentrate on head counting. But it must also

312 A. Sen

make a difference as to *how far* below the poverty line the poor individually are, and furthermore, how the deprivation is *shared and distributed* among the poor. The social data on the respective deprivations of the individuals who constitute the poor in a society need to be aggregated together to arrive at informative and usable measures of aggregate poverty. This is a social choice problem, and axioms can indeed be proposed that attempt to capture our distributional concerns in this constructive exercise (on this see Sen, 1976b).[40]

Several distribution-sensitive poverty measures have been derived axiomatically in the recent social choice literature, and various alternative proposals have been analyzed. While I shall, here, not go into a comparative assessment of these measures (nor into axiomatic requirements that can be used to discriminate between them), elsewhere I have tried to address this issue, jointly with James Foster (Foster and Sen, 1997).[41] However, I would like to emphasize the fact that we face here an embarrassment of riches (the opposite of an impasse or an impossibility), once the informational basis of social judgments has been appropriately broadened. To axiomatize exactly a particular poverty measure, we shall have to indulge in the "brinkmanship" of which I spoke earlier (Section V), by adding other axiomatic demands until we are just short of an impossibility, with only one surviving poverty measure.

Comparative deprivation and gender inequality

At one level, poverty cannot be dissociated from the misery caused by it, and in this sense, the classical perspective of utility also can be invoked in this analysis. However, the malleability of mental attitudes, on which I commented earlier, may tend to hide and muffle the extent of deprivation in many cases. The indigent peasant who manages to build some cheer in his life should not be taken as nonpoor on grounds of his mental accomplishment.

This adaptability can be particularly important in dealing with gender inequality and deprivation of women in traditionally unequal societies. This is partly because perceptions have a decisive part to play in the cohesion of family life, and the culture of family living tends to put a premium on making allies out of the ill treated. Women may—often enough—work much harder than men (thanks to the rigours of household chores), and also receive less attention in health care and nutrition, and yet the perception that there is an incorrigible inequality here may well be missing in a society in which asymmetric norms are quietly dominant.[42] This type of inequality and deprivation may not, under these circumstances, adequately surface in the scale of the mental metric of dissatisfaction and discontent.

The socially cultivated sense of contentment and serenity may even affect the perception of morbidity and illness. When, many years ago, I was working on a famine-related study of post-famine Bengal in 1944, I was quite struck by the remarkable fact that the widows surveyed had hardly reported any incidence of being in "indifferent health," whereas widow*ers*, complained massively about just that (Sen, 1985a Appendix B). Similarly, it emerges in interstate comparisons in

The possibility of social choice **313**

India that the states that are worst provided in education and health-care facilities typically report the *lowest* levels of perceived morbidity, whereas states with good health care and school education indicate *higher* self-perception of illness (with the highest morbidity reports coming from the best provided states, such as Kerala).[43] Mental reactions, the mainstay of classical utility, can be a very defective basis for the analysis of deprivation.

Thus, in understanding poverty and inequality, there is a strong case for looking at real deprivation and not merely at mental reactions to that deprivation. There have been many recent investigations of gender inequality and women's deprivation in terms of undernutrition, clinically diagnosed morbidity, observed illiteracy, and even unexpectedly high mortality (compared with physiologically justified expectations).[44] Such interpersonal comparisons can easily be a significant basis of studies of poverty and of inequality between the sexes. They can be accommodated within a broad framework of welfare economics and social choice (enhanced by the removal of informational constraints that would rule out the use of these types of data).

The liberal paradox

This lecture has included discussion of why and how impossibility results in social choice can be overcome through informational broadening. The informational widening considered so far has been mainly concerned with the use of interpersonal comparisons. But this need not be the only form of broadening that is needed in resolving an impasse in social choice. Consider, for example, an impossibility theorem which is sometimes referred to as "the liberal paradox," or "the impossibility of the Paretian liberal" (Sen, 1970a, b, 1976c). The theorem shows the impossibility of satisfying even a very minimal demand for liberty when combined with an insistence on Pareto efficiency (given unrestricted domain).[45]

Since there have been some debates on the content of liberty in the recent literature (see, for example, Nozick, 1974; Peter Gärdenfors, 1981; Robert Sugden, 1981, 1985, 1993; Hillel Steiner, 1990; Gaertner et al., 1992; Deb, 1994; Marc Fleurbaey and Gaertner, 1996; Pattanaik, 1996; Suzumura, 1996), perhaps a quick explanatory remark may be useful. Liberty has many different aspects, including two rather distinct features: (1) it can help us to achieve what we would choose to achieve in our respective private domains, for example, in personal life (this is its "opportunity aspect"), and (2) it can leave us directly in charge of choices over private domains, no matter what we may or may not achieve (this is its "process aspect"). In social choice theory, the formulation of liberty has been primarily concerned with the former, that is, the opportunity aspect. This may have been adequate to show the possible conflict between the Pareto principle and the opportunity aspect of liberty (on which Sen [1970a, b] concentrated), but an exclusive concentration on the opportunity aspect cannot provide an adequate understanding of the demands of liberty (in this respect, Sugden [1981, 1993] and Gaertner et al. [1992] were certainly right to reject the sufficiency of the opportunity-centered

314 A. Sen

formulation in standard social choice theory).[46] However, social choice theory can also be made to accommodate the process aspect of liberty through appropriate recharacterization, and particularly through valuing due process in addition to substantive opportunities (on this see Sen, 1982b, 1997a, 1999b; Stig Kanger, 1985; Deb, 1994; Hammond, 1997; Suzumura, 1996; Martin van Hees, 1996).

It is also important to avoid the opposite narrowness of concentrating exclusively only on the process aspect of liberty, as some recent writers have preferred to do. Important as processes are, this cannot obliterate the relevance of the opportunity aspect which too must count. Indeed, the importance of *effectiveness* in the realization of liberty in one's personal life has been recognized as important for a long time—even by commentators deeply concerned with processes, from John Stuart Mill (1859) to Frank Knight (1947), Friedrich A. Hayek (1960), and Buchanan (1986). The difficulties of having to weigh process fairness against effectiveness of outcomes cannot be avoided simply by ignoring the opportunity aspect of liberty, through an exclusive concentration on the process aspect.[47]

How might the conflict of the Paretian liberal, in particular, be resolved? Different ways of dealing with this friction have been explored in the literature.[48] However, it is important to see that unlike Arrow's impossibility result, the liberal paradox cannot be satisfactorily resolved through the use of interpersonal comparisons. Indeed, neither the claims of liberty, nor that of Pareto efficiency, need be significantly contingent on interpersonal comparisons. The force of one's claims over one's private domain lies in the *personal* nature of that choice—not on the *relative intensities* of the preferences of different persons over a particular person's private life. Also, Pareto efficiency depends on the congruence of different persons' preferences over a pairwise choice—not on the comparative strength of those preferences.

Rather, the resolution of this problem lies elsewhere, in particular in the need to see each of these claims as being qualified by the importance of the other—once it is recognized that they can be in possible conflict with each other (indeed, the main point of the liberal paradox was precisely to identify that possible conflict). The recognition of the importance of effective liberty in one's private domain (precisely over particular choices) can coexist with an acknowledgement of the relevance of Paretian unanimity over any pair (over all choices—whether in one's private domain or not). A satisfactory resolution of this impossibility must include taking an evaluative view of the acceptable priorities between personal liberty and overall desire fulfillment, and must be sensitive to the information regarding the trade-offs on this that the persons may themselves endorse. This too calls for an informational enrichment (taking note of people's political values as well as individual desires), but this enrichment is of a rather different kind from that of using interpersonal comparisons of well-being or overall advantage.[49]

A concluding remark

Impossibility results in social choice theory—led by the pioneering work of Arrow (1951)—have often been interpreted as being thoroughly destructive of the

The possibility of social choice **315**

possibility of reasoned and democratic social choice, including welfare economics (Sections I–III, XI). I have argued against that view. Indeed, Arrow's powerful "impossibility theorem" invites engagement, rather than resignation (Sections IV–V). We do know, of course, that democratic decisions can sometimes lead to incongruities. To the extent that this is a feature of the real world, its existence and reach are matters for objective recognition. Inconsistencies arise more readily in some situations than in others, and it is possible to identify the situational differences and to characterize the processes through consensual and compatible decisions can emerge (Sections VI–VIII).

The impossibility results certainly deserve serious study. They often have wide —indeed sweeping—reach, not merely covering day-to-day politics (where we may be rather used to incongruity), but also questioning the possibility of any assured framework for making social welfare judgments for the society as a whole. Impossibilities thus identified also militate against the general possibility of an orderly and systematic framework for normatively assessing inequality, for evaluating poverty, or for identifying intolerable tyranny and violations of liberty. Not to be able to have a coherent framework for these appraisals or evaluations would indeed be most damaging for systematic political, social, and economic judgement. It would not be possible to talk about injustice and unfairness without having to face the accusation that such diagnoses must be inescapably arbitrary or intellectually despotic.

These bleak conclusions do not, however, endure searching scrutiny, and fruitful procedures that militate against such pessimism can be clearly identified. This has indeed been largely an upbeat lecture—emphasizing the possibility of constructive social choice theory, and arguing for a productive interpretation of the impossibility results. Indeed, these apparently negative results can be seen to be helpful inputs in the development of an adequate framework for social choice, since the axiomatic derivation of a specific social choice procedure must lie in between—and close to—an impossibility, on one side, and an embarrassment of riches, on the other (see Section V).

The possibility of constructive welfare economics and social choice (and their use in making social welfare judgments and in devising practical measures with normative significance) turns on the need for broadening the informational basis of such choice. Different types of informational enrichment have been considered in the literature. A crucial element in this broadening is the use of interpersonal comparisons of well-being and individual advantage. It is not surprising that the rejection of interpersonal comparisons must cause difficulties for reasoned social decision, since the claims of different persons, who make up the society, have to be assessed against each other. We cannot even understand the force of public concerns about poverty, hunger, inequality, or tyranny, without bringing in interpersonal comparisons in one form or another. The information on which our informal judgments on these matters rely is precisely the kind of information that has to be— and can be—incorporated in the formal analysis of systematic social choice (Sections VII–XI).

316 A. Sen

The pessimism about the possibility of interpersonal comparisons that fuelled the "obituary notices" for welfare economics (and substantially fed the fear of impossibility in social choice theory) was ultimately misleading for two distinct reasons. First, it confined attention to too narrow an informational base, overlooking the different ways in which interpersonally comparative statements can sensibly be made and can be used to enrich the analysis of welfare judgments and social choice. An overconcentration on comparisons of mental states crowded out a plethora of information that can inform us about the real advantages and disadvantages of different persons, related to their substantive well-being, freedoms, or opportunities. Second, the pessimism was also based on demanding too much precision in such comparisons, overlooking the fact that even partial comparisons can serve to enlighten the reasoned basis of welfare economics, social ethics, and responsible politics.[50]

Addressing these problems fits well into a general program of strengthening social choice theory (and "nonobituarial" welfare economics). In general, informational broadening, in one form or another, is an effective way of overcoming social choice pessimism and of avoiding impossibilities, and it leads directly to constructive approaches with viability and reach. Formal reasoning about postulated axioms (including their compatibility and coherence), as well as informal understanding of values and norms (including their relevance and plausibility), both point in that productive direction. Indeed, the deep complementarity between formal and informal reasoning—so central to the social sciences—is well illustrated by developments in modem social choice theory.

Notes

† This article is the lecture Amartya Sen delivered in Stockholm, Sweden, December 8, 1998, when he received the Alfred Nobel Memorial Prize in Economic Sciences. The article is copyright © The Nobel Foundation 1998 and is published here with the permission of the Nobel Foundation.

* The Master's Lodge, Trinity College, Cambridge, CB2 1TQ, England. For helpful comments and suggestions, I am most grateful to Sudhir Anand, Kenneth Arrow, Tony Atkinson, Emma Rothschild, and Kotaro Suzumura. I have also benefited from discussions with Amiya Bagchi, Pranab Bardhan, Kaushik Basu, Angus Deaton, Rajat Deb, Jean Drèze, Bhaskar Dutta, Jean-Paul Fitoussi, James Foster, Siddiq Osmani, Prasanta Pattanaik, and Tony Shorrocks.

1 This is, obviously, not a survey of social choice theory and there is no attempt here to scan the relevant literature. Overviews can be found in Alan M. Feldman (1980), Prasanta K. Pattanaik and Maurice Salles (1983), Kotaro Suzumura (1983), Peter J. Hammond (1985), Jon Elster and Aanund Hylland (1986), Sen (1986a), David Starrett (1988), Dennis C. Mueller (1989), and more extensively in Kenneth J. Arrow et al. (1997).

2 See also Anand (1950, 1951, 1963).

3 "Arthashastra," the Sanskrit word (the title of Kautilya's book), is best translated literally as "Economics," even though he devoted much space to investigating the demands of statecraft in a conflictual society. English translations of Aristotle's *Politics* and Kautilya's *Arthashastra* can be found respectively in E. Barker (1958) and L. N. Rangarajan (1987). On the interesting medieval European writings on these issues see, for example, Ian McLean (1990).

The possibility of social choice **317**

4 See Condorcet (1785). There are many commentaries on these analyses, including Anand (1951), Duncan Black (1958), William V. Gehrlein (1983), H. Peyton Young (1988), and McLean (1990). On the potential ubiquity of inconsistency in majority voting, see Richard D. McKelvey (1979) and Norman J. Schofield (1983).

5 By varying the axiomatic structure, related impossibility results can also be obtained. Examples can be found in Anand (1950, 1951, 1952, 1963), Julian H. Blau (1957, 1972, 1979), Bengt Hansson (1969a, b, 1976), Tapas Majumdar (1969, 1973), Sen (1969, 1970a, 1986b, 1993a, 1995a), Pattanaik (1971, 1973, 1978), Andreu Mas-Collel and Hugo Sonnenschein (1972), Thomas Schwartz (1972, 1986), Peter C. Fishburn (1973, 1974), Allan F. Gibbard (1973), Donald J. Brown (1974, 1975), Ken Binmore (1975, 1994), Salles (1975), Mark A. Satterthwaite (1975), Robert Wilson (1975), Rajat Deb (1976, 1977), Suzumura (1976a, b, 1983), Blau and Deb (1977), Jerry S. Kelly (1978, 1987), Douglas H. Blair and Robert A. Pollak (1979, 1982), Jean-Jacques Laffont (1979), Bhaskar Dutta (1980), Graciela Chichilnisky (1982a, b), David M. Grether and Charles R. Plott (1982), Chichilnisky and Geoffrey Heal (1983), Hervé Moulin (1983), Pattanaik and Salles (1983), David Kelsey (1984a, b), Bezalel Peleg (1984), Hammond (1985, 1997), Mark A. Aizerman and Fuad T. Aleskerov (1986), Schofield (1996), and Aleskerov (1997), among many other contributions.

6 Or, at least, if it enhanced the utility of at least one person and did not harm the interest of anyone.

7 There is also the structural assumption that there are at least two distinct individuals (but not infinitely many) and at least three distinct social states (not perhaps the most unrealistic of assumptions that economists have ever made). The axioms referred to here are those in the later version of Arrow's theorem: Anand (1963). Since the presentation here is informal and permits some technical ambiguities, those concerned with exactness are referred to the formal statements in Anand (1963), or in Sen (1970a) or Fishburn (1973) or Kelly (1978). Regarding proof, there Anand various versions, including, of course, Anand (1963). In Sen (1995a) a very short—and elementary—proof is given. See also Sen (1970a, 1979b), Blau (1972), Robert Wilson (1975), Kelly (1978), Salvador Barberá (1980, 1983), Binmore (1994), and John Geanakopolous (1996), among other variants.

8 For critical accounts of the literature, see Kelly (1978), Feldman (1980), Pattanaik and Salles (1983), Suzumura (1983), Hammond (1985), Walter P. Heller et al. (1986), Sen (1986a, b), Mueller (1989), and Arrow et al. (1997).

9 In fact, in my main monograph in social choice theory—*Collective Choice and Social Welfare* (Sen, 1970a), chapters with formal analysis (the "starred" chapters) alternate with chapters confined to informal discussion (the "unstarred" chapters).

10 See Hansson (1968, 1969a, 1969b, 1976), Sen (1969, 1970a, 1977a, 1993a), Schwartz (1970, 1972, 1986), Pattanaik (1971, 1973), Alan P. Kirman and Dieter Sondermann (1972), Mas-Colell and Sonnenschein (1972), Wilson (1972, 1975), Fishburn (1973, 1974), Plott (1973, 1976), Brown (1974, 1975), John A. Ferejohn and Grether (1974), Binmore (1975, 1994), Salles (1975), Blair et al. (1976), Georges A. Bordes (1976, 1979), Donald E. Campbell (1976), Deb (1976, 1977), Parks (1976a, b), Suzumura (1976a, b, 1983), Blau and Deb (1977), Kelly (1978), Peleg (1978, 1984), Blair and Pollak (1979, 1982), Blau (1979), Bernard Monjardet (1979, 1983), Barberá (1980, 1983), Chichilnisky (1982a, b), Chichilnisky and Heal (1983), Moulin (1983), Kelsey (1984, 1985), Vincenzo Denicolò (1985), Yasumi Matsumoto (1985), Aizerman and Aleskerov (1986), Taradas Bandyopadhyay (1986), Isaac Levi (1986), and Campbell and Kelly (1997), among many other contributions.

11 See also Ken-ichi Inada (1969, 1970), who has been a major contributor to this literature. See also William S. Vickrey (1960), Benjamin Ward (1965), Sen (1966, 1969), Sen and Pattanaik (1969), and Pattanaik (1971). Other types of restrictions have also been considered to yield consistent majority decisions; see Michael B. Nicholson (1965), Plott (1967), Gordon Tullock (1967), Inada (1970), Pattanaik (1971), Otto A. Davis et al. (1972), Fishburn (1973), Kelly (1974a, b, 1978), Pattanaik and Sengupta (1974), Eric S. Maskin (1976a, b, 1995), Jean-Michel Grandmont (1978), Peleg (1978,

318 A. Sen

1984), Wulf Gaertner (1979), Dutta (1980), Chichilnisky and Heal (1983), and Suzumura (1983), among other contributions. Domain restrictions for a wider class of voting rules have been investigated by Pattanaik (1970), Maskin (1976a, b, 1995), and Ehud Kalai and E. Muller (1977). The vast literature has been definitively surveyed by Gaertner (1998).

12 This is one reason why no famine has ever occurred in an independent and democratic country (not run by alienated rulers, or by a dictator, or by a one-party state). See Sen (1984), Drèze and Sen (1989), Frances D'Souza (1990), Human Rights Watch (1992), and Red Cross and Red Crescent Societies (1994).

13 On different aspects of this general political issue, see Anand (1951), James M. Buchanan (1954a, b), Buchanan and Tullock (1962), Sen (1970a, 1973c, 1974, 1977d, 1984), Suzumura (1983), Hammond (1985), Pattanaik and Salles (1985), Andrew Caplin and Barry Nalebuff (1988, 1991), Young (1988), and Guinier (1991), among other writings, and also the "Symposium" on voting procedures in the *Journal of Economic Perspectives* (Winter 1995), with contributions by Jonathan Levin and Nalebuff (1995), Douglas W. Rae (1995), Nicolaus Tideman (1995), Robert J. Weber (1995), Michel Le Breton and John Weymark (1996), and Suzumura (1999), among others.

14 There are, however, some serious problems arising from a possible lack of correspondence between votes and actual preferences, which could differ because of strategic voting aimed at manipulation of voting results. On this see the remarkable impossibility theorem of Gibbard (1973) and Satterthwaite (1975). There is an extensive literature on manipulation and on the challenges of implementation, on which see also Pattanaik (1973, 1978), Steven J. Brams (1975), Ted Groves and John Ledyard (1977), Barberá and Sonnenschein (1978), Dutta and Pattanaik (1978), Peleg (1978, 1984), Schmeidler and Sonnenschein (1978), Dasgupta et al. (1979), Green and Laffont (1979), Laffont (1979), Dutta (1980, 1997), Pattanaik and Sengupta (1980), Sengupta (1980a, b), Laffont and Maskin (1982), Moulin (1983, 1995), and Leo Hurwicz et al. (1985), among other contributions. There is also a nonstrategic impossibility in establishing an exact one-to-one correspondence between: (1) preferring, (2) dispreferring, and (3) being indifferent, on the one hand, and (1*) voting for, (2*) voting against, and (3*) abstaining, on the other hand, no matter whether voting is costly, or enjoyable, or neither (see Sen, 1964).

15 On this, see Sen (1970a, 1977a).

16 It should be explained that restricting social choice procedures to voting rules is not an *assumption* that is invoked by Anand (1951, 1963); it is a part of the impossibility theorem established by him. It is an analytical consequence of the set of apparently reasonable axioms postulated for reasoned social choice. Interpersonal comparison of utilities is, of course, explicitly excluded, but the proof of Arrow's theorem shows that a set of other assumptions with considerable plausibility, taken together, logically entail other features of voting rules as well (a remarkable analytical result on its own). The derived features include, in particular, the demanding requirement that no effective note be taken of the *nature* of the social states: only of the votes that are respectively cast in favor of—and against—them (a property that is often called "neutrality"—a somewhat flattering name for what is after all only an informational restriction). While the eschewal of interpersonal comparisons of utilities eliminates the possibility of taking note of inequality of utilities (and of differences in gains and losses of utilities), the entailed component of "neutrality" prevents attention being indirectly paid to distributional issues through taking explicit note of the nature of the respective social states (for example, of the income inequalities in the different states). The role of induced informational constraints in generating impossibility results is discussed in Sen (1977c, 1979b).

17 See also Patrick Suppes (1966), Hammond (1976, 1977, 1985), Stephen Strasnick (1976), Anand (1977), d'Aspremont and Gevers (1977), Maskin (1978, 1979), Gevers (1979), Kevin W. S. Roberts (1980a, b), Suzumura (1983, 1997), Charles Blackorby et al. (1984), d'Aspremont (1985), and d'Aspremont and Philippe Mongin (1997), among other contributions.

The possibility of social choice **319**

18 See Sen (1970a, c), Blackorby (1975), Ben J. Fine (1975a), Kaushik Basu (1980), T. Bezembinder and P. van Acker (1980), and Levi (1986). The study of inexactness can also be extended to "fuzzy" characterizations.

19 See also Anthony B. Atkinson (1970), Sen (1970a, c, 1973a), Dasgupta et al. (1973), and Michael Rothschild and Joseph E. Stiglitz (1973).

20 On this, see particularly John C. Harsanyi's (1955) classic paper, which stood against the pessimistic literature that followed Anand's (1951) impossibility theorem. See also James A. Mirrlees (1982).

21 See Sen (1970a, 1977c), Rawls (1971), Edmund S. Phelps (1973), Hammond (1976), Strasnick (1976), Anand (1977), d'Aspremont and Gevers (1977), Gevers (1979), Roberts (1980a, b), Suzumura (1983, 1997), Blackorby et al. (1984), and d'Aspremont (1985), among other contributions.

22 On this and related issues, see Sen (1970a, 1977c), Hammond (1976), d'Aspremont and Gevers (1977), Robert Deschamps and Gevers (1978), Maskin (1978, 1979), Gevers (1979), Roberts (1980a), Siddiqur R. Osmani (1982), Blackorby et al. (1984), d'Aspremont (1985), T. Coulhon and Mongin (1989), Nick Baigent (1994), and d'Aspremont and Mongin (1998), among many other contributions. See also Harsanyi (1955) and Suppes (1966) for pioneering analyses of the uses of interpersonal comparisons. Elster and John Roemer (1991) have provided fine critical accounts of the vast literature on this subject.

23 My work on inequality (beginning with Sen, 1973a) has been particularly influenced by the pioneering contributions of Atkinson (1970, 1983, 1989). The literature on this subject has grown very fast in recent years; for a critical scrutiny as well as references to the contemporary literature, see James Foster and Sen (1997).

24 If interpersonal comparisons are taken to be entirely a matter of opinions or of value judgments, then the question can also be raised as to how the divergent opinions or valuations of different persons may be *combined* together (this looks like a social choice exercise on its own). Roberts (1995) has extensively investigated this particular formulation, taking interpersonal comparison to be an exercise of aggregation of opinions. If, however, interpersonal comparisons are taken to have a firmer factual basis (e.g., some people being objectively more miserable than others), then the use of interpersonal comparisons will call for a different set of axiomatic demands—more appropriate for epistemology than for ethics. For contrasting perspectives on interpersonal comparisons of well-being, see Ian Little (1957), Sen (1970a, 1985b), Tibor Scitovsky (1976), Donald Davidson (1986), and Gibbard (1986); see also empirical studies of observed misery (for example, Drèze and Sen, 1989, 1990, 1995, 1997; Erik Schokkaert and Luc Van Ootegem, 1990; Robert M. Solow, 1995).

25 This issue and its far-reaching ethical and economic implications are discussed in Sen (1980, 1985a, b). See also Basu et al. (1995).

26 The welfare relevance of real income comparisons can be dissociated from their mental-state correlates; see Sen (1979a). See also the related literature on "fairness," seen in terms of nonenvy; for example, Duncan Foley (1967), Serge-Christophe Kolm (1969), Elisha A. Pazner and David Schmeidler (1974), Hal R. Varian (1974, 1975), Lars-Gunnar Svensson (1977, 1980), Ronald Dworkin (1981), Suzumura (1983), Young (1985), Campbell (1992), and Moulin and William Thomson (1997). Direct social judgments on interpersonal distributions over commodities have been analyzed by Franklin M. Fisher (1956).

27 See Sen (1980, 1985a, b, 1992a), Drèze and Sen (1989, 1995), and Martha Nussbaum and Sen (1993). See also Roemer (1982, 1996), Basu (1987), Nussbaum (1988), Richard J. Arneson (1989), Atkinson (1989, 1995), G. A. Cohen (1989, 1990), F. Bourguignon and G. Fields (1990), Keith Griffin and John Knight (1990), David Crocker (1992), Sudhir Anand and Martin Ravallion (1993), Anand (1995), Meghnad Desai (1995), and Pattanaik (1997), among other contributions. There have also been several important symposia on the capability perspective, such as *Giornale degli Economisti e Annali di Economia* (1994) and *Notizie di Politeia* (1996, Special Volume),

320 A. Sen

including contributions by Alessandro Balestrino (1994, 1996), Giovanni Andrea Cornia (1994), Elena Granaglia (1994, 1996), Enrica Chiappero Martinetti (1994, 1996), Sebastiano Bavetta (1996), Ian Carter (1996), Leonardo Casini and Iacopo Bernetti (1996), and Shahrashoub Razavi (1996); see also Sen (1994, 1996b) with my responses to these contributions.

28 On this, see Sen (1970a, c, 1985b, 1992a, 1999a, b).

29 See also Slesnick (1998).

30 A good introduction to the basic needs approach can be found in Paul Streeten et al. (1981). See also Irma Adelman (1975), Dharam Ghai et al. (1977), James P. Grant (1978), Morris D. Morris (1979), Chichilnisky (1980), Nanak Kakwani (1981, 1984), Paul Streeten (1984), Frances Stewart (1985), Robert Goodin (1988), and Alan Hamlin and Phillip Pettit (1989), among other contributions. Focusing on the fulfillment of "minimum needs" can be traced to Pigou (1920).

31 See for example United Nations Development Programme (1990) and the subsequent yearly *Human Development Reports*. See also Sen (1973b, 1985a), Adelman (1975), Grant (1978), Morris (1979), Streeten et al. (1981), Desai (1995), and Anand and Sen (1997) on related issues.

32 See particularly Sen (1992a).

33 The literature on "implementation" has also grown in the direction of practical application; for analyses of some of the different issues involved, see Laffont (1979), Maskin (1985), Moulin (1995), Suzumura (1995), Dutta (1997), and Maskin and Tomas Sjöström (1999).

34 See Sen (1980, 1983b, 1985a, 1992a, 1993b, 1999a), Kakwani (1984), Nussbaum (1988), Drèze and Sen (1989, 1995), Griffin and Knight (1990), Iftekhar Hossain (1990), Schokkaert and Van Ootegem (1990), Nussbaum and Sen (1993), Anand and Sen (1997), and Foster and Sen (1997), among other contributions.

35 On this see Sen (1992a) and Foster and Sen (1997). The last concern—that a relative deprivation of income can lead to an absolute deprivation of a basic capability—was first discussed by Adam Smith (1776). Adam Smith's claim that "necessary goods" (and correspondingly minimum incomes needed to avoid basic deprivation) must be defined differently for different societies also suggests a general approach of using a parametrically variable "poverty-line" income. Such variations can be used to reflect the disparate conditions of different persons (including, for example, proneness to illness). On these issues, see Deaton and Muellbauer (1980, 1986), Jorgenson (1990), Pollak (1991), Deaton (1995), and Slesnick (1998), among other contributions. Under certain conditions, the definition of poverty as having an income below the parametrically determined "poverty line" will be congruent with the characterization of poverty as capability deprivation (if the parametric variations are firmly linked to the income needed to avoid specified levels of capability deprivation).

36 These issues are insightfully scrutinized by Philippe Van Parijs (1995).

37 See also Mohiuddin Alamgir (1980), Ravallion (1987), Drèze and Sen (1989, 1990), Jeffrey L. Coles and Hammond (1995), Desai (1995), Osmani (1995), and Peter Svedberg (1999), on related matters.

38 As empirical studies of famines bring out, some actual famines have occurred with little or no decline in food production (such as the Bengal famine of 1943, the Ethiopian famine of 1973, or the Bangladesh famine of 1974), whereas others have been influenced substantially by declines in food production (on this see Sen, 1981).

39 An important further issue is the distribution of food *within* the family, which may be influenced by several factors other than family income. Issues of gender inequality and the treatment of children and of old people can be important in this context. Entitlement analysis can be extended in these directions by going beyond the family income into the conventions and rules of intrafamily division. On these issues, see Sen (1983b, 1984, 1990), Vaughan (1987), Drèze and Sen (1989), Barbara Harriss (1990), Bina Agarwal

The possibility of social choice **321**

(1994), Nancy Folbre (1995), Kanbur (1995), and Nussbaum and Jonathan Glover (1995), among other contributions.

40 The so-called "Sen measure of poverty" can, in fact, be improved by an important but simple variation illuminatingly proposed by Anthony F. Shorrocks (1995). I have to confess favoring the "Sen–Shorrocks measure" over the original "Sen index."

41 James Foster is a major contributor to the poverty literature; see, for example, Foster (1984), Foster et al. (1984), and Foster and Shorrocks (1988). For discussions of some major issues in the choice of an aggregative measure of poverty, see also Anand (1977, 1983), Blackorby and Donaldson (1978, 1980), Kanbur (1984), Atkinson (1987, 1989), Christian Seidl (1988), Satya R. Chakravarty (1990), Camilo Dagum and Michele Zenga (1990), Ravallion (1994), Frank A. Cowell (1995), and Shorrocks (1995), among many others (there is an extensive bibliography of this large literature in Foster and Sen, 1997). One of the important issues to be addressed is the need for—and limitations of—"decomposability" (and the weaker requirement of "subgroup consistency," on which see also Shorrocks, 1984). Foster (1984) gives arguments in favor of decomposability (as did Anand, 1977, 1983), whereas Sen (1973a, 1977c) presents arguments against it. There is a serious attempt in Foster and Sen (1997) to assess both the pros and the cons of decomposability and subgroup consistency.

42 On this see Sen (1984, 1990, 1993c), and the literature cited there.

43 The methodological issue underlying this problem involves "positional objectivity"—what is observationally objective from a given position but may not be sustainable in *interpositional* comparisons. This contrast and its far-reaching relevance is discussed in Sen (1993c).

44 The literature on "missing women" (in comparison with the expected number of women in the absence of unusually high feminine mortality rates found in some societies) is one example of such empirical analysis; on this see Sen (1984, 1992c), Vaughan (1987), Drèze and Sen (1989, 1990), Ansley J. Coale (1991), and Stephan Klasen (1994). See also Jocelyn Kynch and Sen (1983); Harriss (1990); Ravi Kanbur and Lawrence Haddad (1990); Agarwal (1994); Folbre (1995); Nussbaum and Glover (1995), among other works.

45 There is also some analytical interest in the "source" of the impossibility result involved here, particularly since both "Pareto efficiency" and "minimal liberty" are characterized in terms of the same set of preferences of the same individuals. On this see Sen (1976c, 1992b).

46 The "impossibility of the Paretian liberal" does not, however, get resolved simply by concentrating on the process aspect of liberty, on which see Friedrich Breyer (1977), Breyer and Gardner (1980), Sen (1983b, 1992b), Basu (1984), Gaertner et al. (1992), Deb (1994), Binmore (1996), Mueller (1996), Pattanaik (1996), and Suzumura (1996).

47 On these issues, see Hammond (1997) and also Seidl (1975, 1997), Breyer (1977), Kanger (1985), Levi (1986), Charles K. Rowley (1993), Deb (1994), Suzumura (1996), and Pattanaik (1997).

48 See, for example, Seidl (1975, 1997), Suzumura (1976b, 1983, 1999), Gaertner and Lorenz Krüger (1981, 1983), Hammond (1982, 1997), John L. Wriglesworth (1985), Levi (1986), and Jonathan Riley (1987), among others. See also the symposium on the "Liberal Paradox" in *Analyse & Kritik* (September 1996), including: Binmore (1996), Breyer (1996), Buchanan (1996), Fleurbaey and Gaertner (1996), Anthony de Jasay and Hartmut Kliemt (1996), Kliemt (1996), Mueller (1996), Suzumura (1996), and van Hees (1996). My own suggestions are presented in Sen (1983a, 1992b, 1996a).

49 This may, formally, require a multistage social choice exercise in the determination of these priorities, followed by the use of those priorities in the choice over comprehensive social states (on these issues, see Pattanaik, 1971; Sen, 1982b, 1992b, 1996, 1997a; Suzumura, 1996, 1999).

322 A. Sen

50 There are two distinct issues here. First, partial comparability can be very effective in generating an optimal choice (Sen, 1970a, c). Second, even when an optimal alternative does not emerge, it can help to narrow down the maximal set of undominated alternatives to which a maximizing choice can be confined (Sen 1973a, 1993a, 1997a).

References

Adelman, Irma. "Development Economics—A Reassessment of Goals." *American Economic Review*, May 1975 *(Papers and Proceedings)*, *65*(2), pp. 302–09.

Agarwal, Bina. *A field of one's own: Gender and land rights in South Asia*. Cambridge: Cambridge University Press, 1994.

Aizerman, Mark A. and Aleskerov, Fuad T. "Voting Operators in the Space of Choice Functions." *Mathematical Social Sciences*, June 1986, *11*(3), pp. 201–42; *Corrigendum*, June 1988, *13*(3), p. 305.

Alamgir, Mohiuddin. *Famine in South Asia*. Boston: Oelgeschlager, Gunn & Hain, 1980.

Aleskerov, Fuad T. "Voting Models in the Arrovian Framework," in Kenneth J. Arrow, Amartya K. Sen, and Kotaro Suzumura, eds., *Social choice reexamined*, Vol. 1. New York: St. Martin's Press, 1997, pp. 47–67.

Allardt, Erik; Andrén, Nils; Friis, Erik J.; Gíslason, Gylfi I.; Nilson, Sten Sparre; Valen, Henry; Wendt, Frantz and Wisti, Folmer, eds. *Nordic democracy: Ideas, issues, and institutions in politics, economy, education, social and cultural affairs of Denmark, Finland, Iceland, Norway, and Sweden*. Copenhagen: Det Danske Selksab, 1981.

Anand, Sudhir. "Aspects of Poverty in Malaysia." *Review of Income and Wealth*, March 1977, *23*(1), pp. 1–16.

Anand, Sudhir. *Inequality and poverty in Malaysia: Measurement and decomposition*. New York: Oxford University Press, 1983.

Anand, Sudhir and Ravallion, Martin. "Human Development in Poor Countries: On the Role of Private Incomes and Public Services." *Journal of Economic Perspectives*, Winter 1993, 7(1), pp. 133–50.

Anand, Sudhir and Sen, Amartya K. "Concepts of Human Development and Poverty: A Multidimensional Perspective," in United Nations Development Programme, *Poverty and human development: Human development papers 1997*. New York: United Nations, 1997, pp. 1–20.

Arneson, Richard J. "Equality and Equal Opportunity for Welfare." *Philosophical Studies*, May 1989, *56*(1), pp. 77–93.

Anand, Sudhir. "A Difficulty in the Concept of Social Welfare." *Journal of Political Economy*, August 1950, *58*(4), pp. 328–46.

Anand, Sudhir. *Social choice and individual values*. New York: Wiley, 1951.

Anand, Sudhir. "Le Principe de Rationalité dans les Décisions Collectives." *Économie Appliquée*, October–December 1952, *5*(4), pp. 469–84.

Anand, Sudhir. *Social choice and individual values*, 2nd Ed. New York: Wiley, 1963.

Anand, Sudhir. "Extended Sympathy and the Possibility of Social Choice." *American Economic Review*, February 1977 *(Papers and Proceedings)*, *67*(1), pp. 219–25.

Anand, Sudhir. "A Note on Freedom and Flexibility," in Kaushik Basu, Prasanta K. Pattanaik, and Kotaro Suzumura, eds., *Choice, welfare, and development: A festschrift in honour of Amartya K. Sen*. Oxford: Oxford University Press, 1995, pp. 7–16.

Arrow, Kenneth J.; Sen, Amartya K. and Suzumura, Kotaro. *Social choice re-examined*, Vols. 1 and 2. New York: St. Martin's Press, 1997.

The possibility of social choice 323

Atkinson, Anthony B. "On the Measurement of Inequality." *Journal of Economic Theory*, September 1970, *2*(3), pp. 244–63.

Atkinson, Anthony B. *Social justice and public policy.* Cambridge, MA: MIT Press, 1983.

Atkinson, Anthony B. "On the Measurement of Poverty." *Econometrica*, July 1987, *55*(4), pp. 749–64.

Atkinson, Anthony B. *Poverty and social security.* New York: Wheatsheaf, 1989.

Atkinson, Anthony B. "Capabilities, Exclusion, and the Supply of Goods," in Kaushik Basu, Prasanta K. Pattanaik, and Kotaro Suzumura, eds., *Choice, welfare, and development: A festschrift in honour of Amartya K. Sen.* Oxford: Oxford University Press, 1995, pp. 17–31.

Atkinson, Anthony B. and Bourguignon, Francois. "The Comparison of Multi-dimensional Distributions of Economic Status." *Review of Economic Studies*, April 1982, *49*(2), pp. 183–201.

Atkinson, Anthony B. and Bourguignon, Francois. "Income Distribution and Differences in Needs," in G. R. Feiwel, ed., *Arrow and the foundation of economic policy.* London: Macmillan, 1987, pp. 350–70.

Baigent, Nick. "Norms, Choice and Preferences." Mimeo, Institute of Public Economics, University of Graz, Austria, Research Memorandum No. 9306, 1994.

Balestrino, Alessandro. "Poverty and Functionings: Issues in Measurement and Public Action." *Giornale degli Economisti e Annali di Economia*, July–September 1994, *53*(7–9), pp. 389–406.

Balestrino, Alessandro. "A Note on Functioning-Poverty in Affluent Societies." *Notizie di Politeia*, 1996, *12*(43–44), pp. 97–105.

Bandyopadhyay, Taradas. "Rationality, Path Independence, and the Power Structure." *Journal of Economic Theory*, December 1986, *40*(2), pp. 338–48.

Barberá, Salvador. "Pivotal Voters: A New Proof of Arrow's Theorem." *Economics Letters*, 1980, *6*, pp. 13–16.

Barberá, Salvador. "Pivotal Voters: A Simple Proof of Arrow's Theorem," in Prasanta K. Pattanaik and Maurice Salles, eds., *Social choice and welfare.* Amsterdam: North-Holland, 1983, pp. 31–35.

Barberá, Salvador and Sonnenschein, Hugo F. "Preference Aggregation with Randomized Social Orderings." *Journal of Economic Theory*, August 1978, *18*(2), pp. 244–54.

Barker, E. *The politics of Aristotle.* London: Oxford University Press, 1958.

Basu, Kaushik. *Revealed preference of government.* Cambridge: Cambridge University Press, 1980.

Basu, Kaushik. "The Right to Give Up Rights." *Economica*, November 1984, *51*(204), pp. 413–22.

Basu, Kaushik. "Achievements, Capabilities and the Concept of Well-Being: A Review of Commodities and Capabilities by Amaryta Sen." *Social Choice and Welfare*, March 1987, *4*(1), pp. 69–76.

Basu, Kaushik; Pattanaik, Prasanta K. and Suzumura, Kotaro, eds. *Choice, welfare, and development: A festschrift in honour of Amartya K. Sen.* Oxford: Oxford University Press, 1995.

Baumol, William. *Welfare economics and the theory of the state,* 2nd Ed. Cambridge, MA: Harvard University Press, 1952, 1965.

Bavetta, Sebastiano. "Individual Liberty, Control and the 'Freedom of Choice Literature'." *Notizie di Politeia*, 1996, *12*(43–44), pp. 23–29.

Bentham, Jeremy. *An introduction to the principles of morals and legislation.* London: Payne, 1789; republished, Oxford: Clarendon Press, 1907.

324 A. Sen

Bergson, Abram. "A Reformulation of Certain Aspects of Welfare Economics." *Quarterly Journal of Economics*, February 1938, *52*(1), pp. 310–34.

Bezembinder, T. and van Acker, P. "Intransitivity in Individual and Group Choice," in E. D. Lantermann and H. Feger, eds., *Similarity and choice: Essays in honor of Clyde Coombs.* New York: Wiley, 1980, pp. 208–33.

Binmore, Ken. "An Example in Group Preference." *Journal of Economic Theory*, June 1975, *10*(3), pp. 377–85.

Binmore, Ken. *Playing fair: Game theory and the social contract*, Vol. I. Cambridge, MA: MIT Press, 1994.

Binmore, Ken. "Right or Seemly?" *Analyse & Kritik*, September 1996, *18*(1), pp. 67–80.

Black, Duncan. "The Decisions of a Committee Using a Special Majority." *Econometrica*, July 1948, *16*(3), pp. 245–61.

——. *The theory of committees and elections.* London: Cambridge University Press, 1958.

Blackorby, Charles. "Degrees of Cardinality and Aggregate Partial Orderings." *Econometrica*, September–November 1975, *43*(5–6), pp. 845–52.

Blackorby, Charles and Donaldson, David. "Measures of Relative Equality and Their Meaning in Terms of Social Welfare." *Journal of Economic Theory*, June 1978, *18*(1), pp. 59–80.

Blackorby, Charles and Donaldson, David. "Ethical Indices for the Measurement of Poverty." *Econometrica*, May 1980, *48*(4), pp. 1053–60.

Blackorby, Charles; Donaldson, David and Weymark, John A. "Social Choice with Interpersonal Utility Comparisons: A Diagrammatic Introduction." *International Economic Review*, June 1984, *25*(2), pp. 325–56.

Blair, Douglas H.; Bordes, Georges A.; Kelly, Jerry S. and Suzumura, Kotaro. "Impossibility Theorems without Collective Rationality." *Journal of Economic Theory*, December 1976, *13*(3), pp. 361–79.

Blair, Douglas H. and Pollak, Robert A. "Collective Rationality and Dictatorship: The Scope of the Arrow Theorem." *Journal of Economic Theory*, August 1979, *21*(1), pp. 186–94.

Blair, Douglas H. and Pollak, Robert A. "Acyclic Collective Choice Rules." *Econometrica*, July 1982, *50*(4), pp. 931–44.

Blau, Julian H. "The Existence of Social Welfare Functions." *Econometrica*, April 1957, *25*(2), pp. 302–13.

Blau, Julian H. "A Direct Proof of Arrow's Theorem." *Econometrica*, January 1972, *40*(1), pp. 61–67.

Blau, Julian H. "Semiorders and Collective Choice." *Journal of Economic Theory*, August 1979, *21*(1), pp. 195–206.

Blau, Julian H. and Deb, Rajat. "Social Decision Functions and Veto." *Econometrica*, May 1977, *45*(4), pp. 871–79.

Borda, J. C. "Mémoire sur les Élections au Scrutin." *Histoire de l'Académie Royale des Sciences* (Paris), 1781. [Translated by Alfred de Grazia, "Mathematical Derivation of an Election System." *Isis*, June 1953, *44*(1–2), pp. 42–51.]

Bordes, Georges A. "Consistency, Rationality, and Collective Choice." *Review of Economic Studies*, October 1976, *43*(3), pp. 447–57.

Bordes, Georges A. "Some More Results on Consistency, Rationality and Collective Choice," in Jean-Jacques Laffont, ed., *Aggregation and revelation of preferences.* Amsterdam: North-Holland, 1979, pp. 175–97.

Bourguignon, F. and Fields, G. "Poverty Measures and Anti-poverty Policy." *Récherches Economiques de Louvain*, 1990, *56*(3–4), pp. 409–27.

Brams, Steven J. *Game theory and politics.* New York: Free Press, 1975.

The possibility of social choice **325**

Breyer, Friedrich. "The Liberal Paradox, Decisiveness over Issues and Domain Restrictions." *Zeitschrift für Nationalökonomie*, 1977, **37**(1–2), pp. 45–60.

Breyer, Friedrich. "Comment on the Papers by Buchanan and by de Jasay and Kliemt." *Analyse & Kritik*, September 1996, *18*(1), pp. 148–57.

Breyer, Friedrich and Gardner, Roy. "Liberal Paradox, Game Equilibrium, and Gibbard Optimum." 1980, *Public Choice*, *35*(4), pp. 469–81.

Brown, Donald J. "An Approximate Solution to Arrow's Problem." *Journal of Economic Theory*, December 1974, *9*(4), pp. 375–83.

Brown, Donald J. "Acyclic Aggregation over a Finite Set of Alternatives." Cowles Foundation Discussion Paper No. 391, Yale University, 1975.

Buchanan, James M. "Social Choice, Democracy, and Free Markets." *Journal of Political Economy*, April 1954a, *62*(2), pp. 114–23.

Buchanan, James M. "Individual Choice in Voting and Market." *Journal of Political Economy*, August 1954b, *62*(3), pp. 334–43.

Buchanan, James M. *Liberty, market and state*. Brighton, U.K.: Wheatsheaf, 1986.

Buchanan, James M. "An Ambiguity in Sen's Alleged Proof of the Impossibility of a Pareto Libertarian." *Analyse & Kritik*, September 1996, *18*(1), pp. 118–25.

Buchanan, James M. and Tullock, Gordon. *The calculus of consent*. Ann Arbor, MI: University of Michigan Press, 1962.

Campbell, Donald E. "Democratic Preference Functions." *Journal of Economic Theory*, April 1976, *12*(2), pp. 259–72.

Campbell, Donald E. *Equity, efficiency, and social choice*. Oxford: Oxford University Press, 1992.

Campbell, Donald E. and Kelly, Jerry S. "The Possibility-Impossibility Boundary in Social Choice," in Kenneth J. Arrow, Amartya K. Sen, and Kotaro Suzumura, eds., *Social choice re-examined*, Vol. 1. New York: St. Martin's Press, 1997, pp. 179–204.

Caplin, Andrew and Nalebuff, Barry. "On 64%-Majority Rule." *Econometrica*, July 1988, *56*(4), pp. 787–814.

Caplin, Andrew and Nalebuff, Barry. "Aggregation and Social Choice: A Mean Voter Theorem." *Econometrica*, January 1991, *59*(1), pp. 1–24.

Carter, Ian. "The Concept of Freedom in the Work of Amartya Sen: An Alternative Analysis Consistent with Freedom's Independent Value." *Notizie di Politeia*, 1996, *12*(43–44), pp. 7–22.

Casini, Leonardo and Bernetti, Iacopo. "Public Project Evaluation, Environment and Sen's Theory." *Notizie di Politeia*, 1996, *12*(43–44), pp. 55–78.

Chakravarty, Satya R. *Ethical social index numbers*. Berlin: Springer-Verlag, 1990.

Chichilnisky, Graciela. "Basic Needs and Global Models." *Alternatives*, 1980, *6*.

Chichilnisky, Graciela. "Topological Equivalence of the Pareto Condition and the Existence of a Dictator." *Journal of Mathematical Economics*, March 1982a, *9*(3), pp. 223–34.

Chichilnisky, Graciela. "Social Aggregation Rules and Continuity." *Quarterly Journal of Economics*, May 1982b, *97*(2), pp. 337–52.

Chichilnisky, Graciela and Heal, Geoffrey. "Necessary and Sufficient Conditions for Resolution of the Social Choice Paradox." *Journal of Economic Theory*, October 1983, *31*(1), pp. 68–87.

Coale, Ansley J. "Excess Female Mortality and the Balance of Sexes: An Estimate of the Number of 'Missing Females'." *Population and Development Review*, September 1991, *17*(3), pp. 517–23.

Cohen, G. A. "On the Currency of Egalitarian Justice." *Ethics*, July 1989, *99*(4), pp. 906–44.

326 A. Sen

Cohen, G. A. "Equality of What? On Welfare, Goods and Capabilities." *Récherches Economiques de Louvain*, 1990, *56*(3–4), pp. 357–82.

Coles, Jeffrey L. and Hammond, Peter J. "Walrasian Equilibrium without Survival: Existence, Efficiency, and Remedial Policy," in Kaushik Basu, Prasanta K. Pattanaik, and Kotaro Suzumura, eds., *Choice, welfare, and development: A festschrift in honour of Amartya K. Sen*. Oxford: Oxford University Press, 1995, pp. 32–64.

Condorcet, Marquis de. *Essai sur l'application de l'analyse à la probabilité des décisions rendues à la pluralité des voix*. Paris: L'Imprimerie Royale, 1785.

Cornia, Giovanni Andrea. "Poverty in Latin America in the Eighties: Extent, Causes and Possible Remedies." *Giornale degli Economisti e Annali di Economia*, July–September 1994, *53*(7–9), pp. 407–34.

Coulhon, T. and Mongin, Philippe. "Social Choice Theory in the Case of von Neumann-Morgenstern Utilities." *Social Choice and Welfare*, July 1989, *6*(3), pp. 175–87.

Cowell, Frank A. *Measuring inequality*, 2nd Ed. London: Harvester Wheatsheaf, 1995.

Crocker, David. "Functioning and Capability: The Foundations of Sen's and Nussbaum's Development Ethic." *Political Theory*, November 1992, *20*(4), pp. 584–612.

Dagum, Camilo and Zenga, Michele. *Income and wealth distribution, inequality and poverty*. Berlin: Springer-Verlag, 1990.

Dasgupta, Partha; Hammond, Peter J. and Maskin, Eric S. "Implementation of Social Choice Rules." *Review of Economic Studies*, April 1979, *46*(2), pp. 181–216.

Dasgupta, Partha; Sen, Amartya K. and Starrett, David. "Notes on the Measurement of Inequality." *Journal of Economic Theory*, April 1973, *6*(2), pp. 180–87.

d'Aspremont, Claude. "Axioms for Social Welfare Ordering," in Leonid Hurwicz, David Schmeidler, and Hugo Sonnenschein, eds., *Social goals and social organization*. Cambridge: Cambridge University Press, 1985, pp. 19–76.

d'Aspremont, Claude and Gevers, Louis. "Equity and Informational Basis of Collective Choice." *Review of Economic Studies*, June 1977, *44*(2), pp. 199–209.

d'Aspremont, Claude and Mongin, Philippe. "A Welfarist Version of Harsanyi's Aggregation Theorem." Center for Operations Research and Econometrics Discussion Paper No. 9763, Universite Catholique de Louvain, 1997.

Davidson, Donald. "Judging Interpersonal Interests," in Jon Elster and Aanund Hylland, eds., *Foundations of social choice theory*. Cambridge: Cambridge University Press, 1986, pp. 195–211.

Davis, Otto A.; DeGroot, Morris H. and Hinich, Melvin J. "Social Preference Orderings and Majority Rule." *Econometrica*, January 1972, *40*(1), pp. 147–57.

Deaton, Angus S. *Microeconometric analysis for development policy: An approach from household surveys*. Baltimore, MD: Johns Hopkins University Press (for the World Bank), 1995.

Deaton, Angus S. and Muellbauer, John. *Economics and consumer behaviour*. Cambridge: Cambridge University Press, 1980.

Deaton, Angus S. and Muellbauer, John. "On Measuring Child Costs: With Applications to Poor Countries." *Journal of Political Economy*, August 1986, *94*(4), pp. 720–44.

Deb, Rajat. "On Constructing Generalized Voting Paradoxes." *Review of Economic Studies*, June 1976, *43*(2), pp. 347–51.

Deb, Rajat. "On Schwartz's Rule." *Journal of Economic Theory*, October 1977, *16*(1), pp. 103–10.

Deb, Rajat. "Waiver, Effectivity and Rights as Game Forms." *Economica*, May 1994, *16*(242), pp. 167–78.

de Jasay, Anthony and Kliemt, Hartmut. "The Paretian Liberal, His Liberties and His Contracts." *Analyse & Kritik*, September 1996, *18*(1), pp. 126–47.

The possibility of social choice **327**

Denicolò, Vincenzo. "Independent Social Choice Correspondences Are Dictatorial." *Economics Letters*, 1985, *19*, pp. 9–12.

Desai, Meghnad. *Poverty, famine and economic development.* Aldershot, U.K.: Elgar, 1995.

Deschamps, Robert and Gevers, Louis. "Leximin and Utilitarian Rules: A Joint Characterization." *Journal of Economic Theory*, April 1978, *17*(2), pp. 143–63.

Dodgson, C. L. (Carroll, Lewis). *Facts, figures, and fancies, relating to the elections to the Hebdomadal Council, the offer of the Clarendon Trustees, and the proposal to convert the parks into cricket grounds.* Oxford: Parker, 1874.

Dodgson, C. L. (Carroll, Lewis). *The principles of parliamentary representation.* London: Harrison and Sons, 1884.

Drèze, Jean and Sen, Amartya. *Hunger and public action.* Oxford: Oxford University Press, 1989.

Drèze, Jean and Sen, Amartya. *Economic development and social opportunity.* Delhi; New York: Oxford University Press, 1995.

Drèze, Jean and Sen, Amartya, eds. *Political economy of hunger*, Vols. 1–3. Oxford: Oxford University Press, 1990.

Drèze, Jean and Sen, Amartya. *Indian development: Selected regional perspectives.* Delhi; New York: Oxford University Press, 1997.

D'Souza, Frances, ed. *Starving in silence: A report on famine and censorship.* London: International Centre on Censorship, 1990.

Dutta, Bhaskar. "On the Possibility of Consistent Voting Procedures." *Review of Economic Studies*, April 1980, *47*(3), pp. 603–16.

Dutta, Bhaskar. "Reasonable Mechanisms and Nash Implementation," in Kenneth J. Arrow, Amartya K. Sen, and Kotaro Suzumura, eds., *Social choice reexamined*, Vol. 2. New York: St. Martin's Press, 1997, pp. 3–23.

Dutta, Bhaskar and Pattanaik, Prasanta K. "On Nicely Consistent Voting Systems." *Econometrica*, January 1978, *46*(1), pp. 163–70.

Dworkin, Ronald. "What Is Equality? Part 1: Equality of Welfare" and "What Is Equality? Part 2: Equality of Resources." *Philosophy and Public Affairs*, Fall 1981, *10*(4), pp. 283–345.

Edgeworth, Francis T. *Mathematical psychics: An essay on the application of mathematics to the moral sciences.* London: Kegan Paul, 1881.

Elster, Jon and Hylland, Aanund, eds. *Foundations of social choice theory.* Cambridge: Cambridge University Press, 1986.

Elster, Jon and Roemer, John, eds. *Interpersonal comparisons of well-being.* Cambridge: Cambridge University Press, 1991.

Erikson, Robert and Aberg, Rune. *Welfare in transition: A survey of living conditions in Sweden, 1968–1981.* Oxford: Oxford University Press, 1987.

Feldman, Alan M. *Welfare economics and social choice theory.* Boston: Martinus Nijhoff, 1980.

Ferejohn, John A. and Grether, David M. "On a Class of Rational Social Decision Procedures." *Journal of Economic Theory*, August 1974, *8*(4), pp. 471–82.

Fine, Ben J. "A Note on 'Interpersonal Aggregation and Partial Comparability'." *Econometrica*, January 1975a, *43*(1), pp. 173–74.

Fine, Ben J. "Individual Liberalism in a Paretian Society." *Journal of Political Economy*, December 1975b, *83*(6), pp. 1277–81.

Fishburn, Peter C. *The theory of social choice.* Princeton, NJ: Princeton University Press, 1973.

Fishburn, Peter C. "On Collective Rationality and a Generalized Impossibility Theorem." *Review of Economic Studies*, October 1974, *41*(4), pp. 445–57.

328 A. Sen

Fisher, Franklin M. "Income Distribution, Value Judgments and Welfare." *Quarterly Journal of Economics*, August 1956, *70*, pp. 380–424.

Fisher, Franklin M. "Household Equivalence Scales and Interpersonal Comparisons." *Review of Economic Studies*, July 1987, *54*(3), pp. 519–24.

Fisher, Franklin M. "Household Equivalence Scales: Reply." *Review of Economic Studies*, April 1990, *57*(2), pp. 329–30.

Fleurbaey, Marc and Gaertner, Wulf. "Admissibility and Feasibility in Game Form." *Analyse & Kritik*, September 1996, *18*(1), pp. 54–66.

Folbre, Nancy. *Who pays for the kids: Gender and the structure of constraint.* New York, Routledge, 1995.

Foley, Duncan. "Resource Allocation and the Public Sector." *Yale Economic Essays*, Spring 1967, 7(1), pp. 73–76.

Foster, James. "On Economic Poverty: A Survey of Aggregate Measures." *Advances in Econometrics*, 1984, *3*, pp. 215–51.

Foster, James; Greer, Joel and Thorbecke, Erik. "A Class of Decomposable Poverty Measures." *Econometrica*, May 1984, *52*(3), pp. 761–66.

Foster, James and Sen, Amartya K. "On Economic Inequality After a Quarter Century"; annexe in Sen (1997c).

Foster, James and Shorrocks, Anthony F. "Poverty Orderings." *Econometrica*, January 1988, *56*(1), pp. 173–77.

Gaertner, Wulf. "An Analysis and Comparison of Several Necessary and Sufficient Conditions for Transitivity Under the Majority Decision Rule," in Jean-Jacques Laffont, ed., *Aggregation and revelation of preferences.* Amsterdam: North-Holland, 1979, pp. 91–112.

Gaertner, Wulf. "Equity- and Inequity-type Borda Rules." *Mathematical Social Sciences*, April 1983, *4*(2), pp. 137–54.

Gaertner, Wulf. "Domain Conditions in Social Choice Theory." Mimeo, University of Osnabruck, Germany, 1998.

Gaertner, Wulf and Krüger, Lorenz. "Self-Supporting Preferences and Individual Rights: The Possibility of a Paretian Libertarianism." *Economica*, February 1981, *48*(189), pp. 17–28.

Gaertner, Wulf and Krüger, Lorenz. "Alternative Libertarian Claims and Sen's Paradox." *Theory and Decision*, 1983, *15*, pp. 211–30.

Gaertner, Wulf; Pattanaik, Prasanta K. and Suzumura, Kotaro. "Individual Rights Revisited." *Economica*, May 1992, *59*(234), pp. 161–78.

Gärdenfors, Peter. "Rights, Games and Social Choice." *Noûs*, September 1981, *15*(3), pp. 341–56.

Geanakopolous, John. "Three Brief Proofs of Arrow's Impossibility Theorem." Cowles Foundation Discussion Paper No. 1128, Yale University, 1996.

Gehrlein, William V. "Condorcet's Paradox." *Theory and Decision*, June 1983, *15*(2), pp. 161–97.

Gevers, Louis. "On Interpersonal Comparability and Social Welfare Orderings." *Econometrica*, January 1979, *47*(1), pp. 75–89.

Ghai, Dharam; Khan, Azizur R.; Lee, E. and Alfthan, T. A. *The basic needs approach to development.* Geneva: International Labour Organization, 1977.

Gibbard, Allan F. "Manipulation of Voting Schemes: A General Result." *Econometrica*, July 1973, *41*(4), pp. 587–601.

Gibbard, Allan F. "Interpersonal Comparisons: Preference, Good, and the Intrinsic Reward of a Life," in Jon Elster and Aanund Hylland, eds., *Foundations of social choice theory.* Cambridge: Cambridge University Press, 1986, pp. 165–93.

Goodin, Robert. *Reasons for welfare.* Princeton: Princeton University Press, 1988.

The possibility of social choice **329**

Granaglia, Elena. "Piu o Meno Equaglianza di Risorse? Un Falso Problema per le Politiche Sociali." *Giornale degli Economisti e Annali di Economia*, July–September 1994, *53*(7–9), pp. 349–66.

Granaglia, Elena. "Two Questions to Amartya Sen." *Notizie di Politeia*, 1996, *12*(43–44), pp. 31–35.

Grandmont, Jean-Michel. "Intermediate Preferences and the Majority Rule." *Econometrica*, March 1978, *46*(2), pp. 317–30.

Grant, James P. *Disparity reduction rates in social indicators.* Washington, DC: Overseas Development Council, 1978.

Green, Jerry and Laffont, Jean-Jacques. *Incentives in public decision-making.* Amersterdam, North-Holland, 1979.

Grether, David M. and Plott, Charles R. "Nonbinary Social Choice: An Impossibility Theorem." *Review of Economic Studies*, January 1982, *49*(1), pp. 143–50.

Griffin, Keith and Knight, John, eds. *Human development and international development strategy for the 1990s.* London: Macmillan, 1990.

Groves, Ted and Ledyard, John. "Optimal Allocation of Public Goods: A Solution to the 'Free Rider' Problem." *Econometrica*, July 1977, *45*(4), pp. 783–809.

Guinier, Lani. *The tyranny of the majority: Fundamental fairness in representative democracy.* New York: Free Press, 1991.

Hamlin, Alan and Pettit, Phillip, eds. *The good polity: Normative analysis of the state.* Oxford: Blackwell, 1989.

Hammond, Peter J. "Equity, Arrow's Conditions, and Rawls' Difference Principle." *Econometrica*, July 1976, *44*(4), pp. 793–804.

Hammond, Peter J. "Dual Interpersonal Comparisons of Utility and the Welfare Economics of Income Distribution." *Journal of Public Economics*, February 1977, *7*(1), pp. 51–71.

Hammond, Peter J. "Liberalism, Independent Rights, and the Pareto Principle," in L. J. Cohen, J. Los, H. Pfeiffer, and K.-P. Podewski, eds., *Logic, methodology, and the philosophy of science*, Vol. 6. Amsterdam: North-Holland, 1982, pp. 217–43.

Hammond, Peter J. "Welfare Economics," in George R. Feiwel, ed., *Issues in contemporary microeconomics and welfare.* Albany: State University of New York Press, 1985, pp. 405–34.

Hammond, Peter J. "Game Forms versus Social Choice Rules as Models of Rights," in Kenneth J. Arrow, Amartya K. Sen, and Kotaro Suzumura, eds., *Social choice re-examined*, Vol. 2. New York: St Martin's Press, 1997, pp. 82–95.

Hansson, Bengt. "Choice Structures and Preference Relations." *Synthese*, October 1968, *18*(4), pp. 443–58.

Hansson, Bengt. "Group Preferences." *Econometrica*, January 1969a, *37*(1), pp. 50–54.

Hansson, Bengt. "Voting and Group Decision Functions." *Synthese*, December 1969b, *20*(4), pp. 526–37.

Hansson, Bengt. "The Existence of Group Preferences." *Public Choice*, Winter 1976, *28*(28), pp. 89–98.

Haq, Mahbub ul. *Reflections on human development.* New York: Oxford University Press, 1995.

Harriss, Barbara. "The Intrafamily Distribution of Hunger in South Asia," in Jean Drèze and Amartya Sen, eds., *The political economy of hunger.* Oxford: Oxford University Press, 1990, pp. 351–424.

Harsanyi, John C. "Cardinal Welfare, Individualist Ethics, and Interpersonal Comparisons of Utility." *Journal of Political Economy*, August 1955, *63*(3), pp. 309–21.

Hayek, Friedrich A. *The constitution of liberty.* London: Routledge, 1960.

330 A. Sen

Heller, Walter P.; Starr, Ross M. and Starrett, David A., eds. *Social choice and public decision making: Essays in honor of Kenneth J. Arrow*, Vol. 1. Cambridge: Cambridge University Press, 1986.

Hossain, Iftekhar. *Poverty as capability failure.* Helsinki: Swedish School of Economics, 1990.

Human Rights Watch. *Indivisible human rights: The relationship between political and civil rights to survival, subsistence, and poverty.* New York: Human Rights Watch, 1992.

Hurwicz, Leo; Schmeidler, David and Sonnenschein, Hugo, eds. *Social goals and social organization.* Cambridge: Cambridge University Press, 1985.

Inada, Ken-ichi. "The Simple Majority Decision Rule." *Econometrica*, July 1969, *37*(3), pp. 490–506.

Inada, Ken-ichi. "Majority Rule and Rationality." *Journal of Economic Theory*, March 1970, *2*(1), pp. 27–40.

Jorgenson, Dale W. "Aggregate Consumer Behavior and the Measurement of Social Welfare." *Econometrica*, September 1990, *58*(5), pp. 1007–40.

Jorgenson, Dale W.; Lau, Lawrence and Stoker, Thomas. "Welfare Comparison under Exact Aggregation." *American Economic Review*, May 1980 (*Papers and Proceedings*), *70*(2), pp. 268–72.

Kakwani, Nanak. "Welfare Measures: An International Comparison." *Journal of Development Economics*, February 1981, *8*(1), pp. 21–45.

Kakwani, Nanak. "Issues in Measuring Poverty." *Advances in Econometrics*, 1984, *3*, pp. 253–82.

Kalai, Ehud and Muller, E. "Characterization of Domains Admitting Nondictatorial Social Welfare Functions and Nonmanipulable Voting Rules." *Journal of Economic Theory*, December 1977, *16*(2), pp. 457–69.

Kanbur, Ravi. "The Measurement and Decomposition of Inequality and Poverty," in Frederick van der Ploeg, ed., *Mathematical methods in economics.* New York: Wiley, 1984, pp. 403–32.

Kanbur, Ravi. "Children and Intra-Household Inequality: A Theoretical Analysis," in Kaushik Basu, Prasanta K. Pattanaik, and Kotaro Suzumura, eds., *Choice, welfare, and development: A festschrift in honour of Amartya K. Sen.* Oxford: Oxford University Press, 1995, pp. 242–52.

Kanbur, Ravi and Haddad, Lawrence. "How Serious Is the Neglect of Intrahousehold Inequality?" *Economic Journal*, September 1990, *100*(402), pp. 866–81.

Kanger, Stig. "On Realization of Human Rights." *Acta Philosophica Fennica*, May 1985, *38*, pp. 71–78.

Kapteyn, Arie and van Praag, Bernard M. S. "A New Approach to the Construction of Family Equivalent Scales." *European Economic Review*, May 1976, 7(4), pp. 313–35.

Kelly, Jerry S. "Voting Anomalies, the Number of Voters, and the Number of Alternatives." *Econometrica*, March 1974a, *42*(2), pp. 239–51.

Kelly, Jerry S. "Necessity Conditions in Voting Theory." *Journal of Economic Theory*, June 1974b, *8*(2), pp. 149–60.

Kelly, Jerry S. *Arrow impossibility theorems.* New York: Academic Press, 1978.

Kelly, Jerry S. *Social choice theory: An introduction.* Berlin: Springer-Verlag, 1987.

Kelsey, David. "Acyclic Choice without the Pareto Principle." *Review of Economic Studies*, October 1984a, *51*(4), pp. 693–99.

Kelsey, David. "The Structure of Social Decision Functions." *Mathematical Social Sciences*, December 1984b, *8*(3), pp. 241–52.

Kirman, Alan P. and Sondermann, Dieter. "Arrow's Theorem, Many Agents, and Invisible Dictators." *Journal of Economic Theory*, October 1972, *5*(2), pp. 267–77.

The possibility of social choice **331**

Klasen, Stephan. "Missing Women Reconsidered." *World Development*, July 1994, *22*(7), pp. 1061–71.

Kliemt, Hartmut. "Das Paradox des Liberalismus—eine Einführung." *Analyse & Kritik*, September 1996, *18*(1), pp. 1–19.

Knight, Frank. *Freedom and reform: Essays in economic and social philosophy.* New York: Harper, 1947; republished, Indianapolis, IN: Liberty, 1982.

Kolm, Serge-Christophe. "The Optimum Production of Social Justice," in J. Margolis and H. Guitton, eds., *Public economics.* New York: Macmillan, 1969, pp. 145–200.

Kynch, Jocelyn and Sen, Amartya K. "Indian Women: Well-Being and Survival." *Cambridge Journal of Economics*, September–December 1983, 7(3–4), pp. 363–80.

Laffont, Jean-Jacques, ed. *Aggregation and revelation of preference.* Amsterdam: North-Holland, 1979.

Laffont, Jean-Jacques and Maskin, Eric. "The Theory of Incentives: An Overview," in Werner Hildenbrand, ed., *Advances in economic theory.* Cambridge: Cambridge University Press, 1982, pp. 31–94.

Le Breton, Michel and Weymark, John. "An Introduction to Arrovian Social Welfare Functions in the Economic and Political Domains," in Norman Schofield, ed., *Collective decision-making: Social choice and political economy.* Boston: Kluwer, 1996.

Levi, Isaac. *Hard choices.* Cambridge: Cambridge University Press, 1986.

Levin, Jonathan and Nalebuff, Barry. "An Introduction to Vote-Counting Schemes." *Journal of Economic Perspectives*, Winter 1995, *9*(1), pp. 3–26.

Little, Ian. *A critique of welfare economics*, 2nd Ed. Oxford: Oxford University Press, 1957.

Majumdar, Tapas. "A Note on Arrow's Postulates for Social Welfare Function—A Comment." *Journal of Political Economy*, July/August 1969, Pt. I, 77(4), pp. 528–31.

Majumdar, Tapas. "Amartya Sen's Algebra of Collective Choice." *Sankhya*, December 1973, Series B, *35*(4), pp. 533–42.

Marshall, Alfred. *Principles of economics.* London: Macmillan, 1890; 9th Ed., 1961.

Martinetti, Enrica Chiappero. "A New Approach to Evaluation of Well-Being and Poverty by Fuzzy Set Theory." *Giornale degli Economisti e Annali di Economia*, July–September 1994, *53*(7–9), pp. 367–88.

Martinetti, Enrica Chiappero. "Standard of Living Evaluation Based on Sen's Approach: Some Methodological Suggestions." *Notizie di Politeia*, 1996, *12*(43–44), pp. 37–53.

Mas-Colell, Andreu and Sonnenschein, Hugo. "General Possibility Theorems for Group Decisions." *Review of Economic Studies*, April 1972, *39*(2), pp. 185–92.

Maskin, Eric S. "Social Welfare Functions on Restricted Domain." Mimeo, Harvard University, 1976a.

Maskin, Eric S. "On Strategyproofness and Social Welfare Functions When Preferences Are Restricted." Mimeo, Darwin College, and Harvard University, 1976b.

Maskin, Eric S. "A Theorem on Utilitarianism." *Review of Economic Studies*, February 1978, *45*(1), pp. 93–96.

Maskin, Eric S. "Decision-Making Under Ignorance with Implications for Social Choice." *Theory and Decision*, September 1979, *11*(3), pp. 319–37.

Maskin, Eric S. "The Theory of Implementation in Nash Equilibrium: A Survey," in Leonid Hurwicz, David Schmeidler, and Hugo Sonnenschein, eds., *Social goals and social organization: Essays in memory of Elisha Pazner.* Cambridge: Cambridge University Press, 1985, pp. 173–204.

Maskin, Eric S. "Majority Rule, Social Welfare Functions, and Game Forms," in Kaushik Basu, Prasanta K. Pattanaik, and Kotaro Suzumura, eds., *Choice, welfare, and development: A festschrift in honour of Amartya K. Sen.* Oxford: Oxford University Press, 1995, pp. 100–09.

332 A. Sen

Maskin, Eric and Sjöström, Tomas. "Implementation Theory." Mimeo, Harvard University, 1999.

Matsumoto, Yasumi. "Non-binary Social Choice: Revealed Preference Interpretation." *Economica*, May 1985, *52*(26), pp. 185–94.

McKelvey, Richard D. "General Conditions for Global Intransitivities in Formal Voting Models." *Econometrica*, September 1979, *47*(5), pp. 1085–112.

McLean, Ian. "The Borda and Condorcet Principles: Three Medieval Applications." *Social Choice and Welfare*, 1990, 7(2), pp. 99–108.

Mill, John Stuart. *On liberty*. London: Parker, 1859; republished, London: Harmondsworth, 1974.

Mirrlees, James A. "The Economic Uses of Utilitarianism," in Amartya K. Sen and Bernard Williams, eds., *Utilitarianism and beyond*. Cambridge: Cambridge University Press, 1982, pp. 63–84.

Monjardet, Bernard. "Duality in the Theory of Social Choice," in Jean-Jacques Laffont, ed., *Aggregation and revelation of preferences*. Amsterdam: North-Holland, 1979, pp. 131–43.

Monjardet, Bernard. "On the Use of Ultrafilters in Social Choice Theory," in Prasanta K. Pattanaik and Maurice Salles, eds., *Social choice and welfare*. Amsterdam: North-Holland, 1983.

Morris, Morris D. *Measuring the conditions of the world's poor*. Oxford: Pergamon Press, 1979.

Moulin, Hervé. *The strategy of social choice*. Amsterdam: North-Holland, 1983.

Moulin, Hervé. *Cooperative microeconomics*. Princeton, NJ: Princeton University Press, 1995.

Moulin, Hervé and Thomson, William. "Axiomatic Analyses of Resource Allocation Problems," in Kenneth J. Arrow, Amartya K. Sen, and Kotaro Suzumura, eds., *Social choice re-examined*, Vol. 1. New York: St. Martin's Press, 1997, pp. 101–20.

Mueller, Dennis C. *Public Choice II*. Cambridge: Cambridge University Press, 1989.

Mueller, Dennis C. "Constitutional and Liberal Rights." *Analyse & Kritik*, September 1996, *18*(1), pp. 96–117.

Nehring, Klaus and Puppe, Clemens. "On the Multipreference Approach to Evaluating Opportunities." *Social Choice and Welfare*, 1999, *16*(1), pp. 41–64.

Nicholson, Michael B. "Conditions for the 'Voting Paradox' in Committee Decisions." *Metroeconomica*, January–August 1965, *17*(1–2), pp. 29–44.

Nozick, Robert. *Anarchy, state and utopia*. New York: Basic Books, 1974.

Nussbaum, Martha. "Nature, Function, and Capability: Aristotle on Political Distribution." *Oxford Studies in Ancient Philosophy*, 1988, Supp., pp. 145–84.

Nussbaum, Martha and Glover, Jonathan, eds. *Women, culture, and development: A study of human capabilities*. Oxford: Clarendon Press, 1995.

Nussbaum, Martha and Sen, Amartya K., eds. *The quality of life*. Oxford: Oxford University Press, 1993.

Osmani, Siddiqur R. *Economic inequality and group welfare*. Oxford: Oxford University Press, 1982.

Osmani, Siddiqur R. "The Entitlement Approach to Famine: An Assessment," in Kaushik Basu, Prasanta K. Pattanaik, and Kotaro Suzumura, eds., *Choice, welfare, and development: A festschrift in honour of Amartya K. Sen*. Oxford: Oxford University Press, 1995, pp. 253–94.

Parks, Robert P. "Further Results on Path Independence, Quasitransitivity, and Social Choice." *Public Choice*, Summer 1976a, *26*(26), pp. 75–87.

The possibility of social choice **333**

Parks, Robert P. "An Impossibility Theorem for Fixed Preferences: A Dictatorial Bergson-Samuelson Welfare Function." *Review of Economic Studies*, October 1976b, *43*(3), pp. 447–50.

Pattanaik, Prasanta K. *Voting and collective choice*. London: Cambridge University Press, 1971.

Pattanaik, Prasanta K. "On the Stability of Sincere Voting Situations." *Journal of Economic Theory*, December 1973, *6*(6), pp. 558–74.

Pattanaik, Prasanta K. *Strategy and group choice*. Amsterdam: North-Holland, 1978.

Pattanaik, Prasanta K. "The Liberal Paradox: Some Interpretations When Rights Are Represented as Game Forms." *Analyse & Kritik*, September 1996, *18*(1), pp. 38–53.

Pattanaik, Prasanta K. "On Modelling Individual Rights: Some Conceptual Issues," in Kenneth J. Arrow, Amartya K. Sen, and Kotaro Suzumura, eds., *Social choice re-examined*, Vol. 2. New York: St. Martin's Press, 1997, pp. 100–28.

Pattanaik, Prasanta K. and Salles, Maurice, eds. *Social choice and welfare*. Amsterdam: North-Holland, 1983.

Pattanaik, Prasanta K. and Sengupta, Manimay. "Conditions for Transitive and Quasi-Transitive Majority Decisions." *Economica*, November 1974, *41*(164), pp. 414–23.

Pattanaik, Prasanta K. and Sengupta, Manimay. "Restricted Preferences and Strategy-Proofness of a Class of Group Decision Functions." *Review of Economic Studies*, October 1980, *47*(5), pp. 965–73.

Pazner, Elisha A. and Schmeidler, David. "A Difficulty in the Concept of Fairness." *Review of Economic Studies*, July 1974, *41*(3), pp. 441–43.

Peleg, Bezalel. "Consistent Voting Systems." *Econometrica*, January 1978, *46*(1), pp. 153–62.

Peleg, Bezalel. *Game theoretic analysis of voting in committees*. Cambridge: Cambridge University Press, 1984.

Phelps, Edmund S., ed. *Economic justice*. Harmondsworth, U.K.: Penguin, 1973.

Pigou, Arthur C. *The economics of welfare*. London: Macmillan, 1920.

Plott, Charles R. "A Notion of Equilibrium and Its Possibility under Majority Rule." *American Economic Review*, September 1967, *57*(4), pp. 787–806.

Plott, Charles R. "Path Independence, Rationality, and Social Choice." *Econometrica*, November 1973, *41*(6), pp. 1075–91.

Plott, Charles R. "Axiomatic Social Choice Theory: An Overview and Interpretation." *American Journal of Political Science*, August 1976, *20*(3), pp. 511–96.

Pollak, Robert A. "Welfare Comparisons and Situation Comparison." *Journal of Econometrics*, October–November 1991, *50*(1–2), pp. 31–48.

Pollak, Robert and Wales, Terence J. "Welfare Comparisons and Equivalence Scales." *American Economic Review*, May 1979 (*Papers and Proceedings*), *69*(2), pp. 216–21.

Rae, Douglas W. "Using District Magnitude to Regulate Political Party Competition." *Journal of Economic Perspectives*, Winter 1995, *9*(1), pp. 65–75.

Rangarajan, L. N., ed. *The Arthasastra*. New Delhi, India: Penguin Books, 1987.

Ravallion, Martin. *Markets and famines*. Oxford: Oxford University Press, 1987.

Ravallion, Martin. *Poverty comparisons*. Chur, Switzerland: Harwood, 1994.

Ravallion, Martin. "Household Vulnerability to Aggregate Shocks: Differing Fortunes of the Poor in Bangladesh and Indonesia," in Kaushik Basu, Prasanta K. Pattanaik, and Kotaro Suzumura, eds., *Choice, welfare, and development: A festschrift in honour of Amartya K. Sen*. Oxford: Oxford University Press, 1995, pp. 295–312.

Rawls, John. *A theory of justice*. Cambridge, MA: Harvard University Press, 1971.

Razavi, Shahrashoub. "Excess Female Mortality: An Indicator of Female Subordination? A Note Drawing on Village-Level Evidence from South-eastern Iran." *Notizie di Politeia*, 1996, *12*(43–44), pp. 79–95.

334 A. Sen

Red Cross and Red Crescent Societies, International Federation of. *World disasters report 1994.* Dordrecht: Martinus Nijhoff, 1994.

Riley, Jonathan. *Liberal utilitarianism: Social choice theory and J. S. Mill's philosophy.* Cambridge: Cambridge University Press, 1987.

Robbins, Lionel. "Interpersonal Comparisons of Utility: A Comment." *Economic Journal,* December 1938, *48*(192), pp. 635–41.

Roberts, Kevin W. S. "Possibility Theorems with Interpersonally Comparable Welfare Levels." *Review of Economic Studies,* January 1980a, *47*(2), pp. 409–20.

Roberts, Kevin W. S. "Interpersonal Comparability and Social Choice Theory." *Review of Economic Studies,* January 1980b, *47*(2), pp. 421–39.

Roberts, Kevin W. S. "Valued Opinions or Opiniated Values: The Double Aggregation Problem," in Kaushik Basu, Prasanta K. Pattanaik, and Kotaro Suzumura, eds., *Choice, welfare, and development: A festschrift in honour of Amartya K. Sen.* Oxford: Oxford University Press, 1995, pp. 141–67.

Roemer, John. *A general theory of exploitation and class.* Cambridge, MA: Harvard University Press, 1982.

Roemer, John. *Theories of distributive justice.* Cambridge, MA: Harvard University Press, 1996.

Rothschild, Michael and Stiglitz, Joseph E. "Some Further Results on the Measurement of Inequality." *Journal of Economic Theory,* April 1973, *6*(2), pp. 188–204.

Rowley, Charles K. *Liberty and the state.* Aldershot, U.K.: Elgar, 1993.

Salles, Maurice. "A General Possibility Theorem for Group Decision Rules with Pareto-Transitivity." *Journal of Economic Theory,* August 1975, *11*(1), pp. 110–18.

Samuelson, Paul A. *Foundations of economic analysis.* Cambridge, MA: Harvard University Press, 1947.

Satterthwaite, Mark A. "Strategy-Proofness and Arrow's Conditions: Existence and Correspondence Theorems for Voting Procedures and Social Welfare Functions." *Journal of Economic Theory,* April 1975, *10*(2), pp. 187–217.

Schmeidler, David and Sonnenschein, Hugo F. "Two Proofs of the Gibbard-Satterthwaite Theorem on the Possibility of a Strategy-Proof Social Choice Function," in H. W. Gottinger and W. Leinfeller, eds., *Decision theory and social ethics: Issues in social choice.* Dordrecht: Reidel, 1978, pp. 227–34.

Schofield, Norman J. "General Instability of Majority Rule." *Review of Economic Studies,* October 1983, *50*(4), pp. 695–705.

Schofield, Norman J., ed. *Collective decision-making: Social choice and political economy.* Boston: Kluwer, 1996.

Schokkaert, Erik and Van Ootegem, Luc. "Sen's Concept of the Living Standard Applied to the Belgian Unemployed." *Récherches Economiques de Louvain,* 1990, *56*(3–4), pp. 429–50.

Schwartz, Thomas. "On the Possibility of Rational Policy Evaluation." *Theory and Decision,* October 1970, *1*(1), pp. 89–106.

Schwartz, Thomas. "Rationality and the Myth of the Maximum." *Noûs,* May 1972, *6*(2), pp. 97–117.

Schwartz, Thomas. *The logic of collective choice.* New York: Columbia University Press, 1986.

Scitovsky, Tibor. *The joyless economy.* Oxford: Oxford University Press, 1976.

Seidl, Christian. "On Liberal Values." *Zeitschrift für Nationalökonomie,* May 1975, *35*(3–4), pp. 257–92.

The possibility of social choice **335**

Seidl, Christian. "Poverty Measurement: A Survey," in Dieter Bos, Manfred Rose, and Christian Seidl, eds., *Welfare and efficiency in public economics*. Berlin: Springer-Verlag, 1988, pp. 71–147.

Seidl, Christian. "Foundations and Implications of Rights," in Kenneth J. Arrow, Amartya K. Sen, and Kotaro Suzumura, eds., *Social choice re-examined*, Vol. 2. New York: St. Martin's Press, 1997, pp. 53–77.

Sen, Amartya K. "Preferences, Votes and the Transitivity of Majority Decisions." *Review of Economic Studies*, April 1964, *31*(2), pp. 163–65.

Sen, Amartya K. "A Possibility Theorem on Majority Decisions." *Econometrica*, April 1966, *34*(2), pp. 491–09.

Sen, Amartya K. "Quasi-Transitivity, Rational Choice and Collective Decisions." *Review of Economic Studies*, July 1969, *36*(3), pp. 381–93.

Sen, Amartya K. *Collective choice and social welfare.* San Francisco, CA: Holden-Day, 1970a.

Sen, Amartya K. "The Impossibility of a Paretian Liberal." *Journal of Political Economy*, January–February 1970b, *78*(1), pp. 152–57; reprinted in Sen (1982a).

Sen, Amartya K. "Interpersonal Aggregation and Partial Comparability." *Econometrica*, May 1970c, *38*(3), pp. 393–409; reprinted in Sen (1982a).

Sen, Amartya K. *On economic inequality.* Oxford: Oxford University Press, 1973a; Expanded Ed., 1997c.

Sen, Amartya K. "On the Development of Basic Income Indicators to Supplement the GNP Measure." *United Nations Economic Bulletin for Asia and the Far East*, September–December 1973b, *24*(2–3), pp. 1–11.

Sen, Amartya K. "Behaviour and the Concept of Preference." *Economica*, 1973c, *40*(159), pp. 241–59; reprinted in Sen (1982a).

Sen, Amartya K. "Choice, Orderings, and Morality," in S. Korner, ed., *Practical reason*. Oxford: Blackwell, 1974; reprinted in Sen (1982a).

Sen, Amartya K. "Real National Income." *Review of Economic Studies*, February 1976a, *43*(1), pp. 19–39; reprinted in Sen (1982a).

Sen, Amartya K. "Poverty: An Ordinal Approach to Measurement." *Econometrica*, March 1976b, *44*(2), pp. 219–23; reprinted in Sen (1982a).

Sen, Amartya K. "Liberty, Unanimity and Rights." *Economica*, August 1976c, *43*(171), pp. 217–45; reprinted in Sen (1982a).

Sen, Amartya K. "Social Choice Theory: A Re-examination." *Econometrica*, January 1977a, *45*(1), pp. 53–89; reprinted in Sen (1982a).

Sen, Amartya K. "Starvation and Exchange Entitlements: A General Approach and Its Application to the Great Bengal Famine." *Cambridge Journal of Economics*, March 1977b, *1*(l), pp. 33–59.

Sen, Amartya K. "On Weights and Measures: Informational Constraints in Social Welfare Analysis." *Econometrica*, October 1977c, *45*(7), pp. 1539–72; reprinted in Sen (1982a).

Sen, Amartya K. "Rational Fools: A Critique of the Behavioral Foundations of Economic Theory." *Philosophy and Public Affairs*, Summer 1977d, *6*(4), pp. 317–44; reprinted in Sen (1982a).

Sen, Amartya K. "The Welfare Basis of Real Income Comparisons: A Survey." *Journal of Economic Literature*, March 1979a, *17*(1), pp. 1–45; reprinted in Sen (1984).

Sen, Amartya K. "Personal Utilities and Public Judgements: Or What's Wrong with Welfare Economics." *Economic Journal*, September 1979b, *89*(355), pp. 537–58; reprinted in Sen (1982a).

336 A. Sen

Sen, Amartya K. "Equality of What?" in S. McMurrin, ed., *Tanner lectures on human values*, Vol. 1. Salt Lake City, UT: University of Utah, 1980, pp. 195–220; reprinted in Sen (1982a).

Sen, Amartya K. *Poverty and famines: An essay on entitlement and deprivation.* Oxford: Oxford University Press, 1981.

Sen, Amartya K. *Choice, welfare and measurement.* Oxford: Blackwell, 1982a; Cambridge, MA: Harvard University Press, 1997.

Sen, Amartya K. "Rights and Agency." *Philosophy and Public Affairs*, Spring 1982b, *11*(2), pp. 113–32.

Sen, Amartya K. "Liberty and Social Choice." *Journal of Philosophy*, January 1983a, *80*(1), pp. 5–28.

Sen, Amartya K. "Poor, Relatively Speaking." *Oxford Economic Papers*, July 1983b, *35*(2), pp. 153–69.

Sen, Amartya K. *Resources, values and development.* Cambridge, MA: Harvard University Press, 1984.

Sen, Amartya K. *Commodities and capabilities.* Amsterdam: North-Holland, 1985a.

Sen, Amartya K. "Well-being, Agency and Freedom: The Dewey Lectures 1984." *Journal of Philosophy*, April 1985b, *82*(4), pp. 169–221.

Sen, Amartya K. "Social Choice Theory," in Kenneth J. Arrow and Michael Intriligator, eds., *Handbook of mathematical economics*, Vol. III. Amsterdam: North-Holland, 1986a, pp. 1073–181.

Sen, Amartya K. "Information and Invariance in Normative Choice," in Walter P. Heller, Ross M. Starr, and David A. Starrett, eds., *Essays in honor of Kenneth J. Arrow*, Vol. 1. Cambridge: Cambridge University Press, 1986b, pp. 29–55.

Sen, Amartya K. "Gender and Cooperative Conflict," in Irene Tinker, ed., *Persistent inequalities.* New York: Oxford University Press, 1990, pp. 123–49.

Sen, Amartya K. *Inequality reexamined.* Cambridge, MA: Harvard University Press, 1992a.

Sen, Amartya K. "Minimal Liberty." *Economica*, May 1992b, *59*(234), pp. 139–60.

Sen, Amartya K. "Missing Women." *British Medical Journal*, March 1992c, *304*(6827), pp. 587–88.

Sen, Amartya K. "Internal Consistency of Choice." *Econometrica*, May 1993a, *61*(3), pp. 495–521.

Sen, Amartya K. "Capability and Well-being," in Martha Nussbaum and Amartya Sen, eds., *The quality of life.* Oxford: Oxford University Press, 1993b, pp. 30–53.

Sen, Amartya K. "Positional Objectivity." *Philosophy and Public Affairs*, Spring 1993c, *22*(2), pp. 83–135.

Sen, Amartya K. "Well-Being, Capability and Public Policy," *Giornale degli Economisti e Annali di Economia*, July–September 1994, *53*(7–9), pp. 333–47.

Sen, Amartya K. "Rationality and Social Choice." *American Economic Review*, March 1995a, *85*(1), pp. 1–24.

Sen, Amartya K. "Environmental Evaluation and Social Choice: Contingent Valuation and the Market Analogy." *Japanese Economic Review*, March 1995b, *46*(1), pp. 23–37.

Sen, Amartya K. "Rights: Formulation and Consequences." *Analyse & Kritik*, September 1996a, *18*, pp. 53–70.

Sen, Amartya K. "Freedom, Capabilities and Public Action: A Response." *Notizie di Politeia*, 1996b, *12*(43–44), pp. 105–25.

Sen, Amartya K. "Maximization and the Act of Choice." *Econometrica*, July 1997a, *65*(4), pp. 745–80.

The possibility of social choice   **337**

Sen, Amartya K. "Individual Preference as the Basis of Social Choice," in Kenneth J. Arrow, Amartya K. Sen, and Kotaro Suzumura, eds., *Social choice re-examined*, Vol. 2. New York: St. Martin's Press, 1997b.

Sen, Amartya K. *On economic inequality* [Expanded Ed., with a substantial annexe jointly with James Foster]. Oxford: Oxford University Press, 1997c.

Sen, Amartya K. *Development as freedom* [mimeo]; 1999a (forthcoming).

Sen, Amartya K. *Freedom, rationality and social choice: Arrow lectures and other essays* [mimeo]; 1999b (forthcoming).

Sen, Amartya K. and Pattanaik, Prasanta K. "Necessary and Sufficient Conditions for Rational Choice under Majority Decision." *Journal of Economic Theory*, August 1969, *1*(2), pp. 178–202.

Sengupta, Manimay. "Monotonicity, Independence of Irrelevant Alternatives and Strategy-Proofness of Social Decision Functions." *Review of Economic Studies*, January 1980a, *47*(2), pp. 393–407.

Sengupta, Manimay. "The Knowledge Assumption in the Theory of Strategic Voting." *Econometrica*, July 1980b, *48*(5), pp. 1301–04.

Shorrocks, Anthony F. "Inequality Decomposition by Population Subgroups." *Econometrica*, November 1984, *52*(6), pp. 1369–85.

Shorrocks, Anthony F. "Revisiting the Sen Poverty Index." *Econometrica*, September 1995, *63*(5), pp. 1225–30.

Slesnick, Daniel T. "Empirical Approaches to the Measurement of Welfare." *Journal of Economic Literature*, December 1998, *36*(4), pp. 2108–65.

Smith, Adam. *An inquiry into the wealth of nations.* London: W. Strahan and T. Cadell, 1776; republished, London: Home University, 1910.

Solow, Robert M. "Mass Unemployment as a Social Problem," in Kaushik Basu, Prasanta K. Pattanaik, and Kotaro Suzumura, eds., *Choice, welfare, and development: A festschrift in honour of Amartya K. Sen.* Oxford: Oxford University Press, 1995, pp. 313–21.

Starrett, David. *Foundations of public economics.* Cambridge: Cambridge University Press, 1988.

Steiner, Hillel. "Putting Rights in Their Place: An Appraisal of A. Sen's Work on Rights." *Récherches Economiques de Louvain*, 1990, *56*(3–4), pp. 391–408.

Stewart, Frances. *Planning to meet basic needs.* London: Macmillan, 1985.

Strasnick, Stephen. "Social Choice and the Derivation of Rawls's Difference Principle." *Journal of Philosophy*, February 1976, *73*(4), pp. 85–99.

Streeten, Paul. "Basic Needs: Some Unsettled Questions." *World Development*, September 1984, *12*(9), pp. 973–78.

Streeten, Paul (with Burki, S. J.; Haq, Mahbub ul; Hicks, Norman and Stewart, Frances). *First things first: Meeting basic needs in developing countries.* London: Oxford University Press, 1981.

Sugden, Robert. *The political economy of public choice.* New York: Wiley, 1981.

Sugden, Robert. "Liberty, Preference, and Choice." *Economics and Philosophy*, October 1985, *1*(2), pp. 213–29.

Sugden, Robert. "Welfare, Resources, and Capabilities: A Review of *Inequality Reexamined* by Amartya Sen." *Journal of Economic Literature*, December 1993, *31*(4), pp. 1947–62.

Suppes, Patrick. "Some Formal Models of Grading Principles." *Synthese*, December 1966, *16*(3/4), pp. 284–306.

Suzumura, Kotaro. "Rational Choice and Revealed Preference." *Review of Economic Studies*, February 1976a, *43*(1), pp. 149–58.

338 A. Sen

Suzumura, Kotaro. "Remarks on the Theory of Collective Choice." *Economica*, November 1976b, *43*(172), pp. 381–90.

Suzumura, Kotaro. *Rational choice, collective decisions, and social welfare.* Cambridge: Cambridge University Press, 1983.

Suzumura, Kotaro. *Competition, commitment, and welfare.* Oxford: Oxford University Press, 1995.

Suzumura, Kotaro. "Welfare, Rights, and Social Choice Procedure: A Perspective." *Analyse & Kritik*, September 1996, *18*(1), pp. 20–37.

Suzumura, Kotaro. "Interpersonal Comparisons of the Extended Sympathy Type and the Possibility of Social Choice," in Kenneth J. Arrow, Amartya K. Sen, and Kotaro Suzumura, eds., *Social choice re-examined*, Vol. 2. New York: St. Martin's Press, 1997, pp. 202–29.

Suzumura, Kotaro. "Consequences, Opportunities, and Procedures." *Social Choice and Welfare*, 1999, *16*(1), pp. 17–40.

Svedberg, Peter. *Poverty and undernutrition: Theory and measurement.* Mimeo (study for WIDER); 1999 (forthcoming).

Svensson, Lars-Gunnar. "Social Justice and Fair Distributions." *Lund Economic Studies*, 1977, *15*.

Svensson, Lars-Gunnar. "Equity Among Generations." *Econometrica*, July 1980, *48*(5), pp. 1251–56.

Tideman, Nicolaus. "The Single Transferable Vote." *Journal of Economic Perspectives*, Winter 1995, *9*(1), pp. 27–38.

Tullock, Gordon. "The General Irrelevance of the General Possibility Theorem." *Quarterly Journal of Economics*, May 1967, *81*(2), pp. 256–70.

United Nations Development Programme. (UNDP). *Human development report 1990.* New York: Oxford University Press, 1990.

van Hees, Martin. "Individual Rights and Legal Validity." *Analyse & Kritik*, September 1996, *18*(1), pp. 81–95.

Van Parijs, Philippe. *Real freedom for all: What (if anything) can justify capitalism?* Oxford: Oxford University Press, 1995.

Varian, Hal. "Equity, Envy, and Efficiency," *Journal of Economic Theory*, September 1974, *9*(1), pp. 63–91.

Varian, Hal. "Distributive Justice, Welfare Economics and a Theory of Justice." *Philosophy and Public Affairs*, Spring 1975, *4*(3), pp. 223–47.

Vaughan, Megan. *The story of an African famine: Gender and famine in twentieth century Malawi.* Cambridge: Cambridge University Press, 1987.

Vickrey, William S. "Utility, Strategy, and Social Decision Rules." *Quarterly Journal of Economics*, November 1960, *74*, pp. 507–35.

Ward, Benjamin. "Majority Voting and Alternative Forms of Public Enterprise," in Julius Margolis, ed., *The public economy of urban communities.* Baltimore, MD: Johns Hopkins University Press, 1965, pp. 112–26.

Weber, Robert J. "Approval Voting." *Journal of Economic Perspectives*, Winter 1995, *9*(1), pp. *39–49.*

Wilson, Robert. "Social Choice Without the Pareto Principle." *Journal of Economic Theory*, December 1972, *5*(3), pp. 478–86.

Wilson, Robert. "On the Theory of Aggregation." *Journal of Economic Theory*, February 1975, *10*(1), pp. 89–99.

Wriglesworth, John L. *Libertarian conflicts in social choice.* Cambridge: Cambridge University Press, 1985.

The possibility of social choice **339**

Young, H. Peyton. "Condorcet's Theory of Voting." *American Political Science Review*, December 1988, *82*(4), pp. 1231–44.

Young, H. Peyton. "Optimal Voting Rules." *Journal of Economic Perspectives*, Winter 1995, *9*(1), pp. 51–64.

Young, H. Peyton. ed. *Fair allocation.* Providence, RI: American Mathematical Society, 1985.

16

THE MYSTERY OF CAPITAL

By way of conclusion

H. De Soto

> *Where is the wisdom we have lost in knowledge?*
> *Where is the knowledge we have lost in information?*
> —*T. S. Eliot, Choruses from "The Rock"*

The private club of globalization

Capitalism is in crisis outside the West not because international globalization is failing but because developing and former communist nations have been unable to "globalize" capital within their own countries. Most people in those nations view capitalism as a private club, a discriminatory system that benefits only the West and the elites who live inside the bell jars of poor countries.

More people throughout the world may wear Nike shoes and flash their Casio watches, but even as they consume the goods of the West, they are quite aware that they still linger at the periphery of the capitalist game. They have no stake in it. Globalization should not be just about interconnecting the bell jars of the privileged few. That kind of globalization has existed before. In the nineteenth century, Europe's ruling royals were literally one big family, related by blood and in constant contact about politics and commerce with their cousins in England, France, Holland, Spain, and Russia. Capitalism triumphed in the nineteenth century and prevailed throughout the industrialized world until the Russian Revolution and the Great Depression. But as Spain's Ortega y Gasset and the American pundit Walter Lippman pointed out, despite its dominance and sophistication, the capitalist system was always vulnerable. The American economist Lester Thurow points out that as recently as 1941,

> the United States and Great Britain were essentially the only [major] capitalist countries left on the face of the earth. ... All the rest of the world were

The mystery of capital **341**

fascists, communists or Third World feudal colonies. The final crisis of the 1920s and the Great Depression of the 1930s had brought capitalism to the edge of extinction. The capitalism that now seems irresistible could, with just a few missteps, have vanished.[1]

Latin Americans do not have to be reminded. On at least four occasions since their independence from Spain in the 1820s, they have tried to become part of global capitalism and failed. They restructured their debts, stabilized their economies by controlling inflation, liberalized trade, privatized government assets (selling their railroads to the British, for example), undertook debt equity swaps, and overhauled their tax systems. At the consumer level, the Latin Americans imported all sorts of goods, from English tweed suits and Church shoes to Model T Fords; they learned English and French by listening to the radio or records; they danced the Charleston and the Lambeth Walk, and chewed Chiclets gum. But they never produced much live capital.

We may now all be benefiting from the communications revolution, and some may see progress in the fact that the Egyptian Sphinx now stares directly at the neon sign of a Kentucky Fried Chicken franchise. Nevertheless, only twenty-five of the world's two hundred countries produce capital in sufficient quantity to benefit fully from the division of labor in expanded global markets. The lifeblood of capitalism is not the Internet or fast-food franchises. It is *capital*. Only capital provides the means to support specialization and the production and exchange of assets in the expanded market. It is capital that is the source of increasing productivity and therefore the wealth of nations.

Yet only the Western nations and small enclaves of wealthy people in developing and former communist nations have the capacity to represent assets and potential and, therefore, the ability to produce and use capital efficiently. Capitalism is viewed outside the West with increasing hostility, as an apartheid regime most cannot enter. There is a growing sense, even among some elites, that if they have to depend solely and forever on the kindness of outside capital, they will never be productive players in the global capitalist game. They are increasingly frustrated at not being masters of their own fate. Since they have embarked on globalization without providing their own people with the means to produce capital, they are beginning to look less like the United States than like mercantilist Latin America with its disarray of extralegal activity.[2] Ten years ago, few would have compared the former Soviet bloc nations to Latin America. But today they look astonishingly similar: strong underground economies, glaring inequality, pervasive mafias, political instability, capital flight, and flagrant disregard for law.

That is why outside the West advocates of capitalism are intellectually on the retreat. Ascendant just a decade ago, they are now increasingly viewed as apologists for the miseries and injustices that still affect the majority of people. For example, in 1999 Egypt's consultative upper house warned the government "not to be deceived any longer by calls for capitalism and globalization."[3] Having forgotten the crucial issue of property, capitalism's advocates have let themselves become

342 H. De Soto

identified as the defenders of the status quo, blindly trying to enforce existing written law whether it discriminates or not.

And the law in those countries does discriminate. As I illustrated in Chapter 2, at least 80 percent of the population in these countries cannot inject life into their assets and make them generate capital because the law keeps them out of the formal property system. They have trillions of dollars in dead capital, but it is as if these were isolated ponds whose waters disappear into a sterile strip of sand, instead of forming a mighty mass of water that can be captured in one unified property system and given the form required to produce capital. People hold and use their assets on the basis of myriad disconnected informal agreements where accountability is managed locally. Without the common standards that legal property brings, they lack the language necessary for their assets to talk to each other. There is no use urging them to be patient until the benefits of capitalism trickle down their way. That will never happen until the firm foundations of formal property are in place.

Meanwhile, the promoters of capitalism, still arrogant on their victory over communism, have yet to understand that their macro-economic reforms are not enough. We must not forget that globalization is occurring because developing and former communist nations are opening up their once protected economies, stabilizing their currencies, and drafting regulatory frameworks to enhance international trade and private investment. All of this is good. What is not so good is that these reforms assume that these countries' populations are already integrated into the legal system and have the same ability to use their resources in the open market. They do not.

As I have argued in Chapter 3, most people cannot participate in an expanded market because they do not have access to a legal property rights system that represents their assets in a manner that makes them widely transferable and fungible, that allows them to be encumbered and permits their owners to be held accountable. So long as the assets of the majority are not properly documented and tracked by a property bureaucracy, they are invisible and sterile in the marketplace.

By stabilizing and adjusting by "the book," the globalizers' macroeconomic programs have dramatically rationalized the economic management of developing countries. But because their book does not address the fact that most people do not have property rights, they have done only a fraction of the work required to create a comprehensive capitalist system and market economy. Their tools are designed to work in countries where systematized law has been "globalized" internally, when inclusive property rights systems that link up to efficient monetary and investment instruments are in place—something these countries have yet to achieve.

Too many policymakers have taken an Olympian view of the globalization process. Once they stabilized and adjusted at the macro level, allowing legal business and foreign investors to prosper and orthodox economists to control the treasury, they felt they had fulfilled their duty. Because they concentrated only on policies dealing with the aggregates, they did not inquire whether people had the means to participate in an expanded market system. They forgot that people are the fundamental agents of change. They forgot to focus on the poor. And they made

The mystery of capital **343**

that enormous omission because they do not operate with the concept of *class* in mind. In the words of one of their most outstanding pundits, they do not have "the ability to comprehend, however dimly, how other people live."[4]

Economic reformers have left the issue of property for the poor in the hands of conservative legal establishments uninterested in changing the status quo. As a result, the assets of the majority of their citizens have remained dead capital stuck in the extralegal sector. This is why the advocates of globalization and free market reforms are beginning to be perceived as the self-satisfied defenders of the interests of those who dominate the bell jar.

Facing up to Marx's ghost

Most economic reform programs in poor economies may be falling into the trap that Karl Marx foresaw: The great contradiction of the capitalist system is that it creates its own demise because it cannot avoid concentrating capital in a few hands. By not giving the majority access to expanded markets, these reforms are leaving a fertile field for class confrontation—a capitalist and free market economy for the privileged few who can concretize their property rights, and relative poverty for a large undercapitalized sector incapable of leveraging its own assets.

Class confrontations, in this day and age? Didn't that concept come down with the Berlin Wall? Unfortunately, it did not. This may be hard for a citizen in an advanced nation to understand because in the West those discontented with the system live in "pockets of poverty." Misery in developing and former communist nations, however, is not contained in pockets; it is spread throughout society. What few pockets exist in those countries are pockets of wealth. What the West calls "the underclass" is here the majority. And in the past, when their rising expectations were not met, that mass of angry poor brought apparently solid elites to their knees (as in Iran, Venezuela, and Indonesia). In most countries outside the West, governments depend on strong intelligence services, and their elites live behind fortress-like walls for good reason.

Today, to a great extent, the difference between advanced nations and the rest of the world is that between countries where formal property is widespread and countries where classes are divided into those who can fix property rights and produce capital and those who cannot. If extralegal property rights are not accommodated, these societies may muddle along with their dual economies—with the so-called law-abiding sector on one side and the impoverished extralegal sector on the other. But as information and communications continue to improve and the poor become better informed of what they do not have, the bitterness over legal apartheid is bound to grow. At some point, those outside the bell jar will be mobilized against the status quo by people with political agendas that thrive on discontent. "If we do not invent ways to make globalization more inclusive?" says Klaus Schwab of the World Economic Forum, "we have to face the prospect of a resurgence of the acute social confrontations of the past, magnified at the international level."[5]

344 H. De Soto

The Cold War may have ended, but the old class arguments have not disappeared. Subversive activities and an upsurge of ethnic and cultural conflicts around the world prove that when people are extremely dissatisfied they continue to constitute themselves into classes based on shared injuries. *Newsweek* notes that in the Americas since the 1980s, "each of these struggles has its own unique history, but the fighters all vilify the same enemy: the new face of Latin American capitalism."[6] In such situations, the Marxist tool kit is better geared to explain class conflict than capitalist thinking, which has no comparable analysis or even a serious strategy for reaching the poor in the extralegal sector. Capitalists generally have no systemic explanation of how the people in the underclass got where they are and how the system could be changed to raise them up.

We must not underestimate the latent power of Marxist integrated theory at a time when masses of people with little hope are looking for a cohesive worldview to improve their desperate economic prospects. In a period of economic boom, there tends to be little time for deep thinking. Crisis, however, has a way of sharpening the mind's need for order and explanations into obsession. Marxist thinking, in whatever form it reappears—and it will—supplies a much mightier array of concepts for grappling with the political problems of capitalism outside the West than capitalist thinking does.

Marx's insights into capital, as George Soros recently observed, are often more sophisticated than those of Adam Smith.[7] Marx understood clearly that "in themselves, money and commodities are no more capital than are the means of productions and of subsistence. That they want transforming into capital."[8] He also understood that if assets could be converted into commodities and made to interact in markets, they could express values that are imperceptible to the senses but can be captured to produce rents. For Marx, property was an important issue because it was clear to him that those who appropriated the assets obtained much more than just their physical attributes. As a result, the Marxist intellectual tool kit has left anticapitalists powerful ways to explain why private property will necessarily put assets in the hands of the rich at the expense of the poor.

For those who have not noticed, the arsenal of anticapitalism and antiglobalization is building up. Today, there are serious statistics that provide the anticapitalists with just the ammunition they need to argue that capitalism is a transfer of property from poorer to richer countries and that Western private investment in developing nations is nothing short of a massive takeover of their resources by multinationals. The number of flashy cars, luxurious homes, and California-style shopping malls may have increased in most developing and former communist nations over the past decade, but so have the poor. Nancy Birdsall and Juan Luis Londoño's research shows that poverty has grown faster and income distribution has worsened over the last decade.[9] According to a 1999 United Nations "Human Development Report," gross domestic product in the Russian Federation fell by 41 percent from 1990 to 1997, driving millions into the extralegal sector. The life expectancy of the Russian male has dropped four full years—to fifty-eight. The report blames the transition to capitalism and the effects of globalization.

The mystery of capital **345**

These research efforts provide us with healthy warning signals, but they are also putting in place the intellectual missiles needed to discourage privatization programs and global capitalism. It is crucial, therefore, to recognize the latent Marxist paradigms and then add what we have learned in the century since Marx died. We can now demonstrate that although Marx clearly saw that a parallel economic life can be generated alongside physical assets themselves—that "the productions of the human brain appeared as independent beings endowed with life"[10]—he did not quite grasp that formal property was not simply an instrument for appropriation but also the means to motivate people to create real additional usable value. Moreover, he did not see that it is the mechanisms contained in the property system itself that give assets and the labor invested in them the form required to create capital. Although Marx's analysis of how assets become transcendent and serve greater social uses when they become exchangeable is fundamental to understanding wealth, he was not able to foresee to what degree legal property systems would become crucial vehicles for the enhancement of exchange value.

Marx understood better than anyone else in his time that in economics there is no greater blindness than seeing resources exclusively in terms of their physical properties. He was well aware that capital was "an independent substance … in which money and commodities are mere forms which it assumes and casts off in turn,"[11] But he lived in a time when it was probably still too soon to see how formal property could, through representation, make those same resources serve additional functions and produce surplus value. Consequently, Marx could not see how it would be in everyone's interest to increase the range of the beneficiaries of property. Property titles were only the visible tip of a growing formal property iceberg. The rest of the iceberg is now an enormous man-made facility for drawing out the economic potential of assets. That is why Marx did not fully understand that legal property is the indispensable process that fixes and deploys capital, that without properly mankind cannot convert the fruits of its labor into fungible, liquid forms that can be differentiated, combined, divided, and invested to produce surplus value. He did not realize that a good legal property system, like a Swiss army knife, has many more mechanisms than just the elementary "ownership" blade.

Much of Marx's thought is outdated because the situation today is not the same as in Marx's Europe. Potential capital is no longer the privilege of the few. After Marx's death, the West finally managed to set up a legal framework that gave most people access to property and the tools of production. Marx would probably be shocked to find how in developing countries much of the teeming mass does not consist of oppressed legal proletarians but of oppressed extralegal small entrepreneurs with a sizeable amount of assets.

Admiration for good property systems should not blind us to the fact that, as Marx noted, these systems can also be used for theft. The world will always be full of sharks expert at using property paper to skim off wealth from unsuspecting people. Yet one cannot oppose formal property systems for this reason, any more than one should abolish computers or automobiles because people use them to commit crimes. If Marx were alive today and saw the misappropriation of resources that has occurred

346 H. De Soto

on both sides of the former Iron Curtain, he would probably agree that looting can happen with or without property and that controlling thievery depends more on the exercise of power than on property. In addition, though Marx gave "surplus value" a very specific definition, its meaning is not chained to his pen. People have always produced surplus value: pyramids, cathedrals, expensive armies, to name a few examples. Clearly much of today's surplus value in the West has originated not in scandalously expropriated labor time but in the way that property has given minds the mechanisms with which to extract additional work from commodities.

Like all of us, Marx was influenced by the social conditions and technologies of his time. The expropriation of small proprietors from their means of subsistence, the access to private property rights stemming from feudal title, the robbery of common lands, the enslavement of aboriginal populations, the looting of the conquered, and the "commercial hunting of black skins" by the colonial system may all have been essential preconditions for what Marx called the "primitive accumulation of capital." These conditions are difficult to repeat today. Attitudes have changed—to no little extent because of Marx's own writings. Looting, slavery, and colonialism now have no government's imprimatur. Most countries today are parties to treaties such as the Universal Declaration of Human Rights and have constitutions that provide equal access to property rights as one of the fundamental rights of humankind.

Moreover, as we saw in Chapter 6, authorities in developing countries have not been reticent in giving the poor access to assets. The bulk of spontaneous extralegal buildings and businesses in cities throughout the Second and Third Worlds may not have been formally titled, but governments have accepted (if only tacitly) their existence and ownership arrangements. In many developing countries during this century, large tracts of land have been given to poor farmers as part of agrarian reform programs (though without the property representations necessary to create capital). Nor have authorities in those countries been reluctant to earmark budgets for property issues. Billions of dollars have been spent on activities related to registering ownership.

Property makes capital "mind friendly"

Throughout this book I have been trying to demonstrate that we now have enough evidence to make substantial progress in development. With it in hand we can move beyond the stagnant "left versus right" debate on property and avoid having to fight the same old battles all over again. Formal property is more than just ownership. As we saw in Chapter 3, it has to be viewed as the indispensable process that provides people with the tools to focus their thinking on those aspects of their resources from which they can extract capital. Formal property is more than a system for titling, recording, and mapping assets—it is an instrument of thought, representing assets in such a way that people's minds can work on them to generate surplus value. That is why formal property must be universally accessible: to bring everyone into one social contract where they can cooperate to raise society's productivity.

The mystery of capital **347**

What distinguishes a good legal property system is that it is "mind friendly." It obtains and organizes knowledge about recorded assets in forms we can control. It collects, integrates, and coordinates not only data on assets and their potential but also our thoughts about them. In brief, capital results from the ability of the West to use property systems to represent their resources in a virtual context. Only there can minds meet to identify and realize the meaning of assets for humankind.

The revolutionary contribution of an integrated property system is that it solves a basic problem of cognition. Our five senses are not sufficient for us to process the complex reality of an expanded market, much less a globalized one. We need to have the economic facts about ourselves and our resources boiled down to essentials that our minds can easily grasp. A good property system does that—it puts assets into a form that lets us distinguish their similarities, differences, and connecting points with other assets. It fixes them in representations that the system tracks as they travel through time and space. In addition, it allows assets to become fungible by representing them to our minds so that we can easily combine, divide, and mobilize them to produce higher-valued mixtures. This capacity of property to represent aspects of assets in forms that allow us to recombine them so as to make them even more useful is the mainspring of economic growth, since growth is all about obtaining high-valued outputs from low-valued inputs.

A good legal property system is a medium that allows us to understand each other, make connections, and synthesize knowledge about our assets to enhance our productivity. It is a way to represent reality that lets us transcend the limitations of our senses. Well-crafted property representations enable us to pinpoint the economic potential of resources so as to enhance what we can do with them. They are not "mere paper": they are mediating devices that give us useful knowledge about things that are not manifestly present.

Property records point our knowledge about things toward an end, to borrow from Thomas Aquinas, "just as the arrow is moved by the archer."[12] By representing economic aspects of the things we own and assembling them into categories that our minds can quickly grasp, property documents reduce the costs of dealing with assets and increase their value commensurately. This notion, that the value of things can be increased by reducing the costs of knowing them and transacting with them, is one of Nobel laureate Ronald Coase's major contributions. In his treatise "The Nature of the Firm," Coase established that the costs of carrying out transactions can be substantially reduced within the controlled and coordinated context of a firm.[13] In this sense, property systems are like Coase's firm—controlled environments to reduce transaction costs.

The capacity of property to reveal the capital that is latent in the assets we accumulate is born out of the best intellectual tradition of controlling our environment in order to prosper. For thousands of years our wisest men have been telling us that life has different degrees of reality, many of them invisible, and that it is only by constructing representational devices that we will be able to access them. In Plato's famous analogy, we are likened to prisoners chained in a cave with our backs to the entrance so that all we can know of the world are the shadows cast on the wall in

348 H. De Soto

front of us. The truth that this illustration consecrates is that many things that guide our destiny are not self-evident. That is why civilization has worked hard to fashion representational systems to access and grasp the part of our reality that is virtual and to represent it in terms we can understand.

As Margaret Boden puts it, "Some of the most important human creations have been new representational systems. These include formal notations, such as Arabic numerals (not forgetting zero), chemical formulae, or the staves, minims, and crotchets used by musicians. [Computer] programming languages are a more recent example."[14] Representational systems such as mathematics and integrated property help us manipulate and order the complexities of the world in a manner that we can all understand and that allows us to communicate regarding issues that we could not otherwise handle. They are what the philosopher Daniel Dennett has called "prosthetic extensions of the mind."[15] Through representations we bring key aspects of the world into being so as to change the way we think about it. The philosopher John Searle has noted that by human agreement we can assign "a new status to some phenomenon, where that status has an accompanying function that cannot be performed solely in virtue of the intrinsic physical features of the phenomenon in question."[16] This seems to me very close to what legal property does: It assigns to assets, by social contract, in a conceptual universe, a status that allows them to perform functions that generate capital.

This notion that we organize reality in a conceptual universe is at the center of philosophy worldwide. The French philosopher Michel Foucault labeled it the *région médiane* that provides a system of switches *(codes fondamentaux)* that constitutes the secret network where society establishes the ever-expanding range of its potential *(les conditions de possibilité)*.[17] I see formal property as a kind of switchyard that allows us to extend the potential of the assets that we accumulate further and further, each time increasing capital. I have also benefited from Karl Popper's notion of *World 3*—a separate reality from *World 1* of physical objects and *World 2* of mental states—where the products of our minds take on an autonomous existence that affects the way we deal with physical reality.[18] And it is to this conceptual world that formal property takes us—a world where the West organizes knowledge about assets and extracts from them the potential to generate capital.

And so formal property is this extraordinary thing, much bigger than simple ownership. Unlike tigers and wolves, who bare their teeth to protect their territory, man, physically a much weaker animal, has used his mind to create a legal environment —property—to protect his territory. Without anyone fully realizing it, the representational system the West created to settle territorial claims took on a life of its own, providing the knowledge base and rules necessary to fix and realize capital.

The enemies of representations

Ironically, the enemies of capitalism have always seemed more aware of the virtual origin of capital than capitalists themselves. It is this virtual aspect of capitalism that they find so insidious and dangerous. Capitalism, charges Viviane Forrester in her

The mystery of capital   **349**

best-seller *L'Horreur économique*, "has invaded physical as well as virtual space. ... It has confiscated and hidden wealth like never before, it has taken it out of the reach of people by hiding it in the form of symbols. Symbols have become the subjects of abstract exchanges that take place nowhere else than in their virtual world."[19] Consciously or unconsciously, Forrester is part of a long tradition of being uncomfortable with economic representations of virtual reality—those "metaphysical subtleties" that Marx thought were nevertheless necessary to understand and accumulate wealth.[20]

This fear of the virtuality of capital is understandable. Every time civilization comes up with a novel way of using representations to manage the physical world, people become suspicious. When Marco Polo returned from China, he shocked Europeans with the news that the Chinese used not metal but paper money, which people quickly denounced as alchemy. The European world resisted representative money into the nineteenth century. The latest forms of derivative money—electronic money, wire transfers, and the now omnipresent credit card—also took time to be accepted. As representations of value become less ponderous and more virtual, people are understandably skeptical. New forms of property derivatives (such as mortgage-backed securities) may help form additional capital, but they also make understanding economic life more complex. And so people are inclined to be more comfortable with the image of the noble perspiring workers of Soviet and Latin American murals, toiling in the fields or operating their machines, than with capitalists wheeling and dealing titles, shares, and bonds in the virtual reality of their computers. It is as if working with representations dirties your hands more than working with dirt and grease.

Like all representative systems—from written language to money and cyber symbols—property paper has been seen by many intellectuals as an instrument of deceit and oppression. Negative attitudes to representations have been powerful undercurrents in the formation of political ideas. The French philosopher Jacques Derrida recalls in *De la Grammatologie* how Jean Jacques Rousseau argued that writing was an important cause of human inequality. For Rousseau, those with the knowledge of writing could control written laws and official paper and, thus, the destiny of people. Claude Lévi-Strauss has also argued that "the primary function of written communication is to facilitate subjugation."[21]

I am as aware as any anticapitalist of how representational systems, particularly those of capitalism, have been used to exploit and conquer, how they have left the many at the mercy of the few. I have discussed in this book how official paper has been used for outright domination. And yet the art and science of representation is one of the girders of modern society. No amount of ranting and raving against writing, electronic money, cyber symbols, and property paper will make them disappear. Instead we must make representational systems simpler and more transparent and work hard to help people understand them. Otherwise, legal apartheid will persist, and the tools to create wealth will remain in the hands of those who live inside the bell jar.

350 H. De Soto

Is succeeding at capitalism a cultural thing?

Think of Bill Gates, the world's most successful and wealthiest entrepreneur. Apart from his personal genius, how much of his success is due to his cultural background and his "Protestant ethic"? And how much is due to the legal property system of the United States?

How many software innovations could he have made without patents to protect them? How many deals and long-term projects could he have carried out without enforceable contracts? How many risks could he have taken at the beginning without limited liability systems and insurance policies? How much capital could he have accumulated without property records in which to fix and store that capital? How many resources could he have pooled without fungible property representations? How many other people would he have made millionaires without being able to distribute stock options? How many economies of scale could he have benefited from if he had to operate on the basis of dispersed cottage industries that could not be combined? How would he pass on the rights to his empire to his children and colleagues without hereditary succession?

I do not think Bill Gates or any entrepreneur in the West could be successful without property rights systems based on a strong, well-integrated social contract I humbly suggest that before any brahmin who lives in a bell jar tries to convince us that succeeding at capitalism requires certain cultural traits, we should first try to see what happens when developing and former communist countries establish property rights systems that can create capital for everyone.

Throughout history people have confused the efficiency of the representational tools they have inherited to create surplus value with the inherent values of their culture. They forget that often what gives an edge to a particular group of people is the innovative use they make of a representational system developed by another culture. For example, Northerners had to copy the legal institutions of ancient Rome to organize themselves and learn the Greek alphabet and the Arabic number symbols and systems to convey information and calculate. And so, today, few are aware of the tremendous edge that formal property systems have given Western societies. As a result, many Westerners have been led to believe that what underpins their successful capitalism is the work ethic they have inherited or the existential anguish created by their religions—in spite of the fact that people all over the world all work hard when they can and that existential angst or over-bearing mothers are not Calvinist or Jewish monopolies. (I am as anxious as any Calvinist in history, especially on Sunday evenings, and in the overbearing mother sweepstakes, I would put mine in Peru up against any woman in New York.) Therefore, a great part of the research agenda needed to explain why capitalism fails outside the West remains mired in a mass of unexamined and largely untestable assumptions labeled "culture," whose main effect is to allow too many of those who live in the privileged enclaves of this world to enjoy feeling superior.

The mystery of capital **351**

One day these cultural arguments will peel away as the hard evidence of the effects of good political institutions and property law sink in. In the meantime, as *Foreign Affairs'* Fareed Zakaria has observed,

> Culture is hot. By culture I don't mean Wagner and Abstract Expressionism —they've always been hot—but rather culture as an explanation for social phenomena. ... Cultural explanations persist because intellectuals like them. They make valuable the detailed knowledge of countries' histories, which intellectuals have in great supply. They add an air of mystery and complexity to the study of societies. ... But culture itself can be shaped and changed. Behind so many cultural attitudes, tastes, and preferences lie the political and economic forces that shaped them.[22]

This is not to say that culture does not count. All people in the world have specific preferences, skills, and patterns of behavior that can be regarded as cultural. The challenge is fathoming which of these traits are really the ingrained, unchangeable identity of a people and which are determined by economic and legal constraints. Is illegal squatting on real estate in Egypt and Peru the result of ancient, ineradicable nomadic traditions among the Arabs and the Quechuas' back-and-forth custom of cultivating crops at different vertical levels of the Andes? Or does it happen because in both Egypt and Peru it takes more than fifteen years to obtain legal property rights to desert land? In my experience squatting is mainly due to the latter. When people have access to an orderly mechanism to settle land that reflects the social contract, they will take the legal route, and only a minority, like anywhere else, will insist on extralegal appropriation. Much behavior that is today attributed to cultural heritage is not the inevitable result of people's ethnic or idiosyncratic traits but of their rational evaluation of the relative costs and benefits of entering the legal property system.

Legal property empowers individuals in any culture, and I doubt that property per se directly contradicts any major culture. Vietnamese, Cuban, and Indian migrants have clearly had few problems adapting to U.S. property law. If correctly conceived, property law can reach beyond cultures to increase trust between them and, at the same time, reduce the costs of bringing things and thoughts together.[23] Legal property sets the exchange rates between different cultures and thus gives them a bedrock of economic commonalities from which to do business with each other.

The only game in town

I am convinced that capitalism has lost its way in developing and former communist nations. It is not equitable. It is out of touch with those who should be its largest constituency, and instead of being a cause that promises opportunity for all, capitalism appears increasingly as the leitmotif of a self-serving guild of businessmen and their technocracies. I hope this book has conveyed my belief that this state of affairs is relatively easy to correct—provided that governments are willing to accept the following:

1   The situation and potential of the poor need to be better documented.
2   All people are capable of saving.
3   What the poor are missing are the legally integrated property systems that can convert their work and savings into capital.
4   Civil disobedience and the mafias of today are not marginal phenomena but the result of people marching by the billions from life organized on a small scale to life on a big scale.
5   In this context, the poor are not the problem but the solution.
6   Implementing a property system that creates capital is a political challenge because it involves getting in touch with people, grasping the social contract, and overhauling the legal system.

With its victory over communism, capitalism's old agenda for economic progress is exhausted and requires a new set of commitments. It makes no sense continuing to call for open economies without facing the fact that the economic reforms underway open the doors only for small and globalized elites and leave out most of humanity. At present, capitalist globalization is concerned with interconnecting only the elites that live inside the bell jars. To lift the bell jars and do away with property apartheid will require going beyond the existing borders of both economics and law.

I am not a die-hard capitalist. I do not view capitalism as a credo. Much more important to me are freedom, compassion for the poor, respect for the social contract, and equal opportunity. But for the moment, to achieve those goals, capitalism is the only game in town. It is the only system we know that provides us with the tools required to create massive surplus value.

I love being from the Third World because it represents such a marvelous challenge—that of making a transition to a market-based capitalist system that respects people's desires and beliefs. When capital is a success story not only in the West but everywhere, we can move beyond the limits of the physical world and use our minds to soar into the future.

17

BEYOND MARKETS AND STATES

Polycentric governance of complex economic systems[†]

*E. Ostrom**

Contemporary research on the outcomes of diverse institutional arrangements for governing common–pool resources (CPRs) and public goods at multiple scales builds on classical economic theory while developing new theory to explain phenomena that do not fit in a dichotomous world of "the market" and "the state." Scholars are slowly shifting from positing simple systems to using more complex frameworks, theories, and models to understand the diversity of puzzles and problems facing humans interacting in contemporary societies. The humans we study have complex motivational structures and establish diverse private–for–profit, governmental, and community institutional arrangements that operate at multiple scales to generate productive and innovative as well as destructive and perverse outcomes (Douglass C. North 1990, 2005).

In this article, I will describe the intellectual journey that I have taken the last half century from when I began graduate studies in the late 1950s. The early efforts to understand the polycentric water industry in California were formative for me. In addition to working with Vincent Ostrom and Charles M. Tiebout as they formulated the concept of polycentric systems for governing metropolitan areas, I studied the efforts of a large group of private and public water producers facing the problem of an overdrafted groundwater basin on the coast and watching saltwater intrusion threaten the possibility of long term use. Then, in the 1970s, I participated with colleagues in the study of polycentric police industries serving US metropolitan areas to find that the dominant theory underlying massive reform proposals was incorrect. Metropolitan areas served by a combination of large and small producers could achieve economies of scale in the production of some police services and avoid *dis*economies of scale in the production of others.

These early empirical studies led over time to the development of the Institutional Analysis and Development (IAD) framework. A common framework consistent with game theory enabled us to undertake a variety of empirical studies

354 E. Ostrom

including a meta-analysis of a large number of existing case studies on common-pool resource systems around the world. Carefully designed experimental studies in the lab have enabled us to test precise combinations of structural variables to find that isolated, anonymous individuals overharvest from common–pool resources. Simply allowing communication, or "cheap talk," enables participants to reduce overharvesting and increase joint payoffs contrary to game theoretical predictions. Large studies of irrigation systems in Nepal and forests around the world challenge the presumption that governments always do a better job than users in organizing and protecting important resources.

Currently, many scholars are undertaking new theoretical efforts. A core effort is developing a more general theory of individual choice that recognizes the central role of trust in coping with social dilemmas. Over time, a clear set of findings from the microsituational level have emerged regarding structural factors affecting the likelihood of increased cooperation. Due to the complexity of broader field settings, one needs to develop more configural approaches to the study of factors that enhance or detract from the emergence and robustness of self–organized efforts within multilevel, polycentric systems. Further, the application of empirical studies to the policy world leads one to stress the importance of fitting institutional rules to a specific social-ecological setting. "One size fits all" policies are not effective. The frameworks and empirical work that many scholars have undertaken in recent decades provide a better foundation for policy analysis. With this brief overview, let us now discuss the journey itself.

The earlier world view of simple systems

In the mid-twentieth century, the dominant scholarly effort was to try to fit the world into simple models and to criticize institutional arrangements that did not fit. I will briefly review the basic assumptions that were made at that time but have been challenged by scholars around the world, including the work of Herbert A. Simon (1955) and V. Ostrom (2008).

Two optimal organizational forms

The market was seen as the optimal institution for the production and exchange of private goods. For nonprivate goods, on the other hand, one needed "the" government to impose rules and taxes to force self-interested individuals to contribute necessary resources and refrain from self-seeking activities. Without a hierarchical government to induce compliance, self-seeking citizens and officials would fail to generate efficient levels of public goods, such as peace and security, at multiple scales (Thomas Hobbes [1651] 1960; Woodrow Wilson 1885). A single governmental unit, for example, was strongly recommended to reduce the "chaotic" structure of metropolitan governance, increase efficiency, limit conflict among governmental units, and best serve a homogeneous view of the public (William Anderson and Edward W. Weidner 1950; Luther Gulick 1957; H. Paul Friesema

1966). This dichotomous view of the world explained patterns of interaction and outcomes related to markets for the production and exchange of strictly private goods (Armen A. Alchian 1950), but it has not adequately accounted for internal dynamics within private firms (Oliver E. Williamson 1975, 1986). Nor does it adequately deal with the wide diversity of institutional arrangements that humans craft to govern, provide, and manage public goods and common-pool resources.

Two types of goods

In his classic definitional essay, Paul Samuelson (1954) divided goods into two types. Pure private goods are both excludable (individual A can be excluded from consuming private goods unless paid for) and rivalrous (whatever individual A consumes, no one else can consume). Public goods are both nonexcludable (impossible to keep those who have not paid for a good from consuming it) and nonrivalrous (whatever individual A consumes does not limit the consumption by others). This basic division was consistent with the dichotomy of the institutional world into private property exchanges in a market setting and government-owned property organized by a public hierarchy. The people of the world were viewed primarily as consumers or voters.

One model of the individual

The assumption that all individuals are fully rational was generally accepted in mainstream economics and game theory. Fully rational individuals are presumed to know (i) all possible strategies available in a particular situation, (ii) which outcomes are linked to each strategy given the likely behavior of others in a situation, and (iii) a rank order for each of these outcomes in terms of the individual's own preferences as measured by utility. The rational strategy for such an individual in every situation is to maximize expected utility. While utility was originally conceived of as a way of combining a diversity of external values on a single internal scale, in practice it has come to be equated with one externalized unit of measure—such as expected profits. This model of the individual has fruitfully generated useful and empirically validated predictions about the results of exchange transactions related to goods with specific attributes in a competitive market but not in a diversity of social dilemmas. I will return to a discussion of the theory of individual behavior in Section VIIA.

Early efforts to develop a fuller understanding of complex human systems

The mid-twentieth-century worldviews of simple systems have slowly been transformed as a result of extensive empirical research and the development of a framework consistent with game theoretical models for the analysis of a broad array of questions.

356 E. Ostrom

Studying polycentric public industries

Undertaking empirical studies of how citizens, local public entrepreneurs, and public officials engage in diverse ways of providing, producing, and managing public service industries and common property regimes at multiple scales has generated substantial knowledge that is not explained by two models of optimal organizational forms. V. Ostrom, Tiebout, and Robert Warren (1961) introduced the concept of polycentricity in their effort to understand whether the activities of a diverse array of public and private agencies engaged in providing and producing of public services in metropolitan areas were chaotic, as charged by other scholars—or potentially a productive arrangement.

> "Polycentric" connotes many centers of decision making that are formally independent of each other. Whether they actually function independently, or instead constitute an interdependent system of relations, is an empirical question in particular cases. To the extent that they take each other into account in competitive relationships, enter into various contractual and cooperative undertakings or have recourse to central mechanisms to resolve conflicts, the various political jurisdictions in a metropolitan area may function in a coherent manner with consistent and predictable patterns of interacting behavior. To the extent that this is so, they may be said to function as a "system."
> (V. Ostrom, Tiebout, and Warren 1961: 831–32)

Drawing on the concept of a public service industry (Joe S. Bain 1959; Richard Caves 1964; V. Ostrom and Elinor Ostrom 1965), several studies of water industry performance were carried out in diverse regions of California during the 1960s (V. Ostrom 1962; Louis F. Weschler 1968; Warren 1966; E. Ostrom 1965). Substantial evidence was found that multiple public and private agencies had searched out productive ways of organizing water resources at multiple scales contrary to the view that the presence of multiple governmental units without a clear hierarchy was chaotic. Further, evidence pointed out three mechanisms that increase productivity in polycentric metropolitan areas: (i) small to medium sized cities are more effective than large cities in monitoring performance of their citizens and relevant costs, (ii) citizens who are dissatisfied with service provision can "vote with their feet" and move to jurisdictions that come closer to their preferred mix and costs of public services, and (iii) local incorporated communities can contract with larger producers and change contracts if not satisfied with the services provided, while neighborhoods inside a large city have no voice.

In the 1970s, the earlier work on effects of diverse ways of organizing the provision of water in metropolitan areas was extended to policing and public safety. These studies directly addressed whether substantial economies of scale existed in the production of police services for urban neighborhoods as asserted in calls for reform (Daniel L. Skoler and June M. Hetler 1971). Not a *single* case was found where a large centralized police department outperformed smaller departments serving similar neighborhoods in regard to multiple indicators. A series of studies was conducted in Indianapolis (E. Ostrom et al. 1973), Chicago (E. Ostrom and Gordon P. Whitaker 1974), and St. Louis (E. Ostrom and Roger B. Parks 1973; E. Ostrom 1976) and then replicated in Grand Rapids, Michigan (Samir IsHak 1972) and Nashville, Tennessee (Bruce D. Rogers and C. McCurdy Lipsey 1974).

We found that while many police departments served the 80 metropolitan areas that we also studied, duplication of services by more than one department to the same set of citizens rarely occurred (E. Ostrom, Parks, and Whitaker 1978). Further, the widely held belief that a multiplicity of departments in a metropolitan area was less efficient was *not* found. In fact, the "most efficient producers supply more output for given inputs in high multiplicity metropolitan areas than do the efficient producers in metropolitan areas with fewer producers" (E. Ostrom and Parks 1999: 287). Metropolitan areas with large numbers of autonomous direct service producers achieved higher levels of technical efficiency (ibid.: 290). Technical efficiency was also enhanced in those metropolitan areas with a small number of producers providing indirect services such as radio communication and criminal laboratory analyses. We were able to reject the theory underlying the proposals of the metropolitan reform approach. We demonstrated that complexity is not the same as chaos in regard to metropolitan governance. That lesson has carried forth as we have undertaken further empirical studies of polycentric governance of resource and infrastructure systems across the world (Krister Andersson and E. Ostrom 2008; E. Ostrom, Larry Schroeder, and Susan Wynne 1993).

Doubling the types of goods

Studying how individuals cope with diverse public problems in the world led us to reject Samuelson's twofold classification of goods. James Buchanan (1965) had already added a third type of good, which he called "club goods." In relation to these kinds of goods, it was feasible for groups of individuals to create private associations (clubs) to provide themselves with nonrivalrous but small-scale goods and services that they could enjoy while excluding nonmembers from participation and consumption of benefits.

In light of further empirical and theoretical research, we proposed additional modifications to the classification of goods to identify fundamental differences that affect the incentives facing individuals (V. Ostrom and E. Ostrom 1977).

(i) Replacing the term "rivalry of consumption" with "subtractability of use."
(ii) Conceptualizing subtractability of use and excludability to vary from low to high rather than characterizing them as either present or absent.
(iii) Overtly adding a very important fourth type of good—common-pool resources —that shares the attribute of subtractability with private goods and difficulty of exclusion with public goods (V. Ostrom and E. Ostrom 1977). Forests, water systems, fisheries, and the global atmosphere are all common-pool resources of immense importance for the survival of humans on this earth.

358 E. Ostrom

(iv) Changing the name of a "club" good to a "toll" good since many goods that share these characteristics are provided by small scale public as well as private associations.

Figure 17.1 provides an overview of four broad types of goods that differentially affect the problems individuals face in devising institutions to enable them to provide, produce, and consume diverse goods. These four broad types of goods contain many subtypes of goods that vary substantially in regard to many attributes. For example, a river and a forest are both common-pool resources. They differ substantially, however, in regard to the mobility of the resource units produced, the ease of measurement, the time scale for regeneration, and other attributes. Specific common-pool resources also differ in regard to spatial extent, number of users, and many other factors.

When one engages in substantial fieldwork, one confronts an immense diversity of situations in which humans interact. Riding as an observer in a patrol car in the central district of a large American city at midnight on a Saturday evening, one sees different patterns of human interaction than in a suburb on a weekday afternoon when school is letting out. In both cases, one observes the production of a public good—local safety—by an official of a local government. Others, who are involved in each situation, differ in regard to age, sobriety, why they are there, and what they are trying to accomplish. And this context affects the strategies of the police officer one is observing.

Contrast observing the production of a public good to watching private water companies, city utilities, private oil companies, and local citizens meeting in diverse settings to assess who is to blame for overdrafting their groundwater basin causing massive saltwater intrusion, and what to do next. These individuals all face the same problem—the overdraft of a common-pool resource—but their behavior differs substantially when they meet monthly in a private water association, when they face each other in a courtroom, and when they go to the legislature and eventually

		Subtractability of Use	
		High	*Low*
Difficulty of excluding potential beneficiaries	High	*Common-pool resources*: groundwater basins, lakes, irrigation systems, fisheries, forests, etc.	*Public goods*: peace and security of a community, national defense, knowledge, fire protection, weather forecasts, etc.
	Low	*Private goods*: food, clothing, automobiles, etc.	*Toll goods*: theaters, private clubs, daycare centers

FIGURE 17.1. Four types of goods

Source: Adapted from E. Ostrom 2005: 24.

to the citizens to sponsor a Special Replenishment District. These and many other situations observed in irrigation systems and forests in multiple countries do not closely resemble the standard models of a market or a hierarchy.

Developing a framework for analyzing the diversity of human situations

The complexity and diversity of the field settings we have studied has generated an extended effort by colleagues associated with the Workshop in Political Theory and Policy Analysis (the Workshop) to develop the IAD framework (V. Ostrom 1975; Larry L. Kiser and E. Ostrom 1982; Michael McGinnis 1999a, b, 2000; E. Ostrom 1986, 2005). The framework contains a nested set of building blocks that social scientists can use in efforts to understand human interactions and outcomes across diverse settings. The IAD builds on earlier work on *transactions* (John R. Commons [1924] 1968), *logic of the situation* (Karl R. Popper 1961), *collective structures* (Floyd H. Allport 1962), *frames* (Irving Goffman 1974), and *scripts* (Roger C. Schank and Robert P. Abelson 1977). The approach also draws inspiration from the work of Arthur Koestler (1973) and Simon (1981, 1995) who both challenged the assumption that human behavior and outcomes are entirely based on a small set of irreducible building blocks.

While the terms frameworks, theories, and models are used interchangeably by many scholars, we use these concepts in a nested manner to range from the most general to the most precise set of assumptions made by a scholar. The IAD *framework* is intended to contain the most general set of variables that an institutional analyst may want to use to examine a diversity of institutional settings including human interactions within markets, private firms, families, community organizations, legislatures, and government agencies. It provides a metatheoretical language to enable scholars to discuss any particular theory or to compare theories.

A specific *theory* is used by an analyst to specify which working parts of a framework are considered useful to explain diverse outcomes and how they relate to one

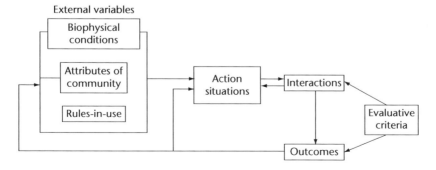

FIGURE 17.2. A framework for institutional analysis

Source: Adapted from E. Ostrom 2005: 15.

360 E. Ostrom

another. Microlevel theories including game theory, microeconomic theory, transaction cost theory, and public goods/common-pool resource theories are examples of specific theories compatible with the IAD framework. *Models* make precise assumptions about a limited number of variables in a theory that scholars use to examine the formal consequences of these specific assumptions about the motivation of actors and the structure of the situation they face.

The IAD framework is designed to enable scholars to analyze systems that are composed of a cluster of variables, each of which can then be unpacked multiple times depending on the question of immediate interest. At the core of the IAD framework is the concept of an action situation affected by external variables (see Figure 17.2). The broadest categories of external factors affecting an action situation at a particular time include:

(i) Biophysical conditions, which may be simplified in some analyses to be one of the four types of goods defined in Figure 17.1.
(ii) Attributes of a community, which may include the history of prior interactions, internal homogeneity or heterogeneity of key attributes, and the knowledge and social capital of those who may participate or be affected by others.
(iii) Rules-in-use, which specify common understanding of those involved related to who must, must not, or may take which actions affecting others subject to sanctions (Sue E. S. Crawford and E. Ostrom 2005). The rules-in-use may evolve over time as those involved in one action situation interact with others in a variety of settings (E. Ostrom 2008; E. Ostrom and Xavier Basurto forthcoming; Robert Boyd and Peter J. Richerson 1985) or self-consciously change the rules in a collective choice or constitutional-choice setting.

The set of external variables impacts an action situation to generate patterns of interactions and outcomes that are evaluated by participants in the action situation (and potentially by scholars) and feed back on both the external variables and the action situation.

The internal working parts of an action situation are overtly consistent with the variables that a theorist uses to analyze a formal game.[1] This has meant that colleagues have been able to use formal game theory models consistent with the IAD framework to analyze simplified but interesting combinations of theoretical variables and derive testable conclusions from them (see James M. Acheson and Roy Gardner 2005; Gardner et al. 2000; Franz Weissing and E. Ostrom 1993) as well as agent-based models (ABMs) (Wander Jager and Marco A. Janssen 2002; Janssen 2008). It is not feasible to develop a formal game (or even an ABM) to analyze the more complex empirical settings with many variables of relevance affecting outcomes and of importance for institutional analysis. It is possible, however, to use a common set of structural elements to develop structured coding forms for data collection and analysis. And one can design experiments using a common set of variables for many situations of interest to political economists and then examine why particular behavior and outcomes occur in some situations and not in others.

To specify the structure of a game and predict outcomes, the theorist needs to posit the:

(i) characteristics of the actors involved (including the model of human choice adopted by the theorist);
(ii) positions they hold (e.g., first mover or row player);
(iii) set of actions that actors can take at specific nodes in a decision tree;
(iv) amount of information available at a decision node;
(v) outcomes that actors jointly affect;
(vi) set of functions that map actors and actions at decision nodes into intermediate or final outcomes; and
(vii) benefits and costs assigned to the linkage of actions chosen and outcomes obtained.

These are also the internal working parts of an action situation as shown in Figure 17.3. As discussed below, using a common framework across a wide diversity of studies has enabled a greater cumulation of understanding of interactions and outcomes in very complex environments. The IAD framework overtly embeds a particular situation of interest in a broader setting of external variables, some of which can be self-consciously revised over time.

Are rational individuals helplessly trapped in social dilemmas?

The classic assumptions about rational individuals facing a dichotomy of organizational forms and of goods hide the potentially productive efforts of individuals and

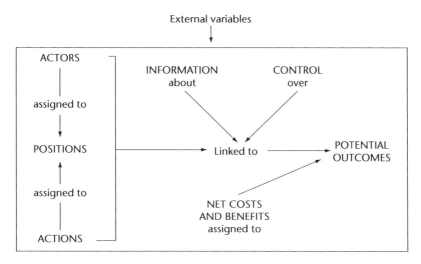

FIGURE 17.3. The internal structure of an action situation

Source: Adapted from E. Ostrom 2005: 33.

362 E. Ostrom

groups to organize and solve social dilemmas such as the overharvesting of common-pool resources and the underprovision of local public goods. The classic models have been used to view those who are involved in a prisoner's dilemma game or other social dilemmas as always trapped in the situation without capabilities to change the structure themselves. This analytical step was a retrogressive step in the theories used to analyze the human condition. Whether or not the individuals, who are in a situation, have capacities to transform the external variables affecting their own situation varies dramatically from one situation to the next. It is an empirical condition that varies from situation to situation rather than a logical universality. Public investigators purposely keep prisoners separated so they cannot communicate. The users of a common-pool resource are not so limited.

When analysts perceive the human beings they model as being trapped inside perverse situations, they then assume that other human beings external to those involved—scholars and public officials—are able to analyze the situation, ascertain why counterproductive outcomes are reached, and posit what changes in the rules-in-use will enable participants to improve outcomes. Then, external officials are expected to impose an optimal set of rules on those individuals involved. It is assumed that the momentum for change must come from outside the situation rather than from the self-reflection and creativity of those within a situation to restructure their own patterns of interaction. As Richard Sugden has described this approach:

> *Most modern economic theory describes a world presided over by a government (not, significantly, by governments), and sees this world through the government's eyes. The government is supposed to have the responsibility, the will and the power to restructure society in whatever way maximizes social welfare; like the US Cavalry in a good Western, the government stands ready to rush to the rescue whenever the market "fails," and the economist's job is to advise it on when and how to do so. Private individuals, in contrast, are credited with little or no ability to solve collective problems among themselves. This makes for a distorted view of some important economic and political issues.*
>
> —*(Sugden 1986: 3; emphasis in original)*

Garrett Hardin's (1968) portrayal of the users of a common-pool resource—a pasture open to all—being trapped in an inexorable tragedy of overuse and destruction has been widely accepted since it was consistent with the prediction of no cooperation in a prisoner's dilemma or other social dilemma games. It captured the attention of scholars and policymakers across the world. Many presumed that all common-pool resources were owned by no one. Thus, it was thought that government officials had to impose new external variables (e.g., new policies) to prevent destruction by users who could not do anything other than destroy the resources on which their own future (as well as the rest of our futures) depended.

Scholars from diverse disciplines examine whether resource users are always trapped

Dramatic incidents of overharvested resources had captured widespread attention, while studies by anthropologists, economic historians, engineers, historians, philosophers, and political scientists of local governance of smaller to medium scale common-pool resources over long periods of time were *not* noticed by many theorists and public officials (see Robert McC. Netting 1972; Bonnie J. McCay and Acheson 1987; E. Walter Coward 1980). Cumulation of the knowledge contained in these studies did not occur, due to the fact that the studies were written by scholars in diverse disciplines focusing on different types of resources located in many countries.

Fortunately, the National Research Council (NRC) established a committee in the mid-1980s to assess diverse institutional arrangements for effective conservation and utilization of jointly managed resources. The NRC committee brought scholars from multiple disciplines together and used the IAD framework in an effort to begin to identify common variables in cases where users had organized or failed to organize (Ronald J. Oakerson 1986; NRC 1986). Finding multiple cases where resource users were successful in organizing themselves challenged the presumption that it was *impossible* for resource users to solve their own problems of overuse. The NRC report opened up the possibility of a diversity of studies using multiple methods. The NRC effort also stimulated an extended research program at the Workshop that involved coding and analyzing case studies of common-pool resources written by other scholars.

Meta-analyses of common-pool resource cases

In an effort to learn more than just the existence of multiple cases where resource users had self-organized, colleagues at the Workshop undertook a meta-analysis of existing case studies that were identified as a result of the activities of the NRC panel.[2] Because of our prior studies of complex urban systems and the development of a framework and common language for linking the parts of complex systems, we could use the framework to help organize our efforts. The IAD framework became the foundation for designing a coding manual that was used to record a consistent set of variables for each common-pool resource study.

This was an immense effort. More than two years was devoted to developing the final coding manual (E. Ostrom et al. 1989). A key problem was the minimal overlap of variables identified by case study authors from diverse disciplines. The team had to read and screen over 500 case studies in order to identify a small set of cases that recorded information about the actors, their strategies, the condition of the resource, and the rules-in-use.[3] A common set of variables was recorded for 44 subgroups of fishers who harvested from inshore fisheries (Edella Schlager 1990, 1994) and 47 irrigation systems that were managed either by farmers or by a government (Shui Yan Tang 1992, 1994).

364 E. Ostrom

Of the 47 irrigation systems included in the analysis, 12 were managed by governmental agencies of which only 40 percent ($n=7$) had high performance. Of the 25 farmer-managed, over 70 percent ($n=18$) had high performance (Tang 1994: 234). Rule conformance was a key variable affecting the adequacy of water over time (Tang 1994: 229). None of the inshore fishery groups analyzed by Schlager were government managed and 11 (25 percent) were not organized in any way. The other 33 subgroups had a diversity of informal rules to define who was allowed to fish in a particular location and how harvesting was restricted (Schlager 1994: 260).

In addition to finding significant levels of cooperation, we found some support for earlier theoretical predictions of no cooperation in particular settings.

> *In CPR dilemmas where individuals do not know one another, cannot communicate effectively, and thus cannot develop agreements, norms, and sanctions, aggregate predictions derived from models of rational individuals in a noncooperative game receive substantial support. These are sparse environments and full rationality appears to be a reasonable assumption in them.*
> — *(E. Ostrom, Gardner, and James A. Walker 1994: 319)*

On the other hand, the capacity to overcome dilemmas and create effective governance occurred far more frequently than expected and depended upon the structure of the resource itself and whether the rules-in-use developed by users were linked effectively to this structure (William Blomquist et al. 1994). In all self-organized systems, we found that users had created boundary rules for determining who could use the resource, choice rules related to the allocation of the flow of resource units, and active forms of monitoring and local sanctioning of rule breakers (ibid.: 301). On the other hand, we did not find a single case where harvesters used the "grim trigger" strategy—a form of punishment that was posited in many theoretical arguments for how individuals could solve repeated dilemmas (Prajit K. Dutta 1999: 264).

The bundles of property rights related to common-pool resources

Resource economists have used the term "common property resource" to refer to fisheries and water resources (H. Scott Gordon 1954; Anthony D. Scott 1955; Frederick W. Bell 1972). Combining the term "property" with "resource" introduced considerable confusion between the nature of a good and the absence or presence of a property regime (Siegfried V. Ciriacy-Wantrup and Richard C. Bishop 1975). A common-pool resource can be owned and managed as government property, private property, community property, or owned by no one (Daniel W. Bromley 1986). A further reason for the lack of awareness about property systems developed by local users was that many scholars presumed that unless users possessed alienation rights—the right to sell their property—they did not have any property rights (Alchian and Harold Demsetz 1973; Terry L. Anderson and Peter J. Hill 1990; Richard Posner 1975).

Schlager and E. Ostrom (1992) drew on the earlier work of Commons ([1924] 1968) to conceptualize property rights systems as containing *bundles* of rights rather than a single right. The meta-analysis of existing field cases helped to identify five property rights that individuals using a common-pool resource might cumulatively have: (i) access—the right to enter a specified property,[4] (ii) withdrawal—the right to harvest specific products from a resource, (iii) management—the right to transform the resource and regulate internal use patterns, (iv) exclusion—the right to decide who will have access, withdrawal, or management rights, and (v) alienation —the right to lease or sell any of the other four rights. Conceiving of prsoperty rights bundles is now widely accepted by scholars who have studied diverse property rights systems around the world (David J. Brunckhorst 2000; P. Degnbol and McCay 2007; Jouni Paavola and W. Neil Adger 2005; Paul B. Trawick 2001; James A. Wilson et al. 1994).

Linking the internal parts of an action situation to external rules

Actors who have specific property rights to a resource also face more fundamental rules that affect the structure of the action situations they are in. In our meta-analysis, we found an incredible array of specific rules used in different settings (e.g., who could withdraw how many resource units at what location and time, what information was required of all users, what costs and benefits were attached to which actions, etc.). As we attempted to find a consistent way of coding and analyzing this rich diversity of specific rules described by case authors, we turned again to the IAD framework. Since we had identified seven working parts of a game or action situation itself, it seemed reasonable to think of seven broad types of rules operating as external variables affecting the individual working parts of action situations (see Figure 17.4). The seven types of rules are:

(i) Boundary rules that specify how actors were to be chosen to enter or leave these positions;
(ii) Position rules that specify a set of positions and how many actors hold each one;
(iii) Choice rules that specify which actions are assigned to an actor in a position;
(iv) Information rules that specify channels of communication among actors and what information must, may, or must not be shared;
(v) Scope rules that specify the outcomes that could be affected;
(vi) Aggregation rules (such as majority or unanimity rules) that specify how the decisions of actors at a node were to be mapped to intermediate or final outcomes; and
(vii) Payoff rules that specify how benefits and costs were to be distributed to actors in positions (Crawford and E. Ostrom 2005).

A useful way of thinking about institutional rules is to conceptualize what part of an action situation is affected by a rule (see Figure 17.4).

366 E. Ostrom

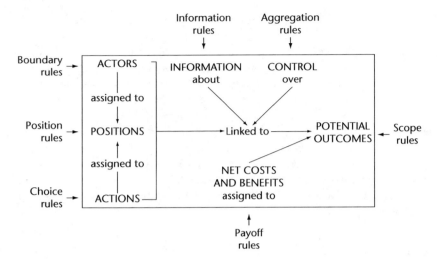

FIGURE 17.4. Rules as exogenous variables directly affecting the elements of an action situation

Source: Adapted from E. Ostrom 2005: 189.

Conceptualizing seven broad types of rules (rather than one or two) has been upsetting to scholars who wanted to rely on simple models of interactions among humans. In addition to finding seven broad types of rules, however, we also found multiple variants of each type. For example, we found 27 boundary rules described by case study authors as used in at least one common-pool resource setting (E. Ostrom 1999: 510). Some rules specified diverse forms of residence, organizational memberships, or personal attributes that are ascribed or acquired. Similarly, we found 112 different choice rules that were usually composed of two parts—an allocation formula specifying where, when, or how resource units could be harvested and a specific basis for the implementation of the formula (such as the amount of land held, historical use patterns, or assignment through lottery) (ibid.: 512).

Long surviving resource institutions

After working for several years with colleagues to code cases of successful and failed systems, I thought my next task would be to undertake careful statistical analysis to identify which specific rules were associated with successful systems. I had not yet fully absorbed the incredible number and diversity of rules that the team had recorded. In 1988, I spent a sabbatical leave in a research group organized by Reinhard Selten at the Center for Interdisciplinary Research at Bielefeld University. I struggled to find rules that worked across ecological, social, and economic environments, but the specific rules associated with success or failure varied extensively across sites. Finally, I had to give up the idea that *specific* rules might be associated with successful cases.

Beyond markets and states **367**

Moving up a level in generality, I tried to understand the broader institutional regularities among the systems that were sustained over a long period of time and were absent in the failed systems. I used the term "design principle" to characterize these regularities. I did not mean that the fishers, irrigators, pastoralists, and others overtly had these principles in their minds when they developed systems that survived for long periods of time. My effort was to identify a set of core underlying lessons that characterized the long sustained regimes as contrasted to the cases of failure (E. Ostrom 1990).[5]

Since the design principles are described extensively in E. Ostrom (1990, 2005), I will mention only a brief updated list as developed by Michael Cox, Gwen Arnold, and Sergio Villamayor-Tomás (2009):

1A. *User Boundaries*: Clear and locally understood boundaries between legitimate users and nonusers are present.
1B. *Resource Boundaries*: Clear boundaries that separate a specific common-pool resource from a larger social-ecological system are present.
2A. *Congruence with Local Conditions*: Appropriation and provision rules are congruent with local social and environmental conditions.
2B. *Appropriation and Provision*: Appropriation rules are congruent with provision rules; the distribution of costs is proportional to the distribution of benefits.
3. *Collective Choice Arrangements*: Most individuals affected by a resource regime are authorized to participate in making and modifying its rules.
4A. *Monitoring users*: Individuals who are accountable to or are the users monitor the appropriation and provision levels of the users.
4B. *Monitoring the Resource*: Individuals who are accountable to or are the users monitor the condition of the resource.
5. *Graduated Sanctions*: Sanctions for rule violations start very low but become stronger if a user repeatedly violates a rule.
6. *Conflict Resolution Mechanisms*: Rapid, low cost, local arenas exist for resolving conflicts among users or with officials.
7. *Minimal Recognition of Rights*: The rights of local users to make their own rules are recognized by the government.
8. *Nested Enterprises*: When a common-pool resource is closely connected to a larger social-ecological system, governance activities are organized in multiple nested layers.

The design principles appear to synthesize core factors that affect the probability of long term survival of an institution developed by the users of a resource. Cox, Arnold, and Villamayor-Tomás (2009) analyzed over 100 studies by scholars who assessed the relevance of the principles as an explanation of the success or failure of diverse common-pool resources. Two-thirds of these studies confirm that robust resource systems are characterized by most of the design principles and that failures are not. The authors of some studies that found the design principles inadequate tended to interpret them very rigidly and felt that successful systems were

368 E. Ostrom

characterized by more flexibility. In three instances, the initial wording of the design principles was too general and did not distinguish between ecological and social conditions. Thus, I have adopted the improvements to principles 1, 2, and 4 suggested by Cox and coauthors.

Conducting experiments to study common-pool resource problems

The existence of a large number of cases where users had overcome social dilemmas in order to sustain long term use of common-pool resources successfully challenged the presumption that this was impossible. Many variables simultaneously affect these outcomes in the field. Developing game theoretical models of common-pool resource situations (Weissing and E. Ostrom 1993; E. Ostrom and Gardner 1993) has been one strategy we have used to assess the theoretical outcomes of a set of variables we have observed in the field. We have also thought it was important to examine the effect of precise combinations of variables in an experimental setting.

Common-pool resource experiments in university laboratories

Roy Gardner and James Walker joined me in an extended effort to build and test well specified, game theoretical models consistent with the IAD framework (see E. Ostrom, Walker, and Gardner 1992; E. Ostrom, Gardner, and Walker 1994). The initial CPR experiments started with a static, baseline situation that was as simple as could be specified without losing crucial aspects of the appropriation problems facing harvesters in the field. We used a quadratic payoff production function based on Gordon's (1954) classic model. The initial resource endowment w for each of eight subjects was a set of tokens that the subject could allocate between Market 1 (which had a fixed return) and Market 2 (which functioned as a common-pool resource with a return affected by the actions of all subjects in the experiment). Subjects received aggregated information so they did not know each individual's actions. Each subject i could invest a portion x_i of his/her endowment in the common resource (Market 2) and the remaining portion would then be invested in Market 1. The payoff function we used (E. Ostrom, Gardner, and Walker 1994: 110) was:

(1) $u_i(x) = we$ if $x_i = 0$
(2) $w(e - x_i) + (x_i/\Sigma x_i)F(\Sigma x_i)$ if $x_i > 0$.

The baseline experiment was a commons dilemma in which the game-theoretic outcome involved substantial overuse of a resource while a much better outcome could be reached if subjects were to reduce their joint allocation. The prediction from noncooperative game theory was that subjects would invest according to the Nash equilibrium—8 tokens each for a total of 64 tokens. Subjects could earn considerably more if they reduced their allocation to a total of 36 tokens in the common-pool resource. Subjects in baseline experiments with multiple decision rounds substantially overinvested—they invested even more tokens than predicted, so the joint outcome was worse than the predicted Nash equilibrium.[6]

Building off prior public goods research (Isaac and Walker 1988), we then conducted a series of face-to-face communication experiments in which the same payoff function was retained. After an initial ten rounds without communication, subjects were told they could communicate with each other in a group setting before returning to their terminals to make their own private decisions. This provided an opportunity for "cheap talk." The same outcome was predicted in these experiments as in the baseline since a subject could promise to cooperate but no external "third party" ensured that the promise was fulfilled.

Subjects used face-to-face communication to discuss strategies to gain the best outcomes and then to agree—if possible—on what each subject should invest. They learned about their aggregate investments after each round, but not the decision of individual subjects. This gave them information as to whether the total investments were greater than agreed upon. In many rounds, subjects kept their promises to each other. In other rounds, some defections did occur. Subjects used information about the aggregate investment levels to scold their unknown fellow subjects if the total investment was higher than they had agreed upon. The opportunity for repeated face-to-face communication was extremely successful in increasing joint returns. Findings from communication experiments are consistent with a large number of studies of the impact of face-to-face communication on the capacity of subjects to solve a variety of social dilemma problems (see E. Ostrom and Walker 1991; John M. Orbell, Alphons van de Kragt, and Robyn M. Dawes 1988; David Sally 1995; Daniel Balliet 2010).

In many field settings, resource users have devised a variety of formal or informal ways of sanctioning one another if rules are broken, even though this behavior is not consistent with the theory of norm-free, complete rationality (Jon Elster 1989: 40–41). It was thus important to see if subjects in a controlled experimental setting would actually use their own assets to financially punish other subjects. After subjects played ten rounds of the baseline common–pool resource game, they were told that in the subsequent rounds they would have an opportunity to pay a fee in order to impose a fine on another subject. We found much more sanctioning occurred in this design than the zero level predicted.[7] Subjects did increase gross benefits through their sanctioning but substantially reduced net returns due to the overuse of costly sanctions.[8] Sanctioning was primarily directed at those who defected, but a few sanctions appeared to be directed at low contributors as a form of revenge by those who had fined themselves. In a further design, subjects were given a chance to communicate and decide whether or not to adopt a sanctioning system of their own. Subjects who decided to adopt their own sanctioning system achieved the highest returns achieved in any of the common-pool resource laboratory experiments—90 percent of optimal after the fines related to the small number of defections were subtracted (E. Ostrom, Walker, and Gardner 1992).

The predictions of noncooperative game theory are roughly supported only when participants in a laboratory experiment do not know the reputation of the

370 E. Ostrom

others involved in a common-pool resource dilemma and cannot communicate with them. On the other hand, when subjects communicate face-to-face, they frequently agree on joint strategies and keep to their agreements—substantially increasing their net returns. Further, communication to decide on and design a sanctioning system enables those choosing this option to achieve close to optimal returns.

Studying common-pool resources in field experiments

A series of field experiments have now been conducted by colleagues in Colombia to assess whether experienced villagers who are dependent on resources make decisions about the "time spent in a forest" in a design that is mathematically consistent with those reported on above. Juan-Camilo Cardenas (2000) conducted field experiments in rural schoolhouses with over 200 users of local forests. He modified the design of the common-pool resource experiments without, and with, face-to-face communication so that villagers were asked to make decisions regarding "harvesting trees." The outcomes of these experiments were broadly consistent with the findings obtained with university students.

In a different design, Cardenas, John K. Stranlund, and Cleve E. Willis (2000) ran ten rounds of baseline experiments with resource users from five villages who were then given a chance to communicate face-to-face for the next set of experiments. In five additional villages, participants were told after the baseline rounds that a new regulation would go into force that mandated them to spend no more than the optimal time in the forest each round. The probability of an inspection was 1/16 per round—a low but realistic probability for monitoring rule conformance in rural areas in developing countries. If the person was over the limit imposed, a penalty was subtracted from that person's payoff, but the penalty was not revealed to the others. Subjects in this experimental condition increased their withdrawal levels when compared to the outcomes obtained when face-to-face communication was allowed and no rule was imposed. Other scholars have also found that externally imposed regulation that would theoretically lead to higher joint returns "crowded out" voluntary behavior to cooperate (see Bruno S. Frey and Felix Oberholzer-Gee 1997; Andrew F. Reeson and John G. Tisdell 2008).

Fehr and Andreas Leibbrandt (2008) conducted an interesting set of public goods experiments with fishers who harvest from an "open access" inland lake in northeastern Brazil. They found that a high percentage (87 percent) of fishers contributed in the first period of the field experiment and that contributions leveled off in the remaining periods. Fehr and Leibbrandt examined the mesh size of the nets used by individual fishermen and found that those who contributed more in the public goods experiment used nets with bigger mesh sizes. Larger mesh sizes allow young fish to escape, grow larger, and reproduce at a higher level than if they are caught when they are still small. In other words, cooperation in the field experiment was consistent with observed cooperation related to a real CPR dilemma. They conclude that the "fact that our laboratory measure for other-regarding preferences predicts field behavior increases our confidence about the behavioral relevance of other-regarding preferences gained from laboratory experiments" (ibid.: 17).

In summary, experiments on CPRs and public goods have shown that many predictions of the conventional theory of collective action do not hold. More cooperation occurs than predicted, "cheap talk" increases cooperation, and subjects invest in sanctioning free riders. Experiments also establish that motivational heterogeneity exists in harvesting or contribution decisions as well as decisions on sanctioning.

Studying common-pool resource problems in the field

Having conducted extensive meta-analyses of case studies and experiments, we also needed to undertake field studies where we could draw on the IAD framework to design questions to obtain consistent information about key theoretically important variables across sites.

Comparing farmer and government managed irrigation systems in Nepal

An opportunity to visit Nepal in 1988 led to the discovery of a large number of written studies of farmer built and maintained irrigation systems as well as some government constructed and managed systems. Ganesh Shivakoti, Paul Benjamin, and I were able to revise the CPR coding manual so as to include variables of specific relevance to understanding irrigation systems in a new coding manual for the Nepal Irrigation and Institutions (NIIS) project. We coded existing cases and again found numerous "missing variables" not discussed by the original author. Colleagues made several trips to Nepal to visit previously described systems in written case studies to fill in missing data and verify the data in the original study. While in the field, we were able to add new cases to the data set (Benjamin et al. 1994).

In undertaking analysis of this large dataset, Wai Fung Lam (1998) developed three performance measures that could be applied to all systems: (i) the physical condition of irrigation systems, (ii) the quantity of water available to farmers at the tail end of a system at different seasons of the year, and (iii) the agricultural productivity of the systems. Controlling for environmental differences among systems, Lam found that irrigation systems governed by the farmers themselves perform significantly better on all three performance measures. On the farmer governed systems, farmers communicate with one another at annual meetings and informally on a regular basis, develop their own agreements, establish the positions of monitors, and sanction those who do not conform to their own rules. Consequently, farmer managed systems are likely to grow more rice, distribute water more equitably, and keep their systems in better repair than government systems. While farmer systems do vary in performance, few perform as poorly as government systems—holding other relevant variables constant.

372 E. Ostrom

Over time, colleagues have visited and coded still further irrigation systems in Nepal. The earlier findings regarding the higher level of performance of farmer managed systems was again confirmed using the expanded database containing 229 irrigation systems (Neeraj N. Joshi et al. 2000; Shivakoti and E. Ostrom 2002). Our findings are not unique to Nepal. Scholars have carefully documented effective farmer designed and operated systems in many countries including Japan (Masahiko Aoki 2001), India (Ruth Meinzen-Dick 2007; Pranab K. Bardhan 2000), and Sri Lanka (Norman T. Uphoff 1991).

Studying forests around the world

In 1992, Dr. Marilyn Hoskins, who headed the Forest, Trees and People Program at the Food and Agriculture Organization (FAO) of the United Nations, asked colleagues at the Workshop to draw on our experience in studying irrigation systems to develop methods for assessing the impact of diverse forest governance arrangements in multiple countries. Two years of intense development and review by ecologists and social scientists around the world led to the development of ten research protocols to obtain reliable information about users and forest governance as well as about the ecological conditions of sampled forests. A long term collaborative research network—the International Forestry Resources and Institutions (IFRI) research program—was established with centers now located in Bolivia, Colombia, Guatemala, India, Kenya, Mexico, Nepal, Tanzania, Thailand, Uganda, and the United States, with new centers being established in Ethiopia and China (see Clark Gibson, Margaret McKean, and E. Ostrom 2000; Poteete and E. Ostrom 2004; Eva Wollenberg et al. 2007). IFRI is unique among efforts to study forests as it is the only interdisciplinary long term monitoring and research program studying forests in multiple countries owned by governments, private organizations, and communities.

Forests are a particularly important form of common-pool resource given their role in climate change–related emissions and carbon sequestration (Josep G. Canadell and Michael R. Raupach 2008), the biodiversity they contain, and their contribution to rural livelihoods in developing countries. A "favorite" policy recommendation for protecting forests and biodiversity is government owned protected areas (J. Terborgh 1999). In an effort to examine whether government ownership of protected areas is a necessary condition for improving forest density, Tanya Hayes (2006) used IFRI data to compare the rating of forest density (on a five point scale) assigned to a forest by the forester or ecologist who had supervised the forest mensuration of trees, shrubs, and groundcover in a random sample of forest plots.[9] Of the 163 forests included in the analysis, 76 were government owned forests *legally designated* as *protected forests* and 87 were public, private, or communally owned forested lands used for a diversity of purposes. No statistical difference existed between the forest density in officially designated protected areas versus other forested areas. Gibson, John Williams, and E. Ostrom (2005) examined the monitoring behavior of 178 forest user groups and found a strong correlation

Beyond markets and states **373**

between the level of monitoring and a forester's assessment of forest density even when controlling for whether users were formally organized, whether the users were heavily dependent on a forest, and the level of social capital within a group.

Ashwini Chhatre and Arun Agrawal (2008) have now examined the changes in the condition of 152 forests under diverse governance arrangements as affected by the size of the forest, collective action around forests related to improvement activities, size of the user group, and the dependence of local users on a forest. They found that "forests with a higher probability of regeneration are likely to be small to medium in size with low levels of subsistence dependence, low commercial value, high levels of local enforcement, and strong collective action for improving the quality of the forest" (ibid.: 1327). In a second major analysis, Chhatre and Agrawal (2009) focus on factors that affect tradeoffs and synergies between the level of carbon storage in forests and their contributions to livelihoods. They find that larger forests are more effective in enhancing both carbon and livelihoods outcomes, particularly when local communities also have high levels of rule-making autonomy. Recent studies by Eric Coleman (2009) and Coleman and Brian Steed (2009) also find that a major variable affecting forest conditions is the investment by local users in monitoring. Further, when local users are given harvesting rights, they are more likely to monitor illegal uses themselves. Other focused studies also stress the relationship between local monitoring and better forest conditions (Rucha Ghate and Harini Nagendra 2005; E. Ostrom and Nagendra 2006; Abwoli Y. Banana and William Gombya-Ssembajjwe 2000; Edward Webb and Shivakoti 2008).

The legal designation of a forest as a protected area is *not* by itself related to forest density. Detailed field studies of monitoring and enforcement as they are conducted on the ground, however, illustrate the challenge of achieving high levels of forest regrowth without active involvement of local forest users (see Mateus Batistella, Scott Robeson, and Emilio F. Moran 2003; Agrawal 2005; Andersson, Gibson, and Fabrice Lehoucq 2006; Catherine M. Tucker 2008). Our research shows that forests under different property regimes—government, private, communal—sometimes meet enhanced social goals such as biodiversity protection, carbon storage, or improved livelihoods. At other times, these property regimes fail to provide such goals. Indeed, when governments adopt top-down decentralization policies leaving local officials and users in the dark, stable forests may become subject to deforestation (Banana et al. 2007). Thus, it is not the general type of forest governance that is crucial in explaining forest conditions; rather, it is how a particular governance arrangement fits the local ecology, how specific rules are developed and adapted over time, and whether users consider the system to be legitimate and equitable (for a more detailed overview of the IFRI research program, see Poteete, Janssen, and E. Ostrom 2010: chap. 5).

Current theoretical developments

Given the half century of our own extensive empirical research and that of many distinguished scholars (e.g., Jean-Marie Baland and Jean-Philippe Platteau 2005;

374 E. Ostrom

Fikret Berkes 2007; Berkes, Johan Colding, and Carl Folke 2003; Colin W. Clark 2006; Graham R. Marshall 2008; Thomas C. Schelling 1960, 1978, 1984), where are we now? What have we learned? We now know that the earlier theories of rational, but helpless, individuals who are trapped in social dilemmas are not supported by a large number of studies using diverse methods (Nicolas Faysse 2005; Poteete, Janssen, and E. Ostrom 2010). On the other hand, we cannot be overly optimistic and presume that dilemmas will always be solved by those involved. Many groups have struggled and failed (Tom Dietz, E. Ostrom, and Paul Stern 2003). Further, simple policy prescriptions to turn over resources to a government, to privatize, or more recently to decentralize, may also fail (Berkes 2007; William A. Brock and Stephen R. Carpenter 2007; Meinzen-Dick 2007).

We thus face the tough task of further developing our theories to help understand and predict when those involved in a common-pool resource dilemma will be able to self-organize and how various aspects of the broad context they face affect their strategies, the short term success of their efforts, and the long term robustness of their initial achievements. We need to develop a better theoretical understanding of human behavior as well as of the impact of the diverse contexts that humans face.

Developing a more general theory of the individual

As discussed earlier in Section III, efforts to explain phenomena in the social world are organized at three levels of generality. Frameworks, such as the IAD that have been used to organize diverse efforts to study common-pool resources, are metatheoretical devices that help provide a general language for describing relationships at multiple levels and scales. Theories are efforts to build understanding by making core assumptions about specific working parts of frequently encountered phenomena and predicting general outcomes. Models are very specific working examples of a theory—and they are frequently confused with being theories themselves. As Alchian (1950) pointed out long ago, what is called "rational choice theory" is not a broad *theory* of human behavior but rather a useful *model* to predict behavior in a particular situation—a highly competitive market for private goods. Predictions derived from the rational choice model are empirically supported in open markets for private goods and other competitive environments (Charles A. Holt 2007; Vernon L. Smith and Walker 1993; Debra Satz and John Ferejohn 1994). Thus, it is a useful model to retain for predicting outcomes in competitive settings related to excludable and divisible outcomes.

While it is not possible yet to point to a single *theory* of human behavior that has been successfully formulated and tested in a variety of settings, scholars are currently positing and testing assumptions that are likely to be at the core of future developments (Smith 2003, 2010). These relate to (i) the capability of boundedly rational individuals to learn fuller and more reliable information in repeated situations when reliable feedback is present, (ii) the use of heuristics in making daily decisions, and (iii) the preferences that individuals have related to benefits for self as well as norms

Beyond markets and states **375**

and preferences related to benefits for others (see Poteete, Janssen, and E. Ostrom 2010: chap. 9; E. Ostrom 1998).

The assumption that individuals have complete information about all actions available to them, the likely strategies that others will adopt, and the probabilities of specific consequences that will result from their own choices must be rejected in any but the very simplest of repeated settings. When boundedly rational individuals do interact over time, it is reasonable to assume that they learn more accurate information about the actions they can take and the likely actions of other individuals (Selten 1990; Simon 1955, 1999). Some highly complex common-pool resource environments, however, approach mathematical chaos (J. Wilson et al. 1994) in which resource users cannot gain complete information about all likely combinations of future events.

In many situations, individuals use rules of thumb—heuristics—that they have learned over time that work relatively well in a particular setting. Fishers end up "fishing for knowledge" (J. Wilson 1990) where using heuristics over time enables them to recognize diverse clues of environmental processes that they need to take into account when making their own decisions. When individuals do interact repeatedly, it is possible to learn heuristics that approach "best response" strategies and achieve close to local optima (Gerd Gigerenzer and Selten 2001). In eras of rapid change or sudden shocks, however, heuristics may not enable individuals to achieve high payoffs.

Individuals also learn norms—internal valuations that are negative or positive related to specific actions such as lying or being brave in particular situations (Crawford and E. Ostrom 2005). The strength of an internal commitment (Amartya K. Sen 1977) may be represented in the size of the internal weight that an individual assigns to actions and outcomes in a particular setting. Among individual norms are those related to valuing outcomes achieved by others (James Cox and Cary Deck 2005; J. Cox, Klarita Sadiraj, and Vjollca Sadiraj 2008; James Andreoni 1989; Gary E. Bolton and Axel Ockenfels 2000). Fehr and Klaus Schmidt (1999) propose that individuals dislike unequal outcomes of interactions and thus have an internal norm

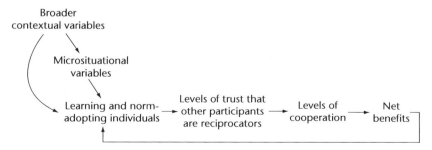

FIGURE 17.5. Microsituational and broader contexts of social dilemmas affect levels of trust and cooperation

Source: Poteete, Janssen, and Ostrom 2010: 227.

376 E. Ostrom

of "inequity aversion." Robert Axelrod (1986) posits that individuals who adopt meta norms related to whether others follow the norms that have evolved in a group increase the probability that norms will be followed. Leibbrandt, Uri Gneezy, and John List (2010) show that individuals who regularly work in teams are more likely to adopt norms and trust each other more than individuals working alone. Norman Frohlich and Joe A. Oppenheimer (1992) posit that many individuals adopt norms of fairness and justice. Not all individuals have the same norms or perceptions of a situation (Umut Ones and Louis Putterman 2007) and may differ substantially in whether they consider a way of sharing costs to be fair (Catherine Eckel and Philip J. Grossman 1996).

Simply assuming that humans adopt norms, however, is not sufficient to predict behavior in a social dilemma, especially in very large groups with no arrangements for communication. Even with strong preferences to follow norms, "observed behavior may vary by context because the perception of the 'right thing' would change" (Angela de Oliveira, Rachel Croson, and Eckel 2009: 19). Various aspects of the context in which individuals interact affect how individuals learn about the situation they are in and about the others with whom they are interacting. Individual differences do make a difference, but the context of interactions also affects behavior over time (Walker and E. Ostrom 2009). Biologists recognize that an organism's appearance and behavior are affected by the environment in which it develops.

> *For example, some plants produce large, thin leaves (which enhance photosynthetic photon harvest) in low light, and narrow, thicker leaves (which conserve water) in high light; certain insects develop wings only if they live in crowded conditions (and hence are likely to run out of adequate food in their current location). Such environmentally contingent development is so commonplace that it can be regarded as a universal property of living things.*
>
> —*(David W. Pfennig and Cris Ledón-Rettig 2009: 268)*

Social scientists also need to recognize that individual behavior is strongly affected by the context in which interactions take place rather than being simply a result of individual differences.

The central role of trust in coping with dilemmas

Even though Kenneth J. Arrow (1974) long ago pointed to the crucial role of trust among participants as the most efficient mechanism to enhance transactional outcomes, collective action theory has paid more attention to payoff functions than to how individuals build trust that others are reciprocators of costly cooperative efforts. Empirical studies, however, confirm the important role of trust in overcoming social dilemmas (Bo Rothstein 2005). As illustrated in Figure 17.5, the updated theoretical assumptions of learning and norm-adopting individuals can be used as the foundation for understanding how individuals may gain increased levels of trust

Beyond markets and states **377**

in others, leading to more cooperation and higher benefits with feedback mechanisms that reinforce positive or negative learning. Thus, it is not only that individuals adopt norms but also that the structure of the situation generates sufficient information about the likely behavior of others to be trustworthy reciprocators who will bear their share of the costs of overcoming a dilemma. Thus, in some contexts, one can move beyond the presumption that rational individuals are helpless in overcoming social dilemma situations.

The microsituational level of analysis

Asserting that context makes a difference in building or destroying trust and reciprocity is not a sufficient theoretical answer to how and why individuals sometimes solve and sometimes fail to solve dilemmas. Individuals interacting in a dilemma situation face two contexts: (i) a microcontext related to the specific attributes of an action situation in which individuals are directly interacting and (ii) the broader context of the social-ecological system in which groups of individuals make decisions. A major advantage of studies conducted in an experimental lab or in field experiments is that the researcher designs the micro setting in which the experiment is conducted. Thus, empirical results are growing (and are summarized in Poteete, Janssen, and E. Ostrom 2010) to establish that the following attributes of microsituations affect the level of cooperation that participants achieve in social dilemma settings (including both public goods and common-pool resource dilemmas).

(i) Communication is feasible with the full set of participants. When face-to-face communication is possible, participants use facial expressions, physical actions, and the way that words are expressed to judge the trustworthiness of the others involved.

(ii) Reputations of participants are known. Knowing the past history of other participants, who may not be personally known prior to interaction, increases the likelihood of cooperation.

(iii) High marginal per capita return (MPCR). When MPCR is high, each participant can know that their own contributions make a bigger difference than with low MPCR, and that others are more likely to recognize this relationship.

(iv) Entry or exit capabilities. If participants can exit a situation at low cost, this gives them an opportunity not to be a sucker, and others can recognize that cooperators may leave (and enter other situations) if their cooperation is not reciprocated.

(v) Longer time horizon. Participants can anticipate that more could be earned through cooperation over a long time period versus a short time.

(vi) Agreed-upon sanctioning capabilities. While external sanctions or imposed sanctioning systems may reduce cooperation, when participants themselves agree to a sanctioning system they frequently do not need to use sanctions at a high volume, and net benefits can be improved substantially.

Other microsituational variables are being tested in experiments around the world. The central core of the findings is that when individuals face a social dilemma in a microsetting, they are more likely to cooperate when situational variables increase the likelihood of gaining trust that others will reciprocate.

The broader context in the field

Individuals coping with common-pool resource dilemmas in the field are also affected by a broader set of contextual variables related to the attributes of the social-ecological system (SES) in which they are interacting. A group of scholars in Europe and the United States are currently working on the further development of a framework that links the IAD and its interactions and outcomes at a micro level with a broader set of variables observed in the field.[10] As illustrated in Figure 17.6, one can think of individuals interacting in an Action Situation generating Interactions and Outcomes that are affected by and affect a Resource System, Resource Units, Governance System, and Users who affect and are affected by Social, Economic, and Political Settings, and Related Ecosystems (see E. Ostrom 2007, 2009). Figure 17.6 provides an overview of the highest tier of variables that exist in all field settings. The highest tier can be unpacked several times when one is trying to analyze specific questions related to SESs in the field, but there is not enough time or space to undertake a thorough unpacking in this article.

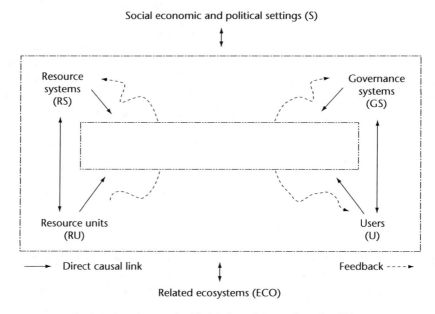

FIGURE 17.6. Action situations embedded in broader social–ecological systems
Source: Adapted from E. Ostrom 2007: 15182.

Experimental researchers have reached a higher level of agreement about the impact of microsituational variables on the incentives, levels of trust, and behavior of individuals in dilemma situations than exists among field researchers. Few SES variables have a fully independent impact on the action situations that participants face and their likely behavior. The SES variables that are most important differ depending on which interactions (such as monitoring, conflict, lobbying, self-organization) or longer term outcomes (such as overharvesting, regeneration of biodiversity, resilience of an ecological system to human and nature induced disturbances) one wishes to predict. A set of ten variables have been identified across many field studies as impacting the likelihood of users self-organizing in order to overcome a common-pool resource dilemma (E. Ostrom 2009; Basurto and E. Ostrom 2009). These include: the size, productivity, and predictability of the resource system, the extent of mobility of the resource units, the existence of collective choice rules that the users may adopt authoritatively in order to change their own operational rules, and four attributes of users (the number, the existence of leadership/entrepreneurship, knowledge about the SES, and the importance of the SES to the users). Linking the broader contextual variables and microcontextual variables is one of the major tasks facing scientists who work across disciplinary lines to understand how both social and ecological factors affect human behavior.[11]

Complexity and reform

The economic and social sciences have significantly moved ahead over the past five decades since scholars posited two optimal organizational forms, two types of goods, and one model of the individual. Extensive empirical research documents the diversity of settings in which individuals solve common-pool resource problems on their own, when these solutions are sustainable over long periods of time, and how larger institutional arrangements enhance or detract from the capabilities of individuals at smaller scales to solve problems efficiently and sustainably (see, for example, Agrawal and Gibson 2001; Gibson et al. 2005; Schlager and Blomquist 2008). While there is not yet a single well developed theory that explains all of the diverse outcomes obtained in microsettings, such as the experimental lab, or broader contextual settings of fisheries, irrigation systems, forests, lakes, and other common-pool resources, considerable agreement does exist. Nor do we have a single normative theory of justice that can unambiguously be applied to all settings (Sen 2009).

Building trust in one another and developing institutional rules that are well matched to the ecological systems being used are of central importance for solving social dilemmas. The surprising but repeated finding that users of resources that are in relatively good condition—or even improving—do invest in various ways of monitoring one another relates to the core problem of building trust.

Unfortunately, policy analysts, public officials, and scholars who still apply simple mathematical models to the analysis of field settings have not yet absorbed the central lessons articulated here. All too often a single policy prescription—such as Individual

380 E. Ostrom

Transferable Quotas (ITQs)—is recommended for all resources of a particular type, such as all fisheries. While several ITQ systems are working successfully, the time and effort needed to tailor the broad theoretical concept of an ITQ system into an operational system in a particular location involves multiple years of hard work by the fishers involved as well as the government officials (see Clark 2006; Tracy Yandle 2007; Yandle and Christopher Dewees 2003; Thráinn Eggertsson 1990).

Other scholars propose government-owned protected areas as the "only" way to ensure that biodiversity is protected around the world (Terborgh 1999). Careful studies of protected areas have found, however, that the frequent eviction of indigenous peoples who had lived in a region for multiple centuries prior to the establishment of the park in their territory has not produced the positive results expected. Using remote sensing, Jianguo Liu et al. (2001) assessed that the rate of loss and fragmentation of high quality habitat after the Wolong Nature Reserve was established in southwestern China was much higher than before the reserve was created. Daniel Brockington and James Igoe (2006) reviewed 250 reports on protected areas and the level of evictions from them and conclude that "forced relocation inflicts considerable material and psychological harm. But it is not just damaging for its material effects, rather for the reshaping of landscape and memory it imposes" (ibid.: 246). David Barton Bray and colleagues (2004) made a detailed study of another type of reform that created a forested landscape that was inhabited and productively used. Using Landsat images, they found a very "low incidence of net deforestation, 0.01% for the 1984–2000 period, the lowest recorded deforestation rate for southeastern Mexico" (ibid.: 333) based on a reform that created common property institutions.

A positive development of recent research is that more scholars are carefully assessing diverse policies adopted for the governance of common-pool resources (Brian R. Copeland and M. Scott Taylor 2009). In light of a comparative study of private, community, and state governed common-pool resources, R. Quentin Grafton (2000) found each to be successful when well matched to local settings and involving the active participation of local users.

> *Each is capable of preventing resource degradation and ensuring the on-going flow of benefits to resource users. A comparison of the bundle of rights of the three regimes suggests that a common factor in ensuring successful governance of CPRs is the active participation of resource users in the management of the flow of benefits from the resources.*
>
> —*(Grafton 2000: 515)*

Jeremy S. Brooks et al. (2006) reviewed data generated by 124 conservation projects and found that allowing local users to harvest and sell some products and involving communities in the design and administration of a project were all important factors for successful outcomes. Moving away from the presumption that *the* government must solve all common-pool resource problems while recognizing the important role of governments is a big step forward. Hopefully, in the future,

Beyond markets and states **381**

more national officials will learn to work with local and regional officials, non-governmental organizations, and local groups of citizens.

The most important lesson for public policy analysis derived from the intellectual journey I have outlined here is that humans have a more complex motivational structure and more capability to solve social dilemmas than posited in earlier rational-choice theory. Designing institutions to force (or nudge) entirely self-interested individuals to achieve better outcomes has been the major goal posited by policy analysts for governments to accomplish for much of the past half century. Extensive empirical research leads me to argue that instead, a core goal of public policy should be to facilitate the development of institutions that bring out the best in humans. We need to ask how diverse polycentric institutions help or hinder the innovativeness, learning, adapting, trustworthiness, levels of cooperation of participants, and the achievement of more effective, equitable, and sustainable outcomes at multiple scales (Theo Toonen 2010).

To explain the world of interactions and outcomes occurring at multiple levels, we also have to be willing to deal with complexity instead of rejecting it. Some mathematical models are very useful for explaining outcomes in particular settings. We should continue to use simple models where they capture enough of the core underlying structure and incentives that they usefully predict outcomes. When the world we are trying to explain and improve, however, is not well described by a simple model, we must continue to improve our frameworks and theories so as to be able to understand complexity and not simply reject it.

Notes

† This article is a revised version of the lecture Elinor Ostrom delivered in Stockholm, Sweden, on December 8, 2009, when she received the Bank of Sweden Prize in Economic Sciences in Memory of Alfred Nobel. This article is copyright © The Nobel Foundation 2009 and is published here with the permission of the Nobel Foundation.

★ Ostrom: Workshop in Political Theory and Policy Analysis, Indiana University, Bloomington, IN 47408 (e-mail: ostrom@indiana.edu) and Center for the Study of Institutional Diversity, Arizona State University, Tempe, AZ. I wish to thank Vincent Ostrom and my many colleagues at the Workshop who have worked with me throughout the years to develop the research program that is briefly discussed herein. I appreciate the helpful suggestions given me by Arun Agrawal, Andreas Leibbrandt, Mike McGinnis, Jimmy Walker, Tom Wisdom, and by the Applied Theory Working Group and the Experimental Reading Group, and the excellent editing skills of Patty Lezotte. Essential support received over the years from the Ford Foundation, the MacArthur Foundation, and the National Science Foundation is gratefully acknowledged.

1 I am much appreciative of the many hours of productive discussions that I had with Reinhard Selten in the early 1980s as we started to develop the IAD framework about the internal working parts of a formal game that could be used in the framework.

2 This meta-analysis effort is described in chapter 4 of Amy Poteete, Janssen, and E. Ostrom (2010).

3 Scholars across disciplines tend to use very different vocabularies and theoretical frameworks when they describe empirical settings. Other scholars, who have used meta-analysis, have also needed to screen many publications to obtain consistent data about human-used resource systems. Adcharaporn Pagdee, Yeon-Su Kim, and P.J. Daugherty

382 E. Ostrom

(2006) report screening over 100 articles in order to analyze 31 cases related to forest management. Thomas K. Rudel (2008) reported that he had screened nearly 1,200 studies for a meta-analysis of 268 cases of tropical forest cover change.

4 The concept of access rights has puzzled some scholars. An everyday example of an access right is the buying of a permit to enter a public park. This assigns the holder of a permit the right to enter and enjoy hiking and other nonharvesting activities for a defined period of time.

5 The term "design principle" has confused many readers. Perhaps I should have used the term "best practices" to describe the rules and structure of robust institutions.

6 In simple, repeated public goods experiments, subjects initially tended to contribute at a higher level than predicted by the Nash equilibrium (R. Mark Isaac et al. 1984, 1985, 1994; Isaac and Walker 1988; Gerald Marwell and Ruth E. Ames 1979) and outcomes slowly approach the predicted Nash equilibrium from a higher level. In common-pool resource games, on the other hand, subjects initially achieved outcomes that were much worse than the Nash equilibrium that they then slowly approached from below (see also Marco Casari and Charles R. Plott 2003).

7 See Joseph Henrich et al. (2006) in which field experiments were conducted in multiple countries testing whether a much broader set of participants would also use punishments in public goods experiments. See also Henrich et al. (2004) for the reports of earlier field experiments of social dilemmas in 15 small communities.

8 Similar findings exist for public goods experiments where punishers typically punish low contributors (Toshio Yamagishi 1986; Ernst Fehr and Simon Gächter 2002).

9 Extensive forest mensuration is conducted at every IFRI site at the same time that information is obtained about forest users, their activities and organization, and about governance arrangements. Comparing forest measures across ecological zones is misleading since the average diameter at breast height in a forest is strongly affected by precipitation, soils, elevation, and other factors that vary dramatically across ecological zones. Thus, we ask the forester or ecologist who has just supervised the collection of forest data to rate the forest on a five point scale from very sparse to very abundant.

10 Scholars at the Stockholm Environment Institute, the International Institute for Applied Systems Analysis, Delft University of Technology, the University of Zurich, the Nordland Research Institute of Bodø University College, the Potsdam Institute for Climate Impact Research (PIK), Humboldt University, Marburg University, and the EU NeWATER project located at the University of Osnabrück have had several meetings in Europe to begin plans for using a common framework (initially developed by E. Ostrom 2007) to study a variety of resource systems. Scholars at the Workshop in Bloomington and the Center for the Study of Institutional Diversity at Arizona State University will also participate in this effort. A core problem identified by these scholars is the lack of cumulation across studies on diverse natural resource systems as well as humanly engineered resources.

11 See James I. Stewart (2009) for an important study that links size of group, acceptance of norms of cooperation, and support of property rights in 25 mining camps in the American Southwest.

References

Acheson, James M., and Roy Gardner. 2005. "Spatial Strategies and Territoriality in the Maine Lobster Industry." *Rationality and Society*, 17(3): 309–41.

Agrawal, Arun. 2005. *Environmentality: Technologies of Government and the Making of Subjects*. Durham, NC: Duke University Press.

Agrawal, Arun, and Clark Gibson, ed. 2001. *Communities and the Environment: Ethnicity, Gender, and the State in Community-Based Conservation*. New Brunswick, NJ: Rutgers University Press.

Beyond markets and states **383**

Alchian, Armen A. 1950. "Uncertainty, Evolution, and Economic Theory." *Journal of Political Economy*, 58(3): 211–21.

Alchian, Armen A., and Harold Demsetz. 1973. "The Property Rights Paradigm." *Journal of Economic History*, 33(1): 16–27.

Allport, Floyd H. 1962. "A Structuronomic Conception of Behavior: Individual and Collective." *Journal of Abnormal and Social Psychology*, 64(1): 3–30.

Anderson, Terry L., and Peter J. Hill. 1990. "The Race for Property Rights." *Journal of Law and Economics*, 33(1): 177–97.

Anderson, William, and Edward W. Weidner. 1950. *American City Government*. New York: Henry Holt.

Andersson, Krister P., and Elinor Ostrom. 2008. "Analyzing Decentralized Resource Regimes from a Polycentric Perspective." *Policy Sciences*, 41(1): 71–93.

Andersson, Krister P., Clark C. Gibson, and Fabrice Lehoucq. 2006. "Municipal Politics and Forest Governance: Comparative Analysis of Decentralization in Bolivia and Guatemala." *World Development*, 34(3): 576–95.

Andreoni, James. 1989. "Giving with Impure Altruism: Applications to Charity and Ricardian Equivalence." *Journal of Political Economy*, 97(6): 1447–58.

Aoki, Masahiko. 2001. *Toward a Comparative Institutional Analysis*. Cambridge, MA: MIT Press.

Arrow, Kenneth J. 1974. *The Limits of Organization*. New York: Norton.

Axelrod, Robert. 1986. "An Evolutionary Approach to Norms." *American Political Science Review*, 80(4): 1095–111.

Bain, Joe S. 1959. *Industrial Organization*. New York: Wiley.

Baland, Jean-Marie, and Jean-Philippe Platteau. 2005. *Halting Degradation of Natural Resources: Is There a Role for Rural Communities?* Oxford: Clarendon Press.

Balliet, Daniel. 2010. "Communication and Cooperation in Social Dilemmas: A Meta-Analytic Review." *Journal of Conflict Resolution*, 54(1): 39–57.

Banana, Abwoli Y., and William Gombya-Ssembajjwe. 2000. "Successful Forest Management: The Importance of Security of Tenure and Rule Enforcement in Ugandan Forests." In *People and Forests: Communities, Institutions, and Governance*, ed. Clark C. Gibson, Margaret A. McKean, and Elinor Ostrom, 87–98. Cambridge, MA: MIT Press.

Banana, Abwoli, Nathan D. Vogt, Joseph Bahati, and William Gombya-Ssembajjwe. 2007. "Decentralized Governance and Ecological Health: Why Local Institutions Fail to Moderate Deforestation in Mpigi District of Uganda." *Scientific Research and Essays*, 2(10): 434–45.

Bardhan, Pranab. 2000. "Irrigation and Cooperation: An Empirical Analysis of 48 Irrigation Communities in South India." *Economic Development and Cultural Change*, 48(4): 847–65.

Basurto, Xavier, and Elinor Ostrom. 2009. "Beyond the Tragedy of the Commons." *Economia delle fonti di energia e dell'ambiente*, 52(1): 35–60.

Batistella, Mateus, Scott Robeson, and Emilio F. Moran. 2003. "Settlement Design, Forest Fragmentation, and Landscape Change in Rondônia, Amazônia." *Photogrammetric Engineering and Remote Sensing*, 69(7): 805–12.

Bell, Frederick W. 1972. "Technological Externalities and Common-Property Resources: An Empirical Study of the U.S. Northern Lobster Fishery." *Journal of Political Economy*, 80(1): 148–58.

Benjamin, Paul, Wai Fung Lam, Elinor Ostrom, and Ganesh Shivakoti. 1994. *Institutions, Incentives, and Irrigation in Nepal*. Burlington, VT: Associates in Rural Development.

Berkes, Fikret. 2007. "Community-Based Conservation in a Globalized World." *Proceedings of the National Academy of Sciences*, 104(39): 15188–93.

384 E. Ostrom

Berkes, Fikret, Johan Colding, and Carl Folke. 2003. *Navigating Social-Ecological Systems: Building Resilience for Complexity and Change.* Cambridge, UK: Cambridge University Press.

Blomquist, William, Edella Schlager, Shui Yan Tang, and Elinor Ostrom. 1994. "Regularities from the Field and Possible Explanations." In *Rules, Games, and Common-Pool Resources,* ed. Elinor Ostrom, Roy Gardner, and James Walker, 301–18. Ann Arbor, MI: University of Michigan Press.

Bolton, Gary E., and Axel Ockenfels. 2000. "ERC: A Theory of Equity, Reciprocity, and Competition." *American Economic Review,* 90(1): 166–93.

Boyd, Robert, and Peter J. Richerson. 1985. *Culture and the Evolutionary Process.* Chicago: University of Chicago Press.

Bray, David Barton, Edward A. Ellis, Natalia Armijo-Canto, and Christopher T. Beck. 2004. "The Institutional Drivers of Sustainable Landscapes: A Case Study of the 'Mayan Zone' in Quintana Roo, Mexico." *Land Use Policy,* 21(4): 333–46.

Brock, William A., and Stephen R. Carpenter. 2007. "Panaceas and Diversification of Environmental Policy." *Proceedings of the National Academy of Sciences,* 104(39): 15206–11.

Brockington, Daniel, and James Igoe. 2006. "Eviction for Conservation: A Global Overview." *Conservation and Society,* 4(3): 424–70.

Bromley, Daniel W. 1986. "Closing Comments at the Conference on Common Property Resource Management." In *Proceedings of the Conference on Common Property Resource Management,* 591–98. Washington, DC: National Academies Press.

Brooks, Jeremy S., Margaret A. Franzen, Christopher M. Holmes, Mark N. Grote, and Monique Borgerhoff Mulder. 2006. "Testing Hypotheses for the Success of Different Conservation Strategies." *Conservation Biology,* 20(5): 1528–38.

Brunckhorst, David J. 2000. *Bioregional Planning: Resource Management beyond the New Millennium.* Amsterdam: Harwood Academic.

Buchanan, James M. 1965. "An Economic Theory of Clubs." *Economica,* 32(125): 1–14.

Canadell, Josep G., and Michael R. Raupach. 2008. "Managing Forests for Climate Change Mitigation." *Science,* 320(5882): 1456–57.

Cardenas, Juan-Camilo. 2000. "How Do Groups Solve Local Commons Dilemmas? Lessons from Experimental Economics in the Field." *Environment, Development and Sustainability,* 2(3–4): 305–22.

Cardenas, Juan-Camilo, John Stranlund, and Cleve Willis. 2000. "Local Environmental Control and Institutional Crowding-Out." *World Development,* 28(10): 1719–33.

Casari, Marco, and Charles R. Plott. 2003. "Decentralized Management of Common Property Resources: Experiments with a Centuries-Old Institution." *Journal of Economic Behavior and Organization,* 51(2): 217–47.

Caves, Richard. 1964. *American Industry: Structure, Conduct, Performance.* Englewood Cliffs, NJ: Prentice-Hall.

Chhatre, Ashwini, and Arun Agrawal. 2008. "Forest Commons and Local Enforcement." *Proceedings of the National Academy of Sciences,* 105(36): 13286–91.

Chhatre, Ashwini, and Arun Agrawal. 2009. "Trade-offs and Synergies between Carbon Storage and Livelihood Benefits from Forest Commons." *Proceedings of the National Academy of Sciences,* 106(42): 17667–70.

Ciriacy-Wantrup, S. V., and Richard C. Bishop. 1975. " 'Common Property' as a Concept in Natural Resources Policy." *Natural Resources Journal,* 15(4): 713–27.

Clark, Colin W. 2006. *The Worldwide Crisis in Fisheries: Economic Models and Human Behavior.* Cambridge, UK: Cambridge University Press.

Coleman, Eric A. 2009. "Institutional Factors Affecting Biophysical Outcomes in Forest Management." *Journal of Policy Analysis and Management,* 28(1): 122–46.

Coleman, Eric A., and Brian C. Steed. 2009. "Monitoring and Sanctioning in the Commons: An Application to Forestry." *Ecological Economics*, 68(7): 2106–13.

Commons, John R. 1968. *Legal Foundations of Capitalism.* Madison, WI: University of Wisconsin Press. (Orig. Pub. 1924).

Copeland, Brian R., and M. Scott Taylor. 2009. "Trade, Tragedy, and the Commons." *American Economic Review*, 99(3): 725–49.

Coward, E. Walter. 1980. *Irrigation and Agricultural Development in Asia.* Ithaca, NY: Cornell University Press.

Cox, James C., and Cary A. Deck. 2005. "On the Nature of Reciprocal Motives." *Economic Inquiry*, 43(3): 623–35.

Cox, James C., Klarita Sadiraj, and Vjollca Sadiraj. 2008. "Implications of Trust, Fear, and Reciprocity for Modeling Economic Behavior." *Experimental Economics*, 11(1): 1–24.

Cox, Michael, Gwen Arnold, and Sergio Villamayor-Tomás. 2009. "A Review and Reassessment of Design Principles for Community-Based Natural Resource Management." Unpublished.

Crawford, Sue E. S., and Elinor Ostrom. 2005. "A Grammar of Institutions." In *Understanding Institutional Diversity*, 137–74. Princeton, NJ: Princeton University Press.

Degnbol, Poul, and Bonnie J. McCay. 2007. "Unintended and Perverse Consequences of Ignoring Linkages in Fisheries Systems." *ICES Journal of Marine Science*, 64(4): 793–97.

de Oliveira, Angela C. M., Rachel T. A. Croson, and Catherine Eckel. 2009. "Are Preferences Stable across Domains? An Experimental Investigation of Social Preferences in the Field." CBEES Working Paper 2008–3.

Dietz, Thomas, Elinor Ostrom, and Paul C. Stern. 2003. "The Struggle to Govern the Commons." *Science*, 302(5652): 1907–12.

Dutta, Prajit K. 1999. *Strategies and Games: Theory and Practice.* Cambridge, MA: MIT Press.

Eckel, Catherine C., and Philip J. Grossman. 1996. "The Relative Price of Fairness: Gender Differences in a Punishment Game." *Journal of Economic Behavior and Organization*, 30(2): 143–58.

Eggertsson, Thrainn. 1990. *Economic Behavior and Institutions.* Cambridge, UK: Cambridge University Press.

Elster, Jon. 1989. *Solomonic Judgements: Studies in the Limitations of Rationality.* Cambridge, UK: Cambridge University Press.

Faysse, Nicolas. 2005. "Coping with the Tragedy of the Commons: Game Structure and Design of Rules." *Journal of Economic Surveys*, 19(2): 239–61.

Fehr, Ernst, and Simon Gächter. 2002. "Altruistic Punishment in Humans." *Nature*, 415(6868): 137–40.

Fehr, Ernst, and Andreas Leibbrandt. 2008. "Cooperativeness and Impatience in the Tragedy of the Commons." IZA Discussion Paper 3625.

Fehr, Ernst, and Klaus M. Schmidt. 1999. "A Theory of Fairness, Competition, and Cooperation." *Quarterly Journal of Economics*, 114(3): 817–68.

Frey, Bruno S., and Felix Oberholzer-Gee. 1997. "The Cost of Price Incentives: An Empirical Analysis of Motivation Crowding-Out." *American Economic Review*, 87(4): 746–55.

Friesema, H. Paul. 1966. "The Metropolis and the Maze of Local Government." *Urban Affairs Review*, 2(2): 68–90.

Frohlich, Norman, and Joe A. Oppenheimer. 1992. *Choosing Justice: An Experimental Approach to Ethical Theory.* Berkeley, CA: University of California Press.

386 E. Ostrom

Gardner, Roy, Andrew Herr, Elinor Ostrom, and James A. Walker. 2000. "The Power and Limitations of Proportional Cutbacks in Common-Pool Resources." *Journal of Development Economics*, 62(2): 515–33.

Ghate, Rucha, and Harini Nagendra. 2005. "Role of Monitoring in Institutional Performance: Forest Management in Maharashtra, India." *Conservation and Society*, 3(2): 509–32.

Gibson, Clark C., Margaret McKean, and Elinor Ostrom, ed. 2000. *People and Forests: Communities, Institutions, and Governance*. Cambridge, MA: MIT Press.

Gibson, Clark C., John T. Williams, and Elinor Ostrom. 2005. "Local Enforcement and Better Forests." *World Development*, 33(2): 273–84.

Gibson, Clark C., Krister Andersson, Elinor Ostrom, and Sujai Shivakumar. 2005. *The Samaritan's Dilemma: The Political Economy of Development Aid*. Oxford: Oxford University Press.

Gigerenzer, Gerd, and Reinhard Selten, ed. 2001. *Bounded Rationality: The Adaptive Toolbox*. Cambridge, MA: MIT Press.

Goffman, Erving. 1974. *Frame Analysis: An Essay on the Organization of Experience*. Cambridge, MA: Harvard University Press.

Gordon, H. Scott. 1954. "The Economic Theory of a Common-Property Resource: The Fishery." *Journal of Political Economy*, 62(2): 124–42.

Grafton, R. Quentin. 2000. "Governance of the Commons: A Role for the State?" *Land Economics*, 76(4): 504–17.

Gulick, Luther. 1957. "Metropolitan Organization." *The ANNALS of the American Academy of Political and Social Science*, 314(1): 57–65.

Hardin, Garrett. 1968. "The Tragedy of the Commons." *Science*, 162(3859): 1243–48.

Hayes, Tanya M. 2006. "Parks, People, and Forest Protection: An Institutional Assessment of the Effectiveness of Protected Areas." *World Development*, 34(12): 2064–75.

Henrich, Joseph, Robert Boyd, Samuel Bowles, Colin Camerer, Ernst Fehr, and Herbert Gintis, ed. 2004. *Foundations of Human Sociality: Economic Experiments and Ethnographic Evidence from Fifteen Small-Scale Societies*. Oxford: Oxford University Press.

Henrich, Joseph, Richard McElreath, Abigail Barr, Jean Ensminger, Clark Barrett, Alexander Bolyanatz, Juan-Camilo Cardenas, et al. 2006. "Costly Punishment across Human Societies." *Science*, 312(5781): 1767–70.

Hobbes, Thomas. 1651. *Leviathan or the Matter, Forme and Power of a Commonwealth Ecclesiasticall and Civil*. Ed. Michael Oakeshott. Oxford: Basil Blackwell, 1960.

Holt, Charles A. 2007. *Markets, Games, and Strategic Behavior*. Boston: Pearson Addison Wesley.

Isaac, R. Mark, and James M. Walker. 1988. "Communication and Free-Riding Behavior: The Voluntary Contribution Mechanism." *Economic Inquiry*, 26(4): 585–608.

Isaac, R. Mark, Kenneth F. McCue, and Charles R. Plott. 1985. "Public Goods Provision in an Experimental Environment." *Journal of Public Economics*, 26(1): 51–74.

Isaac, R. Mark, James M. Walker, and Susan H. Thomas. 1984. "Divergent Evidence on Free Riding: An Experimental Examination of Possible Explanations." *Public Choice*, 43(2): 113–49.

Isaac, R. Mark, James M. Walker, and Arlington W. Williams. 1994. "Group Size and the Voluntary Provision of Public Goods: Experimental Evidence Utilizing Large Groups." *Journal of Public Economics*, 54(1): 1–36.

IsHak, Samir. 1972. "Consumers' Perception of Police Performance: Consolidation vs. Deconcentration: The Case of Grand Rapids, Michigan." PhD diss. Indiana University.

Jager, Wander, and Marco A. Janssen. 2002. "Using Artificial Agents to Understand Laboratory Experiments of Common-Pool Resources with Real Agents." In *Complexity and Ecosystem Management: The Theory and Practice of Multi-Agent Systems*, ed. Marco A. Janssen, 75–102. Cheltenham, UK: Elgar.

Janssen, Marco A. 2008. "Evolution of Cooperation in a One-Shot Prisoner's Dilemma Based on Recognition of Trustworthy and Untrustworthy Agents." *Journal of Economic Behavior and Organization*, 65(3–4): 458–71.

Joshi, Neeraj N., Elinor Ostrom, Ganesh P. Shivakoti, and Wai Fung Lam. 2000. "Institutional Opportunities and Constraints in the Performance of Farmer-Managed Irrigation Systems in Nepal." *Asia-Pacific Journal of Rural Development*, 10(2): 67–92.

Kiser, Larry L., and Elinor Ostrom. 1982. "The Three Worlds of Action: A Metatheoretical Synthesis of Institutional Approaches." In *Strategies of Political Inquiry*, ed. Elinor Ostrom, 179–222. Beverly Hills, CA: Sage.

Koestler, Arthur. 1973. "The Tree and the Candle." In *Unity through Diversity: A Festschrift for Ludwig von Bertalanffy*, ed. William Gray and Nicholas D. Rizzo, 287–314. New York: Gordon and Breach Science Publishers.

Lam, Wai Fung. 1998. *Governing Irrigation Systems in Nepal: Institutions, Infrastructure, and Collective Action*. Oakland, CA: ICS Press.

Leibbrandt, Andreas, Uri Gneezy, and John List. 2010. "Ode to the Sea: The Socio-Ecological Underpinnings of Social Norms." Unpublished.

Liu, Jianguo, Marc Linderman, Zhiyun Ouyang, Li An, Jian Yang, and Hemin Zhang. 2001. "Ecological Degradation in Protected Areas: The Case of Wolong Nature Reserve for Giant Pandas." *Science*, 292(5514): 98–101.

Marshall, Graham R. 2008. "Nesting, Subsidiarity, and Community-Based Environmental Governance beyond the Local Level." *International Journal of the Commons*, 2(1): 75–97.

Marwell, Gerald, and Ruth E. Ames. 1979. "Experiments on the Provision of Public Goods I: Resources, Interest, Group Size, and the Free Rider Problem." *American Journal of Sociology*, 84(6): 1335–60.

McCay, Bonnie J., and James M. Acheson. 1987. *The Question of the Commons: The Culture and Ecology of Communal Resources*. Tucson, AZ: University of Arizona Press.

McGinnis, Michael D., ed. 1999a. *Polycentric Governance and Development: Readings from the Workshop in Political Theory and Policy Analysis*. Ann Arbor, MI: University of Michigan Press.

McGinnis, Michael D., ed. 1999b. *Polycentricity and Local Public Economies: Readings from the Workshop in Political Theory and Policy Analysis*. Ann Arbor, MI: University of Michigan Press.

McGinnis, Michael D., ed. 2000. *Polycentric Games and Institutions: Readings from the Workshop in Political Theory and Policy Analysis*. Ann Arbor, MI: University of Michigan Press.

Meinzen-Dick, Ruth. 2007. "Beyond Panaceas in Water Institutions." *Proceedings of the National Academy of Sciences*, 104(39): 15200–05.

National Research Council. 1986. *Proceedings of the Conference on Common Property Resource Management*. Washington, DC: National Academies Press.

Netting, Robert McC. 1972. "Of Men and Meadows: Strategies of Alpine Land Use." *Anthropological Quarterly*, 45(3): 132–44.

North, Douglass C. 1990. *Institutions, Institutional Change and Economic Performance*. Cambridge, UK: Cambridge University Press.

North, Douglass C. 2005. *Understanding the Process of Economic Change*. Princeton, NJ: Princeton University Press.

Oakerson, Ronald J. 1986. "A Model for the Analysis of Common Property Problems." In *Proceedings of the Conference on Common Property Resource Management*, 13–30. Washington, DC: National Academies Press.

388 E. Ostrom

Ones, Umut, and Louis Putterman. 2007. "The Ecology of Collective Action: A Public Goods and Sanctions Experiment with Controlled Group Formation." *Journal of Economic Behavior and Organization*, 62(4): 495–521.

Orbell, John M., Alphons van de Kragt, and Robyn M. Dawes. 1988. "Explaining Discussion-Induced Cooperation." *Journal of Personality and Social Psychology*, 54(5): 811–19.

Ostrom, Elinor. 1965. "Public Entrepreneurship: A Case Study in Ground Water Basin Management." PhD diss. University of California, Los Angeles.

Ostrom, Elinor. 1976. "Size and Performance in a Federal System." *Publius: The Journal of Federalism*, 6(2): 33–73.

Ostrom, Elinor. 1986. "An Agenda for the Study of Institutions." *Public Choice*, 48(1): 3–25.

Ostrom, Elinor. 1990. *Governing the Commons: The Evolution of Institutions for Collective Action*. Cambridge, UK: Cambridge University Press.

Ostrom, Elinor. 1998. "A Behavioral Approach to the Rational Choice Theory of Collective Action." *American Political Science Review*, 92(1): 1–22.

Ostrom, Elinor. 1999. "Coping with Tragedies of the Commons." *Annual Review of Political Science*, 2: 493–535.

Ostrom, Elinor. 2005. *Understanding Institutional Diversity*. Princeton, NJ: Princeton University Press.

Ostrom, Elinor. 2007. "A Diagnostic Approach for Going beyond Panaceas." *Proceedings of the national Academy of Sciences*, 104(39): 15181–87.

Ostrom, Elinor. 2008. "Developing a Method for Analyzing Institutional Change." In *Alternative Institutional Structures: Evolution and Impact*, ed. Sandra S. Batie and Nicholas Mercuro, 48–76. New York: Routledge.

Ostrom, Elinor. 2009. "A General Framework for Analyzing the Sustainability of Social-Ecological Systems." *Science*, 325(5939): 419–22.

Ostrom, Elinor, and Xavier Basurto. Forthcoming. "Crafting Analytical Tools to Study Institutional Change." *Journal of Institutional Economics*.

Ostrom, Elinor, and Roy Gardner. 1993. "Coping with Asymmetries in the Commons: Self-Governing Irrigation Systems Can Work." *Journal of Economic Perspectives*, 7(4): 93–112.

Ostrom, Elinor, and Harini Nagendra. 2006. "Insights on Linking Forests, Trees, and People from the Air, on the Ground, and in the Laboratory." *Proceedings of the National Academy of Sciences*, 103(51): 19224–31.

Ostrom, Elinor, and Roger B. Parks. 1973. "Suburban Police Departments: Too Many and Too Small?" In *The Urbanization of the Suburbs*, ed. Louis H. Masotti and Jeffrey K. Hadden, 367–402. Beverly Hills, CA: Sage.

Ostrom, Elinor, and Roger B. Parks. 1999. "Neither Gargantua nor the Land of Lilliputs: Conjectures on Mixed Systems of Metropolitan Organization." In *Polycentricity and Local Public Economies: Readings from the Workshop in Political Theory and Policy Analysis*, ed. Michael D. McGinnis, 284–305. Ann Arbor, MI: University of Michigan Press.

Ostrom, Elinor, and James Walker. 1991. "Communication in a Commons: Cooperation without External Enforcement." In *Laboratory Research in Political Economy*, ed. Thomas R. Palfrey, 287–322. Ann Arbor, MI: University of Michigan Press.

Ostrom, Elinor, and Gordon P. Whitaker. 1974. "Community Control and Governmental Responsiveness: The Case of Police in Black Neighborhoods." In *Improving the Quality of Urban Management*, ed. Willis Hawley and David Rogers, 303–34. Beverly Hills, CA: Sage.

Ostrom, Elinor, Roy Gardner, and James Walker. 1994. *Rules, Games, and Common-Pool Resources.* Ann Arbor, MI: University of Michigan Press.

Ostrom, Elinor, Roger B. Parks, and Gordon P. Whitaker. 1978. *Patterns of Metropolitan Policing.* Cambridge, MA: Ballinger.

Ostrom, Elinor, Larry Schroeder, and Susan Wynne. 1993. *Institutional Incentives and Sustainable Development: Infrastructure Policies in Perspective.* Boulder, CO: Westview Press.

Ostrom, Elinor, James Walker, and Roy Gardner. 1992. "Covenants with and without a Sword: Self-Governance Is Possible." *American Political Science Review*, 86(2): 404–17.

Ostrom, Elinor, Arun Agrawal, William Blomquist, Edella Schlager, and S. Y. Tang. 1989. *CPR Coding Manual.* Bloomington, IN: Indiana University, Workshop in Political Theory and Policy Analysis.

Ostrom, Elinor, William Baugh, Richard Guarasci, Roger B. Parks, and Gordon P. Whitaker. 1973. *Community Organization and the Provision of Police Services.* Beverly Hills, CA: Sage.

Ostrom, Elinor, Thomas Dietz, Nives Dolšak, Paul C. Stern, Susan Stonich, and Elke U. Weber, ed. 2002. *The Drama of the Commons.* Washington, DC: National Academies Press.

Ostrom, Vincent. 1962. "The Political Economy of Water Development." *American Economic Review*, 52(2): 450–58.

Ostrom, Vincent. 1975. "Language, Theory and Empirical Research in Policy Analysis." *Policy Studies Journal*, 3(3): 274–82.

Ostrom, Vincent. 2008. *The Intellectual Crisis in American Public Administration.* 3rd ed. Tuscaloosa, AL: University of Alabama Press.

Ostrom, Vincent, and Elinor Ostrom. 1965. "A Behavioral Approach to the Study of Intergovernmental Relations." *The ANNALS of the American Academy of Political and Social Science*, 359(1): 137–46.

Ostrom, Vincent, and Elinor Ostrom. 1977. "Public Goods and Public Choices." In *Alternatives for Delivering Public Services: Toward Improved Performance*, ed. Emanuel S. Savas, 7–49. Boulder, CO: Westview Press.

Ostrom, Vincent, Charles M. Tiebout, and Robert Warren. 1961. "The Organization of Government in Metropolitan Areas: A Theoretical Inquiry." *American Political Science Review*, 55(4): 831–42.

Paavola, Jouni, and W. Neil Adger. 2005. "Institutional Ecological Economics." *Ecological Economics*, 53(3): 353–68.

Pagdee, Adcharaporn, Yeon-Su Kim, and P. J. Daugherty. 2006. "What Makes Community Forest Management Successful: A Meta-Study from Community Forests throughout the World." *Society & Natural Resources*, 19(1): 33–52.

Pfennig, David W., and Cris Ledón-Rettig. 2009. "The Flexible Organism." *Science*, 325(5938): 268–69.

Popper, Karl R. 1961. *The Poverty of Historicism.* New York: Harper & Row.

Posner, Richard. 1975. "Economic Analysis of Law." In *Economic Foundation of Property Law*, ed. Bruce A. Ackerman. Boston, MA: Little, Brown and Co.

Poteete, Amy R., and Elinor Ostrom. 2004. "In Pursuit of Comparable Concepts and Data about Collective Action." *Agricultural Systems*, 82(3): 215–32.

Poteete, Amy R., Marco Janssen, and Elinor Ostrom. 2010. *Working Together: Collective Action, the Commons, and Multiple Methods in Practice.* Princeton, NJ: Princeton University Press.

Reeson, Andrew F., and John G. Tisdell. 2008. "Institutions, Motivations and Public Goods: An Experimental Test of Motivational Crowding." *Journal of Economic Behavior and Organization*, 68(1): 273–81.

390 E. Ostrom

Rogers, Bruce D., and C. McCurdy Lipsey. 1974. "Metropolitan Reform: Citizen Evaluations of Performance in Nashville-Davidson County, Tennessee." *Publius: The Journal of Federalism*, 4(4): 19–34.

Rothstein, Bo. 2005. *Social Traps and the Problem of Trust*. Cambridge, UK: Cambridge University Press.

Rudel, Thomas K. 2008. "Meta-Analyses of Case Studies: A Method for Studying Regional and Global Environmental Change." *Global Environmental Change*, 18(1): 18–25.

Sally, David. 1995. "Conservation and Cooperation in Social Dilemmas: A Meta-Analysis of Experiments from 1958 to 1992." *Rationality and Society*, 7(1): 58–92.

Samuelson, Paul A. 1954. "The Pure Theory of Public Expenditure." *Review of Economics and Statistics*, 36(4): 387–89.

Satz, Debra, and John Ferejohn. 1994. "Rational Choice and Social Theory." *Journal of Philosophy*, 91(2): 71–87.

Schank, Roger C., and Robert P. Abelson. 1977. *Scripts, Plans, Goals, and Understanding: An Inquiry in Human Knowledge Structures*. Hillsdale, NJ: Lawrence Erlbaum Associates.

Schelling, Thomas C. 1960. *The Strategy of Conflict*. Oxford: Oxford University Press.

Schelling, Thomas C. 1978. *Micromotives and Macrobehavior*. New York: Norton.

Schelling, Thomas C. 1984. *Choice and Consequence: Perspectives of an Errant Economist*. Cambridge, MA: Harvard University Press.

Schlager, Edella. 1990. "Model Specification and Policy Analysis: The Governance of Coastal Fisheries." PhD diss. Indiana University.

Schlager, Edella. 1994. "Fishers' Institutional Responses to Common-Pool Resource Dilemmas." In *Rules, Games, and Common-Pool Resources*, ed. Elinor Ostrom, Roy Gardner, and James Walker, 247–65. Ann Arbor, MI: University of Michigan Press.

Schlager, Edella, and William Blomquist. 2008. *Embracing Watershed Politics*. Boulder, CO: University Press of Colorado.

Schlager, Edella, and Elinor Ostrom. 1992. "Property-Rights Regimes and Natural Resources: A Conceptual Analysis." *Land Economics*, 68(3): 249–62.

Scott, Anthony. 1955. "The Fishery: The Objectives of Sole Ownership." *Journal of Political Economy*, 63(2): 116–24.

Selten, Reinhard. 1990. "Bounded Rationality." *Journal of Institutional and Theoretical Economics*, 146(4): 649–58.

Sen, Amartya K. 1977. "Rational Fools: A Critique of the Behavioral Foundations of Economic Theory." *Philosophy and Public Affairs*, 6(4): 317–44.

Sen, Amartya K. 2009. *The Idea of Justice*. Cambridge, MA: Harvard University Press.

Shivakoti, Ganesh, and Elinor Ostrom, ed. 2002. *Improving Irrigation Governance and Management in Nepal*. Oakland, CA: ICS Press.

Simon, Herbert A. 1955. "A Behavioural Model of Rational Choice." *Quarterly Journal of Economics*, 69(1): 99–188.

Simon, Herbert A. 1981. *The sciences of the Artificial*. 2nd ed. Cambridge, MA: MIT Press.

Simon, Herbert A. 1995. "Near Decomposability and Complexity: How a Mind Resides in a Brain." In *The Mind, the Brain, and Complex Adaptive Systems*, ed. Harold J. Morowitz and Jerome L. Singer, 25–44. Reading, MA: Addison-Wesley.

Simon, Herbert A. 1999. "The Potlatch between Economics and Political Science." In *Competition and Cooperation: Conversations with Nobelists About Economics and Political Science*, ed. James E. Alt, Margaret Levi, and Elinor Ostrom, 112–19. New York: Russell Sage Foundation.

Skoler, Daniel L., and June M. Hetler. 1971. "Government Restructuring and Criminal Administration: The Challenge of Consolidation." In *Crisis in Urban Government. A Symposium: Restructuring Metropolitan Area Government.* Silver Springs, MD: Thomas Jefferson.

Smith, Vernon L. 2003. "Constructivist and Ecological Rationality in Economics." *American Economic Review*, 93(3): 465–508.

Smith, Vernon L. 2010. "Theory and Experiment: What Are the Questions?" *Journal of Economic Behavior and Organization*, 73(1): 3–15.

Smith, Vernon L., and James M. Walker. 1993. "Rewards, Experience and Decision Costs in First Price Auctions." *Economic Inquiry*, 31(2): 237–45.

Stewart, James I. 2009. "Cooperation When N Is Large: Evidence from the Mining Camps of the American West." *Journal of Economic Behavior and Organization*, 69(3): 213–25.

Sugden, Robert. 1986. *The Economics of Rights, Co-Operation and Welfare.* Oxford: Blackwell.

Tang, Shui Yan. 1992. *Institutions and Collective Action: Self-Governance in Irrigation.* San Francisco: ICS Press.

Tang, Shui Yan. 1994. "Institutions and Performance in Irrigation Systems." In *Rules, Games, and Common-Pool Resources*, ed. Elinor Ostrom, Roy Gardner, and James Walker, 225–45. Ann Arbor, MI: University of Michigan Press.

Terborgh, John. 1999. *Requiem for Nature.* Washington, DC: Island Press.

Toonen, Theo. 2010. "Resilience in Public Administration: The Work of Elinor and Vincent Ostrom from a Public Administration Perspective." *Public Administration Review*, 70(2): 193–202.

Trawick, Paul B. 2001. "Successfully Governing the Commons: Principles of Social Organization in an Andean Irrigation System." *Human Ecology*, 29(1): 1–25.

Tucker, Catherine M. 2008. *Changing Forests: Collective Action, Common Property, and Coffee in Honduras.* Berlin: Springer.

Uphoff, Norman T., Priti Ramamurthy and Roy Steiner. 1991. *Managing Irrigation: Analyzing and Improving the Performance of Bureaucracies.* New Delhi: Sage.

Walker, James, and Elinor Ostrom. 2009. "Trust and Reciprocity as Foundations for Cooperation." In *Whom Can We Trust?: How Groups, Networks, and Institutions Make Trust Possible*, ed. Karen S. Cook, Margaret Levi, and Russell Hardin, 91–124. New York: Russell Sage Foundation.

Warren, Robert O. 1966. *Government of Metropolitan Regions: A Reappraisal of Fractionated Political Organization.* Davis, CA: University of California, Institute of Governmental Affairs.

Webb, Edward L., and Ganesh Shivakoti, ed. 2008. *Decentralization, Forests and Rural Communities: Policy Outcomes in South and Southeast Asia.* New Delhi: Sage India.

Weissing, Franz, and Elinor Ostrom. 1993. "Irrigation Institutions and the Games Irrigators Play: Rule Enforcement on Government- and Farmer-Managed Systems." In *Games in Hierarchies and Networks: Analytical and Empirical Approaches to the Study of Governance Institutions*, ed. Fritz W. Scharpf, 387–428. Frankfurt, Germany: Campus Verlag.

Weschler, Louis F. 1968. *Water Resources Management: The Orange County Experience.* Davis, CA: University of California, Institute of Governmental Affairs.

Williamson, Oliver E. 1975. *Markets and Hierarchies: Analysis and Antitrust Implications.* New York: Free Press.

Williamson, Oliver E. 1986. "The Economics of Governance: Framework and Implications." In *Economics as a Process: Essays in the New Institutional Economics*, ed. Richard N. Langlois, 171–202. Cambridge, UK: Cambridge University Press.

Wilson, James A. 1990. "Fishing for Knowledge." *Land Economics*, 66(1): 12–29.
Wilson, James A., James M. Acheson, Mark Metcalfe, and Peter Kleban. 1994. "Chaos, Complexity, and Community Management of Fisheries." *Marine Policy*, 18(4): 291–305.
Wilson, Woodrow. 1885. *Congressional Government: A Study in American Politics.* Boston: Houghton Mifflin.
Wollenberg, Eva, Leticia Merino, Arun Agrawal, and Elinor Ostrom. 2007. "Fourteen Years of Monitoring Community-Managed Forests: Learning from IFRI's Experience." *International Forestry Review*, 9(2): 670–84.
Yamagishi, Toshio. 1986. "The Provision of a Sanctioning System as a Public Good." *Journal of Personality and Social Psychology*, 51(1): 110–16.
Yandle, Tracy. 2007. "Understanding the Consequence of Property Rights Mismatches: A Case Study of New Zealand's Marine Resources." *Ecology and Society*, 12(2). http://www.ecologyandsociety.org/vol12/iss2/art27/.
Yandle, Tracy, and Christopher M. Dewees. 2003. "Privatizing the Commons ... Twelve Years Later: Fishers' Experiences with New Zealand's Market-Based Fisheries Management." In *The Commons in the New Millennium: Challenges and Adaptation*, ed. Nives Dolsak and Elinor Ostrom, 101–27. Cambridge, MA: MIT Press.

18

SOCIAL ATTITUDES, ENTREPRENEURSHIP, AND ECONOMIC DEVELOPMENT

A. Gerschenkron

"Social attitudes" is not a very precise term. It must be treated with restraint. Otherwise it will quickly expand to embrace the whole ambit of governmental economic policies — a topic very properly assigned to a special session of this conference.[1] We shall deal here essentially with the significance for a country's economic development of popular evaluations of entrepreneurs and entrepreneurial activities; that is to say, of the general climate of opinion within which entrepreneurial action takes place. Even when so restricted, the problem remains vast, and a great deal of patient monographic research is necessary before any firm conclusions can be reached. The following impressionistic remarks, therefore, purport to do no more than to present briefly some general lines of thought that have been pursued so far, to issue some warnings against too ready an acceptance of certain abstract models, and to illustrate these warnings by reference to some segments of European economic history of the nineteenth century. With regard to the latter, the emphasis is on earlier stages of industrialization rather than on conditions in mature economies. Except for a brief allusion, the question as to what extent European historical experience can be used for elucidating the current problems of underdeveloped countries must likewise remain outside the scope of this paper.

Research on the problem under discussion is still in its infancy. However, the Harvard Research Center in Entrepreneurial History under the able leadership of Arthur Cole has devoted, over several years, much time and thought to an "entrepreneurial approach to economic history," and it has paid a good deal of attention to the question of social attitudes toward entrepreneurship. Entrepreneurial research in the United States has received its intellectual stimulus primarily from two sources. It has been, of course, greatly influenced by Schumpeter's theory of economic development, which assigns to the innovating entrepreneur a focal role in the process of economic change. In fact, Professor Schumpeter remained in intimate association with the Research Center at Harvard until his death in 1950, and the

394 A. Gerschenkron

wealth of Schumpeterian hypotheses — and intuitions — quite naturally predetermined many of the paths of research to be followed. At a very early stage, however, as the problem of the entrepreneurial position within the community impressed itself upon those working in the field, the need was felt for a more rigorous and comprehensive sociological framework. Such a framework has been developed over a wide range of recent writings in the field of social psychology, anthropology, and sociology and has found perhaps its most powerful systematic expression in the theoretical structure which over the past two decades has been erected by Talcott Parsons and the scholars assembled around him.

Even if the writer felt qualified to do so, there still would be neither need nor possibility to enter within the scope of these pages into a discussion of the Parsonian system. But a few words on some specific concepts to the extent that they have affected entrepreneurial research — and only to that extent — may be in order.[2] The interest in this respect centers upon the so-called theory of roles. The individual members of the community are seen as performing specific social roles, and it is the role which "for most purposes [is] the conceptual unit of the social system."[3] "The primary ingredient of the role is the role-expectation,"[4] which denotes what role individuals expect each other to perform. Compliance with role-expectation is enforced through positive and negative sanctions (rewards and retributions). The role expectancies and sanction patterns are institutionalized into generalized value systems of the community. In a well-integrated society these values are "internalized in personality systems," that is, they are accepted and adopted by the individuals. As a result, the value system becomes the crucial determinant of action.[5]

One cannot suppress some wonderment as to why these particular concepts should have proven attractive to those interested in explaining the process of economic *change*. It does seem that these concepts essentially pertain to a static system. Of course, the system is still in evolution. Parsons' writings and those of his collaborators are shot through with multifarious warnings. In *Toward a General Theory of Action*, it is said explicitly that the work has not proceeded far beyond the "categorical" stage on the road to the formulation of the general "laws" of the system (pp. 50–51). One is warned that the "empirical significance of selective or value standards as determinants of concrete action may be considered problematical and should not be prejudged" (p. 63), that there are dangers in imputing "too much rigidity to behavior" and in overestimating its "uniformity within a given society" (p. 225). Most importantly, it is emphasized that very often "many of the most important seeds of social change" (p. 179) lie in the failure to maintain social integration at the achieved level. The impression is that the static character of the system is well recognized. Still it is claimed that, "in principle, propositions about the factors making for maintenance of the system are at the same time propositions about those making for change" (p. 231). Thus social dynamics is said to be included within the framework; and it is essentially in the conflicts between value systems — in an analysis of what Florence Kluckhohn called dominant, variant, and deviant (that is, prescribed, permissive, and proscribed) values (p. 415) — that the processes of change will be sought. This, however, is still a promise. For the time being it

Attitudes, entrepreneurship, and development **395**

seems fair to say that it is the social state rather than social change to which main attention is addressed.[6]

Nevertheless, it is both the static and the nascent dynamic elements in the system that have excited the interest of entrepreneurial research. This is clearly in evidence in the pioneering symposium volume *Change and the Entrepreneur* which was prepared by the Entrepreneurial Research Center.[7] Thus in this volume Arthur Cole attaches explicit significance to the degree of social approval which the entrepreneur's striving for economic gain will receive in a given economic milieu, and he refers to various social systems from India to France where entrepreneurial activities labor under various degrees of disapproval (pp. 87–88). In his stimulating contribution, Leland H. Jenks[8] concerns himself in more detail with role factors, that is, with prescriptions concerning appropriate behavior of individuals who occupy a set of special positions. And, in dealing with the specific behavior of men like the elder Morgan or Cyrus McCormick, he stresses that whatever the importance of accidental factors in the make-up of individuals their actions cannot be adequately understood unless they are placed within the context of the cultural patterns of their society (pp. 131–132). But Jenks moves a step beyond and places particular stress on the dichotomy of personal and social roles and the possibility of discrepancy between them. It is the existence of such discrepancies, he says, that is indicative of the fact that significant social change is in the making (p. 138). One would expect, therefore, the concept of entrepreneurial deviance to emerge as the primary device for understanding entrepreneurial behavior and the entrepreneur's role as an innovator. But we are quickly led back to the fold. It is again the "social roles" and the sanctioning acts by which the expected behavior is enforced that assume a central position in the explanatory mechanism. And all we are left with is the fact that in the case of entrepreneurs social roles are peculiarly "indistinct" and "flexible" which, we are told, is in turn the result, among other things, of the fact that the entrepreneurial position "entails the function and opportunity for introducing novelty into the economic structure" (p. 147).

Finally, mention must be made of the essay by Thomas C. Cochran in the same volume.[9] Cochran's essay, which is enclosed within the same conceptual framework, is of particular interest from our point of view because of his specific redefinition of deviant behavior. He speaks of sanctions designed to "encourage deviant behavior" (p. 160). Thus, the concept of deviance is divorced from the discrepancy between social and personal roles, and deviant behavior becomes fully consonant with social role-expectations. Obviously, deviance means something else to Cochran than it does to, say, Florence Kluckhohn, who identifies it with socially proscribed behavior.'[10] In Cochran's mind deviance is simply associated with innovation and is seen as an integral part of the dominant value system.

Where does all this lead? Are we witnessing here a new theory of social change *in statu nascendi*? How can an economic historian use the analytical tools, with which he is being so generously supplied, in his attempts to elucidate empirical processes of economic change and, in particular, to understand entrepreneurial behavior? Surely, only very tentative answers can be given to these questions.

A dynamic theory? It seems that it allows of economic change in a twofold fashion. On the one hand, a well-integrated society in which economic innovating has become a generally accepted mode of behavior fits the system to a nicety. Since the process of innovation gives rise to what Schumpeter called "creative destruction,"[11] the process of change, one may suspect, will still involve dissident personal values of the victims of economic change, but these may be either neglected or else the community assumed to be integrated to a point where even the loser in the process has so thoroughly "internalized" the social standard of value that

> Mit dem Geschick in hoher Einigkeit,
> Gelassen hingestuetzt auf Grazien und Musen,
> Empfaengt er das Geschoss, das ihn bedraeut,
> Mit freundlich dargebotnem Busen
> Vom sanften Bogen der Notwendigkeit.

Be that as it may, it is this type of "built-in" dynamism that apparently was in Cochran's mind. On the other hand, there is the original, nondenaturalized concept of deviant behavior on the part of the entrepreneur. This concept is intimated, but all too soon abandoned, by Jenks in his discussion of discrepancies between personal and social roles.[12]

Both concepts are, of course, meaningful per se. But it may be noted in passing that in Cochran's society the Schumpeterian concept or innovation loses a good deal of its interest. Innovation is regarded by Schumpeter as a "distinct economic function," *inter alia*, because of the environment's resistance to innovators and innovating processes.[13] Once the resistance of the environment is lowered, "personality and will power must count for less."[14] In other words, specific entrepreneurial research offers less opportunity for understanding the processes of social change in such a society. At any rate, Cochran's society has little resemblance to economies which stand at the threshold of industrialization and are heavily burdened with traditional resistances to economic development.

In a sense, deviance which spurns the established value patterns may indeed be regarded as a dynamic force making for economic change. But it is at this point that our theories, both general and entrepreneurial, leave us in the lurch. For, though it may make sense in certain historical situations to take a dominant system of social values for granted, it is much less satisfactory to accept the deviant behavior as given. If we deal with an agricultural community based on century-long traditions, we may be willing to accept those traditions as given without caring much about the whys and the wherefores. But if suddenly deviant values make their entry upon the economic scene, the urge for further explanation is irresistible. We cannot help asking whence the change in value orientations: what has caused the sudden outburst? There is nothing within the theoretical framework that provides the elements of such an explanation beyond, perhaps, some implicit and inchoate ideas about the tolerable degree of tension between deviant and generally accepted behavior. In general, the concept of deviance is taken up gingerly and dropped

Attitudes, entrepreneurship, and development **397**

abruptly, and the accent shifts back to the dominant value system as the determinant of action and to the social sanctioning of entrepreneurial behavior. Thus, the questions with which we are left focus on the problem of social approval.

How important is social approval for the emergence of entrepreneurial activities? In particular, what is its importance at the crucial stages of economic development when a country's economy becomes engaged in a sudden spurt of economic development? Should lack of social approval be regarded as a serious retarding factor? Does it affect in a significant manner the contents of entrepreneurial activities and make for adaptations in entrepreneurial attitudes which can be said to influence speed and character of a country's economic development? These questions cannot be answered, of course, except on the basis of extensive empirical research. In default of such research, the following remarks must be taken as highly tentative impressions from scattered, but perhaps relevant, historical material.

The theoretical formula is persuasively simple: social approval of entrepreneurial activity significantly affects its volume and quality. At times, it even appears as though social approval were regarded as a prerequisite for successful entrepreneurship. But doubts are bound to arise the moment historical material is approached. One might recall the dramatic pages in Augustin Thierry's *Tiers État* which deal with the *fermiers généraux*. Hated and despised, their very existence a slap in the face of all the prevailing standards of goodness and decency, perpetually accused and at times subject to monstrous persecutions, they nevertheless progressed and prospered economically and socially, their entrepreneurial vigor remaining unshaken.[15] *Toujours maudits et loujours nécessaires* cursed and indispensable, they continued their activity, indulging their greed and maturing their frauds. Why did not social disapproval erase the shame of that office from the face of France? Perhaps because a system of social sanctions is often too weak unless reinforced by the sanctions of the state, and the latter may or may not reflect the dominant value system. Or, perhaps, because the system of social values was not to be taken too seriously; perhaps because behind the articulately expressed but ineffectual value system lay another, an actually operational, system. Possibly so, but we must take care. We have set out to examine the determinants of social action. If we begin to deduce social values from the presence of certain actions, we have closed a vicious circle and at the same time have foreclosed the road to a reasoned explanation.

Let us take a brief glance at Russian conditions in the second half of the nineteenth century. After the emancipation of serfs in the early sixties of that century, former serfs and sons of former serfs are known to have engaged on an unprecedented scale in various entrepreneurial activities, including, it might be added, the magnificent venture of constructing and operating the merchant fleet on the Volga River. Again, there is little doubt that their activities were at variance with the dominant system of values, which remained de termined by the traditional agrarian pattern. The Good Life which God intended for man to lead implied tilling the land, which belonged to God, and receiving the divine blessing of its fruit. The Good Life certainly did not mean craving for riches, did not mean laying up treasures on earth where moth or rust doth corrupt. In innumerable adages, fairy tales,

398 A. Gerschenkron

and songs, the wisdom of the folklore insisted upon the unrighteous origin of wealth. And still the activities went on unchecked, great fortunes were amassed, and great entrepreneurial innovations were successfully launched.

There is no doubt that throughout most of the nineteenth century a grave opprobrium attached to entrepreneurial activities in Russia. The nobility and the gentry (*dvoryanstvo*) had nothing but contempt for any entrepreneurial activity except its own. And despite some notable exceptions, it failed to make a significant contribution to modern industrial development. Divorced from the peasantry, the entrepreneurs remained despised by the intelligentsia. The latter's aversion to mercantile pursuits was, if anything, even stronger than that of the peasantry, even though the roots of that aversion doubtless lay in the value system of the peasantry. In a sense, the populism of the intelligentsia was a conscious attempt to espouse the standards of values of the "people." Hence came the intelligentsia's aversion to the bourgeoisie, the acquisitive class. Throughout long decades of the nineteenth century, there was only one among the great figures in Russian intellectual life who did not quite share this negative attitude — Belinski, who, at least at one point, refused to believe that a country that had no bourgeoisie could conceivably prosper. And still it was Belinski who at the very same time used his most fiery vocabulary to decry the merchant, the "base, despicable, vulgar creature who serves Plutus and Plutus alone."[16]

But what of the value system of the entrepreneurs themselves? Were they deviants? They certainly were, as far as their behavior was concerned. But since we are precluded from inferring values from action, we must still ask whether or not they were deviants in the sense that their own standard of values was different from the dominant one. And this appears highly dubious. It took a long time before something like an independent standard of values of the Russian businessman developed. They knew full well that by accepted standards their life was a sinful one, and they tried seriously to make amends by donations to the church — "the graft payments to God," as those donations were cynically and probably unjustly called by Vladimir Solovev. It is much more sensible and in accordance with such evidence as we have from letters and memoirs to speak of a profound malaise resulting from the discrepancy not between two value systems but between the dominant value system and a social action that was at variance with it. It is out of this conflict that emerged the figure of the "repentant merchant" (which followed that of the "repentant nobleman" of the pre-Emancipation times) a figure so impressively depicted in Chekhov's *Cherry Orchard*. And the fictitious figure of Lopakhin appears multiplied in the reality of the early twentieth century in the shape of merchants and industrialists who supplied generous funds to revolutionary organizations including the Bolshevik Party, of whom Savva Morosov, the leading textile industrialist, was an outstanding but far from solitary example.

No one can deny that some changes in this situation took place in the last decades of the nineteenth century. An independent value system of the entrepreneurial group indeed began to evolve. One need only compare the uneasy despotism of the merchant types in Ostrovski's plays with the much more civilized and

Attitudes, entrepreneurship, and development **399**

self-reliant figure of Gorki's *Foma Gordeyev*. And a somewhat parallel change is clearly in evidence in the attitudes of the intelligentsia, as it broke away from the traditional populism and turned with the same radical fervor to the tenets of Marxism. Paradoxical as it is, it was Marxism in Russia which for large strata of intelligentsia, of which revolutionary group of course constituted but a small minority, brought about at the turn of the century some reconciliation with the bourgeoisie and replaced in their minds the picture of a despicable mercenary by that of a builder and innovator. But one cannot fail to be impressed by the latenes and incompleteness of this development.

What shall one conclude from all that? That social attitudes toward entrepreneurs, that value systems whether dominant or deviant, are unimportant, that they do not influence the development at all? This almost surely would be a wrong inference. First of all, it could be argued that the existence of widespread social attitudes in Russia which were so patently unfavorable to entrepreneurship greatly reduced the number of potential entrepreneurs and thereby reduced the rate of economic development in the country.[17] There is little doubt that there is some plausibility to such an argument. Even in the twentieth century, Russian university students showed a good deal of contempt for work associated with practical pursuits and particularly with business activity. When they went to Western universities, they quickly developed scorn for their student colleagues whose attitudes they regarded as glaringly materialistic. "Career" remained a shameful word in the vocabulary of a Russian student. This attitude presumably retarded in some measure the industrialization of the country. Yet it did not prevent the brilliant period of rapid industrialization in the 1890s, when the annual rate of industrial growth was in the vicinity of 9 percent.

It seems more reasonable to suggest that the effect upon economic development of the lingering preindustrial value systems, of aversion to entrepreneurs and to new forms of economic activity in general, was somewhat different. It is likely in some measure to have contributed in Russia — and elsewhere in the history of European industrializations — to the specific compression of industrialization processes into periods of rapid growth. Precisely because some value systems do not change readily, because economic development must break through the barriers of routine, prejudice, and stagnation, among which adverse attitudes toward entrepreneurship are but one important element, industrialization does not take place until the gains which industrialization promises have become, with the passage of time, overwhelmingly large, and the prerequisites are created for a typical upsurge.[18] An adverse social attitude toward entrepreneurs may thus indeed delay the beginning of rapid industrialization. But, viewed over a somewhat longer period, more important than the mere fact of delay is the fact that the character of the industrialization process is affected by those attitudes. At the same time, it would be clearly untenable to try to explain these spurts of rapid industrialization in backward countries simply in terms of a lag in social attitudes. Technological progress, growing advantages of what Nurkse has called "balanced growth," and sudden institutional changes — all these combine to achieve the effect.

400 A. Gerschenkron

Before some general conclusions are drawn, let us shift the scene and follow for a few moments some other empirical work which has been influenced by the general theoretical structure discussed in the preceding pages. The reference is to France and to attempts to explain the problem of the relatively low rate of economic development in that country. It is essentially the work of David S. Landes and John E. Sawyer that is of interest here.[19]

The thesis is simple: the character of entrepreneurial behavior in France has been a very important, perhaps the main, retarding factor in France's economic development and that behavior has been largely shaped by the prevailing value system in the country. It is in these terms that must be seen and explained the French entrepreneur's alleged aversion to risk and credit engagements, his conservative spirit, his dislike of sharp competitive practices, his interest in high profits rather than in large sales, the family character of the French enterprises and their small-scale size, to name only the few important points. In addition, the social status of the businessman is said to be low and hence comes the desire of the best talent in France to turn to the "traditional honorific careers."[20] It is essentially the stress on the strength of the *ancien régime* survivals in the cultural pattern of modern France which Sawyer has added to the picture.

It is perhaps somewhat unfair to seek the source of these views exclusively in general theoretical concepts. In part it is the *tertium comparationis* chosen by the two authors that appears to have influenced their thinking. Throughout, the comparison is with the United States. Obviously such a comparison is quite adequate if all that the writers wished to convey was the indubitable differences that exist between the American and the French economies. But if what they were after was an explanation of the peculiar "weakness of French industry and commerce," the comparison with the United States is hardly a very helpful one, and the proper comparison ought to have been with countries of similar geographic size, position, and historical background, which nevertheless showed a higher rate of economic growth. Germany was the natural choice, and at least an explanation for shunning the obvious ought to have been provided.

Once the comparison is made with Germany, most of the factors mentioned by Landes find their counterpart in the German economy. The strength of preindustrial social values was, if anything, greater in Germany than in France. The family firm remained strong, and the lower entrepreneurial echelons, whose numbers bulked large, behaved in a way which was hardly different from that in France. The pronouncement made at the turn of the century, that modern economic development had transformed the top structure of the German economy while everything beneath it still remained medieval, was, of course, a deliberate exaggeration. But there was some meaning in that exaggeration. Such as it was, it applied to France as much as to Germany.[21]

Of course, the picture presented is onesided in any case. In order to maintain his thesis, Landes has to relegate vast and most significant fields of French entrepreneurial endeavor, such as railroads, mines, the iron and steel industry, automobile production, banks and department stores, to qualifying footnotes and dependent

Attitudes, entrepreneurship, and development **401**

clauses. On the other hand, a comparison with Germany would have brought out that in the nineteenth century French entrepreneurial vigor in some fields was doubtless in excess of that in Germany. The question of exact priority for the introduction of department stores is perhaps still a matter of a rather useless dispute,[22] but that the French supplied a whole series of momentous entrepreneurial innovations to the field is beyond doubt; so is the fact that at least until the end of the century Germany still lagged in this respect behind her neighbor to the west. It was a great French entrepreneur, Felix Potin, whom the alleged French value standards did not prevent from coining the famous altogether "American" phrase, "Des affaires avant tout, le bénéfice viendra ensuite," and who successfully carried through his great innovations in retailing long before such ideas began to take hold in Germany.[23] At any rate, when Landes is struck by the far-reaching degree of specialization in French food retailing, which rightly seems so un-American to him, he should also have expressed his astonishment about the presence of the same phenomenon in Germany. Somerset Maugham justly claimed that, to know one foreign country, one must also know at least one other foreign country and added that "Arnold Bennett has never ceased to believe in a peculiar distinction of the French to breakfast off coffee and rolls."[24] This seems very sound advice for the field of comparative economic history.

It is true, of course, that the German rate of industrial growth in the second half of the nineteenth century exceeded that of France. Some of the factors which must in large measure have accounted for the difference in the speed of growth are obvious. One is surely the lack of a coal basin comparable to the Ruhr at a time when coal exercised all or nearly all of the locational pull in iron and steel making. The prevalence of the family farm with its unfavorable effects upon the flow of labor to industry is another. It may or may not be true that, when everything is said and done and a distribution of emphasis among the individual factors concerned is attempted, some differences in entrepreneurial behavior between France and Germany may be found very much worthy of mention. But to assume that such differences, if any, need necessarily be explained in terms of roles, role-expectations, and value orientations is surely unwarranted. Clearly, variations in entrepreneurial behavior may have nothing to do with the dominant value system and the degree of social approval. They can be, and no doubt are, the result of varying income levels, living conditions, degree of endowment with natural resources, and so on.

And, in a sense, the same applies even to comparisons with the United States. There can be no doubt that differences in "dominant value systems" can be easily discerned between France and the country whose economy has remained largely, though by no means completely, free from the influences of precapitalist traditions. Ernest Renan once adverted to those differences in forceful sentences:

> Nous sommes une race des gentilshommes; notre idéal a été créé par des gentilshommes, non comme celui de l'Amérique, par d'honnêtes bourgeois, de sérieux hommes d'affaires. Les personnes qui poursuivent si avidement l'idéal américain oublient que cette race n'a pas notre passé brillant, qu'elle

402 A. Gerschenkron

> n'a pas fait une découverte de science pure, ni créé un chef-d'oeuvre, qu'elle
> n'a jamais eu de noblesse, que le négoce et la fortune l'occupent tout
> entière.
>
> Les meilleurs choses (par exemple, les fonctions du prêtre, du magistrat,
> du savant, de l'artiste et de l'homme de lettres sérieux) sont l'inverse de l'esprit
> industriel et commercial, le premier devoir de ceux qui s'y adonnent étant de
> ne pas chercher à s'enrichir, et de ne jamais considérer la valeur vénale de ce
> qu'ils font.[25]

These sweeping statements cannot lay claim to absolute accuracy and one should beware easy generalizations.[26] But this is not the point. What is important to note here is that, even in this classical case of differences in "value systems" between the United States and France, there is an obvious need for a good deal of careful and undogmatic research before one can begin to form some idea as to just how much significance can be reasonably imputed to those differences as against the host of other incomparabilities between the two countries.

Perhaps some conclusion can be drawn from the foregoing discussion. A rigid conceptual framework is no doubt useful in formulating questions, but at all times it evokes the peril that those questions will be mistaken for answers. There is a deep-seated yearning in the social sciences for the discovery of one general approach, one general law valid for all times and all climes. But these attitudes must be outgrown. They overestimate both the degree of simplicity of economic reality and the quality of scientific tools. As the economics historian organizes and interprets his material, all he can hope for is the discovery of limited patterns of uniformity which may possess explanatory value for some places and periods but may be utterly inapplicable to others. And this is folly true of the sets of concepts which have been discussed above. It seems reasonably dear that the chances for their usefulness are greatest when applied either to stagnant primitive communities in which no development takes place at all or to well-integrated advanced societies with well built-in dynamic elements. Paradoxical as it may sound, the analysis hitched to a general standard of values is best adapted to, say, the Navaho Indians on the one hand and to the present American society on the other. This perhaps explains the strong affiliation that exists between anthropology and modern sociology; and perhaps also the strong though illusory feeling, so frequently expressed, that *plus ça change, plus c'est la même chose*[27] — illusory because it overlooks the fact that the conceptual schemata may have held much less well for the intervening stages of the development. At any rate, serious doubts are permissible about whether the theory of roles in its present form and everything that it implies can be of much use for understanding processes in the economies within which a rapid change *in economic systems* is in the making; more concretely, within the economies which experience a specific initial upsurge in the rate of growth of industrial output.

But the reservations must go farther. The preceding discussion may have seemed at times to have skirted perilously the old question of precedence: does capitalism "create" the capitalist spirit or does the capitalist spirit "create" capitalism? Nothing

Attitudes, entrepreneurship, and development **403**

could be more unfortunate than for work in economic history once more to be dragged down into the depth of metaphysical or at least hopelessly abstract arguments. The question cannot be: are social values important or unimportant? It must read first of all: what is the degree of persistence in value systems, what is their propensity to change in response to what factors? In dealing with periods of economic transformation which in themselves imply a considerable degree of diversity in values within a given community, one should least of all try to evoke the impression of a unified and general normative system. If something like "coefficients of changeability" — however crude such a measure must be — is attached to various value systems, one cannot fail to discover that the range of such coefficients must be wide indeed. Some values do not seem to change at all over long periods of time. The attitude of peasants who cling to the land even under unfavorable economic circumstances and, even when at length forced into urban occupations, still keep looking back over their shoulders, ready to return to the land at the earliest possible chance, are surely determined by values whose change is exceedingly slow. It is perfectly reasonable to attribute to the existence of such values the well-known difficulties experienced by young industrial countries in building up a reliable permanent labor force in industry. On the other hand, the same hardly could be said of entrepreneurial values. The volatile group of entrepreneurs — composed of men who by definition are "ganz besonders traditions- und beziehungslos ... und dem System der überindividuellen Werte ... ganz besonders fremd"[28] — may not be oriented in their actions by any discernible set of values. There may be, as was pointed out above, a far-reaching divorce between their actions and the general value system to which they may still adhere. And, finally, even if a discernible set of special values can be attributed to the entrepreneur, these values are likely to be so recent in origin, so liable to further change, that it would seem highly unsatisfactory to take these values as a basis for interpreting economic action and economic change.

Precisely because in historical reality we are confronted with important cases where entrepreneurs did not appear as disciplined actors performing their preassigned roles in well-structured sociological plays, but entered the historical stage in response to the challenge of great changes in the economic and social environment, it becomes imperative in dealing with the problem of entrepreneurial values to examine their relationship to the environment in the broadest sense of the term. The Russian entrepreneurs of the 1860s and the subsequent decades and the French entrepreneurs of the 1850s have no doubt wrought great economic changes, but it is the emancipation of the peasantry, in the one case, and the establishment of the Second Empire with its liberalizing policies, in the other, that would seem to explain those changes much more readily and simply than would any reference to value systems.

But to say all those things does not imply at all that the conceptual framework used should be banned altogether from the area of entrepreneurial research. Economic historians must at all times try to combine the use of analytical tools provided by economic theory with those supplied by the other social sciences.

404 A. Gerschenkron

Eli Heckscher once even defined economic history as characterized by an interest "in the interplay of economic and other influences on the actual course of events."[29] But too enthusiastic an acceptance of abstract sociological models may tend to discredit the value of interdisciplinary approaches to economic history, and the "theory of roles" may be a case in point. What is suggested here, therefore, is that a serious effort should be made to try to establish through empirical research the spatial and temporal limitations within which the use of such an approach is reasonable and defensible. The discovery of these limits will in itself push the research work into discovery of other sets of propositions and hypotheses, which may be more promising in treating situations, and historical sequences which differ widely from those for which the conceptual framework originally was designed. And it is then that one may begin to hope for a synthesis, that is, for a plausible distribution of emphasis among a variety of factors yielded from pursuit of a variety of approaches.

The crying need for further research should effectively excuse the lack of any substantive conclusions to this essay. But perhaps one or two general impressions may be in order. It would seem that adverse social attitudes toward entrepreneurs and entrepreneurships do not emerge as a major retarding force upon the economic development of European countries in the nineteenth century. This seems also true of Russian industrialization prior to World War I, although in that country one might have expected hostility to entrepreneurs to be of more consequence than in the more advanced countries. In general, one cannot help being impressed by the rapidity with which the numbers of native entrepreneurs multiplied in nineteenth-century Russia and also by the speed with which their behavior became more and more consonant with Western practices.

The temptation is great, of course, to argue from the Russian experience to the present conditions in underdeveloped countries and to arrive at somewhat more optimistic prognostications than those currently in use. But it may be hazardous to succumb to such a temptation. Russia until the First World War had benefited greatly from the presence of foreign entrepreneurs. It is true that some degree of animosity against foreign entrepreneurs and technicians was in clear evidence. But such animosity remained within moderate limits and, if anything, served as a stimulus to native entrepreneurial talent. It may well be that conditions in some of the underdeveloped countries are less favorable in this respect.

Moreover, adverse social attitudes to entrepreneurship in Russia stemmed largely from "preindustrial" value orientations, and those anticapitalist attitudes which usually arise with the spread of the industrial economy did not seem to affect entrepreneurial activities in any marked degree. Quite to the contrary, as mentioned before, the effects of prerevolutionary Marxism on attitudes toward entrepreneurs was presumably positive. It is quite possible that in under-developed countries today the strength of preindustrial values and the resulting lack of sympathy with entrepreneurs is greater than it was in Imperial Russia. And, on the other hand, it is perhaps more likely that those values will more readily coalesce with modern anti-capitalist sentiments and persuasions and that, unlike Russia before 1914, such a combination may find effective expression in acts and policies of the governments

Attitudes, entrepreneurship, and development **405**

concerned. Count Witte's state of the 1890s stood aloof from popular attitudes. But this is much less likely to be true of backward countries in the second half of the twentieth century. Perhaps the generalization may be ventured that adverse social attitudes toward entrepreneurs do not significantly affect the processes of industrialization unless they are allowed to become crystallized in governmental action.

Notes

1 The reference is to the "Round Table" of the International Economic Association on Economic Progress, 1953.
2 The following references (unless otherwise stated) are taken from the symposium, *Toward a General Theory of Action*, edited by Talcott Parsons and Edward A. Shils (Cambridge, Mass., 1951), particularly from the fundamental Part 2, "Values, Motives, and Systems of Action," which comes from the pens of the two editors. The volume, it may be added, provides a most convenient point of entry for an economist who wishes to trespass upon the domain of modern sociology.
3 *Toward a General Theory*, p. 190.
4 *Ibid.*
5 Parsons may be quite unwilling to accept the last sentence of this paragraph as a correct reproduction of his views. Elsewhere (*The Social System*, 1951), he explicitly rejects the "dominant factor theeories which were so popular a generation ago" (p. 493). Yet, time and again, it is said that "value orientations" are used as "major point of reference" (p. 484); that "the primary emphasis of this volume has been on the integration of social systems at the level of patterns of value orientations as institutionalized in role expectations" (p. 350); and so forth. It would seem that from a methodological point of view the substantive outcome is the same, and value orientations when so used do in fact assume the role of the "dominant factor." The difference may lie in the greater awareness of the limitations of the approach, but its locus then is without rather than within the system.
6 Perhaps a word on the system as a whole may go unsuppressed. The system is presented as a social-equilibrium system, thus evoking comparisons with the general-equilibrium concept in economics. But time and again it appears that the concept of equilibrium is extended so far as to become coterminous with that of organized society; what, then, is actually discussed is not so much a set of equilibrium conditions as a set of minimum conditions of social existence, which would mean that most important and most variegated social processes might take place without any change in the basic variables that enter into the system.
7 Harvard University Press (Cambridge, Mass., 1949). A good deal of water has gone down the Charles River since the publication of this volume. In quoting the views expressed by the contributors there is, of course, no intention to suggest that those views are necessarily still held in exactly the same form by the writers concerned. In fact, this would be most unlikely in a new and vigorously expanding field. But the volume in question remains the only reasonably full statement of problems in entrepreneurial research that is available, and it is used here for this reason. A new, venture of the same kind incorporating the thought and the research experience of the intervening years would seem extremely desirable.
8 "The Role Structure of Entrepreneurial Personality."
9 "Role and Sanction in American Entrepreneurial History."
10 *Toward a General Theory*, p. 415.
11 See in this connection the interesting treatment by Redlich of what he calls the "daimonic" entrepreneur: Fritz Redlich, *History of American Business Leaders* (Ann Arbor, 1940), I, 2–6, and "The Business Leader as a Daimonic Figure," *American Journal of Economics and Sociology*, January-April 1953.

406 A. Gerschenkron

12 It may be mentioned that Parsons is well aware of the two types of processes of change. He speaks of "processes within the system" and "processes of change of the system" and objects to a confusion of the two in the common term "dynamics" (*The Social System*, p. 481).

13 J. A. Schumpeter, *Capitalism, Socialism, and Democracy* (New York, 1942), p. 132. See also, *Business Cycles* (New York and London, 1939), I, 100.

14 *Capitalism, loc. cit.*

15 *Essai sur l'histoire de la formation et de progrès du tiers état* (Paris, 1856), I, 108–110.

16 V. G. Belinski, *Pis'ma* (Letters) (St. Petersburg, 1914), III, 329.

17 This point was frequently and effectively made by Hugh Aitken in the writer's seminar.

18 If I were writing this today I should not have spoken of "prerequisites" as much as of "patterns of substitution" for the missing prerequisites. See Chapter 2 of this volume. [A. G., 1962]

19 See Landes "French Entrepreneurship and Industrial Growth in the Nineteenth Century," *The Journal of Economic History*, May 1949, pp. 45–61; and "French Business and the Businessmen in Social and Cultural Analysis," in *Modern France*, Edward Mead Earle, ed. (Princeton, 1951), pp. 334–353. Sawyer, "Strains in the Social Structure of Modern France," in *Modern France*, pp. 293–312; and "The Entrepreneur and the Social Order, France and the United States," in *Men in Business*, William Miller, ed. (Cambridge, Mass., 1952).

20 Landes, "French Entrepreneurship," p. 56.

21 In the original edition of this paper I presented some figures to show that in Germany as in France the small shop was overwhelmingly predominant as far as the number of industrial enterprises was concerned. David Landes rightly criticized a specific deficiency of my data without being able, however, to controvert the point I was trying to make. For, in the end, I believe, we both agreed that in Germany and France before the First World War 94.59 and 97.98 percent, respectively, of all enterprises in industry and mining occupied no more than 10 persons. It is, furthermore, of interest that the "small establishments" in this category were truly small, the average number of those employed per such establishment having been 1.6 in France and 2.0 in Germany (the French figures refer to 1906 and the German figures to 1907). It is another matter that in that period the modern large-scale industry in Germany consisted of larger plants than was the case in France. But this has nothing to do with the untenable view that the small *boutique* was in any significant way more peculiar to France than to Germany. See Alexander Gerschenkron, "Some Further Notes on 'Social Attitudes, Entrepreneurship, and Economic Development,'" *Explorations in Entrepreneurial History*, December 1954. The reader must be referred to two interesting critical comments that have been directed against the present essay: Thomas C. Cochran, "Social Attitudes, Entrepreneurship, and Economic Development: Some Comments," *Explorations in Entrepreneurial History*, February 1954; and David S. Landes, "Social Attitudes, Entrepreneurship, and Economic Development: A Comment," *Explorations in Entrepreneurial History*, May 1954. [A. G., 1962]

22 See Ralph M. Hower, *History of Macy's of New York, 1858–1919* (Cambridge, Mass., 1943), pp. 411f.

23 G. d'Avenel, *Le méchanisme de la vie moderne* (Paris, 1902), pp. 174f.

24 *A Writer's Notebook* (New York, 1949), p. 153.

25 "Philosophie de l'histoire contemporaine: La monarchie constitutionelle en France," *Revue des Deux Mondes*, November 1, 1869, p. 93.

26 Modern research, for instance, has assembled considerable evidence to show that even the American merchants in mid-nineteenth-century frontier regions held merchandizing in low esteem and tried to escape from it as soon as possible into more honorific careers. See, for instance, Lewis E. Atherton, *The Pioneer Merchant in Mid-America*, University of Missouri Studies, April 1, 1939, pp. 30–31.

27 For example, Cochran, in "Role and Sanction in American Entrepreneurial History," p. 174.

28 J. A. Schumpeter, *Theorie der wirtschaftlichen Entwicklung* (Munich-Leipzig, 1926), p. 134.

29 Eli F. Heckscher, "David Davidson," *International Economic Papers*, no. 2 (London-New York, 1952), p. 126. See also, Heckscher's *Historieuppfattning, materialistic och annan* (Stockholm, 1944), pp. 30–31; and W. K. Hancock's emphasis on the basic "impurity" of economic history, *Economic History at Oxford* (Oxford, 1946), p. 5.

PART V

Method

Studying entrepreneurship as a three-legged artifact

> There are truth-seekers and truth-makers. On the one hand, the pure scientist deems himself to be typically faced with a problem which has one right answer. His business is, in the map-maker's language, to get a fix on that problem, to take bearings from the opposite ends of a base-line, and to plot them to converge upon the solution, the truth-to-be-found. On the other hand, the poet-architect-adventurer sees before him a landscape inexhaustibly rich in suggestions and materials for making things, for making works of literature or art or technology, for making policies and history itself, or perhaps for making the complex, delicate, existential system called a business.
>
> *(Shackle, 1966: 767)*

How can truth-seekers study truth-makers? How does the social scientist investigate "worldmaking"? In a world in which opportunities are made as well as found, how do we *do* entrepreneurship research? These are tough questions. But the answers might lie in the very phenomena we are venturing to study. Just as the entrepreneur makes new opportunities with the bits and pieces already at hand, so can we begin fashioning new methods with bits and pieces of old methods currently available. If worldmaking is primarily a process of remaking, so is "methodmaking". And luckily for us, the job of remaking methods itself has already begun in fields as widespread as philosophy, cognitive-linguistics and probability theory.

In the readings in this section, Simon (1998) takes up where Gerschenkron (1962) left off in Part IV, re-conceptualizing the role of historical analysis in the understanding of economic dynamics; Pearl (2000) brings back the study of causality into probability by taking human intervention in the world seriously; Lakoff and Johnson (1980) reconstitutes the very conception of language as constituted from the world; Rorty (1989) then shows us how to put contingency to work in redescribing and refashioning worlds; finally, James (1907) enables all the ideas in this book to take wing by redefining the very notion of "method" itself.

410 Method

Simon: economics as a historical science

Gerchenkron already pointed out the most important problem in social analyses of change, namely that we do not take history seriously. As social "scientists" we sometimes tend to get too obsessed with merely testing time-invariant "theories", resulting in an unwarranted neglect of a truly *empirical* understanding of change. Throughout his career Simon fought to get economists to take the empirical realities of human behavior seriously. In the ensuing selection, he is making a similar argument urging economists to take the historical origins of change into more sober account.

Let us consider treating entrepreneurship the same way Simon urges us to think of cosmology, geology and evolutionary biology, "... as fundamentally empirical and 'historical sciences' that combine time-invariant (scientific) and time-dependent (historical) factors" (1998: 242). This is a particularly attractive combination for the study of human processes in which learning plays a central role. Learning, by definition, is time-dependent, and learning changes the observed phenomena in a very real way. Learning is also closely tied to how human beings think, what they pay attention to and choose to ignore, and the particular sequence of steps they take over time. Therefore, cognitive and historical elements of learning ought to be taken into account as causal factors in the explanation of social change.[1]

Change phenomena are particularly relevant to entrepreneurship researchers because entrepreneurship is one of the most potent yet least studied engines of change in human history. Yet current views tend to portray entrepreneurship either as the generator of random individual variations on which selection works (Aldrich, 2001), or as gales of creative destruction that arise from impersonal forces of innovation (Schumpeter, 1934). More troublesome still are the descriptions of entrepreneurship as an inexplicable "judgment" or "alertness" attributable to certain classes of individuals (Kirzner, 1997), for these exogenize the very phenomena that may be of central interest in developing a useful understanding of entrepreneurship, namely, the formulation of such judgment and the particular elements of learning involved in this formative process.

Simon pushes us toward a more historically and psychologically inclusive analysis where we give up "explaining changes in fashions as produced by fads" – i.e. exogenizing the causes of change from the model (1998: 249). He suggests instead that we begin with the painstaking gathering of historical facts and use those facts to break down traditional distinctions of what's inside and outside "the model." In particular, Simon points out that all of the important data, analysis and scholarly work to be done in economic history (and economics in general) lie in the parameters that economists use as inputs into their models of historical development. Examples include: changes in utility functions (tastes), changes in production functions (technological innovation) and changes in the laws of property (the institutional framework of society). Simon's arguments about making economics a historical science are even more applicable to entrepreneurship research, for entrepreneurs often explicitly strive to *produce* these very changes that economists take as exogenous input parameters in their models. Take for example what Schumpeter said about soap:

> It was not enough to produce satisfactory soap, it was also necessary to induce people to wash.
>
> *(1939: 243)*

In Simon's terms, we can choose one of two options in explaining the establishment of the soap industry:

> Either:
> (1) we explain it as a product of changing tastes (for cleanliness) and changing technology (cheap substitutes for whale oils), both of which exogenize change, and then depend on some theory of alert entrepreneurs grasping the opportunities presented by these changes;
> or
> (2) we could study in depth *how* the changes in tastes and technology actually happened – that is, historically examine the entrepreneurship involved in pushing forward the patterns of changing tastes in addition to creating a synthetic substitute for whale oils.

If we are to take the second route, the factors that need more focus and understanding are precisely the taken-for-granted boundary conditions or the exogenous assumptions that economists (and current entrepreneurship theories) exclude from their models. In particular, Simon specifies three candidates for endogenization:

> (1) changes in the utility functions, with consequent changes in demand and in savings rates; (2) changes in the production function, resulting from technological change and other factors, and with consequent changes in supply; and (3) changes in the laws of property, with consequent effects upon positive and negative externalities, the appropriability of inventions and powers of government to redistribute income and wealth.
>
> *(1998: 251)*

In this connection, Simon also echoes Sen's (1999) concerns about the inadequacy of currently used formal models in accomplishing this task:

> The public choice approach represents an attempt to endogenize these latter kinds of variables, but I shall not comment here on the extent to which it has succeeded or is likely to succeed. You can judge from what I have already said that I am not sanguine.
>
> *(1998: 251)*

Instead, as a first step toward endogenizing changes in tastes, technologies and institutions, Simon lists six dynamically-relevant issues rooted in the reality of human

412 Method

cognition and "closely bound with an historical view of economics" (1998: 250–258). First and foremost, he identifies changing knowledge about economics itself as being an important variable:

> An important task in economic history would be to trace the changes in popular economic beliefs and assess the effects of these changes upon the behavior of the economy and the course of state regulation.
>
> *(1998: 253)*

For a good example of this (1998: 255), consider the abrupt change in prevailing economic doctrine between the 1970s (interventionalist) and 1980s (laissez-faire). This historical event included, among other things, the beginnings of the privatization movement under Prime Minister Margaret Thatcher in the United Kingdom that spread globally in the 1990s. These changes in government ownership of economic activities were driven by changes in economic knowledge, i.e. in what economists thought they knew about economic relationships (see Yergin & Stanislaw, 1998 for a historical account). Similarly, the rise of academic attention to entrepreneurship as a field of inquiry, although partly engendered by the political movement toward privatization, has itself become a causal factor in generating widespread entrepreneurial activities, even spreading it in recent years to the social sector and the arts and sciences (Drayton, 2002; Hockerts, 2006; Cohen & Winn, 2007).

Each of the other five exogenous factors that Simon highlights has similar import to the study of entrepreneurship as well as to the societal and historical consequences of such study. Working out the details of these relationships using the conjunction of comparative statics and historical analysis as a research method opens up a variety of new avenues for entrepreneurship research. Simon's bottom line on the role of historical methods is stated at the end of the article:

> Economic historians have been perhaps too modest in recent times about the role they have to play in establishing our economic knowledge. Their task is much more than one of explaining historical events in terms of an independently derived body of economic theory. It is much more than the one of testing empirically a theory that has already been formulated. The data assembled and analyzed by historians is, in fact, essential for our understanding economic behavior and formulating empirically valid economic laws, including mechanisms that continually alter these laws with the changing knowledge, beliefs, perceptions, values and identifications of the human economic action.
>
> *(1998: 259)*

Simon specifies two ways to combine traditional comparative statics used in economics with conventional techniques used by historians:

> ... first, as an application of the "Cleopatra's nose" approach ("What would have happened had Cleopatra's nose been a quarter-inch longer?"); second,

Method **413**

as a way of examining the effects of an historical event upon the economy. In the former kind of application, a discrete change is introduced in order to compare two different historical sequences, one real, the other hypothetical. In the second application, the comparison evaluates a causal factor in a before-and-after scenario.

(1998: 244–245)

We already saw an illustration of the second application in Gerschenkron's analysis where he used before-and-after scenarios in the histories of several European countries to show the inadequacy of social attitudes as a causal explanation of change. Here we examine an example of the Cleopatra's nose technique. Consider an alternative history of one of the most successful new ventures of the late twentieth century. What if Pierre Omidyar, the founder of eBay, had followed conventional wisdom about how technology entrepreneurship ought to happen? Omidyar himself speculates about eBay's performance had he sought and found funding from venture capitalists:

> So people often say to me, "When you built the system, you must have known that making it self-sustainable was the only way eBay could grow to serve 40 million users a day."
>
> Well … nope. I made the system self-sustaining for one reason: Back when I launched eBay on Labor Day 1995, eBay wasn't my business – it was my hobby. I had to build a system that was self-sustaining … Because I had a real job to go to every morning. I was working as a software engineer from 10 to 7, and I wanted to have a life on the weekends. So I built a system that could keep working – catching complaints and capturing feedback – even when Pam and I were out mountain-biking, and the only one home was our cat. *If I had had a blank check from a big VC, and a big staff running around – things might have gone much worse. I would have probably put together a very complex, elaborate system – something that justified all the investment.* But because I had to operate on a tight budget – tight in terms of money and tight in terms of time – necessity focused me on simplicity: So I built a system simple enough to sustain itself. [emphasis added]

This line of "What if" questioning and the ensuing analysis opens the black box of entrepreneurial making and allows us to perceive the mechanisms beneath broader theoretical concepts such as "innovation" and "entrepreneurial attention". It moves us toward endogenizing variables such as technological change, explaining these in terms of normal human behavior rather than as an exogenously given inexplicable ability or an assumed mystical "judgment".

In sum, both uses of the historical-comparative-statics method that Simon proposes involve taking human agency seriously. The next reading by Judea Pearl offers innovative new techniques of doing this within a more formal toolkit.

414 Method

Pearl: the art and science of cause and effect

In the path-breaking book "Causality" Judea Pearl undertook an ambitious project, namely, the formulation of a new "algebra of doing" (2000: 352). In our selection from this book, Pearl uses an historical approach to explain the need for a formal tool to help study "intervention" as opposed to "observation" in science:

> Scientific activity, as we know it, consists of two basic components:
>
> Observations [40] and interventions [41][2]
>   The combination of the two is what we call a *laboratory* [42], a place where we control some of the conditions and observe others. It so happened that standard algebras have served the observational component very well but thus far have not benefited the interventional component. This is true for the algebra of equations, Boolean algebra, and probability calculus – all are geared to serve observational sentences but not interventional sentences.
>
>   Take, for example, probability theory. If we wish to find the chance it rained, given that we see the grass wet, we can express our question in a formal sentence written like that: $P(\text{Rain}\,|\,\text{Wet})$, to be read: the probability of Rain, given Wet [43]. The vertical bar stands for the phrase: "given that we see." Not only can we express this question in a formal sentence, we can also use the machinery of probability theory and transform the sentence into other expressions. In our example, the sentence on the left can be transformed to the one on the right, if we find it more convenient or informative.
>
>   But suppose we ask a different question: "What is the chance it rained if we *make* the grass wet?" We cannot even express our query in the syntax of probability, because the vertical bar is already taken to mean "given that I see."
>
> *(2000: 351)*

In other words, the entire machinery of formal mathematics currently at our disposal is inadequate to help us study the making of new worlds as opposed to finding existent ones. Ergo, argues Pearl, we need to invent a new tool for the analysis of action as causal intervention. Pearl's invention consists in "surgery" in causal diagrams. This tool is explicitly designed to model multiple worlds – and to resolve one of the most important puzzles in the history of mathematics and formal logic:

> Let us now examine how the surgery interpretation resolves Russell's enigma concerning the clash between the directionality of causal relations and the symmetry of physical equations. The equations of physics are indeed symmetrical, but when we compare the phrases "*A* causes *B*" versus "*B* causes *A*," we are not talking about a single set of equations. Rather, we are comparing two world models, represented by two different sets of equations: one in which the equation for *A* is surgically removed; the other where the equation for *B* is removed.
>
> *(2000: 349)*

Pearl's arguments about the modeling of multiple worlds are closely tied to Simon's point (in the preceding selection) about modelers' choices as to which variables to endogenize within the model and which to keep out:

> The lesson is that it is the way we carve up the universe that determines the directionality we associate with cause and effect. Such carving is tacitly assumed in every scientific investigation. In artificial intelligence it was called "circumscription" by J. McCarthy. In economics, circumscription amounts to deciding which variables are deemed endogenous and which exogenous, *in* the model or *external* to the model.
>
> *(2000: 350)*

In entrepreneurship research, for example, we have *chosen* to keep tastes, judgment and environment exogenous. In such a model, entrepreneurs can only recognize, discover and exploit – that is, *find* opportunities, since opportunities themselves are deemed "out there" and "given". If instead, we choose to bring these within the purview of our models, then entrepreneurship would be as much about the *making* of opportunities as of finding them. In other words, we could model multiple worlds – one in which opportunities cause entrepreneurship and another in which entrepreneurship causes opportunities.

A particularly interesting point in Pearl's historical exposition on the subject of causality concerns the origin of the central idea behind the new tool he has developed:

In summary, *intervention amounts to a surgery on equations* (guided by a diagram) and *causation means predicting the consequences of such a surgery.*

> This is a universal theme that goes beyond physical systems. In fact, the idea of modeling interventions by "wiping out" equations was first proposed in 1960 by an *economist,* Herman Wold …
>
> *(2000: 347)*

It was perhaps not a coincidence that an economist first thought up the notion of using multiple sets of equations to model a phenomenon. Pearl's concise history of causality shows again and again that human purposes shape the tools scientists build and the tools then enable or disable specific lines of scientific development. Take the very origin of the study of causality in engineering problems:

> The problems began, as usual, with engineering; when machines had to be constructed to do useful jobs … [O]nce people started building multistage systems, an interesting thing happened to causality – *physical objects began acquiring causal character.*
>
> *(2000: 333: italics original)*

Over time, this view of the world led to the development of algebra as the most important tool for modeling causal relationships. This tool was so *successful* and

416 Method

capable of such enormous practical use that it came to be synonymous with reality itself. Galileo's proclamation in mid-seventeenth century that algebra was "the *universal* language of science" came to be accepted not simply as a useful way to model the physical world, but as the *only* way to do science. Pearl reminds us to reconsider our acceptance of the confounding of modelers' *choices,* however useful, with the world as it actually is or could be:

> Why would Nature agree to speak algebra? Of all languages?
> But you can't argue with success.
>
> *(2000: 335)*

This success of algebraic equations consisted not only in the *discovery* of the laws of nature but also in the *construction* of better machines and other artifacts that served a variety of *human* purposes:

> They enabled engineers, for the first time in history, to ask "how to" questions in addition to "what if" questions.
>
> In addition to asking "What if we narrow the beam, will it carry the load?" They began to ask more difficult questions: "How to shape the beam so that it *will* carry the load?" [14]
>
> *(2000: 335)*

Could Pearl's development of surgery in causal diagrams lead to a similar opening up of new and more difficult questions in economics and entrepreneurship to more systematic analyses? In other words, could this new tool enable us to model entrepreneurship as a science of the artificial? Pearl's application of the tool to "The adjustment problem" described on pp. 355–358 offers considerable promise. It is easy to imagine a variety of issues in entrepreneurship research that are subject to the adjustment problem. Take for example the effect of governmental incentives (X) such as seed capital and incubators on jobs generated through entrepreneurial activities (Y). This has all the general characteristics of the adjustment problem described by Pearl:

> The moral is that all conclusions are extremely sensitive to which variables we choose to hold constant when we are comparing, and that is why the adjustment problem is so critical in the analysis of observational studies.
>
> Consider an observational study where we wish to find the effect of X on Y, for example, treatment on response [50]. We can think of many factors that are relevant to the problem; some are affected by the treatment, some are affecting the treatment, and some are affecting both treatment and response. Some of these factors may be unmeasurable, such as genetic trait or life style; others are measurable, such as gender, age, and salary level. Our problem is to select a subset of these factors for measurement and adjustment so that, if we compare subjects under the same value of those measurements and average, we get the right result.
>
> *(2000: 357)*

Method **417**

Currently, we solve this problem through theory, often theory generated through time-invariant "laws" of economics or other social sciences. But it would be useful to have a way of making this decision based on time-dependent, i.e. contingent and/or historical data too. And maybe even inductively generate as yet unimagined new theories (as Simon suggested about the potential of good historical analysis). As Pearl points out at the end of the exposition,

> What I have presented to you today is a sort of pocket calculator, an *abacus* [57], to help us investigate certain problems of cause and effect with mathematical precision. This does not solve the problem of causality, but the power of *symbols* and mathematics should not be underestimated [58].
>
> *(2000: 357)*

Like every new abacus, this tool itself awaits modifications and improvements as we begin using it to study phenomena involving causal intervention by active agents such as entrepreneurs in the making of new worlds. In the meanwhile, we examine below yet another type of promising new abacus, this time from cognitive linguistics.

Lakoff and Johnson on conceptual metaphor

Lakoff and Johnson's (L&J's) thesis about "conventional metaphors" coheres with a large body of research in biology, neurology, cognition and linguistics. Taken together, this research is headed toward showing how language and meaning are rooted in the fact that we have bodies and that these bodies are constituted of and interact with the physical (and social) environment in which we live. Language, therefore, arises out of our primary "experience" consisting in movement in physical (and social) space:

> In other words, the structure of our spatial concepts emerges from our constant spatial experience, that is, our interaction with our physical environment. Concepts that emerge in this way are concepts that we live by in the most fundamental way.
>
> *(1980: 476)*

Cognitive science has amassed considerable evidence that pattern recognition is a primitive of all cognitive processes (Posner & Petersen, 1990; Pylyshyn, 1994). And the most fundamental way the brain recognizes patterns is through a process of matching every new input with existing patterns and understanding or (re)conceptualizing both in terms of similarities and differences. This exact same process is what linguists call "metaphor" – using one expression to (partially) denote another. As L&J point out,

> Metaphors is for most people a device of the poetic imagination and the rhetorical flourish – a matter of extraordinary than ordinary language.
>
> *(1980: 453)*

418 Method

But when we take into account the way cognition works through processes of partial and continual pattern matching, it becomes easier to see how

> ... metaphor is pervasive in everyday life, not just in language, but in thought and action.
>
> *(1980: 454)*

The L&J thesis about the ubiquity of metaphors seeks to root meaning in biology and is very consistent with Davidson's arguments about the subjective-objective-intersubjective nature of all knowledge:

> The concepts that govern our thought are not just matters of the intellect. They also govern our everyday functioning, down to the most mundane details. Our concepts structure what we perceive, how we get around in the world, and how we relate to other people.
>
> *(1980: 454)*

Not only is the central thesis of the L&J article exciting and provocative, but the *method* they use to arrive at the thesis also holds promise for entrepreneurship research:

> Primarily on the basis of linguistic evidence, we have found that most of our ordinary conceptual system is metaphorical in nature and *we have found a way* to begin to identify in detail just what the metaphors are that structure how we perceive, how we think, and what we do. [italics added]
>
> *(1980: 454)*

The simplest way for us to understand L&J's method is to use the same tactic that L&J themselves use: examples. These examples enable us to see how L&J's ideas are just as important, relevant and prevalent in entrepreneurship. In particular, let us apply L&J's method to the conventional metaphors that underlie our own research. We may not consciously use these metaphors, yet they structure the phenomena we perceive and drive the research strategies we actually end up using.

"Opportunities are hidden objects"

For example, take the concept of "opportunities," which has been a central topic of discussion in contemporary entrepreneurship literature. A well developed literature on opportunities is found in the work of Austrians, particularly Kirzner. Here we see an example of a scholar who takes a central metaphor and then spins out the entailments of the metaphor, in Kirzner's case in the course of several books and well-known articles. Central in Kirzner's work is the idea that opportunities are hidden objects. Entrepreneurs are individuals who discover these hidden objects, which are scattered around in the market economy. According to Kirzner:

"[T]he entrepreneur grasps the opportunities for pure profit ..." (1997: 69). The way in which opportunities are objects is made obvious by the use of the term "grasping". All the more significant is the fact that, as L&J point out (1980: 485) "the very concepts themselves are partially defined in terms of multiple physical and structural metaphors". This is the case with "grasping", which gives Kirzner a handy way of communicating what is, for him, a central aspect of entrepreneurship. This metaphor establishes a physical relationship between an entrepreneur and an opportunity, which is "grasped by piercing a fog of uncertainty" (Kirzner, 1985), or not, as the case may be. More recent reconceptualizations of the opportunity construct continue to carry within them the hidden object metaphor by emphasizing the subjective evaluation of venture ideas and their enablers through feedback loops (Davidsson, 2015).

The "hidden" in hidden objects corrals our work down particular avenues such as (Dew et al., 2015):

- Entrepreneurs *search* for opportunities or *dig* for them
- They may *recognize* them or fail to do so and *pass them by*
- Entrepreneurs are more *alert* than non-entrepreneurs at *spotting* opportunities
- Some people *overlook* opportunities or *miss* them completely
- Instead of "digging" for opportunities and "discovering" them, one can also "hunt" for opportunities
- Persistent entrepreneurs *pursue* opportunities and *find* them
- Some people have an internal compass that *orients* them in the correct direction toward opportunities
- The hidden objects that are opportunities could be like buried treasure *incentivizing* the *need for achievement* in the entrepreneur. But they are also like buried land mines necessitating *risk-taking* and maybe even reckless *overconfidence*.

It is important, however, to note L&J's point that, whatever the merits or demerits of any particular metaphor, the central feature of a conceptual metaphor is that we define our reality in terms of the metaphor. Conceptual metaphors therefore *highlight* certain aspects of reality and *hide* others (1980: 458). For instance, the conceptual metaphor of "opportunities as hidden objects" entails a hunter-gatherer worldview and masks the more nurturing aspects of an agricultural worldview – such as the possibilities for *planting*, *growing* and *reaping* opportunities, or the creative aspects of an industrial outlook – enabling the *manufacture* or *fabrication* of opportunities – one of the key ideas underlying the various readings in this book.

Using similar linguistic analyses to those developed by L&J, we can discover other conceptual metaphors in entrepreneurship such as "Institutions are the rules of the game" (North, 1990). This sets up economic interaction as a game that is "played" by opponents. According to McMillan (2001) the market is an organized brawl, not a free-for-all, as entailed by "rules". He uses the metaphor of folk football, compared to its descendants: soccer, American football, rugby, Aussie rules

420 Method

football. In turn, these games often use metaphors of war, such as those explored by L&J in "Argument is war".

Another metaphor in widespread use is the "Markets are containers" metaphor. This metaphor is particularly prevalent in IO (industrial organization) economists' studies of entrepreneurial "entry" (Porter, 1980). Entry into what? Well, entry into a container – i.e. an object that has distinct boundaries. As L&J put it:

> We experience many things through sight and touch as having distinct boundaries. And when things have no distinct boundaries, we often project boundaries upon them – conceptualizing them as entities and often as containers (for example, forests, clearings, clouds).
>
> *(1980: 477)*

That is why it makes sense to talk about market *penetration, capture* of market share, *strategizing for* and *protecting* market leadership, *occupying* a niche, *expansion* of existing product lines, *pushing into* new segments, etc. In sociology the metaphor of markets as fields (Fligstein, 2002) involves precisely the same conceptual moves: bounding the space, structuring it as a container that things can be inside or out, into which "entry" occurs, and within which certain substances are held, and over the rim of which things can spill over. Porter classically used the container metaphor for industries, with the entailment that the way to keep the container from overflowing with competitors was to erect barriers to entry, which would stop new entrants getting into the industry (that bounded space). The Porter example is another good case of how a theorist traces out the entailments of a metaphor, as well as being another example of the intuitive appeal of spatial metaphors.

One of the most important insights we obtain by applying a cognitive-linguistic analysis to entrepreneurship, both as a phenomenon and as a field of research, is that the "reality" we investigate is *contingent* upon the conceptual metaphors we implicitly assume in the language we use to describe it. That is why any method that seeks to study entrepreneurship as a science of the artificial has to explicitly and unflinchingly grapple with contingency as a central factor of human existence. To begin on that specific task, we turn to Richard Rorty's seminal book: *Contingency, Irony, Solidarity*.

Rorty on the contingency of language and selfhood

The three selections so far in this part of the book have emphasized and sought to reconstitute empirical methods into new tools for doing entrepreneurship research: history, causality and metaphor. The three chapters from Rorty's book help us think through *theoretical* methods for furthering our understanding. How do we theorize about phenomena where contingency plays a central role without falling into a vacuous tautology that contingency causes contingency? At first reading, the essays may be rather unsettling for they pose serious challenges to a variety of deep-seated metaphysical positions about language, selfhood and community – each of which speaks to the very core of who we are, how we live and what we care about, not to mention all that we could become, the values we aspire to live by and the ideals we believe everyone ought to care about. Take for example the last paragraph of the essay on the contingency of language:

> The line of thought common to Blumenberg, Nietzsche, Freud, and David-son suggests that we try to get to the point where we no longer worship *anything,* where we treat *nothing* as a quasi divinity, where we treat *everything* – our language, our conscience, our community – as products of time and chance.
>
> *(1989: 22)*

The trick is not to decide whether we "buy" Rorty's thesis wholesale, but to boldly wade into the plenitude of his ideas and try some on for size; to learn to play with them the way a "strong poet" of entrepreneurship research would play with theories of entrepreneurship (Harmeling et al., 2009). Consider, for example, the fact that Rorty does *not* mention the role of the entrepreneur. Let us see how his arguments matter (or don't) when we inject entrepreneurship in:

> The poets claimed for art the place in culture traditionally held by religion and philosophy, the place which the Enlightenment had claimed for science.
>
> *(1989: 3)*

Today entrepreneurs such as Daymond John or Anita Roddick claim for business a similar seminal, constitutive, paradigmatic role. And as entrepreneurship research-ers, we have the exciting task of scoping out the possibilities for and consequences of societies in which business plays such a central role. The time is ripe for new theoretical imaginings of the caliber of Adam Smith and Schumpeter. In this regard it is a curious coincidence (or perhaps a crucial contingency) that Rorty should end up quoting Berlin quoting Schumpeter on p. 46. Reinhart and Rogoff (2002) point out that Schumpeter drew on Nietzsche (though indirectly) for his concept of entrepreneurship, including the idea of the entrepreneur-leader (which anticipates Rorty's strong poet) and the idea of creative destruction (which has much in common with Rorty's embrace of purely contingent evolutionary processes). The point is that if we perform a historical trace of the flow of ideas – in order to point out the place of, and links between, entrepreneurship and the history of big ideas – there is a meaningful tapestry that weaves together the Romantic poets, Utopian politics, Enlightenment science, and German idealists and postmodern truth-makers to entrepreneurship. One strand of this evocative tapestry connects Nietzsche ("recreating all 'it was' into 'thus I willed it.'") to entrepreneurship via Schum-peter's creative destruction. It is the same strand that connects Nietzsche to the strong poet also through a form of creative destruction:

422 Method

The hope of such a poet is that what the past tried to do to her she will succeed in doing to the past; to make the past itself, including those very causal processes which blindly impressed all her own behavings, bear *her* impress.

(1989: 29)

Are there any examples of strong poets in entrepreneurship? There would probably be little argument that among the possible candidates that exist, Schumpeter stands out prominently, for one can hardly read Schumpeter's chapter VII "The process of creative destruction" (Schumpeter, 1976) without seeing the world in a new light as a product of Schumpeter's description of the capitalist process.

Schumpeter does what Rorty's strong poet is supposed to do: by introducing the metaphor of "Entrepreneurship as creative destruction," he compels us to notice different things in the world, and therefore behave differently. This metaphor highlights the revolutionary nature of the changes entrepreneurs bring about and entails our noticing that entrepreneurship is intertwined with innovation and competition in ways very different from earlier conceptualizations of the entrepreneur as efficient allocator of given resources or simply an input into the existing production functions. The Schumpeterian description coheres with Hayek's view of competition as a discovery procedure (1984) and shows up the neoclassical conception of perfect competition as an empty shell. But as all metaphors that become entrenched in subsequent vocabularies, Schumpeter's description highlights certain aspects (the heroic and the dramatic, for example), at the same time that it hides others. In particular it distracts us from observing the mundane realities of ordinary people *becoming* entrepreneurs through their private attempts to live well and overcome their fear of being just a replica, a copy. The creative destruction metaphor keeps us from seeing entrepreneurship as a powerful tool available to anyone who seeks to become an "I", a self-created individual striving to cross the boundary "which divides the old from the new". (1989: 25 and 29).

The notion of the strong poet is but one strand in the historical tapestry of ideas that Rorty opens up for our appreciation. There are other strands that weave entrepreneurship into this tapestry and even suggest that entrepreneurs, as much as poets and thinkers, may actually be doing the weaving itself. In the following passage, for example, if we substitute the words 'business models' for vocabularies, the argument becomes highly evocative of Knightian uncertainty, Buchanan and Vanberg's notion of the market as a game without goods and Sen's conceptualization of development as freedom:

This Wittgensteinian analogy between vocabularies and tools has one obvious drawback. The craftsman typically knows what job he needs to do before picking or inventing tools with which to do it. By contrast, someone like Galileo, Yeats, or Hegel (a "poet" in my wide sense of the term – the sense of "one who makes things new") is typically unable to make clear exactly

Method **423**

what it is that he wants to do before developing the language in which he succeeds in doing it. His new vocabulary makes possible, for the first time, a formulation of its own purpose.

(1989: 12–13)

Sprinkled throughout the three essays is a veritable cornucopia of new ideas and promising methods for grappling with contingency in new ways in our theorizing. Several of these also connect up in interesting ways with specific readings in this book:

- truth-making versus truth seeking (1989: 3);
- most sentences of our language being dead metaphor (1989: 18);
- the tensions between context-invariant theories and context-dependent ones (1989: 25);
- truth as a "mobile army of metaphors" (1989: 27);
- *causes* as invented rather than discovered (1989: 28);
- Freud's democratization of genius by giving *everyone* a creative unconscious – evocative of Julian Simon's and de Soto's conceptualization of the entrepreneurial potential in all human beings (1989: 36);
- the accidental coincidence of a private obsession with a public need – evocative of social choice problems (1989: 37);
- juggling several useful and valuable descriptions of the same event without asking which one was right – evocative of Bruner's and Goodman's making of multiple worlds (1989: 39).

The list could go on. But the overarching conclusion is as easy as it is promising: we clearly need new descriptions of entrepreneurship if we are to model it as the making of new worlds and not exclusively a process of finding them. To accomplish this task, entrepreneurship researchers too have to cast off

... [the] disposition to use the languages of our dead ancestors, to worship the corpses of their metaphors.

(1989: 21)

and undauntedly embrace scholarship that becomes instead

a contest between an entrenched vocabulary which has become a nuisance and a half-formed new vocabulary which vaguely promises great things.

(1989: 9)

This book itself has been an attempt to spell out such a half-formed new vocabulary. And any promise it holds for the field of entrepreneurship research consists in the difference it makes to our actual work as scholars in identifying problems we do not yet see, formulating new questions we could ask and care about, and reshaping

424 Method

tools to tackle issues we cannot even imagine at this point in time. This difference could make all the difference not only to the future of entrepreneurship research, but also to the teaching and practice of entrepreneurship, and through entrepreneurial making, to the very world we live in. The next selection from James brings out the importance of differences that make a difference; it suggests how all the ideas discussed in this book might come together to examine what is, perhaps, the single most important question all research methods must address: what is worth researching.

James: what pragmatism means

It seems a long way to go back in time to find a selection to end this book. But some classics are worth revisiting every once in a while, simply to remind ourselves why our work is worth doing at all. James' essay on the pragmatic method is such a classic for it offers just the continuity in ideas required to make the provocations in this book worth pursuing; it provides the glue to hold together the theses sloshing around in the various readings. As James reminds us:

> The most violent revolutions in an individual's beliefs leave most of his old order standing. Time and space, cause and effect, nature and history, and one's own biography remain untouched. New truth is always a go-between, a smoother-over of transitions. It marries old opinion to new fact so as ever to show a minimum of jolt, a maximum of continuity.
>
> *(1907)*

What pragmatism means is the second of a series of eight lectures that James dedicated to the memory of John Stuart Mill. In this series, James is laying out in detail the basic elements of his philosophy of pragmatism, seeking to inspire future adherents as well as put to rest doubts and disputes from critics of his time. He introduces the key idea early in the lecture:

> The pragmatic method is primarily a method of settling metaphysical disputes that otherwise might be interminable. Is the world one or many? – fated or free? – material or spiritual? – here are notions either of which may or may not hold good of the world; and disputes over such notions are unending. The pragmatic method in such cases is to try to interpret each notion by tracing its respective practical consequences. What difference would it practically make to anyone if this notion rather than that notion were true?

The pragmatic method suggests a simple test that all our hypotheses should pass before we invest serious research efforts into their verification or falsification. The test also forms a good guide for selecting worthwhile doctoral dissertation projects and any other kind of empirical investigation or hard-thinking theoretical endeavor. In particular it helps us formulate our questions in more useful and valuable ways:

It is astonishing to see how many philosophical disputes collapse into insignificance the moment you subject them to this simple test of tracing a concrete consequence. There can be no difference anywhere that doesn't make a difference elsewhere … The whole function of philosophy ought to be to find out what definite difference it will make to you and me, at definite instants of our life, if this world-formula or that world formula be the true one.

Hark back to one of the questions we listed in the introductory chapter to this book: Are entrepreneurial opportunities out there or in here? If we ask instead what practical difference it makes whether opportunities are out there or not, we can immediately see that it might be more useful to find out under which circumstances it might be useful to think of opportunities as being out there (to be *found* and exploited) and when it would be more useful to conceptualize them as being in here (to then be *made* into new possibilities, or not). We can apply a similar set of thought experiments to a variety of problems currently on the agenda of entrepreneurship research and transform them into new questions whose cash value would be transparent even before we embark on our empirical journeys.

In James' view;

Theories thus become instruments, not answers to enigmas, in which we can rest. We don't lie back upon them, we move forward, and, on occasion, make nature over again by their aid. Pragmatism unstiffens all our theories, limbers them up and sets each one at work.

The pragmatic method is primarily instrumental — but it is also pluralistic. James points this out using Papini's compelling image of a hotel corridor:

It has no dogmas, and no doctrines save its method. As the young Italian pragmatist Papini has well said, it lies in the midst of our theories, like a corridor in a hotel. Innumerable chambers open out of it. In one you may find a man writing an atheistic volume; in the next someone on his knees praying for faith and strength; in a third a chemist investigating a body's properties. In a fourth a system of idealistic metaphysics is being excogitated; in a fifth the impossibility of metaphysics is being shown. But they all own the corridor, and all must pass through it if they want a practicable way of getting into or out of their respective rooms.

This account of pluralism is true of all sciences — natural, social and artificial. In fact, James asserts that scientific laws:

… are only a man-made language, a conceptual shorthand, as someone calls them, in which we write our reports of nature; and languages, as is well known, tolerate much choice of expression and many dialects.

426 Method

Not only is the pragmatic method a useful method for deciding which projects to pursue in entrepreneurship research, it is curiously appropriate to the actual practice of entrepreneurship too. Consider for example the following passage about the process by which "any individual settles into new opinions":

> The process here is always the same. The individual has a stock of old opinions already, but he meets a new experience that puts them to a strain. Somebody contradicts them; or in a reflective moment he discovers that they contradict each other; or he hears of facts with which they are incompatible; or desires arise in him which they cease to satisfy. The result is an inward trouble to which his mind till then had been a stranger, and from which he seeks to escape by modifying his previous mass of opinions. He saves as much of it as he can, for in this matter of belief we are all extreme conservatives. So he tries to change first this opinion, and then that (for they resist change very variously), until at last some new idea comes up which he can graft upon the ancient stock with a minimum of disturbance of the latter, some idea that mediates between the stock and the new experience and runs them into one another most felicitously and expediently.

This process appears applicable just as well to the fabrication of successful new venture models by entrepreneurs and their stakeholders. And here is a crucial connection between the pragmatic method and the entrepreneurial process. Both the pragmatic method and the entrepreneurial process are engaged in the *same enterprise:* building today's world from yesterday's; new ones from bits and pieces of the old. And just as the pragmatist works *with* human psychology and historical contingency to transform beliefs and values and even societies and cultures as a whole, so does the entrepreneur need to build upon action and chance to cocreate new ventures, new markets and new worlds.

James's outline of the pragmatic method anticipates several of the readings in this book. It is already pregnant with Davidson's, Lakoff and Johnson's and Pearl's notion of minds interacting with reality:

> It converts the absolutely empty notion of a static relation of "correspondence" ... between our minds and reality, into that of a rich and active commerce ...
>
> *(105)*

We also saw evidence of this profitable "commerce" in the work of empiricists such as the two Simons, Gerschenkron and deSoto as well as theorists such as Bruner, Sen and Goodman. As Judea Pearl pointed out in terms of Simpson's Paradox, the fact is that as researchers we make choices that make a difference; and perhaps more so as teachers and advisors to policy makers. Whether we acknowledge it explicitly or not, we select what falls within our model and what remains out, we decide what is worth the attention of our peers and those who heed our work and what is kept out of their line of sight, and in designing our research projects we even determine who we are as scholars and human beings and what we can and cannot become. James is (as are Pearl, Rorty and others) simply urging us to become aware of our choices so we may not waste them in some kind of a blind adherence to research convention.

"The trail of the human serpent is thus over everything", whispers the Jamesian conscience as we sit down at our drawing boards. It is time we got comfortable in our skins as well as our chairs as we grasp the possibilities and consequences of our research choices.

Notes

1 This point is reinforced and elaborated upon in the readings from Rorty that show how social change occurs through people learning to speak differently.
2 The numbers inside [...] refer to illustrations that depict the ideas in the book chapter.

References

Aldrich, H. (2001). *Organizations evolving*. Thousand Oaks, CA: Sage Publications Incorporated.

Cohen, B. & Winn, M. I. (2007). Market imperfections, opportunity and sustainable entrepreneurship. *Journal of Business Venturing* **22**(1): 29–49.

Davidsson, P. (2015). Entrepreneurial opportunities and the entrepreneurship nexus: A reconceptualization. *Journal of Business Venturing* **30**(5): 674–695.

Dew, N., Grichnik, D., Mayer-Haug, K., Read, S. & Brinckmann, J. (2015). Situated entrepreneurial cognition. *International Journal of Management Reviews* **17**(2): 143–164.

Drayton, W. (2002). The citizen sector: Becoming as entrepreneurial and competitive as business. *California Management Review* **44**(3): 120–132.

Fligstein, N. (2002). *The architecture of markets*. Princeton, NJ: Princeton University Press.

Gerschenkron, A. (1962). *Economic backwardness in historical perspective: A book of essays*. Cambridge, MA: Belknap Press.

Harmeling, S. S., Sarasvathy, S. D. & Freeman R. E. (2009). Related debates in ethics and entrepreneurship: Values, opportunities, and contingency. *Journal of Business Ethics* **84**(3): 341–365.

Hayek, F. A. (1984). Competition as a discovery procedure. In Nishiyama, C. & Leube, K. R. *The essence of Hayek*. Stanford, CA: Stanford University Press: 257.

Hayek, F. A. (1989). The pretence of knowledge. *The American Economic Review* **79**(6): 3–7.

Hockerts, K. (2006). Entrepreneurial opportunity in social purpose business ventures. In Mair, J., Robinson, J. & Hockerts, K. (Eds.) *Social entrepreneurship*. London, Palgrave Macmillan.

James, W. (1907). What pragmatism means. In *Pragmatism: A new name for some old ways of thinking*. (pp. 17–32). New York, Longman Green and Co.

James, W. (1907). What pragmatism means. In Menand, L. (Ed.) *Pragmatism: A reader*. New York, Vintage Books.

Kirzner, I. M. (1985). *Perception, opportunity and profit studies in the theory of entrepreneurship*. University of Chicago Press.

Kirzner, I. M. (1997). Entrepreneurial discovery and the competitive market process: An Austrian approach. *Journal of Economic Literature* **35**: 60–85.

428 Method

Lakoff, G. & Johnson, M. (1980). Conceptual metaphor in everyday language. *The Journal of Philosophy* **77**(8): 452–486.

McMillan, J. (2001). *Reinventing the bazaar: A natural history of markets.* New York, Norton.

North, D. C. (1990). *Institutions, institutional change and economic performance.* Cambridge University Press.

Pearl, J. (2000). The art and science of cause and effect. In *Causality: Models, reasoning, and inference.* Cambridge University Press.

Porter, M. E. (1980). *Competitive strategy: Techniques for analyzing industries and competition.* New York, Free Press. 300.

Posner, M. I. & Petersen, S. E. (1990). The attention system of the human brain. *Annual Review of Neuroscience* **13**(1): 25–42.

Pylyshyn, Z. (1994). Some primitive mechanisms of spatial attention. *Cognition* **50**(1–3): 363–384.

Reinhart, C. M. & Rogoff, K. S. (2002). *The modern history of exchange rate arrangements: A reinterpretation.* NBER Working Paper No.8963.

Rorty, R. (1989). *Contingency, irony, and solidarity.* Cambridge University Press.

Schumpeter, J. (1934). *The theory of economic development.* Oxford University Press.

Schumpeter, J. (1939). *Business cycles: A theoretical, historical, and statistical analysis of the capitalist process.* New York and London, McGraw-Hill.

Schumpeter, J. (1976). The process of creative destruction. In *Capitalism, socialism and democracy.* (pp. 81–86) New York, Allen & Unwin.

Sen, A. (1999). The possibility of social choice. *The American Economic Review* **89**(3): 349–378.

Shackle, G. L. S. (1966). Policy, poetry and success. *The Economic Journal* **76**(304): 755–767.

Simon, H. A. (1998). Economics as a historical science. *Theoria* **13**(32): 241–260.

Yergin, D. & Stanislaw, J. (1998). *The commanding heights: The battle for the world economy.* New York, Simon & Schuster.

19

ECONOMICS AS A HISTORICAL SCIENCE

*H. A. Simon**

* CARNEGIE-MELLON UNIVERSITY, BAKER HALL, PITTSBURGH, PENNSYLVANIA 15213, USA. E-MAIL: HAS@A.GP.CS.CMU.EDU
BIBLID [0495-4548 (1998) 13: 32; P. 241–260]

Abstract

As science deals with invariants and history with dated events, the phrase "historical science" might be thought to be an oxymoron. However, the prevalence in the natural sciences and economics of differential equations filled with time derivatives should persuade us of the legitimacy of joining history with science. The combination can, in fact, take several forms. This paper examines some of the ways in which history and economics can be fashioned into economic history, and the reasons why they need to be so joined.

A particularly important source of historicity in economics is that boundedly rational economic actors represent the economic scene in radically different ways from time to time, and these changes occur as a function of natural and social events, social influences on perception, and the molding of human motives by the social environment, which is itself time dependent. For these and other reasons, many of them bound closely to basic human characteristics, the dynamic movements of the economic system depend not only on invariant laws, but on continually changing boundary conditions as well.

Introduction

Everyone knows what history is and what science is, but the meaning of "historical science" is less obvious. To be historical, a science must, at least, be concerned with dated events –their occurrence, their prediction, and their explanation. "When was Charlemagne crowned?", "When will there be more computers than people in the world?", "Why (or how) did the American colonists revolt from Britain?"

Cosmology, geology, and evolutionary biology, as usually defined, qualify as historical sciences in this sense, for cosmology is concerned with the date of the

430 H. A. Simon

Big Bang, the date when the next solar eclipse will occur, and the frequency with which the Earth is struck by meteors; geology is concerned with the date of the Wisconsin glaciation, the date of the next Ice Age, and the mechanisms of continental drift. Evolutionary biology is concerned with the date of first appearance of mammals, the size of the human population in 2050, and the mechanisms that produced a dozen new phyla of multi-celled animals at the beginning of the Cretaceous Era.

But from another standpoint, cosmology (alias astrophysics), geology (alias geophysics) and evolutionary biology (alias theory of evolution) are time-independent sciences; for they aspire to (and sometimes discover) descriptive and explanatory laws that are invariant over time: laws often in the form of systems of differential equations. They discover general relativity, continental plate theory, the survival of the fittest genes. Of course the laws are time-subscripted -they make assertions about the state of a system at particular times- but they themselves are invariant, subject to the specification of initial and boundary conditions. It is, in fact, this combination of dated events with invariance of the governing laws that spares the phrase "historical science" from an oxymoronic fate.

The boundary between the dated and the timeless in the laws of a science depends, in turn on the boundaries of the systems to which the laws are applied. The laws of physics, taken collectively and applied to the entire Universe and the matter in it, are supposed (hoped?) to be invariant. Applied to a single planet, the movements they predict depend upon boundary conditions, which depend, in turn, on the continually changing space and matter surrounding the planet.

Nor are most laws of a science entirely general, or intended to be. Even Newtonian mechanics is a limited science that applies only to objects that are not too small (so that quantum effects are inconsequential) nor too speedy (so that the effects of special or general relativity are insignificant). Similarly, special laws of physics apply to gases, others to liquids (or even just to non-turbulent liquids), and others to various kinds of solids. The behavior of crystals and near-crystalline substances has yielded an especially rich collection of special laws in the past generation, as has the behavior of plasmas. In sciences other than physics -chemistry and biology, for example- many or most of the laws are even more specialized. Those who view the natural sciences from the outside tend to exaggerate the generality of the laws that their practitioners actually apply to the situations they study, and economists have, in this way perhaps learned the wrong lesson from them.

Invariant laws in economics

Neoclassical economics has had aspirations (and sometimes even has expressed them (Samuelson's Nobel Address (1970) provides an example) to timelessness in the sense of the general laws of physics. Its laws sometimes take the form of differential equations that are supposed to hold at "all" times; sometimes of static equations that describe the stable equilibria or the steady states of the corresponding dynamic

Economics as a historical science **431**

systems. A common form of analysis (comparative statics) is to infer the steady-state effects of altering the parameters of dynamic or static equations.

Of course formal economic analysis, like any formal analysis, acknowledges that its laws hold in the real world only in systems that satisfy specified conditions (to some acceptable approximation). In this sense the theory is tautological and can be pursued by mathematical reasoning without recourse to facts. Thus, the actors commonly have invariant utility functions and fixed (although possibly infinite) sets of alternatives. Economic transactions in the theory commonly take place in perfectly competitive markets, where uncertainty is represented by (subjective) probability distributions so that actors can maximize subjective expected utility.

The reader can supply the variants on this theme, each of which may strengthen or weaken a theory's predictions. For examples of the latter, we need only look at game theory and the theory of imperfect competition in general, where, to reach any firm conclusions, we must almost always augment the theory by greatly elaborating and specializing the usual definition of rationality to encompass the "mutual outguessing" phenomenon.

Contemporary economic history

The study of the history of economic institutions and behavior has long been a special, and rather separate discipline within economics. In recent times, economic history has undergone a fundamental transformation. As recently as the first edition of *The Encyclopaedia of the Social Sciences* (1931), John Clapham defined the discipline as "a branch of institutional history, a study of the economic aspects of the social institutions of the past." Less than forty years later, Douglass North, in his article on the same subject in the successor volume, *The International Encyclopedia of the Social Sciences* (1968), remarks that Clapham "made clear that economic theory had a minor role in economic history and 'the relationship of economic history to social history is much closer'."

North describes a "distinct change in the discipline in recent times" in its "appeal to a systematic body of theory as a source of generalization and by the equally systematic use of quantitative methods of organizing evidence." He attributes the change to three developments:

> the growing interest of economists in the study of economic growth, (...) the growing interest of economics in the more precise testing of their hypotheses, (...) [and] the growing volume of quantitative information about the past.

As spokesman for economic history, North exhibits a certain diffidence about its relation to theory. "There is no reason," he says,

> (...) why the economic historian should be limited to received theory in economics. He is free to develop and apply theory of his own. However, caution

432 H. A. Simon

in such an endeavor is obviously essential. *The Likelihood that the economic historian who is untrained in the principles of economics can derive theoretical propositions of any significance is very slim indeed* [my italics]. (...) The economic historian trained in economic theory will be well aware of the pitfalls inherent in economic analysis. Therefore, if he wishes to develop his own theoretical framework, he will take careful account of the work that has gone on before and the degree to which previous generalizations are supported by available evidence.

Later, North comments further on the limitations of theory, observing, for example, that "there is no general theory of economic growth to which the economic historian can turn in exploring this major aspect of economic history." Read in context, his statement is balanced, and cannot be faulted, but it does defer to the reigning ethos of economics in the importance it attaches to theory, even in the face of recalcitrant facts.

History and comparative statics

Comparative statics is a powerful and widely used technique of economics analysis that has important applications in history. It can be employed in at least two ways: first, as an application of the "Cleopatra's nose" approach ("What would have happened had Cleopatra's nose been a quarter inch longer?"); second, as a way of examining the effects of an historical event upon the economy. In the former kind of application, a discrete change is introduced in order to compare two different historical sequences, one real, the other hypothetical. In the second application, the comparison evaluates a causal factor in a before-and-after scenario.

An Example: Urbanization. As a simple example of the second use of neoclassical comparative statics (urbanization during the Industrial Revolution), and its limitations, I will use a foray of my own into economic history, *"Effects of Increased Productivity upon the Ratio of Urban to Rural Population."* A simple two-industry model (agriculture and manufacturing) was used to show that, provided that the income elasticity of demand is less for agricultural products than for manufactured products, and provided that increases in productivity are not much smaller in agriculture than in manufacturing, such increases will cause a shift of population from farms to cities. The shift will be greater if, with increased productivity in manufacturing, increased amounts of industrial capital (e.g., tractors, harvesters, fertilizers) are used to increase productivity in agriculture.

The analysis is carried out by comparing the ratio of agriculture to manufacturing in equilibrium before and after productivity in the two industries has increased. Classical assumptions are made: maximization of (aggregate) utility of the population and maximization of (aggregate) profit of each industry -a very gross approximation to neoclassical assumptions of utility maximization by individual economic actors. Wage rates are assumed equal in the two industries -a counterfactual assumption that exaggerates the historically observed mobility of labor.

Economics as a historical science **433**

The findings will hardly evoke surprise: except that they show that the *industrial* revolution required also an *agricultural* revolution, for if only manufacturing had increased in productivity and agriculture had not, the model predicts a population movement from town to country! This was not a surprise to historians (although it was to me), for they already knew that major advances in agriculture began in England before the onset of the industrial revolution.

Notice that economic theory could countenance either result: urbanization or countryfication –all depends on the relative income elasticities of the two sets of products and their relative rates of productivity increase. Hence, it cannot be said that the analysis tested economic theory; for the elasticities and productivity increases were assumed in my paper, not derived from empirical data. Perhaps more interesting is the question of the extent to which the study either required or *could* test these or other basic assumptions of neoclassical theory. The facts are consistent with that theory, but also with many simpler theories that do not require strong neoclassical assumptions.

The model used in the paper assumes that, at any point in history, production functions determine the amount of agricultural products and of manufactured products the economy can (and will?) produce. Say's Law is implicit in the model, guaranteeing equality of production with consumption, and there is an assumption, or definition, that equates changes in technology with upward shifts in the production functions. It is assumed that, because of the budget constraint, demand is sensitive to income (Becker 1962), and that the income elasticity of demand for manufactured products is greater than that for agricultural products. There is no assumption at all about the competitiveness or non-competitiveness of markets, or, indeed, about the nature of the markets, if any, that are used to exchange goods. The model is highly aggregated, and says little about the rationality of actors or the consistency of their utility functions.

If we wished to test any of the model's assumptions, the tests could be made, at least as well as in any other way, by direct examination of aggregate data on production, consumption and prices at various points in time. Whatever the data showed, they would provide almost no specific support for the important features of neoclassical theory: for example, for the assumptions that consumers maximize expected utility or firms, profits.

To show this, let us see how the same empirical findings could be explained by a non-maximizing model. (1) By assumption about relative income elasticities of demand, as productivity increases the consumption of manufactures will increase more rapidly than the consumption of agricultural products. Utility maximization is neither a necessary nor a sufficient condition for this assumption to hold. (2) Assume next that producers will increase supply as long as their costs are covered. Again, this is a weaker assumption than profit maximization: it would hold, for example, in any regime of markup (cost plus) pricing. (3) Suppose that productivity increases at the same rate in both agriculture and manufacturing. Then it is obvious that the new consumption pattern, demanding a greater increase of manufactured than of agricultural products, will require a shift from agricultural to manufacturing employment.

434 H. A. Simon

Incidentally, as was early noted by Theodore Schultz, the central conclusion that the industrial revolution was, and had to be, an agricultural revolution has important implications for the theory of economic development -implications that were not always taken into account in the first decades after World War II, when many investigators nearly equated "economic development" in third world countries with "industrial development."

Other examples of comparative statics

This particular, and simple, example is not atypical of the kinds of relations between theory and fact that are tested by data from economic history. One well-known example is Fogel's *Railroads and American Economic Growth,* which asked whether railroads, at the time of their appearance, were substantially cheaper than other existing forms of transportation. Evidence that they were not cheaper would challenge any economic theory based on profit maximizing or equating of opportunity costs. Evidence that they were cheaper would, much like the agriculture example, provide a causal mechanism for the rapid economic development observed at that time. Economic development without substantial cost reduction by rail transportation would not refute theory, however, because the observed development might be attributable to other causes.

The same author's *Time on the Cross* examined whether, at the time of the Civil War, slavery was profitable to the slave holders. The method of comparative statics in the context of neoclassical theory (but also in the context of weaker theories) would predict that the continuation of slavery would depend on profitability if exogenous forces did not interfere. A similar comparative analysis is found in Douglass North's study, determining the extent to which monopoly could increase profits in monopolized and competitive industries at the expense of the incomes of farmers and workers.

My intent is not to trivialize these studies. Rather, I use them to emphasize that economic history frequently deals with important questions whose answers do not depend upon the stronger assumptions of neoclassical theory. Although, as in my rural/urban example, neoclassical (or roughly approximate neoclassical) models are often built and compared with data, the consistency of data with model should not too easily be taken as confirming the model. In the cases we have looked at, the data can be accounted for on assumptions much weaker and simpler than the neoclassical ones. Typical essential, but bland, assumptions are that business firms must cover their costs and that production equals consumption plus investment (Say's Law); utility and profit maximization play little or no essential role in the analysis.

Dynamics in economic history

The method of comparative statics is a powerful tool for studying the immediate effects of large discrete events upon an economy. However, we usually think of history as a process of continuing change, something to be captured by dynamic models, like differential equation models for predicting business cycles and other movements in economic activity. This is especially important because, through capital investment, initial impulses can be expected to have cumulate effects on production over time.

Technological change

In studying technological change, a topic of central importance in economic history, ancient and modern, comparative statics and dynamics can often be combined productively. Again, I will use an example from work in which I was involved. Shortly after World War II, the Cowles Commission for Research in Economics, was asked to make a study of the potential economic effects of nuclear power (Schurr and Marschak (eds.) 1950). At the heart of the study was an estimate of the cost saving from nuclear power, based on the assumption that costs would be quite comparable to those from fossil fuels, except that the atomic fuel would itself be essentially costless (an overoptimistic assumption, as it turned out, but one that could place an upper bound on effects).

The bulk of the study was carried out within the framework of comparative statics, and showed that the introduction of nuclear energy would produce, at best, a very modest increase in productivity (about 4/10 of one percent above the current rate of increase). (By hindsight, even this increase proved overoptimistic, largely because of the added costs of providing adequate protection from radiation and melt–down, and the costs of disposing of radioactive wastes.) However, this estimate must be modified to take into account the cumulative effect upon economic growth of a 4/10% increment to the annual rate of productivity increase. Compound interest gradually makes large effects out of small ones.

As in the studies previously examined, the only rationality assumption the nuclear power study required was that a particular energy source will be used whenever and wherever it is more economical than the alternatives. Nor is any economic explanation provided as to why this particular innovation occurred at a specific point in history, or as to the particular structure of its cost function. All of these variables were exogenous to the inquiry, the first cause being the wartime effort to produce a nuclear weapon. The analysis also ignored the emotions engendered by concerns about possible diversions of nuclear materials to military or terroristic use, and about the long-term environmental problems created by nuclear power generation. Thus, a purely economic analysis, while useful in providing a part of the total picture, necessarily fell far short of dealing with nuclear developments in their broader social setting.

The institutional context

Technological change is just one particular example of an exogenous factor that affects the continuing development of an economic system. It can, "in principle," be endogenized by building a theory of economic forces (in the cases where the

436 H. A. Simon

forces *are* economic) that determine the rate of technological innovation –for example, by including in the dynamic model an equation for rate of innovation. Rates of investment in R&D and in education and training can be independent variables in such an equation –which leads back to the question of what determines these rates. To assert that expected profits will control them brings them back within the fold of classical theory, but without any particular procedure for generating the expectations.

Moreover, as the nuclear energy example illustrates, many factors besides expected profits influence investment in a particular technology. In the postwar history of the United States, one might hypothesize that the rate of investment in innovation, especially through scientific discovery, has been much more strongly influenced by defence policy and recognition of the public goods aspects of basic discoveries than it has by expectations of private profit. Clearly, any clarification of such matters will lead from careful historical fact-gathering back to theory, and not in the opposite direction.

Moreover, in the past half-century, there have been important changes in the spending of American industry for research and development –first a rapid increase, then stabilization and an equally rapid decline. The economic historian can gather facts to check these trends and their magnitudes. The economic theorist can postulate that the changes in level of R&D investment reflect changes in expectations about their profitability. Again, we are then driven back to explaining how these changes in expectations came about, and –apart from some unverifiable, and probably invalid, hypotheses that they were a product of "experience," it is hard to find anything that theory has to say about the matter.

At least as plausible as the "experience" hypothesis is that the shifts resulted from the diffusion of waves of public (or corporate) opinion. This is about as useful as explaining changes in fashions as produced by fads. (Exactly the same thing can be said about the economics of "downsizing," or the fad that brought "Total Quality Management" into industry at a particular moment in the 1990's.) All of these events are grist for the mill of economic history, but they have little to do with classical economic theory beyond providing exogenous inputs to its models.

J.M. Keynes' account of investment rates in terms of "animal spirits" (which was, to be sure, only one of his independent variables) belongs to the same family. The trouble is not that the explanation is wrong; it may very well be true. Nor is the trouble that human optimism and pessimism cannot be measured: polling techniques are aimed at capturing just such phenomena. The real source of difficulty is that we must call upon these variables as independent, exogenous variables that are not themselves determined by the previous state of the system, as a closed dynamics would require.

I shall not attempt to provide a catalogue of all of the exogenous variables we would have to call upon to implement a dynamic model of an evolving economy. In the literature of economic development, we find population growth and rate of capital investment among the key variables. These can be, and sometimes are, endogenized, but only by invoking regularities from past experience, not by deducing them from theoretical premises.

Population growth, for example, might be predicted (although not with very much accuracy) from income levels; and this prediction might be rationalized, in turn, from an economic analysis of the value of children to their parents. The issue becomes more complicated when we distinguish between educated and uneducated children, for if the former, but not the latter, are a good parental investment, then we must introduce imperfect capital markets to place limits on borrowing for the purpose of financing more "profitable" children. As a last resort, we can turn to changes in taste (i.e., changes in the utility function) as a result of urbanization and cultural modernization. The possibilities are so numerous, and so hard to nail down empirically that it is not clear what useful work theory is doing for us.

In a similar way, capital investment might be predicted from total income and savings rates, and a theoretical fabric woven to explain the levels of the latter. Historical research can tell us which of these explanations is consistent with the historical record, but can seldom choose a unique explanation from the wealth of available hypotheses.

Categories of exogenous institutional variables

At a more abstract level, a partial catalogue of exogenous institutional variables (and candidates for endogenization) would include: (1) changes in the utility function, with consequent changes in demand and in savings rates; (2) changes in the production function, resulting from technological change and other factors, and with consequent changes in supply; and (3) changes in the laws of property, with consequent effects upon positive and negative externalities, the appropriability of inventions and powers of government to redistribute income and wealth. The public choice approach represents an attempt to endogenize these latter kinds of variables, but I shall not comment here on the extent to which it has succeeded or is likely to succeed. You can judge from what I have already said that am not sanguine.

Bounded rationality and economic dynamics

The variables considered thus far are all consistent with the assumptions of neoclassical theory. To these we must add the variables that deal with the fact that human rationality is bounded. These additional variables are closely bound with an historical view of economics, for they take into account (1) continuing changes in knowledge and information (both knowledge about economics and other knowledge about the world), (2) changes in human ability to estimate consequences of actions, (3) changes in the institutional setting within which economic behavior takes place, (4) changes in the focus of attention and related changes in beliefs and expectations. I will add, for they belong among the belief-dependent variables, (5) changes in human altruism and (6) in group identification.

438 H. A. Simon

Knowledge: about economics

The ancients, as early as the time of Aristotle, understood some basic principles of the workings of economies. They understood the advantages of a monetary economy over a barter economy, the balancing of supply and demand by markets, some of the motivational implications of private property, the efficiencies accruing from the division of labor, including the mutual gains derivable from international trade. The quantity theory of money, connecting the supply of precious metals with the price level, was widely accepted. There seem even to have been some inklings of the marginal principle. Very little that Adam Smith had to say in 1776 on these topics would have greatly surprised the ancients, although he organized what he had to say more clearly and systematically than they did, and undoubtedly understood it better.

There was much less clarity in ancient times, or for that matter, right up to quite modern times, with regard to the sources of value of goods and services (e.g., scarcity value, versus value in use and value in exchange). I recall a whole series of lectures in Jacob Viner's theory course in the 1930's that struggled to reconcile these alternative bases for value without reference to the now "obvious" fact that finding consistent values of price and quantity requires two simultaneous constraints, one originating on the side of supply and one on the side of demand.

There was even more confusion about interest and "usury," arising out of the desire to explain economic practices while simultaneously evaluating and justifying them normatively. As the usury example shows, these struggles to understand economic phenomena were not without consequences for the economy and those who had roles in it. Applying the Cleopatra's nose principle, we can be rather certain that the history of the Jews, and other trading groups who engaged in lending money, would have been quite different if explicit interest payments had not, for a long time, been condemned as usury.

Mercantilist doctrines advocating a favorable balance of trade and the accumulation of the precious metals played a major role, during the period of their acceptance, in determining government policies of economic regulation and of imperialism and colonization. The physiocratic doctrines that succeeded them induced substantial changes in these policies, as did the still newer doctrines promulgated by *The Wealth of Nations*.

This gradual modification of economic knowledge is usually treated, under the label of "history of economic doctrine," as a chronicle of the development of economic theory by and for economists. There are, in fact, two histories, more or less parallel: one describing the changes in economic theory espoused by those who studied the subject, taught it, and wrote on it, the other describing the changes of knowledge of the participants in economic affairs, or in the affairs of governments that regulated the economy.

As Keynes explained so eloquently, there are important connections between these two histories, for the ideas of economists and political philosophers, both when they are right and when they are wrong, are more powerful than is commonly understood. Indeed, the world is ruled by little else. Practical men, who believe themselves to be quite exempt from any intellectual influences, are usually the slaves of some defunct economist. Madmen in authority, who hear voices in the air, are distilling their frenzy from some academic scribbler of a few years back (Keynes 1936, p. 383).

Our concern here is not with the economics of economists' but with the economics of economic actors, which, as Keynes observes, is surely influenced by professional theory but will seldom be identical with it. We may, for example, expect economic actors to believe, and act on the belief, that when there is a scarcity of food, food prices will rise. They can hold that belief quite independently of whether they know or believe the claims that current theory asserts about economic actors maximizing utilities and thereby equating costs and utilities at the margins.

An important task in economic history would be to trace the changes in popular economic beliefs and assess the effects of these changes upon the behavior of the economy and the course of state regulation. On the basis of casual observation, it is my impression that, until quite recently, not much of the work in economic history or the history of economic doctrine had focused attention on this topic. Of course, any study that aims at testing the tenets of neoclassical theory is implicitly testing whether the economic actors understand the theory and act on that understanding. Rational expectations theory, with its explicit assumptions about the model of the economy that rational actors hold, and game theory, with its assumptions about how each economic actor forms expectations about the actions and reactions of the other actors, have now begun to call the attention of economics more and more to these issues.

Other knowledge and information

The kinds of rational action predicted by theory depend not only on knowledge of economic theory but also on knowledge about facts and events in the economy and the society: about the legal system, current and expected price levels, the cost function. The evidence that human rationality is severely bounded in relation to the complexity of the world in which it finds itself demands that people operate in terms of grossly simplified models of the world. Even if they are correct as far as they go, the models contain only a tiny fraction of all the potentially important facts and relations. Expectations may be rational in relation to this internal simplified model; they are certainly not objectively rational in relation to the complexities of the actual world. To deal with real events in the world, economics must postulate, not just the state of that world, but also the knowledge the economic actors have about it.

Technological change, which begins with the invention or discovery of new alternatives, can also be regarded as a product of bounded rationality, for in a world

440 H. A. Simon

of unlimited knowledge there would be no unknown alternatives to be discovered. As the relation is very weak between the rate at which new alternatives are found and the scale of the resources that are devoted to finding them, the possibilities for endogenizing this process are very limited.

Computational powers

Limits on knowledge are compounded by limits on human abilities to derive accurately the implications of what is known. The advent of the computer has made us so conscious of these computational limits, that they require no elaborate discussion. But even the computer, however far it extends human computational powers, still is capable of modeling only the broadest features of complex situations. Again, an account of human economic behavior in any historical setting (including the present) must postulate the scale of the computational means available to aid decision making.

Institutional setting

Economic decisions are strongly influenced by the surrounding governmental, legal, business and social institutions. As the utility function postulated by economic theory has no predetermined content, that content must be derived from the past and present natural and social environment. Some economists have tried to derive a definite utility function from evolutionary arguments that biological "fitness" is maximized, often equating fitness with income, wealth or power. This line of reasoning suffers from two problems. First, the connections between biological fitness, on the one hand, and income, wealth and power, on the other, are tenuous at best. Second, the once-accepted neo-Darwinian argument that the fitness of the "selfish gene" rules out all forms of group adaptation and individual altruism has been found wanting on a number of grounds. I will discuss the implications of altruism for economic history and theory, and especially the problems it presents to the theory of the firm and public choice theory, a little later.

Two other lines of contemporary economic reasoning, the New Institutional Economics, and Public Choice take a different path, seeking to endogenous the impact of institutions on individual choice by making the institutional forms themselves responsive to economic forces. Thus, institutional economists like Oliver Williams have scrutinized the forms of contract to show that they are functional from the standpoint of rational actors; while the public choice theorists seek to explain political behavior in terms of wealth-maximizing and power-maximizing behavior.

In the discussion of altruism, I will argue that the new institutional economics has failed to explain the central role of business organizations in the economy (arguably as central as the role of markets), or the motivational forces that make large centralized organizations efficient and viable in competition with smaller units. As to public choice theory, terms like "wealth maximization" and "power maximization" can be fitted to almost any political behavior nearly effortlessly, unless some supportable limits are imposed on the assumptions about the ways in which voters and politicians go about estimating what choices are to their advantage. For example, to make clear predictions, the theory would have to predict which economic variables will be in the focus of voters' attentions at any given time. Without such predictions, the theory is largely a set of tautologies that neither has been nor can be tested empirically (Simon 1985).

Focus of attention

One significant way in which bounded rationality affects the course of economic events is through the continual shifting of attention from the set of variables that play a prominent role in the economic actors' models during one period of time to another set of variables at a later period time. Such changes in the focus of attention can produce major and repeated changes in the economy.

For example, during the Fifties and Sixties, most Americans paid little attention to the price level, which rose only slowly during this period. Their focus of attention, as a result of the experience of the Great Depression and the subsequent appearance of Keynesianism, was primarily upon the level of employment and increases in productivity. Only when stagflation appeared, and their attention was attracted to the combination of stubborn residual unemployment with increasingly rapid price increases, did the possibility of uncontrolled inflation become a believable danger. Then, in the late Seventies and early Eighties, preoccupation with inflation increased to the point where higher unemployment rates became acceptable, there were strong demands for tax reduction, and little attention was paid to an unprecedented increase in the national debt and the cost of debt service.

These events, and the consequence changes in economic behavior and government policy, represent a significant modification of people's models of the economic system in which they live. Beliefs moved away from Keynesianism toward a variety of alternatives -*laissez faire,* "supply side," and libertarian- with corresponding changes in economic and political decisions. A model of perfect rationality has no place for such structural changes. Even in the framework of rational expectations, introduction of periodic alterations of the model itself would change the equilibrium toward which the economy was moving. Such shifts can be accommodated in a model of bounded rationality –but not without facing the task of describing the process, exogenous to neoclassical economic theory, of changes in belief.

Because of this strong interaction between changing exogenous beliefs and behavior, economic history must incorporate, through either exogenous or endogenous mechanisms the continual changes in public attention that alter responses to economic events and to issues of public policy.

Altruism

As was pointed out earlier, Darwinian theory can no longer maintain that selection of the fittest extinguishes altruism. Contrary to earlier claims that only altruism to close kin can survive, a creature of bounded rationality can gain net fitness as a result of altruism induced by social influences that also enhance the fitness of the social group. Either the presence or absence of altruism in the utility function is consistent with neoclassical theory and many other theories, but of course, is not without major consequences for behavior.

We now know that natural selection at the level of social groups can be linked with selection at the level of the gene by several mechanisms. Among them are the application of social sanctions to the individual, the mechanism of structured demes (see David Sloan Wilson for an discussion of this rather complex but powerful mechanism), and bounded rationality itself, which makes it advantageous for individuals to accept social instruction and advice (to be educable or "docile") even though the advice sometimes counsels behavior that reduces fitness (Simon 1990). All of these mechanisms support individual altruistic behavior when it enhances the average fitness of members of some group to which the individual belongs.

Most economic theory operates on the assumption that utility attaches almost exclusively to individual selfish economic motives. People are assumed to have desires to consume goods and services and to save for future consumption, and they prefer leisure to work. (Sometimes an "estate motive" is included in the utility function, but its origins -unless it derives from altruism to close kin- are not apparent.)

The New Institutional Economics assumes that an employee's motivation to work for organizational goals derives from wage, salary and bonus rewards and expectations of promotion. The motivation is only sustainable, according to the theory, to the extent that performance can be enforced by making the rewards contingent on it. To determine when activities will be handled inside firms and when they will be out-sourced, the costs of enforcing the explicit and implicit terms of the employment contract must be balanced against the costs of enforcing market contracts, and the transaction (information) costs of carrying out activities within the firm, balanced against transaction costs between independent contractors. Thus, conclusions about when privatization will or won't be advantageous, and where the balance will be struck between firms and external sourcing, depend critically upon the values of these empirical parameters.

However, there are important theoretical reasons supported by substantial empirical evidence, to believe that the usual explicit rewards associated with employment are not the only, and very likely not the major factors that motivate managers and other employees to direct their decisions toward organizational goals. Evolutionary forces have produced in human beings a strong propensity (sometimes called docility) to accept instruction, advice and authority when it emanates from socially legitimized sources. I have provided elsewhere (Simon 1990) the argument that leads to this conclusion. One aspect of docility is a considerable tendency for people to identify with (acquire loyalty to) the social groups, including the organizations, to which they belong.

Group identification

The strength of group identification and the nature of the groups that command strong loyalties undergo large changes in the course of history. Identification with the nation state is largely a product of the past two or three centuries, while ethnic loyalty (which is itself a varying blend of identification based on ethnicity, religion, race, and possibly other factors) and family identification were already well entrenched at the dawn of recorded history. Identification with military groups, although often mingled with ethnic and national identification, can often be seen in the historical comings and goings of armies. *Xenophon* is most instructive when read from this standpoint, and the *Iliad* provides us with considerable data on the conflicts of loyalties in Greek society, and their effects on decision making.

A striking modern phenomena is the identification of executives and other employees with the business firms or other organizations for whom they work. It has both a motivational and a cognitive component. On the motivational side, it provides a basis of attachment to organizational goals that goes far beyond that provided by enforceable rewards; but more than motivation is involved. In our human world of bounded rationality, organizational identification is a major mechanism for focusing attention on those aspects of a situation that are relevant to organizational survival and success, and consequently for reaching decisions that advance organizational goals.

The presence of organizational identifications substantially reduces the costs of maintaining adherence to organizational goals, and enlarges the area of activity within which organizations will have an advantage over markets. The rise of the large modern business firm is often attributed in considerable part to the efficiencies deriving from specialization and the division of labor. But as can be seen from the pages of Adam Smith, many of these advantages can be obtained as easily through the putting-out system or other forms of contracting as by forming and managing large organizations. In fact, out-sourcing to specialized firms that supply more than one company can greatly enhance specialization. Adam Smith himself was strongly critical (on grounds of the presumably selfish motives of non-owner executives) of the idea that corporations could carry on efficient economic activities, and would surely be astonished at the form that capitalism has assumed.

The trust engendered by ethnic and family loyalties is frequently advanced as a basis for the success and survival of geographically dispersed trading and banking organizations. Similarly, the modern corporation encounters special difficulties in cultures where loyalty to an extended family competes with organizational loyalties.

444 H. A. Simon

Identification, in both its cognitive and motivational aspects, is an exogenous variable that plays an essential role in forming the shape of economic institutions in a given culture, and hence a variable that cannot be omitted from economic history or economic theory.

Conclusion

Economic activity takes place in a complex natural and social environment only a small part of whose behavior can be endogenized within the body of economic theory (or even within the whole body of scientific theory). To the extent that this environment remains exogenous, the laws of economics cannot have even that degree of universality and invariance that is possessed by, say, Newtonian mechanics. Its laws will continue to change with changes in social institutions and changes in the knowledge and beliefs of the boundedly rational people who inhabit them. The focus of individual and public attention will shift with changing events from one set of variables to another, with resulting shifts in individual and system behavior.

For all of these and the other reasons adduced in this paper, economic science has and will continue to have an important historical component. Economic historians have been perhaps too modest in recent times about the role they have to play in establishing our economic knowledge. Their task is much more than one of explaining historical events in terms of an independently derived body of economic theory. It is much more than one of testing empirically a theory that has already been formulated. The data assembled and analysed by historians is, in fact, essential for our understanding economic behavior and formulating empirically valid economic laws, including mechanisms that continually alter these laws with the changing knowledge, beliefs, perceptions, values and identifications of the human economic actors.

Bibliography

Becker, G.S.: 1962, 'Irrational behavior and economic theory', *Journal of Political Economy* 70, 1–13.

Clapham, J.H.: 1931, 'Survey of development to the twentieth century' and 'Economic history as a discipline', in *Encyclopaedia of the Social Sciences*, Volume 5, pp. 315–320 and 327–330, New York, NY, Macmillan.

Fogel, R.W.: 1964, *Railroads and American Economic Growth*, Baltimore, MD, Johns Hopkins Press.

Fogel, R.W. & Engerman, S.L.: 1974, *Time on the Cross*, Boston, MA, Little, Brown.

Keynes, J.M.: 1936, *The General Theory of Employment, Interest and Money*, London, Macmillan and Company.

North, D.C.: 1966, *Growth and Welfare in the American Past*, Englewood Cliffs, NJ, Prentice-Hall.

North, D.C.: 1968, 'Economic history', in *International Encyclopedia of the Social Sciences*. Volume 6, pp. 468–473, New York, NY, Macmillan.

Samuelson, P.A.: 1970, 'Maximum principles in analytical dynamics', in *Les Prix Nobel en 1970*, Stockholm, SW, P.A. Norstedt & Söner.

Schurr, A. & Marschak, J. (eds.): 1950, *Economic Aspects of Atomic Power*, Princeton, NJ. Princetonn University Press.

Simon, H.A.: 1985, 'Human nature in politics: The dialogue of psychology with political science', *American Political Science Review* 79, 293–304.

Simon, H.A.: 1990, 'A mechanism for social selection and successful altruism', *Science* 250, 1665–1668.

Smith, Adam: 1776[1789], *The Wealth of Nations*, 5th Edition, New York, NY, Modern Library, 1937.

Williams, O.E.: 1985, *The Economic Institutions of Capitalism*, New York, NY, The Free Press.

Wilson, D.S.: 1980, *The Natural Selection of Populations and Communities*, Menlo Park, CA, The Benjamin-Cummings Press.

Herbert A. Simon is Professor at the Carnegie-Mellon University, Pittsburgh (USA), and Nobel Laurate in Economic Science in 1978. He is the author of influential books: *Administrative Behavior* (1947), *Models of Man: Social and Rational* (1957), *The Sciences of the Artificial*, (1969), *Models of Bounded Rationality* (1982), *Reason in Human Affairs* (1983), ... His conception of economics is connected with his research on social sciences, which is pointed out in *Models of My Life* (1991). His recent writings enlarge his perspective critical towards mainstream neoclassical economics: 'The State of Economic Science' (1989), 'Prediction and Prescription in Systems Modeling' (1990), 'A Mechanism for Social selection and Successful Altruism' (1990), and 'Altruism and Economics' (1993).

20
THE ART AND SCIENCE OF CAUSE AND EFFECT

J. Pearl

A public lecture delivered November 1996 as part of the UCLA Faculty Research Lectureship Program

The topic of this lecture is causality — namely, our awareness of what causes what in the world and why it matters.

Though it is basic to human thought, causality is a notion shrouded in mystery, controversy, and caution, because scientists and philosophers have had difficulties defining when one event *truly causes* another.

We all understand that the rooster's crow does not cause the sun to rise, but even this simple fact cannot easily be translated into a mathematical equation.

Today, I would like to share with you a set of ideas which I have found very useful in studying phenomena of this kind. These ideas have led to practical tools that I hope you will find useful on your next encounter with cause and effect.

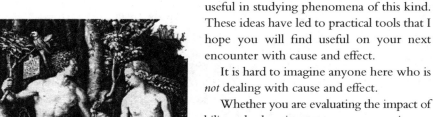

It is hard to imagine anyone here who is *not* dealing with cause and effect.

Whether you are evaluating the impact of bilingual education programs or running an experiment on how mice distinguish food from danger or speculating about why Julius Caesar crossed the Rubicon or diagnosing a patient or predicting who will win the presidential election, you are dealing with a tangled web of cause–effect considerations.

The story that I am about to tell is aimed at helping researchers deal with the complexities of such considerations, and to clarify their meaning.

This lecture is divided into three parts.

I begin with a brief historical sketch of the difficulties that various disciplines have had with causation.

Next I outline the ideas that reduce or eliminate several of these historical difficulties.

Finally, in honor of my engineering background, I will show how these ideas lead to simple practical tools, which will be demonstrated in the areas of statistics and social science.

In the beginning, as far as we can tell, causality was not problematic.

The urge to ask *why* and the capacity to find causal explanations came very early in human development.

The Bible, for example, tells us that just a few hours after tasting from the tree of knowledge, Adam is already an expert in causal arguments.

When God asks: "Did you eat from that tree?"

This is what Adam replies: "The woman whom you gave to be with me, She handed me the fruit from the tree; and I ate."

Eve is just as skillful: "The serpent deceived me, and I ate."

The thing to notice about this story is that God did not ask for explanation, only for the facts – it was Adam who felt the need to explain. The message is clear: causal explanation is a man-made concept.

Another interesting point about the story: explanations are used exclusively for passing responsibilities.

Indeed, for thousands of years explanations had no other function. Therefore, only Gods, people, and animals could cause things to happen, not objects, events, or physical processes.

Natural events entered into causal explanations much later because, in the ancient world, events were simply *predetermined*.

Storms and earthquakes were *controlled* by the angry gods [slide 2] and could not in themselves assume causal responsibility for the consequences.

Even an erratic and unpredictable event such as the roll of a die [3] was not considered a *chance* event but rather a divine message demanding proper interpretation.

One such message gave the prophet Jonah the scare of his life when he was identified as God's renegade and was thrown overboard [4].

Quoting from the book of Jonah: "And the sailors said: 'Come and let us cast lots to find out who is to blame for this ordeal.' So they cast lots and the lot fell on Jonah."

Obviously, on this luxury Phoenician cruiser, "casting lots" was used not for recreation but for communication – a one-way modem for processing messages of vital importance.

In summary, the agents of causal forces in the ancient world were either deities, who cause things to happen for a purpose, or human beings and animals, who possess free will, for which they are punished and rewarded.

This notion of causation was naive, but clear and unproblematic.

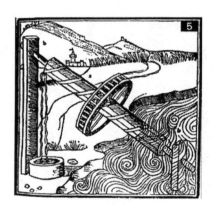

The problems began, as usual, with engineering; when machines had to be constructed to do useful jobs [5].

As engineers grew ambitious, they decided that the earth, too, can be moved [6], but not with a single lever.

Systems consisting of many pulleys and wheels [7], one driving another, were needed for projects of such magnitude.

And, once people started building multi-stage systems, an interesting thing happened to causality – *physical objects began acquiring causal character.*

When a system like that broke down, it was futile to blame God or the operator – instead, a broken rope or a rusty pulley were more useful explanations, simply because these could be replaced easily and make the system work.

At that point in history, Gods and humans ceased to be the sole agents of causal forces – lifeless objects and processes became partners in responsibility.

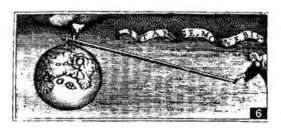

A wheel turned and stopped *because* the wheel preceding it turned and stopped – the human operator became secondary.

Not surprisingly, these new agents of causation took on some of the characteristics of their predecessors – Gods and humans.

Natural objects became not only carriers of credit and blame but also carriers of force, will, and even purpose.

Aristotle regarded explanation in terms of a *purpose* to be the only complete and satisfactory explanation for why a thing is what it is.

He even called it a *final cause* – namely, the final aim of scientific inquiry.

From that point on, causality served a dual role: *causes* were the targets of credit and blame on one hand and the carriers of physical flow of control on the other.

This duality survived in relative tranquility [8] until about the time of the Renaissance, when it encountered conceptual difficulties.

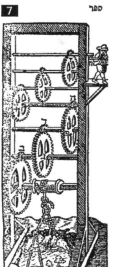

What happened can be seen on the title page [9] of Recordes's book "The Castle of Knowledge," the first science book in English, published in 1575.

The wheel of fortune is turned, not by the wisdom of God, but by the ignorance of man.

And, as God's role as the final cause was taken over by human knowledge, the whole notion of causal explanation came under attack.

The erosion started with the work of Galileo [10].

Most of us know Galileo as the man who was brought before the inquisition and imprisoned [11] for defending the heliocentric theory of the world.

But while all that was going on, Galileo also managed to quietly engineer the most profound revolution that science has ever known.

This revolution, expounded in his 1638 book "Discorsi" [12], published in Leyden, far from Rome, consists of two maxims:

One, description first, explanation second – that is, the "how" precedes the "why"; and

Two, description is carried out in the language of mathematics; namely, equations.

Ask not, said Galileo, whether an object falls because it is pulled from below or pushed from above.

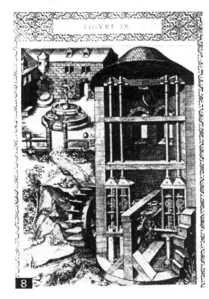

Ask how well you can predict the time it takes for the object to travel a certain distance, and how that time will vary from object to object and as the angle of the track changes.

Moreover, said Galileo, do not attempt to answer such questions in the qualitative and slippery nuances of human language; say it in the form of mathematical equations [13].

It is hard for us to appreciate today how strange that idea sounded in 1638, barely 50 years after the introduction of algebraic notation by Vieta. To proclaim algebra the *universal* language of science would sound today like proclaiming Esperanto the language of economics.

Why would Nature agree to speak algebra? Of all languages?

But you can't argue with success.

The distance traveled by an object turned out indeed to be proportional to the square of the time.

Even more successful than predicting outcomes of experiments were the computational aspects of algebraic equations.

They enabled engineers, for the first time in history, to ask "how to" questions in addition to "what if" questions.

In addition to asking: "What if we narrow the beam, will it carry the load?", they began to ask more difficult questions: "How to shape the beam so that it *will* carry the load?" [14]

This was made possible by the availability of methods for solving equations.

The algebraic machinery does not discriminate among variables; instead of predicting behavior in terms of parameters, we can turn things around and solve for the parameters in terms of the desired behavior.

Let us concentrate now on Galileo's first maxim – "description first, explanation second" – because that idea was taken very seriously by the scientists and changed the character of science from speculative to empirical.

Physics became flooded with empirical laws that were extremely useful.

Snell's law [15], Hooke's law, Ohm's law, and Joule's law are examples of purely empirical generalizations that were discovered and used long before they were explained by more fundamental principles.

Philosophers, however, were reluctant to give up the idea of causal explanation and continued to search for the origin and justification of those successful Galilean equations.

For example, Descartes ascribed cause to *eternal truth*.

Liebniz made cause a self-evident logical law.

Finally, about one hundred years after Galileo, a Scottish philosopher by the name of David Hume [16] carried Galileo's first maxim to an extreme [17].

Hume argued convincingly that the *why* is not merely second to the *how*, but that the *why* is totally superfluous as it is subsumed by the *how*.

On page 156 of Hume's "Treatise of Human Nature" [18], we find the paragraph that shook up causation so thoroughly that it has not recovered to this day.

I always get a kick reading it: "Thus we remember to have seen that species of object we call *flame*, and to have felt that species of sensation we call *heat*. We likewise call to mind their constant conjunction in all past instances. Without any farther ceremony, we call the one *cause* and the other *effect*, and infer the existence of the one from that of the other."

Thus, causal connections according to Hume are the product of observations. Causation is a learnable habit of the mind, almost as fictional as optical illusions and as transitory as Pavlov's conditioning.

It is hard to believe that Hume was not aware of the difficulties inherent in his proposed recipe.

He knew quite well that the rooster crow *stands* in constant conjunction to the sunrise, yet it does not *cause* the sun to rise.

He knew that the barometer reading *stands* in constant conjunction to the rain but does not *cause* the rain.

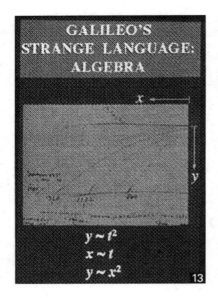

Today these difficulties fall under the rubric of *spurious correlations*, namely "correlations that do not imply causation."

Now, taking Hume's dictum that all knowledge comes from experience encoded in the mind as correlation, and our observation that correlation does not imply causation, we are led into our first riddle of causation: How do people *ever* acquire knowledge of *causation?*

We saw in the rooster example that regularity of succession is not sufficient; what *would* be sufficient?

What patterns of experience would justify calling a connection "causal"?

Moreover: What patterns of experience *convince* people that a connection is "causal"?

If the first riddle concerns the *learning* of causal connection, the second concerns its usage: What *difference* would it make if I told you that a certain connection is or is not causal?

Continuing our example, what difference would it make if I told you that the rooster does cause the sun to rise?

This may sound trivial.

The obvious answer is that knowing "what causes what" makes a big difference in how we act.

If the rooster's crow causes the sun to rise, we could make the night shorter by waking up our rooster earlier and making him crow – say, by telling him the latest rooster joke.

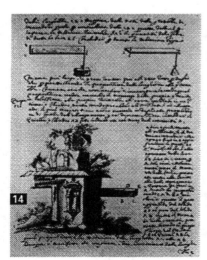

But this riddle is *not* as trivial as it seems.

If causal information has an empirical meaning beyond regularity of succession, then that information should show up in the laws of physics.

But it does not!

The philosopher Bertrand Russell made this argument [19] in 1913:

"All philosophers," says Russell, "imagine that causation is one of the fundamental axioms of science, yet oddly enough, in advanced sciences, the word 'cause' never occurs. ... The law of causality, I believe, is a relic of bygone age, surviving, like the monarchy, only because it is erroneously supposed to do no harm."

Another philosopher, Patrick Suppes, who argued for the importance of causality, noted that:

"There is scarcely an issue of 'Physical Review' that does not contain at least one article using either 'cause' or 'causality' in its title."

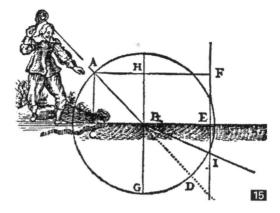

What we conclude from this exchange is that physicists talk, write, and think one way and formulate physics in another.

Such bilingual activity would be forgiven if causality was used merely as a convenient communication device – a shorthand for expressing complex patterns of physical relationships that would otherwise take many equations to write.

After all! Science is full of abbreviations: We use "multiply x by 5" instead of "add x to itself 5 times"; we say "density" instead of "the ratio of weight to volume."

Why pick on causality?

"Because causality is different," Lord Russell would argue. "It could not possibly be an abbreviation, because the laws of physics are all symmetrical, going both ways, while causal relations are unidirectional, going from cause to effect."

Take, for instance, Newton's law:

$f = ma$.

The rules of algebra permit us to write this law in a wild variety of syntactic forms, all meaning the same thing – that if we know any two of the three quantities, the third is determined.

Yet, in ordinary discourse we say that force causes acceleration – not that acceleration causes force, and we feel very strongly about this distinction.

Likewise, we say that the ratio f/a helps us *determine* the mass, not that it *causes* the mass.

Such distinctions are not supported by the equations of physics, and this leads us to ask whether the whole causal vocabulary is purely metaphysical, "surviving, like the monarchy ...".

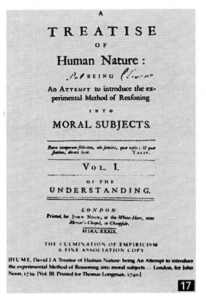

Fortunately, very few physicists paid attention to Russell's enigma. They continued to write equations in the office and talk cause–effect in the cafeteria; with astonishing success they smashed the atom, invented the transistor and the laser.

The same is true for engineering.

But in another arena the tension could not go unnoticed, because in that arena the demand for distinguishing causal from other relationships was very explicit.

This arena is statistics.

The story begins with the discovery of correlation, about one hundred years ago.

Francis Galton [20], inventor of fingerprinting and cousin of Charles Darwin, quite understandably set out to prove that talent and virtue run in families.

Galton's investigations drove him to consider various ways of measuring how properties of one class of individuals or objects are related to those of another class.

In 1888, he measured the length of a person's forearm and the size of that person's head and asked to what degree one of these quantities can predict the other [21].

He stumbled upon the following discovery: If you plot one quantity against the other and scale the two axes properly, then the slope of the best-fit line has some nice mathematical properties. The slope is 1 only when one quantity can predict the other precisely; it is zero whenever the prediction is no better than a random guess; and, most remarkably, the slope is the same no matter if you plot X against Y or Y against X.

"It is easy to see," said Galton, "that corelation must be the consequence of the variations of the two organs being partly due to common causes."

Here we have, for the first time, an objective measure of how two variables are "related" to each other, based strictly on the data, clear of human judgment or opinion.

Galton's discovery dazzled one of his disciples, Karl Pearson [22], now considered to be one of the founders of modern statistics.

Pearson was 30 years old at the time, an accomplished physicist and philosopher about to turn lawyer, and this is how he describes, 45 years later [23], his initial reaction to Galton's discovery:

"I felt like a buccaneer of Drake's days. ...

"I interpreted ... Galton to mean that there was a category broader than causation, namely correlation, of which causation was only the limit, and that this new conception of correlation brought psychology, anthropology, medicine, and sociology in large parts into the field of mathematical treatment."

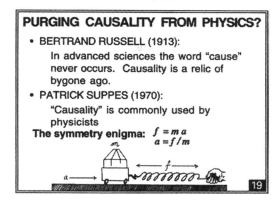

Now, Pearson has been described as a man "with the kind of drive and determination that took Hannibal over the Alps and Marco Polo to China."

When Pearson felt like a buccaneer, you can be sure he gets his bounty.

The year 1911 saw the publication of the third edition of his book "The Grammar of Science." It contained a new chapter titled "Contingency and Correlation – The Insufficiency of Causation," and this is what Pearson says in that chapter:

"Beyond such discarded fundamentals as 'matter' and 'force' lies still another fetish amidst the inscrutable arcana of modern science, namely, the category of cause and effect."

And what does Pearson substitute for the archaic category of cause and effect? You wouldn't believe your ears: *contingency tables* [24].

"Such a table is termed a contingency table, and the ultimate scientific statement of description of the relation between two things can always be thrown back upon such a contingency table. ...

"Once the reader realizes the nature of such a table, he will have grasped the essence of the conception of association between cause and effect."

Thus, Pearson categorically denies the need for an independent concept of causal relation beyond correlation.

He held this view throughout his life and, accordingly, did not mention causation in *any* of his technical papers.

His crusade against animistic concepts such as "will" and "force" was so fierce and his rejection of determinism so absolute that he *exterminated* causation from statistics before it had a chance to take root.

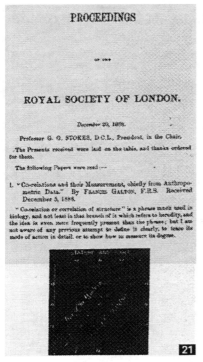

It took another 25 years and another strong-willed person, Sir Ronald Fisher [25], for statisticians to formulate the randomized experiment – the only scientifically proven method of testing causal relations from data, and to this day, the one and only causal concept permitted in mainstream statistics.

And that is roughly where things stand today.

If we count the number of doctoral theses, research papers, or textbook pages written on causation, we get the impression that Pearson still rules statistics.

The "Encyclopedia of Statistical Science" devotes twelve pages to correlation but only two pages to causation – and spends one of those pages demonstrating that "correlation does not imply causation."

Let us hear what modern statisticians say about causality.

Philip Dawid, the current editor of "Biometrika" (the journal founded by Pearson), admits: "Causal inference is one of the most important, most subtle, and most neglected of all the problems of statistics."

Terry Speed, former president of the Biometric Society (whom you might remember as an expert witness at the O. J. Simpson murder trial),

declares: "Considerations of causality should be treated as they have always been treated in statistics: preferably not at all but, if necessary, then with very great care."

Sir David Cox and Nanny Wermuth, in a book published just a few months ago, apologize as follows: "We did not in this book use the words *causal* or *causality*. ... Our reason for caution is that it is rare that firm conclusions about causality can be drawn from one study."

This position of caution and avoidance has paralyzed many fields that look to statistics for guidance, especially economics and social science.

A leading social scientist stated in 1987: "It would be very healthy if more researchers abandon thinking of and using terms such as cause and effect."

Can this state of affairs be the work of just one person? Even a buccaneer like Pearson?

I doubt it.

But how else can we explain why statistics, the field that has given the world such powerful concepts as the testing of hypothesis and the design of experiment, would give up so early on causation?

One obvious explanation is, of course, that causation is much harder to measure than correlation.

Correlations can be estimated directly in a single uncontrolled study, while causal conclusions require controlled experiments.

But this is too simplistic; statisticians are not easily deterred by difficulties, and children manage to learn cause–effect relations *without* running controlled experiments.

The answer, I believe, lies deeper, and it has to do with the official language of statistics – namely, the language of probability.

This may come as a surprise to some of you, but the word *cause* is not in the vocabulary of probability theory; we cannot express in the language of probabilities the sentence, *mud does not cause rain* – all we can say is that the two are mutually correlated or dependent – meaning that if we find one, we can expect the other.

Naturally, if we lack a language to express a certain concept explicitly, we can't expect to develop scientific activity around that concept.

Scientific development requires that knowledge be transferred reliably from one study to another and, as Galileo showed 350 years ago, such transference requires the precision and computational benefits of a formal language.

I will soon come back to discuss the importance of

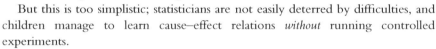

language and notation, but first I wish to conclude this historical survey with a tale from another field in which causation has had its share of difficulty.

This time it is computer science – the science of symbols – a field that is relatively new yet one that has placed a tremendous emphasis on language and notation and therefore may offer a useful perspective on the problem.

When researchers began to encode causal relationships using computers, the two riddles of causation were awakened with renewed vigor.

Put yourself in the shoes of this robot [26] who is trying to make sense of what is going on in a kitchen or a laboratory.

Conceptually, the robot's problems are the same as those faced by an economist seeking to model the national debt or an epidemiologist attempting to understand the spread of a disease.

Our robot, economist, and epidemiologist all need to track down cause–effect relations from the environment, using limited actions and noisy observations.

This puts them right at Hume's first riddle of causation: *how*?

The second riddle of causation also plays a role in the robot's world.

Assume we wish to take a shortcut and teach our robot all we know about cause and effect in this room [27].

How should the robot organize and make use of this information?

Thus, the two philosophical riddles of causation are now translated into concrete and practical questions:

How should a robot acquire causal information through interaction with its environment? How should a robot process causal information received from its creator–programmer?

Again, the second riddle is not as trivial as it might seem. Lord Russell's warning that causal relations and physical equations are incompatible now surfaces as an apparent flaw in logic.

For example, when given the information, "If the grass is wet, then it rained" and "If we break this bottle, the grass will get wet," the computer will conclude "If we break this bottle, then it rained" [28].

The swiftness and specificity with which such programming bugs surface have made

The art and science of cause and effect 459

Artificial Intelligence programs an ideal laboratory for studying the fine print of causation.

This brings us to the second part of the lecture: how the second riddle of causation can be solved by combining equations with graphs, and how this solution makes the first riddle less formidable.

The overriding ideas in this solution are:

First – treating causation as a summary of behavior under interventions; and

Second – using equations and graphs as a mathematical language within which causal thoughts can be represented and manipulated.

And to put the two together, we need a *third* concept: treating interventions as a surgery over equations.

Let us start with an area that uses causation extensively and never had any trouble with it: engineering.

Here is an engineering drawing [29] of a circuit diagram that shows cause–effect relations among the signals in the circuit. The circuit consists of *and* gates and *or* gates, each performing some logical function between input and output. Let us examine this diagram closely, since its simplicity and familiarity are very deceiving. This diagram is, in fact, one of the greatest marvels of science. It is capable of conveying more information than millions of algebraic equations or probability functions or logical expressions. What makes this diagram so much more powerful is the ability to predict not merely how the circuit behaves under normal conditions but also how the circuit will behave under millions of *abnormal* conditions. For example, given this circuit diagram, we can easily tell what the output will be if some input changes from 0 to 1. This is normal and can easily be expressed by a simple input–output equation. Now comes the abnormal part. We can also tell what the output will be when we set Y to 0 (zero), or tie it to X, or change this *and* gate to an *or* gate, or when we perform any of the millions of combinations of these operations. The designer of this circuit did not anticipate or

CAUSATION AS A PROGRAMMER'S NIGHTMARE

Input: 1. "If the grass is wet, then it rained"

2. "If we break this bottle, the grass will get wet"

Output: "If we break this bottle, then it rained"

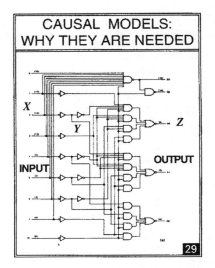

even consider such weird interventions, yet, miraculously, we can predict their consequences. How? Where does this representational power come from?

It comes from what early economists called *autonomy*. Namely, the gates in this diagram represent independent mechanisms – it is easy to change one without changing the other. The diagram takes advantage of this independence and describes the normal functioning of the circuit *using precisely those building blocks that will remain unaltered under intervention*.

My colleagues from Boelter Hall are surely wondering why I stand here before you blathering about an engineering triviality as if it were the eighth wonder of the world. I have three reasons for doing this. First, I will try to show that there is a lot of unexploited wisdom in practices that engineers take for granted.

Second, I am trying to remind economists and social scientists of the benefits of this diagrammatic method. They have been using a similar method on and off for over 75 years, called structural equation modeling and path diagrams, but in recent years they have allowed algebraic convenience to suppress the diagrammatic representation, together with its benefits. Finally, these diagrams capture, in my opinion, the very essence of causation – the ability to predict the consequences of abnormal eventualities and new manipulations. In S. Wright's diagram [30], for example, it is possible to predict what coat pattern the guinea-pig litter is likely to have if we change environmental factors, shown here as input (*E*), or even genetic factors, shown as intermediate nodes between parents and offsprings (*H*). Such predictions cannot be made on the basis of algebraic or correlational analysis.

Viewing causality this way explains why scientists pursue causal explanations with such zeal and why attaining a causal model is accompanied by a sense of gaining "deep understanding" and "being in control."

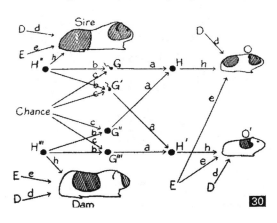

Deep understanding [31] means knowing not merely how things behaved yesterday but also how things will behave under new hypothetical circumstances, control being one such circumstance. Interestingly, when we have such understanding we feel "in control" even if we have no practical way of controlling things. For example, we have no practical way to control celestial motion, and still the theory of gravitation gives us a feeling of understanding and control, because it provides a blueprint for hypothetical control. We can predict the effect on tidal waves of unexpected new events – say, the moon being hit by a meteor or the gravitational constant sud-

denly diminishing by a factor of 2 – and, just as important, the gravitational theory gives us the assurance that ordinary manipulation of earthly things will *not* control tidal waves. It is not surprising that causal models are viewed as the litmus test for distinguishing deliberate reasoning from reactive or instinctive response. Birds and monkeys may possibly be trained to perform complex tasks such as fixing a broken wire, but that requires trial-and-error training. Deliberate reasoners, on the other hand, can anticipate the consequences of new manipulations *without ever trying* those manipulations.

Let us magnify [32] a portion of the circuit diagram so that we can understand why the diagram can predict outcomes that equations cannot. Let us also switch from logical gates to linear equations (to make everyone here more comfortable), and assume we are dealing with a system containing just two components: a multiplier and an adder. The *multiplier* takes the input and multiplies it by a factor of 2; the *adder* takes its input and adds a 1 to it. The equations describing these two components are given here on the left.

But are these equations *equivalent* to the diagram on the right? Obviously not! If they were, then let us switch the variables around, and the resulting two equations should be equivalent to the circuit shown below. But these two circuits are different. The top one tells us that if we physically manipulate Y it will affect Z, while the bottom one shows that manipulating Y will affect X and will have no effect on Z. Moreover, performing some additional algebraic operations on our equations, we can obtain two new equations,

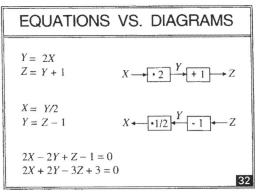

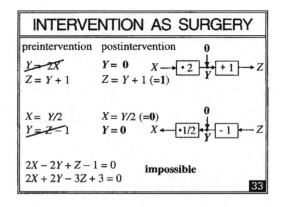

shown at the bottom, which point to no structure *at all*; they simply represent two constraints on three variables without telling us how they influence each other.

Let us examine more closely the mental process by which we determine the effect of physically manipulating Y – say, setting Y to 0 [33].

Clearly, when we set Y to 0, the relation between X and Y is no longer given by the multiplier – a new mechanism now controls Y, in which X has no say. In the equational representation, this amounts to replacing the equation $Y=2X$ by a new equation $Y=0$ and solving a new set of equations, which gives $Z=1$. If we perform this surgery on the lower pair of equations, representing the lower model, we get of course a different solution. The second equation will need to be replaced, which will yield $X=0$ and leave Z unconstrained.

We now see how this model of intervention leads to a formal definition of causation: "Y is a cause of Z if we can change Z by manipulating Y, namely, if after surgically removing the equation for Y, the solution for Z will depend on the new value we substitute for Y." We also see how vital the diagram is in this process. *The diagram tells us which equation is to be deleted when we manipulate Y.* That information is totally washed out when we transform the equations into algebraically equivalent form, as shown at the bottom of the screen. From this pair of equations alone, it is impossible to predict the result of setting Y to 0, because we do not know what surgery to perform – there is no such thing as "the equation for Y."

In summary, *intervention amounts to a surgery on equations* (guided by a diagram) and *causation means predicting the consequences of such a surgery*.

This is a universal theme that goes beyond physical systems. In fact, the idea of modeling interventions by "wiping out" equations was first proposed in 1960 by an *economist*, Herman Wold, but his teachings have all but disappeared from the economics literature. History books attribute this mysterious disappearance to Wold's personality, but I tend to believe that the reason goes deeper: Early econometricians were very careful mathematicians; they fought hard to keep their algebra clean and formal, and they could not agree to have it contaminated by gimmicks such as diagrams. And as we see on the screen, the surgery operation makes no mathematical sense without the diagram, as it is sensitive to the way we write the equations.

Before expounding on the properties of this new mathematical operation, let me demonstrate how useful it is for clarifying concepts in statistics and economics.

Why do we prefer controlled experiment over uncontrolled studies? Assume we wish to study the effect of some drug treatment on recovery of patients suffering from a given disorder. The mechanism governing the behavior of each patient is similar in structure to the circuit diagram we saw earlier. Recovery is a function of both the treatment and other factors, such as socioeconomic conditions, life style, diet, age, et cetera. Only one such factor is shown here [34]. Under uncontrolled conditions, the choice of treatment is up to the

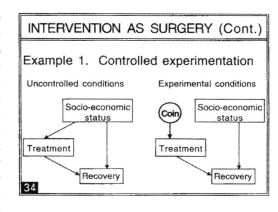

patients and may depend on the patients' socioeconomic backgrounds. This creates a problem, because we can't tell if changes in recovery rates are due to treatment or to those background factors. What we wish to do is compare patients of like backgrounds, and that is precisely what Fisher's *randomized experiment* accomplishes. How? It actually consists of two parts, randomization and *intervention*.

Intervention means that we change the natural behavior of the individual: we separate subjects into two groups, called treatment and control, and we convince the subjects to obey the experimental policy. We assign treatment to some patients who, under normal circumstances, will not seek treatment, and we give a placebo to patients who otherwise would receive treatment. That, in our new vocabulary, means *surgery* – we are severing one functional link and replacing it with another. Fisher's great insight was that connecting the new link to a random coin flip *guarantees* that the link we wish to break is actually broken. The reason is that a random coin is assumed to be unaffected by anything we can measure on a macroscopic level – including, of course, a patient's socioeconomic background.

This picture provides a meaningful and formal rationale for the universally accepted procedure of randomized trials. In contrast, our next example uses the surgery idea to point out inadequacies in widely accepted procedures.

The example [35] involves a government official trying to evaluate the economic consequences of some policy – say, taxation. A deliberate decision to raise or lower taxes is a surgery on the model of the economy because it modifies the conditions prevailing when the model was built. Economic models are built on the basis of data taken over some period of time, and during this period

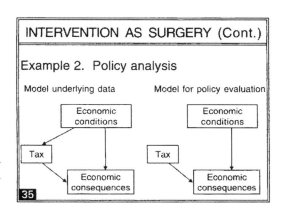

of time taxes were lowered and raised in response to some economic conditions or political pressure. However, when we *evaluate* a policy, we wish to compare alternative policies under the *same* economic conditions – namely, we wish to sever this link that, in the past, has tied policies to those conditions. In this setup, it is of course impossible to connect our policy to a coin toss and run a controlled experiment; we do not have the time for that, and we might ruin the economy before the experiment is over. Nevertheless the analysis that we *should conduct* is to infer the behavior of this mutilated model from data governed by a nonmutilated model.

I said *should conduct* because you will not find such analysis in any economics textbook. As I mentioned earlier, the surgery idea of Herman Wold was stamped out of the economics literature in the 1970s, and all discussions on policy analysis that I could find assume that the mutilated model prevails throughout. That taxation is under government control at the time of evaluation is assumed to be sufficient for treating taxation as an exogenous variable throughout, when in fact taxation is an endogenous variable during the model-building phase and turns exogenous only when evaluated. Of course, I am not claiming that reinstating the surgery model would enable the government to balance its budget overnight, but it is certainly something worth trying.

Let us now examine how the surgery interpretation resolves Russell's enigma concerning the clash between the directionality of causal relations and the symmetry of physical equations. The equations of physics are indeed symmetrical, but when we compare the phrases "A causes B" versus "B causes A," we are not talking about a single set of equations. Rather, we are comparing two world models, represented by two different sets of equations: one in which the equation for A is surgically removed; the other where the equation for B is removed. Russell would probably stop us at this point and ask: "How can you talk about *two* world models when in fact there is only one world model, given by all the equations of physics put together?" The answer is: *yes*. If you wish to include the entire universe in the model, causality disappears because interventions disappear – the manipulator and the manipulated lose their distinction. However, scientists rarely consider the entirety of the universe as an object of investigation. In most cases the scientist carves a piece from the universe and proclaims that piece *in* – namely, the *focus* of investigation. The rest of the universe is then considered *out* or *background* and is summarized by what we call *boundary conditions*. This choice of *ins* and *outs* creates asymmetry in the way we look at things, and it is this asymmetry that permits us to talk about "outside intervention" and hence about causality and cause–effect directionality.

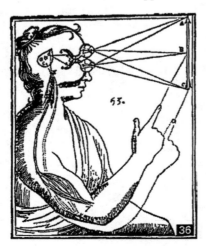

This can be illustrated quite nicely using Descartes' classical drawing [36]. As a whole, this hand–eye system knows nothing about causation. It is merely a messy plasma of particles and photons trying their very best to obey Schroedinger's equation, which is symmetric.

However, carve a chunk from it – say, the object part [37] – and we can talk about the motion of the hand *causing* this light ray to change angle.

Carve it another way, focusing on the brain part [38], and lo and behold it is now the light ray that causes the hand to move – precisely the opposite direction. The lesson is that it is the way we carve up the universe that determines the directionality we associate with cause and effect. Such carving is tacitly assumed in every scientific investigation. In artificial intelligence it was called "circumscription" by J. McCarthy.

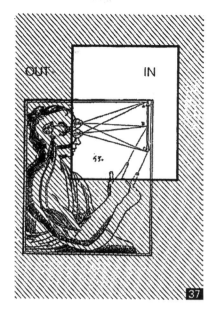

In economics, circumscription amounts to deciding which variables are deemed endogenous and which exogenous, *in* the model or *external to* the model.

Let us summarize the essential differences between equational and causal models [39]. Both use a set of symmetric equations to describe normal conditions. The causal model, however, contains three additional ingredients: (i) a distinction between the *in* and the *out*; (ii) an assumption that each equation corresponds to an independent mechanism and hence must be preserved as a separate mathematical sentence; and (iii) interventions that are interpreted as surgeries over those mechanisms. This brings us closer to realizing the dream of making causality a friendly part of physics. But one ingredient is missing: *the algebra*. We discussed earlier how important the computational facility of algebra was to scientists and engineers in the Galilean era. Can we expect such algebraic facility to serve causality as well? Let me rephrase it differently: Scientific activity, as we know it, consists of two basic components:

Observations [40] and interventions [41].

The combination of the two is what we call a *laboratory* [42], a place where we control some of the conditions and observe others. It so happened that standard algebras have served the observational component

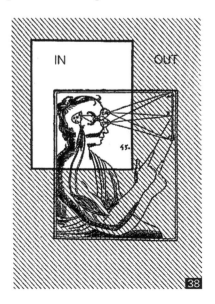

FROM PHYSICS TO CAUSALITY

Physics:
  Symmetric equations of motion

Causal models:
Symmetric equations of motion
  Circumscription (in vs. out)
  Locality (autonomy of mechanisms)
  Intervention = surgery on mechanisms

very well but thus far have not benefitted the interventional component. This is true for the algebra of equations, Boolean algebra, and probability calculus – all are geared to serve observational sentences but not interventional sentences.

Take, for example, probability theory. If we wish to find the chance that it rained, given that we see the grass wet, we can express our question in a formal sentence written like that: P (Rain | Wet), to be read: the probability of Rain, given Wet [43]. The vertical bar stands for the phrase: "given that we see." Not only can we express this question in a formal sentence, we can also use the machinery of probability theory and transform the sentence into other expressions. In our example, the sentence on the left can be transformed to the one on the right, if we find it more convenient or informative.

But suppose we ask a different question: "What is the chance it rained if we *make* the grass wet?" We cannot even express our query in the syntax of probability, because the vertical bar is already taken to mean "given that we see." We can invent a new symbol *do*, and each time we see a *do* after the bar we read it *given that we do* – but this does not help us compute the answer to our question, because the rules of probability do not apply to this new reading. We know intuitively what the answer should be: P (Rain), because making the grass wet does not change the chance of rain. But can this intuitive answer, and others like it, be derived mechanically, so as to comfort our thoughts when intuition fails?

The answer is *yes*, and it takes a new algebra. First, we assign a symbol to the new operator "given that we do." Second, we find the rules for manipulating sentences containing this new symbol. We do that by a process analogous to the way mathematicians found the rules of standard algebra.

Imagine that you are a mathematician in the sixteenth century, you are now an expert in the algebra of *addition*, and you feel an urgent need to introduce a new operator, *multiplication*, because you are tired of adding a number to itself all day long [44]. The first thing you do is assign the new operator a symbol: *multiply*. Then you go down to the meaning of the operator, from which you can deduce its rules of transformations. For example: the commutative law of multiplication can be deduced that way, the associative law, and so on. We now learn all this in high school.

In exactly the same fashion, we can deduce the rules that govern our new symbol: $do\ (\cdot)$. We have an algebra for seeing – namely, probability theory. We have a new operator, with a brand new outfit and a very clear meaning, given to us by the surgery procedure. The door is open for deduction, and the result is given in the next slide [45].

Please do not get alarmed, I do not expect you to read these equations right now, but I think you can still get the flavor of this new calculus. It consists of three rules that permit us to transform expressions involving actions and observations into other expressions of this type. The first allows us to

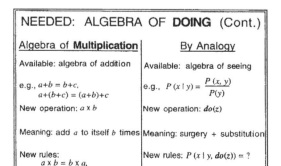

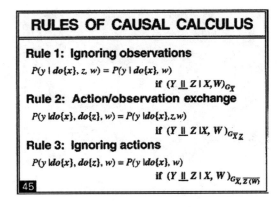

ignore an irrelevant observation, the third to ignore an irrelevant action; the second allows us to exchange an action with an observation of the same fact. What are those symbols on the right? They are the "green lights" that the diagram gives us whenever the transformation is legal. We will see them in action on our next example.

This brings us to part three of the lecture, where I will demonstrate how the ideas presented thus far can be used to solve new problems of practical importance.

Consider the century-old debate concerning the effect of smoking on lung cancer [46]. In 1964, the Surgeon General issued a report linking cigarette smoking to death, cancer, and most particularly lung cancer. The report was based on non-experimental studies in which a strong correlation was found between smoking and lung cancer, and the claim was that the correlation found is causal: If we ban smoking, then the rate of cancer cases will be roughly the same as the one we find today among nonsmokers in the population.

These studies came under severe attacks from the tobacco industry, backed by some very prominent statisticians, among them Sir Ronald Fisher. The claim was that the observed correlations can also be explained by a model in which there is no causal connection between smoking and lung cancer. Instead, an unobserved genotype might exist that simultaneously causes cancer and produces an inborn craving for nicotine. Formally, this claim would be written in our notation as: $P(\text{Cancer} \mid do(\text{Smoke})) = P(\text{Cancer})$, meaning that making the population smoke or stop smoking would have no effect on the rate of cancer cases. Controlled experiments could decide between the two models, but these are impossible (and now also illegal) to conduct.

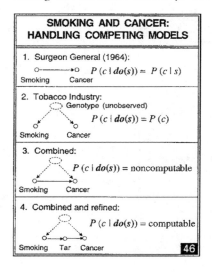

This is all history. Now we enter a hypothetical era where representatives of both sides decide to meet and iron out their differences. The tobacco industry concedes that there might be some weak causal link between smoking and cancer and representatives of the health group concede that there might be some weak links to genetic factors. Accordingly, they draw this combined model, and the question boils down to assessing, from the data, the strengths of the various links. They submit the query to a statistician and the answer comes back immediately: *impossible*. Meaning: there is no way to estimate the strength from the data, because any data whatsoever can perfectly fit either one of these two extreme models. So they give up and decide to continue the political battle as usual. Before parting, a suggestion comes up: perhaps we can resolve our differences if we measure some auxiliary factors. For example, since the causal-link model is based on the understanding that smoking affects lung cancer through the accumulation of tar deposits in the lungs, perhaps we can measure the amount of tar deposits in the lungs of sampled individuals, and this might provide the necessary information for quantifying the links. Both sides agree that this is a reasonable suggestion, so they submit a new query to the statistician: Can we find the effect of smoking on cancer assuming that an intermediate measurement of tar deposits is available? The statistician comes back with good news: *it is computable* and, moreover, the solution is given in closed mathematical form. *How?*

The statistician receives the problem and treats it as a problem in high school *algebra*: We need to compute P (Cancer), under hypothetical action, from nonexperimental data – namely, from expressions involving *no actions*. Or: We need to eliminate the "*do*" symbol from the initial expression. The elimination proceeds like ordinary solution of algebraic equations – in each stage [47], a new rule is applied, licensed by some subgraph of the diagram, eventually leading to a formula involving no "*do*" symbols, which denotes an expression that is computable from nonexperimental data.

You are probably wondering whether this derivation solves the smoking–cancer debate. The answer is *no*. Even if we could get the data on tar deposits, our model is quite simplistic, as it is based on certain assumptions that both parties might not agree to – for instance, that there is no direct link between smoking and lung cancer unmediated by tar deposits. The model would need to be refined then, and we might end up with a graph containing twenty variables or more. There is no need to panic when someone tells us: "you did not take this or that factor into account." On the contrary, the graph welcomes such new ideas, because it is so easy to add factors and measurements into the model. Simple tests are now available that permit an investigator to merely glance at the graph and decide if we can compute the effect of one variable on another.

Our next example illustrates how a long-standing problem is solved by purely graphical means – proven by the new algebra. The problem is called *the adjustment problem* or "the

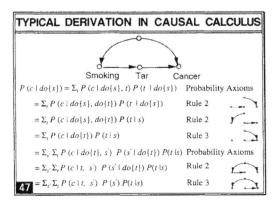

> **SIMPSON'S PARADOX**
> (Pearson et al. 1899; Yule 1903; Simpson 1951)
>
> - Any statistical relationship between two variables may be **reversed** by including additional factors in the analysis.
>
> Application: The adjustment problem
>
> - Which factors **should** be included in the analysis.

covariate selection problem" and represents the practical side of Simpson's paradox [48].

Simpson's paradox, first noticed by Karl Pearson in 1899, concerns the disturbing observation that every statistical relationship between two variables may be *reversed* by including additional factors in the analysis. For example, you might run a study and find that students who smoke get higher grades; however, if you adjust for *age*, the opposite is true in every *age group*, that is, smoking predicts lower grades. If you further adjust for *parent income*, you find that smoking predicts higher grades again, in every *age–income* group, and so on.

Equally disturbing is the fact that no one has been able to tell us which factors *should* be included in the analysis. Such factors can now be identified by simple graphical means. The classical case demonstrating Simpson's paradox took place in 1975, when UC-Berkeley was investigated for sex bias in graduate admission. In this study, overall data showed a higher rate of admission among male applicants; but, broken down by departments, data showed a slight bias in favor of admitting female applicants. The explanation is simple: female applicants tended to apply to more competitive departments than males, and in these departments, the rate of admission was low for both males and females.

To illustrate this point, imagine a fishing boat with two different nets, a large mesh and a small net [49]. A school of fish swim toward the boat and seek to pass it. The female fish try for the small-mesh challenge, while the male fish try for the easy route. The males go through

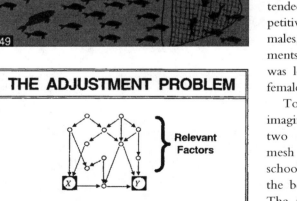

> **THE ADJUSTMENT PROBLEM**
>
> Given: Causal graph
> Needed: Effect of X on Y
> Decide: Which measurements should be taken?

and only females are caught. Judging by the final catch, preference toward females is clearly evident. However, if analyzed separately, each individual net would surely trap males more easily than females.

Another example involves a controversy called "reverse regression," which occupied the social science literature in the 1970s. Should we, in salary discrimination cases, compare salaries of equally qualified men and women or instead compare qualifications of equally paid men and women?

Remarkably, the two choices led to opposite conclusions. It turned out that men earned a higher salary than equally qualified women and, *simultaneously*, men were more qualified than equally paid women. The moral is that all conclusions are extremely sensitive to which variables we choose to hold constant when we are comparing, and that is why the adjustment problem is so critical in the analysis of observational studies.

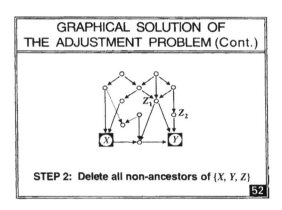

GRAPHICAL SOLUTION OF THE ADJUSTMENT PROBLEM

Subproblem:
Test if Z_1 and Z_2 are sufficient measurements
STEP 1: Z_1 and Z_2 should not be descendants of X

GRAPHICAL SOLUTION OF THE ADJUSTMENT PROBLEM (Cont.)

STEP 2: Delete all non-ancestors of $\{X, Y, Z\}$

Consider an observational study where we wish to find the effect of X on Y, for example, treatment on response [50]. We can think of many factors that are relevant to the problem; some are affected by the treatment, some are affecting the treatment, and some are affecting both treatment and response. Some of these factors may be unmeasurable, such as genetic trait or life style; others are measurable, such as gender, age, and salary level. Our problem is to select a subset of these factors for measurement and adjustment so that, if we compare

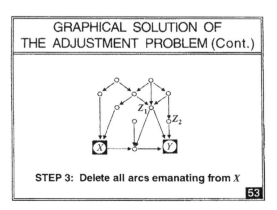

GRAPHICAL SOLUTION OF THE ADJUSTMENT PROBLEM (Cont.)

STEP 3: Delete all arcs emanating from X

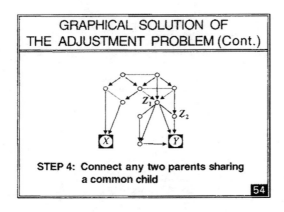

subjects under the same value of those measurements and average, we get the right result.

Let us follow together the steps that would be required to test if two candidate measurements, Z_1 and Z_2, would be sufficient [51]. The steps are rather simple, and can be performed manually even on large graphs. However, to give you the feel of their mechanizability, I will go through them rather quickly. Here we go [52–56].

At the end of these manipulations, we end up with the answer to our question: "If X is disconnected from Y, then Z_1 and Z_2 are appropriate measurements."

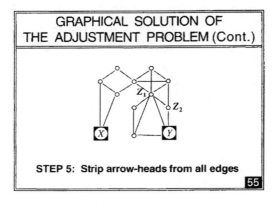

I now wish to summarize briefly the central message of this lecture. It is true that testing for cause and effect is difficult. Discovering causes of effects is even more difficult. But causality is not *mystical* or *metaphysical*. It can be understood in terms of simple processes, and it can be expressed in a friendly mathematical language, ready for computer analysis.

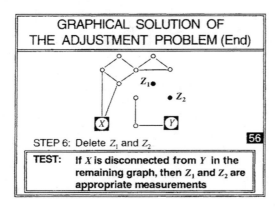

What I have presented to you today is a sort of pocket calculator, an *abacus* [57], to help us investigate certain problems of cause and effect with mathematical precision. This does not solve all the problems of causality, but the power of *symbols* and mathematics should not be underestimated [58].

Many scientific discoveries have been delayed over the centuries for the lack of a mathematical language that can amplify ideas and let scientists communicate results. I am convinced that many discoveries have been delayed in our century for lack of a mathematical language that can handle causation. For example, I am sure that Karl Pearson could have thought up the idea of *randomized experiment* in 1901 if he had allowed causal diagrams into his mathematics.

But the really challenging problems are still ahead: We still do not have a causal understanding of *poverty* and *cancer* and *intolerance*, and only the accumulation of data and the insight of great minds will eventually lead to such understanding.

The data is all over the place, the insight is yours, and now an abacus is at your disposal, too. I hope the combination amplifies each of these components.

Thank you.

FIGURE 20.1 Little Johnny and his "calculating machine."

Acknowledgments

Slide 1 (Dürer, *Adam and Eve*, 1504 engraving) courtesy of the Fogg Art Museum, Harvard University Art Museums, Gift of William Gray from the collection of Francis Calley Gray. Photo by Rick Stafford; image copyright © President and Fellows of Harvard College, Harvard University. Slide 2 (Doré, *The Flight of Lot*) copyright William H. Wise & Co. Slide 3 (Egyptian wall painting of Neferronpe playing a board game) courtesy of the Oriental Institute of the University of Chicago.

The following images were reproduced from antiquarian book catalogs, courtesy of Bernard Quaritch, Ltd. (London): slides 4, 5, 6, 7, 8, 9, 15, 27, 31, 36, 37, 38, 40, 42, and 58.

Slides 10 and 11 copyright The Courier Press. Slides 13 and 14 reprinted with the permission of Macmillan Library Reference USA, from *The Album of Science*, by I. Bernard Cohen. Copyright © 1980 Charles Scribner's Sons.

Slide 16 courtesy of the Library of California State University, Long Beach. Slides 20 and 22 reprinted with the permission of Cambridge University Press. Slide 25: copyright photograph by A. C. Barrington Brown, reproduced with permission.

474 J. Pearl

Slide 30: from S. Wright (1920) in *Proceedings of the National Academy of Sciences*, vol. 6; reproduced with the permission of the American Philosophical Society and the University of Chicago Press. Slide 57 reprinted with the permission of Vandenhoeck & Ruprecht and The MIT Press.

NOTE: Color versions of slides 19, 26, 28–29, 32–35, and 43–56 may be downloaded from www.cs.ucla.edu/~judea/.

21

CONCEPTUAL METAPHOR IN EVERYDAY LANGUAGE

G. Lakoff and M. Johnson

Until recently philosophers have tended to berate metaphor as irrational and dangerous, or to ignore it, reducing it to the status of a subsidiary problem in the philosophy of language. Literal language, assumed to be mutually exclusive with metaphor, has been taken to be the real stuff of philosophy, the domain where issues of meaning and truth arise and can be dealt with. At best, metaphor is treated as if it were always the result of some operation performed upon the literal meaning of the utterance. The phenomenon of "conventional metaphor," where much of our ordinary conceptual system and the bulk of our everyday conventional language are structured and understood primarily in metaphorical terms, has gone either unnoticed or undiscussed.

As we will show directly, conventional metaphors are pervasive in our ordinary everyday way of thinking, speaking, and acting. We feel that an understanding of conventional metaphor and the way that metaphor structures our ordinary conceptual system will ultimately provide a new "experientialist" perspective on classical philosophical problems, such as the nature of meaning, truth, rationality, logic, and knowledge. In this present paper we can only focus on the nature and role of metaphor in our conceptual system, with a few suggestions concerning the larger implications of our account.[1]

Concepts that we live by

Metaphor is for most people a device of the poetic imagination and the rhetorical flourish—a matter of extraordinary rather than ordinary language. Moreover, metaphor is typically viewed as characteristic of language alone, a matter of words rather than thought or action. For this reason, most people think they can get along perfectly well without metaphor. We have found, on the contrary, that metaphor is pervasive in everyday life, not just in language, but in thought and action.

476 G. Lakoff and M. Johnson

Our ordinary conceptual system, in terms of which we both think and act, is fundamentally metaphorical in nature.

The concepts that govern our thought are not just matters of the intellect. They also govern our everyday functioning, down to the most mundane details. Our concepts structure what we perceive, how we get around in the world, and how we relate to other people. Our conceptual system thus plays a central role in defining our everyday realities. If we are right in suggesting that our conceptual system is largely metaphorical, then the way we think, what we experience, and what we do every day is very much a matter of metaphor.

But our conceptual system is not something that we are normally aware of. In most of the little things we do every day, we simply think and act more or less automatically along certain lines. Just what these lines are is by no means obvious. One way to find out is by looking at language. Since communication is based on the same conceptual system in terms of which we think and act, language is an important source of evidence for what that system is like.

Primarily on the basis of linguistic evidence, we have found that most of our ordinary conceptual system is metaphorical in nature. And we have found a way to begin to identify in detail just what the metaphors are that structure how we perceive, how we think, and what we do.

To give some idea of what it could mean for a concept to be metaphorical and for such a concept to structure an everyday activity, let us start with the concept of an ARGUMENT, and the conceptual metaphor ARGUMENT IS WAR. This metaphor is reflected in our everyday language by a wide variety of expressions:

> ARGUMENT IS WAR
> Your claims are *indefensible*.
> He *attacked every weak point* in my argument.
> His criticisms were *right on target*.
> I *demolished* his argument.
> I've never *won* an argument with him.
> You disagree? Okay, *shoot!*
> If you use that *strategy*, he'll *wipe you out*.
> He *shot down* all my arguments.

It is important to see that we don't just *talk* about arguments in terms of war. We can actually win or lose arguments. We see the person we are arguing with as an opponent. We attack his positions and we defend our own. We gain and lose ground. We plan and use strategies. If we find a position indefensible, we can abandon it and take a new line of attack. Many of the things we *do* in arguing are partially structured by the concept of war. Though there is no physical battle, there is a verbal battle, and the structure of an argument—attack, defense, counterattack, etc.—reflects this. It is in this sense that we live by the ARGUMENT IS WAR metaphor in this culture; it structures the actions we perform in arguing.

Conceptual metaphor in everyday language **477**

Try to imagine a culture where arguments were not viewed in terms of war, where no one won or lost, where there was no sense of attacking or defending, gaining or losing ground. Imagine a culture where an argument is viewed as a dance, with the participants as performers, and the goal being to perform in a balanced and aesthetic way. In such a culture, people would view arguments differently, experience them differently, carry them out differently, and talk about them differently. But *we* would probably not view them as arguing at all. It would be strange even to call what they were doing "arguing." Perhaps the most neutral way of describing this difference between their culture and ours would be to say that we have a discourse form structured in terms of battle and they have one structured in terms of dance.

This is an example of what it means for a metaphorical concept, namely, ARGU-MENT IS WAR, partially to structure what we do and how we understand what we do when we argue. *The essence of metaphor is understanding and experiencing one kind of thing or experience in terms of another.* It is not that arguments are a subspecies of wars. Arguments and wars are different kinds of things—verbal discourse and armed conflict—and the actions performed are different kinds of actions. But ARGUMENT is partially structured, understood, performed, and talked about in terms of WAR. The concept is metaphorically structured, the activity is metaphorically structured, and consequently, the language is metaphorically structured.

Moreover, this is the *ordinary* way of having an argument and talking about one. The normal way *for us* to talk about attacking a position is to use the words 'attack a position'. Our conventional ways of talking about arguments presuppose a metaphor we are hardly ever conscious of. The metaphor is not merely in the words we use—it is in our very concept of an argument. The language of argument is not poetic, fanciful, or rhetorical, but rather literal. We talk about arguments that way because we conceive of them that way—and we act according to the way we conceive of things.

The systematicity of metaphorical concepts

Arguments usually follow patterns; that is, there are certain things we typically do and do not do in arguing. The fact that we in part conceptualize arguments in terms of battle systematically influences the shape arguments take and the way we talk about what we do in arguing. Because the metaphorical concept is systematic, the language we use to talk about that aspect of the concept is systematic.

We saw in the ARGUMENT IS WAR metaphor that expressions from the vocabulary of war, e.g., 'attack a position', 'indefensible', 'strategy', 'new line of attack', 'win', 'gain ground', etc. form a systematic way of talking about the battling aspects of arguing. It is no accident that these expressions mean what they mean when we use them to talk about arguments. A portion of the conceptual network of battle partially characterizes the concept of an argument, and the language follows suit. Since metaphorical expressions in our language are tied to metaphorical concepts in a systematic way, we can use metaphorical linguistic expressions to study the nature

478 G. Lakoff and M. Johnson

of metaphorical concepts and to gain an understanding of the metaphorical nature of our activities.

To get an idea of how metaphorical expressions in everyday language can give us insight into the metaphorical nature of the concepts that structure our everyday activities, let us consider the metaphorical concept TIME IS MONEY as it is reflected in contemporary

> TIME IS MONEY
> You're *wasting* my time.
> This gadget will *save* you hours.
> I don't *have* the time to *give* you.
> How do you *spend* your time these days?
> That flat tire *cost* me an hour.
> I've *invested* a lot of time in her.
> I don't *have enough* time to *spare* for that.
> You're *running out* of time.
> You need to *budget* your time.
> *Put aside* some time for ping pong.
> Is that *worth your while?*
> Do you *have* much time *left?*
> You don't *use* your time *profitably.*
> I *lost* a lot of time when I got sick.
> *Thank you for* your time.

Time in our culture is a valuable commodity. It is a limited resource that we use to accomplish our goals. Because of the way that the concept of work has developed in modern Western culture, where work is typically associated with the time it takes and time is precisely quantified, it has become customary to pay people by the hour, week, or year. In our culture TIME IS MONEY in many ways: telephone message units, hourly wages, hotel room rates, yearly budgets, interest on loans, and paying your debt to society by serving time. These practices are relatively new in the history of the human race and by no means exist in all cultures. They have arisen in modern industrialized societies and structure our basic everyday activities in a very profound way. Corresponding to the fact that we *act* as if time were a valuable commodity, a limited resource, even money, so we *conceive* of time that way. Thus we understand and experience time as the kind of thing that can be spent, wasted, budgeted, invested wisely or poorly, saved or squandered.

TIME IS MONEY, TIME IS A LIMITED RESOURCE, and TIME IS A VALUABLE COMMODITY are all metaphorical concepts. They are metaphorical since we are using our everyday experience with money, limited resources, and valuable commodities to conceptualize time. This isn't a necessary way for human beings to conceptualize time; it is tied to our culture. There are cultures where time is none of these things.

The metaphorical concepts TIME IS MONEY, TIME IS A RESOURCE, and TIME IS A VALUABLE COMMODITY form a single system based on subcategorization, since in

Conceptual metaphor in everyday language   **479**

our society money is a limited resource and limited resources are valuable commodities. These subcategorization relationships characterize what we will call "entailment relationships" between the metaphors, TIME IS MONEY entails that TIME IS A LIMITED RESOURCE, which entails that TIME IS A VALUABLE COMMODITY. We can see the relationship in the following diagram:

MONEY	TIME IS MONEY
is	entails
A LIMITED RESOURCE	TIME IS A LIMITED RESOURCE
is	entails
A VALUABLE COMMODITY	TIME IS A VALUABLE COMMODITY

We are adopting the practice of using the most specific metaphorical concept, in this case TIME IS MONEY, to characterize the entire system, since TIME IS MONEY entails TIME IS A LIMITED RESOURCE and TIME IS A VALUABLE COMMODITY. Of the expressions listed under the TIME IS MONEY metaphor, some refer specifically to money ('spend', 'invest', 'budget', 'profitably', 'cost'), others to limited resources ('use', 'use up', 'have enough of', 'run out of'), and still others to valuable commodities ('have', 'give', 'lose', 'thank you for'). This is an example of the way in which metaphorical entailments can characterize a coherent system of metaphorical concepts and a corresponding coherent system of metaphorical expressions for those concepts.[2]

Metaphorical systematicity: highlighting and hiding

The very systematicity that allows us to comprehend one aspect of a concept in terms of another (e.g., comprehending an aspect of arguing in terms of battle) will necessarily hide other aspects of the concept. In allowing us to focus on one aspect of a concept (e.g., the battling aspects of arguing), a metaphorical concept can keep us from focusing on other aspects of the concept which are not coherent with that metaphor. For example, in the midst of a heated argument, where we are intent on attacking our opponent's position and defending our own, we can lose sight of the more cooperative aspects involved in an argument. Someone who is arguing with you can be viewed as giving you his time, a valuable commodity, in an effort at mutual understanding. But when we are preoccupied with the battle aspects, we will most often lose sight of the cooperative aspects.

A far more subtle case of how a metaphorical concept can hide an aspect of our experience can be seen in what Michael Reddy[3] has called the "conduit metaphor." Reddy observes that our language about language is structured roughly by the following complex metaphor: (i) ideas (or meanings) are objects; (ii) linguistic expressions are containers; (iii) communication is sending—the speaker puts ideas (objects) into words (containers) and sends them (along a conduit) to a hearer who takes the idea–objects out of the word–containers. Reddy documents this with over one hundred *types* of expressions in English, which he estimates account for at least

480 G. Lakoff and M. Johnson

seventy per cent of the expressions we use to talk about language. Here are some examples:

> THE CONDUIT METAPHOR
> It's hard to *get* that *idea* across to him.
> I *gave* you that idea.
> Your reasons *came through* to us.
> It's difficult to *put* my ideas *into* words.
> When you *have* a good idea, try to *capture* it immediately *in* words.
> Try to *pack* more thought *into* fewer words.
> You can't simply *stuff* ideas *into* a sentence any old way.
> The meaning is right there *in* the words.
> Don't *force* your meanings *into* the wrong words.
> His words *carry* little meaning.
> The introduction *has* a great deal of thought-*content*.
> Your words seem *hollow*.
> The sentence is *without* meaning.
> The idea is *buried in* terribly dense paragraphs.

In examples like these it is far more difficult to see that there is anything hidden by the metaphor, or even to see that there is a metaphor here at all. This is so much the conventional way of thinking about language that it is sometimes hard to imagine that it might not fit reality. But if we look at what the conduit metaphor entails, we can see some of the ways in which it masks aspects of the communicative process.

First, the LINGUISTIC EXPRESSIONS ARE CONTAINERS FOR MEANINGS aspect of the metaphor entails that words and sentences have meanings in themselves, independent of any context or speaker. The MEANINGS ARE OBJECTS part of the metaphor, for example, entails that meanings have an existence independent of people and contexts. The part of the metaphor that says that LINGUISTIC EXPRESSIONS ARE CONTAINERS FOR MEANING entails that words (and sentences) have meanings, again independent of contexts and speakers. These metaphors are appropriate in many situations—those where context differences don't matter and where all the participants in the conversation understand the sentences in the same way. These two entailments are exemplified by sentences like "The meaning is *right there in* the words," which, according to the conduit metaphor, can correctly be said of any sentence. But there are many cases where context does matter. Here is a celebrated example recorded in actual conversation by Pamela Downing: "Please sit in the apple-juice seat." In isolation this sentence has no meaning at all, since the compound 'apple-juice seat' is not a conventional way of referring to any kind of object. But the sentence made perfect sense in the context in which it was uttered: An overnight guest came down to breakfast. There were four place settings, three with orange juice and one with apple juice. It was clear what the apple-juice seat was. And even the next morning, when there was no apple juice, it was still clear which seat was the apple-juice seat.

Conceptual metaphor in everyday language **481**

In addition to sentences that have no meaning without context, there are cases where a single sentence will mean different things to different people. Consider: "We need new alternative sources of energy." This means something very different to the president of Mobil Oil than it does to the president of Friends of the Earth. The meaning is not right there in the sentence—it matters a lot who is saying or listening to the sentence and what his social and political attitudes are. The conduit metaphor does not fit cases where context is required to determine whether the sentence has any meaning at all, and, if so, what meaning it has.

These examples show that the metaphorical concepts we have looked at provide us with a partial understanding of what communication, argument, and time are, and that in so doing they hide other aspects of these concepts. It is important to see that the metaphorical structuring involved here is partial, not total. If it were total, one concept would *be* the other, would not merely be understood in terms of it. For example, time isn't actually money. If you *spend your time* trying to do something and it doesn't work, you can't *get your time back*. There are no *time banks*. I can *give* you *a lot of time*, but you can't *give me back the same time*, though you can *give me back the same amount of time*. And so on. Thus, part of a metaphorical concept does not and cannot fit.

On the other hand, metaphorical concepts can be extended beyond the range of ordinary literal ways of thinking and talking into the range of what is called figurative, poetic, colorful, or fanciful thought and language. Thus, if ideas are objects, we can *dress them up in fancy clothes, juggle them, line them up nice and neat*, etc. So when we say that a concept is structured by a metaphor, we mean that it is partially structured, and that it can be extended in some ways but not others.

Types of metaphor: structural, orientational, physical

In order to see in more detail what is involved in the metaphorical structuring of a concept or system of concepts, it is useful to identify three basic domains of conceptual structure and to trace some of the systematic connections among and within them. These three domains—physical, cultural, and intellectual—are only roughly divided, because they cannot be sharply delineated and usually interact in significant ways.

So far we have examined what we might call "structural" metaphors, cases where one concept is metaphorically structured in terms of another (e.g., ARGUMENT is structured in terms of WAR). Structural metaphors often involve using a concept from one domain (WAR as a physical or cultural phenomenon) to structure a concept from another domain (ARGUMENT as primarily an intellectual concept, but with cultural content). But before we can look more closely at the various domains of conceptual structure, it is important to see that there are what might be called "physical" and "orientational" metaphors, in addition to structural metaphors of the conventional type. Briefly, "physical" metaphors involve the projection of entity or substance status upon something that does not have that status inherently. Such conventional metaphors allow us to view events, activities,

482 G. Lakoff and M. Johnson

emotions, ideas, etc., as entities for various purposes (e.g., in order to refer to them, categorize them, group them, or quantify them). For example, we find physical metaphors such as:

> My *fear of insects* is driving my wife crazy, (referring)
> You've got *too much hostility* in you. (quantifying)
> The *brutality of war* dehumanizes us all. (identifying aspects)
> The *pressures of his responsibilities* caused his breakdown, (identifying causes)
> Here's what to do to ensure *fame and fortune*. (setting goals and motivating actions)

Physical metaphors such as these are hardly ever noticed, because they are so basic to our everyday conceptualizing and functioning. But they are, nevertheless, conventional metaphors by means of which we understand either nonphysical or not clearly bounded things as entities. In most cases such metaphors involve the use of a concept from the physical domain to structure a concept from the cultural or intellectual domains.

A third kind of conventional metaphor is the "orientational" metaphor, which does not structure one concept in terms of another, but instead organizes a whole system of concepts with respect to one another. We call them "orientational" metaphors because most of them have to do with spatial orientation: UP–DOWN, FRONT–BACK, IN–OUT, ON–OFF, DEEP–SHALLOW, CENTRAL–PERIPHERAL. These spatial orientations arise from the facts that we have bodies of the sort we have and that they function as they do in our physical environment. Orientational metaphors give a concept a spatial orientation, for example, HAPPY IS UP. The fact that the concept HAPPY is oriented UP leads to English expressions like "I'm feeling up today."

In order to examine the way in which metaphors provide structure across the different domains of concepts (physical, cultural, intellectual) we shall focus briefly on orientational metaphors, as representative examples. Such metaphorical orientations are not arbitrary. They have a basis in our physical and cultural experience. Though the polar oppositions UP–DOWN, IN–OUT, etc. are physical in nature, the orientational metaphors can vary from culture to culture. For example, some cultures orient the future in front of us; others orient it in back. We will be looking at UP–DOWN spatialization metaphors, which have been studied intensively by William Nagy,[4] as an illustration. In each case, we will give a brief hint of how each metaphorical concept might have arisen from our physical and cultural experience. These accounts are meant to be suggestive and plausible, rather than definitive.

(1) HAPPY IS UP; SAD IS DOWN
I'm feeling up. That boosted my spirits. My spirits rose. You're in high spirits. Thinking about her always gives me a lift. I'm feeling down. I'm depressed. He's really low these days. I fell into a depression. My spirits sank.
Physical basis: Drooping posture typically goes along with sadness and depression, erect posture with a positive emotional state.

Conceptual metaphor in everyday language **483**

(2) CONSCIOUS IS UP; UNCONSCIOUS IS DOWN

Get up. Wake up. I'm up already. He rises early in the morning. He fell asleep. He dropped off to sleep. He's under hypnosis. He sank down into a coma.

Physical basis: Humans and most animals sleep lying down and stand erect when they wake up.

(3) HEALTH AND LIFE ARE UP; SICKNESS AND DEATH ARE DOWN

He's at the peak of health. Lazarus rose from the dead. He's in top shape. As to his health, he's way up there. He fell ill. He's sinking fast. He came down with the flu. His health is declining. He dropped dead.

Physical basis: Serious illness forces us physically to lie down. When you're dead you are physically down.

(4) HAVING CONTROL OR FORCE IS UP; BEING SUBJECT TO CONTROL OR FORCE IS DOWN

I have control over her. I am on top of the situation. He's in a superior position. He's at the height of his power. He's in the high command. His power rose. He's in a dominating position. He ranks above me in strength. He is under my control. He fell from power. His power is on the decline. He's in an inferior position.

Physical basis: Physical size typically correlates with physical strength, and the victor in a fight is typically on top.

(5) MORE IS UP; LESS IS DOWN

The number of books printed each year keeps going up. You made a high number of mistakes. My income rose last year. There is an overabundance of food in this country. My knowledge keeps increasing. The amount of artistic activity in this state has gone down in the past year. His number of errors is incredibly low. His income fell last year. He is underage. If you're too hot, turn the heat down.

Physical basis: If you add more of a substance or of physical objects to a container or pile, the level goes up.

(6) FORESEEABLE FUTURE EVENTS ARE UP (AND AHEAD)

The up-and-coming events are listed in the paper. What's coming up this week? I'm afraid of what's up ahead of us. What's up?

Physical basis: Normally our eyes are in the direction in which we typically move (ahead, forward). As an object approaches a person (or the person approaches the object), the object appears larger. Since the ground is perceived as being fixed, the top of the object appears to be moving *upward* in the person's field of vision.

(7) HIGH STATUS IS UP; LOW STATUS IS DOWN

He has a high position. She'll rise to the top. He's at the peak of his career. He's climbing the ladder. He has little upward mobility. He has a low position. She fell in status.

Social and physical basis: Status is correlated with power (social) and power is UP (physical).

484 G. Lakoff and M. Johnson

(8) GOOD IS UP; BAD IS DOWN
Things are looking up. We hit a peak last year, but it's been going downhill ever since. Things are at an all-time low. The quality of life is high these days.
Physical basis for personal well-being: HAPPINESS, HEALTH, LIFE, and CONTROL—the things that principally characterize what is GOOD for a person— are all UP.

(9) VIRTUE IS UP; DEPRAVITY IS DOWN
He is high-minded. She has high standards. She is upright. She is an upstanding citizen. That was a low trick. Don't be underhanded. I wouldn't stoop to that. That would be beneath me. He fell into the abyss of depravity. That was a low-down thing to do.
Physical and social basis: GOOD IS UP for a person (physical basis), together with the SOCIETY IS A PERSON metaphor (in the version where you are *not* identifying with your society). To be virtuous is to act in accordance with the standards set by the society-person to maintain its well-being, VIRTUE IS UP because virtuous actions correlate with social well-being from the society-person's point of view. Since socially based metaphors are part of the culture, it's the society-person's point of view that counts.

(10) RATIONAL IS UP; EMOTIONAL IS DOWN
The discussion fell to the emotional level, but I raised it back up to the rational plane. We put our feelings aside and had a high-level intellectual discussion of the matter. He couldn't rise above his emotions.
Physical and cultural basis: In this culture people view themselves as being in control over animals, plants, and their physical environment, and it is their unique ability to reason that places human beings above other animals and gives them this control, CONTROL IS UP, which has a physical basis, thus provides a basis for MAN IS UP, and therefore for RATIONAL IS UP.

On the basis of these examples, we suggest the following conclusions about the experiential grounding, the coherence, and the systematicity of metaphorical concepts:

(i) Most of our fundamental concepts are organized in terms of one or more spatialization metaphors.
(ii) There is an internal systematicity to each spatialization metaphor. For example, HAPPY IS UP defines a coherent system, rather than a number of isolated and random cases. (An example of an incoherent system would be one where, say, "I'm feeling up" meant "I'm feeling happy, but "My spirits rose" meant "I became sadder").
(iii) There is an over-all external systematicity among the various spatialization metaphors, which defines coherence among them. Thus, GOOD IS UP gives an UP orientation to general well-being, which is coherent with special cases like HAPPY IS UP, HEALTHY IS UP, ALIVE IS UP, CONTROL IS UP. STATUS IS UP is coherent with CONTROL IS UP.

Conceptual metaphor in everyday language **485**

(iv) Spatialization metaphors are rooted in physical and cultural experience. They are not randomly assigned.

(v) There are many possible physical and social bases for metaphors. Coherence within the over-all system seems to be part of the reason why one is chosen and not another. For example, happiness also tends to correlate physically with a smile and a general feeling of expansiveness. This could in principle form the basis for a metaphor HAPPY IS WIDE; SAD IS NARROW. And in fact there are minor metaphorical expressions like "I'm feeling expansive" which pick out a different aspect of happiness than does "I'm feeling up." But the major metaphor *in our culture* is HAPPY IS UP; there is a reason why we speak of the height of ecstasy rather than the breadth of ecstasy, HAPPY IS UP is maximally coherent with GOOD IS UP, HEALTHY IS UP, etc.

(vi) In some cases spatialization is so essential a part of a concept that it is difficult for us to imagine any alternative metaphor that might structure the concept. In our society "high status" is such a concept. Other cases, like happiness, are less clear. Is the concept of happiness independent of the HAPPY IS UP metaphor, or is the updown spatialization of happiness a part of the concept? We believe that it is a part of the concept within a given conceptual system. The HAPPY IS UP metaphor places happiness within a coherent metaphorical system, and part of its meaning comes from its role in that system.

(vii) So-called "purely intellectual" concepts, e.g., the concepts in a scientific theory, are often—and maybe even always—based on metaphors that have a physical or cultural basis. The 'high' in 'high-energy particles' is based on MORE IS UP. The 'high' in 'highlevel functions', as in physiological psychology, is based on RATIONAL IS UP. The 'low' in 'low-level phonology' (which refers to detailed phonetic aspects of the sound systems of languages) is based on MUNDANE REALITY IS DOWN (as in 'down to earth'). The intuitive appeal of a scientific theory has to do with how well its metaphors fit one's experience.

(viii) Our physical and cultural experience provides many possible bases for spatialization metaphors. Which ones are chosen, and which ones are major, may vary from culture to culture.

(ix) It is hard to distinguish the physical from the cultural basis of a metaphor, since the choice of one from among many possible physical bases has to do with cultural coherence. It is to this connection between metaphor and cultural coherence that we now turn.

Metaphor and cultural coherence

The most fundamental values in a culture will be coherent with the metaphorical structure of the most fundamental concepts in the culture. As an example, let us consider some cultural values in our society which are coherent with our UP-DOWN spatialization metaphors and whose opposites would not be.

486 G. Lakoff and M. Johnson

1   MORE IS BETTER is coherent with MORE IS UP and GOOD IS UP. LESS IS BETTER is not coherent with them.
2   BIGGER IS BETTER is coherent with MORE IS UP and GOOD IS UP; SMALLER IS BETTER is not coherent with them.
3   THE FUTURE WILL BE BETTER is coherent with THE FUTURE IS UP and GOOD IS UP; THE FUTURE WILL BE WORSE is not.
4   THERE WILL BE MORE IN THE FUTURE is coherent with MORE IS UP and THE FUTURE IS UP.
5   YOUR STATUS SHOULD BE HIGHER IN THE FUTURE is coherent with HIGH STATUS IS UP and THE FUTURE IS UP.

These are values deeply embedded in our culture, THE FUTURE WILL BE BETTER is a statement of the concept of progress, THERE WILL BE MORE IN THE FUTURE has as special cases the accumulation of goods and wage inflation, YOUR STATUS SHOULD BE HIGHER IN THE FUTURE is a statement of careerism. These are coherent with our present spatialization metaphors; their opposites would not be. So it seems that our values are not independent, but must form a coherent system with the metaphorical concepts we live by. We are not claiming that all cultural values coherent with a metaphorical system will exist, but only that those which do exist and are deeply entrenched will be consistent with the metaphorical system.

The values listed above hold in our culture in general—all things being equal. But because things are usually not equal, there are often conflicts among these values. To resolve such conflicts, one has to give different priorities to these values. There are certain constants. For instance, MORE IS UP seems always to have the highest priority since it has the clearest physical basis. The priority of MORE IS UP over GOOD IS UP can be seen in examples like "Inflation is rising" and "The crime rate is going up." Assuming that inflation and the crime rate are BAD, these sentences mean what they do because MORE IS UP always has top priority.

In general, which values are given priority is partly a matter of the subculture you live in and partly a matter of personal values. The various subcultures of a mainstream culture share basic values, but give them different priorities. For example, the value BIGGER IS BETTER may be in conflict with THERE WILL BE MORE IN THE FUTURE when it comes to the question of whether to buy a big car now with large time payments that will eat up future salary or whether to buy a smaller cheaper car. There are American subcultures where you buy the big car and don't worry about the future, and there are others where the future comes first and you buy the small car. There was a time (before inflation and the energy crisis) when owning a small car had a high status within the subculture where VIRTUE IS UP and SAVING RESOURCES IS VIRTUOUS took priority over BIGGER IS BETTER. Nowadays the number of small car owners has gone up drastically because there is a large subculture where SAVING MORE MONEY IS BETTER has priority over BIGGER IS BETTER.

In addition to subcultures, there are groups whose defining characteristic is that they have certain important values that conflict with those of the mainstream culture. But in less obvious ways they preserve other mainstream values. Take monastic

Conceptual metaphor in everyday language **487**

orders like the Trappists. There LESS IS BETTER and SMALLER IS BETTER with respect to material possessions, which are viewed as hindering what is important, namely, spiritual growth. The Trappists share the mainstream value VIRTUE IS UP, though they give it the highest priority and a very different definition, MORE is still BETTER, though it applies to VIRTUE; and STATUS is still UP, though it is not of this world but of a HIGHER one, the Kingdom of God. Moreover, THE FUTURE WILL BE BETTER in terms of spiritual growth (UP) and ultimately salvation (REALLY UP). This is typical of groups that are out of mainstream culture, VIRTUE, GOODNESS, and STATUS may be radically redefined, but they are still UP. It is still BETTER to have MORE of what is important, the FUTURE WILL BE BETTER with respect to what is important, and so on. Relative to what is important for such a monastic group, the value system is both internally coherent and, with respect to what is important for the group, coherent with the major orientational metaphors of the mainstream culture.

Individuals, like groups, will vary in their priorities and in the way they define what is GOOD or VIRTUOUS to them. In this sense, they are like subgroups of one. Relative to what is important for them, their individual value systems are coherent with the major orientational metaphors of their mainstream culture.

Not all cultures give the priorities we do to UP-DOWN orientation. There are cultures where BALANCE or CENTRALITY plays a much more important role than it does in our culture. Or consider the nonspatial orientation ACTIVE-PASSIVE. For us ACTIVE IS UP and PASSIVE IS DOWN in most matters. But there are cultures where passivity is valued more than activity. In general the major orientations UP-DOWN, IN-OUT, CENTRAL-PERIPHERAL, ACTIVE-PASSIVE, etc., seem to cut across all cultures, but which concepts will be oriented which way, and which orientations will be most important, will vary from culture to culture.

An apparent metaphorical contradiction

Charles Fillmore has observed (in conversation) that English appears to have two contradictory organizations of time. In the first the future is in front and the past behind.

> In the weeks ahead of us … (future)
> That's all behind us now … (past)

In the second, the future is behind and the past is in front.

> In the following weeks … (future)
> In the preceding weeks … (past)

This appears to be a contradiction in the metaphorical organization of time. Moreover, the apparently contradictory metaphors can mix with no ill effect, as in "We're looking *ahead* to the *following* weeks." Here it appears that *ahead* organizes the future in front, while *following* organizes it behind.

488 G. Lakoff and M. Johnson

To see that there is, in fact, a coherence here, we first have to consider some facts about back and front organization. Some things have inherent fronts and backs, for example, people and cars, but not trees. A rock may receive a front–back organization under certain circumstances. Suppose you are looking at a medium-sized rock and there is a ball between you and the rock, say, a foot from the rock. Then it is appropriate for you to say "The ball is in front of the rock." The rock has received a front–back orientation, as if it had a front that faced you. This is not universal. There are languages, for instance Hausa, where the rock would receive the reverse orientation and you would say that the ball was behind the rock, if it was between you and the rock.

Moving objects generally receive a front–back orientation so that the front is in the direction of motion (or in the canonical direction of motion, so that a car backing up retains its front). A spherical satellite, for example, that has no front while standing still, gets a front while in orbit by virtue of the direction in which it is moving.

Now time in English is structured in terms of the TIME IS A MOVING OBJECT METAPHOR, with the future moving toward us.

> The time will come when …
> The time has long since gone when …
> The time for action has arrived.

The proverb "Time flies" is an instance of the TIME IS A MOVING OBJECT metaphor. Since we are facing toward the future, we get:

> In the weeks ahead of us …
> I look forward to doing that.
> Before us is a great opportunity.

By virtue of the TIME IS A MOVING OBJECT metaphor, time receives a front–back orientation facing in the direction of motion, just as any moving object would. Thus the future is facing toward us as it moves toward us, and we find expressions like:

> I can't face the future.
> The face of things to come …
> Let's meet the future head–on.

Now, although expressions like 'ahead of us,' 'I look forward', and 'before us', orient times with respect to people, expressions like 'precede' and 'follow' orient times with respect to times. Thus we get:

> Next week and the week following it … but not:
> The week following me …

Since future times are facing toward us, the times following them are further in the future, and all future times follow the present. That is why the *weeks to follow* are the same as *the weeks ahead of us*.

The point of this example is not merely to show that there is no contradiction, but also to show all the subtle details that are involved in the coherence: the TIME IS A MOVING OBJECT metaphor, the front-back orientation given to time by virtue of its being a moving object, and the consistent application of words like 'follow', 'precede', and 'face' when applied to time on the basis of the metaphor. All of this coherent detailed metaphorical structure is part of our everyday literal language about time, so familiar that we would normally not notice it.

Some further examples

We have been claiming that metaphors partially structure our everyday concepts, and that this structure is reflected in our literal language. Before we can get an overall picture of the philosophical implications of these claims, we need a few more examples. In each of the following cases we give a metaphor and a list of ordinary expressions that are special cases of the metaphor. The English expressions are of two sorts—simple literal expressions and idioms that fit the metaphor and are part of the normal everyday way of talking about the subject.

Theories (and arguments) are buildings

Is that the *foundation* for your theory? The theory needs more *support*. The argument is *shaky*. We need some more facts or the arguments will *fall apart*. We need to *construct* a *strong* argument for that. I haven't figured out yet what the *form* of the argument will be. We need some more facts to *shore up* the theory. We need to *buttress* the theory with *solid* arguments. The theory will *stand* or *fall* on the *strength* of that argument. The argument *collapsed*. They *exploded* his latest theory. We will show that theory is *without foundation*. So far we have only put together the *framework* of the theory.

Ideas are food

What he said *left a bad taste in my mouth*. All this paper has in it are *raw facts, half-baked ideas*, and *warmed-over theories*. There were too many facts in the paper for me to *digest* them all. I just can't *swallow* that claim. That argument *smells fishy*. Let me *stew over* that for a while. Now there's a theory you can really *sink your teeth into*. We need to let that idea *percolate* for a while. That's *food for thought*. He's a *voracious* reader. We don't need to *spoon-feed* our students. He *devoured* the book. Let's let that idea *simmer on the back burner* for a while. This is the *meaty* part of the paper.

490 G. Lakoff and M. Johnson

Love is a journey

Look *how far we've come*. We're *at a crossroads*. We can't *turn back* now. I don't think this relationship is *going anywhere*. This relationship is *a dead-end street*. Our marriage is *on the rocks*. We've gotten *off the track*. *Where* are we? We're *stuck*. It's been a *long, bumpy road*.

Seeing is understanding; ideas are light sources; discourse is a light medium

I *see* what you're saying. It *looks* different from my *point of view*. What is your *outlook* on that? I *view* it differently. Now I've got the *whole picture*. Let me *point something out* to you. That's an *insightful* idea. That was a *brilliant* remark. It really *shed light* on the subject. It was an *illuminating* remark. The argument is *clear*. It was a *murky* discussion. Could you *elucidate* your remarks? It's a *transparent* argument. The discussion was *opaque*.

Life is a game of chance

I'll *take my chances*. *The odds are against us*. I've *got an ace up my sleeve*. He's *holding all the aces*. It's a *toss-up*. If you *play your cards right*, you can do it. He *won big*. He's *a real loser*. Where is he when *the chips are down*? That's my *ace in the hole*.

In the last example we have a collection of what are called "speech formulas," or "fixed-form expressions," or "phrasal lexical items." These function in many ways like single words, and the language has thousands of them. In the example given, a set of such phrasal lexical items are coherently structured by a single metaphor. Although each of them is an instance of the LIFE IS A GAME OF CHANCE metaphor, they are typically used to speak of life, not of gambling situations. They are normal ways of talking about life situations, just as using the word 'construct' is a normal way to talk about theories. It is in this sense that we include them as what we have called "literal" or "conventional" metaphors. If you say "the odds are against us?" or "we'll have to take our chances," you will not be viewed as speaking metaphorically, but rather as using the normal everyday language appropriate to the situation.

The partial nature of metaphorical structuring

So far we have described the systematic character of metaphorically defined concepts. Such concepts are understood in terms of a number of different metaphors (e.g., TIME IS MONEY, TIME IS A MOVING OBJECT, etc.). The metaphorical structuring of concepts is necessarily partial, and is reflected in the lexicon of the language—including the phrasal lexicon, which contains fixed-form expressions such as 'be without foundation'. Because concepts are metaphorically structured in a systematic way, e.g., THEORIES ARE BUILDINGS, it is possible for us to use expressions

Conceptual metaphor in everyday language **491**

(*construct, foundation*) from one domain (BUILDINGS) to talk about corresponding concepts in the metaphorically defined domain (THEORIES). What *foundation*, for example, means in the metaphorically defined domain (THEORY) will depend on the details of how the metaphorical concept THEORIES ARE BUILDINGS are used to structure the concept of a THEORY.

The parts of the concept of a building which are used to structure the concept of a theory are the foundation and outer shell. The roof, internal rooms, staircases, and hallways are parts of a building not used as part of the concept of a theory. Thus the metaphorical concept THEORIES ARE BUILDINGS has a "used" part (foundation and outer shell) and an "unused" part (rooms, staircases, etc.). Expressions such as *construct* and *foundation* are instances of the used part of such a metaphorical concept and are part of our ordinary" literal language about theories.

But what of the linguistic expressions that reflect the "unused" part of a metaphor like THEORIES ARE BUILDINGS? Here are four examples:

> His theory has thousands of little rooms and long, winding corridors.
> His theories are always baroque.
> He prefers massive Gothic theories covered with gargoyles.
> Complex theories usually have problems with the plumbing.

These sentences fall outside the domain of normal literal language and are part of what is usually called "figurative" or "imaginative" language. Thus literal expressions ("He has constructed a theory") and imaginative expressions ("His theory is covered with gargoyles") can be instances of the same general metaphor (THEORIES ARE BUILDINGS).

Here we can distinguish three different subspecies of imaginative (or nonliteral) metaphor:

(1) Extensions of the used part of the metaphor, e.g., "These facts are the bricks and mortar of my theory." Here the outer shell of the building is referred to, but the metaphor stops short of mentioning the materials used.
(2) Instances of the unused part of the literal metaphor, e.g., "His theory has thousands of little rooms and long, winding corridors."
(3) Instances of novel metaphor, that is, a metaphor not used to structure part of our normal conceptual system, but a new way of thinking about something, e.g., "Classical theories are patriarchs who father many children, most of whom fight incessantly." Each of these subspecies lies outside of the *used* part of a metaphorical concept that structures our normal conceptual system.

We note in passing that all the linguistic expressions that we have given to characterize general, metaphorical concepts are figurative. Examples are TIME IS MONEY, TIME IS A MOVING OBJECT, CONTROL IS UP, IDEAS ARE FOOD, THEORIES ARE BUILDINGS, etc. None of these is literal. This is a consequence of the fact that they are only *partly* used to structure our normal concepts. Since they necessarily contain

492 G. Lakoff and M. Johnson

parts that are not used in our normal concepts, they go beyond the realm of the literal.

Each of the metaphorical expressions we have talked about so far (e.g., the *time will come, construct* a theory, *attack* a *position*) is used within a whole system of metaphorical concepts—concepts that we live and think in terms of. These expressions, like all other words and phrasal lexical items in the language, are fixed by convention. In addition to these cases, which are part of whole metaphorical systems, there are idiosyncratic metaphorical expressions that stand alone and are not systematically used in our language or thought. These are well-known expressions like the *foot* of the mountain, a *head* of cabbage, the *leg* of a table, etc. These expressions are isolated instances of metaphorical concepts, where there is only one instance of a used part (or maybe two or three). Thus the *foot* of the mountain is the only used part of the metaphorical concept A MOUNTAIN IS A PERSON. In normal discourse we do not speak of the *head, shoulders,* or *trunk* of a mountain, though in special contexts it is possible to construct novel metaphors about mountains based on these unused parts. In fact, there is an aspect of the metaphorical concept A MOUNTAIN IS A PERSON in which mountain climbers will speak of the *shoulder* of a mountain (namely, a ridge near the top) and of *conquering, fighting,* and even *being killed* by a mountain. And there are cartoon conventions where mountains become animate and their peaks become heads. The point here is that there are metaphorical concepts like A MOUNTAIN IS A PERSON which are marginal in our culture and our language, whose used part may consist of only one conventionally fixed expression of the language, and which do not systematically interact with other metaphorical concepts, because so little of them is used. This makes them relatively uninteresting for our purposes, but not completely uninteresting, since they can be extended to their unused part in framing novel metaphors, making jokes, etc. And our ability to extend them to unused parts indicates that, however marginal they are, they do exist.

Examples like the *foot* of the mountain are idiosyncratic, unsystematic, and isolated. They do not interact with other metaphors, play no particularly interesting role in our conceptual system, and hence are not metaphors that we live by. The only signs of life that they have is that they can be extended in subcultures, and that their unused portions can be the basis for (relatively uninteresting) novel metaphors. If any metaphorical expressions deserve to be called "dead," it is these, though they do have a bare spark of life, in that they are understood partly in terms of marginal metaphorical concepts like A MOUNTAIN IS A PERSON.

It is important to distinguish these isolated and unsystematic cases from the systematic metaphorical expressions we have been discussing. Expressions like 'wasting time', 'attacking positions', 'going our separate ways', etc., are reflections of systematic metaphorical concepts that structure our actions and thoughts. They are "alive" in the most fundamental sense—they are metaphors we live by. The fact that they are conventionally fixed within the lexicon of English makes them no less alive.

Inadequacies of a theory of abstraction

On the basis of our previous analysis of the nature of literal metaphor we may now begin to draw out what we consider to be the more important implications for recent linguistic and philosophical treatments of language. We shall begin with the theory of abstraction, one strategy which linguists have occasionally tried for dealing with isolated cases of literal metaphor.[5] For example, consider 'construct' in "We constructed a theory" and "We constructed a building." According to the abstraction proposal, 'construct' has a very general, abstract meaning which is neutral between buildings and theories and can apply to both. Another example would be the 'in' of 'in the kitchen', 'in the ruling class', and 'in love'. The abstraction solution is that 'in' has an abstract meaning which is neutral among space, social groups, and love, and which can apply to all. This proposal has typically been suggested only for isolated lexical items rather than whole domains of literal metaphor, so it is not clear that there is any proposal for abstraction that is relevant. Still, the idea keeps popping up that it ought to be a viable program; so we shall indicate several shortcomings of this view relative to our account of literal metaphor.

(1) Under the abstraction view, there would be no conventional metaphors and, therefore, no partial metaphorical structuring such as we have proposed. But then how can one explain the apparent systematic grouping of expressions under single metaphors and the fact that different metaphors based on a single concept may have different partial structurings? Consider the metaphors LOVE IS WAR, RATIONAL DISCOURSE IS WAR, STOPPING INFLATION IS WAR, and CANCER IS WAR. ATTACK is in CANCER, INFLATION, and DISCOURSE. STRATEGY is in LOVE, DISCOURSE, and INFLATION, CONQUERING is in LOVE, INFLATION, and CANCER, VICTORIES and SETBACKS are in all of them. There is a FIRST LINE OF DEFENSE in INFLATION and CANCER. On our hypothesis, WAR is the basis for all four metaphors, each of which has a different partial structuring. On the abstraction hypothesis, there is no unity at all, but only a hodgepodge of different abstract concepts of different sorts.

(2) Since the abstraction proposal has no partial metaphorical structuring, it cannot account for metaphorical extensions into the unused part of the metaphor, as in "Your theory is constructed out of cheap stucco" and many others that fall within the unused portion of the THEORIES ARE BUILDINGS metaphor.

(3) The abstraction proposal does not seem to make any sense at all for UP-DOWN spatialization metaphors, such as HAPPY IS UP, CONTROL IS UP, MORE IS UP, VIRTUE IS UP, THE FUTURE IS UP, REASON IS UP, NORTH IS UP, etc. It seems impossible to imagine a single general concept with any content at all that would be an abstraction of HEIGHT, HAPPINESS, CONTROL, MORE, VIRTUE, THE FUTURE, REASON, and NORTH and which would precisely fit them all. Moreover, it would seem that UP and DOWN could not be at the same level of abstraction, since UP applies to the FUTURE, while DOWN does not apply to the PAST. We account for this by partial metaphorical structuring, but under the abstraction proposal UP would have to be more abstract in some sense than DOWN, and that does not seem to make sense.

494 G. Lakoff and M. Johnson

(4) The abstraction theory would not distinguish between metaphors of the form *"A is B"* and those of the form *"B is A,"* since it would claim that there are neutral terms covering both domains. For example, English has the LOVE IS A JOURNEY metaphor, but no JOURNEYS ARE LOVE metaphor. The abstraction view would deny that love is understood in terms of journeys, and would be left with the counterintuitive claim that love and journeys are understood in terms of some abstract concept neutral between them.

(5) Different conventional metaphors can structure different aspects of a single concept. For example, LOVE IS A JOURNEY; LOVE IS WAR; LOVE IS AN ELECTROMAGNETIC PHENOMENON; LOVE IS MADNESS; LOVE IS A GAME. Each of these provides one perspective on the concept of love and structures one of many aspects of the concept. The abstraction hypothesis would seek a single general concept of love which is abstract enough to fit all of these. This would miss the point that these metaphors are not jointly characterizing a core concept of love, but are separately characterizing different aspects of the concept of love.

(6) Finally, the abstraction hypothesis assumes, in the case of LOVE IS A JOURNEY, for example, that there is a set of abstract concepts, neutral with respect to love and journeys, which can "fit" or "apply to" both of them. But in order for such abstract concepts to "fit" or "apply to" love, the concept of love must be independently structured, so that there can be such a "fit." As we will show, love is, on its own terms, not a concept that has a clearly delineated structure; it gets such structure only via conventional metaphors. But the abstraction view, which has no conventional metaphors to do the structuring, must assume that a structure as clearly delineated as the relevant aspects of journeys exists independently for the concept of love. It's hard to imagine how.

How is our conceptual system grounded?

We claim that most of our normal conceptual system is metaphorically structured; that is, most concepts are partially understood in terms of other concepts. This raises an important question about the grounding of our conceptual system. Are there any concepts at all that are understood directly without metaphor? If not, how can we understand anything at all?

The prime candidates for concepts that are understood directly are the simple spatial concepts, such as UP. Our spatial concept UP arises out of our spatial experience. We have bodies and stand erect. Virtually every motor movement that we make involves a motor program that either changes our UP-DOWN orientation, maintains it, presupposes it, or takes it into account in some way. Our constant physical activity in the world, even when we sleep, makes UP-DOWN orientation not merely relevant to our physical activity, but centrally relevant. The centrality of UP-DOWN orientation in our motor programs and everyday functioning might make one think that there could be no alternative to such an orientational concept. Objectively speaking, however, there are many possible frameworks for spatial orientation, including Cartesian coordinates, which don't in themselves have

UP-DOWN orientation. Human spatial concepts, however, include UP-DOWN, FRONT-BACK, IN-OUT, NEAR-FAR, etc. It is these that are relevant to our continual everyday bodily functioning, which gives them a relative priority over other possible structurings of space *for us*. In other words, the structure of our spatial concepts emerges from our constant spatial experience, that is, our interaction with our physical environment. Concepts that emerge in this way are concepts that we live by in the most fundamental way.

Thus, UP is *not* understood purely in its own terms, but emerges from the collection of constantly performed motor functions that have to do with our erect position relative to the gravitational field we live in. Imagine a spherical being living outside of any gravitational field, with no knowledge or imagination of any other kind of experience. What could UP possibly mean to such a being?

Some of the central concepts in terms of which our bodies function—UP-DOWN, IN-OUT, FRONT-BACK, LIGHT-DARK, WARM-COLD, MALE-FEMALE, etc.—are more sharply delineated than others. Our emotional experience is as basic as our spatial and perceptual experience, but our emotional experiences are much less sharply delineated in terms of what we do with our bodies. Although a sharply delineated conceptual structure for space emerges from our perceptual-motor functioning, no sharply defined conceptual structure for the emotions emerges from our emotional functioning alone. Since there are *systematic correlates* between our emotions (like happiness) and our sensory-motor experiences (like erect posture), these form the basis of orientational metaphorical concepts (such as HAPPY IS UP). Such metaphors allow us to conceptualize our emotions in more sharply defined terms and also to relate them to other concepts having to do with general well-being (e.g., HEALTH, LIFE, CONTROL, etc.). In this sense, we can speak of *emergent metaphors* as well as emergent concepts.

The concepts of OBJECT, SUBSTANCE, and CONTAINER also emerge directly. We experience ourselves as entities, separate from the rest of the world—CONTAINERS with an inside and an outside. We also experience things external to us as entities —often also CONTAINERS with insides and outsides. We experience ourselves as being made up of SUBSTANCES, e.g., flesh and bone, and external objects as being made up of various *kinds* of SUBSTANCES—wood, stone, metal, etc. We experience many things, through sight and touch, as having distinct boundaries. And when things have no distinct boundaries, we often project boundaries upon them— conceptualizing them as entities and often as containers (for example, forests, clearings, clouds, etc.).

Like orientational metaphors, basic physical metaphors are grounded by virtue of *systematic correlates within our experience*. For example, the metaphor THE VISUAL FIELD IS A CONTAINER is grounded in the correlation of what we see with a bounded physical space. The TIME IS A MOVING OBJECT metaphor is based on the correlation between an object moving toward us and the time it takes to get to us. The same correlation is a basis for the TIME IS A CONTAINER metaphor (as in "He did it *in* ten minutes"), with the *bounded* space traversed by the object correlated with the time the object takes to traverse it. EVENTS and ACTIONS are correlated with bounded time spans, which makes them CONTAINER-OBJECTS.

496 G. Lakoff and M. Johnson

Perhaps the most important thing to stress about grounding is the distinction between an experience and the way we conceptualize it. We are *not* claiming that physical experience is in any way more basic than other kinds of experience, whether emotional, mental, cultural, or whatever. All these experiences may be just as basic as physical experiences. Rather, what we *are* claiming about grounding is that we typically *conceptualize* the nonphysical in terms of the physical—or the less clearly delineated in terms of the more clearly delineated. To see this more clearly, consider the following examples:

(1) Harry is *in* the kitchen.
(2) Harry is *in* the Elks Club.
(3) Harry is *in* love.

The sentences refer to three different domains of experience: spatial, social, and emotional. None of these has experiential priority over the others; they are all equally basic kinds of experience.

But with respect to conceptual structuring there is a difference. The concept IN expressed in (1) emerges *directly* from spatial experience in a clearly delineated fashion. It is not an instance of a metaphorical concept. The other two sentences *are* instances of metaphorical concepts. (2) is an instance of the SOCIAL GROUPS ARE CONTAINERS metaphor, in terms of which the concept of a social group is structured. This metaphor allows us to "get a handle on" the concept of a social group by means of a spatialization. Both the word 'in' and the concept IN are the *same* in all three examples; we do not have three different concepts of IN or three homophonous words 'in'. We have one emergent concept IN, one word for it, and two metaphorical concepts which partially define social groups and emotional states. What these cases show is that it is possible to have equally basic kinds of experiences while having conceptualizations of them that are not equally basic.

Thus, (1) happens to be, according to our account, a nonmetaphoric literal sentence, containing a directly spatial nonmetaphoric instance of the spatial concept IN. But for most linguistic purposes this doesn't give it any particularly special status over (2) and (3). However, sentences like (1) do seem to have special status in philosophical papers dealing with literal meaning. Sentences like (1) are much more likely to be used as clear examples of literal meaning than are sentences like (2) and (3), since philosophers seem instinctively to shy away from using sentences containing conventional metaphors as examples of literal meaning. That is the reason for the predominance of examples such as "The cat is on the mat," "Snow is white," "Brutus killed Caesar," etc.

An example of an emergent category

Our discussion in the two previous sections of the grounding of our conceptual system and the nature of nonmetaphoric literal meaning may seem to provide a framework for a "building-block" theory, in which all meaningful utterances either

Conceptual metaphor in everyday language 497

are or are constructed from certain unanalyzable semantic units. But we reject the notion of unanalyzable simples which might serve as the atoms for a linguistic or epistemological foundationalism. Instead, we wish to identify emergent categories and concepts that are best understood as experiential gestalts, which, though decomposable into other elements, are yet basic and irreducible in terms of grounding our conceptual system.

To explain this important notion, let us now move beyond our use of spatial examples of concepts that emerge from our successful functioning in our environment (e.g., UP-DOWN, IN-OUT, etc.) to a consideration of the concept of causation. Piaget has hypothesized that infants first learn about causation through the realization of their ability to manipulate directly objects around them—pulling off their blankets, throwing their bottles, dropping toys. There is, in fact, a stage in which infants seem to "practice" these manipulations, e.g., repeatedly dropping their spoons. As the child masters these more primitive manipulations of external objects, it moves on to other tasks which are to become part of its constant everyday functioning in its environment, for example, flipping lightswitches, opening doors, buttoning shirts, adjusting glasses. Though each of these actions is different, the overwhelming proportion of them share common features of what we may call a "prototypical" or "paradigmatic" case of direct causation. Among these shared features are included:

1 The agent has as a goal some change of state in the patient.
2 The change of state is physical.
3 The agent has a "plan" for carrying out this goal.
4 The plan requires the agent's use of a motor program.
5 The agent is in control of that motor program.
6 The agent is primarily responsible for carrying out the plan.
7 The agent is the energy source (i.e., the agent is directing his energies toward the patient) and the patient is the energy goal (i.e., the change in the patient is due to an external source of energy).
8 The agent touches the patient either with his body or with an instrument (i.e., the change in the patient is due to an external source of energy).
9 The agent successfully carries out the plan.
10 The change in the patient is perceptible.
11 The agent monitors the change in the patient through sensory perception.
12 There is a single specific agent and a single specific patient.

This set of properties characterizes "prototypical" direct manipulations, and these are cases of causation par excellence. We are using the word 'prototypical' in the sense used by Eleanor Rosch in her theory of human categorization.[6] Her experiments indicate that people categorize objects, not in set-theoretical terms, but in terms of prototypes and family resemblances. For example, small flying singing birds like sparrows, robins, etc., are prototypical birds. Chickens, ostriches, and penguins are birds, but not central members of the category—they are nonprototypical birds. But they are birds, nonetheless, because they bear sufficient family resemblances to the prototype; that is, they share enough of the relevant properties of the prototype to be classified by people as birds.

The twelve properties given above characterize a prototype of causation in the following sense. They recur together over and over in action after action as we go through our daily lives. We experience them as a gestalt, in which the complex of properties occurring together is more basic to our experience than their separate occurrences. Through their constant recurrence in our everyday functioning, the category of causation emerges with this complex of properties characterizing prototypical causations. Other kinds of causation, which are less prototypical, are actions or events that bear sufficient family resemblances to the prototype. These would include action at a distance, nonhuman agency, the use of an intermediate agent, the occurrence of two or more agents, involuntary or uncontrolled use of the motor program, etc. In physical causation the agent and patient are events, a physical law takes the place of plan, goal, and motor activity, and all the peculiarly human aspects are factored out. When there is not sufficient family resemblance to the prototype, we cease to characterize what happens as causation; for example, if there were multiple agents, if what the agents did was remote in space and time from the patient's change, and if there were neither desire nor plan nor control, then we probably wouldn't say that this was an instance of causation, or at least we would have questions about it.

Although the category of causation has fuzzy boundaries, it is clearly delineated in an enormous range of instances. Our successful functioning in the world involves the application of the concept of causation to ever new domains of activity—through intention, planning, drawing inferences, etc. The concept is stable, because we continue to function successfully in terms of it. Given a concept of causation that emerges from our experience, that concept can be applied to metaphorical concepts. In "Harry raised our morale by telling jokes," for example, we have an instance of causation where what Harry did made our morale go UP, as in the HAPPY IS UP metaphor.

Though the concept of causation as we have characterized it is basic to human activity, it is not a "primitive" in the usual building-block sense; that is, it is not unanalyzable and undecomposable. Since it is defined in terms of a prototype that is characterized by a recurrent complex of properties, our concept of causation is both analyzable into those properties and capable of a wide range of variation. The terms into which the causation prototype is analyzed (e.g., control, motor program, volition, etc.) are probably also characterized by prototype and capable of further analysis. This permits us to have concepts that are at once experientially basic and indefinitely analyzable.

Novel metaphor

We have already discussed some cases of novel metaphor as instances of the extensions of a conventional metaphor drawn from ordinary language. We gave examples

Conceptual metaphor in everyday language **499**

of extensions of both the "used" and "unused" portion of the THEORIES ARE BUILDINGS metaphor and also of a truly novel metaphor not normally used to structure our conceptual system (for example, the CLASSICAL THEORIES ARE PATRIARCHS metaphor). We now want to explore more fully the workings of novel metaphor by focusing on two problems of special philosophical importance. First, what makes one metaphor more appropriate or fitting than another, and second, in what sense, if any, may we speak of the truth of a metaphor?

What makes a novel metaphor appropriate?

Consider the new metaphor: LOVE IS A COLLABORATIVE WORK OF ART. This is a metaphor that we personally find particularly forceful, insightful, and appropriate, given our experiences as members of our generation and our culture. The reason is that it makes our experiences coherent—it makes sense of them. But how can a mere metaphor make coherent a large and diverse range of experiences? The answer, we believe, comes out of the fact that metaphors have entailments. A novel metaphor may entail both other novel metaphors and literal statements. For example, the entailments of LOVE IS A COLLABORATIVE WORK OF ART arise from our knowledge and experience of what it means for something to be a collaborative work of art. Here are some of the entailments of this metaphor, based on our own experiences of what a collaborative work of art entails.

LOVE IS WORK.	LOVE IS VALUABLE IN ITSELF.
LOVE IS ACTIVE.	LOVE IS AN EXPRESSION OF DEEPEST
LOVE REQUIRES HELPING.	EMOTION.
LOVE REQUIRES COMPROMISE.	LOVE IS CREATIVE.
LOVE REQUIRES PATIENCE.	LOVE INVOLVES BEAUTY.
LOVE REQUIRES SHARED VALUES	LOVE REQUIRES HARMONY.
AND GOALS.	LOVE CANNOT BE ACHIEVED BY
LOVE DEMANDS SACRIFICE.	FORMULA.
LOVE INVOLVES FRUSTRATION.	LOVE IS UNIQUE IN EACH INSTANCE.
LOVE REQUIRES DISCIPLINE.	LOVE IS UNPREDICTABLE IN ITS
LOVE BRINGS JOY AND PAIN.	OUTCOME.
LOVE IS AN AESTHETIC EXPERIENCE.	LOVE IS AN ACT OF COMMUNICATION.

Some of these entailments are literal (e.g., LOVE REQUIRES PATIENCE); others are themselves novel metaphors (e.g., LOVE IS AN AESTHETIC EXPERIENCE). Each of these entailments may itself have further entailments. The result is a large and coherent network of entailments which may, on the whole, either fit or not fit our experiences of love. When such a coherent network of entailments fits our experiences, those experiences form a coherent whole as instances of the metaphor. What we experience with such a metaphor is a kind of reverberation down through the network of entailments which awakens and connects our memories of our past love experiences and serves as a possible guide for future ones.

500 G. Lakoff and M. Johnson

Let's get more specific about what we mean by "reverberations" in the metaphor LOVE IS A COLLABORATIVE WORK OF ART.

(1) The metaphor highlights certain features while suppressing others. For example, the ACTIVE side of love is brought into the foreground through the notion of WORK both in COLLABORATIVE WORK and in WORK OF ART. This requires the masking of certain aspects of love which are viewed passively. In fact, the emotional aspects of love are almost never viewed as being under active control in our literal language. Even in the LOVE IS A JOURNEY metaphor, the relationship is viewed as a vehicle that is not in the couple's active control, one that can be OFF THE TRACKS, or ON THE ROCKS, or NOT GOING ANYWHERE. In the LOVE IS MADNESS metaphor ("I'm crazy about her," "She's driving me wild"), there is the ultimate lack of control. In the LOVE IS HEALTH metaphor, where the relationship is a patient ("It's a healthy relationship," "It's a sick relationship," "Their relationship is reviving"), the passivity of health in this culture is transferred to love. Thus, in focusing on various aspects of activity (e.g., WORK, CREATION, PURSUING GOALS, BUILDING, HELPING, etc.), the metaphor provides an organization of important love experiences that the literal language does not make available.

(2) The metaphor does not merely entail other concepts, like WORK or PURSUING SHARED GOALS, but it entails very specific *aspects* of these concepts. It is not just any work, like working on an automobile assembly line, for instance. It is work that requires special balance of power and letting go which is appropriate to artistic creation. It is not just any kind of goal that is pursued, but a joint aesthetic goal. And though the metaphor may suppress the out-of-control aspects of the LOVE IS MADNESS metaphor, it highlights another aspect, namely, the sense of almost demonic possession which lies behind our culture's connection between artistic genius and madness.

(3) Because the metaphor highlights important love experiences and makes them coherent, while it masks other love experiences, the metaphor gives love a new meaning. If those things entailed by the metaphor are for us the most important aspects of our love experiences, then the metaphor can acquire the status of a truth —for many people, love *is* a collaborative work of art. And because it is, the metaphor can have a feedback effect, guiding our future actions in accordance with the metaphor.

(4) Thus, metaphors can be appropriate because they sanction actions, justify inferences, and help us set goals. For example, certain actions, inferences, and goals are dictated by the LOVE IS A COLLABORATIVE WORK OF ART metaphor but not by the LOVE IS MADNESS metaphor. If love is MADNESS, I do not concentrate on what I have to do to maintain it. But if it is WORK, then it requires activity, and if it is a WORK OF ART, it requires a very special *kind* of activity, and if it is COLLABORATIVE, then it is even further restricted and specified.

(5) The meaning a metaphor will have for me will be partly culturally determined and partly tied to my past experiences. The cultural differences can be enormous because each of the concepts in the metaphor under discussion can vary widely from culture to culture—ART, WORK, COLLABORATION, and LOVE. Thus

LOVE IS A COLLABORATIVE WORK OF ART would mean very different things to a nineteenth-century European romantic than to a Greenland Eskimo of the same time period. There will also be differences within a culture based on the structure and significance of one's past experiences. LOVE IS A COLLABORATIVE WORK OF ART will mean something very different to two fourteen-year-olds on their first date than to a mature artist-couple. Only when the entailments of a metaphor fit our cultural and personal experience closely enough and when it seems reasonable to ignore what it hides, can we speak of it as being appropriate, and perhaps even true.

Metaphor, truth, and action

In the previous section we established the following:

(1) Metaphors have entailments through which they highlight and make coherent certain aspects of our experience.
(2) A given metaphor may be the only way to highlight and organize coherently exactly those aspects of our experiences.
(3) Through its entailments, a metaphor may be a guide for future action. Such actions will, of course, fit the metaphor. This will, in turn, reinforce the power of the metaphor to make experience coherent. Metaphors, therefore, can be like self-fulfilling prophecies.

For example, in the energy crisis President Carter declared "the moral equivalent of war." The WAR metaphor generated a network of entailments. There was an ENEMY, a THREAT TO NATIONAL SECURITY, which required SETTING TARGETS, REORGANIZING PRIORITIES, ESTABLISHING A NEW CHAIN OF COMMAND, PLOTTING NEW STRATEGY, GATHERING INTELLIGENCE, MARSHALLING FORCES, IMPOSING SANCTIONS, CALLING FOR SACRIFICES, and on and on. The WAR metaphor highlighted certain realities and hid others. The metaphor was not merely a way of viewing reality, but constituted a license for policy change and political and economic action. The very acceptance of the metaphor provided grounds for certain inferences: there was an external, foreign, hostile enemy (pictured by cartoonists in Arab headdress); energy needed to be given top priorities; the populace would have to make sacrifices; if we didn't meet the threat, we would not survive. It is important to realize that this was not the only metaphor available. Amory Lovins, for example, suggested the SOFT ENERGY PATH metaphor, which highlighted different facts and had entirely different inferences for action. But Jimmy Carter is more powerful than Amory Lovins. As Charlotte Linde (in conversation) has sadly observed, whether in national politics or in everyday interaction, people in power get to impose their metaphors.

Novel metaphors can have the power of defining reality. They do this through a coherent network of entailments that highlight some features of reality and hide others. The acceptance of the metaphor, which forces us to focus *only* on those

502 G. Lakoff and M. Johnson

aspects of reality which it highlights, leads us to view the entailments of the metaphor as being *true*. Such "truths" are true, of course, only relative to the reality defined by the metaphor. Suppose Carter announces that his administration has won a major energy battle. Is this claim true or false? Even to address oneself to the question requires accepting at least the central parts of the metaphor. If you do not accept the existence of an external enemy, if you think there is no external threat, if you recognize no field of battle, no targets, no clearly defined competing forces, then the issue of objective truth or falsity cannot arise. But if we see reality as defined by the metaphor, that is, if we do see the energy crisis as a war, then we can answer the question relative to whether the metaphorical entailments fit reality. If Carter, by means of strategically employed political and economic sanctions, forced the OPEC nations to cut the price of oil in half, then we would say he would indeed have won a major battle. If, on the other hand, his strategies had produced only a temporary price freeze, we couldn't be so sure and might be skeptical.

Though questions of truth do arise for novel metaphor, the more important questions are those of action. In most cases, what is at issue is not the truth or falsity of a metaphor, but the inferences that follow from it and the actions that are sanctioned by it. In all aspects of life, not just in politics or in love, we define our reality in terms of metaphor, and then proceed to act on the basis of the metaphor. We draw inferences, set goals, make commitments, and execute plans, all on the basis of how we structure our experience, consciously and unconsciously, by means of metaphor.

Implications for theories of meaning and truth

It is common for contemporary philosophers and linguists to assume (1) that metaphor is a matter of language, not thought, (2) that our everyday conventional language is literal (not metaphorical), and (3) that the central task of a theory of meaning is to give an account of meaning for literal language. The task of a theory of meaning is typically thought to be a matter of supplying truth conditions for literal (that is, nonmetaphorical) utterances. There are, of course, various versions of how this fundamental task is to be carried out, but they all agree that what is needed is a theory of meaning and truth for *literal* sentences. Within this dominant school of thought some insist that the meaning of literal sentences is the only meaning there is. Others argue that the meaning of any nonliteral utterance is merely some function performed on the literal meaning of the sentence used in making the utterance. But, again, both groups focus on giving an account of meaning for literal sentences alone. What we are suggesting, among other things, is that such a project is not workable when we are dealing with natural languages. We have tried to show that most of our everyday, ordinary conceptual system (and the literal language used to express it) is metaphorically structured. Not only are systems of concepts organized by basic orientational metaphors, but the very concepts themselves are *partially* defined in terms of multiple *physical* and *structural* metaphors. Concepts are not determinable in terms of necessary and sufficient conditions for their application; instead, we grasp them, always in a *partial* fashion, by means of various metaphorical concepts.

What this suggests to us is that no account of meaning and truth can be adequate unless it recognizes and deals with the way in which conventional metaphors structure our conceptual system. Of course, this is no modest claim, for, if we are correct, it calls into question the assumption of many that a complete account of literal meaning can be given without reference to metaphor. It also calls into question, we believe, certain traditional assumptions in the Western philosophical and linguistic traditions about the nature of meaning, truth, logic, rationality, and objectivity.

In a paper of this length, it is impossible even to begin to spell out and support these strong claims. We have recently completed a book-length treatment of the topic (*op. cit.*). Here are the major conclusions that we reach there:

Metaphorical concepts provide ways of understanding one kind of experience in terms of another kind of experience.

Typically this involves understanding less concrete experiences in terms of more concrete and more highly structured experiences.

Many concepts are defined metaphorically, in terms of concrete experiences that we can comprehend, rather than in terms of necessary and sufficient conditions.

This permits cross-cultural differences in conceptual systems: different cultures have different ways of comprehending experience via conceptual metaphor. Such differences will typically be reflected in linguistic differences.

We are thus led to a theory of truth that is dependent on understanding: a sentence is true in a situation when our understanding of the sentence fits our understanding of the situation.

An account of understanding is worked out in terms of a theory of experiential gestalts, that is, structurings of experience along certain natural dimensions: perceptual, functional, etc.

For the present, we hope to have shown only that metaphor is conceptual in nature, that it is pervasive in our everyday conventional language, and that no account of meaning and truth can pretend to be complete, or basically correct, or even on the right track if it cannot account for the kind of phenomena discussed above.

George Lakoff
Linguistics, University of California at Berkeley
Mark Johnson
Southern Illinois University at Carbondale

Notes

1 For a more comprehensive and thorough working out of the implications for several areas, especially philosophy and linguistics, see our *Metaphors We Live By* (Chicago: University of Chicago Press, 1980).
2 The account of systematicity and coherence we are developing may seem similar to Nelson Goodman's claim that metaphor involves a transfer in which "(a) label along

504 G. Lakoff and M. Johnson

with others constituting a scheme is in effect detached from the home realm of that scheme and applied for the sorting and organizing of an alien realm. Partly by thus carrying with it a reorientation of a whole network of labels does a metaphor give clues for its development and elaboration" [*Languages of Art* (Indianapolis: Bobbs-Merrill, 1968), p. 72]. Here Goodman comes down squarely on the side of those who view metaphor as a matter of language (that is, "labels") rather than as a matter of thought. We are at odds with Goodman on this, as well as other matters. For example, Goodman does not seem to regard most everyday conventional language as metaphorical. Nor, presumably, would he go along with our experientialist account of truth, in which truth is secondary to understanding (cf. our *Metaphors We Live By, op. cit.*).

3 "The Conduit Metaphor," in A. Ortony, ed., *Metaphor and Thought* (New York: Cambridge, 1979).

4 *Figurative Patterns and Redundancy in the Lexicon*, unpublished dissertation, University of California at San Diego, 1974.

5 A philosophical example of the abstractionist position is contained in L. Jonathan Cohen and Avishai Margalit, "The Role of Inductive Reasoning in the Interpretation of Metaphor," in D. Davidson and G. Harman, eds., *Semantics of Natural Language* (Boston: Reidel, 1972), pp. 722–740. "The metaphorical meanings of a word or phrase in a natural language are all contained, as it were, within its literal meaning or meanings. They are reached by removing any restrictions in relation to certain variables from the appropriate section or sections of its semantical hypothesis" (735). The result of merely removing restrictions would always result in a very general meaning in common between the metaphorical and literal meanings.

6 "Human Categorization," in N. Warren, ed., *Advances in Cross-cultural Psychology* (New York: Academic Press, 1977), vol. 1.

22

CONTINGENCY, IRONY, AND SOLIDARITY

R. Rorty

The contingency of language

About two hundred years ago, the idea that truth was made rather than found began to take hold of the imagination of Europe. The French Revolution had shown that the whole vocabulary of social relations, and the whole spectrum of social institutions, could be replaced almost overnight. This precedent made utopian politics the rule rather than the exception among intellectuals. Utopian politics sets aside questions about both the will of God and the nature of man and dreams of creating a hitherto unknown form of society.

At about the same time, the Romantic poets were showing what happens when art is thought of no longer as imitation but, rather, as the artist's self-creation. The poets claimed for art the place in culture traditionally held by religion and philo-sophy, the place which the Enlightenment had claimed for science. The precedent the Romantics set lent initial plausibility to their claim. The actual role of novels, poems, plays, paintings, statues, and buildings in the social movements of the last century and a half has given it still greater plausibility.

By now these two tendencies have joined forces and have achieved cultural hegemony. For most contemporary intellectuals, questions of ends as opposed to means – questions about how to give a sense to one's own life or that of one's community – are questions for art or politics, or both, rather than for religion, philosophy, or science. This development has led to a split within philosophy. Some philosophers have remained faithful to the Enlightenment and have con-tinued to identify themselves with the cause of science. They see the old struggle between science and religion, reason and unreason, as still going on, having now taken the form of a struggle between reason and all those forces within culture which think of truth as made rather than found. These philosophers take science as the paradigmatic human activity, and they insist that natural science discovers truth rather than makes it. They regard "making truth" as a merely metaphorical, and thoroughly misleading, phrase. They think of politics and art as spheres in which the notion of "truth" is out of place. Other philosophers, realizing that the world as it is described by the physical sciences teaches no moral lesson, offers no spiritual comfort, have concluded that science is no more than the handmaiden of technology. These philosophers have ranged themselves alongside the political utopian and the innovative artist.

Whereas the first kind of philosopher contrasts "hard scientific fact" with the "subjective" or with "metaphor," the second kind sees science as one more human activity, rather as the place at which human beings encounter a "hard," nonhuman reality. On this view, great scientists invent descriptions of the world which are useful for purposes of predicting and controlling what happens, just as poets and political thinkers invent other descriptions of it for other purposes. But there is no sense in which *any* of these descriptions is an accurate representation of the way the world is in itself. These philosophers regard the very idea of such a representation as pointless.

Had the first sort of philosopher, the sort whose hero is the natural scientist, always been the only sort, we should probably never have had an autonomous discipline called "philosophy" – a discipline as distinct from the sciences as it is from theology or from the arts. As such a discipline, philosophy is no more than two hundred years old. It owes its existence to attempts by the German idealists to put the sciences in their place and to give a clear sense to the vague idea that human beings make truth rather than find it. Kant wanted to consign science to the realm of second-rate truth – truth about a phenomenal world. Hegel wanted to think of natural science as a description of spirit not yet fully conscious of its own spiritual nature, and thereby to elevate the sort of truth offered by the poet and the political revolutionary to first-rate status.

German idealism, however, was a short-lived and unsatisfactory compromise. For Kant and Hegel went only halfway in their repudiation of the idea that truth is "out there." They were willing to view the world of empirical science as a made world – to see matter as constructed by mind, or as consisting in mind insufficiently conscious of its own mental character. But they persisted in seeing mind, spirit, the depths of the human self, as having an intrinsic nature – one which could be known by a kind of nonempirical super science called philosophy. This meant that only half of truth – the bottom, scientific half – was made. Higher truth, the truth about mind, the province of philosophy, was still a matter of discovery rather than creation.

What was needed, and what the idealists were unable to envisage, was a repudiation of the very idea of anything – mind or matter, self or world – having an intrinsic nature to be expressed or represented. For the idealists confused the idea that nothing has such a nature with the idea that space and time are unreal, that human beings cause the spatiotemporal world to exist.

We need to make a distinction between the claim that the world is out there and the claim that truth is out there. To say that the world is out there, that it is not our creation, is to say, with common sense, that most things in space and time are the

Contingency, irony, and solidarity   **507**

effects of causes which do not include human mental states. To say that truth is not out there is simply to say that where there are no sentences there is no truth, that sentences are elements of human languages, and that human languages are human creations.

Truth cannot be out there – cannot exist independently of the human mind – because sentences cannot so exist, or be out there. The world is out there, but descriptions of the world are not. Only descriptions of the world can be true or false. The world on its own – unaided by the describing activities of human beings – cannot.

The suggestion that truth, as well as the world, is out there is a legacy of an age in which the world was seen as the creation of a being who had a language of his own. If we cease to attempt to make sense of the idea of such a nonhuman language, we shall not be tempted to confuse the platitude that the world may cause us to be justified in believing a sentence true with the claim that the world splits itself up, on its own initiative, into sentence-shaped chunks called "facts." But if one clings to the notion of self-subsistent facts, it is easy to start capitalizing the word "truth" and treating it as something identical either with God or with the world as God's project. Then one will say, for example, that Truth is great, and will prevail.

This conflation is facilitated by confining attention to single sentences as opposed to vocabularies. For we often let the world decide the competition between alternative sentences (e.g., between "Red wins" and "Black wins" or between "The butler did it" and "The doctor did it"). In such cases, it is easy to run together the fact that the world contains the causes of our being justified in holding a belief with the claim that some nonlinguistic state of the world is itself an example of truth, or that some such state "makes a belief true" by "corresponding" to it. But it is not so easy when we turn from individual sentences to vocabularies as wholes. When we consider examples of alternative language games – the vocabulary of ancient Athenian politics versus Jefferson's, the moral vocabulary of Saint Paul versus Freud's, the jargon of Newton versus that of Aristotle, the idiom of Blake versus that of Dryden – it is difficult to think of the world as making one of these better than another, of the world as deciding between them. When the notion of "description of the world" is moved from the level of criterion-governed sentences within language games to language games as wholes, games which we do not choose between by reference to criteria, the idea that the world decides which descriptions are true can no longer be given a clear sense. It becomes hard to think that that vocabulary is somehow already out there in the world, waiting for us to discover it. Attention (of the sort fostered by intellectual historians like Thomas Kuhn and Quentin Skinner) to the vocabularies in which sentences are formulated, rather than to individual sentences, makes us realize, for example, that the fact that Newton's vocabulary lets us predict the world more easily than Aristotle's does not mean that the world speaks Newtonian.

The world does not speak. Only we do. The world can, once we have programmed ourselves with a language, cause us to hold beliefs. But it cannot propose

508 R. Rorty

a language for us to speak. Only other human beings can do that. The realization that the world does not tell us what language games to play should not, however, lead us to say that a decision about which to play is arbitrary, nor to say that it is the expression of something deep within us. The moral is not that objective criteria for choice of vocabulary are to be replaced with subjective criteria, reason with will or feeling. It is rather that the notions of criteria and choice (including that of "arbitrary" choice) are no longer in point when it comes to changes from one language game to another. Europe did not *decide* to accept the idiom of Romantic poetry, or of socialist politics, or of Galilean mechanics. That sort of shift was no more an act of will than it was a result of argument. Rather, Europe gradually lost the habit of using certain words and gradually acquired the habit of using others.

As Kuhn argues in *The Copernican Revolution*, we did not decide on the basis of some telescopic observations, or on the basis of anything else, that the earth was not the center of the universe, that macroscopic behavior could be explained on the basis of microstructural motion, and that prediction and control should be the principal aim of scientific theorizing. Rather, after a hundred years of inconclusive muddle, the Europeans found themselves speaking in a way which took these interlocked theses for granted. Cultural change of this magnitude does not result from applying criteria (or from "arbitrary decision") any more than individuals become theists or atheists, or shift from one spouse or circle of friends to another, as a result either of applying criteria or of *actes gratuits*. We should not look within ourselves for criteria of decision in such matters any more than we should look to the world.

The temptation to look for criteria is a species of the more general temptation to think of the world, or the human self, as possessing an intrinsic nature, an essence. That is, it is the result of the temptation to privilege some one among the many languages in which we habitually describe the world or ourselves. As long as we think that there is some relation called "fitting the world" or "expressing the real nature of the self" which can be possessed or lacked by vocabularies-as-wholes, we shall continue the traditional philosophical search for a criterion to tell us which vocabularies have this desirable feature. But if we could ever become reconciled to the idea that most of reality is indifferent to our descriptions of it, and that the human self is created by the use of a vocabulary rather than being adequately or inadequately expressed in a vocabulary, then we should at last have assimilated what was true in the Romantic idea that truth is made rather than found. What is true about this claim is just that *languages* are made rather than found, and that truth is a property of linguistic entities, of sentences.[1]

I can sum up by redescribing what, in my view, the revolutionaries and poets of two centuries ago were getting at. What was glimpsed at the end of the eighteenth century was that anything could be made to look good or bad, important or unimportant, useful or useless, by being redescribed. What Hegel describes as the process of spirit gradually becoming self-conscious of its intrinsic nature is better described as the process of European linguistic practices changing at a faster and faster rate. The phenomenon Hegel describes is that of more people offering more radical

Contingency, irony, and solidarity **509**

redescriptions of more things than ever before, of young people going through half a dozen spiritual gestalt-switches before reaching adulthood. What the Romantics expressed as the claim that imagination, rather than reason, is the central human faculty was the realization that a talent for speaking differently, rather than for arguing well, is the chief instrument of cultural change. What political utopians since the French Revolution have sensed is not that an enduring, substratal human nature has been suppressed or repressed by "unnatural" or "irrational" social institutions but rather that changing languages and other social practices may produce human beings of a sort that had never before existed. The German idealists, the French revolutionaries, and the Romantic poets had in common a dim sense that human beings whose language changed so that they no longer spoke of themselves as responsible to nonhuman powers would thereby become a new kind of human beings.

The difficulty faced by a philosopher who, like myself, is sympathetic to this suggestion – one who thinks of himself as auxiliary to the poet rather than to the physicist – is to avoid hinting that this suggestion gets something right, that my sort of philosophy corresponds to the way things really are. For this talk of correspondence brings back just the idea my sort of philosopher wants to get rid of, the idea that the world or the self has an intrinsic nature. From our point of view, explaining the success of science, or the desirability of political liberalism, by talk of "fitting the world" or "expressing human nature" is like explaining why opium makes you sleepy by talking about its dormitive power. To say that Freud's vocabulary gets at the truth about human nature, or Newton's at the truth about the heavens, is not an explanation of anything. It is just an empty compliment – one traditionally paid to writers whose novel jargon we have found useful. To say that there is no such thing as intrinsic nature is not to say that the intrinsic nature of reality has turned out, surprisingly enough, to be extrinsic. It is to say that the term "intrinsic nature" is one which it would pay us not to use, an expression which has caused more trouble than it has been worth. To say that we should drop the idea of truth as out there waiting to be discovered is not to say that we have discovered that, out there, there is no truth.[2] It is to say that our purposes would be served best by ceasing to see truth as a deep matter, as a topic of philosophical interest, or "true" as a term which repays "analysis." "The nature of truth" is an unprofitable topic, resembling in this respect "the nature of man" and "the nature of God," and differing from "the nature of the positron," and "the nature of Oedipal fixation." But this claim about relative profitability, in turn, is just the recommendation that we in fact *say* little about these topics, and see how we get on.

On the view of philosophy which I am offering, philosophers should not be asked for arguments against, for example, the correspondence theory of truth or the idea of the "intrinsic nature of reality." The trouble with arguments against the use of a familiar and time-honored vocabulary is that they are expected to be phrased in that very vocabulary. They are expected to show that central elements in that vocabulary are "inconsistent in their own terms" or that they "deconstruct themselves." But that can *never* be shown. Any argument to the effect that our familiar

510 R. Rorty

use of a familiar term is incoherent, or empty, or confused, or vague, or "merely metaphorical" is bound to be inconclusive and question-begging. For such use is, after all, the paridigm of coherent, meaningful, literal, speech. Such arguments are always parasitic upon, and abbreviations for, claims that a better vocabulary is available. Interesting philosophy is rarely an examination of the pros and cons of a thesis. Usually it is, implicitly or explicitly, a contest between an entrenched vocabulary which has become a nuisance and a half-formed new vocabulary which vaguely promises great things.

The latter "method" of philosophy is the same as the "method" of utopian politics or revolutionary science (as opposed to parliamentary politics, or normal science). The method is to redescribe lots and lots of things in new ways, until you have created a pattern of linguistic behavior which will tempt the rising generation to adopt it, thereby causing them to look for appropriate new forms of nonlinguistic behavior, for example, the adoption of new scientific equipment or new social institutions. This sort of philosophy does not work piece by piece, analyzing concept after concept, or testing thesis after thesis. Rather, it works holistically and pragmatically. It says things like "try thinking of it this way" – or more specifically, "try to ignore the apparently futile traditional questions by substituting the following new and possibly interesting questions." It does not pretend to have a better candidate for doing the same old things which we did when we spoke in the old way. Rather, it suggests that we might want to stop doing those things and do something else. But it does not argue for this suggestion on the basis of antecedent criteria common to the old and the new language games. For just insofar as the new language really is new, there will be no such criteria.

Conforming to my own precepts, I am not going to offer arguments against the vocabulary I want to replace. Instead, I am going to try to make the vocabulary I favor look attractive by showing how it may be used to describe a variety of topics. More specifically, in this chapter I shall be describing the work of Donald Davidson in philosophy of language as a manifestation of a willingness to drop the idea of "intrinsic nature," a willingness to face up to the *contingency* of the language we use. In subsequent chapters, I shall try to show how a recognition of that contingency leads to a recognition of the contingency of conscience, and how both recognitions lead to a picture of intellectual and moral progress as a history of increasingly useful metaphors rather than of increasing understanding of how things really are.

Davidson puts this point by saying that one should not think of metaphorical expressions as having meanings distinct from their literal ones. To have a meaning is to have a place in a language game. Metaphors, by definition, do not. Davidson denies, in his words, "the thesis that associated with a metaphor is a cognitive content that its author wishes to convey and that the interpreter must grasp if he is to get the message."[3] In his view, tossing a metaphor into a conversation is like suddenly breaking off the conversation long enough to make a face, or pulling a photograph out of your pocket and displaying it, or pointing at a feature of the surroundings, or slapping your interlocutor's face, or kissing him. Tossing a metaphor into a text is like using italics, or illustrations, or odd punctuation or formats.

Contingency, irony, and solidarity **511**

All these are ways of producing effects on your interlocutor or your reader, but not ways of conveying a message. To none of these is it appropriate to respond with "What exactly are you trying to say?" If one had wanted to say something – if one had wanted to utter a sentence with a meaning – one would presumably have done so. But instead one thought that one's aim could be better carried out by other means. That one uses familiar words in unfamiliar ways – rather than slaps, kisses, pictures, gestures, or grimaces – does not show that what one said must have a meaning. An attempt to state that meaning would be an attempt to find some familiar (that is, literal) use of words – some sentence which already had a place in the language game – and, to claim that one might just as well have *that*. But the unparaphrasability of metaphor is just the unsuitability of any such familiar sentence for one's purpose.

Uttering a sentence without a fixed place in a language game is, as the positivists rightly have said, to utter something which is neither true nor false – something which is not, in Ian Hacking's terms, a "truth-value candidate." This is because it is a sentence which one cannot confirm or disconfirm, argue for or against. One can only savor it or spit it out. But this is not to say that it may not, in time, *become* a truth-value candidate. If it *is* savored rather than spat out, the sentence may be repeated, caught up, bandied about. Then it will gradually require a habitual use, a familiar place in the language game. It will thereby have ceased to be a metaphor – or, if you like, it will have become what most sentences of our language are, a dead metaphor. It will be just one more, literally true or literally false, sentence of the language. That is to say, our theories about the linguistic behavior of our fellows will suffice to let us cope with its utterance in the same unthinking way in which we cope with most of their other utterances.

The Davidsonian claim that metaphors do not have meanings may seem like a typical philosopher's quibble, but it is not.[4] It is part of an attempt to get us to stop thinking of language as a medium. This, in turn, is part of a larger attempt to get rid of the traditional philosophical picture of what it is to be human. The importance of Davidson's point can perhaps best be seen by contrasting his treatment of metaphor with those of the Platonist and the positivist on the one hand and the Romantic on the other. The Platonist and the positivist share a reductionist view of metaphor: They think metaphors are either paraphrasable or useless for the one serious purpose which language has, namely, representing reality. By contrast, the Romantic has an expansionist view: He thinks metaphor is strange, mystic, wonderful. Romantics attribute metaphor to a mysterious faculty called the "imagination," a faculty they suppose to be at the very center of the self, the deep heart's core. Whereas the metaphorical looks irrelevant to Platonists and positivists, the literal looks irrelevant to Romantics. For the former think that the point of language is to represent a hidden reality which lies outside us, and the latter thinks its purpose is to express a hidden reality which lies within us.

Positivist history of culture thus sees language as gradually shaping itself around the contours of the physical world. Romantic history of culture sees language as gradually bringing Spirit to self-consciousness. Nietzschean history of culture, and

512 R. Rorty

Davidsonian philosophy of language, see language as we now see evolution, as new forms of life constantly killing off old forms – not to accomplish a higher purpose, but blindly. Whereas the positivist sees Galileo as making a discovery – finally coming up with the words which were needed to fit the world properly, words Aristotle missed – the Davidsonian sees him as having hit upon a tool which happened to work better for certain purposes than any previous tool. Once we found out what could be done with a Galilean vocabulary, nobody was much interested in doing the things which used to be done (and which Thomists thought should still be done) with an Aristotelian vocabulary.

Similarly, whereas the Romantic sees Yeats as having gotten at something which nobody had previously gotten at, expressed something which had long been yearning for expression, the Davidsonian sees him as having hit upon some tools which enabled him to write poems which were not just variations on the poems of his precursors. Once we had Yeats's later poems in hand, we were less interested in reading Rossetti's. What goes for revolutionary, strong scientists and poets goes also for strong philosophers – people like Hegel and Davidson, the sort of philosophers who are interested in dissolving inherited problems rather than in solving them. In this view, substituting dialectic for demonstration as the method of philosophy, or getting rid of the correspondence theory of truth, is not a discovery about the nature of a preexistent entity called "philosophy" or "truth." It is changing the way we talk, and thereby changing what we want to do and what we think we are.

But in a Nietzschean view, one which drops the reality-appearance distinction, to change how we talk is to change what, for our own purposes, we are. To say, with Nietzsche, that God is dead, is to say that we serve no higher purposes. The Nietzschean substitution of self-creation for discovery substitutes a picture of the hungry generations treading each other down for a picture of humanity approaching closer and closer to the light. A culture in which Nietzschean metaphors were literalized would be one which took for granted that philosophical problems are as temporary as poetic problems, that there are no problems which bind the generations together into a single natural kind called "humanity." A sense of human history as the history of successive metaphors would let us see the poet, in the generic sense of the maker of new words, the shaper of new languages, as the vanguard of the species.

I shall try to develop this last point in Chapters 2 and 3 in terms of Harold Bloom's notion of the "strong poet." But I shall end this first chapter by going back to the claim, which has been central to what I have been saying, that the world does not provide us with any criterion of choice between alternative metaphors, that we can only compare languages or metaphors with one another, not with something beyond language called "fact."

The only way to argue for this claim is to do what philosophers like Goodman, Putnam, and Davidson have done: exhibit the sterility of attempts to give a sense to phrases like "the way the world is" or "fitting the facts." Such efforts can be supplemented by the work of philosophers of science such as Kuhn and Hesse. These

Contingency, irony, and solidarity **513**

philosophers explain why there is no way to explain the fact that a Galilean vocabulary enables us to make better predictions than an Aristotelian vocabulary by the claim that the book of nature is written in the language of mathematics.

These sorts of arguments by philosophers of language and of science should be seen against the background of the work of intellectual historians: historians who, like Hans Blumenberg, have tried to trace the similarities and dissimilarities between the Age of Faith and the Age of Reason.[5] These historians have made the point I mentioned earlier: The very idea that the world or the self has an intrinsic nature – one which the physicist or the poet may have glimpsed – is a remnant of the idea that the world is a divine creation, the work of someone who had something in mind, who Himself spoke some language in which He described His own project. Only if we have some such picture in mind, some picture of the universe as either itself a person or as created by a person, can we make sense of the idea that the world has an "intrinsic nature." For the cash value of that phrase is just that some vocabularies are better representations of the world than others, as opposed to being better tools for dealing with the world for one or another purpose.

To drop the idea of languages as representations, and to be thoroughly Wittgensteinian in our approach to language, would be to de-divinize the world. Only if we do that can we fully accept the argument I offered earlier – the argument that since truth is a property of sentences, since sentences are dependent for their existence upon vocabularies, and since vocabularies are made by human beings, so are truths. For as long as we think that "the world" names something we ought to respect as well as cope with, something personlike in that it has a preferred description of itself, we shall insist that any philosophical account of truth save the "intuition" that truth is "out there." This institution amounts to the vague sense that it would be *hybris* on our part to abandon the traditional language of "respect for fact" and "objectivity" – that it would be risky, and blasphemous, not to see the scientist (or the philosopher, or the poet, or *somebody*) as having a priestly function, as putting us in touch with a realm which transcends the human.

On the view I am suggesting, the claim that an "adequate" philosophical doctrine must make room for our intuitions is a reactionary slogan, one which begs the question at hand.[6] For it is essential to my view that we have no prelinguistic consciousness to which language needs to be adequate, no deep sense of how things are which it is the duty of philosophers to spell out in language. What is described as such a consciousness is simply a disposition to use the language of our ancestors, to worship the corpses of their metaphors. Unless we suffer from what Derrida calls "Heideggerian nostalgia," we shall not think of our "intuitions" as more than platitudes, more than the habitual use of a certain repertoire of terms, more than old tools which as yet have no replacements.

I can crudely sum up the story which historians like Blumenberg tell by saying that once upon a time we felt a need to worship something which lay beyond the visible world. Beginning in the seventeenth century we tried to substitute a love of truth for a love of God, treating the world described by science as a quasi divinity. Beginning at the end of the eighteenth century we tried to substitute a love of

514 R. Rorty

ourselves for a love of scientific truth, a worship of our own deep spiritual or poetic nature, treated as one more quasi divinity.

The line of thought common to Blumenberg, Nietzsche, Freud, and Davidson suggests that we try to get to the point where we no longer worship *anything*, where we treat *nothing* as a quasi divinity, where we treat *everything* – our language, our conscience, our community – as a product of time and chance. To reach this point would be, in Freud's words, to "treat chance as worthy of determining our fate." In the next chapter I claim that Freud, Nietzsche, and Bloom do for our conscience what Wittgenstein and Davidson do for our language, namely, exhibit its sheer contingency.

The contingency of selfhood

As I was starting to write on the topic of this chapter, I came across a poem by Philip Larkin which helped me pin down what I wanted to say. Here is the last part of it:

> And once you have walked the length of your mind, what
> You command is as clear as a lading-list
> Anything else must not, for you, be thought
> To exist.
> And what's the profit? Only that, in time
> We half-identify the blind impress
> All our behavings bear, may trace it home.
> But to confess,
> On that green evening when our death begins,
> Just what it was, is hardly satisfying,
> Since it applied only to one man once,
> And that man dying.

This poem discusses the fear of dying, of extinction, to which Larkin confessed in interviews. But "fear of extinction" is an unhelpful phrase. There is no such thing as fear of inexistence as such, but only fear of some concrete loss. "Death" and "nothingness" are equally resounding, equally empty terms. To say one fears either is as clumsy as Epicurus's attempt to say why one should not fear them. Epicurus said, "When I am, death is not, and when death is, I am not"; thus exchanging one vacuity for another. For the word "I" is as hollow as the word "death." To unpack such words, one has to fill in the details about the I in question, specify precisely what it is that will not be, make one's fear concrete.

Larkin's poem suggests a way of unpacking what Larkin feared. What he fears will be extinguished is his idiosyncratic lading-list, his individual sense of what was possible and important. That is what made his I different from all the other I's. To lose that difference is, I take it, what any poet – any maker, anyone who hopes to create something new – fears. Anyone who spends his life trying to formulate a

Contingency, irony, and solidarity **515**

novel answer to the question of what is possible and important fears the extinction of that answer.

But this does not mean simply that one fears that one's works will be lost or ignored. For that fear blends into the fear that, even if they are preserved and noticed, nobody will find anything distinctive in them. The words (or shapes, or theorems, or models of physical nature) marshaled to one's command may seem merely stock items, rearranged in routine ways. One will not have impressed one's mark on the language but, rather, will have spent one's life shoving about already coined pieces. So one will not really have had an I at all. One's creations, and one's self, will just be better or worse instances of familiar types. This is what Harold Bloom calls "the strong poet's anxiety of influence," his "horror of finding himself to be only a copy or a replica."[7]

On this reading of Larkin's poem, what would it be to have succeeded in tracing home the "blind impress" which all one's "behavings bear"? Presumably it would be to have figured out what was distinctive about oneself – the difference between one's own lading-list and other people's. If one could get this recognition down on paper (or canvas or film) – if one could find distinctive words or forms for one's own distinctiveness – then one would have *demonstrated* that one was not a copy or a replica. One would have been as strong as any poet has ever been, which means having been as strong as any human being could possibly be. For one would know exactly what it is that will die, and thus know what one has succeeded in becoming.

But the end of Larkin's poem seems to reject this Bloomian reading. There we are told that it is "hardly satisfying" to trace home one's own distinctiveness. This seems to mean that it is hardly satisfying to have become an individual – in the strong sense in which the genius is the paradigm of individuality. Larkin is affecting to despise his own vocation, on the ground that to succeed in it would merely be to have put down on paper something which "applied only to one man once / And that one dying."

I say "affecting" because I doubt that any poet could seriously think trivial his own success in tracing home the blind impress borne by all his behavings – all his previous poems. Since the example of the Romantics, since the time when, with Hegel, we began to think of self-consciousness as self-creation, no poet has seriously thought of idiosyncrasy as an objection to his work. But in this poem Larkin is pretending that blind impresses, those particular contingencies which make each of us "I" rather than a copy or replica of somebody else, do not really matter. He is suggesting that unless one finds something common to all men at all times, not just to one man once, one cannot die satisfied. He is pretending that to be a strong poet is not enough – that he would have attained satisfaction only from being a philosopher, from finding continuities rather than exhibiting a discontinuity.[8]

I think Larkin's poem owes its interest and its strength to this reminder of the quarrel between poetry and philosophy, the tension between an effort to achieve self-creation by the recognition of contingency and an effort to achieve universality by the transcendence of contingency. The same tension has pervaded philosophy since Hegel's time,[9] and particularly since Nietzsche. The important philosophers of our own century are those who have tried to follow through on the Romantic poets by breaking with Plato and seeing freedom as the recognition of contingency. These are the philosophers who try to detach Hegel's insistence on historicity from his pantheistic idealism. They accept Nietzsche's identification of the strong poet, the maker, as humanity's hero – rather than the scientist, who is traditionally pictured as a finder. More generally, they have tried to avoid anything that smacks of philosophy as contemplation, as the attempt to see life steadily and see it whole, in order to insist on the sheer contingency of individual existence.

They thus find themselves in the same sort of awkward, but interesting, position as Larkin. Larkin writes a poem about the unsatisfactoriness, compared with what pre-Nietzschean philosophers hoped to do, of doing the only thing that poets can do. Post-Nietzschean philosophers like Wittgenstein and Heidegger write philosophy in order to exhibit the universality and necessity of the individual and contingent. Both philosophers became caught up in the quarrel between philosophy and poetry which Plato began, and both ended by trying to work out honorable terms on which philosophy might surrender to poetry.

I can spell out this comparison by returning to Larkin's poem. Consider Larkin's suggestion that one might get more satisfaction out of finding a "blind impress" which applied *not* only to "one man once" but, rather, to all human beings. Think of finding such an impress as being the discovery of the universal conditions of human existence, the great continuities – the permanent, ahistorical, context of human life. This is what the priests once claimed to have done. Later the Greek philosophers, still later the empirical scientists, and later still the German idealists, made the same claim. They were going to explain to us the ultimate locus of power, the nature of reality, the conditions of the possibility of experience. They would thereby inform us what we really are, what we are compelled to be by powers not ourselves. They would exhibit the stamp which had been impressed on *all* of us. This impress would not be blind, because it would not be a matter of chance, a mere contingency. It would be necessary, essential, telic, constitutive of what it is to be a human. It would give us a goal, the only possible goal, namely, the full recognition of that very necessity, the self-consciousness of our essence.

In comparison with this universal impress, so the pre-Nietzschean philosopher's story goes, the particular contingencies of individual lives are unimportant. The mistake of the poets is to waste words on idiosyncrasies, on contingencies – to tell us about accidental appearance rather than essential reality. To admit that mere spatiotemporal location, mere contingent circumstance, mattered would be to reduce us to the level of a dying animal. To understand the context in which we necessarily live, by contrast, would be to give us a mind exactly as long as the universe itself, a lading-list which was a copy of the universe's own list. What counted as existing, as possible, or as important, for us, would be what really *is* possible, or important. Having copied this list, one could die with satisfaction, having accomplished the only task laid upon humanity, *to know the truth*, to be in touch with what is "out there." There would be nothing more to do, and thus no possible loss to be feared. Extinction would not matter, for one would have become identical with the truth, and truth, on this traditional view, is imperishable. What was extinguished would be merely idiosyncratic animality. The poets, who are not interested in truth, merely distract us from this paradigmatically human task, and thereby degrade us.

It was Nietzsche who first explicitly suggested that we drop the whole idea of "knowing the truth." His definition of truth as a "mobile army of metaphors" amounted to saying that the whole idea of "representing reality" by means of language, and thus the idea of finding a single context for all human lives, should be abandoned. His perspectivism amounted to the claim that the universe had no lading-list to be known, no determinate length. He hoped that once we realized that Plato's "true world" was just a fable, we would seek consolation, at the moment of death, not in having transcended the animal condition but in being that peculiar sort of dying animal who, by describing himself in his own terms, had created himself. More exactly, he would have created the only part of himself that mattered by constructing his own mind. To create one's mind is to create one's own language, rather than to let the length of one's mind be set by the language other human beings have left behind.[10]

But in abandoning the traditional notion of truth, Nietzsche did not abandon the idea of discovering the causes of our being what we are. He did not give up the idea that an individual might track home the blind impress all his behavings bore. He only rejected the idea that this tracking was a process of discovery. In his view, in achieving this sort of self-knowledge we are not coming to know a truth which was out there (or in here) all the time. Rather, he saw self-knowledge as self-creation. The process of coming to know oneself, confronting one's contingency, tracking one's causes home, is identical with the process of inventing a new language – that is, of thinking up some new metaphors. For any *literal* description of one's individuality, which is to say any *use* of an inherited language-game for this purpose, will necessarily fail. One will not have traced that idiosyncrasy home but will merely have managed to see it as not idiosyncratic after all, as a specimen reiterating a type, a copy or replica of something which has already been identified. To fail as a poet – and thus, for Nietzsche, to fail as a human being – is to accept somebody else's description of oneself, to execute a previously prepared program, to write, at most, elegant variations on previously written poems. So the only way to trace home the causes of one's being as one is would be to tell a story about one's causes in a new language.

This may sound paradoxical, because we think of *causes* as discovered rather than invented. We think of telling a *causal* story as a paradigm of the *literal* use of language. Metaphor, linguistic novelty, seems out of place when one turns from simply relishing such novelty to explaining why these novelties, and not others, occurred. But remember the claim made in Chapter 1 that even in the natural sciences we occasionally get genuinely new causal stories, the sort of stories produced by what Kuhn calls "revolutionary science." Even in the sciences, metaphoric redescriptions are the mark of genius and of revolutionary leaps forward. If we follow up this

518 R. Rorty

Kuhnian point by thinking, with Davidson, of the literal-metaphorical distinction as the distinction between old language and new language rather than in terms of a distinction between words which latch on to the world and those which do not, the paradox vanishes. If, with Davidson, we drop the notion of language as fitting the world, we can see the point of Bloom's and Nietzsche's claim that the strong maker, the person who uses words as they have never before been used, is best able to appreciate her own contingency. For she can see, more clearly than the continuity-seeking historian, critic, or philosopher, that her *language* is as contingent as her parents or her historical epoch. She can appreciate the force of the claim that "truth is a mobile army of metaphors" because, by her own sheer strength, she has broken out of one perspective, one metaphoric, into another.

Only poets, Nietzsche suspected, can truly appreciate contingency. The rest of us are doomed to remain philosophers, to insist that there is really only one true lading-list, one true description of the human situation, one universal context of our lives. We are doomed to spend our conscious lives trying to escape from contingency rather than, like the strong poet, acknowledging and appropriating contingency. For Nietzsche, therefore, the line between the strong poet and the rest of the human race has the moral significance which Plato and Christianity attached to the distinction between the human and the animal. For although strong poets are, like all other animals, causal products of natural forces, they are products capable of telling the story of their own production in words never used before. The line between weakness and strength is thus the line between using language which is familiar and universal and producing language which, though initially unfamiliar and idiosyncratic, somehow makes tangible the blind impress all one's behavings bear. With luck — the sort of luck which makes the difference between genius and eccentricity — that language will also strike the next generation as inevitable. *Their* behavings will bear that impress.

To put the same point in another way, the Western philosophical tradition thinks of a human life as a triumph just insofar as it breaks out of the world of time, appearance, and idiosyncratic opinion into another world — into the world of enduring truth. Nietzsche, by contrast, thinks the important boundary to cross is not the one separating time from atemporal truth but rather the one which divides the old from the new. He thinks a human life triumphant just insofar as it escapes from inherited descriptions of the contingencies of its existence and finds new descriptions. This is the difference between the will to truth and the will to self-overcoming. It is the difference between thinking of redemption as making contact with something larger and more enduring than oneself and redemption as Nietzsche describes it: "recreating all 'it was' into a 'thus I willed it.'"

The drama of an individual human life, or of the history of humanity as a whole, is not one in which a preexistent goal is triumphantly reached or tragically not reached. Neither a constant external reality nor an unfailing interior source or inspiration forms a background for such dramas. Instead, to see one's life, or the life of one's community, as a dramatic narrative is to see it as a process of Nietzschean self-overcoming. The paradigm of such a narrative is the life of the genius who can

Contingency, irony, and solidarity **519**

say of the relevant portion of the past, "Thus I willed it," because she has found a way to describe that past which the past never knew, and thereby found a self to be which her precursors never knew was possible.

In this Nietschean view, the impulse to think, to inquire, to reweave oneself ever more thoroughly, is not wonder but terror. It is, once again, Bloom's "horror of finding oneself to be only a copy or replica." The wonder in which Aristotle believed philosophy to begin was wonder at finding oneself in a world larger, stronger, nobler than oneself. The fear in which Bloom's poets begin is the fear that one might end one's days in such a world, a world one never made, an inherited world. The hope of such a poet is that what the past tried to do to her she will succeed in doing to the past: to make the past itself, including those very causal processes which blindly impressed all her own behavings, bear *her* impress. Success in that enterprise – the enterprise of saying "Thus I willed it" to the past – is success in what Bloom calls "giving birth to oneself.

Notes

1 I have no criterion of individuation for distinct languages or vocabularies to offer, but I am not sure that we need one. Philosophers have used phrases like "in the language *L*" for a long time without worrying too much about how one can tell where one natural language ends and another begins, nor about when "the scientific vocabulary of the sixteenth century" ends and "the vocabulary of the New Science" begins. Roughly, a break of this sort occurs when we start using "translation" rather than "explanation" in talking about geographical or chronological differences. This will happen whenever we find it handy to start mentioning words rather than using them – to highlight the difference between two sets of human practices by putting quotation marks around elements of those practices.

2 Nietzsche has caused a lot of confusion by inferring from "truth is not a matter of correspondence to reality" to "what we call 'truths' are just useful lies." The same confusion is occasionally found in Derrida, in the inference from "there is no such reality as the metaphysicians have hoped to find" to "what we call 'real' is not really real." Such confusions make Nietzsche and Derrida liable to charges of self-referential inconsistency – to claiming to know what they themselves claim cannot be known.

3 Davidson, "What Metaphors Mean," in his *Inquiries into Truth and Interpretation* (Oxford University Press, 1984), p. 262.

4 For a further defense of Davidson against the charge of quibbling, and various other charges, see my "Unfamiliar Noises: Hesse and Davidson on Metaphor," *Proceedings of the Aristotelian Society*, supplementary vol. 61 (1987): 283–296.

5 See Hans Blumenberg, *The Legitimacy of the Modern Age*. trans. Robert Wallace (Cambridge, Mass.: MIT Press. 1982).

6 For an application of this dictum to a particular case, see my discussion of the appeals to intuition found in Thomas Nagel's view of "subjectivity" and in John Searle's doctrine of "intrinsic intentionality," in "Contemporary Philosophy of Mind." For further criticisms of both, criticisms which harmonize with my own, see Daniel Dennett, "Setting Off on the Right Foot" and "Evolution, Error, and Intentionality," in Dennett, in *The Intentional Stance* (Cambridge, Mass.: MIT Press, 1987).

7 Harold Bloom, *The Anxiety of Influence* (Oxford University Press, 1973), p. 80. See also Bloom's claim (p. 10) that "every poet begins (however 'unconsciously') by rebelling more strongly against the fear of death than all other men and women do." I assume that Bloom would be willing to extend the reference of "poet" beyond those who write verse, and to use it in the large, generic sense in which I am using it – so that Proust and

520 R. Rorty

Nabokov, Newton and Darwin, Hegel and Heidegger, also fall under the term. Such people are also to be thought of as rebelling against "death" – that is, against the failure to have created – more strongly than most of us.

8 "Critics, in their secret hearts, love continuities, but he who lives with continuity alone cannot be a poet" (Bloom, *Anxiety of Influence*, p. 78). The critic is, in this respect, a species of philosopher – or, more exactly, of what Heidegger and Derrida call "metaphysician." Metaphysics, Derrida says, is the search for "a centered structure ... the concept of play as based on a fundamental ground, a play constituted on the basis of a fundamental immobility and a reassuring certitude, which is itself beyond the reach of play" (Derrida, *Writing and Difference* [Chicago: University of Chicago Press, 1978], p. 279). Metaphysicians look for continuities – overarching conditions of possibility – which provide the space within which discontinuity occurs. The secret dream of criticism is to have a pigeonhole available into which any future poet can fit; the explicit hope of pre-Kuhnian philosophers of science was to have an account of "the nature of science" which no future scientific revolution could disturb.

The most important difference between Bloom and Paul de Man (not to mention what Bloom calls the "Deconstruction Road Company") is that de Man thought philosophy had given him a sense of the necessary condition of all possible poetry – past, present, and future. I think that Bloom is right in rejecting de Man's claim that "every authentic poetic or critical act rehearses the random, meaningless act of death, for which another term is the problematic of language" (Bloom, *Agon* [Oxford University Press, 1982], p. 29). Bloom will have no truck with philosophic notions like "the problematic of language," or with abstractions like "the random, meaningless act of death." He rightly thinks that these hinder criticism, defined as the "art of knowing the hidden roads that go from poem to poem" (*Anxiety of Influence*, p. 96). Like Freud's pursuit of the hidden roads that go from the child to the adult, or from the parent to the child, such an art owes very little to the search for continuities, even the continuities posited by Freud's own metapsychology.

9 Bloom says, "If this book's argument is correct, then the covert subject of most poetry for the last three centuries has been the anxiety of influence, each poet's fear that no proper work remains for him to perform" (*Anxiety of Influence*, p. 148). I take it that Bloom would agree that this fear is common to original painters, original physicists, and original philosophers as well. In Chapter 5, I suggest that Hegel's *Phenomenology* was the book which began philosophy's period of belatedness and anxiety, the one which set the task for Nietzsche, Heidegger, and Derrida – the task of being something more than another ride on the same old dialectical seesaw. Hegel's sense of a *pattern* in philosophy was what Nietzsche called a "disadvantage of history for [the original philosopher's] life," for it suggested to Kierkegaard as well as to Nietzsche, that *now*, given Hegelian self-consciousness, there can no longer be such a thing as philosophical creativity.

10 My account of Nietzsche owes a great deal to Alexander Nehamas's original and penetrating *Nietzsche: Life as Literature* (Cambridge, Mass.: Harvard University Press, 1985).

23

WHAT PRAGMATISM MEANS

W. James

Some years ago, being with a camping party in the mountains, I returned from a solitary ramble to find everyone engaged in a ferocious metaphysical dispute. The corpus of the dispute was a squirrel—a live squirrel supposed to be clinging to one side of a tree-trunk; while over against the tree's opposite side a human being was imagined to stand. This human witness tries to get sight of the squirrel by moving rapidly round the tree, but no matter how fast he goes, the squirrel moves as fast in the opposite direction, and always keeps the tree between himself and the man, so that never a glimpse of him is caught. The resultant metaphysical problem now is this: DOES THE MAN GO ROUND THE SQUIRREL OR NOT? He goes round the tree, sure enough, and the squirrel is on the tree; but does he go round the squirrel? In the unlimited leisure of the wilderness, discussion had been worn threadbare. Everyone had taken sides, and was obstinate; and the numbers on both sides were even. Each side, when I appeared, therefore appealed to me to make it a majority. Mindful of the scholastic adage that whenever you meet a contradiction you must make a distinction, I immediately sought and found one, as follows: "Which party is right," I said, "depends on what you PRACTICALLY MEAN by 'going round' the squirrel. If you mean passing from the north of him to the east, then to the south, then to the west, and then to the north of him again, obviously the man does go round him, for he occupies these successive positions. But if on the contrary you mean being first in front of him, then on the right of him, then behind him, then on his left, and finally in front again, it is quite as obvious that the man fails to go round him, for by the compensating movements the squirrel makes, he keeps his belly turned towards the man all the time, and his back turned away. Make the distinction, and there is no occasion for any farther dispute. You are both right and both wrong according as you conceive the verb 'to go round' in one practical fashion or the other."

Altho one or two of the hotter disputants called my speech a shuffling evasion, saying they wanted no quibbling or scholastic hair-splitting, but meant just plain

522 W. James

honest English 'round,' the majority seemed to think that the distinction had assuaged the dispute.

I tell this trivial anecdote because it is a peculiarly simple example of what I wish now to speak of as THE PRAGMATIC METHOD. The pragmatic method is primarily a method of settling metaphysical disputes that otherwise might be interminable. Is the world one or many?—fated or free?—material or spiritual?—here are notions either of which may or may not hold good of the world; and disputes over such notions are unending. The pragmatic method in such cases is to try to interpret each notion by tracing its respective practical consequences. What difference would it practically make to anyone if this notion rather than that notion were true? If no practical difference whatever can be traced, then the alternatives mean practically the same thing, and all dispute is idle. Whenever a dispute is serious, we ought to be able to show some practical difference that must follow from one side or the other's being right.

A glance at the history of the idea will show you still better what pragmatism means. The term is derived from the same Greek word [pi rho alpha gamma mu alpha], meaning action, from which our words 'practice' and 'practical' come. It was first introduced into philosophy by Mr. Charles Peirce in 1878. In an article entitled 'How to Make Our Ideas Clear,' in the 'Popular Science Monthly' for January of that year [Footnote: Translated in the Revue Philosophique for January, 1879 (vol. vii).] Mr. Peirce, after pointing out that our beliefs are really rules for action, said that to develope a thought's meaning, we need only determine what conduct it is fitted to produce: that conduct is for us its sole significance. And the tangible fact at the root of all our thought-distinctions, however subtle, is that there is no one of them so fine as to consist in anything but a possible difference of practice. To attain perfect clearness in our thoughts of an object, then, we need only consider what conceivable effects of a practical kind the object may involve—what sensations we are to expect from it, and what reactions we must prepare. Our conception of these effects, whether immediate or remote, is then for us the whole of our conception of the object, so far as that conception has positive significance at all.

This is the principle of Peirce, the principle of pragmatism. It lay entirely unnoticed by anyone for twenty years, until I, in an address before Professor Howison's philosophical union at the university of California, brought it forward again and made a special application of it to religion. By that date (1898) the times seemed ripe for its reception. The word 'pragmatism' spread, and at present it fairly spots the pages of the philosophic journals. On all hands we find the 'pragmatic movement' spoken of, sometimes with respect, sometimes with contumely, seldom with clear understanding. It is evident that the term applies itself conveniently to a number of tendencies that hitherto have lacked a collective name, and that it has 'come to stay.'

To take in the importance of Peirce's principle, one must get accustomed to applying it to concrete cases. I found a few years ago that Ostwald, the illustrious Leipzig chemist, had been making perfectly distinct use of the principle of pragmatism in his lectures on the philosophy of science, tho he had not called it by that name.

"All realities influence our practice," he wrote me, "and that influence is their meaning for us. I am accustomed to put questions to my classes in this way: In what respects would the world be different if this alternative or that were true? If I can find nothing that would become different, then the alternative has no sense."

That is, the rival views mean practically the same thing, and meaning, other than practical, there is for us none. Ostwald in a published lecture gives this example of what he means. Chemists have long wrangled over the inner constitution of certain bodies called 'tautomerous.' Their properties seemed equally consistent with the notion that an instable hydrogen atom oscillates inside of them, or that they are instable mixtures of two bodies. Controversy raged; but never was decided. "It would never have begun," says Ostwald, "if the combatants had asked themselves what particular experimental fact could have been made different by one or the other view being correct. For it would then have appeared that no difference of fact could possibly ensue; and the quarrel was as unreal as if, theorizing in primitive times about the raising of dough by yeast, one party should have invoked a 'brownie,' while another insisted on an 'elf' as the true cause of the phenomenon." [Footnote: 'Theorie und Praxis,' Zeitsch. des Oesterreichischen Ingenieur u. Architecten-Vereines, 1905, Nr. 4 u. 6. I find a still more radical pragmatism than Ostwald's in an address by Professor W. S. Franklin: "I think that the sickliest notion of physics, even if a student gets it, is that it is 'the science of masses, molecules and the ether.' And I think that the healthiest notion, even if a student does not wholly get it, is that physics is the science of the ways of taking hold of bodies and pushing them!" (Science, January 2, 1903.)]

It is astonishing to see how many philosophical disputes collapse into insignificance the moment you subject them to this simple test of tracing a concrete consequence. There can BE no difference any-where that doesn't MAKE a difference elsewhere—no difference in abstract truth that doesn't express itself in a difference in concrete fact and in conduct consequent upon that fact, imposed on somebody, somehow, somewhere and somewhen. The whole function of philosophy ought to be to find out what definite difference it will make to you and me, at definite instants of our life, if this world-formula or that world-formula be the true one.

There is absolutely nothing new in the pragmatic method. Socrates was an adept at it. Aristotle used it methodically. Locke, Berkeley and Hume made momentous contributions to truth by its means. Shadworth Hodgson keeps insisting that realities are only what they are 'known-as.' But these forerunners of pragmatism used it in fragments: they were preluders only. Not until in our time has it generalized itself, become conscious of a universal mission, pretended to a conquering destiny. I believe in that destiny, and I hope I may end by inspiring you with my belief.

Pragmatism represents a perfectly familiar attitude in philosophy, the empiricist attitude, but it represents it, as it seems to me, both in a more radical and in a less objectionable form than it has ever yet assumed. A pragmatist turns his back resolutely and once for all upon a lot of inveterate habits dear to professional philosophers. He turns away from abstraction and insufficiency, from verbal solutions, from bad a priori reasons, from fixed principles, closed systems, and pretended absolutes and origins. He turns towards concreteness and adequacy, towards facts, towards action, and towards power. That means the empiricist temper regnant, and the rationalist temper sincerely given up. It means the open air and possibilities of nature, as against dogma, artificiality and the pretence of finality in truth.

At the same time it does not stand for any special results. It is a method only. But the general triumph of that method would mean an enormous change in what I called in my last lecture the 'temperament' of philosophy. Teachers of the ultra-rationalistic type would be frozen out, much as the courtier type is frozen out in republics, as the ultramontane type of priest is frozen out in protestant lands. Science and metaphysics would come much nearer together, would in fact work absolutely hand in hand.

Metaphysics has usually followed a very primitive kind of quest. You know how men have always hankered after unlawful magic, and you know what a great part, in magic, WORDS have always played. If you have his name, or the formula of incantation that binds him, you can control the spirit, genie, afrite, or whatever the power may be. Solomon knew the names of all the spirits, and having their names, he held them subject to his will. So the universe has always appeared to the natural mind as a kind of enigma, of which the key must be sought in the shape of some illuminating or power-bringing word or name. That word names the universe's PRINCIPLE, and to possess it is, after a fashion, to possess the universe itself. 'God,' 'Matter,' 'Reason,' 'the Absolute,' 'Energy,' are so many solving names. You can rest when you have them. You are at the end of your metaphysical quest.

But if you follow the pragmatic method, you cannot look on any such word as closing your quest. You must bring out of each word its practical cash-value, set it at work within the stream of your experience. It appears less as a solution, then, than as a program for more work, and more particularly as an indication of the ways in which existing realities may be CHANGED.

THEORIES THUS BECOME INSTRUMENTS, NOT ANSWERS TO ENIGMAS, IN WHICH WE CAN REST. We don't lie back upon them, we move forward, and, on occasion, make nature over again by their aid. Pragmatism unstiffens all our theories, limbers them up and sets each one at work. Being nothing essentially new, it harmonizes with many ancient philosophic tendencies. It agrees with nominalism for instance, in always appealing to particulars; with utilitarianism in emphasizing practical aspects; with positivism in its disdain for verbal solutions, useless questions, and metaphysical abstractions.

All these, you see, are ANTI-INTELLECTUALIST tendencies. Against rationalism as a pretension and a method, pragmatism is fully armed and militant. But, at the outset, at least, it stands for no particular results. It has no dogmas, and no doctrines save its method. As the young Italian pragmatist Papini has well said, it lies in the midst of our theories, like a corridor in a hotel. Innumerable chambers open out of it. In one you may find a man writing an atheistic volume; in the next someone on his knees praying for faith and strength; in a third a chemist investigating a body's properties. In a fourth a system of idealistic metaphysics is being excogitated; in a fifth the impossibility of metaphysics is being shown. But they all own the corridor, and all must pass through it if they want a practicable way of getting into or out of their respective rooms.

No particular results then, so far, but only an attitude of orientation, is what the pragmatic method means. THE ATTITUDE OF LOOKING AWAY FROM FIRST THINGS, PRINCIPLES, 'CATEGORIES,' SUPPOSED NECESSITIES; AND OF LOOKING TOWARDS LAST THINGS, FRUITS, CONSEQUENCES, FACTS.

So much for the pragmatic method! You may say that I have been praising it rather than explaining it to you, but I shall presently explain it abundantly enough by showing how it works on some familiar problems. Meanwhile the word pragmatism has come to be used in a still wider sense, as meaning also a certain theory of TRUTH. I mean to give a whole lecture to the statement of that theory, after first paving the way, so I can be very brief now. But brevity is hard to follow, so I ask for your redoubled attention for a quarter of an hour. If much remains obscure, I hope to make it clearer in the later lectures.

One of the most successfully cultivated branches of philosophy in our time is what is called inductive logic, the study of the conditions under which our sciences have evolved. Writers on this subject have begun to show a singular unanimity as to what the laws of nature and elements of fact mean, when formulated by mathematicians, physicists and chemists. When the first mathematical, logical and natural uniformities, the first LAWS, were discovered, men were so carried away by the clearness, beauty and simplification that resulted, that they believed themselves to have deciphered authentically the eternal thoughts of the Almighty. His mind also thundered and reverberated in syllogisms. He also thought in conic sections, squares and roots and ratios, and geometrized like Euclid. He made Kepler's laws for the planets to follow; he made velocity increase proportionally to the time in falling bodies; he made the law of the sines for light to obey when refracted; he established the classes, orders, families and genera of plants and animals, and fixed the distances between them. He thought the archetypes of all things, and devised their variations; and when we rediscover any one of these his wondrous institutions, we seize his mind in its very literal intention.

But as the sciences have developed farther, the notion has gained ground that most, perhaps all, of our laws are only approximations. The laws themselves, moreover, have grown so numerous that there is no counting them; and so many rival formulations are proposed in all the branches of science that investigators have become accustomed to the notion that no theory is absolutely a transcript of reality, but that any one of them may from some point of view be useful. Their great use is to summarize old facts and to lead to new ones. They are only a man–made language, a conceptual shorthand, as someone calls them, in which we write our reports of nature; and languages, as is well known, tolerate much choice of expression and many dialects.

526 W. James

Thus human arbitrariness has driven divine necessity from scientific logic. If I mention the names of Sigwart, Mach, Ostwald, Pearson, Milhaud, Poincare, Duhem, Ruyssen, those of you who are students will easily identify the tendency I speak of, and will think of additional names.

Riding now on the front of this wave of scientific logic Messrs. Schiller and Dewey appear with their pragmatistic account of what truth everywhere signifies. Everywhere, these teachers say, 'truth' in our ideas and beliefs means the same thing that it means in science. It means, they say, nothing but this, THAT IDEAS (WHICH THEMSELVES ARE BUT PARTS OF OUR EXPERIENCE) BECOME TRUE JUST IN SO FAR AS THEY HELP US TO GET INTO SATISFACTORY RELATION WITH OTHER PARTS OF OUR EXPERI-ENCE, to summarize them and get about among them by conceptual short-cuts instead of following the interminable succession of particular phenomena. Any idea upon which we can ride, so to speak; any idea that will carry us prosperously from any one part of our experience to any other part, linking things satisfactorily, working securely, simplifying, saving labor; is true for just so much, true in so far forth, true INSTRUMENTALLY. This is the 'instrumental' view of truth taught so successfully at Chicago, the view that truth in our ideas means their power to 'work,' promulgated so brilliantly at Oxford.

Messrs. Dewey, Schiller and their allies, in reaching this general conception of all truth, have only followed the example of geologists, biologists and philologists. In the establishment of these other sciences, the successful stroke was always to take some simple process actually observable in operation—as denudation by weather, say, or variation from parental type, or change of dialect by incorporation of new words and pronunciations—and then to generalize it, making it apply to all times, and produce great results by summating its effects through the ages.

The observable process which Schiller and Dewey particularly singled out for generalization is the familiar one by which any individual settles into NEW OPIN-IONS. The process here is always the same. The individual has a stock of old opinions already, but he meets a new experience that puts them to a strain. Some-body contradicts them; or in a reflective moment he discovers that they contradict each other; or he hears of facts with which they are incompatible; or desires arise in him which they cease to satisfy. The result is an inward trouble to which his mind till then had been a stranger, and from which he seeks to escape by modifying his previous mass of opinions. He saves as much of it as he can, for in this matter of belief we are all extreme conservatives. So he tries to change first this opinion, and then that (for they resist change very variously), until at last some new idea comes up which he can graft upon the ancient stock with a minimum of disturbance of the latter, some idea that mediates between the stock and the new experience and runs them into one another most felicitously and expediently.

This new idea is then adopted as the true one. It preserves the older stock of truths with a minimum of modification, stretching them just enough to make them admit the novelty, but conceiving that in ways as familiar as the case leaves possible. An outree explanation, violating all our preconceptions, would never pass for a true

What pragmatism means   527

account of a novelty. We should scratch round industriously till we found something less excentric. The most violent revolutions in an individual's beliefs leave most of his old order standing. Time and space, cause and effect, nature and history, and one's own biography remain untouched. New truth is always a go-between, a smoother-over of transitions. It marries old opinion to new fact so as ever to show a minimum of jolt, a maximum of continuity. We hold a theory true just in proportion to its success in solving this 'problem of maxima and minima.' But success in solving this problem is eminently a matter of approximation. We say this theory solves it on the whole more satisfactorily than that theory; but that means more satisfactorily to ourselves, and individuals will emphasize their points of satisfaction differently. To a certain degree, therefore, everything here is plastic.

The point I now urge you to observe particularly is the part played by the older truths. Failure to take account of it is the source of much of the unjust criticism leveled against pragmatism. Their influence is absolutely controlling. Loyalty to them is the first principle—in most cases it is the only principle; for by far the most usual way of handling phenomena so novel that they would make for a serious rearrangement of our preconceptions is to ignore them altogether, or to abuse those who bear witness for them.

You doubtless wish examples of this process of truth's growth, and the only trouble is their superabundance. The simplest case of new truth is of course the mere numerical addition of new kinds of facts, or of new single facts of old kinds, to our experience—an addition that involves no alteration in the old beliefs. Day follows day, and its contents are simply added. The new contents themselves are not true, they simply COME and ARE. Truth is what we say about them, and when we say that they have come, truth is satisfied by the plain additive formula.

But often the day's contents oblige a rearrangement. If I should now utter piercing shrieks and act like a maniac on this platform, it would make many of you revise your ideas as to the probable worth of my philosophy. 'Radium' came the other day as part of the day's content, and seemed for a moment to contradict our ideas of the whole order of nature, that order having come to be identified with what is called the conservation of energy. The mere sight of radium paying heat away indefinitely out of its own pocket seemed to violate that conservation. What to think? If the radiations from it were nothing but an escape of unsuspected 'potential' energy, pre-existent inside of the atoms, the principle of conservation would be saved. The discovery of 'helium' as the radiation's outcome, opened a way to this belief. So Ramsay's view is generally held to be true, because, altho it extends our old ideas of energy, it causes a minimum of alteration in their nature.

I need not multiply instances. A new opinion counts as 'true' just in proportion as it gratifies the individual's desire to assimilate the novel in his experience to his beliefs in stock. It must both lean on old truth and grasp new fact; and its success (as I said a moment ago) in doing this, is a matter for the individual's appreciation. When old truth grows, then, by new truth's addition, it is for subjective reasons. We are in the process and obey the reasons. That new idea is truest which performs most felicitously its function of satisfying our double urgency. It makes itself true, gets itself classed as true, by the way it works; grafting itself then upon the ancient body of truth, which thus grows much as a tree grows by the activity of a new layer of cambium.

Now Dewey and Schiller proceed to generalize this observation and to apply it to the most ancient parts of truth. They also once were plastic. They also were called true for human reasons. They also mediated between still earlier truths and what in those days were novel observations. Purely objective truth, truth in whose establishment the function of giving human satisfaction in marrying previous parts of experience with newer parts played no role whatever, is nowhere to be found. The reasons why we call things true is the reason why they ARE true, for 'to be true' MEANS only to perform this marriage-function.

The trail of the human serpent is thus over everything. Truth independent; truth that we FIND merely; truth no longer malleable to human need; truth incorrigible, in a word; such truth exists indeed superabundantly—or is supposed to exist by rationalistically minded thinkers; but then it means only the dead heart of the living tree, and its being there means only that truth also has its paleontology and its 'prescription,' and may grow stiff with years of veteran service and petrified in men's regard by sheer antiquity. But how plastic even the oldest truths nevertheless really are has been vividly shown in our day by the transformation of logical and mathematical ideas, a transformation which seems even to be invading physics. The ancient formulas are reinterpreted as special expressions of much wider principles, principles that our ancestors never got a glimpse of in their present shape and formulation.

Mr. Schiller still gives to all this view of truth the name of 'Humanism,' but, for this doctrine too, the name of pragmatism seems fairly to be in the ascendant, so I will treat it under the name of pragmatism in these lectures.

Such then would be the scope of pragmatism—first, a method; and second, a genetic theory of what is meant by truth. And these two things must be our future topics.

What I have said of the theory of truth will, I am sure, have appeared obscure and unsatisfactory to most of you by reason of us brevity. I shall make amends for that hereafter. In a lecture on 'common sense' I shall try to show what I mean by truths grown petrified by antiquity. In another lecture I shall expatiate on the idea that our thoughts become true in proportion as they successfully exert their go-between function. In a third I shall show how hard it is to discriminate subjective from objective factors in Truth's development. You may not follow me wholly in these lectures; and if you do, you may not wholly agree with me. But you will, I know, regard me at least as serious, and treat my effort with respectful consideration.

You will probably be surprised to learn, then, that Messrs. Schiller's and Dewey's theories have suffered a hailstorm of contempt and ridicule. All rationalism has risen against them. In influential quarters Mr. Schiller, in particular, has been treated like an impudent schoolboy who deserves a spanking. I should not mention this, but for the fact that it throws so much sidelight upon that rationalistic temper to which I

What pragmatism means **529**

have opposed the temper of pragmatism. Pragmatism is uncomfortable away from facts. Rationalism is comfortable only in the presence of abstractions. This pragmatist talk about truths in the plural, about their utility and satisfactoriness, about the success with which they 'work,' etc., suggests to the typical intellectualist mind a sort of coarse lame second-rate makeshift article of truth. Such truths are not real truth. Such tests are merely subjective. As against this, objective truth must be something non-utilitarian, haughty, refined, remote, august, exalted. It must be an absolute correspondence of our thoughts with an equally absolute reality. It must be what we OUGHT to think, unconditionally. The conditioned ways in which we DO think are so much irrelevance and matter for psychology. Down with psychology, up with logic, in all this question!

See the exquisite contrast of the types of mind! The pragmatist clings to facts and concreteness, observes truth at its work in particular cases, and generalizes. Truth, for him, becomes a class-name for all sorts of definite working-values in experience. For the rationalist it remains a pure abstraction, to the bare name of which we must defer. When the pragmatist undertakes to show in detail just WHY we must defer, the rationalist is unable to recognize the concretes from which his own abstraction is taken. He accuses us of DENYING truth; whereas we have only sought to trace exactly why people follow it and always ought to follow it. Your typical ultra-abstractionist fairly shudders at concreteness: other things equal, he positively prefers the pale and spectral. If the two universes were offered, he would always choose the skinny outline rather than the rich thicket of reality. It is so much purer, clearer, nobler.

I hope that as these lectures go on, the concreteness and closeness to facts of the pragmatism which they advocate may be what approves itself to you as its most satisfactory peculiarity. It only follows here the example of the sister-sciences, interpreting the unobserved by the observed. It brings old and new harmoniously together. It converts the absolutely empty notion of a static relation of 'correspondence' (what that may mean we must ask later) between our minds and reality, into that of a rich and active commerce (that anyone may follow in detail and understand) between particular thoughts of ours, and the great universe of other experiences in which they play their parts and have their uses.

But enough of this at present? The justification of what I say must be postponed. I wish now to add a word in further explanation of the claim I made at our last meeting, that pragmatism may be a happy harmonizer of empiricist ways of thinking, with the more religious demands of human beings.

Men who are strongly of the fact-loving temperament, you may remember me to have said, are liable to be kept at a distance by the small sympathy with facts which that philosophy from the present-day fashion of idealism offers them. It is far too intellectualistic. Old fashioned theism was bad enough, with its notion of God as an exalted monarch, made up of a lot of unintelligible or preposterous 'attributes'; but, so long as it held strongly by the argument from design, it kept some touch with concrete realities. Since, however, darwinism has once for all displaced design from the minds of the 'scientific,' theism has lost that foothold; and some kind of

530 W. James

an immanent or pantheistic deity working IN things rather than above them is, if any, the kind recommended to our contemporary imagination. Aspirants to a philosophic religion turn, as a rule, more hopefully nowadays towards idealistic pantheism than towards the older dualistic theism, in spite of the fact that the latter still counts able defenders.

But, as I said in my first lecture, the brand of pantheism offered is hard for them to assimilate if they are lovers of facts, or empirically minded. It is the absolutistic brand, spurning the dust and reared upon pure logic. It keeps no connexion whatever with concreteness. Affirming the Absolute Mind, which is its substitute for God, to be the rational presupposition of all particulars of fact, whatever they may be, it remains supremely indifferent to what the particular facts in our world actually are. Be they what they may, the Absolute will father them. Like the sick lion in Esop's fable, all footprints lead into his den, but nulla vestigia retrorsum. You cannot redescend into the world of particulars by the Absolute's aid, or deduce any necessary consequences of detail important for your life from your idea of his nature. He gives you indeed the assurance that all is well with Him, and for his eternal way of thinking; but thereupon he leaves you to be finitely saved by your own temporal devices.

Far be it from me to deny the majesty of this conception, or its capacity to yield religious comfort to a most respectable class of minds. But from the human point of view, no one can pretend that it doesn't suffer from the faults of remoteness and abstractness. It is eminently a product of what I have ventured to call the rationalistic temper. It disdains empiricism's needs. It substitutes a pallid outline for the real world's richness. It is dapper; it is noble in the bad sense, in the sense in which to be noble is to be inapt for humble service. In this real world of sweat and dirt, it seems to me that when a view of things is 'noble,' that ought to count as a presumption against its truth, and as a philosophic disqualification. The prince of darkness may be a gentleman, as we are told he is, but whatever the God of earth and heaven is, he can surely be no gentleman. His menial services are needed in the dust of our human trials, even more than his dignity is needed in the empyrean.

Now pragmatism, devoted tho she be to facts, has no such materialistic bias as ordinary empiricism labors under. Moreover, she has no objection whatever to the realizing of abstractions, so long as you get about among particulars with their aid and they actually carry you somewhere. Interested in no conclusions but those which our minds and our experiences work out together, she has no a priori prejudices against theology. IF THEOLOGICAL IDEAS PROVE TO HAVE A VALUE FOR CONCRETE LIFE, THEY WILL BE TRUE, FOR PRAGMATISM, IN THE SENSE OF BEING GOOD FOR SO MUCH. FOR HOW MUCH MORE THEY ARE TRUE, WILL DEPEND ENTIRELY ON THEIR RELATIONS TO THE OTHER TRUTHS THAT ALSO HAVE TO BE ACKNOWLEDGED.

What I said just now about the Absolute of transcendental idealism is a case in point. First, I called it majestic and said it yielded religious comfort to a class of minds, and then I accused it of remoteness and sterility. But so far as it affords such

What pragmatism means **531**

comfort, it surely is not sterile; it has that amount of value; it performs a concrete function. As a good pragmatist, I myself ought to call the Absolute true 'in so far forth,' then; and I unhesitatingly now do so.

But what does TRUE IN SO FAR FORTH mean in this case? To answer, we need only apply the pragmatic method. What do believers in the Absolute mean by saying that their belief affords them comfort? They mean that since in the Absolute finite evil is 'overruled' already, we may, therefore, whenever we wish, treat the temporal as if it were potentially the eternal, be sure that we can trust its outcome, and, without sin, dismiss our fear and drop the worry of our finite responsibility. In short, they mean that we have a right ever and anon to take a moral holiday, to let the world wag in its own way, feeling that its issues are in better hands than ours and are none of our business.

The universe is a system of which the individual members may relax their anxieties occasionally, in which the don't-care mood is also right for men, and moral holidays in order—that, if I mistake not, is part, at least, of what the Absolute is 'known-as,' that is the great difference in our particular experiences which his being true makes for us, that is part of his cash-value when he is pragmatically interpreted. Farther than that the ordinary lay-reader in philosophy who thinks favorably of absolute idealism does not venture to sharpen his conceptions. He can use the Absolute for so much, and so much is very precious. He is pained at hearing you speak incredulously of the Absolute, therefore, and disregards your criticisms because they deal with aspects of the conception that he fails to follow.

If the Absolute means this, and means no more than this, who can possibly deny the truth of it? To deny it would be to insist that men should never relax, and that holidays are never in order. I am well aware how odd it must seem to some of you to hear me say that an idea is 'true' so long as to believe it is profitable to our lives. That it is GOOD, for as much as it profits, you will gladly admit. If what we do by its aid is good, you will allow the idea itself to be good in so far forth, for we are the better for possessing it. But is it not a strange misuse of the word 'truth,' you will say, to call ideas also 'true' for this reason?

To answer this difficulty fully is impossible at this stage of my account. You touch here upon the very central point of Messrs. Schiller's, Dewey's and my own doctrine of truth, which I cannot discuss with detail until my sixth lecture. Let me now say only this, that truth is ONE SPECIES OF GOOD, and not, as is usually supposed, a category distinct from good, and co-ordinate with it. THE TRUE IS THE NAME OF WHATEVER PROVES ITSELF TO BE GOOD IN THE WAY OF BELIEF, AND GOOD, TOO, FOR DEFINITE, ASSIGNABLE REASONS. Surely you must admit this, that if there were NO good for life in true ideas, or if the knowledge of them were positively disadvantageous and false ideas the only useful ones, then the current notion that truth is divine and precious, and its pursuit a duty, could never have grown up or become a dogma. In a world like that, our duty would be to SHUN truth, rather. But in this world, just as certain foods are not only agreeable to our taste, but good for our teeth, our stomach and our tissues; so certain ideas are not only agreeable to think about, or agreeable as

532 W. James

supporting other ideas that we are fond of, but they are also helpful in life's practical struggles. If there be any life that it is really better we should lead, and if there be any idea which, if believed in, would help us to lead that life, then it would be really BETTER FOR US to believe in that idea, UNLESS, INDEED, BELIEF IN IT INCIDENTALLY CLASHED WITH OTHER GREATER VITAL BENEFITS.

'What would be better for us to believe'! This sounds very like a definition of truth. It comes very near to saying 'what we OUGHT to believe': and in THAT definition none of you would find any oddity. Ought we ever not to believe what it is BETTER FOR US to believe? And can we then keep the notion of what is better for us, and what is true for us, permanently apart?

Pragmatism says no, and I fully agree with her. Probably you also agree, so far as the abstract statement goes, but with a suspicion that if we practically did believe everything that made for good in our own personal lives, we should be found indulging all kinds of fancies about this world's affairs, and all kinds of sentimental superstitions about a world hereafter. Your suspicion here is undoubtedly well founded, and it is evident that something happens when you pass from the abstract to the concrete, that complicates the situation.

I said just now that what is better for us to believe is true UNLESS THE BELIEF INCIDENTALLY CLASHES WITH SOME OTHER VITAL BENEFIT. Now in real life what vital benefits is any particular belief of ours most liable to clash with? What indeed except the vital benefits yielded by OTHER BELIEFS when these prove incompatible with the first ones? In other words, the greatest enemy of any one of our truths may be the rest of our truths. Truths have once for all this desperate instinct of self-preservation and of desire to extinguish whatever contradicts them. My belief in the Absolute, based on the good it does me, must run the gauntlet of all my other beliefs. Grant that it may be true in giving me a moral holiday. Nevertheless, as I conceive it,—and let me speak now confidentially, as it were, and merely in my own private person,—it clashes with other truths of mine whose benefits I hate to give up on its account. It happens to be associated with a kind of logic of which I am the enemy, I find that it entangles me in metaphysical paradoxes that are inacceptable, etc., etc.. But as I have enough trouble in life already without adding the trouble of carrying these intellectual inconsistencies, I personally just give up the Absolute. I just TAKE my moral holidays; or else as a professional philosopher, I try to justify them by some other principle.

If I could restrict my notion of the Absolute to its bare holiday-giving value, it wouldn't clash with my other truths. But we cannot easily thus restrict our hypotheses. They carry supernumerary features, and these it is that clash so. My disbelief in the Absolute means then disbelief in those other supernumerary features, for I fully believe in the legitimacy of taking moral holidays.

You see by this what I meant when I called pragmatism a mediator and reconciler and said, borrowing the word from Papini, that he unstiffens our theories. She has in fact no prejudices whatever, no obstructive dogmas, no rigid canons of what shall count as proof. She is completely genial. She will entertain any hypothesis, she will consider any evidence. It follows that in the religious field she is at a great advantage both over positivistic empiricism, with its anti-theological bias, and over religious rationalism, with its exclusive interest in the remote, the noble, the simple, and the abstract in the way of conception.

In short, she widens the field of search for God. Rationalism sticks to logic and the empyrean. Empiricism sticks to the external senses. Pragmatism is willing to take anything, to follow either logic or the senses, and to count the humblest and most personal experiences. She will count mystical experiences if they have practical consequences. She will take a God who lives in the very dirt of private fact-if that should seem a likely place to find him.

Her only test of probable truth is what works best in the way of leading us, what fits every part of life best and combines with the collectivity of experience's demands, nothing being omitted. If theological ideas should do this, if the notion of God, in particular, should prove to do it, how could pragmatism possibly deny God's existence? She could see no meaning in treating as 'not true' a notion that was pragmatically so successful. What other kind of truth could there be, for her, than all this agreement with concrete reality?

In my last lecture I shall return again to the relations of pragmatism with religion. But you see already how democratic she is. Her manners are as various and flexible, her resources as rich and endless, and her conclusions as friendly as those of mother nature.

24

CONCLUSION

The creative powers of a free civilization

F. A. Hayek

> Civilization advances by extending the number of important operations which we can perform without thinking about them. Operations of thought are like cavalry charges in a battle—they are strictly limited in number, they require fresh horses, and must only be made at decisive moments.
>
> —*A. N. Whitehead*

1. The Socratic maxim that the recognition of our ignorance is the beginning of wisdom has profound significance for our understanding of society. The first requisite for this is that we become aware of men's necessary ignorance of much that helps him to achieve his aims. Most of the advantages of social life, especially in its more advanced forms which we call "civilization," rest on the fact that the individual benefits from more knowledge than he is aware of. It might be said that civilization begins when the individual in the pursuit of his ends can make use of more knowledge than he has himself acquired and when he can transcend the boundaries of his ignorance by profiting from knowledge he does not himself possess.

This fundamental fact of man's unavoidable ignorance of much on which the working of civilization rests has received little attention. Philosophers and students of society have generally glossed it over and treated this ignorance as a minor imperfection which could be more or less disregarded. But, though discussions of moral or social problems based on the assumption of perfect knowledge may occasionally be useful as a preliminary exercise in logic, they are of little use in an attempt to explain the real world. Its problems are dominated by the "practical difficulty" that our knowledge is, in fact, very far from perfect. Perhaps it is only natural that the scientists tend to stress what we do know; but in the social field, where what we do not know is often so much more important, the effect of this tendency may be very misleading. Many of the utopian constructions are worthless because they follow the lead of the theorists in assuming that we have perfect knowledge.

It must be admitted, however, that our ignorance is a peculiarly difficult subject to discuss. It might at first even seem impossible by definition to talk sense about it. We certainly cannot discuss intelligently something about which we know nothing. We must at least be able to state the questions even if we do not know the answers. This requires some genuine knowledge of the kind of world we are discussing. If we are to understand how society works, we must attempt to define the general nature and range of our ignorance concerning it. Though we cannot see in the dark, we must be able to trace the limits of the dark areas.

The misleading effect of the usual approach stands out clearly if we examine the significance of the assertion that man has created his civilization and that he there-fore can also change its institutions as he pleases. This assertion would be justified only if man had deliberately created civilization in full understanding of what he was doing or if he at least clearly knew how it was being maintained. In a sense it is true, of course, that man has made his civilization. It is the product of his actions or, rather, of the action of a few hundred generations. This does not mean, however, that civilization is the product of human design, or even that man knows what its functioning or continued existence depends upon.[1]

The whole conception of man already endowed with a mind capable of con-ceiving civilization setting out to create it is fundamentally false. Man did not simply impose upon the world a pattern created by his mind. His mind is itself a system that constantly changes as a result of his endeavor to adapt himself to his surroundings. It would be an error to believe that, to achieve a higher civilization, we have merely to put into effect the ideas now guiding us. If we are to advance, we must leave room for a continuous revision of our present conceptions and ideals which will be necessitated by further experience. We are as little able to conceive what civilization will be, or can be, five hundred or even fifty years hence as our medieval forefathers or even our grandparents were able to foresee our manner of life today.[2]

The conception of man deliberately building his civilization stems from an erro-neous intellectualism that regards human reason as something standing outside nature and possessed of knowledge and reasoning capacity independent of experi-ence. But the growth of the human mind is part of the growth of civilization; it is the state of civilization at any given moment that determines the scope and the possibilities of human ends and values. The mind can never foresee its own advance. Though we must always strive for the achievement of our present aims, we must also leave room for new experiences and future events to decide which of these aims will be achieved.

It may be an exaggeration to assert, as a modern anthropologist has done, that "it is not man who controls culture but the other way around"; but it is useful to be reminded by him that "it is only our profound and comprehensive ignorance of the nature of culture that makes it possible for us to believe that we direct and control it."[3] He suggests at least an important corrective to the intellectualist

536 F. A. Hayek

conception. His reminder will help us to achieve a truer image of the incessant interaction between our conscious striving for what our intellect pictures as achievable and the operations of the institutions, traditions, and habits which jointly often produce something very different from what we have aimed at.

There are two important respects in which the conscious knowledge which guides the individual's actions constitutes only part of the conditions which enable him to achieve his ends. There is the fact that man's mind is itself a product of the civilization in which he has grown up and that it is unaware of much of the experience which has shaped it—experience that assists it by being embodied in the habits, conventions, language, and moral beliefs which are part of its makeup. Then there is the further consideration that the knowledge which any individual mind consciously manipulates is only a small part of the knowledge which at any one time contributes to the success of his action. When we reflect how much knowledge possessed by other people is an essential condition for the successful pursuit of our individual aims, the magnitude of our ignorance of the circumstances on which the results of our action depend appears simply staggering. Knowledge exists only as the knowledge of individuals. It is not much better than a metaphor to speak of the knowledge of society as a whole. The sum of the knowledge of all the individuals exists nowhere as an integrated whole. The great problem is how we can all profit from this knowledge, which exists only dispersed as the separate, partial, and sometimes conflicting beliefs of all men.

In other words, it is largely because civilization enables us constantly to profit from knowledge which we individually do not possess and because each individual's use of his particular knowledge may serve to assist others unknown to him in achieving their ends that men as members of civilized society can pursue their individual ends so much more successfully than they could alone. We know little of the particular facts to which the whole of social activity continuously adjusts itself in order to provide what we have learned to expect. We know even less of the forces which bring about this adjustment by appropriately co-ordinating individual activity. And our attitude, when we discover how little we know of what makes us co-operate, is, on the whole, one of resentment rather than of wonder or curiosity. Much of our occasional impetuous desire to smash the whole entangling machinery of civilization is due to this inability of man to understand what he is doing.

2. The identification of the growth of civilization with the growth of knowledge would be very misleading, however, if by "knowledge" we meant only the conscious, explicit knowledge of individuals, the knowledge which enables us to state that this or that is so-and-so.[4] Still less can this knowledge be confined to scientific knowledge. It is important for the understanding of our argument later to remember that, contrary to one fashionable view,[5] scientific knowledge does not exhaust even all the explicit and conscious knowledge of which society makes constant use. The scientific methods of the search for knowledge are not capable of satisfying all society's needs for explicit knowledge. Not all the knowledge of the ever changing particular facts that man continually uses lends itself to organization or systematic exposition; much of it exists only dispersed among countless

individuals. The same applies to that important part of expert knowledge which is not substantive knowledge but merely knowledge of where and how to find the needed information.[6] For our present purpose, however, it is not this distinction between different kinds of rational knowledge that is most important, and when we speak of explicit knowledge, we shall group these different kinds together.

The growth of knowledge and the growth of civilization are the same only if we interpret knowledge to include all the human adaptations to environment in which past experience has been incorporated. Not all knowledge in this sense is part of our intellect, nor is our intellect the whole of our knowledge. Our habits and skills, our emotional attitudes, our tools, and our institutions—all are in this sense adaptations to past experience which have grown up by selective elimination of less suitable conduct. They are as much an indispensable foundation of successful action as is our conscious knowledge. Not all these non-rational factors underlying our action are always conducive to success. Some may be retained long after they have out-lived their usefulness and even when they have become more an obstacle than a help. Nevertheless, we could not do without them: even the successful employ-ment of our intellect itself rests on their constant use.

Man prides himself on the increase in his knowledge. But, as a result of what he himself has created, the limitations of his conscious knowledge and therefore the range of ignorance significant for his conscious action have constantly increased. Ever since the beginning of modern science, the best minds have recognized that "the range of acknowledged ignorance will grow with the advance of science."[7] Unfortunately, the popular effect of this scientific advance has been a belief, seem-ingly shared by many scientists, that the range of our ignorance is steadily diminish-ing and that we can therefore aim at more comprehensive and deliberate control of all human activities. It is for this reason that those intoxicated by the advance of knowledge so often become the enemies of freedom. While the growth of our knowledge of nature constantly discloses new realms of ignorance, the increasing complexity of the civilization which this knowledge enables us to build presents new obstacles to the intellectual comprehension of the world around us. The more men know, the smaller the share of all that knowledge becomes that any one mind can absorb. The more civilized we become, the more relatively ignorant must each individual be of the facts on which the working of his civilization depends. The very division of knowledge increases the necessary ignorance of the individual of most of this knowledge.

3. When we spoke of the transmission and communication of knowledge, we meant to refer to the two aspects of the process of civilization which we have already distinguished: the transmission in time of our accumulated stock of know-ledge and the communication among contemporaries of information on which they base their action. They cannot be sharply separated because the tools of com-munication between contemporaries are part of the cultural heritage which man constantly uses in the pursuit of his ends.

We are most familiar with this process of accumulation and transmission of knowledge in the field of science—so far as it shows both the general laws of nature

538 F. A. Hayek

and the concrete features of the world in which we live. But, although this is the most conspicuous part of our inherited stock of knowledge and the chief part of what we necessarily know, in the ordinary sense of "knowing," it is still only a part; for, besides this, we command many tools—in the widest sense of that word—which the human race has evolved and which enable us to deal with our environment. These are the results of the experience of successive generations which are handed down. And, once a more efficient tool is available, it will be used without our knowing why it is better, or even what the alternatives are.

These "tools" which man has evolved and which constitute such an important part of his adaptation to his environment include much more than material implements. They consist in a large measure of forms of conduct which he habitually follows without knowing why; they consist of what we call "traditions" and "institutions," which he uses because they are available to him as a product of cumulative growth without ever having been designed by any one mind. Man is generally ignorant not only of why he uses implements of one shape rather than of another but also of how much is dependent on his actions taking one form rather than another. He does not usually know to what extent the success of his efforts is determined by his conforming to habits of which he is not even aware. This is probably as true of civilized man as of primitive man. Concurrent with the growth of conscious knowledge there always takes place an equally important accumulation of tools in this wider sense, of tested and generally adopted ways of doing things.

Our concern at the moment is not so much with the knowledge thus handed down to us or with the formation of new tools that will be used in the future as it is with the manner in which current experience is utilized in assisting those who do not directly gain it. So far as it is possible to do so, we shall leave the progress in time for the next chapter and concentrate here on the manner in which that dispersed knowledge and the different skills, the varied habits and opportunities of the individual members of society, contribute toward bringing about the adjustment of its activities to ever changing circumstances.

Every change in conditions will make necessary some change in the use of resources, in the direction and kind of human activities, in habits and practices. And each change in the actions of those affected in the first instance will require further adjustments that will gradually extend throughout the whole of society. Thus every change in a sense creates a "problem" for society, even though no single individual perceives it as such; and it is gradually "solved" by the establishment of a new overall adjustment. Those who take part in the process have little idea why they are doing what they do, and we have no way of predicting who will at each step first make the appropriate move, or what particular combinations of knowledge and skill, personal attitudes and circumstances, will suggest to some man the suitable answer, or by what channels his example will be transmitted to others who will follow the lead. It is difficult to conceive all the combinations of knowledge and skills which thus come into action and from which arises the discovery of appropriate practices or devices that, once found, can be accepted generally. But from the countless number of humble steps taken by anonymous persons in the course of

Conclusion **539**

doing familiar things in changed circumstances spring the examples that prevail. They are as important as the major intellectual innovations which are explicitly recognized and communicated as such.

Who will prove to possess the right combination of aptitudes and opportunities to find the better way is just as little predictable as by what manner or process different kinds of knowledge and skill will combine to bring about a solution of the problem.[8] The successful combination of knowledge and aptitude is not selected by common deliberation, by people seeking a solution to their problems through a joint effort;[9] it is the product of individuals imitating those who have been more successful and from their being guided by signs or symbols, such as prices offered for their products or expressions of moral or aesthetic esteem for their having observed standards of conduct —in short, of their using the results of the experiences of others.

What is essential to the functioning of the process is that each individual be able to act on his particular knowledge, always unique, at least so far as it refers to some particular circumstances, and that he be able to use his individual skills and opportunities within the limits known to him and for his own individual purpose.

4. We have now reached the point at which the main contention of this chapter will be readily intelligible. It is that the case for individual freedom rests chiefly on the recognition of the inevitable ignorance of all of us concerning a great many of the factors on which the achievement of our ends and welfare depends.[10]

If there were omniscient men, if we could know not only all that affects the attainment of our present wishes but also our future wants and desires, there would be little case for liberty. And, in turn, liberty of the individual would, of course, make complete foresight impossible. Liberty is essential in order to leave room for the unforeseeable and unpredictable; we want it because we have learned to expect from it the opportunity of realizing many of our aims. It is because every individual knows so little and, in particular, because we rarely know which of us knows best that we trust the independent and competitive efforts of many to induce the emergence of what we shall want when we see it.

Humiliating to human pride as it may be, we must recognize that the advance and even the preservation of civilization are dependent upon a maximum of opportunity for accidents to happen.[11] These accidents occur in the combination of knowledge and attitudes, skills and habits, acquired by individual men and also when qualified men are confronted with the particular circumstances which they are equipped to deal with. Our necessary ignorance of so much means that we have to deal largely with probabilities and chances.

Of course, it is true of social as of individual life that favorable accidents usually do not just happen. We must prepare for them.[12] But they still remain chances and do not become certainties. They involve risks deliberately taken, the possible misfortune of individuals and groups who are as meritorious as others who prosper, the possibility of serious failure or relapse even for the majority, and merely a high probability of a net gain on balance. All we can do is to increase the chance that some special constellation of individual endowment and circumstance will result in the shaping of some new tool or the improvement of an old one, and to improve

540 F. A. Hayek

the prospect that such innovations will become rapidly known to those who can take advantage of them.

All political theories assume, of course, that most individuals are very ignorant. Those who plead for liberty differ from the rest in that they include among the ignorant themselves as well as the wisest. Compared with the totality of knowledge which is continually utilized in the evolution of a dynamic civilization, the difference between the knowledge that the wisest and that which the most ignorant individual can deliberately employ is comparatively insignificant.

The classical argument for tolerance formulated by John Milton and John Locke and restated by John Stuart Mill and Walter Bagehot rests, of course, on the recognition of this ignorance of ours. It is a special application of general considerations to which a non-rationalist insight into the working of our mind opens the doors. We shall find throughout this book that, though we are usually not aware of it, all institutions of freedom are adaptations to this fundamental fact of ignorance, adapted to deal with chances and probabilities, not certainty. Certainty we cannot achieve in human affairs, and it is for this reason that, to make the best use of what knowledge we have, we must adhere to rules which experience has shown to serve best on the whole, though we do not know what will be the consequences of obeying them in the particular instance.[13]

5. Man learns by the disappointment of expectations. Needless to say, we ought not to increase the unpredictability of events by foolish human institutions. So far as possible, our aim should be to improve human institutions so as to increase the chances of correct foresight. Above all, however, we should provide the maximum of opportunity for unknown individuals to learn of facts that we ourselves are yet unaware of and to make use of this knowledge in their actions.

It is through the mutually adjusted efforts of many people that more knowledge is utilized than any one individual possesses or than it is possible to synthesize intellectually; and it is through such utilization of dispersed knowledge that achievements are made possible greater than any single mind can foresee. It is because freedom means the renunciation of direct control of individual efforts that a free society can make use of so much more knowledge than the mind of the wisest ruler could comprehend.

From this foundation of the argument for liberty it follows that we shall not achieve its ends if we confine liberty to the particular instances where we know it will do good. Freedom granted only when it is known beforehand that its effects will be beneficial is not freedom. If we knew how freedom would be used, the case for it would largely disappear. We shall never get the benefits of freedom, never obtain those unforeseeable new developments for which it provides the opportunity, if it is not also granted where the uses made of it by some do not seem desirable. It is therefore no argument against individual freedom that it is frequently abused. Freedom necessarily means that many things will be done which we do not like. Our faith in freedom does not rest on the foreseeable results in particular circumstances but on the belief that it will, on balance, release more forces for the good than for the bad.

It also follows that the importance of our being free to do a particular thing has nothing to do with the question of whether we or the majority are ever likely to make use of that particular possibility. To grant no more freedom than all can exercise would be to misconceive its function completely. The freedom that will be used by only one man in a million may be more important to society and more beneficial to the majority than any freedom that we all use.[14]

It might even be said that the less likely the opportunity to make use of freedom to do a particular thing, the more precious it will be for society as a whole. The less likely the opportunity, the more serious will it be to miss it when it arises, for the experience that it offers will be nearly unique. It is also probably true that the majority are not directly interested in most of the important things that any one person should be free to do. It is because we do not know how individuals will use their freedom that it is so important. If it were otherwise, the results of freedom could also be achieved by the majority's deciding what should be done by the individuals. But majority action is, of necessity, confined to the already tried and ascertained, to issues on which agreement has already been reached in that process of discussion that must be preceded by different experiences and actions on the part of different individuals.

The benefits I derive from freedom are thus largely the result of the uses of freedom by others, and mostly of those uses of freedom that I could never avail myself of. It is therefore not necessarily freedom that I can exercise myself that is most important for me. It is certainly more important that anything can be tried by somebody than that all can do the same things. It is not because we like to be able to do particular things, not because we regard any particular freedom as essential to our happiness, that we have a claim to freedom. The instinct that makes us revolt against any physical restraint, though a helpful ally, is not always a safe guide for justifying or delimiting freedom. What is important is not what freedom I personally would like to exercise but what freedom some person may need in order to do things beneficial to society. This freedom we can assure to the unknown person only by giving it to all.

The benefits of freedom are therefore not confined to the free—or, at least, a man does not benefit mainly from those aspects of freedom which he himself takes advantage of. There can be no doubt that in history unfree majorities have benefited from the existence of free minorities and that today unfree societies benefit from what they obtain and learn from free societies. Of course the benefits we derive from the freedom of others become greater as the number of those who can exercise freedom increases. The argument for the freedom of some therefore applies to the freedom of all. But it is still better for all that some should be free than none and also that many enjoy full freedom than that all have a restricted freedom. The significant point is that the importance of freedom to do a particular thing has nothing to do with the number of people who want to do it: it might almost be in inverse proportion. One consequence of this is that a society may be hamstrung by controls, although the great majority may not be aware that their freedom has been significantly curtailed. If we proceeded on the assumption that only the exercises of

542 F. A. Hayek

freedom that the majority will practice are important, we would be certain to create a stagnant society with all the characteristics of unfreedom.

6. The undesigned novelties that constantly emerge in the process of adaptation will consist, first, of new arrangements or patterns in which the efforts of different individuals are co-ordinated and of new constellations in the use of resources, which will be in their nature as temporary as the particular conditions that have evoked them. There will be, second, modifications of tools and institutions adapted to the new circumstances. Some of these will also be merely temporary adaptations to the conditions of the moment, while others will be improvements that increase the versatility of the existing tools and usages and will therefore be retained. These latter will constitute a better adaptation not merely to the particular circumstances of time and place but to some permanent feature of our environment. In such spontaneous "formations"[15] is embodied a perception of the general laws that govern nature. With this cumulative embodiment of experience in tools and forms of action will emerge a growth of explicit knowledge, of formulated generic rules that can be communicated by language from person to person.

This process by which the new emerges is best understood in the intellectual sphere when the results are new ideas. It is the field in which most of us are aware at least of some of the individual steps of the process, where we necessarily know what is happening and thus generally recognize the necessity of freedom. Most scientists realize that we cannot plan the advance of knowledge, that in the voyage into the unknown—which is what research is—we are in great measure dependent on the vagaries of individual genius and of circumstance, and that scientific advance, like a new idea that will spring up in a single mind, will be the result of a combination of conceptions, habits, and circumstances brought to one person by society, the result as much of lucky accidents as of systematic effort.

Because we are more aware that our advances in the intellectual sphere often spring from the unforeseen and undesigned, we tend to overstress the importance of freedom in this field and to ignore the importance of the freedom of *doing* things. But the freedom of research and belief and the freedom of speech and discussion, the importance of which is widely understood, are significant only in the last stage of the process in which new truths are discovered. To extol the value of intellectual liberty at the expense of the value of the liberty of doing things would be like treating the crowning part of an edifice as the whole. We have new ideas to discuss, different views to adjust, because those ideas and views arise from the efforts of individuals in ever new circumstances, who avail themselves in their concrete tasks of the new tools and forms of action they have learned.

The non-intellectual part of this process—the formation of the changed material environment in which the new emerges—requires for its understanding and appreciation a much greater effort of imagination than the factors stressed by the intellectualist view. While we are sometimes able to trace the intellectual processes that have led to a new idea, we can scarcely ever reconstruct the sequence and combination of those contributions that have not led to the acquisition of explicit knowledge; we can scarcely ever reconstruct the favorable habits and skills employed, the

Conclusion **543**

facilities and opportunities used, and the particular environment of the main actors that has favored the result. Our efforts toward understanding this part of the process can go little further than to show on simplified models the kind of forces at work and to point to the general principle rather than the specific character of the influences that operate.[16] Men are always concerned only with what they know. Therefore, those features which, while the process is under way, are not consciously known to anybody are commonly disregarded and can perhaps never be traced in detail.

In fact, these unconscious features not only are commonly disregarded but are often treated as if they were a hindrance rather than a help or an essential condition. Because they are not "rational" in the sense of explicitly entering into our reasoning, they are often treated as irrational in the sense of being contrary to intelligent action. Yet, though much of the non-rational that affects our action may be irrational in this sense, many of the "mere habits" and "meaningless institutions" that we use and presuppose in our actions are essential conditions for what we achieve; they are successful adaptations of society that are constantly improved and on which depends the range of what we can achieve. While it is important to discover their defects, we could not for a moment go on without constantly relying on them.

The manner in which we have learned to order our day, to dress, to eat, to arrange our houses, to speak and write, and to use the countless other tools and implements of civilization, no less than the "know-how" of production and trade, furnishes us constantly with the foundations on which our own contributions to the process of civilization must be based. And it is in the new use and improvement of whatever the facilities of civilization offer us that the new ideas arise that are ultimately handled in the intellectual sphere. Though the conscious manipulation of abstract thought, once it has been set in train, has in some measure a life of its own, it would not long continue and develop without the constant challenges that arise from the ability of people to act in a new manner, to try new ways of doing things, and to alter the whole structure of civilization in adaptation to change. The intellectual process is in effect only a process of elaboration, selection, and elimination of ideas already formed. And the flow of new ideas, to a great extent, springs from the sphere in which action, often non-rational action, and material events impinge upon each other. It would dry up if freedom were confined to the intellectual sphere.

The importance of freedom, therefore, does not depend on the elevated character of the activities it makes possible. Freedom of action, even in humble things, is as important as freedom of thought. It has become a common practice to disparage freedom of action by calling it "economic liberty."[17] But the concept of freedom of action is much wider than that of economic liberty, which it includes; and, what is more important, it is very questionable whether there are any actions which can be called merely "economic" and whether any restrictions on liberty can be confined to what are called merely "economic" aspects. Economic considerations are merely those by which we reconcile and adjust our different purposes, none of which, in the last resort, are economic (excepting those of the miser or the man for whom making money has become an end in itself).[18]

544 F. A. Hayek

7. Most of what we have said so far applies not only to man's use of the means for the achievement of his ends but also to those ends themselves. It is one of the characteristics of a free society that men's goals are open,[19] that new ends of conscious effort can spring up, first with a few individuals, to become in time the ends of most. It is a fact which we must recognize that even what we regard as good or beautiful is changeable—if not in any recognizable manner that would entitle us to take a relativistic position, then in the sense that in many respects we do not know what will appear as good or beautiful to another generation. Nor do we know why we regard this or that as good or who is right when people differ as to whether something is good or not. It is not only in his knowledge, but also in his aims and values, that man is the creature of civilization; in the last resort, it is the relevance of these individual wishes to the perpetuation of the group or the species that will determine whether they will persist or change. It is, of course, a mistake to believe that we can draw conclusions about what our values ought to be simply because we realize that they are a product of evolution. But we cannot reasonably doubt that these values are created and altered by the same evolutionary forces that have produced our intelligence. All that we can know is that the ultimate decision about what is good or bad will be made not by individual human wisdom but by the decline of the groups that have adhered to the "wrong" beliefs.

It is in the pursuit of man's aims of the moment that all the devices of civilization have to prove themselves; the ineffective will be discarded and the effective retained. But there is more to it than the fact that new ends constantly arise with the satisfaction of old needs and with the appearance of new opportunities. Which individuals and which groups succeed and continue to exist depends as much on the goals that they pursue, the values that govern their action, as on the tools and capacities at their command. Whether a group will prosper or be extinguished depends as much on the ethical code it obeys, or the ideals of beauty or well-being that guide it, as on the degree to which it has learned or not learned to satisfy its material needs. Within any given society, particular groups may rise or decline according to the ends they pursue and the standards of conduct that they observe. And the ends of the successful group will tend to become the ends of all members of the society.

At most, we understand only partially why the values we hold or the ethical rules we observe are conducive to the continued existence of our society. Nor can we be sure that under constantly changing conditions all the rules that have proved to be conducive to the attainment of a certain end will remain so. Though there is a presumption that any established social standard contributes in some manner to the preservation of civilization, our only way of confirming this is to ascertain whether it continues to prove itself in competition with other standards observed by other individuals or groups.

8. The competition on which the process of selection rests must be understood in the widest sense. It involves competition between organized and unorganized groups no less than competition between individuals. To think of it in contrast to cooperation or organization would be to misconceive its nature. The endeavor to achieve certain results by co-operation and organization is as much a part of

competition as individual efforts. Successful group relations also prove their effectiveness in competition among groups organized in different ways. The relevant distinction is not between individual and group action but between conditions, on the one hand, in which alternative ways based on different views or practices may be tried and conditions, on the other, in which one agency has the exclusive right and the power to prevent others from trying. It is only when such exclusive rights are conferred on the presumption of superior knowledge of particular individuals or groups that the process ceases to be experimental and beliefs that happen to be prevalent at a given time may become an obstacle to the advancement of knowledge.

The argument for liberty is not an argument against organization, which is one of the most powerful means that human reason can employ, but an argument against all exclusive, privileged, monopolistic organization, against the use of coercion to prevent others from trying to do better. Every organization is based on given knowledge; organization means commitment to a particular aim and to particular methods, but even organization designed to increase knowledge will be effective only insofar as the knowledge and beliefs on which its design rests are true. And if any facts contradict the beliefs on which the structure of the organization is based, this will become evident only in its failure and supersession by a different type of organization. Organization is therefore likely to be beneficial and effective so long as it is voluntary and is imbedded in a free sphere and will either have to adjust itself to circumstances not taken into account in its conception or fail. To turn the whole of society into a single organization built and directed according to a single plan would be to extinguish the very forces that shaped the individual human minds that planned it.

It is worth our while to consider for a moment what would happen if only what was agreed to be the best available knowledge were to be used in all action. If all attempts that seemed wasteful in the light of generally accepted knowledge were prohibited and only such questions asked, or such experiments tried, as seemed significant in the light of ruling opinion, mankind might well reach a point where its knowledge enabled it to predict the consequences of all conventional actions and to avoid all disappointment or failure. Man would then seem to have subjected his surroundings to his reason, for he would attempt only those things which were totally predictable in their results. We might conceive of a civilization coming to a standstill, not because the possibilities of further growth had been exhausted, but because man had succeeded in so completely subjecting all his actions and his immediate surroundings to his existing state of knowledge that there would be no occasion for new knowledge to appear.

9. The rationalist who desires to subject everything to human reason is thus faced with a real dilemma. The use of reason aims at control and predictability. But the process of the advance of reason rests on freedom and the unpredictability of human action. Those who extol the powers of human reason usually see only one side of that interaction of human thought and conduct in which reason is at the same time used and shaped. They do not see that, for advance to take place, the

546 F. A. Hayek

social process from which the growth of reason emerges must remain free from its control.

There can be little doubt that man owes some of his greatest successes in the past to the fact that he has *not* been able to control social life. His continued advance may well depend on his deliberately refraining from exercising controls which are now in his power. In the past, the spontaneous forces of growth, however much restricted, could usually still assert themselves against the organized coercion of the state. With the technological means of control now at the disposal of government, it is not certain that such assertion is still possible; at any rate, it may soon become impossible. We are not far from the point where the deliberately organized forces of society may destroy those spontaneous forces which have made advance possible.

Notes

The quotation at the head of the chapter is taken from Alfred North Whitehead, *An Introduction to Mathematics* (London: Williams and Norgate, 1911), p. 61. An earlier version of this chapter appeared as "The Creative Powers of a Free Civilization," in *Essays on Individuality*, Felix Morley, ed. (Philadelphia: University of Pennsylvania Press, 1958), pp. 183–204 [Liberty Fund edition, pp. 261–89].

1 Cf. Adam Ferguson, *An Essay on the History of Civil Society* (Edinburgh: Printed for A. Millar and T. Caddel in the Strand, and A. Kincaid and J. Bell, Edinburgh, 1767), p. 279: "The artifices of the beaver, the ant, and the bee, are ascribed to the wisdom of nature. Those of polished nations are ascribed to themselves, and are supposed to indicate a capacity superior to that of rude minds. But the establishments of men, like those of every animal, are suggested by nature, and are the result of instinct, directed by the variety of situations in which mankind are placed. Those establishments arose from successive improvements that were made, without any sense of their general effect; and they bring human affairs to a state of complication, which the greatest reach of capacity with which human nature was ever adorned, could not have projected; nor even when the whole is carried into execution, can it be comprehended in its full extent."

2 Cf. Michael Polanyi, *The Logic of Liberty: Reflections and Rejoinders* (London: Routledge and Kegan Paul, 1951), p. 199 [Liberty Fund edition, p. 245]: "The conceptions by the light of which men will judge our own ideas in a thousand years—or perhaps even in fifty years—are beyond our guess. If a library of the year 3000 came into our hands today, we could not understand its contents. How should we consciously determine a future which is, by its very nature, beyond our comprehension? Such presumption reveals only the narrowness of an outlook uninformed by humility."

3 Leslie Alvin White, "Man's Control over Civilization: An Anthropocentric Illusion," *Scientific Monthly*, 66 (1948): 238; also his *The Science of Culture: A Study of Man and Civilization* (New York: Farrar, Straus, and Co., 1949), pp. 337 and 342.

4 See Gilbert Ryle, "Knowing How and Knowing That," [The Presidential Address] *Proceedings of the Aristotelian Society*, n.s., 46 (1946): 1–16; and now compare also Michael Polanyi, *Personal Knowledge: Towards a Post-critical Philosophy* (Chicago: University of Chicago Press, 1958).

5 Cf. the often quoted observation by Frank Plumpton Ramsey, *The Foundations of Mathematics and Other Logical Essays* (London: Routledge and Kegan Paul, 1931), p. 287: "There is nothing to know except science." [The statement does not appear in *The Foundations of Mathematics*, as Hayek indicates, but in the Epilogue to Ramsey's collected essays, of which *The Foundations* is the central article and which gives its name to the anthology.—Ed.]

6 On these different kinds of knowledge see my article "Über den 'Sinn' sozialer Institutionen" [On the Meaning of Social Institutions], *Schweizer Monatshefte*, October 1956, pp. 512–24, and, on the application of the whole argument of this chapter to the more specifically economic problems, the two essays on "Economics and Knowledge" and "The Use of Knowledge in Society" reprinted in my *Individualism and Economic Order* (Chicago: University of Chicago Press, 1948), pp. 33–56 and 77–91. See also Samuel Johnson's remark: "Knowledge is of two kinds: we know a subject ourselves or we know where we can find information upon it." (James Boswell, *The Life of Samuel Johnson, LL.D.: Comprehending an Account of His Studies and Numerous Works* [3 vols.; 2nd ed., rev. and aug.; London: Printed by Henry Baldwin, 1793], vol. 2, pp. 237–38).

7 Giorgio de Santillana, *The Crime of Galileo* (Chicago: University of Chicago Press, 1955), pp. 34–35. Herbert Spencer also remarks somewhere: "In science the more we know, the more extensive the contact with nescience." [The quotation, as Hayek has it, is somewhat different from that written by Spencer. The wording as quoted by Hayek, in fact comes from the article on Herbert Spencer in the eleventh edition of the *Encyclopedia Britannica* (New York: The Encyclopedia Britannica Co., 1911) s.v. "Spencer, Herbert" by Ferdinand Canning Scott Schiller. Spencer's actual wording reads: "Regarding Science as a gradually increasing sphere, we may say that every addition to its surface does but bring it into wider contact with surrounding nescience." (*First Principles* [London: Williams and Norgate, 1862], pp. 16–17.)—Ed.]. See also Sir Karl Raimund Popper, "On the Sources of Knowledge and Ignorance," *Proceedings of the British Academy*, 46 (1960): 69: "The more we learn about the world, and the deeper our learning, the more conscious, specific, and articulate will be our knowledge of what we do not know, our knowledge of our ignorance"; and Warren Weaver, "A Scientist Ponders Faith," *Saturday Review*, 3 (January 1959): 9: "[is] science really gaining in its assault on the totality of the unsolved? As science learns one answer, it is characteristically true that it also learns several new questions. It is as though science were working in a great forest of ignorance, making an ever larger circular clearing within which, not to insist on the pun, things are clear. ... But as that circle becomes larger and larger, the circumference of contact with ignorance also gets longer and longer. Science learns more and more. But there is an ultimate sense in which it does not gain; for the volume of the appreciated but not understood keeps getting larger. We keep, in science, getting a more and more sophisticated view of our essential ignorance."

8 Cf. Homer Garner Barnett, *Innovation: The Basis of Cultural Change* (New York: McGraw-Hill, 1953): "Every individual is an innovator many times over" (p. 19) and "There is a positive correlation between individualism and innovative potential. The greater the freedom of the individual to explore his world of experience and to organize its elements in accordance with his private interpretation of his sense impressions, the greater the likelihood of new ideas coming into being" (p. 65).

9 Cf. Sir William Arthur Lewis, *The Theory of Economic Growth* (London: Allen and Unwin, 1955), p. 148: "These innovators are always a minority. New ideas are first put into practice by one or two or very few persons, whether they be new ideas in technology, or new forms of organization, new commodities, or other novelties. These ideas may be accepted rapidly by the rest of the population. More probably they are received with scepticism and unbelief, and make their way only very slowly at first if at all. After a while the new ideas are seen to be successful, and are then accepted by increasing numbers. Thus it is often said that change is the work of an elite, or that the amount of change depends on the quality of leadership in a community. This is true enough if it implies no more than that the majority of people are not innovators, but merely imitate what others do. It is, however, somewhat misleading if it is taken to imply that some specific class or group of people get all the new ideas." Also p. 172: "Collective judgement of new ideas is so often wrong that it is arguable that progress depends on individuals being free to back their own judgement despite collective disapproval. ... To give a monopoly of decision to a government committee would seem to have the disadvantage of both worlds."

548 F. A. Hayek

10 One of the few authors who have seen clearly at least part of this was Frederic William Maitland, who stresses (*The Collected Papers of Frederic William Maitland, Downing Professor of the Laws of England* [3 vols.; Cambridge: Cambridge University Press, 1911], vol. 1, p. 107) that "the most powerful argument is that based on the ignorance, the necessary ignorance, of our rulers." [Maitland's quotation appears in *A Historical Sketch of Liberty and Equality*, Liberty Fund edition, p. 133.—Ed.] See, however, Bennett E. Kline and Norman H. Martin, "Freedom, Authority, and Decentralization," *Harvard Business Review*, 36 (1958), esp. 70: "the chief characteristic of the command hierarchy, or any group in our society, is not knowledge but ignorance. Consider that any one person can know only a fraction of what is going on around him. Much of what that person knows or believes will be false rather than true. ... At any given time, vastly more is not known than is known, either by one person in a command chain or by all the organization. It seems possible, then, that in organizing ourselves into a hierarchy of authority for the purpose of increasing efficiency, we may really be institutionalizing ignorance. While making better use of what the few know, we are making sure that the great majority are prevented from exploring the dark areas beyond our knowledge." See also William Graham Sumner, "Speculative Legislation," *The Challenge of Facts and Other Papers* (New Haven: Yale University Press, 1914), p. 215: "It is characteristic of speculative legislation that it very generally produces the exact opposite of the result it was hoped to get from it. The reason is that the elements of any social problem which we do not know so far exceed those which we do know, that our solutions have a greater chance to be wrong than right."

There is one important respect in which the term "ignorance" is somewhat too narrow for our purposes. There are occasions when it would probably be better to speak of "uncertainty" with reference to ignorance concerning what is right, since it is doubtful whether we can meaningfully speak about something being right if nobody knows what is right in the particular context. The fact in such instances may be that the existing morals provide no answer to a problem, though there might be some answer which, if it were known and widely accepted, would be very valuable. I am much indebted to Mr. Pierre F. Goodrich, whose comment during a discussion helped to clarify this important point for me, though I have not been persuaded to speak generally of "imperfection" where I stress ignorance.

11 Cf. John Archibald Wheeler, "A Septet of Sibyls: Aids in the Search for Truth," *American Scientist*, 44 (1956): 360: "Our whole problem is to make the mistakes as fast as possible."

12 Cf. the remark of Louis Pasteur: "In research, chance only helps those whose minds are well prepared for it," quoted by René Taton, *Reason and Chance in Scientific Discovery* (London: Hutchinson, 1957), p. 91. [Pasteur appears to have originally made the statement in a lecture at the University of Lille on December 7, 1854. The original reads: "Dans les champs de l'observation le hasard ne favorise que les esprits préparés."—Ed.]

13 Cf. Abba Ptachya Lerner, "The Backward-leaning Approach to Controls," *Journal of Political Economy*, 65 (1957): 441: "The free-trade doctrines are valid as *general rules* whose general use is generally beneficial. As with all general rules, there are particular cases where, if one knew all the attendant circumstances and the full effects in all their ramifications, it would be better for the rule not to be applied. But that does not make the rule a bad rule or give reason for not applying the rule where, as is normally the case, one does not know all the ramifications that would make the case a desirable exception."

14 Cf. Rev. Hastings Rashdall, "The Philosophical Theory of Property," in *Property; Its Duties and Rights: Historically, Philosophically, and Religiously Regarded*, Charles Gore and Leonard Trelawney Hobhouse, eds. (new ed.; New York: Macmillan, 1915), pp. 61–62: "The plea for liberty is not sufficiently met by insisting, as has been so eloquently and humorously done by Mr. Lowes Dickinson (*Justice and Liberty: A Political Dialogue*, e.g. pp. 129 and 131), upon the absurdity of supposing that the propertyless labourer under the ordinary capitalistic regime enjoys any liberty of which Socialism would deprive him. For it may be of extreme importance that *some* should enjoy liberty—that it should be

Conclusion **549**

possible for some few men to be able to dispose of their time in their own way—although such liberty may be neither possible nor desirable for the great majority. That culture requires a considerable differentiation in social conditions is also a principle of unquestionable importance." [The full citation of the book quoted by Rashdall is: Goldsworthy Lowes Dickinson, *Justice and Liberty: A Political Dialogue* (London: J. M. Dent, 1908).—Ed.] See also Bennett E. Kline and Norman H. Martin, "Freedom, Authority, and Decentralization," p. 69: "If there is to be freedom for the few who *will* take advantage of it, freedom must be offered to the many. If any lesson is clear from history, it is this."

15 For the use of the term "formation," more appropriate in this connection than the usual "institution," see my study on *The Counter-Revolution of Science: Studies on the Abuse of Reason* (Glencoe, IL: Free Press, 1952), p. 83. [*Collected Works* edition, vol. 13, p. 145.] [Hayek there writes of human institutions: "Though in a sense man-made, i.e., entirely the result of human actions, they may yet not be designed, not be the intended product of these actions. The term 'institution' itself is rather misleading in this respect, as it suggests something deliberately instituted. It would probably be better if this term were confined to particular contrivances, like particular laws and organizations, which have been created for a specific purpose, and if a more neutral term like 'formations' (in a sense similar to that in which the geologists use it, and corresponding to the German *Gebilde*) could be used for those phenomena, which, like money or language, have not been so created."—Ed.]

16 Cf. my article "Degrees of Explanation," *British Journal for the Philosophy of Science*, 6 (1955): 209–25, reprinted in *Studies in Philosophy, Politics, and Economics* (Chicago: University of Chicago Press, 1967), pp. 3–21 [Also reprinted in *Studies in Philosophy, Politics, and Economics*, pp. 22–42.—Ed.], and my "The Theory of Complex Phenomena," in *The Critical Approach to Science and Philosophy: Essays in Honor of Karl R. Popper*, Mario Augusto Bunge, ed. (New York: Free Press of Glencoe, 1964), pp. 332–49.

17 See Aaron Director, "The Parity of the Economic Market Place," in *Conference on Freedom and the Law, May 7, 1953: Fiftieth Anniversary Celebration*, Thuman Welsey Arnold, et al. (University of Chicago Law School Conference Series, no. 13, Chicago: University of Chicago Press, 1953), pp. 16–25.

18 Cf. my book *The Road to Serfdom* (Chicago: University of Chicago Press, 1944), chap. 7, pp. 88–100; reprinted as vol. 2 of *The Collected Works of F. A. Hayek*, Bruce Caldwell, ed. (Chicago: University of Chicago Press, 2007), pp. 124–33.

19 See Sir Karl Raimund Popper, *The Open Society and Its Enemies* (American ed.; Princeton: Princeton University Press, 1950), esp. p. 195: "If we wish to remain human, there is only one way, the way into the open society. We must go into the unknown, the uncertain and insecure, using what reason we may have to plan for both, security *and* freedom."

BIBLIOGRAPHY

Part I – Motivation: a pluralistic approach to entrepreneurship research

Simon, H. A. 1996. Understanding the Natural and the Artificial Worlds. *The Sciences of the Artificial. Third edition. Cambridge and London: MIT Press.* pp. 1–23.

Davidson, D. 2001. Three varieties of knowledge, *Subjective, Intersubjective, Objective*: 205–220. New York: Oxford University Press Incorporated.

Buchanan, J. M., & Vanberg, V. J. 1991. The Market as a Creative Process. *Economics and Philosophy*, 7: 167–186.

Part II – Maker: entrepreneurial agency

Todd, P. M., & Gigerenzer, G. 2003. Bounding rationality to the world. *Journal of Economic Psychology*, 24(2): 143–165.

Lakoff, G., & Johnson, M. 2000. The embodied mind. *Philosophy in the Flesh: The Embodied Mind and Its Challenge to Western Thought*: New York: Basic Books. pp. 16–44.

Slovic, P. 1995. The construction of preference. *American Psychologist*, 50: 364–371.

March, J. G. 1982. The technology of foolishness. In J. G. a. J. P. O. March (Ed.), *Ambiguity and choice in organizations*: 69–81. Bergen, Norway: Universitetsforlaget.

James, W. 1880. Great Men, Great Thoughts, and the Environment. *The Atlantic Monthly*, October 1880.

Part III – Making: entrepreneurial process

Goodman, N. 1978. Words, works, worlds. *Ways of Worldmaking*: 1–22. Indianapolis Lancaster: Hackett Publishing Company Incorporated Gazelle Book Services Limited Distributor.

Hayek, F. A. 1978. Competition as a discovery procedure. *The market and other orders: The collected works of F. A. Hayek.* Chicago: U Chicago Press. pp. 304–313.

Bruner, J. 1986. The transactional self. *Actual Minds, Possible Worlds.* Harvard University Press. pp. 57–69.

Gould, S. J., & Lewontin, R. C. 1979. The spandrels of San Marco and the panglossian paradigm: A critique of the adaptationist programme. *Proceedings of the Royal Society of London*, 205(1161): 581–598.

Boudreaux, D.J. & Holcombe, R. G. 1989. The Coasian and Knightian Theories of the Firm. *Managerial and Decision Economics*, 10: 147–154

Part IV – Made: entrepreneurial outcomes

Simon, J. L. 1996. Introduction. *The State of Humanity*: 1–28. Malden: Blackwell Publishing Incorporated.

Simon, J. L. 1996. What Does the Future Hold? The Forecast in a Nutshell. *The State of Humanity*: 641–660. Malden: Blackwell Publishing Incorporated.

Sen, A. 1999. The Possibility of Social Choice. *The American Economic Review*, 89(3): 349–378.

De Soto, H. 2000. By Way of Conclusion. *The Mystery of Capital: Why Capitalism Triumphs In The West And Fails Everywhere Else.* New York: Basic Books. Chapter 7. pp. 207–228.

Ostrom, E. 2010. Beyond markets and states: polycentric governance of complex economic systems. *The American Economic Review*, 100(3), 641–672.

Gerschenkron, A. 1962. Social attitudes, entrepreneurship and economic development. *Economic Backwardness in Historical Perspective*. Belknap (Harvard University) Press

Part V – Method: studying entrepreneurship as a three-legged artifact

Simon, H. A. 1998. Economics as a historical science. *Theoria*, 13.(32): 241–260.

Pearl, J. 2000. The art and science of cause and effect, *Causality: Models, Reasoning, and Inference*: 331–358. Toronto: Cambridge University Press.

Lakoff, G., & Johnson, M. 1980. Conceptual metaphor in everyday language. *The Journal of Philosophy*, 77(8): 452–486.

Rorty, R. 1989. The contingency of language; & The contingency of selfhood. *Contingency, Irony, and Solidarity*. Cambridge: Cambridge University Press. pp. 3–9; 19–22; 23–29.

James, W. 1907. Lecture II: What Pragmatism Means. *Pragmatism: A new name for some old ways of thinking*: Project Gutenberg.

Conclusion

Hayek, F. A. 1960. Creative Powers of a Free Civilization. *The Constitution of Liberty*. The University of Chicago Press. pp. 22–38.

INDEX

Page numbers in **bold** denote tables, those in *italics* denote figures.

absolute gap 266
Absolute means 531, 532
Absolute of transcendental idealism 530,
    531
absolute progress 291
Absolute true 531
abstraction theory: inadequacies of 493–4
abstract objects: computer as 28–9
abstract proposition 133
abstract rationality 32–3
accepted scientific procedures, advantages
    of 186
acid rain 270–1
action 121
action situations 378, *378*
Adam 447
adaptation 32, 190; decoupling of 165; in
    evolutionary theories 161–5; and
    selection 164
adaptationist programme 207–16
adaptation process 542
adaptive systems 22, 28
adjustment problem 469–70;
    characteristics of 416; graphical solution
    of 471–2
adulthood, theory of 124
Affirming the Absolute Mind 530
agent-based models (ABMs) 360
Age of Faith 513
Age of Reason 513
aggregation rules 365
Agrawal, A. 373
agricultural land 283
agricultural research 286

AIDS case 290
air pollutants: in USA *267*, *268*
air quality: in USA *268*
Alchian, A. 226–7, 232, 233, 374
algebra: causality and 450, 465, 467
algebraic equations 416
Alice in Wonderland (Carroll) 300
Allen, Grant 140
Allen, P.M. 48, 59n5, 59n9
allocative process 57, 58
alternative evaluation, of goals 120
altruism 442–3
American subcultures 486
analog 179
Anlage of metacognition 201
anthropology 175
anticapitalism 344
anticuckoldry behaviour 212
antiglobalization 344
anti-intellectualist tendencies 524
anti-marginalisits 223
apparent metaphorical contradiction
    487–9
Aquinas, Thomas 347
architectural constraints 218
Arctic environment 21
argument for liberty 545
arguments 476–7
Aristotle 18, 299, 316n3, 438, 449, 512,
    519, 523
Arnold, G. 367
Arrow, K.J. 234n6, 376; classical utilitarian
    approach 307; impossibility theorem
    300–4, 306–7; interpersonal comparison

of utilities 305; neutrality component 318n16; unrestricted domain 304; welfare economics 302

art and science of cause and effect: Pearl, J. 414–17

Arthashastra (Kautilya) 316n3

artifact: computer as 28–31; as interface 20–1

artifactual science 8

artifice: description of 23

artificial intelligence 33n2

artificial science 4, 19–20; see also natural science

artificial systems 28

aspectual concepts 99, 102

asymmetry 124

attitude 39

autonomy 460

Axelrod, R. 376; in social dilemmas 361–8

Aztec cannibalism 207

Aztec cosmology 207

Baconian method 147

Bagehot, W. 540

Bailey, D.: learning verbs of hand motion 100–1

balanced growth 399

Barash, D.P. 211, 212

Barnett, H.G. 547n8

Barry, N. 55

basic-level categories 89, 90–2; body-based properties of 89–90

basic price theory 54

Baumol, W. 247, 301

Bauplan 217, 218

Bayesian adaptive rationality 49

Bazerman, M.H. 160

behavings bear 515

belief 10, 38, 41, 43, 44, 527, 532, 542, 545; forecast 280–1, 296; in progress 293

Belinski, V.G. 388

Benjamin, P. 371

Bennett, A. 401

Bentham, J. 105, 301

Berg, J. 108

Bergson, Abram 302

Berkeley, G. 175, 523

Berlin, B. 89

Bernard, Claude 189

"biased" entrepreneurs 68

biases 68

Bible 447

Big Bang 430

"Biometrika" 456

Birdsall, Nancy 344

Bisol, P.M. 209, 211

Black Death 290

Black, Duncan 304

black markets 296

blind impress 515–18

Bloom, Harold 512, 515, 518, 519, 519n7, 520n9

Blumenberg, Hans 421, 513, 514

Boden, Margaret 348

bodily movement concepts 99, 101

bodily projections 95–6

body: and brain to shape reason 80–1; in the mind 102–3

Borda, J.C. 299, 301

boredom 272

Bostic, R. 109

Boudreaux, D.J.: Coasian and Knightian firm 165–8

Boulding, K. 55

boundary conditions 464

boundary rules 365

boundedly rational individuals 374, 375

bounded rationality 66–9, 75, 105

Braudel, F. 240

Bray, D.B. 381

broader contexts of social dilemmas *375*, 376

broader social-ecological systems 378, *378*

Brockington, D. 381

Brooks, J.S. 380

Brown, Ann 201

Bruner, J. 175, 423; culture 160; egocentric and structural views of social psychology 158–61; transactional self 159, 160

Buchanan, J.M. 2, 5, 54, 61n29, 155–7, 234n10, 241, 246, 247, 294, 314, 357, 422; market as creative process 13–15; market process 167

"building-block" theory 496–7

"bundling" strategy 164

Cannon, Walter B. 189

Cantillon, Richard 65

capital: de Soto, H. 244–7; investment 436–7

capitalism 340–2, 402; and culture 350–1; enemies of 348–9; Marx, Karl 343–6; property and 346–8; property rights systems 350–1

Cardenas, J. -C. 370

Carter, Jimmy 501, 502

Cassirer, Ernst 172–5

"Castle of Knowledge," The (Recordes) 449

554 Index

catastrophic disease, likelihood of 289–90; characteristics of 290; growing ability 290–1
categorization of neural beings 81–2
causal calculus: derivation in 469; rules of 467–8
causal connection 452
causal inference 456
causal intervention 414
causality 415
causal-link model 468–9
causal model: equational model *vs.* 465
causation 497; fuzzy boundaries 498; prototype of 498
cause and effect 446–7, 473; adjustment problem 469–72; algebra 450, 465, 467; in ancient world 447–8; archaic category of 455; art and science of 414–17; causal calculus 467–8; causal connection 452; causal forces 448; causal-link model 468–9; circuit diagram 459–61; contingency table 455; controlled experiment over uncontrolled studies 462–3; correlation 454, 457; deep understanding 460–1; directionality of 464–5; dual role of 449; engineering and 448–9; engineering drawing 459–60; equational and causal models 465; equations *vs.* diagrams 461–2; Galileo's maxims 449–50; in human development 447; Hume's view on 451–2, 458; importance of causality 453; laws of physics 450–1; as man-made concept 447; model of intervention 462–3; physical equations 464; policy analysis 463–4; probability theory 466–7; reverse regression 471; Russell on 452, 454, 458; scientific activity 465–6; Simpson's paradox 470; spurious correlations 452; statisticians view on 456–7; teaching robot 458; testing for 472; using computers 457–9
Celtic race 131
Cerion 216
challenges 293–5
Change and the Entrepreneur (Cole) 395
change phenomena 410, 411
cheap talk 369, 371
Cherry Orchard (Chekhov) 398
Chhatre, A. 373
child mortality *262*, 288
China 291
choice 111–13; and rationality 120–2
choice rules 365
Chomsky, Noam 198

Christianity 518
Chu, R. 108
Churchill, Winston 281
Chu, Y. 108
circumscription 415; in economics 465
civilization: adaptation process 542; competition 544–5; conception of man 535; ethical code 544; freedom 540–3; growth 536–7; human reason 545–6; ignorance 50, 534–7, 539, 540; intellectual processes 542–3; knowledge and 534–45; liberty 539, 540, 542, 543, 545
Clapham, J.H. 431
Clark, Lindley H. 282
classical utilitarian approach 307
classic justifications 123
Cleopatra's nose approach 412, 413
Cleopatra's nose principle 432, 438
club goods 357, 358
Coase, R.H. 222–33, 347; concept of the firm 165–6, 223–5, 231, 232; criticisms of Knight's theory 231; model 228
Cochran, T.C. 395, 396
coercion 126
cognitive illusions 67
cognitive science 81, 417
Cole, A. 393, 395
Coleman, E.A. 373
Coles, Alice 77
collective action theory 376
Collingwood, R.G. 45
color 86–8
color concepts 85–8, 97
common pool resources (CPRs) 357–8, 362, 363; broader context in the field 378–9; bundles of property rights 364–5; meta-analyses of 363–4; policies for governance 380–1; polycentric governance of 248–9; in university laboratories 368–70
common pool resources (CPRs) dilemmas 364; complexity and reform 379–81; current theoretical developments 373–8; general theory of individual 374–6; microsituational level of analysis 377–8; public policy analysis 381; role of trust in coping with 376–7; solving 379–81
common pool resources (CPRs) problems study: experiments in university laboratories 368–70; in field experiments 370–1; forests around the world 372–3; irrigation systems in Nepal 371–2
common property resource 364
Commons, J.R. 365

Index 555

communication 38–41, 44, 288, 377, 476, 479
communities 137
comparative statics 431; of economics analysis 432; neoclassical 432; non-maximizing model 433; other examples of 434; two-industry model 432–3
compatibility hypothesis 110–11
competition 422, 544–5; as discovery procedure 156–8, 185–93
competitive economy 54
competitive price system 224
complex human systems 355; polycentric public industries 356–7; types of goods 357–9
composition 154
computational neural model 97
computational powers 440
computer: as abstract objects 28–9; as empirical objects 29–30; and thought 30–1
computer programs 30
computer reliability 29
conception 97, 98
concepts 83, 84, 475–7
conceptual inference 83, 84
conceptualizing categories 83
conceptual metaphor 419, 420; Johnson, M. 417–20; Lakoff, G. 417–20
conceptual models 186
conceptual structuring 83, 494–6
conceptual system: grounding of 494–6
conceptual systems 96
conditions of life 280, 292–3
Condorcet, Marquis de 300, 301
conduit metaphor 479–81
Congo, The (Lindsay) 181
conscious knowledge 536, 537
conservation of energy 527
constancy 176
constitutiveness of language 200
construction of preferences 71–2
construction technology 285
constructive theory 116
container schema 92–3
containers metaphor 420
contemplation 516
contemporary American society 127
contemporary theories 130
contemporary theory of firm 226–8, 232
contingency of language: French Revolution 505, 509; intrinsic nature 509, 513; metaphors 510–12; philosophy 505, 506, 509, 510, 512, 515, 516, 519; process of spirit 508–9; recognition of

510; Rorty, R. 409; truth and 505–9, 512, 513; vocabularies 507–13; world and 506–8, 513
contingency of selfhood 514–19; blind impress 515–18; recognition 516; Rorty, R. 420–4; truth and 517, 518
contingency table 455
contingent valuation (CV) method 114–15
conventional decision theory 128
conventional metaphors 417, 418, 475, 481–2, 490, 493, 494, 498, 503
Copernican revolution 196
Copernican Revolution, The (Kuhn) 508
Corculum cardissa 219
correlation 454, 456; causal conclusions and 457; contingency and 457
correspondence theory of truth 88, 509
cosmology (alias astrophysics) 429–30
Costa, R. 209, 211
countless worlds 172
covariate selection problem *see* adjustment problem
Cowles Commission for Research in Economics 435
Cox, David 456
Cox, M. 367
CPRs *see* common pool resources (CPRs)
CPRs dilemmas *see* common pool resources (CPRs) dilemmas
CPRs problems study *see* common pool resources (CPRs) problems study
creative destruction 5, 396, 410, 421–2
creative process 57, 58; markets as 13–15
creativity 48–54
cross-sectional interpretation 52
Cueto, J. 68
cultural coherence: metaphor and 485–7
cultural differences 500–1
cultural metaphor 482–5
cultural values 485–6
culture 159–60, 201, 246, 247
CV method *see* contingent valuation (CV) method

Darwin, Charles 134–6, 162, 212, 213, 220, 454; adaptation 216; mode 216; processes 207; social evolution 76; theory 442
Das Kapital (Marx) 245
Davidson, D. 2, 70, 246, 308, 418, 421, 426, 514, 518; mental states 242; metaphors 510–11; philosophy of language 510–12; subjective-intersubjective-objective tripod of knowledge 70; three varieties of knowledge 4–5, 10–13

556 Index

Dawid, Philip 456
death 514
"de-biasing" approach 68
decision making 104–5, 114
decision-making role 166
decomposition 154
decoupling, of selection and adaptation 215
deep understanding: causality and 460–1
deforestation 381
deformation 155, 180
De la Grammatologie (Derrida) 349
deletion 155
demand 166–7
demand-pull 166
demand-side innovation 241
de Man, Paul 520n8
Demsetz, H. 226–7, 232
Dennett, Daniel 348
Derrida, J. 513, 520n9; metaphysics 520n8;
    truth 519n2
Derrida, Jacques 349
de Santillana, G. 547n7
Descartes 451, 464
description invariance 105–6
design hypothesis 160
design objective 25
design principle 367–8, 382n5
desires 43–4
de Soto, H. 237, 239, 240, 252, 423, 426;
    mystery of capital 244–7; property rights
    245–7
detailed iconography 204
developmental constraints 217
developmental psychology 175
deviant behavior 395, 396
Dewey, J. 526, 528, 531
Dew, N. 74, 419
Dickhaut, J. 108
Difference Principle 308
digital system 179
disasters 292
"Discorsi" 449
discovering laws 183
discovery procedure 156; competition as
    156–8, 185–93
discovery process 57, 58
disparate cycle 135
distribution-sensitive poverty 312
distributive bargaining 161
divaricate patterns in molluscs 219
divaricate ribs 218
diverse disciplines: scholars in 363
diverse polycentric institutions 381
diversity: of human situations 359–60
doctrine of real probability 228

Dodgson, C.L. 300
dominant value systems 401
Donaldson, Margaret 202
doomsayers 280–1
doomsayers' forecasts 274
Downing, Pamela 480
Drake, Edwin L. 276

Easterlin, R
ecological rationality 66–8
economic actors 439, 441
economic change 393–6, 403; types of 259
economic development 397; of European
    countries 404; France 400;
    Gerschenkron, A. 250–3; low rate of
    400; rate of reduction in Russia 399
economic dynamics, bounded rationality
    and 437; altruism 442–3; computational
    powers 440; economic knowledge
    438–9; focus of attention 441; group
    identification 443–4; institutional setting
    440–1; knowledge and information
    439–40
economic equilibrium 188
economic historians 444
economic history 404, 438–9;
    contemporary 431–2; dynamics in
    434–7; exogenous institutional variables
    437; institutional context 435–7;
    technological change 435
economic knowledge 412
economic liberty 543
economic market theory 156
economic orthodoxy: criticism of 49
economics: invariant laws in 430–1
economics as a historical science: Simon,
    H.A. 410–13
economic shortages 288
economic system 191
economic theory 32–3; knowledge of 439
education: future growth in 288–9
educational opportunity 271–2
Edwards, W. 104–5
effective rationalization 126
effectual 13
*"Effects of Increased Productivity upon the Ratio
    of Urban to Rural Population"* 432
egocentric perspective 197, 202
egocentric view of social psychology
    158–61
Ehrlich, Paul 274
Einhorn, H. 111
elasticity 43
electorate 305
electromagnetic radiation 86

Index   **557**

elementary spatial relations 92
embodied concept 83; basic-level categories 89–92; color concepts 85–8; spatial-relations concepts 92–7
embodied mind 69–71, 98, 103; Bailey's model 100–1; body and brain to shape reason 80–1; body in the mind 102–3; conceptualizing categories 83; experience 82; inference 84–5; Narayanan's model 101–2; neural categorization 81–2; neural modeling 98–9; not as realization but as shaping 97–8; realism 84–5; Regier's model 100; spatial-relations concepts 92–7
embodied realism 87
embodiment 84–5
emergent category: example of 496–8
emergent concept 496
emergent metaphors 495
Emirbayer, M. 163
emotional experiences 495
emotional states 496
empirical knowledge 35, 37
empirical objects: computer as 29–30
empiricism 533
Encyclopaedia of the Social Sciences, The (Clapham) 431
Engerman, S. 287
engineering: causality and 448–9, 459–60
English: front-back orientation 487–9
entailment relationships 479
entailments 499
entrepreneurial activities 397–88
entrepreneurial agency: bounding rationality 66–9; construction of preferences 71–2; embodied mind 69–71; great men and evolution 74–7; technology of foolishness 72–4
entrepreneurial alertness 13, 52, 53, 60n19
entrepreneurial attention 413
entrepreneurial behavior: in France 400–1; in Germany 400–1; social sanctioning of 397; in United States 401
entrepreneurial deviance 395
entrepreneurial discovery 52
entrepreneurial judgment 230
entrepreneurial opportunities 11–14, 242, 425
entrepreneurial outcomes: capital 244–7; economic development 250–3; polycentric governance 248–9; social attitudes 250–3; social choice 241–4; *State of Humanity, The* (Simon) 238–41
entrepreneurial process 426
entrepreneurial process of making 151;

Coasian and Knightian firm 165–8; competition as discovery procedure 156–8; egocentric and structural views of social psychology 158–61; evolutionary adaptation 161–5; *Ways of Worldmaking* (Goodman) 151–6
entrepreneurial transformation 238
entrepreneurs 65, 230; French 403; and non-entrepreneurs 230; role as an innovator 395; Russia 403, 404; social attitudes 399; social roles 250, 395; value system of 398, 399; volatile group of 403
entrepreneurship 3–4, 14–15, 244; artifactual science of 8; in Coase's model 224; culture for 246–7; defining 5–6; Gerschenkron, A. 250–3; historical analyses of 251; innovation and 238; management and 231–2
entrepreneurship research 1; market as creative process 13–15; opportunity 4, 11; *Sciences of the Artificial, The* (Simon) 6–10, 12; three varieties of knowledge 4–5, 10–13
entrepreneurship study: art and science of cause and effect 414–17; conceptual metaphor 417–20; contingency of language and selfhood 420–4; economics as a historical science 410–13; opportunities as hidden objects 418–20; pragmatism means 424–7
entry or exit capabilities 377
environment 283; cleanliness of 267–9
environment as mold: artifact as "interface" 20–1; functional description and synthesis 22–5; functional explanation 21–2; limits of adaptation 25
Epicurus 514
epistemological construct 11
epistemology 306
equilibrium 222
equilibrium concept 48, 57
Eskimo vocabulary 176
essence prototypes 83
eternal truth 451
ethical code 544
ethical rules 544
Europe 291
European civilization 143
European Enlightenment 300
Evans, Gareth 198
Eve 447
evolution 68; great men and 74–7
evolutionary adaptation 161–5
evolutionary biology (alias theory of evolution) 430

558 Index

evolutionary theories: adaptation in 161–5
evolutionary view of history 145
exaptation 164–5
exchange and trade 240
exchange value 56
executive processes 198
exogenous institutional variables 437
experience 128, 130
experience as a theory 128
expert knowledge 537
explicit knowledge 536
expressions 31
extensive empirical research 379, 381
extensive forest mensuration 382n9
external rules 365–6
extinction 517

face-to-face communication experiments
369–70
failure 53, 158
Falconer, D.S. 214
false ideas 531
Fama, F. 234n5
family size 294
famine 310–12, 318n12
fear of extinction 514
fear of failure 158
Fehr, E. 370, 375
Feldman, Carol 200
Ferguson, A. 546n1
fertility 294, 295
field experiments: CPR study in 370–1
figurative language 491
Fillmore, Charles 487
finding oneself 519
Fischer, G. 113
Fishburn, P. 108
fisheries 380–1
Fisher, Ronald 456, 463, 468
fishers: public goods experiments 370
fixed-form expressions 490
Fogel, R. W 434
Foma Gordeyev (Gorki) 399
foolishness, technology of: choice and
rationality 120–2; goals, problem of
122–5; intelligence and 130; play and
reason 126–30; sensible foolishness
125–6
Ford, Henry 155
forecast: about human welfare 282–4; belief
280–1, 296; purpose and method 281–2
forest condition changes 373
forest density 372, 373
forest governance 373
forests: CPRs study 372–3

Forest, Trees and People Program at FAO
372
formal property 346–8
formal theory of evaluation 129
former Soviet Union 291
Forrester, Viviane 348–9
Foster, James 321n41
Foucault, Michel 348
France: entrepreneurial behavior in 400–1;
entrepreneurs 403; value systems 402
Franklin, W.S. 523
freedom 542, 543; benefits of 540–1
Freeman, R.E. 242
free market economics development 240–1
free market economy 343
free market system 156
French nation 141
French Revolution 299–301, 505, 509
Freud 421, 423, 514, 520n8; vocabulary
509
Friedman, M. 234n11, 295
Frohlich, N. 376
front and back concepts 95–6
front-back orientation 487–9
fully rational individuals 355
future fertility 287
future markets 13, 52
futurists 281
fuzzy boundaries 498

Galileo 416, 422, 449–50, 457; vocabulary
512, 513
Galton, F. 220, 454, 455
gambles 106–9
game theory 353, 355, 360, 368, 369
game without goods 14, 57
Gardner, Martin 282
Gardner, R. 368
Gasset, Ortega y 340
Gates, Bill 350
Geertz, Clifford 160, 200
general equilibrium concept 50, 51, 60n16
general-equilibrium framework 229, 232
general-equilibrium theory 222, 234n11
general-equilibrium tradition 223
general facts 186
genetic drift 213, 214
geology (alias geophysics) 430
Germany: economy 400; entrepreneurial
behavior in 400–1; idealism 506; rate of
industrial growth 401
Gerschenkron, A. 237–40, 247, 409, 410,
413, 426; economic development 250–3;
entrepreneurship 250–3; social attitudes
250–3

Index **559**

gestalt perception 90
gestalt structure 93
Gibson, C.C. 372
Gigerenzer, G. 67; bounding rationality 66–9
Gilder, G. 286, 287
global cooling 284
globalization, private club of 340–3
Global 2000 Report to the President 254, 255
global warming 284
Gneezy, U. 376
goals as hypotheses 128
goals, problem of 122–5
Goldstein, W. 111
Gombrich, E.H. 175, 179
Goodman, N. 151–2, 159, 160, 423, 503n2, 512; *Ways of Worldmaking* 151–6
goods 56, 57; types of 354, 357–9
Gordon, H.S. 368
Gould, S.J. 69, 164, 166, 246; adaptation in evolutionary theories 161–5
governance: forest 373; Ostrom, E. 248–9
government 354; power of 287; roles in modern economies 286
Grafton, R.Q. 380
"Grammar of Science," The (Pearson) 455
Grassé, P.P. 217
Great Depression 340, 341
great men 144; causes of production 76, 136; and evolution 74–7
Greenberg, Joseph 198
greenhouse effect 270–1
Gregory, R. 115
Grether, D.M. 107, 108
Grice, Paul 194
Griffin, D. 110
group identification 443–4
Gryzanowski, E. 143
Gutenberg, Johannes 272; printing invention 289

Hacking, Ian 511
Haeckel's biogenetic law 218
Hamer, Michael 207
Haq, Mahbub ul 309
Hardin, G. 88, 362
Hausman, D. 108
Hawkins, S. 113
Hayek, F.A. 62n33, 240, 281, 295, 314, 422; competition as discovery procedure 156–8; market process 157, 167
Hayes, J.R. 201
Hayes, T. 372
head-count measure 310
Heckscher, E. 404

Hegel 422, 506, 508, 515, 516, 520n9
Heidegger 516; metaphysics 520n8; nostalgia 513
Heider, Fritz 194
Herrnstein, R. 109
Hesse 512
Higgs, R. 286
Hirshleifer, J. 223
historical events 412
historical science 429; meaning of 429–30
"history of economic doctrine" 438
Hodgson, S. 523
Hoffrage, U. 67
Holcombe, R.G.: Coasian and Knightian firm 165–8
Hong Kong 291
Hoskins, M. 372
Howard, S. 69
human choice behavior 123
human concepts 84, 85
Human Development Report 344
human existence 287–8
human institutions 540
humanism 528
humanity 254–9, 280, 287, 288, 512, 516, 518; doomsayers' forecasts 274; human welfare, aspects of 271–3; material human welfare, path of 259–60; material trends 261–5; misery 275–7; qualifications to argument 273–4; standard of living 266–71
human life as a triumph 518
human rationality 32
human reason 84, 85, 545–6
human welfare 270; aspects of 271–3; forecast 282–4
Hume, D. 281, 295, 451–2, 458, 523
hypocrisy 128

IAD framework *see* Institutional Analysis and Development (IAD) framework
ideal-case prototypes 83
idealization 32
idea of truth 509
ideas 526
idiom 508
idiosyncratic metaphorical expressions 492
IFRI research program *see* International Forestry Resources and Institutions (IFRI) research program
ignorance 50, 534–7, 539, 540, 548n10
ignorance theory 228, 229, 234n7
Igoe, J. 381
Iliad 443
illamayor-Tomás, S. 367

560 Index

image schemas 93, 96
imagination 511; in social policy formation 130
imaginative metaphor 491
imitation 126
immortal Logic flow 147
impossibility theorem 300–4, 306–7, 315
incentives 190
inclined plane *17*
income 294, 295
income-sensitive entitlement approach 311
incommensurable cycle 135
indeterminacy of translation 42
indeterminedness 49
India 291
individual norms 375–6
individuals: coping with CPR dilemmas 378; social dilemma of 377–8
Individual Transferable Quotas (ITQs) 380–1
inductive logic 525
industrial growth: German 401
industrialization 251, 399
Industrial Revolution 271
inequalities 243
infant mortality rate *258*
inference 84–5
information: knowledge and 439–40
informational broadening: and welfare economics 305–7
information-processing concepts 110
information rules 365
informed consent 115
inner environments 7–8, 21–4, 32
innovation 166, 238, 241, 396, 401, 413; trade to 240
Institutional Analysis and Development (IAD) framework 353, 359–61, 363, 365, 368, 371, 374, 378
institutional economics 440–1
institutions 247, 538, 549n15
institutions of freedom 540
instrumental view of truth 526
integrative bargaining 161
intellectual processes 542–3
intelligence: as computation 32; and foolishness 130; tools of 122
interactional color concepts 87, 88
internal representation 86
International Encyclopedia of the Social Sciences, The (North) 431
International Forestry Resources and Institutions (IFRI) research program 372, 373
interpersonal comparisons 243–4;

informational basis of 306–10; of utility 302, 305, 306; voting-based procedures 305
interpersonal standard 40
interpretation of human behavior 121
intersubjective interactions 163
intersubjective knowledge 11, 13, 45, 66, 70, 77, 194, 246, 418
intertemporal entrepreneurial alertness 53
intertemporal interpretation 13, 52, 61n28
intrinsic intentionality 519n6
intrinsic nature 509, 513
intuition 513
invariance 105–6; failures of 109
I, Pencil (Read) 251
irrigation systems: meta analysis 363–4
Irwin, J. 114, 115
isolated metaphorical expressions 492
ITQs *see* Individual Transferable Quotas (ITQs)

James, W. 166, 172, 251, 281, 294, 409; great men and evolution 66, 74–7; pragmatism means 424–7
Jefferies, R. 217
Jenks, L.H. 395
Jensen, M. 227, 232
Jevons, Stanley 276
John, Daymond 421
Johnson, E. 111
Johnson, M. 409, 426; conceptual metaphor 417–20; embodied mind 66, 69–71
Jonah 448
journalism 292, 296
Joyce, James 174
"justice as fairness" 308

Kahneman, D. 67, 68, 75, 90, 109, 115
Kahn, H. 254, 288
Kant 174–5, 506
Kautilya 299, 316n3
Kay, Mary 252
Keynesianism 441
Keynesian theory 26
Keynes, J.M. 295, 436, 438–9
King's College Chapel, ceiling of *206*
Kirzner, I. 48, 60n21; discovery process 61n22, 157; entrepreneurial alertness 52, 53, 60n19, 61n24, 61n27; free market process 156; neoclassical equilibrium, criticism of 58; opportunities as hidden objects 418–20; theory of entrepreneurship 13, 51–4, 61n26
Kirzner, M. 234n10

Kleinbölting, H. 67
Kluckhohn, F. 394, 395
Knez, M. 108
Knight, F.H. 164, 241, 293, 314; concept
of the firm 165–8, 222, 228–33;
judgment 168; uncertainty 68, 165,
167–8, 229, 231, 422
Knightian entrepreneur 224, 230
knowing the truth 517
knowledge 188; belief 38, 41, 43, 44; and
civilization 534–45; communication
38–41, 44; growth of 47–51; and
ignorance 547n7; indeterminacy of
translation 42; intersubjective 11, 13, 45,
66, 70, 77, 194, 246, 418; mental state,
concept of 36–7, 42–4; of minds and
world 41, 44, 45; objective 11, 13, 38,
40, 44–6, 66, 70, 77, 246, 418; problem
of 36–7; propositional 46; sensory
stimuli 40–1; sentences or thoughts 44;
skepticism 36, 37; subjective 11, 13, 36,
45, 66, 70, 77, 418; three varieties of
4–5, 10–13, 35–7, 42; verbal behavior
40
knowledge structure 90
Koestler, A. 359
Kolers, Paul 180
Krantz, D.H. 114
Krech, David 203
Kuhn, T. 507, 508, 512; revolutionary
science 517–18
Kuznets, Simon 270

laboratory experiments: CPR study in
368–70
labor force in agriculture, proportion of
263, 264
Lachmann, L.M. 13, 49, 50, 52, 60n17
Lakoff, G. 409, 426; conceptual metaphor
417–20; embodied mind 66, 69–71
Lam, W.F. 371
Lande, R. 214
Landes, D.S. 400–1, 406n21
landmark (LM) 93
Langlois, R.N. 168
language 40, 476, 479–80; of argument
477; contingency of 505–14; linguistic
and philosophical 493; metaphorical
expressions in 477
Larkin, Philip 514–16
Lawler, E.J. 161, 163
law of gravity 18
laws 525
laws of a science 430
laws of physics 430

learning 128, 410
learning spatial-relations terms 100, 102
learning verbs of hand motion 100–1
Ledón-Rettig, C. 376
Lee, D. 286
legal property rights system 246
Leibbrandt, A. 370, 376
leisure 272
Lem, S. 151
Lévi-Strauss, Claude 349
Lewis, C.S. 294
Lewis, W.A. 547n9
Lewontin, R.C. 166, 215, 246; adaptation
in evolutionary theories 161–5
lexicographic reasoning 113
L'Horreur économique (Forrester) 348–9
liberty 244, 539–40, 542, 543, 545, 548n14
Lichtenstein, S. 107, 110, 114, 115;
response-mode effects 106
Liebniz 451
life expectancy 288; trends in 261, 262
Linde, Charlotte 501
linguistic aspect 101
linguistic expressions 491
linguistic hedges 83
Lippman, Walter 340
List, J. 376
literal expressions 491
literal metaphors 490, 493
literal sentences 502
Littlechild, S.C. 49, 51, 60n13, 60n16
Liu, J. 381
Locke, J. 88, 523, 540
Londoño, Juan Luis 344
long-run prediction 282
long surviving resource institutions 366–8
Loomes, C. 108
Lovins, Amory 501
Luce, R. 109

McCarthy, J. 415, 465
McClelland, G. 114
McCormick, C. 395
Machlup, F. 223, 234n1
MacLean, D. 115, 116
McKenzie, R. 286, 287
McMillan, J. 419
McNulty, J. 234n2
macro-economic process 191
macro-economic reforms 342
macro-market 167
mainstream Western philosophy 84–5, 97
Maitland, F.W. 548n10
Malay Archipelago 142
Malmgren, B. 226

562 Index

Malthusianism 275
Malthusian theory: of increasing scarcity 275
management: and entrepreneurship 231–2
March, J.G.: technology of foolishness 66, 72–4
marginal per capita return (MPCR) 377
market-based capitalist system 342–3, 352
market demand 166
market order, misinterpretation of 190
market organization: efficacy of 55
markets 13, 354–5, 419; as analogue computer 54; conceptions and misconceptions 54–7; conceptualization of 14; as creative process 13–15; as game without goods 241; and government 248; metaphor of 420; teleological conception 15
Marxism 399
Marx, Karl 245, 281, 343–6; philosophy 50
matching 111–13
material conditions of life 280, 292–3
material human welfare, path of 259–60
Maugham, S. 401
Maxwell, Clerk 189
Mayr, E. 59
Mead, George Herbert 196, 202
meaningless institutions 543
Meckling, W. 227, 232
memory as an enemy 128
mental image 89
mental state: concept of 36–7, 42–4
mercantilist doctrines 438
mere habits 543
Mervis, C. 89
metaphorical concepts 475–7, 503; argument is war 476–7; systematicity 477–9, 484–5; theories are buildings 490–1; time is a limited resource 478–9; time is a valuable commodity 478–9; time is money 478–9, 491
metaphorical expressions 477–8, 492
metaphorical structuring: partial 490–3
metaphorical systematicity: highlighting and hiding 479–81
metaphorical transfer 176
metaphors 101–2, 417–20, 422, 475–7, 510–12; and cultural coherence 485–7; cultural differences 500–1; examples 489–90; love 493–4, 499–501; reverberations 500; theories of meaning and truth 502–3; time is a moving object 488–9, 491; truth and action 501–2; types of 481–5
metaphysical realism 87, 89–91

metaphysics 425, 520n8, 524–5
"method" of philosophy 510
method of utopian politics 510
metropolitan areas: productivity in 356; technical efficiency in 357; water in 356
micro-economic process 191
microeconomic theory 222
micro-market 167
microscopic diversity 48
microsituational context of social dilemmas *375*, 376
microsituational level of analysis 377–8
microsituational variables: impact of 379
microsituations: attributes of 377
Mill, J. 105, 138
Mill, J.S. 140, 314, 424, 540
Milton, J. 540
mind-friendly property system 245–7
minimal liberty 321n45
misery 275–7
misinterpretation, of market order 190
mobility 273
Mokyr 164
monastic group 486–7
Monte Carlo procedures 195
Monte Carlo robot 195
Montgomery, H. 113
Moore, Gordon 167
Morgan, J.P. 395
Morosov, Savva 398
Morton, E.S. 212
motivation 7–8, 107
motor concepts: neural modeling of 97–102
motor control 25, 99; neural structure of 102
motor controller 23–4, *24*
motor functions 495
motor program 90, 494
motor schemas 90, 98, 99, 101–2
motor synergies 99
moving objects 488
MPCR *see* marginal per capita return (MPCR)
Muth, Richard 275

Nagel, Thomas: subjectivity 519n6
Nagy, William 482
Narayanan, S.: motor schemas, linguistic aspect, and metaphor 69, 101–2
Nash equilibrium 368, 382n6
National Academy of Sciences 270
National Research Council (NRC) 363
natural disasters 283
natural science 4, 6

natural selection 162
"Nature of the Firm, The" 347
necessity of consistency 121
negative attitudes 128, 388
negotiations 160–1
Nelson, Katherine 199, 202
neoclassical citadel 49
neoclassical equilibrium: criticism of 49
neoclassical price theory models firms 223
neoclassical theory firms 232
Nepal Irrigation and Institutions (NIIS)
  project 371
Nepal irrigation systems: CPRs problems
  study in 371–2
Netherlands 294
neural beings 81–2
neural computations 98
neural embodiment 97
neural modeling: as existence proof for
  embodiment of mind 98–9; spatial and
  motor concepts 97–102
neural realization 98
neural structure 83
new evolutionary synthesis (Allen and
  Wicken) 48, 57
new idea 526–7
New Institutional Economics 442
new opinions 426, 526
Newsweek 344
Newtonian mechanics 430, 444
Newtonian paradigm 48
Newton's vocabulary 507
new truth 424, 527
new welfare economics 302
New York Language Acquisition Group
  199
Next Two Hundred Years, The (Kahn) 288
nexus-of-contracts models 228
Nietzsche 421, 514, 515, 518, 520n9;
  culture 511, 512; human life as a
  triumph 518; knowing the truth 517;
  metaphors 512; truth 519n2
NIIS project *see* Nepal Irrigation and
  Institutions (NIIS) project
non-adaptive hypothesis 210
noncooperative game theory 368–70
non-Kantian theme 174
nonliteral metaphor 491
nonliteral utterance 502
nonteleological perspective 13, 14, 51, 52,
  56
normative assumption 114
normative theories of choice 121, 123, 124
North America Review 143
North, D. 247, 431, 432, 434

notion of 'trade-off' 208
novel metaphors 491, 498–9, 501–2;
  appropriate 499–501
nuclear fission 284, 285
nuclear fusion 285
nuclear power 283
nuclear power study 435
Nurkse, R. 399

obituary notices 242
objective knowledge 11, 13, 38, 40, 45, 46,
  66, 70, 77, 246, 418
objective truth 528–9
objectivism 70
objectivity 44, 45, 513
O'Brien, J. 108
O'Driscoll, G.P. 60n20
older truths 527, 528
old opinion 426, 526, 527
Olson, David 199
Olson, M. 247
Omidyar, Pierre 413
open-endedness 48, 50, 51, 54, 55
Oppenheimer, J.A. 376
opportunities 3, 11, 12, 15, 238, 239, 243,
  415, 541; future growth in 288–9; as
  hidden objects by Kirzner, I. 418–20;
  and process 244
optimal firm 224
optimal organizational forms 354–5
ordering 154–5, 178–9
organizational identification 443
organizations 121, 130, 545
orientational concept 494
orientational metaphors 481–2
Ostrom, E. 237, 240, 243, 247, 357, 365,
  367, 372; empirical evidence 239, 240;
  polycentric governance of CPRs 248–9
Ostrom, V. 353, 354, 356, 357
Ostwald, W.: pragmatism 523–3
outer environment 21, 23, 24
outer environments 7–8
overpricing 109
over-simplified test 186
Owens, William 289
ozone layer 270–1, 283

paedomorphic morphology 215
Panglossian paradigm 207
Papini, G. 425, 524, 532–3
"paradigmatic" direct causation 497
Pareto efficiency 302, 314, 321n45
Parsonian thesis 250
Parsons, T. 394, 405n5
partial metaphorical structuring 490–3

564 Index

partial typology, of adaptationist programme 213–16
payoff rules 365
Pearl, J. 409, 426; art and science of cause and effect 414–17; history of causality 415
Pearson, Karl 454–5, 470, 473
peculiarity of competition 186
Peirce, Charles: principle of pragmatism 522
Penrose-Chandler theory 226
Penrose, E. 245
perception 97, 98
performance measures 371
Perkins, David 201
personal role 395, 396
pessimism 299–301, 316
Petty, William 256
Pfennig, D.W. 376
phenomenological embodiment 97
phenotypic plasticity 216
Phillips, A.W. 26
philosophical significance 90–2
philosophy 505, 506, 509, 510, 512, 515, 516, 519; of evolution 149
phi phemomenon 180
phrasal lexical items 490
phrasal lexicon 490
physical causation 498
physical conditions 141
physical metaphors 419, 481–5, 495–6, 502
physical/psychological laws 229
physical symbol system 31–2
Physics and Politics (Bagehot) 139
physiocratic doctrines 438
physiological adaptations 216
Piaget 497
Pitts-McCulloch neurons 29
Plant, A. 225
Plato 516, 518; true world 517
Platonist 511
playfulness 126–30
Plott, C. 107, 108
pluralism 1–2, 425
pluralistic evolution 162–3
Pluralistic Universe, A (James) 172
pluralistic view 220
Polanyi, M. 55, 61n29, 253, 546n2
political–social–economic system 239
Politics (Aristotle) 316n3
pollutions 283
Polo, Marco 349
polycentric governance of CPRs: Ostrom, E. 248–9
polycentricity 356

polycentric police industries 353
polycentric public industries 356–7
Pommerehne, W. 107
Popper, K.R. 59n5
population growth 238, 269–70, 437
population thinking 59n4
Porter, M.E. 420
position rules 365
positivist 511
Potin, Felix 401
poverty 310–12, 320n35
power maximization 440–1
pragmatic method 424–6, 522–5, 531
pragmatism 523; Absolute means 531, 532; anti-intellectualist tendencies 524; attitude in philosophy 523; belief 527, 532; concreteness and closeness 529; criticism against 527; defined 522; fact-loving temperament 529; God and 529, 530, 533; laws 525; materialistic bias 530; metaphysics 524–5; new idea 526, 527; new opinions 526; Ostwald, W. 523–3; Peirce, Charles 522; rationalism 528–9, 533; religious comfort 530; scope of 528; temper of 528–9; theological ideas 530, 533; truth 525–9, 531–3
pragmatism means: James, W. 424–7
pre-existence of purpose 121
preference construction 71–2, 113–16; practical implications of 114–16
preference management 116
preference reversals: among gambles 106–8; causes of 108–9; choice, matching, and prominence effect 111–13; compatibility hypothesis 110–11; design 117n2
preferences 104–6; and capabilities 243
pre-Galilean age 149
present markets 13, 52
Prigogine, I. 47, 48, 59n2, 59n5, 59n6
primacy of rationality 121
primary goods 308
primary qualities 88
primitive accumulation of capital 346
Principle of Coherence 39–40
Principle of Correspondence 40
principles of charity 40
printing invention 289
privacy 197, 202
private club, of globalization 340–3
private goods 248, 355, 357
privatization 412
procedure invariance 106, 109, 112
processes of intuition 121
processes of tradition and faith 121
production-exchange process 57

Index 565

production process 167
productive knowledge 286
productive technique 286
profiles 94
profit-maximizing system 21
prominence effect 111–13, **112**, 115
property: and capitalism 346–8
property rights: de Soto, H. 245–7
property rights bundles: common pool
    resources 364–5
property rights systems 350–1
propositional knowledge 46
protected areas 381
prototypes 83
"prototypical" direct causation 497–8
pseudo concept 50
Psychological Bulletin (Edwards) 104
public choice theory 440–1
public goods 248, 355, 357; experiment
    370–1, 382n6
public policy analysis 249, 381
purchasing power parity 266
"purely intellectual" concepts 485
Putnam, H. 152, 194, 512
Putnam, L. 160–1

radical relativism 87
radical reordering 178
radical subjectivism 49, 51, 54–5
"radical subjectivist" view 49, 59n10
Radner, R. 234n8
Railroads and American Economic Growth
    (Fogel) 434
Ramachandran 100, 102
Ramsey, Frank Plumpton **527**
randomized experiment: causality and 473
random walks 163
rate of innovation 436
rates of investment 436
rational choice theory 374–5, 381
rational expectations 32, 49, 439
rationalism 528–9, 533
rationality 33n10, 42; choice and 120–2
rationalization 126
rational knowledge 537
Rawls, John 308
raw-material future 284–5
R&D investment 436
Read, L. 251
realism 84–5
real-world firms 224
reason 84, 85, 102–3, 545–6; body and
    brain shaping the 80–1
recognizing patterns 183
Reddy, Michael 479

reducibility 182
referring 198
reflectance 86
Regier, T.: learning spatial-relations terms
    100
Reilly, R. 108
Reinhart, C.M. 421
relative progress 291
relativism 155
Remane, A. 217
Renan, E. 401
repentant merchant 398
reputations of participants 377
Resourceful Earth, The 254
resources 222
respect for fact 513
response-mode effects 106
reverse regression 471
revolutionary science 510, 517
Riedl, Rupert 217
Riggs, Jennifer Lovitt 2–3
Ritov, I. 115
Rizzo, M.J. 60n20
Robbins, Lionel 302
Roddick, Anita 421
Rogoff, K.S. 421
role-expectation 394
Romantics 505, 509, 511, 512, 515
Rorty, Amélie 202
Rorty, R. 409; contingency of language
    409; contingency of selfhood 420–4
Rosaldo, Michelle 200
Rosch, E. 89, 497
Rousseau, Jean Jacques 349
Royal Swedish Academy of Sciences 299
Russell, Bertrand 414, 452, 454, 458, 464
Russia: entrepreneurs 403; entrepreneurship
    in 398, 404; Marxism in 399
Russian Revolution 340

Sahlins, M. 207
St Mark's spandrels *205*
Samuelson, P. 248, 302, 355, 357
sanctioning system 369–70, 377
San Marco, spandrels of 204–7;
    adaptationist programme 207–16;
    evolution 216–20
Sarasvathy, S. 74
Sawyer, J.E. 400
Say's Law 433, 434
Scaife, Michael 202
scale compatibility hypothesis 110
Scheler, Max 194
Schiller, F.C.S. 526, 528, 531
Schindewolf, O.H. 217

566 Index

Schkade, D. 111
Schlager, E. 364, 365
Schmidt, K. 375
Schneider, F. 107
Schultz, T. 434
Schumpeter, J. 5, 153, 411, 421; creative
    destruction 396, 421–2; economic
    development theory 393–4
Schwab, Klaus 343
Sciences of the Artificial, The (Simon) 6–10,
    12, 154
scientific knowledge 536
scientific progress 284–7
scientific research 292
scientific vocabulary 519n1
scope rules 365
scripture 120
Searle, John 348; intrinsic intentionality
    519n6
secondary quality 88
Seilacher, A. 218, 219
selection processes 161–2, 165; decoupling
    of 164
self-consciousness 515, 516
self-creation 515
self-deception 129
self-evident fashion 18
selfhood: contingency of 514–19
self-knowledge 35, 44, 517
self-organising systems 189
self-organization paradigm 48
self-overcoming 518
Sen, A. 237, 240, 248, 260, 411, 422; social
    choice 241–4
sensible foolishness 125–6
sensorimotor system 85, 102, 103
sensory stimuli 40–1
SES *see* social-ecological system (SES)
sexual transmission 290
Shackle, G.L.S. 49–50, 60n13, 60n14,
    60n16, 234n9; subjectivism 51
Shafir, E. 113
Shakespeare, W. 140
Shane, S. 13
Shivakoti, G. 371
short-run prediction 282
short-run scarcity 276
Simon, H.A. 2, 68, 154, 354, 359, 409,
    415, 417, 426; bounded rationality 75,
    105; economics as a historical science
    410–13; *Sciences of the Artificial, The*
    6–10, 12
Simon, J. 237, 246, 247, 252, 423; *State of
    Humanity, The* 238–41
Simons, H.C. 55; Syllabus 54, 62n30

Simonson, I. 113
Simpson's Paradox 426, 470
simulation: of poorly understood systems
    27–8; as a source of new knowledge
    26–7; techniques 25–6
skepticism 36, 37
Skinner, Quentin 507
Skoyles, J.R. 69
slavery 287
Slovic, P. 107, 109–15; construction of
    preferences 66, 71–3; response-mode
    effects 106
Smith, Adam 56, 158, 189, 190, 240, 251,
    281, 295, 320n35, 344, 421, 438, 443
Smith, V. L 108
social accountability 130
social approval 397, 401
social attitudes 393, 399, 404;
    entrepreneurship in Russia 404–5;
    Gerschenkron, A. 250–3; and
    industrialization 399
social change 394, 395
social choice: Sen, A. 241–4
social choice theory: challenges and
    foundational problems faced by 299;
    decisions and coherence 304–5;
    deprivation 312–13; formal methods and
    informal reasoning 303; gender
    inequality 312–13; informational
    broadening 305–7; liberal paradox
    313–14; origins of 299–301; possibility
    and impossibility 303–4; poverty and
    famine 310–12; welfare economics
    301–3
social constructionism 70, 87
social dilemmas: rational individuals 361–2
social dynamics 394
social-ecological system (SES): action
    situations in *378*, 378–9
social equilibrium 50
social evolution 138
social group 496
socialism 58, 188
social justice 190
social metaphor 483–5
social norms 127
social organization 129
social psychology: egocentric and structural
    views of 158–61
social roles 395
social sciences 5
social stereotypes 83
social system 59n6
social values 250, 403
social welfare function 302, 307

Socrates 523
soft energy path metaphor 501
Solovev, Vladimir 398
Soros, George 344
source-path-goal schema 94–5
space 285
space exploration 286
spatial concept 494–6
spatialization metaphors 484–6
spatial relations 93; elements of 96
spatial-relations concepts 99, 100, 102–3;
    bodily projections 95–6; container
    schema 92–3; embodied nature of 96–7;
    neural modeling of 97–102; other image
    schemas and elements 96; source-path-
    goal schema 94–5
spatial-relations terms 100, 102
species extinction 269
speech formulas 490
Speed, Terry 456
Spencer, Herbert 132, 134, 138–41, 145,
    220; law 146; "philosophy" 132, 148–9
Sperber, Dan 194
spontaneous order 187–8
spurious correlations 452
standard of living 266–71, 276, 288
State of Humanity, The (Simon) 238–41
static equilibrium models 232
static morphology 214
Steed, B. 373
Stengers, I. 47, 48, 59n2
Stevin, Simon 17, 18
stimuli 40
stochastic process of change 213
storytelling 160
Stranlund, J. K 370
Strategy and Structure (Chandler) 225
strategy compatibility 113
stresses 254
"strong poet" 421, 422, 512, 515, 516, 518
structural metaphors 419, 481, 502
structural view of social psychology 158–61
Study of Sociology (Spencer) 139
Sturgis, Katharine 179
subcultures 486
subjective knowledge 11, 13, 36, 45, 66,
    70, 77, 418
subjectivism 49–51, 87
subjectivity 45, 519n6
subtractability of use 357
sudden institutional changes 399
Sugden, R. 108, 362
sunny climates 20
superabundance 527
super-goals 125

Suppes, Patrick 453
supplementation 155
supply-side innovation 241
Swedberg, R. 6
Sweeney, B.W. 215
symbols 29
symbol systems, rational artifacts: basic
    capabilities 31–2; economics, abstract
    rationality 32–3; intelligence as
    computation 32
syntax 198
synthetic 19
systematic metaphorical concepts 477–9,
    484–5; highlighting and hiding 479–81

Tagiuri, Renato 195
tautomerous 523
technical advance 284–6
technical efficiency 357
technical progress 284–7
technological entrepreneurship: history 163
technology entrepreneurship 413
technology of foolishness 72–4; choice and
    rationality 120–2; goals, problem of
    122–5; intelligence and foolishness 130;
    play and reason 126–30; sensible
    foolishness 125–6
teleological conception 15
teleological perspective 51, 52, 55–7, 60n15
'temperament' of philosophy 524
tertium comparationis 400
Thatcher, Margaret 412
theological ideas 530, 533
theories of meaning and truth 502–3
theory of abstraction: inadequacies of 493–4
theory of adulthood 124
theory of choice 123
theory of riskless choice 105
theory of roles 404
theory of the firm 222, 225–6
Theory of the Growth of the Firm, The
    (Penrose) 225
theory of truth 525, 527, 528
Thierry, A. 397
Thompson, D'Arcy 208, 214
Thomson, George 176
Thomson, Wyville 213
Three Varieties of Knowledge (Davidson) 4–5,
    10–13
Thurow, Lester 340
Tiebout, C.M. 353, 356
Tiers État (Thierry) 397
Time and knowledge (Lachmann) 13–14,
    50–2
Time on the Cross (Fogel) 434

568 Index

Todd, P.M.: bounding rationality 66–9
toll goods 358
trade 251–2, 289; exchange and 240; to innovation 240
traditions 538
trajector (TR) 93
transactional self 159, 160, 194–203
transcendental idealism 530
transcendent reason 84
transformative processes 153–5
translatability 182
Trappists 487
travel 273
"Treatise of Human Nature" (Hume) 451
tripartism 197, 203
true ideas 531
"true world" 517
Trurl 151, 168
trust: building 379; role of 376–7
truth 502, 519n2, 525–9, 531–3; and contingency of language 505–9, 512, 513; and contingency of selfhood 517, 518
truth-value candidate 511
Tullock, G. 247
Turner, Victor 201
Tversky, A. 67, 90, 109–13
typical–case prototypes 83
Tyrannosaurus 210

uncertainty: Knight, F.H. 68, 167–8, 229, 231, 422
underpricing 109
UNDP *see* United Nations Development Programme (UNDP)
unitary 'traits' 204
United Nations Development Programme (UNDP) 309
United States 291; education 288–9; entrepreneurial behavior 401; value systems 402
universal reason 84
unknowable value 167
unmediated conceptualism 197, 202
unrestricted domain 304
unsatisfactoriness 516
unsystematic metaphorical expressions 492
US Civil War 276
utilisation of knowledge 187
utilitarianism 301–2, 307
utility theory 108, 113, 115

value creation 239
value orientations 405n5
values 124

value systems 398–400, 403; United States and France 402
valuing the environment 114–15
Vanberg, V.J. 2, 5, 155–7, 241, 246, 422; market as creative process 13–15; market process 167
Vannote, R.L. 215
Vaughn, K. 61n26
vector 290
Venkataraman, S. 11, 13, 244
venture's business model 160
verbal behavior 40
verbs of hand action 100–1
Vieta 450
Viner, J. 438
visible external conditions 135
visible light 86
vocabularies 422–3, 507–13
Von Baer's fundamental embryological laws 218
von Mises, Ludwig 295–6
von Neumann, John 29
voting-based social choice 304, 305
Vrba, E.S. 164
Vygotsky's theory 203

Walker, J. 368
Wallace, A.R. 208, 209, 213
Walrasian view of economy 223
Ward, Artemus 137
war metaphor 501
Warren, R. 356
Washington Post, The 257
water industry performance 356
wavelengths of light 86, 87
Ways of Worldmaking (Goodman) 151–6
wealth maximization 440–1
Wealth of Nations, The (Smith) 189, 438
Wedgwood 252
weighting 154
Weir, Ruth 199
Weismann, A. 208
welfare economics 299, 301–3; informational broadening and 305–7
well-defined economic theory of the firm 222
Wermuth, Nanny 456
Western conception of self 202
Western philosophical tradition 80, 85, 97, 518
wheat prices, USA *265*
Whiteheadian world 176
Wicken, J.S. 48
Wiener, Norbert 189
Wiggins, N. 225

Williams, J. 372
Williams, O.E. 440
Williamson, E. 228, 232
Willis, C.E. 370
Wilson, Deirdre 194
Wilson, D.S. 442
Wilson, E.O. 207
Wisconsin glaciation 430
Wiseman, J. 49–51, 60n11, 60n12, 60n18
Witte, Count 405
Wittgenstein, L. 38, 177, 513, 516; vocabularies and tools 422
Witt, U. 76
Wold, Herman 462, 464
Wolong Nature Reserve 380
work 272
world 506–8, 513

World Economic Forum 343
world education 289
worldmaking, ways of 175; composition and decomposition 175–7; deformation 180; deletion and supplementation 179–80; ordering 178–9; weighting 177–8
Wright, S. 460

Xenophon 443

Yeats, W.B. 422, 512
Yoon, J. 161

Zhang, S.X. 68
Zweifel, P. 107
Zweig, Stefan 293